Jeff Duntemann Series Editor

HIGH PERFORMANCE DELPHI 3 PROGRAMMING

Don Taylor

Jim Mischel

John Penman

Terence Goggin

CORIOLIS GROUP BOOKS

an International Thomson Publishing company I(T)P®

Albany, NY • Belmont, CA • Bonn • Boston • Cincinnati • Detroit • Johannesburg • London
Madrid • Melbourne • Mexico City • New York • Paris • Singapore • Tokyo • Toronto • Washington

Publisher	Keith Weiskamp
Project Editor	Denise Constantine
Production Project Coordinator	Kim Eoff
Cover Artist	Performance Design/Gary Smith
Cover Design	Tony Stock
Interior Design	Nicole Colón
Compositor	ProImage/Jimmie Young
Copyeditor	Laura Lawrie
Proofreader	Meredith Brittain
Indexer	Laura Lawrie
CD-ROM Development	Robert Clarfield

High Performance Delphi 3 Programming
ISBN: 1-57610-179-7
Copyright © 1997 by The Coriolis Group, Inc.

All rights reserved. This book may not be duplicated in any way without the express written consent of the publisher, except in the form of brief excerpts or quotations for the purposes of review. The information contained herein is for the personal use of the reader and may not be incorporated in any commercial programs, other books, databases, or any kind of software without written consent of the publisher. Making copies of this book or any portion for any purpose other than your own is a violation of United States copyright laws.

Limits of Liability and Disclaimer of Warranty

The author and publisher of this book have used their best efforts in preparing the book and the programs contained in it. These efforts include the development, research, and testing of the theories and programs to determine their effectiveness. The author and publisher make no warranty of any kind, expressed or implied, with regard to these programs or the documentation contained in this book.

The author and publisher shall not be liable in the event of incidental or consequential damages in connection with, or arising out of, the furnishing, performance, or use of the programs, associated instructions, and/or claims of productivity gains.

Trademarks

Trademarked names appear throughout this book. Rather than list the names and entities that own the trademarks or insert a trademark symbol with each mention of the trademarked name, the publisher states that it is using the names for editorial purposes only and to the benefit of the trademark owner, with no intention of infringing upon that trademark.

The Coriolis Group, Inc.
An International Thomson Publishing Company
14455 N. Hayden Road, Suite 220
Scottsdale, Arizona 85260

602/483-0192
FAX 602/483-0193
http://www.coriolis.com

Printed in the United States of America
10 9 8 7 6 5 4 3 2 1

To my benefactor, Jesus of Nazareth. The gift you freely gave I could not possibly have earned in a thousand lifetimes.
—*Don Taylor*

For Dean Bennett and Randy Schafer: good friends and fellow computer junkies.
—*Jim Mischel*

To my darling wife, Jocie, and my wonderful children, David and Diana, for their support. To Mum and Dad for all their love and hard work to bring me to where I am today.
—*John Penman*

To Tim, my brother and my friend.
—*Terence Goggin*

Acknowledgments

My thanks to Marge McRae, friend and good neighbor, for doing a first read on my manuscript, and for suggesting the Marge Reynolds character (who is nothing like the *real* Marge, who doesn't even like polyester all that much).
—*Don Taylor*

It takes an amazing amount of logistic support to put a book together—especially when so many authors are involved (one of whom didn't always get his stuff in on time). Denise Constantine, our Project Editor, did a tremendous job keeping the project on track and coordinating the myriad details that go into producing a book. Thanks, Denise, for keeping me on schedule.
—*Jim Mischel*

I wish to thank Jeff Duntemann for booting my writing career into successful orbit.
—*John Penman*

A Note From Jeff Duntemann

Programmers (especially those just coming up to speed) often challenge one another with questions like, "How good are your tools?" There was a time when this was a valid question. Compilers, debuggers, servers, database engines, and all the rest were just coming out of the Stone Age. There were tremendous variations in quality and power from one tool to another. If you bet on the wrong toolset, you could be working harder than you needed to—or worse.

Today, the more pertinent question might be "How good are *you*?" Relentless competition has given today's developer tools tremendous depth and amazing quality, such that a journeyman programmer is highly unlikely to push such tools to the limit. Long before your tools hit the wall, *you* will—unless you go the distance to learn everything you can about the tools that you use, and refine the skill with which you use them.

The Coriolis Group's High Performance series was designed to help you take your tools *deep*. These books explain the advanced tool features that the intro books just can't cover, and provide heavy-duty projects that force you to think through the development process at an expert's level—using those head muscles that lie behind everything we could call skill.

You could discover this knowledge by beating your head against the technology, and trying things randomly until they work. Or you can benefit from the experience of our authors, who've been up this learning curve before and took notes along the way. We've chosen the topics, the authors, and the approaches carefully to ensure that you don't get mired in introductory material you don't need and irrelevant technology that you can't use.

The goal is to take you and your chosen toolset as far as you choose to go. You've already got high-performance tools. Here's to your success at becoming and remaining a high-performance developer.

—*Jeff Duntemann*

Contents

Introduction   xvii

Chapter 1   32-Bit Console Applications   1

Console Applications   3
Filters   4

Console Applications And Delphi   5
Hello, Delphi   5
Saving A Program Template   7
Console Input And Output   8

Filter Programs In Delphi   9
Your Basic Filter Program   9
Processing The Command Line   10
Command-Line Options   12
A Reusable Command-Line Parser   13
Testing The CmdLine Unit   21

A Note On Program Structure   23

Reading And Writing Files   25
Using The Filter Template   34

A Critique   34

Chapter 2   32-Bit Delphi DLLs— When, Why, And How   37

What's A DLL And Why Do I Want One?   40
How Do I Do It?   41

Building A DLL	**42**
Calling DLL Functions	**43**
Linking DLLs At Runtime 44	
Where Windows Looks For DLLs 49	
DLLs: Disadvantages And Cautions	**49**
Creating Forms In DLLs	**50**
Coding For Flexibility	**53**
Creating The Text Editor 54	
Sharing Memory Between Applications	**60**
The DLLProc Variable 61	
Movin' On!	**64**

Chapter 3 Drag And Drop The Windows Way 65

Drag And Drop	**68**
What To Do With Windows Code 73	
Responding To Windows Messages	**78**
Custom Controls 79	
Subclassing	**81**
Defining The Interface 82	
Implementing The New Interface 84	
Subclassing Revisited	**84**

Chapter 4 Dragging And Dropping With OLE 95

What Is OLE?	**97**
OLE Inheritance And TInterfacedObject 98	

OLE Drag And Drop Requirements — 99
Drop Client Responsibilities 99
How It Works 107
So What? 110

Becoming A Drag And Drop Server — 110
Drop Server Responsibilities 111
IDropSource Interface Requirements 112
IDataObject Holds The Data 112
Implementing The Drop Server 117

OLE! — 127

Chapter 5 The Delphi Winsock Component — 129

What Is Winsock? — 131
Dissecting CsSocket — 132
Running The Resolver32 Application — 172
What's My Name? 176
What's The Address? 176
What's Your Name? 182
Getting The Name Asynchronously 183
Who's At This Address? 189

Canceling A WSAAsync Operation — 190
Resolving Ports And Services — 191
Finding The Service 192

Resolving Protocols — 193
Using Tags — 193
To Block Or Not — 195

Chapter 6 CsShopper: An FTP Client Component — 197

Are You Being Served? — 199
The CsShopper Component — 201
Displaying Output 203
Putting Shopper32 To Work — 203
SHOPPER32 Profiles 227
Connecting In — 229
Closing The Connection — 231
Uploading And Downloading Files — 232
Changing Directories For File Transfers 232
Uploading Files 233
Transfer Of Multiple Files 233
Asynchronous File Transfer — 234
Put That Back On The Shelf! — 239
Gone Shopping — 240

Chapter 7 An FTP Server Component — 241

Opening CsKeeper For Business — 245
Configuring KEEPER32 With The Options Tab 247
Security Settings 249
Informative Messages For Connecting Clients 250
Where And How Settings Are Stored 251
Open And Running! — 255
Showing The Client What's Available 256
Creating A Listening Socket 258
Are You Being Served? — 259
One User At A Time 259
I'll Take One Of Those… 268

Can You Store This For Me? 269
Taking Inventory 270

Chapter 8   3D Fractal Landscapes   271

Bending And Dividing   273
The Shared Edges Problem   273
A Triangular Array   277
Bending   287
Draw, Then Display   288
Generating And Displaying The Landscape   289
The Project() Routine   300
Outline Mode   301
Filled Mode   301
Rendered Mode   303
Create Your Own Worlds   303

Chapter 9   Problems With Persistents, And Other Advice   305

Reading To Write?   307
Reasonable Workarounds   308
A Little Perspective   310
Using RDTSC For Pentium Benchmarking   311
Drag-and-Drop Text For A Delphi Listbox   313
Making String Collections More List-Like   316
Letting Delphi Applications Set Up Themselves   318
Using inherited With Redeclared Properties In Delphi   319
Taking Snapshots Of The Screen With Delphi   322

Delphi RadioGroup Buttons You Can Disable	324
Capturing The System Palette With Delphi	326
Treating The Clipboard Like A Stream	328
Changing Hints On The Fly	331
Using Macros With Delphi's Code Editor	332
Streaming TPersistent	334
Enabling Drag Image Display For Delphi 2 And 3	336

Chapter 10 Models, Views, And Frames 339

Implementing Views As Real Live Code	**344**
Component Templates And Compound Components 344	
Form Inheritance 345	
From Embedded Forms To Views	**347**
The Interfaces Rationale 350	
Interfaced Forms	**351**
Delphi 3's Reference Count Gotcha 354	
Abstract, Valid, And Fickle Views	**356**
Model Editors	**360**
The Sample Model	**365**
Other Applications	**369**

Chapter 11 The Shadowy Math Unit 371

Three Good Reasons To Use The Math Unit	**373**
Dynamic Data And Static Declarations	**374**
Slice To The Rescue 374	
Creating The DBStatistics Component	**375**
Defining The Component's Tasks 375	

Getting Access To The Data   376
Storing Data Locally   376
Extracting Data   377
Making The Data Available   380
Test Driving The DBStatistics Component   381

Bugs In The Delphi 2 Math Unit — 383
Poly: The Function That Got Away — 383
Filling The Pascal Power Gap — 387
Math Unit Function Summary — 387
Trigonometric Functions And Procedures   387
Arithmetic Functions And Procedures   388
Financial Functions And Procedures   389
Statistical Functions And Procedures   390

Chapter 12   Dynamic User Interfaces — 395
An Example "UI-It-Yourself" Application — 396
Building In A "Delphi" For Your Users — 397
Moving Controls   397
Resizing Controls   400
Responding To The Pop-up Menu   402
Abandoning Changes   405
Changing The Tab Order At Runtime   406

Changing Other Properties — 408
Changing Control Fonts At Runtime   408
Changing Properties In An Object Inspector   410

Saving Component Changes Made At Runtime — 412
Snag: Components With Components As Properties   413
Alternate Paths To A Stream   415

Toward More Flexible User Interfaces — 415

Chapter 13 Hierarchical Data In Relational Databases — 417

One-To-Many Hierarchies — 419
Simple Recursive Hierarchical Data — 420
Using TQuery As A Detail DataSet 423
Nested Recursive Hierarchical Data — 425
Hierarchy Navigation 426
Displaying The Data — 428
Using The Data — 430
Finding Rows 432
Using Hierarchical Data In Queries 433
Referential Integrity And Circular References — 434
Using SQL — 435
Solving The Problem Of Arbitrary Nesting 435
Using Stored Procedures — 436
The TreeData Components — 438
TreeData Property Management 439
TreeData Component Internals 440
TreeDataComboBox 441
TreeDataListBox 441
TreeDataOutline And TreeDataUpdate 442
Hierarchical Wisdom — 442

Chapter 14 The Oracle Vanishes — 445

An Evening At The Office — 448
An Urgent Plea — 450

The Disappearance	**451**
At The Sleeveless Arms	**453**
Doing The Old Drag/Drop	**454**
Kind Of A Drag 454	
Dropping The Payload 457	
Packing Paradox And dBASE Tables	**461**
The Packing Demo 465	
Back At Ace's Office	**469**
Different Strokes	**471**
Playing A WAV File	**478**
Some Sound Advice 478	
A Disconcerting Discovery 480	

Chapter 15 A Revelation In The Mud 483

Resizing Forms	**487**
Making A Splash	**493**
Ace Gets An Answer	**504**
Making Data Global To An Application	**506**
An Exciting Discovery!	**513**
Taking Win95 For A Walk	**515**
Just Say "Cheese" 517	
The WalkStuf Unit 519	
Stepping Out 528	

Chapter 16 The Oracle Returns 535

Sharing Event Handlers	**539**
Taking A First Run 540	
Down A Crooked Path 543	

Just One More Thing... 551

Using Memory Files — 553
Before The Beginning 555

Preventing Program Execution — 557

Floating Toolbars — 560

Ace Gets The Goods — 566

Epilogue — 573

Chapter 17 An Age-Old Problem — 575

Facing The Situation — 579
Specifying The Problem 580

Designing The DLL — 583
Startup Code 592
Signals From A Semaphore 593
Shutdown Code 595
Examining The DLL Routines 595

Creating The Sender Component — 597

Creating The Receiver Component — 603
Subclassing The Owner Window 609
Other Interesting Stuff 613

Creating A Receiver Demo — 614

Creating A Sender Demo — 619

A Rude Awakening — 626

Index — 629

Introduction

Way, *way* back in the mid-to-late 80s, the Pascal programming language was the target of a systematic slander attack by C and (later) C++ partisans, who got the ear of the media and said "Pascal is a kiddie language" so often that the media chowderheads took their word for it.

Most of these people knew nothing of Pascal, or perhaps took a college-level course in it from other chowderheads who considered drop-in code portability the sole virtue in all computer science. So the Pascal taught in schools is typically castrated Pascal that can't do much more than iterate arrays and talk to the command line. C is no more portable than Pascal, but…c'mon, already: The whole issue is ridiculous because portability is and always was a myth. Quick, you C gurus: Write me a single, library-free C program that will locate the text cursor to 0,0 on *any* C implementation on *any* platform. See what I mean? *No es posible*. Arguing about portability is about as useful as discussing where UFOs come from.

A better measure of a language is how much it can accomplish—and how productive it makes the programmer. There was a time when C++ had a slight edge in power. But then Borland got hold of Pascal and added everything of value that C++ had. The "kiddie language" now had typecasts, pointers, objects, inline assembly, special hooks for Windows, the "woiks." Those of us who used Pascal immediately leapt on the additional features, and before you knew it there were hordes of highly sophisticated applications everywhere you looked, all written in Borland Pascal.

Sometimes you can't win. The C++ guys snorted and looked the other way, and the media chowderheads still call Pascal a kiddie language. It got so bad that a lot of commercial software vendors were afraid to admit that their applications were written in Pascal.

So Borland did the right thing. They dumped the P-word. Delphi, when it happened, stood on its own merits. It wasn't a language. It was a lean, mean, program-building machine. The sheer *depth* of the Delphi product is astonishing—you can wander for months in the help system and not see the same entry twice.

The potential in all that power was slow to be understood. We're only now starting to appreciate what you can do in Delphi. This book is meant to be a compendium of truly advanced Delphi techniques—stuff you can't do in a kiddie language, and stuff that isn't a cakewalk even in C++. It's proof, now and for all time, that Delphi goes all the way down to the metal and back in creating professional applications for Windows as good as anything you can create in any language you can name.

Having lost the P-word to kick around, the media chowderheads have begun repeating a new mantra, that anything you can do in Delphi takes five or six times as long in C++. It's gotten so bad I've heard tell of MIS shops where managers are forbidding the use of C++ and replacing it with Delphi and Visual Basic.

Hey, pass the chowder. There may yet be justice.

Jeff Duntemann KG7JF
Scottsdale, Arizona
July, 1997

HIGH PERFORMANCE

32-Bit Console Applications

CHAPTER 1

Now that DOS has been stuffed and hung on the wall of Win32 as a minor API, how's a hacker to do command-line text filters? Well, the POSIX fairy waved her magic wand, and Poof! DOS became The Console, and it's deja vu all over again.

32-Bit Console Applications

Jim Mischel

Windows, OS/2, the Macintosh, and other graphical user interfaces have been the darlings of the computer press (both technical and nontechnical) for many years now. With all that attention focused on writing applications for these GUI environments, it's sometimes tough to remember that there is another world out there—a world of command-line tools that perform batch processing with a minimum of user input. These tools aren't especially sexy, but they're certainly useful. Banks, for example, still process your checks, deposits, and loan payments in batches every night. Insurance and credit card companies also perform nightly updates, as do countless other businesses. (And do they use fancy GUI environments? Ask your bank teller. Or guess.)

Command-line tools aren't limited to companies running financial programs on big iron. Windows 95 itself comes with quite a few: ATTRIB, DISKCOPY, FORMAT, FDISK, SORT, and XCOPY among them. Even Delphi comes with some command-line tools. A quick peek in Delphi's BIN directory reveals (among others) the Resource compilers (BRC32.EXE and BRCC32.EXE), the Pascal compiler (DCC32.EXE), and a few others.

Console Applications

Windows 95 and Windows NT support *console applications*—programs that have no GUI presence but instead run in what is commonly referred to as a "DOS box." Although these applications don't have a window, they *do* have access to the Windows API and the full 32-bit Windows address space (including virtual memory). This is in contrast to Windows 3.1, where GUI programs had access to Windows address space, and DOS programs had access to the lower 640K.

In the past, DOS applications got around the 640K limitation through the use of DOS extenders that supported standards like DPMI (DOS Protected Mode Interface) and VCPI (Virtual Control Program Interface). If you had a 16-bit extender, you had access to 16 megabytes of memory. The less common 32-bit extenders gave you access to the full 32-bit address space, and some even supported virtual memory. The problem with DOS extenders is that they are—no matter how well presented—hacks. And many users simply couldn't get their older machines to run the DOS extenders reliably, and some DOS extenders couldn't run in a Windows DOS box.

A console application running under Windows 95, on the other hand, is simply a Windows program without a window. There's no special extender software required, and any computer that can run Windows 95 or Windows NT will support console applications.

So we've got the RAM and we're free of the GUI. What can we *do* with it?

Filters

Probably the most common use of command-line tools in the PC world is the broad category of programs called "filters." A filter can be anything from a very simple line counter to a complex compiler (like Delphi's Pascal compiler), a sorting utility, or a batch update program.

All filters operate basically the same way: They're invoked from the command line and passed arguments that specify options, and input and output files. The filter reads the input, applies some processing (such processing modified by the options specified on the command line), and writes an output file.

Filters typically don't access the mouse, and in fact, rarely accept user input. If they *do* accept user input, it's through a very simple text-oriented interface. Output to the user is normally limited to status reports ("Working, please wait..."), error notifications, and a final "done" message.

In this chapter, we're going to build a relatively simple filter program with Delphi, and construct a filter program "shell" that you can use to quickly build other filter programs. Along the way, we'll learn a thing or two about Delphi's Object Repository, reusable code, and (shudder) *process-oriented* programming.

> *Note: I find it ironic that three years ago I was explaining Windows programming to DOS programmers, telling them how to move away from their process-oriented mindset and move into the wide world of event-driven*

Windows programming. With the advent of visual development tools like Visual Basic and Delphi, many new programmers started with event-oriented programming and haven't ever written a process-oriented command-line tool. Now I'm explaining process-oriented programming to event-oriented programmers. Plus ça change. *One good thing, though: Programmers who understand event-oriented programming have little trouble understanding process-oriented code. The reverse, sadly, is not true.*

Console Applications And Delphi

Although it's possible to write console applications with Delphi, the documentation suspiciously is silent on exactly how such a thing is done. Considering the excellent demo programs that explore so many other facets of Delphi, I found the lack of an example console application surprising. Fortunately, creating a console application with Delphi is not very difficult, although it would have been nice to be informed about a couple of the details. (Trial and error is *such* an inefficient way to learn!)

The simplest console app is, of course, the "Hello world" program. It's not an exciting program, but it's usually the first program I ever write with a new tool because it lets me learn about the tool without having to worry too much about the program itself. And once we've created a simple console app with Delphi, we can save the code in the Object Repository so it can be used as the starting point for other console apps.

Hello, Delphi

Start with a new application (File|New Application). First we need to change some of the project options to tell Delphi that we're creating a console app. Select Project|Options, and on the Linker page of the Project Options dialog box, click on the "Generate console application" check box, and then click on OK to save this change.

Since console applications don't have a main form (or any other form for that matter), we need to remove the Form1 that is automatically created when you start a new application. Select File|Remove From Project, and when the Remove From Project dialog box appears, highlight the line that contains Unit1 and Form1, and click on the OK button. If a message box appears and asks you if you want to save changes to Unit1, say No. You'll be left with a Delphi screen that has only the Object Inspector. No Form or Unit window will be shown. So where do you write the code?

The one thing that's left is the project source file. Select View|Project Source, and Delphi will display a text editor window that contains the source of PROJECT1.DPR. It's this file that we're going to modify in order to create our first console application. Before you do anything else, select File|Save, and save the project as HELLO.DPR.

Modify the project source in the editor so that it resembles Listing 1.1, save your work, and then press F9 to compile and run the program.

Listing 1.1 The "Hello, Delphi" program.

```
{
  HELLO.DPR — Simple Delphi console application

  Author: Jim Mischel
  Last Update: 05/04/97
}
{$APPTYPE CONSOLE}
program Hello;

uses Windows;

begin
  WriteLn ('Hello, Delphi');
  Write ('Press Enter...');
  ReadLn;
end.
```

The first line in Listing 1.1 is a compiler directive that tells Delphi to create a console application, and *must* be included at the top of any console application. This line should be included *only* in programs—not units or Dynamic Link Libraries (DLLs). The **uses** statement isn't necessary for the program (after all, the program isn't making any Windows API calls), but for some reason, Delphi doesn't like to save a project that doesn't have a **uses** statement (see again my comment about trial-and-error learning). Windows seemed like a fairly innocuous unit to list here, and listing a unit doesn't mean that it's linked in—only that Delphi will search that unit if it can't find an identifier in the current unit.

The rest of the program is real simple. The string "Hello, Delphi" is output to the console (that is, the screen), and then you're prompted to press Enter. I included a prompt for the Enter key because, without it, Delphi just displays a console window (DOS box) briefly, runs the program and displays the hello message, and then closes the console window. The prompt lets you see that the program actually works.

Saving A Program Template

The steps required to build a console app aren't especially difficult, but there are a few details to remember. Rather than building from scratch every time (and forgetting a detail or two), let's save our little Hello program in the Object Repository so that we'll have a starting point for other console apps.

Using the Windows Exploder (what we called File Mangler under Windows NT 3.51), create a subdirectory called ConsoleApp in Delphi's Objrepos subdirectory. If you installed Delphi using the standard options, the full path name will be:

```
C:\Program Files\Borland\Delphi 3\Objrepos\ConsoleApp
```

Then, select Project|Save Project As from Delphi's main menu, and save the project as ConsoleApp.dpr (don't you just *love* long file names?) in that new directory.

Once you've saved the project, add it to the repository by selecting Project|Add to Repository, and fill in the Add to Repository dialog box as shown in Figure 1.1.

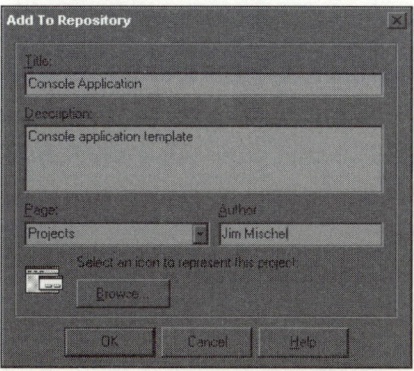

Figure 1.1
Adding the console application template to the repository.

Once you've added the project to the Repository, select File|New from Delphi's main menu, select the Projects page of the New Items dialog box, and double-click on the "Console Application" icon. Delphi will prompt you for a directory and create a new project that has the options set for the console application.

> **Note**: I haven't quite decided if it's a good idea to store your own objects in Delphi's Object Repository directory. Whereas it's a handy place to put things, it's also asking for trouble if you ever upgrade your version of Delphi. If you upgrade, it's quite likely that Delphi's Objrepos directory will be deleted—along with all of your cool objects. You'll have to back up your objects before you upgrade.
>
> You can, if you'd rather, create your own Repository directory that's not a child of Delphi's main directory. Either way, you'll have to again add the projects to Delphi's repository after you upgrade, but with a separate directory you won't run the risk of inadvertently deleting your projects' source code.

Console Input And Output

When a console application is started, the **Input** and **Output** standard text files are automatically associated with the console window. As a result, the **ReadLn** and **WriteLn** procedures work as expected, as do **Eof**, **Eoln**, **Read**, **Write**, and the other text file I/O functions.

There are a number of console-specific I/O functions that can come in handy from time to time. Unfortunately, these console-specific functions are defined in the Windows console interface and there's no convenient Delphi component wrapper to insulate us from the gory details. (Now there's a good shareware project for an enterprising programmer: a Delphi class that encapsulates the Windows console interface.) The Windows console interface is a chapter in itself, so I'm conveniently going to ignore it here. If you're interested in learning more about **PeekConsoleInput**, **WriteConsole**, and the rest of the console API functions, check out the "Console Reference" entry in the WIN32.HLP file that's in Delphi's Help directory. The install program doesn't make a shortcut to this file, so you'll have to locate and load it yourself.

Because we don't have space here to discuss the Console API, we're going to limit our console input and output to the standard text file I/O routines. Don't take this the wrong way. The Console API functions are useful for some applications—just not for the kinds of applications that you'll typically write as console apps. Yeah, I know, it's confusing. It turns out that the Console API is much more useful for GUI programs that want to control a console window than it is for straight console applications controlling themselves.

Console apps aren't limited to a boring old text mode interface. Since you've got access to the full Windows API, you can display message and dialog boxes, control other windows, and even create another console from within your application.

Filter Programs In Delphi

Now that we know how to create a console application, let's put that knowledge to use. The rest of this chapter is concerned with writing filter programs as console apps. After an overview of how filter programs work, we're going to discuss processing the command-line and efficient file operations. We'll be cutting a wide swath through Delphi's standard runtime library, and won't have time to discuss every function in detail. Remember that online help is your friend—use it early and often.

Your Basic Filter Program

As I mentioned at the beginning of this chapter, filter programs typically accept a command line that specifies options and input/output file names, crunch the input as specified by the options, and produce the output file.

Given that general description, there's *lots* of room for improvisation. A line counter program, for example, could accept multiple input file names (including wildcards), and could have options that tell it to report not only the number of text lines in a file, but also the number of words and characters, and possibly a frequency distribution of words and characters. In a more involved program, the output can be a simple transformation of a single input file, a single file that combines multiple input files, or many different files created from a single input file.

Despite the differences in complexity, filters share a large amount of common functionality. They all process the command line, read-input files, and write-output files. Only the intermediate processing step changes significantly from one program to another. Because of this commonality, it's possible to build a group of functions that provides the common functionality and allows you to quickly build a custom filter program by simply defining how the command line is to be parsed and writing the code for the "processing" step. The input, output, and command-line parsing portions are all there. Kind of a dehydrated filter program—just add processing.

Processing The Command Line

Command-line processing sounds so simple. Given a text string that represents the command line, we want to parse out the file names and options, and set the program's variables accordingly. I'm continually amazed at how *difficult* such a simple-sounding thing can be. Fortunately, Object Pascal has two standard functions, **ParamCount** and **ParamStr**, that make things a bit easier.

ParamCount simply returns a count of the parameters on the command line. So if your command line is "MyFilter file1.txt file2.txt", **ParamCount** will return 2. The program name itself isn't counted as a parameter by this function.

ParamStr accepts an integer and returns a string that contains the command-line argument that corresponds to that integer. For example, given the above command line, this statement

```
WriteLn (ParamStr (1));
```

will output "file1.txt" (without the quotes).

If you pass 0 to **ParamStr**, the returned string will contain the full path and file name of the program that's currently being executed.

The Params program shown in Listing 1.2 illustrates the use of **ParamCount** and **ParamStr**. To create this program, select File|New from Delphi's main menu, select the Console Application item from the Projects page of the New Items dialog box, and then tell Delphi where to put your new application. Be sure to save the project as Params.dpr before you modify it.

Listing 1.2 The Params program.

```
{
  PARAMS.DPR—a simple exploration of the ParamCount and
  ParamStr functions

  Author:  Jim Mischel
  Last Update:  05/04/97
}
{$APPTYPE CONSOLE}
program Params;

uses Windows;

Var
  i : Integer;

begin
  WriteLn ('Program:  ', ParamStr (0));
  WriteLn ('ParamCount = ', ParamCount);
  WriteLn ('Parameters');
  WriteLn ('———');

  for i := 1 to ParamCount do
  begin
    WriteLn (ParamStr (i));
  end;

  Write ('Press Enter...');
  ReadLn;
end.
```

If you want to test the program from within Delphi, you need to select Run|Parameters from Delphi's main menu and enter the command line that you want to have passed to the program. For the above example, you'd enter the string "file1.txt file2.txt" (without the quotes) in the Run parameters dialog box.

Simple, no? Unfortunately, not so simple. Back in the days of DOS and Windows 3.1, things really *were* simple. But then along came long file names with embedded spaces. Now we have a problem. You see, **ParamCount** and **ParamStr** assume that command line arguments are separated by spaces. This works fine as long as your files don't have embedded spaces, but try this command line:

```
params c:\program files\borland\delphi 3\readme.txt
```

ParamCount returns 3, and the individual parameters it reports are

```
c:\program
files\borland\delphi
3\readme.txt
```

which is clearly *not* what we intended! (Okay, so maybe long file names aren't all peaches and cream—beer and skittles if you're British. *Warm* beer.)

I won't go into all the possible solutions to this problem. If you want a full discussion of this problem and the possible solutions (none of which are satisfactory, by the way—thank you Microsoft), get a copy of Lou Grinzo's *Zen of Windows 95 Programming*, also published by Coriolis Group Books. The book is ostensibly about C and C++ programming for Windows 95, but there's a wealth of good information in there for all programmers, especially in the way of writing bug-free programs. This book is among the top three programming books I've ever read, along with *Writing Solid Code* and *Debugging the Development Process*, both written by Steve Maguire and published by Microsoft Press.

The only *workable* (although not satisfactory) solution to the embedded spaces problem is to require that file names containing embedded spaces be surrounded by quotation marks. So our sample command line becomes:

```
params "c:\program files\borland\delphi 3\readme.txt"
```

I guess you could require that your users always pass the short version of the file name, but I suspect they'd be more upset having to enter this

```
params c:\progra~1\borland\delphi~1\readme.txt
```

than they would be about the quotation marks.

Command-Line Options

Most (definitely not all) command-line programs get their parameters via the command line. Sometimes you'll see programs that receive their parameters from environment variables or configuration files, and some are hybrids that can accept parameters from the command line or from a configuration file whose name is specified on the command line. Since we don't want to get too bogged down in parameter processing, we're going to ignore the configuration files and environment variables, and concentrate solely on command line parameters.

You've probably used a command-line tool (like DIR) that accepts options prefaced by a slash (/). For example, if you want a listing of files in the current directory and all of its subdirectories, you'd enter the command: DIR /S. Many programs also accept command line parameters prefaced by the dash (or minus sign, -). Both are common, and many programs will accept either.

File names, on the other hand, are specified in many different ways, depending on the tool. COPY, for example, lets you specify the name of the input and output files without prefacing them with option characters. So COPY FILE1 FILE2 copies FILE1 to FILE2. Borland's MAKE program, on the other hand, requires that you preface the input file name with the -f parameter. So, to process BUILD.MAK, you'd enter this command: MAKE -fbuild.mak.

The way MAKE processes command lines is easier, because *everything* is an option. Every option is separated from the others by at least one space, and file names are handled just like other options—there aren't any special cases. This is the model we're going to use for our filter programs.

In general, there are four kinds of command-line options: switches, numbers, strings, and file names. Switches simply turn an option on or off. A text filter, for example, might have a switch option to convert all lower case characters to upper case. Numbers can be integers or floating point, and can be specified in any number of ways, decimal and hexadecimal being the most common. Strings and file names are similar, although file names often are validated to ensure that they're properly formed.

A Reusable Command-Line Parser

If there's anything I dislike about programming, it's slogging through dozens (or hundreds) of lines of code to do something for the tenth (or hundredth) time. Command-line parsing is like that: Every filter program has to process the command line, and command-line parsing is *boring* code after you've written it once or twice. So I keep trying to come up with a generalized command-line parser that will, with a minimum of effort on my part, parse a command line and fill in my program's options structure. That way, I'll have more time to spend on the filter (the real problem, after all) rather than on the command-line parser.

A generalized command-line parser is not an easy piece of code to write, and even a minimal one can be a bit involved. The one we'll develop here is minimal, but functional for many applications.

The basic idea is to define the valid option characters, the type of each option, and the default value for each option. The structure that contains this information is passed to the command-line parser, which chews up the command line and fills in the values for the individual options that it finds. If it finds an error (an invalid option or a number where it expected a switch), it spits out an error message, stops processing, and returns an error status to the calling function. Simple, right? Ahhh...but not so easy.

An individual options record takes the format of the **OptionsRec** structure shown in Listing 1.3. This listing contains the full source of the CmdLine unit. You should create a new file in your editor, and enter and save this code as CMDLINE.PAS.

Listing 1.3   The CmdLine unit.

```
{
  CMDLINE.PAS–Command line parameters parsing

  Author: Jim Mischel
  Last Update:  05/04/97
}
unit cmdline;

interface

type
  OptionType = (otBool, otInt, otString, otFilename);

  pOptionRec = ^OptionRec;
  OptionRec = record
    OptionChar : char;
    case Option : OptionType of
      otBool : (OnOff : Boolean);
      otInt : (Value : Integer);
      otString : (Param : ShortString);
      otFilename : (Filename : ShortString);
  end;

  pOptionsArray = ^OptionsArray;
  OptionsArray = Array [1..1] of OptionRec;
```

```
{
  GetOptionRec—return a pointer to the options record in the
  passed Options array that corresponds to the specified option
  character.  Returns Nil if the option character is not in
  the passed Options array.
}
function GetOptionRec
     (
       Options : pOptionsArray;
       nOptions : Integer;
       OptionChar : char
     ) : pOptionRec;

{
  ProcessCommandLine—process the command line according to the
  parameters list passed in the Options array.  Returns True if
  successful, or False if an error occurred in processing.
}
function ProcessCommandLine
     (
       Options : pOptionsArray;
       nOptions : Integer
     ) : Boolean;

implementation

uses SysUtils;

{
  GetOptionRec—return a pointer to the options record in the
  passed Options array that corresponds to the specified option
  character.  Returns Nil if the option character is not in
  the passed Options array.
}
function GetOptionRec
     (
       Options : pOptionsArray;
       nOptions : Integer;
       OptionChar : char
     ) : pOptionRec;
var
  i : Integer;
begin
  Result := Nil;
  for i := 1 to nOptions do begin
```

```
      if (Options^[i].OptionChar = OptionChar) then begin
        Result := @Options^[i].OptionChar;
        Break;
      end;
    end;
end;

{
  ProcessBool

  Extract the on/off state for a parameter.  If the passed Param
  is a blank string, it is assumed to be On (+).  Otherwise the
  routine expects the string to start with + or -, and sets the
  OnOff variable accordingly.
}
function ProcessBool
      (
        Param : String;
        var OnOff : Boolean
      ) : Boolean;
begin
  Result := True;

  if (Length (Param) = 0) then begin
    OnOff := True;
    Exit;
  end;

  case Param[1] of
    '+' : OnOff := True;
    '-' : OnOff := False;

    else begin
      WriteLn ('Error:  + or - expected');
      Result := False;
    end;
  end;

end;

{
  ProcessInt

  Extract an integer from the passed command line parameter.
}
```

```pascal
function ProcessInt
      (
         Param : String;
         var Value : Integer
      ) : Boolean;
begin
  if (Length (Param) = 0) then begin
    Result := False;
    WriteLn ('Error:  integer expected');
    Exit;
  end;

  Result := True;
  try
    Value := StrToInt (Param);
  except
    WriteLn ('Error:  integer expected');
    Result := False;
  end;
end;

{
  ProcessString

  Copy the passed string to the Option variable.  No error checking
  is performed, and a blank string is considered a valid parameter.
}
function ProcessString
      (
         Param : String;
         var Option : ShortString
      ) : Boolean;
begin
  Option := Param;
  Result := True;
end;

{
  ProcessFilename

  Extract a file name from the passed command-line parameter.
  Currently, this function just calls ProcessString to copy the
  string parameter to the Filename.  It could, in the future,
  check to see if the string represents a valid file name, or it
  could be used to expand a short filename to a full path/file.
}
```

```
function ProcessFilename
      (
        Param : String;
        var Filename : ShortString
      ) : Boolean;
begin
  Result := ProcessString (Param, Filename);
end;

{
  CheckParam

  Check the passed Param, representing one command-line argument, against
  the list of options.  If the option character is valid, then process
  the option based on its type (Boolean, Integer, String, or Filename).

  Returns True if option processed and stored correctly, False otherwise.
}
function CheckParam
      (
        Param : String;
        Options : pOptionsArray;
        nOptions : Integer
      ) : Boolean;
var
  Rec : pOptionRec;
  Option : String;
begin
  Result := False;
  if (Param[1] in ['-', '/']) then begin
    if (Length (Param) < 2) then begin
      WriteLn ('Invalid option');
    end
    else begin
      Rec := GetOptionRec (Options, nOptions, Param[2]);
      if (Rec <> Nil) then begin
        Option := Copy (Param, 3, Length (Param) - 2);
        case Rec^.Option of
          otBool :
            Result := ProcessBool (Option, Rec.OnOff);
          otInt :
            Result := ProcessInt (Option, Rec^.Value);
          otString :
            Result := ProcessString (Option, Rec^.Param);
          otFilename :
```

```
              Result := ProcessFilename (Option, Rec^.Filename);
            else
              WriteLn ('Invalid option specification: ', Param[2]);
          end;
        end
        else begin
          WriteLn ('Invalid option character: ', Param[2]);
        end;
      end;
    end
    else begin
      WriteLn ('Error: options must start with - or /');
    end;
end;

{
  ProcessCommandLine

  Given a list of option characters and parameter types, check each
  command-line argument against the list and set the values in the
  options structure accordingly.

  Returns True if all parameters processed and stored successfully.
}
function ProcessCommandLine
        (
          Options : pOptionsArray;
          nOptions : Integer
        ) : Boolean;

var
  ParamNo : Integer;

begin
  Result := True;

  for ParamNo := 1 to ParamCount do begin
    if (Not CheckParam (ParamStr (ParamNo), Options, nOptions)) then
begin
      Result := False;
      Exit;
    end;
  end;
end;

end.
```

OptionType is an enumerated type that describes the kinds of options that **ProcessCommandLine** knows about. The **OptionRec** record has three fields: the option character, the option type, and a variant portion that has a field that will hold the value for the particular option type. (If you're not familiar with variant records, take a peek at the help topic that discusses record types, or pick up a Pascal primer at your local bookstore.)

The **OptionRec** record, as coded, is a pretty inefficient way to solve this problem because each record, regardless of the type of option, occupies the maximum possible size. A **ShortString** type takes 256 bytes, which means that most of the records are much larger than they need to be. There are several ways around this, probably the most straightforward being to use *pointers* to strings, rather than strings themselves, for string and file name types. I choose not to implement that here because of the extra coding involved.

The other problem with this implementation also has to do with the **ShortString** type. The longest possible string that can be stored in a **ShortString** is 255 characters, which is shorter than the maximum path length Windows will accept (260 bytes). I had hoped to use Delphi's **AnsiString** (i.e., "long string") type for this reason, but long string types can't be stored in the variant portion of a record. Again, the most obvious solution would be to use string pointers.

Even with those problems, CmdLine is quite useful. The extra memory required shouldn't be a problem because most programs have only a handful of options, and there's no silly 64K limit on the size of static data anymore. (It's a wide 32-bit world out there!) The file name length limitation is a bit of a bother, but I don't know too many people (like, none) who're going to be typing 256-character path names into a command-line tool.

The CmdLine unit makes two functions available to calling programs: **GetOptionRec** and **ProcessCommandLine**. **GetOptionRec** will return a pointer to the record that corresponds to the specified option character. If no record exists for that option, then **GetOptionRec** returns **Nil**. **ProcessCommandLine** is the real workhorse. You pass it an array of **OptionRec** structures, and it parses the command line, filling in the value fields for the individual options. If **ProcessCommandLine** processes all of the command-line arguments without encountering an error, it returns **True**. If it encounters an error at any point, it immediately stops processing the command line, displays an error message, and returns **False** to the calling program.

Testing The CmdLine Unit

In order to test the command-line parsing functions, we need a test program. Start a new application using the Console Application template. Save the new project as FILTER.DPR, and copy CMDLINE.PAS (Listing 1.3) to the directory that contains the new project. Then, select File|Add to Project to add the CmdLine unit to your new project.

The Filter project will be the testbed for the CmdLine unit and the file I/O unit that we'll be working on next. When we're done with those units, we're going to save the entire thing in the repository so that we have a template for other filter programs.

To test CmdLine, we need an array of options structures and some code that will call **ProcessCommandLine**. The test program, which you should enter into FILTER.DPR, is shown in Listing 1.4.

Listing 1.4 Testing the CmdLine unit with FILTER.DPR.

```
{
  FILTER.DPR—Filter main program

  Author: Jim Mischel
  Last Update: 05/04/97
}
{$APPTYPE CONSOLE}
program filter;

uses Windows, CmdLine;

const
  nOptions = 4;

  Options : Array [1..nOptions] of OptionRec = (
    (OptionChar : 'i'; Option : otFilename; Filename : ''),
    (OptionChar : 'o'; Option : otFilename; Filename : ''),
    (OptionChar : 'n'; Option : otInt; Value : 36),
    (OptionChar : 'd'; Option : otBool; OnOff : False)
  );

var
  cRslt : Boolean;
  Rec : pOptionRec;
```

```
begin
  cRslt := CmdLine.ProcessCommandLine (@Options, nOptions);
  WriteLn ('ProcessCommandLine returned ', cRslt);

  Rec := CmdLine.GetOptionRec (@Options, nOptions, 'i');
  WriteLn ('i = ', Rec^.Filename);
  Rec := CmdLine.GetOptionRec (@Options, nOptions, 'o');
  WriteLn ('o = ', Rec^.Filename);
  Rec := CmdLine.GetOptionRec (@Options, nOptions, 'n');
  WriteLn ('n = ', Rec^.Value);
  Rec := CmdLine.GetOptionRec (@Options, nOptions, 'd');
  WriteLn ('d = ', Rec^.OnOff);

  Write ('Press Enter...');
  ReadLn;
end.
```

The options table is initialized in the **const** section of the program, and then **ProcessCommandLine** is called to read the command-line arguments and store the options' values in the options table. The program then displays the return result of **ProcessCommandLine**, and also displays the value of each option.

Try this program with a bunch of different command lines. Be sure to try some invalid command lines along with the valid ones, just to make sure that the error handling is working properly. Here are some suggested test cases:

```
-iInFile.txt -oOutFile.txt -n995 -d{valid}
-n8.94   {Error: integer expected}
-x       {Invalid option character: x}
```

The generalized command-line parser provided in CmdLine makes picking out program options very easy. Just fill in a table, pass it to **ProcessCommandLine**, and it's done for you. All you have to do is ensure that any required options are specified, and set your program's internal variables according to the options that the user specified. Believe me, it's *much* easier than writing a custom command-line parser for every different program.

A Note On Program Structure

Before we start writing more involved programs, let's move the processing code from the project (DPR) file to a separate unit. I've found that it's best to keep my own handwritten code out of the project file and in separate units, for several reasons.

For me, the most important point is that Delphi modifies the project file from time to time. I *think* it's only when you change the project name or add a new unit to the project, but I'm not sure. I don't know what Delphi is capable of changing, I haven't seen it fully documented anywhere, and I'd sure be upset if it changed something that I thought was constant. On the flip side, I might inadvertently change something that Delphi put there for a reason. This in itself is reason enough for me. Delphi rarely touches nonform units (to my knowledge, only when you select File|Save As to change the unit name), so I feel safer with my code in separate units.

Another reason is that the project file is difficult to debug. For some reason, I had trouble setting breakpoints and single-stepping through code that was in the DPR file.

Finally, the project file is just that—a project file. From the structure of the example programs and the way that Delphi creates projects, I get the impression that the DPR file was never meant to contain large amounts of executable code. The project file gathers the project's units together for the project manager and at runtime automatically creates specific forms, and then runs the application. Seems to me that we should use the product in the way that it was intended.

So let's split out the processing code and make FILTER.DPR essentially a one-liner. Listing 1.5 is the new FILTER.DPR, and Listing 1.6 contains FILTMAIN.PAS—the module that now contains all of the processing code.

Listing 1.5 The new Filter project file.

```
{
  FILTER.DPR-Filter main program

  Author: Jim Mischel
  Last Update: 05/04/97
}
{$APPTYPE CONSOLE}
program filter;
```

```pascal
uses
  cmdline in 'cmdline.pas',
  filtmain in 'filtmain.pas';

begin
  DoFilter;
end.
```

Listing 1.6 FILTMAIN: the Filter program's processing module.

```pascal
{
  FILTMAIN.PAS—main processing module for Filter program.

  Author:  Jim Mischel
  Last Update:  05/04/97
}
unit filtmain;

interface

{ DoFilter does all the processing }
procedure DoFilter;

implementation

uses CmdLine;

procedure DoFilter;
const
  nOptions = 4;

  Options : Array [1..nOptions] of OptionRec = (
    (OptionChar : 'i'; Option : otFilename; Filename : ''),
    (OptionChar : 'o'; Option : otFilename; Filename : ''),
    (OptionChar : 'n'; Option : otInt; Value : 36),
    (OptionChar : 'd'; Option : otBool; OnOff : False)
  );

var
  cRslt : Boolean;
  Rec : pOptionRec;

begin
  cRslt := CmdLine.ProcessCommandLine (@Options, nOptions);
  WriteLn ('ProcessCommandLine returned ', cRslt);
```

```
    Rec := CmdLine.GetOptionRec (@Options, nOptions, 'i');
    WriteLn ('i = ', Rec^.Filename);
    Rec := CmdLine.GetOptionRec (@Options, nOptions, 'o');
    WriteLn ('o = ', Rec^.Filename);
    Rec := CmdLine.GetOptionRec (@Options, nOptions, 'n');
    WriteLn ('n = ', Rec^.Value);
    Rec := CmdLine.GetOptionRec (@Options, nOptions, 'd');
    WriteLn ('d = ', Rec^.OnOff);

    Write ('Press Enter...');
    ReadLn;
  end;

end.
```

Now the project file contains just what it's supposed to contain—project build information and a "go" command. All of the programmer-written code is in FILTMAIN.PAS.

Reading And Writing Files

Once you've got command-line parsing out of the way, the next big hurdle in a filter program is file I/O. Of course, if you're doing a simple character-by-character (or line-by-line) translation of a text file, you can use **Read** and **Write** (or **ReadLn** and **WriteLn**) in conjunction with **Eof** and **Eoln** to process your file. For example, the **DoFilter** procedure shown in Listing 1.7 copies characters from input to output, translating the lowercase characters to uppercase along the way.

Listing 1.7   Translating characters from uppercase to lowercase.

```
procedure DoFilter;

const
  nOptions = 2;

  Options : Array [1..nOptions] of OptionRec = (
    (OptionChar : 'i'; Option : otFilename; Filename : ''),
    (OptionChar : 'o'; Option : otFilename; Filename : '')
  );

var
  cRslt : Boolean;
  iRec : pOptionRec;
```

```
    oRec : pOptionRec;
    InputFile : Text;
    OutputFile : Text;
    c : char;
begin
    cRslt := CmdLine.ProcessCommandLine (@Options, nOptions);
    if (not cRslt) then
       Halt;

    { make sure input and output files were specified }
    iRec := CmdLine.GetOptionRec (@Options, nOptions, 'i');
    if (iRec^.Filename = '') then begin
       WriteLn ('Error: input file expected');
       Halt;
    end;

    oRec := CmdLine.GetOptionRec (@Options, nOptions, 'o');
    if (oRec^.Filename = '') then begin
       WriteLn ('Error: output file expected');
       Halt;
    end;

    { open input file—no error checking }
    Assign (InputFile, iRec^.Filename);
    Reset (InputFile);

    { create output file—no error checking }
    Assign (OutputFile, oRec^.Filename);
    Rewrite (OutputFile);

    { Read and translate each character }
    while (not Eof (InputFile)) do begin
       Read (InputFile, c);
       c := UpCase (c);
       Write (OutputFile, c);
    end;

    Close (InputFile);
    Close (OutputFile);
end;
```

There are two problems with this version of FILTER. First, it's slow—kinda like a snake crawling out of a refrigerator. If you've got a megabyte-sized text file somewhere and a few minutes to spare, try it. The other problem is that the program only works on text files. That's fine for a one-shot filter application, but we're writing a filter template that's going to be used by many different types of programs, some of which will have to work with nontext files, and they'll all benefit from a speed improvement. What we need is a more general and much faster way to read characters (or bytes) from the file. We have to do our own buffering, which adds some complexity, but the results are well worth the effort.

The **TFilterFile** class shown in Listing 1.8 is designed to give filter programs quick byte-by-byte access to files. It encapsulates all of the buffering and, as much as possible, relieves the programmer from having to remember the mundane details of file handling (although you do still have to **Open** and **Close** your files).

Listing 1.8 The TFilterFile class implemented in FILEIO.PAS.

```
{
  FILEIO.PAS—File input and output for filter programs

  Author:  Jim Mischel
  Last Update:  05/04/97
}
{$I+}  { use exceptions for error handling }
unit fileio;

interface

type
  FileIOMode = (fioNotOpen, fioRead, fioWrite);

  BuffArray = array[0..1] of byte;
  pBuffArray = ^BuffArray;

  TFilterFile = class (TObject)
  private
    FFilename : String;
    F : File;
    FBufferSize : Integer;
    FBuffer : pBuffArray;

    FBytesInBuff : Integer;
    FBuffIndx : Integer;
    FFileMode : FileIOMode;

    function ReadBuffer : boolean;
    function WriteBuffer : boolean;
```

```
    public
      constructor Create (AName : String; ABufSize : Integer);
      destructor Destroy; override;

      function Open (AMode : FileIOMode) : Boolean;
      procedure Close;

      function Eof : Boolean;

      function GetByte : byte;
      function PutByte (b : byte) : boolean;
    end;

implementation

{ TFilterFile }

{ Create—sets up but doesn't actually open the file }
constructor TFilterFile.Create
     (
        AName : String;
        ABufSize : Integer
     );

begin
  inherited Create;
  FFilename := AName;
  FBufferSize := ABufSize;
  FBytesInBuff := 0;
  FBuffIndx := 0;
  FFileMode := fioNotOpen;

  { Assign but don't open }
  Assign (F, FFilename);
  { allocate memory for buffer }
  GetMem (FBuffer, FBufferSize);
end;

{ Destroy—closes the file (if open) and destroys the object }
destructor TFilterFile.Destroy;
begin
  { if the file's open, close it }
  if (FFileMode <> fioNotOpen) then begin
    Self.Close;
  end;
```

```pascal
  { if the buffer's been allocated, free it }
  if (FBuffer <> Nil) then begin
    FreeMem (FBuffer, FBufferSize);
    FBuffer := Nil;
  end;

  inherited Destroy;
end;

{ Open—open the file in the proper mode }
function TFilterFile.Open
      (
        AMode : FileIOMode
      ) : Boolean;
var
  SaveFileMode : Byte;
begin
  Result := True;
  SaveFileMode := FileMode;   { FileMode defined in system unit }

  { try to open the file }
  try
    case AMode of
      fioRead : begin
        FileMode := 0;
        Reset (F, 1);
      end;

      fioWrite : begin
        FileMode := 1;
        Rewrite (F, 1);
      end;
    end;
    FFileMode := AMode;
  except
    Result := False;
  end;

  FBytesInBuff := 0;
  FBuffIndx := 0;

  FileMode := SaveFileMode;
end;

{ Close—close the file, flushing the buffer if needed }
procedure TFilterFile.Close;
```

```
begin
  { if the write buffer has stuff in it, write it out }
  if ((FFileMode = fioWrite) and
      (FBytesInBuff > 0)) then begin
    WriteBuffer;
  end;

  try
    { close the file }
    System.Close (F);
  finally
    FFileMode := fioNotOpen;
  end;
end;

{ ReadBuffer—read a block from the file into the buffer }
function TFilterFile.ReadBuffer : Boolean;
begin
  Result := True;

  if (Self.Eof) then begin
    Result := False;
  end
  else begin
    try
      BlockRead (F, FBuffer^, FBufferSize, FBytesInBuff);
    except
      Result := False;
    end;
  end;

end;

{ GetByte—return next byte in file.  Read buffer if necessary }
function TFilterFile.GetByte : byte;
begin
  if (FBuffIndx >= FBytesInBuff) then begin
    if (not ReadBuffer) then begin
      Result := 0;
      Exit;
    end
    else begin
      FBuffIndx := 0;
    end;
  end;
```

```pascal
    Result := FBuffer^[FBuffIndx];
    Inc (FBuffIndx);
end;

{ WriteBuffer—write block from buffer to file }
function TFilterFile.WriteBuffer : Boolean;
begin
  Result := True;
  try
    BlockWrite (F, FBuffer^, FBytesInBuff);
  except
    Result := False;
  end;
  if (Result = True) then begin
    FBytesInBuff := 0;
  end;
end;

{ PutByte—put byte into buffer.  Write to file if necessary }
function TFilterFile.PutByte (b : byte) : Boolean;
begin
  if (FBytesInBuff = FBufferSize) then begin
    if (not WriteBuffer) then begin
      Result := False;
      Exit;
    end
    else begin
      FBytesInBuff := 0;
    end;
  end;

  FBuffer^[FBytesInBuff] := b;
  Inc (FBytesInBuff);
  Result := True;
end;

{ Eof—return True if at end of input file }
function TFilterFile.Eof : Boolean;
begin
  Result := (FBuffIndx >= FBytesInBuff);
  if Result then begin
    try
      Result := System.Eof (F);
```

```
    except
      Result := True;
    end;
  end;
end;
```

end.

Because **TFilterFile** handles most of the details, using it in place of standard text file I/O is very simple. The performance, though, isn't similar at all. The new **DoFilter** procedure shown in Listing 1.9 uses **TFilterFile** for input and output. The resulting program is *much* faster than the original. The beauty is that the program isn't any harder to read or understand than the slower version.

Listing 1.9 Using TFilterFile in place of standard I/O.

```
{
  FILTMAIN.PAS—main processing module for Filter program.

  Author:  Jim Mischel
  Last Update:   05/04/97
}
unit filtmain;

interface

{ DoFilter does all the processing }
procedure DoFilter;

implementation

uses CmdLine, FileIO;

procedure DoFilter;

const
  nOptions = 2;

  Options : Array [1..nOptions] of OptionRec = (
    (OptionChar : 'i'; Option : otFilename; Filename : ''),
    (OptionChar : 'o'; Option : otFilename; Filename : '')
  );

  BigBufferSize = 65536;
```

```
var
  cRslt : Boolean;
  iRec : pOptionRec;
  oRec : pOptionRec;
  InputFile : TFilterFile;
  OutputFile : TFilterFile;
  c : char;

begin
  cRslt := CmdLine.ProcessCommandLine (@Options, nOptions);
  if (not cRslt) then
    Halt;

  { make sure input and output files were specified }
  iRec := CmdLine.GetOptionRec (@Options, nOptions, 'i');
  if (iRec^.Filename = '') then begin
    WriteLn ('Error: input file expected');
    Halt;
  end;

  oRec := CmdLine.GetOptionRec (@Options, nOptions, 'o');
  if (oRec^.Filename = '') then begin
    WriteLn ('Error: output file expected');
    Halt;
  end;

  { Create and open the input file }
  InputFile := TFilterFile.Create (iRec.Filename, BigBufferSize);
  if (not InputFile.Open (fioRead)) then begin
    WriteLn ('Error opening input file');
    Halt;
  end;

  { Create and open the output file }
  OutputFile := TFilterFile.Create (oRec.Filename, BigBufferSize);
  if (not OutputFile.Open (fioWrite)) then begin
    WriteLn ('Error opening output file');
    Halt;
  end;

  { process and each character }
  while (not InputFile.Eof) do begin
    c := char (InputFile.GetByte);
    c := UpCase (c);
```

```
      if (not OutputFile.PutByte (byte (c))) then begin
        WriteLn ('Write error');
        Halt;
      end;
   end;

   InputFile.Close;
   InputFile.Free;

   OutputFile.Close;
   OutputFile.Free;
end;

end.
```

Using The Filter Template

If you want to add the filter to the Repository, create a new directory under the ObjRepos directory, and save FILTER.DPR, FILTMAIN.PAS, CMDLINE.PAS, and FILEIO.PAS in that directory. Then just select Project|Add to Repository, and fill in the prompts. Next time you have to write a filter, all the tedious stuff is done. Just grab the template, fix up the options, and change the processing loop.

A Critique

Have you ever had the urge, after you've finished a project, to turn around and do it right? Not that there's anything *wrong* with this filter template, but now that it's finished, I look back and see where I could have done things differently.

In all, I'm pretty happy with the way it turned out, and I've used it to create some very useful programs, ranging in complexity from the one-shot quickie to a very useful stream editor.

The command-line parsing is restrictive in its format because all parameters *must* be option-based, and it doesn't allow response (or configuration) files. Requiring options for all parameters isn't too much of a hassle, and it makes the code a lot easier. Adding support for response files would be very useful, and with the current design, shouldn't be terribly difficult. The only other thing I'd change (and mostly from a cosmetic point of view) is the use of **ShortString** in string and file name parameter types. **PString** or maybe **PChar** would be a more efficient choice.

TFilterFile is another story. This class implements the bare minimum required for filter I/O. You probably noticed that it doesn't have a block read or write mechanism, and it doesn't allow random file I/O. Many filter programs require one or both of those features. Block operations are fairly simple to add using an untyped **var** parameter and a byte count, in much the same way that the standard **BlockRead** and **BlockWrite** procedures work. These procedures would have to block copy bytes between the user's data structure and the object's buffer, and be sure to handle reading from and writing to the file as required.

I used methods for the **GetByte** and **PutByte** operations, rather than using properties. With some modest changes to **TFilterFile**, I could have defined these two properties

```
property InByte : byte read GetByte;
property OutByte : byte write PutByte;
```

and made **Eof** a property too, rather than a method. Making this change is appealing in some ways, but I'd be unhappy having to do without a return value from the output function. Since I'd be unhappy with the output being a property, I decided to leave all three as methods. Another alternative would be to handle input/output exceptions with **try-finally** blocks.

I'm unhappy with having to cast the return value of **GetByte** to a char in my program. I could have easily defined **GetChar** and **PutChar** methods in **TFilterFile**, but dang it, a character *is* a byte and I should be able to treat it that way. Here's one case where C gets it right and Object Pascal is too restrictive. It's rare, but it happens. The typecast is okay, I guess, but I normally avoid typecasts because, in general, they are considered "bad programming practice." You're telling the compiler: "Yes, I know I'm breaking the rules. Shut up and do it anyway." Second guessing the compiler is not a habit I'd like to get into.

32-Bit Delphi DLLs—When, Why, And How

HIGH PERFORMANCE

CHAPTER 2

HIGH PERFORMANCE

VCL components are the new and snazzy way to reuse your code, but even ancient mechanisms like those behind Windows DLLs can work miracles when evoked in the proper fashion.

32-Bit Delphi DLLs—When, Why, And How

Jim Mischel

It's been an interesting spring. February was *cold*—it actually snowed here in Austin. The roads iced up and people were smashing their cars right and left. Great amusement unless you happened to be one of those who got smashed. Shortly after the ice storm, the old Bronco's water pump went, along with a head gasket, and we decided it was time to get a new vehicle. Have you priced so-called inexpensive cars these days? Yikes!

Next on the agenda was the pool filter. April is swimming pool month around here, so I uncovered the thing (what an interesting shade of green) and turned on the pump. No dice. Mr. Pool Man came out and did his thing, leaving me that much poorer. And then the septic system backed up because some idiot contractor saved $20 by installing inferior pipe between the tank and the house. Mr. Plumber took more than Mr. Pool Man. All in all, it's been an expensive couple of months here at *chez Mischel.*

I'm not looking for sympathy. The point is that you can't always anticipate what's going to happen, and you'd better be flexible, or a run of bad luck similar to this can throw your life into complete disarray. The same is true of your programs—if you don't build in flexibility, somebody else will, and your program's sales will suffer for it.

In life, the key to flexibility is usually money. When you're talking Windows programming, the key to flexibility is DLLs.

Chapter 2

What's A DLL And Why Do I Want One?

A DLL (Dynamic Link Library) is a Windows-specific executable file that contains code or data designed to be accessed by other programs. DLLs are similar in concept to Delphi's units. Both are prepackaged pieces of code that your programs can call to accomplish all manner of things. The concept is the same—but the implementation, that's another story.

Delphi's units are *statically* linked to your programs. This means that at compile time, a copy of the code in all of the units that your program uses is placed in the program's EXE file. And every program that uses a particular unit has a separate copy of that unit in its EXE file. Normally, this is a good thing—you want your programs to be as self-contained as possible. However, there are at least two good reasons why you might not want code to be statically linked.

If you have a *large* unit, and a lot of different programs that use that unit, you're going to end up with an amazing amount of duplicate code in your programs. With hard drive space going for something like 30¢ per megabyte, that's less of a problem today than it once was (we'll ignore minimum sector size issues in this discussion), but what happens if you want to have four or five of those programs running at the same time? You end up with that many copies of the unit's code in memory. RAM, as inexpensive as it is, still ain't cheap—certainly not cheap enough to waste.

The second reason you may not want static linking is flexibility. Say you've just written the newest whiz-bang word processor and you'd like to be able to import other vendor's document file formats (something you *must* do if you want to compete in the word processor market). You could code up special modules for all of the currently popular formats and send your product out the door. But six months later, when the new version of Word Grinder Max (I hope that's not the name of a real product) comes out with a new format, *your* program is obsolete! The only way to get your program to read the new Word Grinder format is to release an upgrade, which will cost you plenty and gain you little. The size issue comes into play here, too. If you're statically linking code to convert hundreds of different formats, your program has an awful lot of dead weight—code that's going to be used infrequently by a very small number of customers.

The solution to both of these problems is *dynamic* linking. Instead of linking in a copy of a unit's code to the application's main EXE file, a DLL allows you to place

32-Bit Delphi DLLs—When, Why, And How

the reusable code in a separate library file that's loaded at runtime on an as-needed basis. If five different programs need to use functions in the DLL, there's still only one copy of the code on disk and, way better still, only one copy in memory. Rather than linking in a piece of code to the main EXE file, you just link in some instructions that tell the program where to find the code it needs. And rather than linking a gazillion different format-conversion routines into your word processor, you just build in the ability to specify a new format conversion DLL. Your support for new formats becomes a simple matter of writing a DLL and making it available to users on an as-needed basis.

Now *that's* flexibility.

How Do I Do It?

There are two parts to DLLs: building them and using them. You *use* DLLs every day in your normal Windows programming, probably without even knowing it. Darn near all of Windows itself is implemented in DLLs. When you call the Windows **MessageBox** function, for example, you're calling a function that's located in a DLL called USER.EXE (or USER32.DLL—Windows 95 does some funny fooling around with automatic 32-bit to 16-bit thunking, so I'm not always certain exactly what's going on). At any rate, whether you know it or not, you're already using DLLs in your everyday programming.

There are two ways to tell your program to call a function in a DLL. You can build a DLL interface unit that names the DLL and the functions that it contains, and link that interface unit with your Delphi program. This is called (remember, I'm just the messenger) statically linking the DLL. It's also known as compile-time dynamic linking. This is how you access Windows API functions. WINDOWS.DCU, which is linked with your program when you specify the Windows unit in your **uses** statement, is the DLL interface unit that defines these functions.

The other way to call DLL functions is, you guessed it, dynamically. When dynamically loading a DLL, you don't have to link with any DLL interface units. Instead, your program uses the **LoadLibrary** and **GetProcAddress** functions at runtime to locate and link to functions in a DLL. This is also known as runtime dynamic linking. Of the two methods, compile-time dynamic linking is easiest to code—but runtime dynamic linking is much more robust and flexible.

Building A DLL

Logically, a DLL is more like a unit than a program, but the code looks more like a program than a unit. This isn't too surprising when you consider that a DLL is just a special kind of program whose purpose is to provide code or data that other programs can access. Listing 2.1 shows a very simple DLL that supplies just one function: **BeepMe**. This function does nothing more than emit a "beep" when it's called.

Listing 2.1   A simple DLL.

```
{
  BEEPER.DPR-a simple DLL example

  Author: Jim Mischel
  Last Update:  05/12/97
}
library beeper;

uses Windows;

procedure BeepMe; stdcall;
begin
  MessageBeep (0);
end;

Exports
  BeepMe index 1 name 'BeepMe';

begin

end.
```

DLLs start with the reserved word **library** rather than **program** or **unit**. They also have a **uses** statement. You'll notice that, like programs, DLLs don't have separate **interface** and **implementation** sections. You write your procedures and functions in the DLL just as you would in a unit or a program, and then you specifically *export* those functions that you want to be available to other programs.

The **stdcall** reserved word isn't strictly required in DLLs, but it's not a bad idea. Exported DLL functions that are defined with the **stdcall** modifier are compatible with other languages (like C++) that can call DLLs. There's no disadvantage in using

stdcall for your exported functions. I recommend using **stdcall** if there's any chance that you might want C/C++ programs to have access to your exported functions.

The **Exports** statement is what tells the compiler to make specific functions available to other programs. In this example, I've exported the **BeepMe** procedure by name and by ordinal number—both of which are optional. Multiple exported functions should be separated by commas. So if you had another function in the DLL called **PageMe**, your **Exports** statement would look something like this:

```
Exports
   BeepMe index 1 name 'BeepMe',
   PageMe index 2 name 'PageMe';
```

To create the DLL, select File|New and select DLL from the New Items dialog box. Enter the code as shown in Listing 2.1, save it as BEEPER.DPR, and then compile. You can't run the DLL—you need another program to call it.

Calling DLL Functions

Once you've compiled the DLL, save the project and then select File|New Application. We're going to build a quick test program to put it all together.

Drop a button onto the main form and create an event handler that looks like this:

```
procedure TForm1.Button1Click(Sender: TObject);
begin
   BeepMe;
end;
```

Next add **BeepDLL** to the list of units in the form unit's **uses** statement. Don't try to compile—we need to create BEEPDLL.PAS first.

Create a new unit called BEEPDLL.PAS, and enter the code shown in Listing 2.2.

Listing 2.2   The BEEPER.DLL interface unit.

```
{ BEEPDLL.PAS-interface unit for BEEPER.DLL }
unit BeepDLL;

interface
```

```
procedure BeepMe; external 'beeper.dll';
procedure BeepMeTwo; external 'beeper.dll' name 'BeepMe';
procedure BeepMeThree; external 'beeper.dll' index 1;

implementation

end.
```

If you've done everything right, when you compile and run the program, pressing the button should emit a beep (or whatever sound your computer makes in place of a beep).

You probably noticed that I listed three different procedures, all of which are resolved at runtime, to call the **BeepMe** procedure that's in BEEPER.DLL. If you were to change your button's event handler to call **BeepMeThree** rather than **BeepMe**, the results would be the same. This is a contrived example, but there actually are times when you might need to use the **name** or **index** clauses to link to DLL functions. For example, you might run across a DLL (I have) that has a function named something like **XY$FORMAT** that you want to link to. Since **XY$FORMAT** isn't a valid Pascal identifier, you'd be unable to link to that function if you couldn't rename the function. Same goes for the **index** clause: Some DLL functions are exported by ordinal number only—no name!

This is an example of static DLL linkage—compile-time dynamic linking. All the interface unit, BEEPDLL.PAS, does is let the compiler know that the **BeepMe** procedure is to be dynamically linked from the BEEPER.DLL file. No code from BEEPER.DLL is actually linked with your program. If you don't believe it, delete BEEPER.DLL and run the program. If you're running from within the Delphi IDE, Delphi will report an error. If you're running from outside the IDE, Windows will report that the required BEEPER.DLL could not be found.

And *that* error message brings us to the other way of calling DLL functions—runtime dynamic linking.

Linking DLLs At Runtime

Sometimes you really don't *need* a particular DLL in order for your program to work. Take the word processor format conversion DLLs, for example. It's not very often that a user will actually want to convert a file. In fact, most of your users will likely never even once convert a file. It would be criminal for the program to require the format conversion DLLs in order to perform normal editing tasks. But that's what happens with statically linked DLLs. If Windows can't find the DLL when the program's loaded, you get a pretty little error message and Windows shuts down the program.

The other problem with statically linking DLLs is that it doesn't allow flexibility. If your program has to know at compile time what DLLs exist, then you're back in the same boat you were before—the only way to supply a new format conversion is to patch the executable program. Not good.

That's where runtime dynamic linking comes in. Rather than having Windows automatically load and link to your DLL at load time, why not have the program itself explicitly load and link the DLL if it's required? That way, the program will still run if the DLL is missing, it just won't be able to perform whatever function is implemented in the DLL. One neat thing about this approach is that you can tell the user what the problem is and, if he has a copy of the DLL somewhere, he can copy it to the proper place and retry—all without having to shut down the program.

Listing 2.3 is an updated version of the BEEPER.DLL interface unit that can be conditionally compiled for compile-time or runtime dynamic linking.

Listing 2.3   Dynamically linking a DLL at runtime.

```
{
  BEEPDLL.PAS—interface unit for BEEPER.DLL

  Author: Jim Mischel
  Last Update:  05/12/97
}
unit BeepDLL;


{$DEFINE DYNAMIC}   { comment this line for compile-time linkage }

interface

{$IFDEF DYNAMIC}
  { procedure declarations for runtime dynamic linking }
  procedure BeepMe;
  procedure BeepMeTwo;
  procedure BeepMeThree;
```

```pascal
{$ELSE}
  { procedure declarations for compile-time dynamic linking }
  procedure BeepMe; external 'beeper.dll';
  procedure BeepMeTwo; external 'beeper.dll' name 'BeepMe';
  procedure BeepMeThree; external 'beeper.dll' index 1;
{$ENDIF}

implementation

{$IFDEF DYNAMIC}
uses Windows;

type
  BeepMeProc = procedure;

var
  LibInstance : HMODULE;        { DLL module handle (if loaded) }
  BeepMePtr : BeepMeProc;

procedure BeepMe;
begin
  if (LibInstance = 0) then begin
    { DLL not loaded, try to load it }
    LibInstance := LoadLibrary ('beeper.dll');

    { if LoadLibrary returns 0, there's an error }
    if (LibInstance = 0) then begin
      MessageBox (0, 'Can''t load BEEPER.DLL', 'Error',
        MB_ICONEXCLAMATION or MB_OK);
      Exit;
    end;

    { DLL is loaded, try to link to the function }
    BeepMePtr := BeepMeProc (GetProcAddress (LibInstance, 'BeepMe'));
    { if GetProcAddress returns Nil, we've got a problem }
    if (Not Assigned (BeepMePtr)) then begin
      { unload the DLL first so the user can replace it if possible }
      FreeLibrary (LibInstance);
      LibInstance := 0;
      MessageBox (0, 'Can''t find BeepMe function in DLL.', 'Error',
        MB_ICONEXCLAMATION or MB_OK);
      Exit;
    end;
  end;
```

```
    BeepMePtr;
end;

procedure BeepMeTwo;
begin
  BeepMe;
end;

procedure BeepMeThree;
begin
  BeepMe;
end;


initialization
  LibInstance := 0;
  BeepMePtr := Nil;

finalization
  { if the DLL has been loaded, be sure to unload it }
  if (LibInstance <> 0) then begin
    FreeLibrary (LibInstance);
    LibInstance := 0;
  end;

end.
{$ELSE}

end.

{$ENDIF}
```

Hey, I *said* it was more involved!

Yes, runtime dynamic linking is a little more involved. You end up writing code to do what Windows will do automatically at startup if you select compile-time dynamic linking. But there is a serious benefit to all this code—you have much better error recovery. Let's take a moment and examine how this code works.

First of all, the procedure names in the unit aren't exported in the **interface** section, but instead correspond to real procedures that are defined in the **implementation** part of the module. It's the **export** statements in the statically bound interface unit that cause the automatic DLL linkage at program startup, so if you remove them, Windows won't try to load and link to your DLL.

Then, we define a procedure type and two variables:

```
type
  BeepMeProc = procedure;

var
  LibInstance : HMODULE;         { DLL module handle (if loaded) }
  BeepMePtr : BeepMeProc;
```

The procedure type **BeepMeProc** is similar to Delphi's event handler types. A variable of this type (in this case, **BeepMePtr**) contains a pointer to a procedure that takes no parameters. Once we've loaded BEEPER.DLL and located the **BeepMe** procedure, we'll assign its address to **BeepMePtr**.

LibInstance is the module instance handle of BEEPER.DLL, which is returned by **LoadLibrary** if it successfully loads the DLL.

The **BeepMeTwo** and **BeepMeThree** procedures are just aliases for **BeepMe**, so in the dynamic link version of the unit, they just call the unit's **BeepMe** procedure.

BeepMe is where all of the magic is performed. It first checks to see if the DLL has been loaded. If not, it calls Windows' **LoadLibrary** API function, which finds the DLL and attempts to load it—executing the DLL's startup code (more on that later)—and then returns a module handle that uniquely identifies the DLL. If the DLL couldn't be found or Windows encountered an error while loading it, then **LoadLibrary** will return 0 and **BeepMe** will issue an error message.

Assuming that **LoadLibrary** was able to load the DLL, the function then calls **GetProcAddress**, which attempts to locate a function called **BeepMe** in the newly loaded DLL. If the function is found, then its address is placed in **BeepMePtr**. If **GetProcAddress** can't find the function, then it returns **Nil**, causing **BeepMe** to issue an error message and unload the DLL.

If everything worked right—the DLL was loaded and the **BeepMe** procedure was found in the DLL—then it's called through the **BeepMePtr** procedure pointer.

One last note—your program should explicitly unload (by calling **FreeLibrary**) any DLLs that it loads with **LoadLibrary**. That's the purpose of the **initialization** and **finalization** parts of the module. During unit startup, the **initialization** section sets **LibInstance** and **BeepMePtr** to known values that indicate that the DLL isn't loaded. When the program exits, the **finalization** section unloads the DLL if it was loaded.

Where Windows Looks For DLLs

If you're deploying a DLL with your application, you'll usually have your installation program place the DLL in the same directory as your program's executable file. If that's where you put it, then Windows won't have any trouble locating it when it comes time to load your program (or when you call **LoadLibrary** if you're using runtime dynamic linking). If your application installs several executable files in different directories, then you have the option of placing a copy of the DLL in each directory (which kind of defeats the purpose of the DLL), or you can put the DLL into a common directory that Windows will search by default when it tries to load the DLL.

Windows searches for DLLs in these places, in the order shown:

1. The directory from which the application loaded;
2. The current directory;
3. The Windows system directory;
4. Windows NT only: the 16-bit Windows system directory;
5. The Windows directory; and
6. The directories that are listed in the PATH environment variable.

If you're using runtime dynamic linking by explicitly calling **LoadLibrary**, then you can specify a full path name to the DLL, and Windows will *only* look there. This isn't an option if you're counting on Windows to automatically load your DLLs at runtime.

DLLs: Disadvantages And Cautions

Most programmers, once they've grasped a new concept, start acting like a tool addict with a new torque wrench—they just can't *wait* to apply it to something. And they'll apply some amazingly convoluted logic in order to rationalize applying it to a particular situation. I know it's hard, but restrain yourself. DLLs are undoubtedly cool, but they can easily mutate into foot-seeking missles.

Don't even *think* of implementing required program features in a DLL. Your word processor's text formatter, for example, belongs in the program, not in an external DLL. DLLs should be reserved for optional features (including third-party add-ons) and common libraries. That's *it*. If you use a DLL for anything else, you're just begging for trouble.

The biggest disadvantage to using DLLs is type checking—or the lack thereof. When you access a DLL function, using either method of linking to it, you're telling the compiler to call functions that it knows nothing about. For example, in the BEEPDLL.PAS unit, we have this declaration:

```
procedure BeepMe; external 'beeper.dll';
```

This declaration is telling the compiler that there's a procedure called **BeepMe** that's located in the named DLL. So far, so good. Here's the kicker. *The compiler takes your word for it.* There's absolutely no way that the compiler can go find BEEPER.DLL, disassemble it, and verify that the procedure called **BeepMe** actually exists and does indeed expect to be called with no parameters. If the DLL's **BeepMe** procedure is expecting one or more parameters (or in the case of a procedure with parameters, different types of parameters), then all hell will break loose when your program calls **BeepMe**, because it got more, fewer, or different types of parameters than were expected. I guarantee that this will happen to you at some point, and I can tell you from experience that it's a very difficult bug to track down. In fact—and this is very embarrassing to admit—I ran into this problem myself shortly after I wrote that last sentence, while I was working on the code for the next section.

If you want a more detailed (and hair-raising) discussion of possible problems with DLLs, I suggest that you take a look at Lou Grinzo's *Zen of Windows 95 Programming* (Coriolis Group Books, 1995). This is an excellent book that contains a wealth of information about Windows 95 programming, and some very good advice about programming in general. Programming requires a healthy dose of paranoia and a firm belief in Murphy's Law. If you don't believe that now, you will after reading Lou's book.

I'll climb off my soapbox now, but don't say I didn't warn you. Now that you know how to build DLLs, let's take a look at some of the things you can do with them.

Creating Forms In DLLs

Probably the most common use of DLLs in Delphi programming is to store common forms. If you're building a suite of programs, you've probably got dozens of forms that are common across all of the programs. Rather than building all of those forms into each program, you can put them all into a single DLL, which will save you disk space and memory, and (perhaps most important) maintenance problems. A DLL that contains Delphi forms does incur the overhead of the runtime library code (about 100K), but if you put many forms into a single DLL, the overhead isn't a problem.

Accessing a form from a DLL is slightly different from accessing the form in a program. Since you're not linking the unit that contains the form, you can't just show it as you would from within a normal program (that is, by calling **Form1.ShowModal**). Instead, you have to create a wrapper function in the DLL, and then call the wrapper function from the program. The wrapper function creates the form, displays it, gathers any data, destroys the form when it's closed, and returns any required information to the calling program.

Listings 2.4 and 2.5 contain PICKCLR.DPR and COLORFRM.PAS, which implement a color selection form in a DLL.

Listing 2.4   PICKCLR.DPR.

```
{
  PICKCLR.DPR—Color selection form DLL

  Author: Jim Mischel
  Last Update:  05/12/97
}
library pickclr;

uses
  SysUtils,
  Classes,
  ColorFrm in 'colorfrm.pas' {ColorSelectionForm};

Exports
  ColorFrm.PickColors index 1 name 'PickColors';

begin
end.
```

Listing 2.5   COLORFRM.PAS.

```
{
  COLORFRM.PAS—DLL-based color selection form

  Author: Jim Mischel
  Last Update:  05/12/97
}
unit colorfrm;

interface
```

```
uses
  Windows, Messages, SysUtils, Classes, Graphics, Controls, Forms,
  Dialogs, StdCtrls, ColorGrd;

type
  TColorSelectionForm = class(TForm)
    ColorGrid1: TColorGrid;
    BtnOk: TButton;
    BtnCancel: TButton;
  private
    { Private declarations }
  public
    { Public declarations }
    function Execute : boolean;
  end;

function PickColors (var Foreground, Background : TColor) : boolean;
    stdcall; export;

implementation

{$R *.DFM}

function TColorSelectionForm.Execute : boolean;
begin
  Result := (ShowModal = mrOk);
end;

function PickColors (var Foreground, Background : TColor) : boolean;
    stdcall;
var
  ColorForm : TColorSelectionForm;
begin
  ColorForm := TColorSelectionForm.Create (Application);
  Result := ColorForm.Execute;
  if (Result = True) then begin
    Foreground := ColorForm.ColorGrid1.ForegroundColor;
    Background := ColorForm.ColorGrid1.BackgroundColor;
  end;
  ColorForm.Free;
end;

end.
```

You should note that COLORFRM.PAS can be linked with a program or with a DLL without changes. This makes moving forms from programs into DLLs fairly easy. For ease of debugging, you develop the form and test it with a program. Once you've got it working, you add it to a DLL shell that you've set up.

As you can see from Listing 2.4, the project file for a DLL is very simple. The most important part is getting the **Exports** statement right. If you want more forms in the DLL, simply add their unit names to the **uses** statement, and add definitions of their wrapper functions to the **Exports** statement.

A DLL that contains forms should have an interface unit similar to the BEEPDLL.PAS unit shown in Listing 2.3. Like BEEPDLL, the unit can provide compile-time or runtime DLL linkage. For brevity, I haven't included an interface unit for the PICKCLRDLL.

To use a form that's stored in a DLL, you simply link with the DLL's interface unit and call the form's wrapper function, which will display the form and return any required values.

Coding For Flexibility

Many products provide "hooks" to which third parties can hang on additional modules. Windows Help, for example, defines an interface through which developers can add custom macros and embedded windows that provide some very interesting features to Windows Help files. Borland's C++ 5.0 IDE also has an add-on interface that other companies are using to add features. Version control and a Java development add-on are shipped with BC++ 5.0. Both are implemented using the DLL add-on interface.

I've offered the example of word processor format conversion in this chapter as an example of one possible use of DLLs. Let's develop that idea a little further by writing a mini text editor that offers an add-on format conversion interface. The text editor itself is very simple-minded—just a Memo component and menu options to open and save files. That's okay, though. What we're really interested in is the format conversion interface.

Creating The Text Editor

Since we're all programmers here, I'm going to move fairly rapidly through the mechanics of creating the text editor's shell. I'll slow down when we get to the add-on interface.

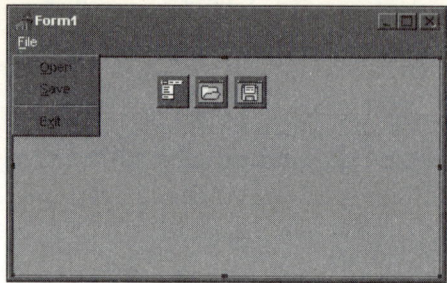

Figure 2.1
The completed text editor form.

Starting with a new project, add a Memo component to the form and set its **Align** property to **alClient** so that it takes up the entire form. Then add MainMenu, OpenDialog, and SaveDialog components to the form. In the Menu Designer, add three items to the menu: Open, Save, and Exit. Save the unit as EDITFORM.PAS and the project file as TEXTEDIT.DPR. The completed form is shown in Figure 2.1, and the complete program listing is shown in Listing 2.6.

Listing 2.6 The text editor form, EDITFORM.PAS.

```
{
  EDITFORM.PAS—Simple text editor to illustrate use of DLLs

  Author: Jim Mischel
  Last Update:  05/12/97
}
unit editform;

interface

uses
  Windows, Messages, SysUtils, Classes, Graphics, Controls, Forms,
  Dialogs, Menus, StdCtrls;

type
  TForm1 = class(TForm)
    Memo1: TMemo;
    OpenDialog1: TOpenDialog;
    SaveDialog1: TSaveDialog;
    MainMenu1: TMainMenu;
```

```
    File1: TMenuItem;
    Open1: TMenuItem;
    Save1: TMenuItem;
    N1: TMenuItem;
    Exit1: TMenuItem;
    procedure Exit1Click(Sender: TObject);
    procedure Open1Click(Sender: TObject);
    procedure Save1Click(Sender: TObject);
  private
    { Private declarations }
    FileName : String;
    procedure OpenFile(Filename: String);
    procedure SaveFile(Filename: String);
  public
    { Public declarations }
  end;

var
  Form1: TForm1;

implementation

{$R *.DFM}

uses IniFiles;

procedure TForm1.Exit1Click(Sender: TObject);
begin
  Close;
end;

procedure TForm1.Open1Click(Sender: TObject);
begin
  if OpenDialog1.Execute then
    OpenFile (OpenDialog1.FileName);
end;

procedure TForm1.Save1Click(Sender: TObject);
begin
  if SaveDialog1.Execute then
    SaveFile (SaveDialog1.FileName);
end;
```

```
procedure TForm1.OpenFile (Filename: String);
begin
  Memo1.Lines.LoadFromFile (Filename);
end;

procedure TForm1.SaveFile (Filename: String);
begin
  Memo1.Lines.SaveToFile (Filename);
end;

end.
```

Test the program and make sure that it'll load and save an ASCII file (any file with a .TXT extension will work, as will .PAS and .DPR).

Now what we want to do is have the program read other file formats, convert to straight text, and display the text. Since we don't know exactly what formats might need to be converted, we need the ability to add new formats as the need arises. Probably the easiest way to do this is with an initialization (INI) file.

The idea is to save a description of the file format, a default extension, and the name of the DLL that contains the format conversion function. An example INI file is shown in Listing 2.7.

Listing 2.7   TEXTEDIT.INI.

```
; TEXTEDIT.INI
; Example of file conversion add-on interface
[Text]
Extension=.TXT
ConvertDLL=textconv.dll

[Word for Windows]
Extension=.DOC
ConvertDLL=wfwconv.dll

[WordCruncher]
Extension=.WCX
ConvertDLL=wcxconv.dll
```

What we do is modify the **OpenFile** procedure so that it examines the extension of the file that you choose to open, and then calls the conversion function in the proper DLL. The DLL reads the file, converts the text, and returns the result in a string list.

All of the conversion functions have a function called **Convert**, which the text editor program calls. Listing 2.8 contains the modified **OpenFile** function (be sure to add IniFiles to the form's **uses** list), and Listings 2.9 and 2.10 contain the code for the text conversion DLL (TEXTCONV.DLL).

Listing 2.8 The new OpenFile function.

```
procedure TForm1.OpenFile (Filename: String);
type
  ConvertFunc = function (Filename: String;
      Strings: TStrings): boolean; stdcall;
var
  ConvertIni : TIniFile;
  ConvertList : TStringList;
  FileExt : String;
  Extension : String;
  DLLName : String;
  x : Integer;
  Found : Boolean;
  LibInstance : HMODULE;
  Converter : ConvertFunc;
  IniFileName : String;

begin
  FileExt := UpperCase (ExtractFileExt (Filename));
  IniFileName := ExtractFileDir (ParamStr (0)) + '\TEXTEDIT.INI';
  ConvertIni := TIniFile.Create (IniFileName);
  ConvertList := TStringList.Create;
  { Read the list of available conversions }
  ConvertList.Add ('Hello, world');
  ConvertIni.ReadSections (ConvertList);

  {
    For each conversion, read the Extension entry and compare it
    against the extension of the selected file.
  }
  x := 0;
  Found := False;
  while ((x < ConvertList.Count) and (Not Found)) do begin
    Extension := ConvertIni.ReadString (
      ConvertList.Strings[x], 'Extension', '');
    if (UpperCase (Extension) = FileExt) then
      Found := True
    else
      x := x + 1;
  end;
```

```
    if Found then begin
      DLLName := ConvertIni.ReadString (
        ConvertList.Strings[x], 'ConvertDLL', '');
      {
        Load the DLL, get the address of the Convert function,
        and call it.
      }
      LibInstance := LoadLibrary (PChar(DLLName));
      if LibInstance = 0 then begin
        Application.MessageBox (
          PChar ('Can''t load DLL '+DLLName),
          'TextEdit',
          MB_ICONEXCLAMATION or MB_OK);
      end
      else begin
        Converter := GetProcAddress (LibInstance, 'Convert');
        if Not Assigned (Converter) then begin
          Application.MessageBox (
            PChar ('Can''t find Convert function in '+DLLName),
            'TextEdit',
            MB_ICONEXCLAMATION or MB_OK);
        end
        else begin
          if not Converter (Filename, Memo1.Lines) then begin
            Application.MessageBox (
              'Error loading file',
              'TextEdit',
              MB_ICONEXCLAMATION or MB_OK);
          end;
        end;
        FreeLibrary (LibInstance);
      end;
    end
    else begin
      Application.MessageBox (
        PChar('No conversion supplied for file type '+FileExt),
        'TextEdit',
        MB_ICONEXCLAMATION or MB_OK);
    end;

    ConvertList.Free;
    ConvertIni.Free;
end;
```

Listing 2.9   TEXTCONV.DPR.

```
{
  TEXTCONV.DPR—Text conversion DLL main module.

  Author: Jim Mischel
  Last Update:   05/12/97
}
library textconv;

{ Important note about DLL memory management: ShareMem must be the
  first unit in your library's USES clause AND your project's (select
  View-Project Source) USES clause if your DLL exports any procedures or
  functions that pass strings as parameters or function results. This
  applies to all strings passed to and from your DLL—even those that
  are nested in records and classes. ShareMem is the interface unit to
  the DELPHIMM.DLL shared memory manager, which must be deployed along
  with your DLL. To avoid using DELPHIMM.DLL, pass string information
  using PChar or ShortString parameters. }

uses
  ShareMem,
  SysUtils,
  Classes,
  textc in 'textc.pas';

Exports
  textc.Convert index 1 name 'Convert';

begin
end.
```

Listing 2.10   TEXTC.PAS.

```
{
  TEXTC.PAS—Text conversion module.  Loads text files from disk.

  Author: Jim Mischel
  Last Update:   05/12/97
}unit textc;

interface

uses Classes;

function Convert (Filename: String; Strings: TStrings) : boolean;
  stdcall; export;
```

```
implementation

function Convert (Filename: String; Strings: TStrings) : boolean;
  stdcall;
begin
  Strings.LoadFromFile (Filename);
  Result := True;
end;

end.
```

Pay particular attention to the note at the top of Listing 2.9 (TEXTCONV.DPR). The really cool thing about this note is that it's placed automatically in your project file when you select File|New|DLL. Truthfully, I'm not sure if I should be referencing the ShareMem unit or not in this case. I've tried the program without ShareMem, and it appears to work okay. And I can make the argument that I'm not passing a class to the **Convert** function—only a *pointer* to a **TStrings** object. I rather suspect, though, that the note applies to pointers to classes as well, so I've included ShareMem in the **uses** list for the program and the DLL. If you do have to use ShareMem, remember to ship the DELPHIMM.DLL file with your application.

Do note that the **OpenFile** function in Listing 2.8 is by no means good enough for a commercial program. This is an *example* that illustrates the concept. A commercial implementation would require that your program actually go read the file to determine what type it is (if possible), and prompt the user for permission to perform the conversion before actually doing anything. This example shows you one way that you could implement an add-on interface to provide support for third-party additions to your products.

Sharing Memory Between Applications

Fortunately for us Delphi programmers, Delphi's DLLs by default allow multiple instances, so there's one less worry. However, just because multiple instances are allowed doesn't mean that it's easy to share information between processes that are using the same DLL. Under Windows 95 and Windows NT, each instance of a DLL has its own data segment. You can't use a simple global variable in a DLL to share information between two running applications. For this, you need to set up a shared memory block in Windows. And to do *that*, you need to understand a little more about how Windows and Delphi load and map DLLs.

The DLLProc Variable

When Delphi loads a DLL, the DLL's startup code (the code between the **begin** and **end** at the bottom of your DLL) is executed. If your DLL needs to load resources, allocate memory, or do any other processing when it's first loaded and before any other functions are called, then that code should be placed here. This code is executed for every application that loads the DLL.

Windows will also notify your DLL when a process or thread attaches to it or detaches from it. But you have to request that notification from Delphi. The way you do that is by setting up a DLL handler function and setting the **DLLProc** variable (defined in the System unit) to point to that function. Your DLL handler function should be defined like this:

```
procedure DLLHandler (Reason: Integer);
```

The Reason parameter will be one of four constants: **DLL_PROCESS_ATTACH**, **DLL_PROCESS_DETACH**, **DLL_THREAD_ATTACH**, or **DLL_THREAD_DETACH**.

To set up a shared memory block, you need to respond to **DLL_PROCESS_ATTACH** messages and call **CreateFileMapping** to create a (or obtain a pointer to an already-created) shared memory block. Your DLL must also respond to **DLL_PROCESS_DETACH** messages and release the memory block so that Windows can release it when no more processes need it.

SHAREME.DPR (Listing 2.11) implements a shared memory block. In this example, the shared memory is just an integer that gets incremented every time a process attaches, and decremented when a process detaches.

Listing 2.11 Implementing shared memory in a DLL.

```
{
  SHAREME.DPR-Example of providing interprocess shared memory

  Author: Jim Mischel
  Last Update:   05/12/97
}
library shareme;
```

```pascal
uses
  Windows,
  SysUtils,
  Classes;

const
  pCounter: ^Longint = nil;

function GetProcessCount : Longint; stdcall; export;
begin
  Result := pCounter^;
end;

procedure MyDLLHandler (Reason: Integer);
const
  hMapObject : THandle = 0;
var
  fInit : Boolean;
begin
  case Reason of
    DLL_PROCESS_ATTACH : begin
      { create a named file mapping object }
      hMapObject := CreateFileMapping (
        $FFFFFFFF,        { use paging file }
        nil,              { no security attributes }
        PAGE_READWRITE,   { read/write access }
        0,                { high 32 bits of size }
        sizeof (longint), { low 32 bits of size }
        'SharedMem'       { name of object }
      );

      { the first process to attach initializes the memory }
      fInit := (GetLastError <> ERROR_ALREADY_EXISTS);

      { get a pointer to the file-mapped shared memory }
      pCounter := MapViewOfFile (
        hMapObject,       { object to map view of }
        FILE_MAP_WRITE,   { read/write access }
        0,                { high 32 bits of offset }
        0,                { low 32 bits of offset }
        0                 { default: map entire file }
      );

      { initialize or increment the count }
      if (fInit) then
        pCounter^ := 1
```

```
      else
        pCounter^ := pCounter^ + 1;
    end;

    DLL_PROCESS_DETACH : begin
      { decrement the count }
      pCounter^ := pCounter^ - 1;

      { unmap shared memory from the process's address space }
      UnmapViewOfFile (pCounter);

      { close the handle to the file-mapping object }
      CloseHandle (hMapObject);
    end;

    (*
      Thread attach and thread detach aren't handled

    DLL_THREAD_ATTACH :
    DLL_THREAD_DETACH :

    *)

  end;
end;

Exports
  GetProcessCount index 1 name 'GetProcessCount';

begin
  DLLProc := @MyDLLHandler;
  MyDLLHandler (DLL_PROCESS_ATTACH);
end.
```

You should take special note of the two lines of code in the DLL's initialization section. The first line of code initializes the System unit's **DLLProc** variable to point to the DLL's handler function. I thought that this was all that was required, but it appears that Delphi won't call the handler with a **DLL_PROCESS_ATTACH** value. So, the library's initialization code calls its own handler function. In my opinion, this is a bug in Delphi's handling of DLL initialization.

To test the shared memory, create a form that calls the DLL's **GetProcessCount** function when the form is created, and have it display the count in a label field on the form. If you run multiple copies of the application, you should see the counter increment once for each process that attaches to the DLL. If you close one or more of the applications and open new ones, the process counter should reflect the net effect (that is, if you opened three, closed one, and then opened another, the last one you open should have a process count of 3).

Global memory handles like those allocated by SHAREME consume valuable Windows resources, so be careful how you allocate them. If you'll be sharing a lot of different fields from a single DLL, you should put them all together into a single memory block (i.e., a record), and allocate just one memory block for the entire structure. This will minimize the Windows resources that the program uses. And be sure that your DLL correctly frees the memory blocks. If your DLL crashes or otherwise exits without freeing the memory block, that memory and the Windows resource will remain allocated until you reboot Windows. There is no way to free it once you've trashed the handle to the memory block.

Movin' On!

If you're interested in digging, there's lots of stuff to learn about DLLs. In this chapter, I've given you enough information for you to go exploring. If you have the Microsoft Developer's Network CD-ROMs, you'll want to look up DLLs in the index and read everything you can find. You also should learn more about **CreateFileMapping** and related file mapping functions, paying special attention to the differences between Windows 95 and Windows NT. You can do a lot of cool things with DLLs, but you've got to be careful. Good luck!

HIGH PERFORMANCE

Drag And Drop The Windows Way

CHAPTER 3

You'd think dragging and dropping your way around the Windows UI would be easier—but they had to leave something around for High Performance programmers to chew on, right?

Drag And Drop The Windows Way

Jim Mischel

There are at least three different drag and drop interfaces that can be supported by Delphi programs. The **TControl** class, of which all Delphi controls are descendents, defines a drag and drop interface between controls. By writing event handlers for the **OnDragDrop**, **OnDragOver**, and other similar events, a Delphi program supports internal drag and drop operations. With some fancy footwork and shared memory, it's possible that this method could be extended to work between two Delphi programs, but it can't be used to support drag and drop between a Delphi application and a non-Delphi program. This interface is well covered in Delphi's documentation and example programs.

Windows' Object Linking and Embedding (OLE) API also defines a drag and drop interface, which Delphi programs can support with the use of the built-in OLE controls. These controls will allow you to build OLE client or OLE server applications that support full drag and drop with OLE objects. In a raw Windows program, OLE is very difficult to use well. Delphi has classes that support OLE and make OLE programming a little easier, and in the next chapter we'll show how to use those classes to implement OLE drag and drop.

The third kind of drag and drop supported by Delphi is the dragging and dropping of files from (as I like to put it) File Mangler (Windows NT 3.5) or Windows Exploder (Windows 95 and NT 4.0). This interface is minimal—the only things you can drag and drop are files—but it's surprisingly useful. *This* interface, which I'll call "File Manager Drag and Drop" (FMDD), is not covered at all in Delphi's documentation, and is the subject of this chapter.

Drag And Drop

FMDD is implemented in Windows through the Shell interface in SHELL32.DLL. The implementation consists of four Windows API functions: **DragAcceptFiles**, **DragQueryFile**, **DragQueryPoint**, and **DragFinish**; and one Windows message: **WM_DROPFILES**. In Delphi, the **WM_DROPFILES** message is defined in the Messages unit, and the API functions are declared in the ShellAPI unit. The documented interface supports FMDD *clients*, but not FMDD *servers*. Your programs can accept dropped files from File Manager, but they can't send files to another program.

A typical implementation of FMDD in a Windows program requires that your code perform the following steps:

1. At program startup, call **DragAcceptFiles**, passing it a window handle and a **True** flag to enable acceptance of dragged files by that window.

2. When the window receives a **WM_DROPFILES** Windows message, perform the following (the **Msg.wParam** field in the Object Pascal message structure is a handle to memory used by the **WM_DROPFILES** message):

    a. Call **DragQueryPoint** to determine if the drop occurred in the client area of the window.

    b. Call **DragQueryFile** with an index value of $FFFFFFFF to retrieve the number of files being dropped.

    c. For each file, call **DragQueryFile** to copy the file name to an internal buffer.

    d. Perform the desired action on each file name.

    e. Free all internal memory allocated during processing of the dropped files.

    f. Call **DragFinish** to free the memory allocated by the FMDD server (i.e., File Mangler).

3. At program shutdown, call **DragAcceptFiles**, passing it a window handle and a **False** flag to discontinue acceptance of dragged files by the window.

Drag1, the first draft of a program that implements FMDD, is shown in Listings 3.1 and 3.2. A screen shot of the completed program is shown in Figure 3.1.

Drag And Drop The Windows Way

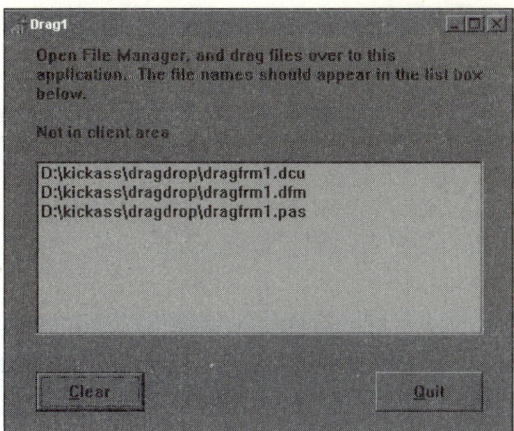

Figure 3.1
The completed Drag1 program.

Listing 3.1   DRAG1.DPR.

```
{
  DRAG1.DPR—First cut at Windows drag and drop

  Author: Jim Mischel
  Last Update:   04/27/97
}program drag1;

uses
  Forms,
  dragfrm1 in 'dragfrm1.pas' {Form1};

{$R *.RES}

begin
  Application.CreateForm(TForm1, Form1);
  Application.Run;
end.
```

Listing 3.2   DRAGFRM1.PAS.

```
{
  DRAGFRM1.PAS—First pass implementation of drag and drop

  Author: Jim Mischel
  Last Update: 04/27/97
}
unit dragfrm1;
```

```
interface

uses
  SysUtils, Windows, Messages, Classes, Graphics, Controls,
  Forms, Dialogs, StdCtrls,
  {
     ShellAPI defines the drag and drop functions.
     The functions are implemented in SHELL32.DLL.
  }
  ShellAPI;

type
  TForm1 = class(TForm)
    ListBox1: TListBox;
    Button1: TButton;
    Button2: TButton;
    Label1: TLabel;
    Label2: TLabel;
    procedure FormCreate(Sender: TObject);
    procedure AppMessage(var Msg: TMsg; var Handled: Boolean);
    procedure FormClose(Sender: TObject; var Action: TCloseAction);
    procedure Button1Click(Sender: TObject);
    procedure Button2Click(Sender: TObject);
  private
    { Private declarations }
    procedure WMDropFiles (hDrop : THandle; hWindow : HWnd);
  public
    { Public declarations }
  end;

var
  Form1: TForm1;

implementation

{$R *.DFM}

procedure TForm1.FormCreate(Sender: TObject);
begin
  Application.OnMessage := AppMessage;
  {
    Call DragAcceptFiles to tell the drag & drop manager
    that you're accepting files.
  }
  DragAcceptFiles (Handle, True);
end;
```

```pascal
procedure TForm1.WMDropFiles (hDrop : THandle; hWindow : HWnd);
Var
  TotalNumberOfFiles,
  nFileLength : Integer;
  pszFileName : PChar;
  pPoint : TPoint;
  i : Integer;
  InClientArea : Boolean;

Begin
  {
    hDrop is a Handle to the internal Windows data
    structure which has information about the dropped files.
  }

  {
    Determine if the files were dropped in the client area
  }
  InClientArea := DragQueryPoint (hDrop, pPoint);
  if InClientArea then
    Label2.Caption := 'In client area'
  else
    Label2.Caption := 'Not in client area';

  {
    Find out total number of files dropped, by passing -1 for
    the index parameter to DragQueryFile
  }
  TotalNumberOfFiles := DragQueryFile (hDrop , $FFFFFFFF, Nil, 0);

  for i := 0 to TotalNumberOfFiles - 1 do begin
    {
      Get the length of a file name by telling DragQueryFile
      which file you're requerying about ( i ), and passing Nil
      for the buffer parameter.  The return value is the length
      of the file name.
    }
    nFileLength := DragQueryFile (hDrop, i , Nil, 0) + 1;
    GetMem (pszFileName, nFileLength);

    {
      Copy a file name.   Tell DragQueryFile the file
      you're interested in (i) and the length of your buffer.
      NOTE: Make sure that the length is 1 more than the file name
      to make room for the nul character!
    }
    DragQueryFile (hDrop , i, pszFileName, nFileLength);
```

```
    Listbox1.Items.Add (StrPas (pszFileName));

    { free the allocated memory... }
    FreeMem (pszFileName, nFileLength);
  end;

  {
   Call DragFinish to release the memory that Shell allocated
   for this handle.
   NOTE: This is a real easy step to forget and could
   explain memory leaks and incorrect program performance.
  }
  DragFinish (hDrop);
end;


{
  AppMessage captures application messages.  Assign this method
  to the Application.OnMessage property in FormCreate.
}
procedure TForm1.AppMessage(var Msg: TMsg; var Handled: Boolean);
begin
  case Msg.Message of
    WM_DROPFILES : begin
      WMDropFiles (Msg.wParam, Msg.hWnd);
      Handled := True;
    end;

    else
      Handled := False;
  end;
end;

procedure TForm1.FormClose (Sender: TObject; var Action: TCloseAction);
begin
  { Don't accept files anymore }
  DragAcceptFiles (Handle, False);
end;

procedure TForm1.Button1Click(Sender: TObject);
begin
  Listbox1.Clear;
end;
```

```
procedure TForm1.Button2Click(Sender: TObject);
begin
  Close;
end;

end.
```

The only real trick in DRAGFRM1.PAS is the line in **TForm1.FormCreate** that reads:

```
Application.OnMessage := AppMessage;
```

This line of code tells Delphi to pass Windows messages on to the **TForm1.AppMessage** procedure. This is the Delphi way of performing traditional handling of Windows messages. We have to do it this way because neither Delphi's **TControl** class, nor any of its descendents (like **TForm**), know anything about **WM_DROPFILES**, so that message isn't wrapped up in a nice Delphi event like **OnDropFiles**. More's the pity.

There's nothing especially *wrong* with the code in Listing 3.2. It works, which is the most important thing, but it's large, it has lots of places where you can make mistakes, and (perhaps worst of all) it's *ugly*. All that icky Windows code in the middle of a pure Delphi program *just ain't right!* (Texans have such colorful ways of mangling the language.)

There's another problem, too, but it's caused by Delphi's message handling machinery. Suppose you have two forms that want to respond to **WM_DROPFILES** messages. If each form assigns its own message handler to the **Application** object's **OnMessage** event, only the second form will get messages. The first form's message handler is overwritten by the second. There are a number of ways around this problem, and we'll discuss some of them after we've taken care of that ugly Windows code.

What To Do With Windows Code

The answer to the question is "encapsulate it." That's what Delphi does, and does very well. The whole *point* of Delphi is to insulate you from the sordid little details of Windows programming so that you can concentrate on the important parts of your application. We'll do the same with FMDD—wrap it up into a pretty little Delphi unit called FMDD.

Rather than have the form handle all of the details of **WM_DROPFILES** processing, we'll define a function in the FMDD unit that the form's **OnMessage** handler can call to retrieve an object that contains all available information about the drag and drop event. This object will include everything that we obtained from the Windows FMDD interface, but it will be all packaged together in a single, more manageable structure that looks like this:

```
TDragDropInfo = class (TObject)
  private
    FNumFiles : UINT;
    FInClientArea : Boolean;
    FDropPoint : TPoint;
    FFileList : TStringList;
  public
    constructor Create (ANumFiles : UINT);
    destructor Destroy; override;

    property NumFiles : UINT read FNumFiles;
    property InClientArea : Boolean read FInClientArea;
    property DropPoint : TPoint read FDropPoint;
    property Files : TStringList read FFileList;
end;
```

In addition to the **TDragDrop** structure, the FMDD unit defines three functions: **AcceptDroppedFiles**, **UnacceptDroppedFiles**, and **GetDroppedFiles**. The first two simply encapsulate the **DragAcceptFiles** function. The third, **GetDroppedFiles**, is called in response to the **WM_DROPFILES** message and returns a **TDropInfo** object. The code for the first pass of this unit, FMDD1.PAS, is shown in Listing 3.3.

Listing 3.3 First pass at the FMDD unit that encapsulates the Drag and Drop interface.

```
{
  FMDD1.PAS-First pass at encapsulating File Mangler Drag and Drop

  Author: Jim Mischel
  Last Update: 04/27/97
}
unit fmdd1;

interface

uses Windows, Classes;
```

```pascal
type
  TDragDropInfo = class (TObject)
  private
    FNumFiles : UINT;
    FInClientArea : Boolean;
    FDropPoint : TPoint;
    FFileList : TStringList;
  public
    constructor Create (ANumFiles : UINT);
    destructor Destroy; override;

    property NumFiles : UINT read FNumFiles;
    property InClientArea : Boolean read FInClientArea;
    property DropPoint : TPoint read FDropPoint;
    property Files : TStringList read FFileList;
  end;

function GetDroppedFiles (hDrop : THandle) : TDragDropInfo;
procedure AcceptDroppedFiles (Handle : HWND);
procedure UnacceptDroppedFiles (Handle : HWND);

implementation

uses ShellAPI;

constructor TDragDropInfo.Create (ANumFiles : UINT);
begin
  inherited Create;
  FNumFiles := ANumFiles;
  FFileList := TStringList.Create;
end;

destructor TDragDropInfo.Destroy;
begin
  FFileList.Free;
  inherited Destroy;
end;

function GetDroppedFiles (hDrop : THandle) : TDragDropInfo;
var
  DragDropInfo : TDragDropInfo;
  TotalNumberOfFiles,
  nFileLength : Integer;
  pszFileName : PChar;
  i : Integer;
```

```
begin
  {
    hDrop is a Handle to the internal Windows data
    structure which has information about the dropped files.
  }
  {
    Find out total number of files dropped, by passing -1 for
    the index parameter to DragQueryFile
  }
  TotalNumberOfFiles := DragQueryFile (hDrop , $FFFFFFFF, Nil, 0);

  DragDropInfo := TDragDropInfo.Create (TotalNumberOfFiles);

  {
    Determine if the files were dropped in the client area
  }
  DragDropInfo.FInClientArea := DragQueryPoint (hDrop,
                                                DragDropInfo.FDropPoint);


  for i := 0 to TotalNumberOfFiles - 1 do begin
    {
      Get the length of a file name by telling DragQueryFile
      which file you're querying about ( i ), and passing Nil
      for the buffer parameter.  The return value is the length
      of the file name.
    }
    nFileLength := DragQueryFile (hDrop, i , Nil, 0) + 1;
    GetMem (pszFileName, nFileLength);

    {
      Copy a file name.   Tell DragQueryFile the file
      you're interested in (i) and the length of your buffer.
      NOTE: Make sure that the length is 1 more than the file name
      to make room for the nul character!
    }
    DragQueryFile (hDrop , i, pszFileName, nFileLength);

    { Add the file to the string list }
    DragDropInfo.FFileList.Add (pszFileName);

    { free the allocated memory... }
    FreeMem (pszFileName, nFileLength);
  end;
```

```
    {
    Call DragFinish to release the memory that Shell allocated
    for this handle.
    NOTE: This is a real easy step to forget and could
    explain memory leaks and incorrect program performance.
    }
    DragFinish (hDrop);
    Result := DragDropInfo;
end;

procedure AcceptDroppedFiles (Handle : HWND);
begin
  DragAcceptFiles (Handle, True);
end;

procedure UnacceptDroppedFiles (Handle : HWND);
begin
  DragAcceptFiles (Handle, False);
end;

end.
```

In order to make the existing test program use the new interface, we just have to change a few lines of code. First, change the reference to unit ShellAPI in the unit's **uses** statement to FMDD1. Then, change the form's event handlers as shown in Listing 3.4. The DRAG2.DPR program and DRAGFRM2.PAS modules on the listings CD-Rom implement these changes.

Listing 3.4 Using the new File Manager Drag and Drop interface.

```
procedure TForm1.FormCreate(Sender: TObject);
begin
  Application.OnMessage := AppMessage;
  FMDD1.AcceptDroppedFiles (Handle);
end;

procedure TForm1.WMDropFiles (hDrop : THandle; hWindow : HWnd);
var
  DragDropInfo : TDragDropInfo;
  i : Integer;

begin
  DragDropInfo := FMDD1.GetDroppedFiles (hDrop);
```

```
  { Determine if in client area }
  if DragDropInfo.InClientArea then
    Label2.Caption := 'In client area'
  else
    Label2.Caption := 'Not in client area';

  { add each file to the list box }
  for i := 0 to DragDropInfo.NumFiles - 1 do begin
    Listbox1.Items.Add (DragDropInfo.Files[i]);
  end;

  { Destroy the DragDropInfo object }
  DragDropInfo.Free;
end;

procedure TForm1.FormClose (Sender: TObject; var Action: TCloseAction);
begin
  { Don't accept files anymore }
  FMDD1.UnacceptDroppedFiles (Handle);
end;
```

I don't know about you, but I find it much easier to use this new interface. In the spirit of Delphi, we've removed the Windows API handling code from our application's code, and we've put it into a unit where we don't have to look at or worry about it. The FMDD unit handles all the mucking around in Windows internals and returns an object—something that we know how to work with. The result is less code (and much cleaner code) that's easier to write and maintain.

Responding To Windows Messages

In most cases, Delphi's interface for handling Windows messages—the **Application** object's **OnMessage** event handler—is sufficient. Programs can define their own **OnMessage** handler, and Delphi dutifully will pass Windows messages on to that procedure. But Delphi doesn't allow you to define multiple **OnMessage** handlers in a single program, making custom processing of Windows messages for multiple windows somewhat of a problem. In our case, it's a real problem—only one control in an application can be accepting dropped files.

The first solution that comes to mind is to have an event handler that knows about all of the controls that need to process Windows messages. This event handler can then compare the **Msg.hwnd** value with the **Handle** properties of each control, passing the message on to the proper control's event handler. This is certainly possible, but it requires that your program know—at compile time—all of the controls that might want to process Windows messages.

A related solution would be to define an **OnMessage** event chaining facility, whereby controls that want to process Windows messages link themselves to a chain of **OnMessage** event handlers, and the chaining facility itself hooks **Application.OnMessage**, and then searches the list of linked controls whenever a message comes in. Controls could then link and unlink themselves from the **OnMessage** chain at will, although your code will have to take care to prevent breaking the chain and leaving some controls hanging without messages.

Both of these solutions have one major drawback—they require that all controls that will be handling Windows messages know about how the main application is handling the message chain. The lower-level portions of your program have to know about the higher-level implementation. This is not a good thing.

Suppose, for example, that your latest masterpiece is finished except for a really cool spreadsheet control. Flipping through the latest copy of *Hacker Monthly*, you find a review of Spreadsheet MAX, the coolest spreadsheet control ever invented. It's *perfect* for your application and you order a copy. When it arrives, you find that it works flawlessly except that it stomps on the **Application.OnMessage** event handler to do its thing—completely wiping out the **OnMessage** chaining that you had set up. How was the spreadsheet supposed to know that you were providing message chaining?

If there's a reliable way to make multiple controls properly handle the **Application.OnMessage** event handler, I certainly haven't found it. So my solution is to forget it—don't use **Application.OnMessage** at all if you have multiple windows that need to process Windows messages. There are alternative methods of defurring felines.

Custom Controls

If you have a special type of control that you want to respond to particular messages, simply write a custom version of the control. For example, if you wanted a **TForm** descendent that responds to **WM_DROPFILES**, you could create the custom **TFMDDForm** control shown in Listing 3.5.

Listing 3.5 The TFMDDForm custom component.

```pascal
{
  FMDDFORM.PAS—implements a form that responds to the
  WM_DROPFILES Windows message

  Author: Jim Mischel
  Last Update:  04/27/97
}
unit fmddform;

interface

uses
  Windows, Messages, SysUtils, Classes, Graphics, Controls,
  Forms, Dialogs, FMDD1;

type
  TFMDDEvent = procedure (Sender: TObject; DragDropInfo : TDragDropInfo)
    of object;
  TFMDDForm = class(TForm)
  private
    { Private declarations }
    FOnFMDD : TFMDDEvent;
    procedure WMDropFiles (var Message: TMessage);
      message WM_DROPFILES;
  protected
    { Protected declarations }
  public
    { Public declarations }
    constructor Create(AOwner: TComponent); override;
    destructor Destroy; override;
  published
    { Published declarations }
    property OnFMDD: TFMDDEvent read FOnFMDD write FOnFMDD;
  end;

procedure Register;

implementation

constructor TFMDDForm.Create(AOwner: TComponent);
begin
  inherited Create (AOwner);
  FMDD1.AcceptDroppedFiles (Handle);
end;
```

```
destructor TFMDDForm.Destroy;
begin
  FMDD1.UnacceptDroppedFiles (Handle);
  inherited Destroy;
end;

procedure TFMDDForm.WMDropFiles (var Message: TMessage);
var
  DragDropInfo : TDragDropInfo;
begin
  if assigned (FOnFMDD) then begin
    DragDropInfo := FMDD1.GetDroppedFiles (Message.wParam);
    FOnFMDD (Self, DragDropInfo);
    DragDropInfo.Free;
  end;
end;

procedure Register;
begin
  RegisterComponents('Samples', [TFMDDForm]);
end;

end.
```

The problem with this approach is that you'd have to create a custom version of *every* form for which you wanted to process **WM_DROPFILES** messages. Even if you had the stomach for it, you couldn't dig into the source for **TWinControl** and create an **OnFMDD** event so that all windowed controls knew about the **WM_DROPFILES** windows message. You can't do this because Delphi itself uses these controls and wouldn't know what to do if you changed them.

And even if you could modify **TWinControl**, it wouldn't do you any good if all of a sudden you want a control to respond to multiple user-defined messages whose values aren't even defined until runtime. We need a more general and more flexible solution.

Subclassing

The problem of custom responses to Windows messages isn't new to Delphi—it's been around for as long as Windows has been around. They've even got a name for the technique: *subclassing*. Technically, there's subclassing, and then there's *superclassing*, the difference being that subclassing restricts a window's response to messages, and superclassing adds to the processing of a window's message. In my mind, they're the same thing simply because you use the same technique to implement either. The technique? Well, it's kind of ugly when compared to the elegance of Delphi (okay, it's *really* ugly), but it works wonders, and we can encapsulate the ugliness so you never see it in your programs.

The idea behind subclassing is pretty simple. Every window has an associated data structure that Windows knows about. Among the many wondrous things in that structure is a pointer to the window's *window procedure*—the procedure that processes Windows messages. When Windows receives a message that's destined for a window, it looks up the address of that window's window procedure and calls it, passing the information pertinent to the particular message. When you subclass a window, you replace the window's window procedure with your custom routine, and save a pointer to the old procedure so you can pass messages on to it. All of this stuff is documented in the Windows SDK manuals, and there are some fairly good examples (all in C—you can't have *everything*). True, it's a bit-twiddling and hackerish kind of thing to do, but sometimes you just have to get your hands dirty. (Have you taken a look at the VCL source code lately? If you want an eye-opening experience, glance at CONTROLS.PAS sometime.)

At any rate, Delphi gives us all the tools we need to subclass a window, and we can use those tools to create a drag and drop interface with which your programs can interact in the normal Delphi fashion. As always, we'll start with the requirements.

Defining The Interface

We want drag and drop to operate as much as possible like a normal Delphi event. Since we're not defining a new custom control, we can't define an **OnFMDD** event that can be assigned at design time. So we have to simulate that behavior at runtime. To do that, we need to:

1. Define a **TFMDDEvent** type for the event handler.

2. Declare an **OnFMDragDrop** event handler in the form's **private** section.

3. When the form is created, pass the address of the event handler to the FMDD interface so the interface knows that we want the form to accept dropped files.

4. When a drag and drop event occurs (that is, when the form receives a **WM_DROPFILES** message), the FMDD interface will call the **OnFMDragDrop** event handler, passing it a **TDragDropInfo** object.

5. When the form is closed, call the FMDD interface to stop accepting dropped files.

That requirements list leads us to the **interface** section shown in Listing 3.6.

Listing 3.6 The interface section of the new FMDD unit.

```
interface

uses Windows, Messages, Classes, Controls;

type
  TDragDropInfo = class (TObject)
  private
    FNumFiles : UINT;
    FInClientArea : Boolean;
    FDropPoint : TPoint;
    FFileList : TStringList;
  public
    constructor Create (ANumFiles : UINT);
    destructor Destroy; override;

    property NumFiles : UINT read FNumFiles;
    property InClientArea : Boolean read FInClientArea;
    property DropPoint : TPoint read FDropPoint;
    property Files : TStringList read FFileList;
  end;

  TFMDDEvent = procedure (DDI : TDragDropInfo) of object;


procedure AcceptDroppedFiles (Control : TWinControl;
                              AOnDrop : TFMDDEvent);
procedure UnacceptDroppedFiles (Control : TWinControl);
```

Note that the **TDragDropInfo** class remains the same. We've removed the **GetDroppedFiles** function and redefined the **AcceptDroppedFiles** and **UnacceptDroppedFiles** procedures. The result is a much cleaner interface than the previous one—one that doesn't expect you to know about ugly little things like window handles and Windows messages. Of course, *somebody* has to know about those things. The details are hidden in FMDD's **implementation** section.

Implementing The New Interface

The devil, as always, is in the details. FMDD has to do a lot of processing behind the scenes. There are three separate, but interrelated, parts to FMDD's processing:

1. **AcceptDroppedFiles** has to save the window handle of the passed control and the **OnDrop** event handler for future use. This procedure also must call **DragAcceptFiles** to enable **WM_DROPFILES** processing for this window, and then subclass the window so that it can respond to the message.

2. We need a Windows message handler that will respond to **WM_DROPFILES** messages by constructing a **TDragDropInfo** object and passing it to the appropriate control.

3. **UnacceptDroppedFiles** should unsubclass the window and call **DragAcceptFiles** to prevent future **WM_DROPFILES** messages from being sent to the window.

Because FMDD should allow multiple windows to accept dropped files, we'll have to keep a list of window handles and their associated event handling procedures. When **AcceptDroppedFiles** is called, it'll save the control's information in the list. The procedure that handles the **WM_DROPFILES** message will look up the window's handle in the list so that it knows to which object it should send an **OnFMDragDrop** event, and then the **UnacceptDroppedFiles** procedure has to remove the control's information from the list. Fortunately, Delphi's **TList** component is tailor-made for list processing, and it's a snap to add items to, delete items from, and look items up in, a **TList**.

The tricky part of the implementation is the subclassing—mostly because it deals with Windows arcana. Previously, I touched briefly on what subclassing is, but purposely left out any discussion of how to do it until we got to the implementation. It's time now to get our hands dirty.

Subclassing Revisited

To subclass a window, you need to obtain and save a pointer to the window's existing window procedure, and then set the new window procedure pointer in the window's data structure. To do this, you call Windows' **GetWindowLong** and **SetWindowLong** API functions, which retrieve and set values in the window's internal data structure.

Once you've subclassed a window successfully, Windows will send all messages destined for that window to the new window procedure. It's this procedure's job to respond to the messages that it's interested in (in our case, **WM_DROPFILES**), and then pass all of the other messages on to the previous window procedure—a pointer to which you saved when you subclassed the window. You can't just call that old window procedure, though. Instead, you have to call the **CallWindowProc** API function and pass it the address of the old window procedure and the parameters that Windows passed to you.

The last part of subclassing is *un*subclassing—putting things back the way you found them. Unsubclassing is a simple matter of calling **SetWindowLong** again, this time replacing the new window procedure with the old one.

It all sounds a little more complicated than it really is, and once you've seen and puzzled over an example and crashed Windows a few times, it becomes as clear as mud (which is about as clear as *any* Windows programming gets).

The new FMDD unit that supports subclassing is shown in Listing 3.7.

Listing 3.7 The new FMDD unit that supports multiple controls.

```
{
  FMDD2.PAS—Fully encapsulated File Mangler Drag and Drop

  Author: Jim Mischel
  Last Update:  04/27/97
}
unit fmdd2;

interface

uses Windows, Messages, Classes, Controls;

type
  TDragDropInfo = class (TObject)
  private
    FNumFiles : UINT;
    FInClientArea : Boolean;
    FDropPoint : TPoint;
    FFileList : TStringList;
```

```pascal
  public
    constructor Create (ANumFiles : UINT);
    destructor Destroy; override;

    property NumFiles : UINT read FNumFiles;
    property InClientArea : Boolean read FInClientArea;
    property DropPoint : TPoint read FDropPoint;
    property Files : TStringList read FFileList;
  end;

  TFMDDEvent = procedure (DDI : TDragDropInfo) of object;


procedure AcceptDroppedFiles (Control : TWinControl;
            AOnDrop : TFMDDEvent);
procedure UnacceptDroppedFiles (Control : TWinControl);

implementation

uses ShellAPI;

type
  {
    TSubclassItem stores information about a subclassed window
  }
  TSubclassItem = class (TObject)
  private
    Handle : HWND;          { the window handle }
    WindowProc : TFNWndProc; { its old window procedure }
    FOnDrop : TFMDDEvent;    { the control's OnFMDragDrop event handler }
  public
    constructor Create (AHandle : HWND;
        AWndProc : TFNWndProc; AOnDrop : TFMDDEvent);
  end;

var
  SubclassList : TList;

constructor TSubclassItem.Create (AHandle : HWND;
              AWndProc : TFNWndProc; AOnDrop : TFMDDEvent);
begin
  inherited Create;
  Handle := AHandle;
  WindowProc := AWndProc;
  FOnDrop := AOnDrop;
end;
```

```pascal
{
  WMDragDrop creates the TDragDropInfo object and calls the
  FOnDrop event handler.
}
procedure WMDragDrop (hDrop : THandle; FOnDrop : TFMDDEvent);
var
  DragDropInfo : TDragDropInfo;
  TotalNumberOfFiles,
  nFileLength : Integer;
  pszFileName : PChar;
  i : Integer;

begin
  if not assigned (FOnDrop) then
    exit;
  {
    hDrop is a Handle to the internal Windows data
    structure which has information about the dropped files.
  }
  {
    Find out total number of files dropped, by passing -1 for
    the index parameter to DragQueryFile
  }
  TotalNumberOfFiles := DragQueryFile (hDrop , $FFFFFFFF, Nil, 0);

  DragDropInfo := TDragDropInfo.Create (TotalNumberOfFiles);

  {
    Determine if the files were dropped in the client area
  }
  DragDropInfo.FInClientArea :=
    DragQueryPoint (hDrop, DragDropInfo.FDropPoint);


  for i := 0 to TotalNumberOfFiles - 1 do begin
    {
      Get the length of a file name by telling DragQueryFile
      which file you're querying about ( i ), and passing Nil
      for the buffer parameter.  The return value is the length
      of the file name.
    }
    nFileLength := DragQueryFile (hDrop, i , Nil, 0) + 1;
    GetMem (pszFileName, nFileLength);

    {
      Copy a file name.  Tell DragQueryFile the file
      you're interested in (i) and the length of your buffer.
```

```
      NOTE: Make sure that the length is 1 more than the file name
      to make room for the nul character!
    }
    DragQueryFile (hDrop , i, pszFileName, nFileLength);

    { Add the file to the string list }
    DragDropInfo.FFileList.Add (pszFileName);

    { free the allocated memory... }
    FreeMem (pszFileName, nFileLength);
  end;

  {
   Call DragFinish to release the memory that Shell allocated
   for this handle.
   NOTE: This is a real easy step to forget and could
   explain memory leaks and incorrect program performance.
  }
  DragFinish (hDrop);

  { call the event handler }
  FOnDrop (DragDropInfo);

  { and destroy the TDragDropInfo object }
  DragDropInfo.Free;
end;


{
  find and return the list item that corresponds to
  the passed window handle.
}
function FindItemInList (Handle : HWND) : TSubclassItem;
var
  i : Integer;
  Item : TSubclassItem;
begin
  for i := 0 to SubclassList.Count - 1 do begin
    Item := SubclassList.Items[i];
    if Item.Handle = Handle then begin
      Result := Item;
      exit;
    end;
  end;
  Result := Nil;
end;
```

```
{
  FMDDWndProc handles WM_DROPFILES messages by calling WMDragDrop.
  All other messages are passed on to the window's old window proc.
}
function FMDDWndProc (
    Handle : HWND; Msg : UINT;
    wparam: WPARAM; lparam: LPARAM) : LRESULT; stdcall;
var
  Item : TSubclassItem;
begin
  Item := FindItemInList (Handle);
  if Item <> Nil then begin
    if Msg = WM_DROPFILES then begin
      WMDragDrop (wparam, Item.FOnDrop);
      Result := 0;
    end
    else
      Result := CallWindowProc (Item.WindowProc,
          Handle, Msg, wparam, lparam)
  end
  else
    Result := 0;
end;

{
  AcceptDroppedFiles subclasses the control's window and saves
  information about the control for future use.
}
procedure AcceptDroppedFiles (Control : TWinControl;
            AOnDrop : TFMDDEvent);
var
  WndProc : TFNWndProc;
begin
  DragAcceptFiles (Control.Handle, True);
  { get the old window procedure }
  WndProc :=
    TFNWndProc(GetWindowLong (Control.Handle, GWL_WNDPROC));
  { attach the new window procedure }
  SetWindowLong (Control.Handle,
    GWL_WNDPROC, Longint (@FMDDWndProc));
  { and add it to the list }
  SubclassList.Add (
    TSubclassItem.Create (Control.Handle, WndProc, AOnDrop));
end;
```

```pascal
{
  UnacceptDroppedFiles unsubclasses the window and removes its
  entry from the subclass list.
}
procedure UnacceptDroppedFiles (Control : TWinControl);
var
  Item : TSubclassItem;
begin
  { stop accepting dropped files }
  DragAcceptFiles (Control.Handle, False);

  Item := FindItemInList (Control.Handle);
  if Item <> Nil then begin
    { restore the old window procedure }
    SetWindowLong (Control.Handle, GWL_WNDPROC,
      Longint (Item.WindowProc));
    { remove the item from the list }
    SubclassList.Remove (Item);
    { and destroy it }
    Item.Free;
  end;
end;

{ TDragDropInfo }
constructor TDragDropInfo.Create (ANumFiles : UINT);
begin
  inherited Create;
  FNumFiles := ANumFiles;
  FFileList := TStringList.Create;
end;

destructor TDragDropInfo.Destroy;
begin
  FFileList.Free;
  inherited Destroy;
end;

initialization
  SubclassList := TList.Create;

finalization
  SubclassList.Free;

end.
```

Drag And Drop The Windows Way

If you've done subclassing before, you may wonder why I didn't store the old window procedure (or even a pointer to the **TSubclassItem** object) in the **GWL_USER- DATA** member of the window's data structure. I thought about it, but I came up against the same arguments I used against chaining **Application.On Message:** There's no telling what some other program's gonna do. If FMDD were to use **GWL_USERDATA**, then any control that wanted to use FMDD couldn't use that field. It seems like an arbitrary restriction, so I went with a **TList** of structures. This provides a more flexible implementation, at only a small cost in runtime efficiency (that is, in the time required to look up the item in the list). Handling Windows messages isn't normally an especially time-critical operation, so the small amount of time required for the lookup won't be noticed. Leave **GWL_USERDATA** for the user data, and find another way to store the saved window procedure pointer.

With the completed FMDD unit, we're now free to create applications that have multiple forms accepting dropped files, or even forms that accept dropped files in two or more different controls. The Drag3 program, shown in Figure 3.2, is one such form. The form itself doesn't accept dropped files—the individual list boxes do. Fire it up and check it out. The form's source code, DRAGFRM3.PAS, is shown in Listing 3.8.

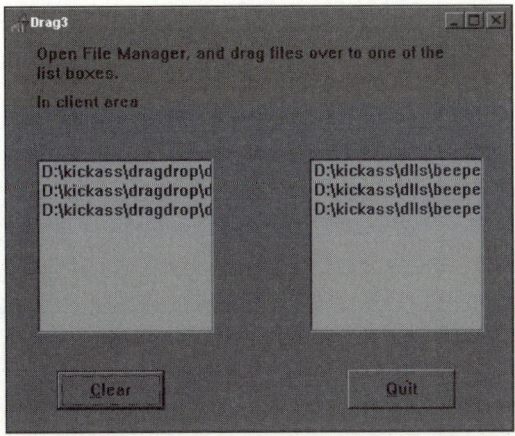

Figure 3.2
A form that accepts dropped files in multiple list boxes.

Chapter 3

Listing 3.8 DRAGFRM3.PAS.

```pascal
{
  DRAGFRM3.PAS-Accepting dragged files in multiple controls

  Author: Jim Mischel
  Last Update:  04/27/97
}
unit dragfrm3;

interface

uses
  SysUtils, Windows, Messages, Classes, Graphics, Controls,
  Forms, Dialogs, StdCtrls,
  {
     FMDD defines the drag and drop interface.
  }
  FMDD2;

type
  TForm1 = class(TForm)
    ListBox1: TListBox;
    Button1: TButton;
    Button2: TButton;
    Label1: TLabel;
    Label2: TLabel;
    ListBox2: TListBox;
    procedure FormCreate(Sender: TObject);
    procedure FormClose(Sender: TObject; var Action: TCloseAction);
    procedure Button1Click(Sender: TObject);
    procedure Button2Click(Sender: TObject);
  private
    { Private declarations }
    procedure OnListbox1FMDragDrop (DragDropInfo : TDragDropInfo);
    procedure OnListbox2FMDragDrop (DragDropInfo : TDragDropInfo);
    procedure ProcessDroppedFiles (lb : TListBox;
                DragDropInfo : TDragDropInfo);
  public
    { Public declarations }
  end;

var
  Form1: TForm1;

implementation
```

```
{$R *.DFM}

procedure TForm1.FormCreate(Sender: TObject);
begin
  FMDD2.AcceptDroppedFiles (Listbox1, OnListbox1FMDragDrop);
  FMDD2.AcceptDroppedFiles (Listbox2, OnListbox2FMDragDrop);
end;


procedure TForm1.ProcessDroppedFiles (lb : TListBox;
             DragDropInfo : TDragDropInfo);
var
  i : Integer;
begin
  { Determine if in client area }
  if DragDropInfo.InClientArea then
    Label2.Caption := 'In client area'
  else
    Label2.Caption := 'Not in client area';

  { add each file to the list box }
  for i := 0 to DragDropInfo.NumFiles - 1 do begin
    lb.Items.Add (DragDropInfo.Files[i]);
  end;
end;

procedure TForm1.OnListbox1FMDragDrop (DragDropInfo : TDragDropInfo);
begin
  ProcessDroppedFiles (Listbox1, DragDropInfo);
end;

procedure TForm1.OnListbox2FMDragDrop (DragDropInfo : TDragDropInfo);
begin
  ProcessDroppedFiles (Listbox2, DragDropInfo);
end;

procedure TForm1.FormClose (Sender: TObject; var Action: TCloseAction);
begin
  { Don't accept files anymore }
  FMDD2.UnacceptDroppedFiles (Listbox1);
  FMDD2.UnacceptDroppedFiles (Listbox2);
end;

procedure TForm1.Button1Click(Sender: TObject);
```

Chapter 3

```
begin
  Listbox1.Clear;
  Listbox2.Clear;
end;

procedure TForm1.Button2Click(Sender: TObject);
begin
  Close;
end;

end.
```

Now *that* is a Delphi program. There's no mucking around with window handles and window procedures. Everything's done with components and event handlers the way Delphi programs were meant to be written. All of the gory details are hidden away in FMDD—out of sight of the application programmer, who's interested in accepting dropped files, but not particularly interested in learning how to navigate through the Windows message loop.

Don't get me wrong, I'm a firm believer in knowledge. As you learn more about how Windows and Delphi work "under the hood," you develop alternate ways of looking at and solving problems. But after you've solved the problem once, why do it again? It takes a little time to design and implement a good wrapper around a Windows feature like drag and drop, but once you've done it, you can use that wrapper for any application that needs the feature, and you don't have to step down into the bowels of Windows to do it.

HIGH PERFORMANCE

Dragging And Dropping With OLE

CHAPTER 4

As it turns out, the File Manager drag and drop implementation is just a special case of the more general OLE drag and drop interface. With the OLE interface your application can be a drag and drop server—sending files and other types of data to other applications.

Dragging And Dropping With OLE

Jim Mischel

Knowledge is a funny thing. Not the knowledge itself, but more the way we acquire it. Trial and error seems to be my default method of learning, although given a choice (or perhaps just better preparation) I'd choose a different school altogether. Building an OLE drag and drop application from scratch using only the scant information provided in the Delphi documentation and the Windows Software Development Kit (SDK) is a full-semester course at Hard Knocks College. I have the scars to prove it.

What Is OLE?

OLE is an acronym for Object Linking and Embedding. It's a technology that lets your applications share information with other applications through well-defined interfaces that can be accessed from a variety of different programming languages. A Delphi program can communicate with Microsoft Word, for example, through an OLE interface, and make Word do all manner of things—load and print files, automatically create documents, or whatever. The Windows documentation calls this OLE Automation. OLE is also used to provide Windows 95 shell extensions, links to files, shortcuts, and just about anything else these days that has two programs talking to each other.

Since its first release several years ago, OLE has gone through quite a few refinements and a number of name changes. In addition to OLE, this technology has been known as OCX, and most recently ActiveX. Whatever you call it, OLE is built on top of an interface specification model called Component Object Model, or COM. And it's COM that's the really interesting thing here. COM is simply a method of defining interfaces that completely hide implementations. A COM interface specification is like the **interface** part of a Delphi unit—you can see *what* the interface does, but not *how* it's accomplished.

Windows' OLE is just a bunch of COM specifications and a handful of implementations. It's important that you understand this. The drag and drop interface, for example, consists of four major interfaces: **IDropTarget**, **IDropSource**, **IDataObject**, and **IEnumFormatEtc**. *But none of these interfaces are implemented!* There are functions that *call* these interfaces, but it's up to you to write the code that actually implements the interfaces and returns the data that the Windows functions expect. OLE defines the edges—you do the dirty work under the hood.

OLE Inheritance And TInterfacedObject

The interfaces I mentioned above, like all of Windows' OLE interfaces, are descended from the **IUnknown** interface. The **IUnknown** interface provides two services to OLE objects: reference counting and identification. The **QueryInterface** function allows clients to determine what interfaces a particular object supports. The **AddRef** and **Release** functions allow the object itself to keep track of how many clients are referencing it. A counter is incremented each time a client calls **AddRef**, and the same counter is decremented when the client calls **Release**. If the count goes to zero, the object can remove itself from memory because nobody's using it.

All OLE objects inherit this behavior from **IUnknown**. However, OLE objects do not necessarily inherit the *implementation* of this behavior. Inheritance in OLE parlance means inheritance of interface specification—not inheritance of code. That all of the OLE interfaces inherit from **IUnknown** simply means that all of the OLE interfaces are expected to implement the three functions that are defined by **IUnknown**. It does not, under any circumstances, imply that implementations of **IDropTarget** and **IDropSource** share the same code in the same way that **TControl** and **TWinControl** share the same code for the **WMLButtonDown** procedure. In fact, if you were to implement these two interfaces in a nonobject-oriented language, each interface implementation would have to have its own **QueryInterface**, **AddRef**, and **Release** functions, each of which *could* call some common code if that's the way you wanted to write it.

As it does with everything else Windows-related, Delphi makes dealing with OLE interfaces much easier. Delphi defines a class, **TInterfacedObject**, that implements the **IUnknown** interface and can serve as a base class for simple OLE objects. It's nice to know how the **IUnknown** interface works but, believe me, it's even nicer not having to worry about it. Our implementations of the four interfaces required for drag and drop will all descend from **TInterfacedObject**.

> **Note**: *Delphi 2 implemented OLE interfaces using the OLE2.PAS unit, which has been provided in Delphi 3 for backward compatibility. But new code should be written using ACTIVEX.PAS and **TInterfacedObject**. You could write your code using OLE2, but it would be much more difficult. You're using a state-of-the-art development tool, so go ahead and use the new technology that goes along with it.*

OLE Drag And Drop Requirements

If your application is going to be a drop target—that is, if it will accept dropped information—then it must implement only the **IDropTarget** interface. If your application will be sourcing drag and drop information, then it must implement the **IDropSource** and **IDataObject** interfaces. The **IDataObject** interface, if implemented correctly, can be reused by code that implements clipboard cut and paste operations.

We're going to implement all three of these interfaces to provide drag client and drag server functionality.

Drop Client Responsibilities

In order to be a drop target, a window must:

1. Initialize the OLE libraries by calling **OleInitialize**.
2. Instantiate an object that implements the **IDropTarget** interface.
3. Lock the instantiated object by calling **CoLockObjectExternal**.
4. Call **RegisterDragDrop**, passing the handle of the window that will acceptdropped data, and the instantiated **IDropTarget** interface object.
5. On exit, unlock the object, call **RevokeDragDrop** to tell OLE that the window no longer accepts dropped data, and call **OleUninitialize** to uninitialize the OLE libraries.

And that's just the stuff that your application has to do in order for OLE to treat it as a drop target. In order to implement the **IDropTarget** interface, you must define the following methods, which are called by OLE during a drag operation:

1. **DragEnter** is called when the mouse cursor is over the window. **DragEnter** must determine the type of data being dragged and return status to indicate whether or not, and how, the window can accept the data. **DragEnter** can also provide visual feedback (changing the cursor, for example) to indicate that the data can or cannot be dropped.

2. **DragLeave** is called if the mouse cursor moves out of the window, or if the user cancels the drag operation. **DragLeave** must release any references it may have to the data being dragged, and must also remove any visual feedback about the drag operation.

3. **DragOver** is called whenever the mouse moves while it's on the window. This function can give visual feedback to the user, and also tell OLE whether or not the data can be dropped at that particular point on the window. **DragOver** is called many times during a drag operation, so it should be a reasonably efficient function with no unnecessary processing going on.

4. **Drop** is called when the user completes the drag and drop operation. **Drop** incorporates the data into the target window, removes any visual feedback, and releases the data object. This function must also return status to OLE so that OLE can tell the drop source object to terminate.

These four methods are declared by the **IDropTarget** interface in ACTIVEX.PAS, and are implemented for a file drop target object in FILEDROP.PAS, shown in Listing 4.1.

Listing 4.1 FILEDROP.PAS implements the TFileDropTarget class.

```
{
  FILEDROP.PAS - implements a simple OLE file drop target

  Author: Jim Mischel
  Last Update: 05/28/97
}
unit FileDrop;

interface
```

```pascal
uses Windows, ActiveX, Classes;
type
  { TDragDropInfo is slightly modified from FMDD2.PAS }
  TDragDropInfo = class (TObject)
  private
    FInClientArea : Boolean;
    FDropPoint : TPoint;
    FFileList : TStringList;
  public
    constructor Create (ADropPoint : TPoint; AInClient : Boolean);
    destructor Destroy; override;
    procedure Add (const s : String);

    property InClientArea : Boolean read FInClientArea;
    property DropPoint : TPoint read FDropPoint;
    property Files : TStringList read FFileList;
  end;

  TFileDropEvent = procedure (DDI : TDragDropInfo) of object;

  { TFileDropTarget knows how to accept dropped files }
  TFileDropTarget = class (TInterfacedObject, IDropTarget)
  private
    FHandle : HWND;
    FOnFilesDropped : TFileDropEvent;
  public
    constructor Create (Handle: HWND; AOnDrop: TFileDropEvent);
    destructor Destroy; override;

    { from IDropTarget }
    function DragEnter(const dataObj: IDataObject; grfKeyState: Longint;
      pt: TPoint; var dwEffect: Longint): HResult; stdcall;
    function DragOver(grfKeyState: Longint; pt: TPoint;
      var dwEffect: Longint): HResult; stdcall;
    function DragLeave: HResult; stdcall;
    function Drop(const dataObj: IDataObject; grfKeyState: Longint; pt:
TPoint; var dwEffect: Longint): HResult; stdcall;

    property OnFilesDropped : TFileDropEvent
      read FOnFilesDropped write FOnFilesDropped;
  end;

implementation
```

```pascal
uses ShellAPI;

{ TDragDropInfo }

constructor TDragDropInfo.Create
    (
        ADropPoint : TPoint;
        AInClient : Boolean
    );
begin
  inherited Create;
  FFileList := TStringList.Create;
  FDropPoint := ADropPoint;
  FInClientArea := AInClient;
end;

destructor TDragDropInfo.Destroy;
begin
  FFileList.Free;
  inherited Destroy;
end;

procedure TDragDropInfo.Add
    (
        const s : String
    );
begin
  Files.Add (s);
end;

{ TFileDropTarget }

constructor TFileDropTarget.Create
    (
        Handle: HWND;
        AOnDrop: TFileDropEvent
    );
begin
  inherited Create;
  _AddRef;
  FHandle := Handle;
  FOnFilesDropped := AOnDrop;
  ActiveX.CoLockObjectExternal(Self, true, false);
  ActiveX.RegisterDragDrop (FHandle, Self);
end;
```

Dragging And Dropping With OLE

```
{ Destroy unlocks and disassociates an object. }
destructor TFileDropTarget.Destroy;
var
  WorkHandle: HWND;
begin
  {
    If FHandle is not 0, then we're still associated with
    a window.  Note that we must set FHandle to 0 before
    doing anything else because CoLockObjectExternal and
    RevokeDragDrop both call Release, which could call Free,
    putting us into an infinite loop here.

    I've a feeling that this isn't entirely safe.  If this
    object is freed before the reference count goes to 0,
    it's possible that this function will raise an exception.
  }
  if (FHandle <> 0) then
  begin
    WorkHandle := FHandle;
    FHandle := 0;
    ActiveX.CoLockObjectExternal (Self, false, true);
    ActiveX.RevokeDragDrop (WorkHandle);
  end;

  inherited Destroy;
end;


function TFileDropTarget.DragEnter
    (
      const dataObj: IDataObject;
      grfKeyState: Longint;
      pt: TPoint;
      var dwEffect: Longint
    ): HResult; stdcall;
begin
  dwEffect := DROPEFFECT_COPY;
  Result := S_OK;
end;

function TFileDropTarget.DragOver
    (
      grfKeyState: Longint;
      pt: TPoint;
      var dwEffect: Longint
    ): HResult; stdcall;
```

```
begin
  dwEffect := DROPEFFECT_COPY;
  Result := S_OK;
end;

function TFileDropTarget.DragLeave: HResult; stdcall;
begin
  Result := S_OK;
end;

{
  Data's been dropped.  Handle it.
}
function TFileDropTarget.Drop
    (
       const dataObj: IDataObject;
       grfKeyState: Longint;
       pt: TPoint;
       var dwEffect: Longint
    ): HResult; stdcall;
var
  Medium : TSTGMedium;
  Format : TFormatETC;
  NumFiles: Integer;
  i : Integer;
  rslt : Integer;
  DropInfo : TDragDropInfo;
  szFilename : array [0..MAX_PATH] of char;
  InClient : Boolean;
  DropPoint : TPoint;
begin
  dataObj._AddRef;
  {
    Get the data.  The TFormatETC structure tells
    dataObj.GetData how to get the data and in which
    format it should be stored.  It's stored in the
    TSTGMedium structure.
  }
  Format.cfFormat := CF_HDROP;
  Format.ptd      := Nil;
  Format.dwAspect := DVASPECT_CONTENT;
  Format.lindex   := -1;
  Format.tymed    := TYMED_HGLOBAL;

  { Get data into the Medium structure }
  rslt := dataObj.GetData (Format, Medium);
```

```
    {
      If we were successful, then treat it like a File Mangler
      drag and drop operation.
    }
    if (rslt = S_OK) then
    begin
      { Get number of files and other info }
      NumFiles := DragQueryFile (Medium.hGlobal, $FFFFFFFF, NIL, 0);
      InClient := DragQueryPoint (Medium.hGlobal, DropPoint);

      { create the TDragDropInfo object }
      DropInfo := TDragDropInfo.Create (DropPoint, InClient);

      { add each file to the list }
      for i := 0 to NumFiles - 1 do
      begin
        DragQueryFile (Medium.hGlobal, i, szFilename, sizeof(szFilename));
        DropInfo.Add (szFilename);
      end;

      { if a drop event handler was specified, call it }
      if (Assigned (FOnFilesDropped)) then
      begin
        FOnFilesDropped (DropInfo);
      end;

      DropInfo.Free;
    end;

    if (Medium.unkForRelease = nil) then
      ReleaseStgMedium (Medium);

  dataObj._Release;
  dwEffect := DROPEFFECT_COPY;
  result := S_OK;
end;


initialization
  OleInitialize (Nil);

finalization
  OleUninitialize;

end.
```

Note here that the **OleInitialize** and **OleUninitialize** functions are called in the **initialization** and **finalization** sections, respectively, of the unit. This ensures that the OLE libraries are properly initialized before anything in the DragDrop module accesses them, and uninitialized after everything that accesses them has been shut down.

Before we talk any more about this implementation, let's build a simple form that uses the **TOleDropTarget** object to accept dropped data. This form is much like the samples we used in the last chapter. The form's only component is a list box into which you can drop files from Windows Explorer. The form's few simple methods are shown in Listing 4.2.

Listing 4.2 DRAGFRM1.PAS uses the TFileDropTarget object to accept dropped files.

```
{
  DRAGFRM1.PAS - Accepting files the OLE way

  Author:   Jim Mischel
  Last Update:  05/28/97
}
unit dragfrm1;

interface

uses
  Windows, Messages, SysUtils, Classes, Graphics, Controls, Forms,
Dialogs, StdCtrls, FileDrop;

type
  TForm1 = class(TForm)
    ListBox1: TListBox;
    procedure FormCreate(Sender: TObject);
    procedure FormClose(Sender: TObject; var Action: TCloseAction);
  private
    { Private declarations }
    FDropTarget: TFileDropTarget;
    procedure OnFilesDropped (DropInfo: TDragDropInfo);
  public
    { Public declarations }
  end;
```

```
var
  Form1: TForm1;

implementation

{$R *.DFM}

procedure TForm1.FormCreate(Sender: TObject);
begin
  { Create a drop target }
  FDropTarget := TFileDropTarget.Create (Listbox1.Handle,
                                         OnFilesDropped);
end;

procedure TForm1.FormClose(Sender: TObject; var Action: TCloseAction);
begin
  FDropTarget.Free;
end;

{
  OnFilesDropped is called if files are received by the
  TFileDropTarget object.
}
procedure TForm1.OnFilesDropped (DropInfo: TDragDropInfo);
var
  i : Integer;
begin
  { add each file to the list box }
  for i := 0 to DropInfo.Files.Count-1 do begin
    Listbox1.Items.Add (DropInfo.Files[i]);
  end;
end;

end.
```

When you compile and run this program, you should be able to drag a file or files from Windows Explorer or File Manager onto the list box and have the file names appear in the list box, just as we did with the example programs in the last chapter.

How It Works

Listing 4.1 actually implements two classes. The first, **TDragDropInfo**, you probably recognize from the last chapter. I've beefed it up a little here because it's going to need a little more functionality in order to be used for drop sourcing, but in general it's the same object that we used for the File Manager Drag and Drop example.

The other class, **TFileDropTarget**, is an implementation of the **IDropTarget** interface. If you look at the definition of this class, you see:

```
class TFileDropTarget = class (TInterfacedObject, IDropTarget)
```

If you're deep into C++, don't get your hopes up. And if you think multiple inheritance is the manifest work of the devil, don't run screaming for the hills. This is *not* multiple inheritance. This odd-looking bit of code says, "**TFileDropTarget** is a descendent of **TInterfacedObject**, and implements the **IDropTarget** interface." It's true that a single class can implement multiple interfaces, but that's a far cry from multiple inheritance.

If you take a peek at the ACTIVEX.PAS file, which is installed in Delphi's Source\RTL\WIN directory, you'll see the following declaration for the **IDropTarget** interface:

```
IDropTarget = interface(IUnknown)
   ['{00000122-0000-0000-C000-000000000046}']
   function DragEnter(const dataObj: IDataObject; grfKeyState: Longint;
     pt: TPoint; var dwEffect: Longint): HResult; stdcall;
   function DragOver(grfKeyState: Longint; pt: TPoint;
     var dwEffect: Longint): HResult; stdcall;
   function DragLeave: HResult; stdcall;
   function Drop(const dataObj: IDataObject; grfKeyState: Longint; pt:
              TPoint;
     var dwEffect: Longint): HResult; stdcall;
 end;
```

The first line just says that **IDropTarget** is an interface that inherits from **IUnknown**. The next line defines the interface's Globally Unique Identifier (GUID). A GUID is a 128-bit number that is supposed to be unique for each different object type. Microsoft assigned GUIDs to the standard OLE interfaces, and there are programs (and even a Windows API call) that can generate a GUID. Statistically, it's highly unlikely that two generated GUIDs will ever be the same. At any rate, you don't really need to understand GUIDs to use already defined OLE interfaces, but if you're going to be building your own interfaces you'll have to understand how to generate and use a GUID.

The rest of the code just declares the interface's methods. A class that implements this interface must implement all of the declared methods, although it can return error codes for those methods that aren't supported.

Interfaces, then, are similar to classes in that they describe what is expected. But, unlike classes, interfaces don't have storage classes (**private**, **public**, **protected**, and so on), and they can't declare variables or properties. Also (and again, unlike classes) **interface**s don't have corresponding implementations. Nowhere in ACTIVEX.PAS (or anywhere else) do you see a line of code that reads:

```
function IDropTarget.DragLeave : HResult;
```

The only really weird part of the drop target implementation in Listing 4.1 is the **TFileDropTarget.Drop** method, which is called by OLE when the user drops the files onto the destination. This function must then get the data from the data object and incorporate it into the window. Incorporating it into the window is taken care of by the **FOnFilesDropped** event procedure, which **Drop** calls after it gets the data. This function and the way it's handled are very similar to the **TFMDDEvent** handling presented in the previous chapter.

Getting the data, on the other hand, is a bit more involved.

In order to get the dropped data, **Drop** fills in a **TFormatETC** structure that describes how the data should be presented, and passes that structure and a **TStgMedium** structure to the data object's **GetData** method. **GetData** formats the data as requested by the contents of the **TFormatETC** structure, and returns the data in the **TStgMedium** structure. **Drop** can then work with the data, which in this case means building the **TDragDropInfo** structure. When **Drop** is done with the data, it must free the **TStgMedium** structure. This last point is *very* important—especially when you're implementing the drop source half. The *client* is responsible for freeing data. This means that your data object's implementation of **GetData** has to provide a copy of the data—not the data itself. This may sound obvious now, and it's certainly obvious to me after I spent a day and a half debugging!

What I found most surprising about this drop target implementation is that it's less complicated than the drag and drop implementation in Chapter 3—which perhaps goes to show that things aren't always as hard as we think they are. I must admit, though, that wrapping my head around COM and **TInterfacedObject** took a while—quite a bit longer than it took to understand **WM_DROPFILES**.

So What?

So I've given you yet another method of accepting dropped files. As it turns out, this new method can in most cases completely replace the code that I presented in the last chapter. The important thing here, though, is that we've taken a process that we understand very well—accepting dropped files—and implemented it using a new (to us) technology: COM/OLE. And we learned how to use COM/OLE in the process. *Now* we can apply that new knowledge to implementing something new, different, and *much* more involved—a drag and drop server.

Becoming A Drag And Drop Server

Unlike the drop client, which went together fairly painlessly once I understood the whole COM interface idea, building the server was an exercise in frustration. At first, it seemed like I was having to implement the whole kitchen sink just to get a simple drag server going. Building a drag and drop server requires that you implement three interfaces—and you can't test any one of the interfaces until they've all been coded. This makes for an interesting debugging environment in that you can't ever be certain which part of the program is causing a particular problem.

> **Note**: I'm sure that part of my troubles stems from my inexperience with OLE and COM, but I'm equally convinced that the largest part of the confusion was due to the needless complexity of the interface and the less-than-adequate documentation. Do realize that I work in C and C++, so I'm not daunted by the obvious slant of the Windows SDK documentation, whose quality ranges from nonexistent through somewhat helpful. The SDK example programs, on the other hand, are not especially clear or helpful even to an experienced C++ programmer. Simple programs that illustrate concepts in a straightforward, no-frills manner would be much more helpful than the convoluted OLE sample programs that try to do everything and do nothing especially well. I learned more from the OLECTNRS.PAS file (in Delphi's Source\VCL directory) than I did from all of the Microsoft SDK examples that I studied.

Drop Server Responsibilities

From far enough away, implementing a drag and drop server doesn't look much more difficult than implementing the client's side. And, in my opinion, it shouldn't be. But whoever designed the OLE drag and drop interface didn't ask my opinion. Here's what a drag and drop server has to do:

1. Determine, based on the user's input, the data that's been selected for dragging.

2. Call **OleInitialize** to initialize the OLE libraries.

3. Instantiate an object that implements the **IDropSource** interface. This object controls the user interface during the drag operation.

4. Instantiate an object that implements the **IDataObject** interface. This object carries the data that is being dragged.

5. Initiate the drag operation by calling the OLE **DoDragDrop** function, passing it the **IDropSource** and **IDataObject** objects. **DoDragDrop** controls the drag operation and calls methods in the **IDropSource** object and in the **IDropTarget** object of any window that's been registered with **RegisterDragDrop** and over which the mouse cursor passes during the drag operation.

6. Generate visual feedback during the drag operation, such as setting the cursor shape as it moves across the screen.

7. Perform any action on the original data, based on the results of the drag operation. For example, you may have to delete the original data after a drag move operation completes.

8. When **DoDragDrop** returns, destroy the instantiated **IDataObject** and **IDropSource** objects.

9. Call **OleUninitialize** to shut down the OLE libraries.

Those are just the basic steps. There are *lots* of details to be managed. The application program's responsibilities are pretty simple: initialize stuff, instantiate a couple of objects, and call **DoDragDrop**. It's the implementations of **IDropSource**, **IDataObject**, and **IEnumFormatEtc** that get complicated in a hurry. All of which means that you should have a good understanding of what's expected on the server side before you start coding. Let's take a look at how all these pieces fit together and how they relate to each other.

IDropSource Interface Requirements

Of the three interfaces required for a drag and drop server, **IDropSource** is the easiest to implement. The **IDropSource** implementation has two responsibilities:

1. Respond to changes in mouse buttons or keyboard input to determine whether the drag operation should continue, be completed, or be canceled.

2. Respond to changes in mouse location by changing the cursor or providing other visual feedback.

These two responsibilities are handled by **IDropSource**'s two methods: **QueryContinueDrag** and **GiveFeedback**. Their declarations are shown in this **interface** specification:

```
IDropSource = interface(IUnknown)
   ['{00000121-0000-0000-C000-000000000046}']
    function QueryContinueDrag(fEscapePressed: BOOL;
      grfKeyState: Longint): HResult; stdcall;
    function GiveFeedback(dwEffect: Longint): HResult; stdcall;
 end;
```

QueryContinueDrag is called by the **DoDragDrop** function whenever it detects a change in the keyboard or mouse button state during the drag operation. **QueryContinueDrag** determines whether the operation should be continued, canceled, or deleted based on the values of the **fEscapePressed** and **grfKeyState** variables.

GiveFeedback is called by the **DoDragDrop** function for every change in the mouse state during a drag operation. **GiveFeedback**'s job is to provide visual feedback about the state of the drag operation. Most of the time, this visual feedback is just a change in the cursor's shape. **GiveFeedback** is called by **DoDragDrop** after it calls the **IDropSource** methods **DragEnter**, **DragLeave**, or **DragOver**, and is passed the **DROPEFFECT** value that was returned by the **IDropTarget** method.

IDropSource is normally very simple, especially because OLE defines default behavior that's easy to implement.

IDataObject Holds The Data

IDataObject defines an interface that controls the data being dragged, and also knows how to present that data in a format that a requesting **IDropTarget** object will understand. **IDataObject** is used in drag and drop implementations, and also in implementations of clipboard data transfer. Once you have an **IDataObject** interface working with one type of data transfer, making it work with the other is painless. But getting it to work the first time is difficult. Sometimes. And convoluted. Mostly.

The **IDataObject** interface provides data transfer capabilities and change notification. Defined methods can set the object's data, retrieve the object's data in a number of (possibly device-specific) formats, return information about the supported data formats, and provide notification to other objects if the data object's data changes. Although only three of the **IDataObject** methods must be fully implemented in order to support dragging and dropping files onto the Windows Explorer or File Manager, those three methods make up a very large chunk of code.

The three **IDataObject** methods that you must implement in order to make a file drop server work are **QueryGetData**, **GetData**, and **EnumFormatEtc**. And implementation of **EnumFormatEtc**, as you'll see, requires that you also implement the **IEnumFormatEtc** interface. I told you this was going to get complicated.

QueryGetData is called by a drop target and passed a **TFormatEtc** structure that describes how the drop target wants data to be returned. It's up to **QueryGetData** to tell the drop target if the data object is capable of providing the data in the specified format. The return value of **QueryGetData** is S_OK if there's a reasonable certainty that a subsequent call to **GetData** would be successful. In some cases (such as out of memory), the subsequent **GetData** call may still fail.

GetData is called when a drop target wants to receive the data. The drop target passes a **TFormatEtc** structure that describes the desired data format, and a **TStgMedium** structure into which **GetData** will render the data. It's the caller's (that is, the drop target's) responsibility to free the **TStgMedium** structure once it's finished with the data. This is very important to remember. Since the client is freeing data returned by **GetData**, **GetData** must provide a *copy* of the data object's data. If **GetData** were to return the actual data, the client would free it, causing big problems the next time a client (or the data object itself) wanted to access the data.

The **EnumFormatEtc** function reports on the formats that the data object is capable of rendering. The data returned is in the form of an **IEnumFormatEtc** object, which means that we have to implement **IEnumFormatEtc** in order to implement

IDataObject. The OLE SDK samples provide a number of **IEnumFormatEtc** implementations—all in C or C++, and all more than just a little complicated. Fortunately, the implementation of the **TOleForm** and **TOleContainer** classes in OLECTNRS.PAS includes a much more straightforward implementation which served as the template for my own implementation. Looking at the OLE SDK example implementations of **IEnumFormatEtc** makes sense now, but I'd still be ripping my hair out had I not seen the implementation in OLECTNRS.PAS.

IEnumFormatEtc defines four methods, **Next**, **Skip**, **Reset**, and **Clone**, which allow applications to step through and examine the supported data formats, and also to copy the list of supported formats. A general implementation of **IEnumFormatEtc** gets very complex because it must be able to dynamically allocate **TFormatEtc** structures and copy the internal data contained by the structures. Our needs aren't that involved so our implementation assumes that the **TFormatEtc** array to which it points is static data. This is good enough for our purposes, but would be much too restrictive for many applications. Our implementation of **IEnumFormatEtc** is shown in Listing 4.3.

Listing 4.3 ENUMFMT.PAS: a simple implementation of the IEnumFormatEtc interface.

```
{
  ENUMFMT.PAS - Implementation of IEnumFormatEtc interface

  Author: Jim Mischel
  Last Update:  05/30/97

  Note that this isn't an especially robust implementation of
  IEnumFormatEtc in that it expects the FormatList maintained
  by the TEnumFormatEtc object to be a static array.  This
  works fine for simple objects like the file drop server,
  but would be an extreme constraint on many applications.
}
unit EnumFmt;

interface

uses Windows, ActiveX;

type
  { TFormatList is an array of TFormatEtc records }
```

```
    PFormatList = ^TFormatList;
    TFormatList = array[0..1] of TFormatEtc;

    TEnumFormatEtc = class (TInterfacedObject, IEnumFormatEtc)
    private
      FFormatList: PFormatList;
      FFormatCount: Integer;
      FIndex: Integer;
    public
      constructor Create
        (FormatList: PFormatList; FormatCount, Index: Integer);
      { IEnumFormatEtc }
      function Next
        (celt: Longint; out elt; pceltFetched: PLongint): HResult; stdcall;
      function Skip (celt: Longint) : HResult; stdcall;
      function Reset : HResult; stdcall;
      function Clone (out enum : IEnumFormatEtc) : HResult; stdcall;
    end;

implementation

constructor TEnumFormatEtc.Create
    (
      FormatList: PFormatList;
      FormatCount, Index : Integer
    );
begin
  inherited Create;
  FFormatList := FormatList;
  FFormatCount := FormatCount;
  FIndex := Index;
end;


{
  Retrieve the specified number of TFormatEtc structures
  into the passed elt array.
  This retrieves celt items starting at the current list pointer.
}
function TEnumFormatEtc.Next
    (
      celt: Longint;
      out elt;
      pceltFetched: PLongint
    ): HResult;
var
  i : Integer;
```

```
    eltout : TFormatList absolute elt;
begin
  i := 0;

  while (i < celt) and (FIndex < FFormatCount) do
  begin
    eltout[i] := FFormatList[FIndex];
    Inc (FIndex);
    Inc (i);
  end;

  if (pceltFetched <> nil) then
    pceltFetched^ := i;

  if (I = celt) then
    Result := S_OK
  else
    Result := S_FALSE;
end;

{
  Skips over celt items in the list, setting the current list pointer
  to (CurrentPointer + celt) or to <End of list> if overflow
  occurs.
}
function TEnumFormatEtc.Skip
    (
      celt: Longint
    ): HResult;
begin
  if (celt <= FFormatCount - FIndex) then
  begin
    FIndex := FIndex + celt;
    Result := S_OK;
  end else
  begin
    FIndex := FFormatCount;
    Result := S_FALSE;
  end;
end;

{ Reset the current pointer to the head of the list }
function TEnumFormatEtc.Reset: HResult;
```

```
begin
  FIndex := 0;
  Result := S_OK;
end;

{ Make a copy of the list of structures }
function TEnumFormatEtc.Clone
    (
      out enum: IEnumFormatEtc
    ): HResult;
begin
  enum := TEnumFormatEtc.Create (FFormatList, FFormatCount, FIndex);
  Result := S_OK;
end;

end.
```

Implementing The Drop Server

OLE drop targets that accept dropped files expect data to be delivered in a clipboard format called **CF_HDROP**. This is the format that the first example program in this chapter expects, and is also the format that the **WM_DROPFILES** implementation expects, although it hides that expectation behind the **DragQueryFile** and other API calls. Since we're implementing a drag server, we need a way to create **CF_HDROP** data from our list of files. We already have a class, **TDragDropInfo**, that keeps track of a list of files, so it makes sense to add such a method to this class. This new method, **TDragDropInfo.CreateHDrop**, is shown in Listing 4.4.

Listing 4.4   TDragDropInfo.CreateHDrop converts the dragged file data.

```
function TDragDropInfo.CreateHDrop : HGlobal;
var
  RequiredSize : Integer;
  i : Integer;
  hGlobalDropInfo : HGlobal;
  DropFiles : PDropFiles;
  c : PChar;
begin
  {
    Build a TDropFiles structure in GlobalAlloc'd memory.
    This is globally allocated and shared because it's
    probably being passed to another process.
  }
```

```
  { Determine required structure size }
  RequiredSize := sizeof (TDropFiles);
  for i := 0 to Self.Files.Count-1 do
  begin
    { Length of each string, plus 1 byte for terminator }
    RequiredSize := RequiredSize + Length (Self.Files[i]) + 1;
  end;
  { 1 byte for final terminator }
  inc (RequiredSize);

  hGlobalDropInfo := GlobalAlloc
      ((GMEM_SHARE or GMEM_MOVEABLE or GMEM_ZEROINIT), RequiredSize);
  if (hGlobalDropInfo <> 0) then
  begin
    { Lock the memory so we can access it }
    DropFiles := GlobalLock (hGlobalDropInfo);

    { Fill in DropFiles structure fields }
    {
      pFiles is an offset from the start of the structure
      to the first byte of the file names array.
    }
    DropFiles.pFiles := sizeof (TDropFiles);
    DropFiles.pt := Self.FDropPoint;
    DropFiles.fNC := Self.InClientArea;
    DropFiles.fWide := False;

    {
      Copy each file name into the buffer.
      The buffer starts at DropFiles + DropFiles.pFiles..
      that is, after the last structure member.
    }
    c := PChar (DropFiles);
    c := c + DropFiles.pFiles;
    for i := 0 to Self.Files.Count-1 do
    begin
      StrCopy (c, PChar (Self.Files[i]));
      c := c + Length (Self.Files[i]);
    end;

    { Release our lock }
    GlobalUnlock (hGlobalDropInfo);
  end;

  Result := hGlobalDropInfo;
end;
```

This function simply computes the required data size (which is the size of a **TDropFiles** record—defined in the ShlObj unit—plus the combined length of all of the file names), allocates memory, and then fills in the structure. The memory is allocated on Windows' global heap and is made sharable so that it can be passed to other applications. The allocated memory is referenced by a handle of type **HGlobal**. It is this handle that we return to the caller. And it's the caller's responsibility to free the data (by calling Windows' **GlobalFree** API function) when it's done with the data.

The **IDropSource** and **IDataObject** interfaces are implemented in DRAGDROP.PAS (Listing 4.5) by **TFileDropSource** and **THDropDataObject**, respectively. The **TFileDropSource** object is very simple. Its constructor simply calls the constructor for **TInterfacedObject**, and then calls **_AddRef** to set the initial reference count. The **GiveFeedback** function just instructs **DoDragDrop** to use the default cursor shapes, and **QueryContinueDrag** checks the escape key pressed flag and the mouse buttons to determine if the operation should be completed, continued, or canceled. There's nothing fancy here.

THDropDataObject is a bit more involved. The constructor creates a **TDragDropInfo** object that has an empty files list. The caller then adds files to the list by calling the **Add** method. The object's destructor frees the **TDragDropInfo** object if it exists. Of the **IDataObject** interface methods, only **GetData**, **QueryGetData**, and **EnumFormatEtc** are implemented. The others return values to indicate that this object does not support those methods.

QueryGetData simply examines the passed **TFormatEtc** record to verify that it's asking for the data in the format that we can supply. If it is, the return value indicates that **GetData** can probably render the data. **EnumFormatEtc** creates and returns an **IEnumFormatEtc** object from the static, single-item array of **TFormatEtc** structures. The **GetData** function ensures that the requested format is valid (again, by calling **QueryGetData**), makes sure that there's some data to render, and then calls **TDragDropInfo.CreateHDrop** to create the global memory object that it returns to the caller in the passed **TStgMedium** record. The caller is responsible for freeing the data.

Listing 4.5 DRAGDROP.PAS: the interfaces required for a drag and drop server.

```
{
  DRAGDROP.PAS — OLE Drag and Drop implementation
```

```
    Author: Jim Mischel
    Last Update: 05/30/97
}
unit DragDrop;

interface

uses Windows, ActiveX, Classes, FileDrop;

type
  { TFileDropSource sources dropped files }
  TFileDropSource = class (TInterfacedObject, IDropSource)
    constructor Create;
    function QueryContinueDrag(fEscapePressed: BOOL;
      grfKeyState: Longint): HResult; stdcall;
    function GiveFeedback(dwEffect: Longint): HResult; stdcall;
  end;


  { THDropDataObject is a data object that contains dropped file name
    info }
  THDropDataObject = class(TInterfacedObject, IDataObject)
  private
    FDropInfo : TDragDropInfo;
  public
    constructor Create(ADropPoint : TPoint; AInClient : Boolean);
    destructor Destroy; override;
    procedure Add (const s : String);
    { from IDataObject }
    function GetData(const formatetcIn: TFormatEtc;
      out medium: TStgMedium): HResult; stdcall;
    function GetDataHere(const formatetc: TFormatEtc;
      out medium: TStgMedium): HResult; stdcall;
    function QueryGetData(const formatetc: TFormatEtc): HResult; stdcall;
    function GetCanonicalFormatEtc(const formatetc: TFormatEtc;
      out formatetcOut: TFormatEtc): HResult; stdcall;
    function SetData(const formatetc: TFormatEtc; var medium: TStgMedium;
      fRelease: BOOL): HResult; stdcall;
    function EnumFormatEtc(dwDirection: Longint; out enumFormatEtc:
      IEnumFormatEtc): HResult; stdcall;
    function DAdvise(const formatetc: TFormatEtc; advf: Longint;
      const advSink: IAdviseSink; out dwConnection: Longint): HResult;
stdcall;
    function DUnadvise(dwConnection: Longint): HResult; stdcall;
    function EnumDAdvise(out enumAdvise: IEnumStatData): HResult;
stdcall;
  end;
```

```pascal
implementation

uses EnumFmt;

{ TFileDropSource }
constructor TFileDropSource.Create;
begin
  inherited Create;
  _AddRef;
end;

{
  Determine proper action.  This function assumes that only the left
  button is used for dragging.
}
function TFileDropSource.QueryContinueDrag
    (
      fEscapePressed: BOOL;
      grfKeyState: Longint
    ): HResult;
begin
  if (fEscapePressed) then
  begin
    Result := DRAGDROP_S_CANCEL;
  end
  else if ((grfKeyState and MK_LBUTTON) = 0) then
  begin
    Result := DRAGDROP_S_DROP;
  end
  else
  begin
    Result := S_OK;
  end;
end;

function TFileDropSource.GiveFeedback
   (
     dwEffect: Longint
   ): HResult;
begin
  case dwEffect of
    DROPEFFECT_NONE,
    DROPEFFECT_COPY,
    DROPEFFECT_LINK,
    DROPEFFECT_SCROLL : Result := DRAGDROP_S_USEDEFAULTCURSORS;
```

```
    else
      Result := S_OK;
  end;
end;

{ THDropDataObject }
constructor THDropDataObject.Create
    (
      ADropPoint : TPoint;
      AInClient : Boolean
    );
begin
  inherited Create;
  _AddRef;
  FDropInfo := TDragDropInfo.Create (ADropPoint, AInClient);
end;


destructor THDropDataObject.Destroy;
begin
  if (FDropInfo <> nil) then
    FDropInfo.Free;
  inherited Destroy;
end;


procedure THDropDataObject.Add
    (
      const s : String
    );
begin
  FDropInfo.Add (s);
end;



function THDropDataObject.GetData
    (
      const formatetcIn: TFormatEtc;
      out medium: TStgMedium
    ): HResult;
begin
  Result := DV_E_FORMATETC;
  { must set all medium values to 0 (nil) in case of error }
  medium.tymed := 0;
  medium.hGlobal := 0;
  medium.unkForRelease := nil;
```

```
    { If it's a supported format, create the data and return it }
    if (QueryGetData (formatetcIn) = S_OK) then
    begin
      if (FDropInfo <> nil) then
      begin
        medium.tymed := TYMED_HGLOBAL;
        { The caller is responsible for freeing this! }
        medium.hGlobal := FDropInfo.CreateHDrop;
        Result := S_OK;
      end;
    end;
end;

function THDropDataObject.GetDataHere
    (
      const formatetc: TFormatEtc;
      out medium: TStgMedium
    ): HResult;
begin
  Result := DV_E_FORMATETC;  { Sorry, not supported }
end;

function THDropDataObject.QueryGetData
    (
      const formatetc: TFormatEtc
    ): HResult;
begin
  Result := DV_E_FORMATETC;
  with formatetc do
    if dwAspect = DVASPECT_CONTENT then
      if (cfFormat = CF_HDROP) and (tymed = TYMED_HGLOBAL) then
        Result := S_OK;
end;

function THDropDataObject.GetCanonicalFormatEtc
    (
      const formatetc: TFormatEtc;
      out formatetcOut: TFormatEtc
    ): HResult;
begin
  formatetcOut.ptd := nil;
  Result := E_NOTIMPL;
end;

function THDropDataObject.SetData
    (
```

```
      const formatetc: TFormatEtc;
      var medium: TStgMedium;
      fRelease: BOOL
    ): HResult;
begin
  Result := E_NOTIMPL;
end;

{ Return list of supported formats }
function THDropDataObject.EnumFormatEtc
    (
      dwDirection: Longint;
      out enumFormatEtc:
      IEnumFormatEtc
    ): HResult;
const
  DataFormats: array [0..0] of TFormatEtc =
  (
    (
      cfFormat : CF_HDROP;
      ptd      : Nil;
      dwAspect : DVASPECT_CONTENT;
      lindex   : -1;
      tymed    : TYMED_HGLOBAL;
    )
  );
  DataFormatCount = 1;

begin
  { Only Get is supported.  We can't set data }
  if dwDirection = DATADIR_GET then
  begin
    enumFormatEtc := TEnumFormatEtc.Create
      (@DataFormats, DataFormatCount, 0);
    Result := S_OK;
  end else
  begin
    enumFormatEtc := nil;
    Result := E_NOTIMPL;
  end;
end;

{ Advise functions are not supported }
function THDropDataObject.DAdvise
    (
```

```
        const formatetc: TFormatEtc;
        advf: Longint;
        const advSink: IAdviseSink;
        out dwConnection: Longint
    ): HResult;
begin
  Result := OLE_E_ADVISENOTSUPPORTED;
end;

function THDropDataObject.DUnadvise
    (
        dwConnection: Longint
    ): HResult;
begin
  Result := OLE_E_ADVISENOTSUPPORTED;
end;

function THDropDataObject.EnumDAdvise
    (
        out enumAdvise: IEnumStatData
    ): HResult;
begin
  Result := OLE_E_ADVISENOTSUPPORTED;
end;

initialization
  OleInitialize (Nil);

finalization
  OleUninitialize;

end.
```

The last thing we have to do is create a form that can use this new module. I've taken drag form 1 from the previous example and added a label component whose caption is "D:\TESTO.TXT". When you click on this component, an OLE drag-and-drop operation is started. You can then drag and drop the file onto the form's list box, or onto Windows Explorer. The program's list box should just display the file name. Windows Explorer should copy the file to the destination. The procedure that provides this capability, **TForm1.Label1MouseDown**, is shown in Listing 4.6.

Listing 4.6 Initiating a drag-and-drop operation.

```
procedure TForm1.Label1MouseDown(Sender: TObject; Button: TMouseButton;
  Shift: TShiftState; X, Y: Integer);
var
  DropSource : TFileDropSource;
  DropData : THDropDataObject;
  rslt : HRESULT;
  dwEffect : DWORD;
  DropPoint : TPoint;
begin
  if (Button = mbLeft) then
  begin
    { create drop source object }
    DropSource := TFileDropSource.Create;

    { And the drop data object }
    DropPoint.x := 0;
    DropPoint.y := 0;
    DropData := THDropDataObject.Create (DropPoint, True);
    DropData.Add (Label1.Caption);

    {
      DoDragDrop takes over and calls the appropriate IDropSource and
      IDropTarget functions as required.
    }
    rslt := DoDragDrop (DropData, DropSource, DROPEFFECT_COPY, dwEffect);

    if ((rslt <> DRAGDROP_S_DROP) and
        (rslt <> DRAGDROP_S_CANCEL)) then
    begin
      case rslt of
        E_OUTOFMEMORY : ShowMessage ('Out of memory');
        else ShowMessage ('Something bad happened');
      end;
    end;

    { and free stuff then we're done }
    DropSource.Free;
    DropData.Free;
  end;
end;
```

OLE!

And that, in a nutshell, is how you do drag and drop. Whole books have been written on the ins and outs of the different OLE interfaces, and there's even a lot more to know about drag and drop. But the hardest part for most programmers is wrapping their brains around the idea of COM, and the fact that OLE is mostly about defining *interfaces* for which application programmers (that is, you and I) have to provide implementations. Some of the interfaces (like **IStorage**) are also implemented by Windows, but most of the interfaces are defined so that your applications can provide information to Windows or to other applications.

We've only scratched the surface of OLE in this chapter. If you want to learn more about the predefined interfaces, you need to pick up one of the many OLE references available in any bookstore. You might also want to pick up a copy of the Windows SDK, which describes all of Windows' OLE interfaces and the implemented functions, although if you're not conversant with C, the SDK might not do you much good.

For more information about creating and using your own (or others') OLE interfaces, you'll want to study Delphi's **TComObject** and **TActiveXControl** objects, and the information in Chapter 25 of the Delphi 3 *User's Guide*, and all of Part IV, "Working with COM and ActiveX," in the Delphi 3 *Developer's Guide*. And, as always, the online help is your friend.

There's a lot to be said for the COM model of programming. If you can define a complete, but minimal, interface for an object—an interface that doesn't rely on the client knowing anything about the internal data representation—then you've probably got a very good idea of what your object does. And you've been able to draw the line between the *what* and the *how*. I'm finding that as programs get more complex, defining the interfaces between the parts of the program is the most important part of my job. If I design easy-to-use interfaces, then implementing the interfaces is easier and putting the pieces together is easier. The result is a more clearly defined program that has fewer bugs and is much easier to maintain. The interfaces don't have to be defined using COM, but the *idea* of all communication between objects taking place through well-defined interfaces has proven to be very powerful indeed.

HIGH PERFORMANCE

The Delphi Winsock Component

CHAPTER 5

Objects are good...but components are better. Let's make Internet access for Delphi a plug-and-play proposition by putting all our Winsock baggage into a VCL component.

The Delphi Winsock Component

John Penman

The Internet—and networked environments in general—becomes more popular every day. It's natural, therefore, for programmers to want to integrate network services into their applications. Under Microsoft Windows, the Winsock API is the *lingua franca* for Internet access. Using the Winsock component described in this chapter as a starting point, you'll soon be implementing many familiar TCP/IP-based programs such as FINGER, FTP, SMTP, POP3, and ECHO applications.

What Is Winsock?

Winsock is an abbreviation for Windows Sockets, an interface layer between a Windows application and an underlying TCP/IP network. The sockets interface originated with Berkeley Unix as the API to its TCP/IP network stack. Winsock is based on the Berkeley Sockets API and includes most of the standard BSD API functions, as well as some Windows-specific extensions. Adding TCP/IP networking capability to your Windows programs is as simple as using the Winsock API and dynamically linking with WINSOCK.DLL, the library that implements Winsock.

The easiest way for a Delphi programmer to interface with the Winsock API is as a component. In this chapter, we'll do just that by creating the CsSocket component, encapsulating the Winsock API. This produces several immediate benefits:

- The API becomes part of the Delphi VCL;
- Encapsulation promotes easier code reuse; and
- The client application sees a clean interface using properties and methods.

The CsSocket component is certainly Delphi-friendly, but it's not comprehensive. CsSocket provides the framework you'll use to create daughter components designed to handle any particular Internet protocol. A Winsock component already equipped to handle every conceivable Internet protocol would be a fat and complicated component. Instead, we'll use the CsSocket component as the basis for new components that deal specifically with a particular protocol.

For example, creating a component for the Hypertext Transfer Protocol (HTTP) involves three steps:

1. Derive a new component from CsSocket.
2. Set the **Service** property to HTTP in the new component's constructor.
3. Add the appropriate methods and properties for handling HTTP.

We'll go through these steps in the next chapter to create a specific component for anFTP client application.

Dissecting CsSocket

The CsSocket component is based on the nonvisual **TCsSocket** class that, in turn, descends from **TComponent**. Because it's nonvisual, **TCsSocket** is like a foundation of a house, normally hidden from view. The **TComponent** class provides the necessary methods and properties that CsSocket requires—but no more. Had I used **TGraphicControl** as an ancestor, the resulting **TCsSocket** class would be more powerful, but with a corresponding increase in complexity and overhead. CsSocket provides the basic framework to set up and maintain a TCP/IP connection and supports both stream (TCP) and datagram (UDP) sockets.

To simplify the task of building TCP/IP networking components for Internet applications, our ideal Winsock component must perform the following basic housekeeping functions:

- Start and stop Winsock;
- Resolve host names and perform other conversion operations;
- Create, maintain and destroy a connection (both TCP and UDP); and
- Send and receive data over a connection.

The Delphi Winsock Component

Like all networking life forms, our Winsock component must initialize, clean up after itself, and report errors. Listing 5.1 shows the **TCsSocket** class that performs these functions and much more. The majority of methods are in the protected section in the **TCsSocket** class so that scion components can use them. These methods remain invisible to the client applications.

Listing 5.1 The TCsSocket Definition.

```
(* CsSocket Unit
   A simple Winsock interface unit
   Developed for High Performance Delphi 3 Programming—John Penman 1997
*)

{$H+}
unit CsSocket;

interface

uses
  Windows, Messages, SysUtils, Classes, Graphics, Controls, Forms,
  Dialogs;

{$INCLUDE CsSOCKINT.PAS}

const
  winsocket       = 'wsock32.dll';

  WSockVersionNo : String = '2.0';
  WSockBuildDate : String = '7 May 97';

  SOCK_EVENT      = WM_USER + 1;
  ASYNC_EVENT     = SOCK_EVENT + 1;

type

  TConditions  = (Success, Failure, None);

  THostAddr    = (HostAddr, IPAddr);

  TOperations  = (SendOp, RecvOp, NoOp);

  TAccess      = (Blocking, NonBlocking);

  TSockTypes   = (SockStrm, SockDgram, SockRaw);
```

```
TServices     = (NoService, Echo, Discard,
                 Systat, Daytime, Netstat,
                 Qotd, Chargen, ftp, telnet,
                 smtp, time, rlp, nameserver,
                 whois, domain, mtp, tftp, rje,
                 finger, http, link, supdup,
                 hostnames, ns, pop2, pop3,
                 sunrpc, auth, sftp,
                 uucp_path, nntp);

TProtoTypes = (IP, ICMP, GGP, TCP, PUP, UDP);

TAsyncTypes = (AsyncName, AsyncAddr, AsyncServ,
               AsyncPort, AsyncProtoName, AsyncProtoNumber);

const

  NULL : Char    = #0;

  CRLF : array[0..2] of char = #13#10#0;

  MaxBufferSize  = MAXGETHOSTSTRUCT;

  {strings for services property}
  ServiceStrings : array[TServices] of String[10]
               = ('No Service',
                  'echo        ',
                  'discard     ',
                  'systat      ',
                  'daytime     ',
                  'netstat     ',
                  'qotd        ',
                  'chargen     ',
                  'ftp         ',
                  'telnet      ',
                  'smtp        ',
                  'time        ',
                  'rlp         ',
                  'nameserver',
                  'whois       ',
                  'domain      ',
                  'mtp         ',
                  'tftp        ',
                  'rje         ',
                  'finger      ',
```

```
                         'http      ',
                         'link      ',
                         'supdup    ',
                         'hostnames ',
                         'ns        ',
                         'pop2      ',
                         'pop3      ',
                         'sunrpc    ',
                         'auth      ',
                         'sftp      ',
                         'uucp-path ',
                         'nntp      ');
  { protocol strings }
  ProtoStrings : array[TProtoTypes] of String[4] =
                   ('ip  ',
                    'icmp',
                    'gcmp',
                    'tcp ',
                    'pup ',
                    'udp ');

type

  CharArray   = array[0..MaxBufferSize] of char;

  TAddrTypes  = (AFUnspec,     { unspecified }
                 AFUnix,       { local to host (pipes, portals) }
                 AFInet,       { internetwork: UDP, TCP, etc. }
                 AFImpLink,    { arpanet imp addresses }
                 AFPup,        { pup protocols: e.g. BSP }
                 AFChaos,      { mit CHAOS protocols }
                 AFNs,         { XEROX NS protocols }
                 AFIso,        { ISO protocols }
                 AFOsi,        { OSI is ISO }
                 AFEcma,       { European computer manufacturers }
                 AFDatakit,    { data kit protocols }
                 AFCcitt,      { CCITT protocols, X.25 etc. }
                 AFSna,        { IBM SNA }
                 AFDecNet,     { DECnet }
                 AFDli,        { Direct data link interface }
                 AFLat,        { LAT }
                 AFHyLink,     { NSC Hyperchannel }
                 AFAppleTalk,  { AppleTalk }
                 AFNetBios,    { NetBios-style addresses }
                 AFMax);
```

```
const
 ServDefault     =   NoService;
 ProtoDefault    =   TCP;
 SockDefault     =   SockStrm;
 AddrDefault     =   AFINET;
 PortNoDefault   =   0;


type
{$LONGSTRINGS ON}

 ECsSocketError = class(Exception);


 TLookUpOp      = (resHostName, resIpAddress, resService, resPort,
resProto, resProtoNo);


 TAsyncOpEvent  = procedure(Sender : TObject; sSocket : TSocket) of
object;
 TCleanUpEvent  = procedure(Sender : TObject; CleanUp : Boolean) of
object;
 TConnEvent     = procedure(Sender : TObject; sSocket : TSocket) of
object;
 TDisConnEvent  = procedure(Sender : TObject; sSocket : TSocket) of
object;
 TInfoEvent     = procedure(Sender : TObject; Msg : String) of object;
 TErrorEvent    = procedure(Sender : TObject; Status : TConditions; Msg :
String) of object;
 TAbortEvent    = procedure(Sender : TObject) of object;
 TBusyEvent     = procedure(Sender : TObject; BusyFlag : Boolean) of
object;
 TStatusEvent   = procedure(Sender : TObject; Mode, Status : String) of
object;
 TLookUpEvent   = procedure(Sender : TObject; LookUpOp : TLookUpOp; Value
: String; Result : Boolean) of object;
 TSendDataEvent = procedure(Sender : TObject; sSocket : TSocket) of
object;
 TRecvDataEvent = procedure(Sender : TObject; sSocket : TSocket) of
object;
 TTimeOutEvent  = procedure(Sender : TObject; sSocket : TSocket; TimeOut
: LongInt) of object;

 TCsSocket = class(TComponent)
   private
```

```
{ Private declarations }
FOnCleanUpEvent          : TCleanUpEvent;
FOnConnEvent             : TConnEvent;
FOnDisConnEvent          : TDisConnEvent;
FOnInfoEvent             : TInfoEvent;
FOnErrorEvent            : TErrorEvent;
FOnAbortEvent            : TAbortEvent;
FOnBusyEvent             : TBusyEvent;
FOnStatusEvent           : TStatusEvent;
FOnLookUpEvent           : TLookUpEvent;
FOnSendDataEvent         : TSendDataEvent;
FOnRecvDataEvent         : TRecvDataEvent;
FOnTimeOutEvent          : TTimeOutEvent;
FOnAsyncOpEvent          : TAsyncOpEvent;
FValidSocket             : u_int;
FParent                  : TComponent;
FSockType                : TSockTypes;
FService                 : TServices;
FProtocol                : TProtoTypes;
FAddrType                : TAddrTypes;
FAsyncType               : TAsyncTypes;
FLookUpOp                : TLookUpOp;
FCleanUp                 : Boolean;
FData,
FRemoteName,
FAsyncRemoteName,
FAsyncService,
FAsyncPort,
FAsyncProtocol,
FAsyncProtoNo,
FLocalName,
FInfo                    : String;
FBusy,
FCancelAsyncOp,
FOKToDisplayErrors       : Boolean;
FStatus                  : TConditions;
FAccess                  : TAccess;
FConnected               : Boolean;
FTaskHandle              : THandle;
FHomeHostName            : String;
FWSALastError,
FTimeOut                 : Integer;
FRC                      : Integer;
FVendor,
FWSVersion,
FMaxNoSockets,
```

```
    FMaxUDPPSize,
    FWSStatus,
    FServiceName,
    FPortName,
    FProtocolName,
    FProtocolNo           : String;
    FAsyncBuff            : array[0..MAXGETHOSTSTRUCT-1] of char;
    FNoOfBlockingTasks    : Integer;
  protected
    { Protected declarations }
    FPortNo               : Integer;
    FHost                 : pHostent;
    FServ                 : pServent;
    FProto                : pProtoEnt;
    FHostEntryBuff,
    FProtoName,
    FServName             : CharArray;
    Fh_addr               : pChar;
    FpHostBuffer,
    FpHostName            : array[0..MAXGETHOSTSTRUCT-1] of char;
    FAddress              : THostAddr;
    FMsgBuff              : CharArray;
    FSocket               : TSocket;
    FSockAddress          : TSockAddrIn;
    FHandle               : THandle;
    FStarted              : Boolean;
    FHwnd,
    FAsyncHWND            : HWND;
// methods
    procedure ConnEvent;
    procedure CleanUpEvent; dynamic;
    procedure DisConnEvent; dynamic;
    procedure InfoEvent(Msg : String); dynamic;
    procedure ErrorEvent(Status : TConditions; Msg : String); dynamic;
    procedure StatusEvent; dynamic;
    procedure BusyEvent; dynamic;
    procedure LookUpEvent(Value : TLookUpOp; Msg : String; Result :
                          Boolean); dynamic;
    procedure SendDataEvent; dynamic;
    procedure RecvDataEvent; dynamic;
    procedure TimeOutEvent; dynamic;
    procedure AbortEvent; dynamic;
    procedure AsyncOpEvent; dynamic;
    function  GetLocalName : String;
    procedure SetRemoteHostName(NameReqd : String);
    function  GetDataBuff  : String;
    procedure SetDataBuff(DataReqd : String);
```

```
    function  GetDatagram  : String;
    procedure SetDatagram(DataReqd : String);
    procedure SetUpPort;
    procedure SetPortName(ReqdPortName : String);
    procedure SetServiceName(ReqdServiceName : String);
    {Winsock calls}
    procedure GetProt(Protocol : PChar);
    procedure ConnectToHost;
    function  GetOOBData : String;
    procedure SetOOBData(ReqdOOBData : String);
    function  StartUp : Boolean;
    procedure CleanUp;
    procedure SetUpAddr; virtual;
    procedure SetUpAddress; virtual;
    procedure GetHost;
    procedure GetServ;
    function  CreateSocket : TSocket;
    function  WSAErrorMsg : String;
    function  GetInfo : String; virtual;
    procedure SetInfo(InfoReqd : String); virtual;
    procedure SetProtocolName(ReqdProtoName : String);
    procedure SetProtoNo(ReqdProtoNo : String);
    procedure WMTimer(var Message : TMessage); message wm_Timer;
    procedure StartAsyncSelect; virtual;
    procedure AsyncOperation(var Mess : TMessage);
    function  GetAsyncHostName : String;
    procedure SetAsyncHostName(ReqdHostName : String);
    function  GetAsyncService : String;
    procedure SetAsyncService(ReqdService : String);
    function  GetAsyncPort : String;
    procedure SetAsyncPort(ReqdPort : String);
    function  GetAsyncProtoName : String;
    procedure SetAsyncProtoName(ReqdProtoName : String);
    function  GetAsyncProtoNo : String;
    procedure SetAsyncProtoNo(ReqdProtoNo : String);
    procedure CancelAsyncOperation(CancelOp : Boolean);
    function CheckConnection : Boolean;
public
    { Public declarations }
    procedure GetServer;
    procedure QuitSession;
    procedure Cancel;
    constructor Create(AOwner : TComponent); override;
    destructor Destroy; override;
    { Public properties }
    property WSVendor      : String      read FVendor;
```

```
    property WSVersion       : String        read FWSVersion;
    property WSMaxNoSockets: String           read FMaxNoSockets;
    property WSMaxUDPPSize : String           read FMaxUDPPSize;
    property WSStatus        : String         read FWSStatus;
    property Info            : String         read FInfo
                                              write FInfo;
    property WSErrNo         : Integer        read FWSALastError
                                              default 0;
    property Connected       : Boolean        read FConnected
                                              write FConnected default FALSE;
    property LocalName       : String         read GetLocalName
                                              write FLocalName;
    property Status          : TConditions    read FStatus
                                              write FStatus default None;
    property HostName        : String         read FRemoteName
                                              write SetRemoteHostName;
    property WSService       : String         read FServiceName
                                              write SetServiceName;
    property WSPort          : String         read FPortName
                                              write SetPortName;
    property WSProtoName     : String         read FProtocolName
                                              write SetProtocolName;
    property WSProtoNo       : String         read FProtocolNo
                                              write SetProtoNo;
    property Data            : String         read GetDataBuff
                                              write SetDataBuff;
    property Datagram        : String         read GetDatagram
                                              write SetDatagram;
    property OOBData         : String         read GetOOBData
                                              write SetOOBData;
    property CancelAsyncOP : Boolean          read FCancelAsyncOp
                                              write CancelAsyncOperation;
published
  { Published declarations }
    property OkToDisplayErrors : Boolean      read FOKToDisplayErrors
                                              write FOKToDisplayErrors
                                              default TRUE;
    property HomeServer        : String       read FHomeHostName
                                              write FHomeHostName;
    property SockType          : TSockTypes   read FSockType
                                              write FSockType
                                              default SOCKSTRM;
    property Service           : TServices    read FService
                                              write FService
                                              default NoService;
```

```
    property Protocol         : TProtoTypes      read FProtocol
                                                 write FProtocol
                                                 default TCP;
    property AddrType         : TAddrTypes       read FAddrType
                                                 write FAddrType
                                                 default AFInet;
    property Access           : TAccess          read FAccess
                                                 write FAccess
                                                 default blocking;
    property OnConnect        : TConnEvent       read FOnConnEvent
                                                 write FOnConnEvent;
    property OnClose          : TDisConnEvent    read FOnDisConnEvent
                                                 write FOnDisConnEvent;
    property OnCleanUp        : TCleanUpEvent    read FOnCleanUpEvent
                                                 write FOnCleanUpEvent;
    property OnInfo           : TInfoEvent       read FOnInfoEvent
                                                 write FOnInfoEvent;
    property OnError          : TErrorEvent      read FOnErrorEvent
                                                 write FOnErrorEvent;
    property OnLookup         : TLookUpEvent     read FOnLookUpEvent
                                                 write FOnLookUpEvent;
    property OnStatus         : TStatusEvent     read FOnStatusEvent
                                                 write FOnStatusEvent;
    property OnSendData       : TSendDataEvent   read FOnSendDataEvent
                                                 write FOnSendDataEvent;
    property OnRecvData       : TRecvDataEvent   read FOnRecvDataEvent
                                                 write FOnRecvDataEvent;
    property OnTimeOut        : TTimeOutEvent    read FOnTimeOutEvent
                                                 write FOnTimeOutEvent;
    property OnAbort          : TAbortEvent      read FOnAbortEvent
                                                 write FOnAbortEvent;
    property OnAsyncOp        : TAsyncOpEvent    read FOnAsyncOpEvent
                                                 write FOnAsyncOpEvent;
  end;

procedure Register;

implementation

var
 myWsaData   : TWSADATA;

function TCsSocket.StartUp : Boolean;
var
 VersionReqd : WordRec;
```

```
begin
 with VersionReqD do
 begin
  Hi := 1;
  Lo := 1;
 end;
 Result := WSAStartUp(Word(VersionReqD),myWsaData) = 0;
 if not Result then
 begin
  FStatus := Failure;
  raise ECsSocketError.Create('Cannot start WinSock!');
  Exit;
 end
 else
 begin
  with myWsaData do
  begin
   FVendor       := StrPas(szDescription);
   FWSVersion    :=
Concat(IntToStr(Hi(wVersion)),'.',(intToStr(Lo(wVersion))));
   FWSStatus     := StrPas(szSystemStatus);
   FMaxNoSockets := IntToStr(iMaxSockets);
   FMaxUDPPSize  := IntToStr(iMaxUDPDg);
  end;
  InfoEvent('Started WinSock');
 end;
end;

procedure TCsSocket.CleanUp;
begin
 if FStarted then
 begin
  FStarted := False;
  if WSACleanUp = SOCKET_ERROR then
   raise ECsSocketError.create('Cannot close WinSock!');
 end;
end;

constructor TCsSocket.Create(AOwner : TComponent);
begin
 inherited Create(AOwner);
 FParent      := AOwner;
 FValidSocket := INVALID_SOCKET;
 FSockType    := SockDefault;
 FAddrType    := AddrDefault;
```

```
  FService        := ServDefault;
  FProtocol       := ProtoDefault;
  with FSockAddress do
  begin
   sin_family     := PF_INET;
   sin_addr.s_addr := INADDR_ANY;
   sin_port       := 0;
  end;
  FSocket         := INVALID_SOCKET;
  FLocalName      := '';
  FInfo           := '';
  FAccess         := Blocking;
  FStarted        := StartUp;
  if not FStarted then
  begin
   inherited Destroy;
   Exit;
  end;
  FHomeHostName    := 'local';
  FOKToDisplayErrors := TRUE;
  FConnected       := FALSE;
  FWSALastError    := 0;
  FTimeOut         := 0;
  FNoOfBlockingTasks := 0;
  InfoEvent(Concat('Version ',WSockVersionNo));
  FAsyncHWND       := AllocateHWND(AsyncOperation);
end;

destructor TCsSocket.Destroy;
begin
 DeallocateHWND(FAsyncHWND);
 CleanUp;
 inherited Destroy;
end;

procedure TCsSocket.SetUpPort;
begin
 {Now, we need to determine the port no from the Service}
 case FService of
   NoService  : FPortNo := 0;
   echo       : FPortNo := 7;
   discard    : FPortNo := 9;
   systat     : FPortNo := 11;
   daytime    : FPortNo := 13;
   netstat    : FPortNo := 15;
```

```pascal
    qotd        : FPortNo := 17;
    chargen     : FPortNo := 19;
    ftp         : FPortNo := 21;
    telnet      : FPortNo := 23;
    smtp        : FPortNo := 25;
    time        : FPortNo := 37;
    rlp         : FPortNo := 39;
    nameserver  : FPortNo := 42;
    whois       : FPortNo := 43;
    domain      : FPortNo := 53;
    mtp         : FPortNo := 57;
    tftp        : FPortNo := 69;
    rje         : FPortNo := 77;
    finger      : FPortNo := 79;
    http        : FPortNo := 80;
    link        : FPortNo := 87;
    supdup      : FPortNo := 95;
    hostnames   : FPortNo := 101;
    ns          : FPortNo := 105;
    pop2        : FPortNo := 109;
    pop3        : FPortNo := 110;
    sunrpc      : FPortNo := 111;
    auth        : FPortNo := 113;
    sftp        : FPortNo := 115;
    uucp_path   : FPortNo := 117;
    nntp        : FPortNo := 119;
  end;{case}
end;

function TCsSocket.GetLocalName : String;
var
  LocalName : array[0..MaxBufferSize] of Char;
begin
  if gethostname(LocalName, SizeOf(LocalName)) = 0 then
    Result := StrPas(LocalName)
  else
    Result := '';
end;

function TCsSocket.GetInfo : String;
begin
  GetInfo := FInfo;
end;

procedure TCsSocket.SetInfo(InfoReqd : String);
```

```pascal
begin
 FInfo := InfoReqd;
end;

function TCsSocket.CreateSocket: TSocket;
begin
 case FSockType of
  SOCKSTRM  : FSocket := socket(PF_INET, SOCK_STREAM, IPPROTO_IP);
  SOCKDGRAM : FSocket := socket(PF_INET, SOCK_DGRAM,  IPPROTO_IP);
  SOCKRAW   : FSocket := socket(PF_INET, SOCK_RAW,    IPPROTO_IP);
 end;
 if FSocket = INVALID_SOCKET then
 begin { Failure to create a socket }
  FStatus := Failure;
  ErrorEvent(FStatus, WSAErrorMsg);
  Result := INVALID_SOCKET;
  if FOkToDisplayErrors then
   raise ECsSocketError.create(WSAErrorMsg);
  Exit;
 end;
 FStatus := Success;
 Result := FSocket;
 InfoEvent('Socket ' + IntToStr(Result) + ' created...');
end;

procedure TCsSocket.SetUpAddress;
begin
 with FSockAddress.sin_addr do
 begin
  S_un_b.s_b1   := Fh_addr[0];
  S_un_b.s_b2   := Fh_addr[1];
  S_un_b.s_b3   := Fh_addr[2];
  S_un_b.s_b4   := Fh_addr[3];
 end;
end;

procedure TCsSocket.SetUpAddr;
begin
 with FSockAddress do
 begin
  sin_family           := AF_INET;
  sin_port             := FServ^.s_port;
 end;
end;
```

```
procedure TCsSocket.GetServ;
var
 ProtoStr,
 ServStr : String;
begin
 ProtoStr := Copy(ProtoStrings[TProtoTypes(FProtocol)],1,Pos(' ',
             ProtoStrings[TProtoTypes(FProtocol)])-1);
 StrPCopy(FProtoName, ProtoStr);
 GetProt(FProtoName);
 if FProto = NIL then
 begin { No service available }
  FStatus := Failure;
  ErrorEvent(FStatus, WSAErrorMsg);
  InfoEvent(ProtoStr + ' not available!');
  if FOkToDisplayErrors then
   raise ECsSocketError.create(WSAErrorMsg);
  Exit;
 end;
 if FService = NoService then
  Exit;
 ServStr   := Copy(ServiceStrings[TServices(FService)],1,Pos(' ',
             ServiceStrings[TServices(FService)])-1);
 StrPCopy(FServName, ServStr);
 FServ := getservbyname(FServName,FProtoName);
 if FServ = NIL then
 begin { No service available }
  FStatus := Failure;
  ErrorEvent(FStatus, WSAErrorMsg);
  InfoEvent(ServStr + ' not available!');
  if FOkToDisplayErrors then
   raise ECsSocketError.create(WSAErrorMsg);
  Exit;
 end;
 FStatus := Success;
end;

procedure TCsSocket.GetProt(Protocol : PChar);
begin
 FProto := getprotobyname(Protocol);
 if FProto = NIL then
 begin
  FStatus := Failure;
  ErrorEvent(FStatus, WSAErrorMsg);
  LookUpEvent(resProto, StrPas(Protocol) + ' not available!', FALSE);
```

```pascal
      if FOkToDisplayErrors then
        raise ECsSocketError.create(StrPas(Protocol) + ' not available!');
      Exit;
    end;
    FStatus := Success;
    LookUpEvent(resProto, StrPas(FProto.p_name), TRUE);
  end;

  procedure TCsSocket.WMTimer(var Message : TMessage);
  begin
    KillTimer(FHandle,10);
    if WSAIsBlocking then
    begin
      if WSACancelBlockingCall <> SOCKET_ERROR then
        InfoEvent('Timed out. Call cancelled')
      else
      begin
        ErrorEvent(Failure, WSAErrorMsg);
        if FOkToDisplayErrors then
          raise ECsSocketError.create(WSAErrorMsg);
      end;
    end;
  end;

  procedure TCsSocket.ConnectToHost;
  begin
    InfoEvent('Connecting to ' + FRemoteName);
    case SockType of
      SOCKSTRM : begin
                   if connect( FSocket, FSockAddress, SizeOf(TSockAddrIn)) =
                              SOCKET_ERROR then
                   begin
                     if WSAGetLastError <> WSAEWOULDBLOCK then
                     begin
                       ErrorEvent(Failure, WSAErrorMsg);
                       FConnected := FALSE;
                       closesocket(FSocket);
                       if FOkToDisplayErrors then
                         raise ECsSocketError.create(WSAErrorMsg);
                       Exit;
                     end;
                   end;
                   FStatus := Success;
                   FConnected := TRUE;
                 end;
      SOCKDGRAM : begin
```

```
            end;
    end;{case}
end;

procedure TCsSocket.GetHost;
begin
  if Length(HostName) = 0 then
  begin
    MessageDlg('No host name given!', mtError,[mbOk],0);
    FStatus := Failure;
    Exit;
  end;
  CreateSocket;
  if FStatus = Failure then
    Exit;
  GetServ;
  if FStatus = Failure then
  begin
    raise ECsSocketError.create('Failed to resolve host : '+ HostName);
    Exit;
  end;
  SetUpAddress;
  if FService = NoService then
    FSockAddress.sin_family := AF_INET (* for apps that require no port*)
  else
    SetUpAddr;
  if FStatus = Failure then
    Exit;
  FRemoteName := StrPas(inet_ntoa(FSockAddress.sin_addr));
  if SockType = SockStrm then
    ConnectToHost
  else
  begin
    {Because we are dealing with packets, assume there is a connection}
    FConnected := TRUE;
  end;
end;

procedure TCsSocket.GetServer;
begin
  GetServ;
  if Status = Failure then Exit;
  FSockAddress.sin_family          := PF_INET;
  FSockAddress.sin_port            := FServ^.s_port;
  FSockAddress.sin_addr.s_addr     := htonl(INADDR_ANY);
```

```
    FRemoteName                      := LocalName;
    FSocket                          := CreateSocket;
end;

procedure TCsSocket.QuitSession;
begin
  if FConnected then
  begin
    if WSAIsBlocking then
      WSACancelBlockingCall;
    closesocket(FSocket);
    FConnected := FALSE;
  end;
end;

function TCsSocket.WSAErrorMsg : String;
begin
  FWSALastError := WSAGetLastError;
  case FWSALastError of
    WSAEINTR           : Result := 'Interrupted system call';{WSAEINTR}
    WSAEBADF           : Result := 'Bad file number'; {WSAEBADF}
    WSAEACCES          : Result := 'Permission denied'; {WSAEACCES}
    WSAEFAULT          : Result := 'Bad address';{WSAEFAULT}
    WSAEINVAL          : Result := 'Invalid argument';{WSAEINVAL}
    WSAEMFILE          : Result := 'Too many open files';{WSAEMFILE}
    WSAEWOULDBLOCK     : Result := 'Operation would block';{WSAEWOULDBLOCK}
    WSAEINPROGRESS     : Result := 'Operation now in
                                    progress';{WSAEINPROGRESS}
    WSAEALREADY        : Result := 'Operation already in
                                    progress';{WSAEALREADY}
    WSAENOTSOCK        : Result := 'Socket operation on
                                    nonsocket';{WSAENOTSOCK}
    WSAEDESTADDRREQ    : Result := 'Destination address
                                    required';{WSAEDESTADDRREQ}
    WSAEMSGSIZE        : Result := 'Message too long';{WSAEMSGSIZE}
    WSAEPROTOTYPE      : Result := 'Protocol wrong type for
                                    socket';{WSAEPROTOTYPE}
    WSAENOPROTOOPT     : Result := 'Protocol not
                                    available';{WSAENOPROTOOPT}
    WSAEPROTONOSUPPORT : Result := 'Protocol not
                                    supported';{WSAEPROTONOSUPPORT}
    WSAESOCKTNOSUPPORT : Result := 'Socket not
                                    supported';{WSAESOCKTNOSUPPORT}
    WSAEOPNOTSUPP      : Result := 'Operation not supported on
                                    socket';{WSAEOPNOTSUPP}
```

```
WSAEPFNOSUPPORT       : Result := 'Protocol family not
                                   supported';{WSAEPFNOSUPPORT}
WSAEAFNOSUPPORT       : Result := 'Address family not
                                   supported';{WSAEAFNOSUPPORT}
WSAEADDRINUSE         : Result := 'Address already in use';{WSAEADDRINUSE}
WSAEADDRNOTAVAIL      : Result := 'Can''t assign requested
                                   address';{WSAEADDRNOTAVAIL}
WSAENETDOWN           : Result := 'Network is down';{WSAENETDOWN}
WSAENETUNREACH        : Result := 'Network is
                                   unreachable';{WSAENETUNREACH}
WSAENETRESET          : Result := 'Network dropped connection on
                                   reset';{WSAENETRESET}
WSAECONNABORTED       : Result := 'Software caused connection
                                   abort';{WSAECONNABORTED}
WSAECONNRESET         : Result := 'Connection reset by
                                   peer';{WSAECONNRESET}
WSAENOBUFS            : Result := 'No buffer space available';{WSAENOBUFS}
WSAEISCONN            : Result := 'Socket is already
                                   connected';{WSAEISCONN}
WSAENOTCONN           : Result := 'Socket is not connected';{WSAENOTCONN}
WSAESHUTDOWN          : Result := 'Can''t send after socket
                                   shutdown';{WSAESHUTDOWN}
WSAETOOMANYREFS       : Result := 'Too many references:can''t
                                   splice';{WSAETOOMANYREFS}
WSAETIMEDOUT          : Result := 'Connection timed out';{WSAETIMEDOUT}
WSAECONNREFUSED       : Result := 'Connection refused';{WSAECONNREFUSED}
WSAELOOP              : Result := 'Too many levels of symbolic
                                   links';{WSAELOOP}
WSAENAMETOOLONG       : Result := 'File name is too
                                   long';{WSAENAMETOOLONG}
WSAEHOSTDOWN          : Result := 'Host is down';{WSAEHOSTDOWN}
WSAEHOSTUNREACH       : Result := 'No route to host';{WSAEHOSTUNREACH}
WSAENOTEMPTY          : Result := 'Directory is not empty';{WSAENOTEMPTY}
WSAEPROCLIM           : Result := 'Too many processes';{WSAEPROCLIM}
WSAEUSERS             : Result := 'Too many users';{WSAEUSERS}
WSAEDQUOT             : Result := 'Disk quota exceeded';{WSAEDQUOT}
WSAESTALE             : Result := 'Stale NFS file handle';{WSAESTALE}
WSAEREMOTE            : Result := 'Too many levels of remote in
                                   path';{WSAEREMOTE}
WSASYSNOTREADY        : Result := 'Network subsystem is
                                   unusable';{WSASYSNOTREADY}
WSAVERNOTSUPPORTED    : Result := 'Winsock DLL cannot support this
                                   application';{WSAVERNOTSUPPORTED}
WSANOTINITIALISED     : Result := 'Winsock not
                                   initialized';{WSANOTINITIALISED}
```

```delphi
    WSAHOST_NOT_FOUND    : Result := 'Host not found';{WSAHOST-NOT-FOUND}
    WSATRY_AGAIN         : Result := 'Non authoritative - host not
                                      found';{WSATRY_AGAIN}
    WSANO_RECOVERY       : Result := 'Non recoverable error';
    WSANO_DATA           : Result := 'Valid name, no data record of requested
                                      type'
    else Result := 'Not a Winsock error';
  end;
  FStatus := Failure;
end;

procedure TCsSocket.SetRemoteHostName(NameReqd : String);
var
 P : Pointer;
 IPAddress : LongInt;
begin
 FRemoteName := NameReqd;
 if Length(NameReqd) = 0 then
 begin
  FStatus := Failure;
  ErrorEvent(FStatus, 'No host name given!');
  case FLookUpOp of
   resHostName   : LookUpEvent(resHostName,FRemoteName, FALSE);
   resIPAddress  : LookUpEvent(resIPAddress,FRemoteName, FALSE);
  end;// case
  raise ECsSocketError.Create('No host name given!');
  Exit;
 end;
 if FAccess = NonBlocking then
  SetAsyncHostName(FRemoteName)
 else
 begin
  InfoEvent('Resolving host');
  StrPCopy(FpHostName, FRemoteName);
  { check what type of address has been entered }
  IPAddress := inet_addr(FpHostName);
  if IPAddress <>INADDR_NONE then {this is a dotted address}
  begin
   FLookUpOp := resHostName;
   FAddress := IPAddr;
   P := addr(IPAddress);
   case AddrType of
    AFINET : FHost := gethostbyaddr(P, 4, AF_INET);
   end;
  end
```

```
    else {no, it looks like a human readable hostname}
    begin
     FLookUpOp := resIPAddress;
     FAddress  := HostAddr;
     FHost     := gethostbyname(FpHostName);
    end;
    if FHost = NIL then
    begin{Unknown host, so aborting...}
     LookUpEvent(FLookUpOp, '', FALSE);
     FStatus := Failure;
     if FOkToDisplayErrors then
      raise ECsSocketError('Unable to resolve ' + FpHostName);
     Exit;
    end;
    InfoEvent('Host found');
    FStatus := Success;
    Move(FHost^.h_addr_list^, Fh_addr, SizeOf(FHost^.h_addr_list^));
    if FAddress = HostAddr then
    begin
     SetUpAddress;
     FRemoteName := StrPas(inet_ntoa(FSockAddress.sin_addr));
    end
    else
    if FAddress = IPAddr then
    begin
     FRemoteName := StrPas(FHost^.h_name);
     InfoEvent('Host found...');
    end;
    case FLookUpOp of
     resHostName  : LookUpEvent(resHostName,FRemoteName, TRUE);
     resIPAddress : LookUpEvent(resIPAddress,FRemoteName, TRUE);
    end;// case
   end;
end;

function TCsSocket.GetDataBuff : String;
var
 Response : Integer;
 Buffer : CharArray;
begin
 Response := recv(FSocket, Buffer, MaxBufferSize, 0);
 if Response = SOCKET_ERROR then
 begin
  if WSAGetLastError <> WSAEWOULDBLOCK then{this is a real error!}
```

```
    begin
     FStatus := Failure;
     ErrorEvent(FStatus, WSAErrorMsg);
     Result := '';
     if FOKToDisplayErrors then
       raise ECsSocketError.create(WSAErrorMsg);
     Exit;
    end else Exit;
  end
  else
  if Response = 0 then{no more data from the host}
  begin
   Result := '';
   Exit;
  end;
  Buffer[Response] := NULL;
  FData := StrPas(Buffer);
  Result := FData;
end;

procedure TCsSocket.SetDataBuff(DataReqd : String);
var
 Data : CharArray;
 Response : Integer;
begin
 FData := DataReqd;
 StrPCopy(Data, FData);
 StrCat(Data, CRLF);
 Response := send(FSocket, Data, StrLen(Data), 0);
 if Response = SOCKET_ERROR then
 begin { Error sending data to remote host }
   if WSAGetLastError <> WSAEWOULDBLOCK then{this is a real error!}
   begin
     FStatus := Failure;
     ErrorEvent(FStatus, WSAErrorMsg);
     if FOKToDisplayErrors then
       raise ECsSocketError.create(WSAErrorMsg);
     Exit;
   end
 end;
end;

function  TCsSocket.GetDatagram : String;
var
 Size       : Integer;
 Response   : Integer;
```

```
  MsgBuff    : CharArray;
begin
 Size := SizeOf(TSockAddrIn);
 Response := recvfrom(FSocket, MsgBuff, SizeOf(MsgBuff), 0,
                     FSockAddress, Size);
 if Response = SOCKET_ERROR then
  begin { Error receiving data from remote host }
   if WSAGetLastError <> WSAEWOULDBLOCK then{this is a real error!}
   begin
    FStatus := Failure;
    ErrorEvent(FStatus, WSAErrorMsg);
    if FOKToDisplayErrors then
     raise ECsSocketError.create(WSAErrorMsg);
    Exit;
   end
  end;
  Result := StrPas(MsgBuff);
end;

procedure TCsSocket.SetDatagram(DataReqd : String);
var
 Response : Integer;
 MsgBuff   : CharArray;
begin
 StrpCopy(MsgBuff,DataReqd);
 StrCat(MsgBuff,@NULL);
 Response := sendto(FSocket, MsgBuff, SizeOf(MsgBuff), MSG_DONTROUTE,
                    FSockAddress, SizeOf(TSockAddrIn));
 if Response = SOCKET_ERROR then
  begin { Error sending data to remote host }
   if WSAGetLastError <> WSAEWOULDBLOCK then{this is a real error!}
   begin
    FStatus := Failure;
    ErrorEvent(FStatus, WSAErrorMsg);
    if FOKToDisplayErrors then
     raise ECsSocketError.create(WSAErrorMsg);
    Exit;
   end
 end else InfoEvent('Data sent...');
end;

function TCsSocket.GetOOBData : String;
var
  Response: integer;
  Data : CharArray;
```

```pascal
begin
 if FSocket <> INVALID_SOCKET then
 begin
  Response := recv(FSocket,Data,255,MSG_OOB);
  if Response < 0 then
  begin
   ErrorEvent(Failure, WSAErrorMsg);
   if FOKToDisplayErrors then
    raise ECsSocketError.create(WSAErrorMsg);
   FStatus := Failure;
   Exit;
  end;
  Data[Response] := NULL;
  Result := StrPas(Data);
 end
 else Result := '';
end;

procedure TCsSocket.SetOOBData(ReqdOOBData : String);
var
 Data : CharArray;
 Response : Integer;
begin
 if WSAIsBlocking then
  if WSACancelBlockingCall <> SOCKET_ERROR then
  begin
   StrPCopy(Data, ReqdOOBData);
   StrCat(Data, CRLF);
   Response := send(FSocket, Data, StrLen(Data), MSG_OOB);
   if Response = SOCKET_ERROR then
   begin { Error sending data to remote host }
    FStatus := Failure;
    ErrorEvent(Failure,WSAErrorMsg);
    if FOKToDisplayErrors then
     raise ECsSocketError.create(WSAErrorMsg);
    Exit;
   end;
  end;
end;

procedure TCsSocket.Cancel;
begin
 if WSAIsBlocking then
  if WSACancelBlockingCall = SOCKET_ERROR then
```

```pascal
    begin
      FStatus := Failure;
      ErrorEvent(FStatus,WSAErrorMsg);
      if FOKToDisplayErrors then
        raise ECsSocketError.create(WSAErrorMsg);
    end;
end;

{ Start of Asynchronous code }

procedure TCsSocket.StartAsyncSelect;
begin
  FRC := WSAAsyncSelect(FSocket, FHwnd, SOCK_EVENT, FD_READ
                        or FD_CONNECT or FD_WRITE or FD_CLOSE);
  if FRC =  SOCKET_ERROR then
  begin
   FStatus := Failure;
   ErrorEvent(FStatus,WSAErrorMsg);
   InfoEvent('Cannot get WSAAsyncSelect');
    if FOKToDisplayErrors then
      raise ECsSocketError.create(WSAErrorMsg);
   Exit;
  end;
end;

procedure TCsSocket.SetPortName(ReqdPortName : String);
var
 ProtocolName : String;
 ProtoName : CharArray;
begin
  if Length(ReqdPortName) = 0 then
  begin
   FStatus     := Failure;
   LookUpEvent(resPort,'',FALSE);
   raise ECsSocketError.create('No port number given!');
   Exit;
  end;
  if ReqdPortName[1] in ['a'..'z', 'A'..'Z'] then
  begin
   FStatus     := Failure;
   LookUpEvent(resPort,'',FALSE);
   raise ECsSocketError.create('You must enter a number for a port!');
   Exit;
  end;
  if FAccess = NonBlocking then
   SetAsyncPort(ReqdPortName)
```

The Delphi Winsock Component

```
    else
    begin
      FPortName    := ReqdPortName;
      ProtocolName := ProtoStrings[FProtocol];
      ProtocolName := Copy(ProtocolName,1, Pos(' ',ProtocolName)-1);
      StrPCopy(ProtoName, ProtocolName);
      FServ := getservbyport(htons(StrToInt(FPortName)),ProtoName);
      if FServ = NIL then
      begin
        FStatus := Failure;
        FPortName := 'no service';
        LookUpEvent(resPort, '', FALSE);
        if FOKToDisplayErrors then
          raise ECsSocketError.create('Cannot get service');
      end else
      begin
        FStatus := Success;
        FPortName := StrPas(Fserv^.s_name);
        LookUpEvent(resPort, FPortName, TRUE);
      end;
    end;
end;

procedure TCsSocket.SetServiceName(ReqdServiceName : String);
var
  ProtoName, ServName : CharArray;
  ProtocolName : String;
begin
  if Length(ReqdServiceName) = 0 then
  begin
    FStatus := Failure;
    LookUpEvent(resService, '', FALSE);
    raise ECsSocketError.create('No service name given!');
    Exit;
  end;
  if FAccess = NonBlocking then
    SetAsyncService(ReqdServiceName) else
  begin
    FServiceName :=  ReqdServiceName;
    StrPCopy(ServName, FServiceName);
    ProtocolName := ProtoStrings[FProtocol];
    ProtocolName := Copy(ProtocolName,1, Pos(' ',ProtocolName)-1);
    StrPCopy(ProtoName, ProtocolName);
    FServ := getservbyname(ServName,ProtoName);
    if FServ = NIL then
```

```
  begin
   FStatus := Failure;
   LookUpEvent(resService, '', FALSE);
   if FOKToDisplayErrors then
    raise ECsSocketError.create(WSAErrorMsg);
  end else
  begin
   FStatus := Success;
   FPortName := IntToStr(LongInt(abs(ntohs(FServ^.s_port))));
   LookUpEvent(resService, FPortName, TRUE);
  end;
 end;
end;

procedure TCsSocket.SetProtocolName(ReqdProtoName : String);
var
 ProtoName : CharArray;
begin
 if Length(ReqdProtoName) = 0 then
 begin
  FStatus := Failure;
  LookUpEvent(resProto,'No protocol number given!',FALSE);
  raise ECsSocketError.create('No protocol number given!');
  Exit;
 end;
 if FAccess = NonBlocking then
  SetAsyncProtoName(ReqdProtoName)
 else
 begin
  StrPCopy(ProtoName, ReqdProtoName);
  FProto := getprotobyname(ProtoName);
  if FProto = NIL then
  begin
   InfoEvent(StrPas(ProtoName) + ' not available!');
   LookUpEvent(resProto, '', FALSE);
   FStatus := Failure;
   if FOKToDisplayErrors then
    raise ECsSocketError.create(WSAErrorMsg);
   Exit;
  end;
  FStatus := Success;
  FProtocolNo := IntToStr(FProto^.p_proto);
  LookUpEvent(resProto, FProtocolNo, TRUE)
 end;
end;
```

```
procedure TCsSocket.SetProtoNo(ReqdProtoNo : String);
var
 ProtoNo : Integer;
begin
 if Length(ReqdProtoNo) = 0 then
 begin
  FStatus := Failure;
  raise ECsSocketError.create('No protocol number given!');
  Exit;
 end;
 if FAccess = NonBlocking then
  SetAsyncProtoNo(ReqdProtoNo)
 else
 begin
  ProtoNo := StrToInt(ReqdProtoNo);
  FProto := getprotobynumber(ProtoNo);
  if FProto = NIL then
  begin
   InfoEvent(IntToStr(ProtoNo) + ' not available!');
   LookUpEvent(resProtoNo, '', FALSE);
   FStatus := Failure;
   if FOKToDisplayErrors then
    raise ECsSocketError.create(WSAErrorMsg);
   Exit;
  end;
  FStatus := Success;
  FProtocolName := StrPas(FProto^.p_name);
  LookUpEvent(resProtoNo,FProtocolName, TRUE);
 end;
end;

procedure TCsSocket.CancelAsyncOperation(CancelOP : Boolean);
begin
 if WSACancelAsyncRequest(THandle(FTaskHandle)) = SOCKET_ERROR then
 begin
  FStatus := Failure;
  ErrorEvent(FStatus,WSAErrorMsg);
  if FOKToDisplayErrors then
   raise ECsSocketError.create(WSAErrorMsg);
 end
 else
 begin
  FStatus := Success;
  InfoEvent('WSAAsync lookup cancelled!');
 end;
end;
```

Chapter 5

```pascal
procedure TCsSocket.AsyncOperation(var Mess : TMessage);
var
 MsgErr : Word;
begin
 if Mess.Msg = ASYNC_EVENT then
 begin
  MsgErr := WSAGetAsyncError(Mess.lparam);
  if MsgErr <> 0 then
  begin
   FStatus := Failure;
   ErrorEvent(FStatus,WSAErrorMsg);
   if FOKToDisplayErrors then
    raise ECsSocketError.create(WSAErrorMsg);
   Exit;
  end
  else
  begin
   FStatus := Success;
   InfoEvent('WSAAsync operation succeeded!');
   case FAsyncType of
    AsyncName,
    AsyncAddr        : begin
                        FHost := pHostent(@FAsyncBuff);
                        if (FHost^.h_name = NIL) then
                        begin{Unknown host, so aborting...}
                         FStatus := Failure;
                         if FAsyncType = AsyncName then
                          LookUpEvent(resIPAddress,'',FALSE)
                         else
                          LookUpEvent(resHostName,'',FALSE);
                         if FOKToDisplayErrors then
                          raise ECsSocketError.create('Unable to resolve
                                                          host');
                         Exit;
                        end;
                        if length(StrPas(FHost^.h_name)) = 0 then
                        begin
                         InfoEvent('Host lookup failed!');
                         FStatus := Failure;
                         if FAsyncType = AsyncName then
                          LookUpEvent(resIPAddress,'',FALSE)
                         else
                          LookUpEvent(resHostName,'',FALSE);
```

```
                         if FOKToDisplayErrors then
                           raise ECsSocketError.create('Unknown host');
                         Exit;
                       end;
                       case FAddress of
                        IPAddr   : begin
                                    Move(FHost^.h_addr_list^, Fh_addr,
                                    SizeOf(FHost^.h_addr_list^));
                                    FAsyncRemoteName :=
                                    StrPas(FHost^.h_name);
                                    LookUpEvent(resHostName,
                                    FAsyncRemoteName, TRUE);
                                  end;
                        HostAddr : begin
                                    Move(FHost^.h_addr_list^, Fh_addr,
                                    SizeOf(FHost^.h_addr_list^));
                                    SetUpAddress;
                                    FAsyncRemoteName:=
                                    StrPas(inet_ntoa(FSockAddress.
                                    sin_addr));
                                   LookUpEvent(resIPAddress,FAsyncRemoteName,
                                       TRUE);
                                  end;
                        end;{case}
                      end;
AsyncServ           : begin
                        FServ := pServent(@FAsyncBuff);
                        if FServ^.s_name = NIL then
                        begin { No service available }
                          FStatus := Failure;
                          LookUpEvent(resService,'',FALSE);
                          if FOKToDisplayErrors then
                            raise ECsSocketError.create(WSAErrorMsg);
                          Exit;
                        end;
                        FAsyncPort := IntToStr(ntohs(FServ^.s_port));
                        LookUpEvent(resService, FAsyncPort, TRUE);
                      end;
AsyncPort           : begin
                        FServ := pServent(@FAsyncBuff);
                        if FServ^.s_name = NIL then
                        begin { No service available }
                          FStatus := Failure;
                          LookUpEvent(resPort,'',FALSE);
                          if FOKToDisplayErrors then
                            raise ECsSocketError.create(WSAErrorMsg);
                          Exit;
```

```
                               end;
                               FAsyncService := StrPas(FServ^.s_name);
                               LookUpEvent(resPort, FAsyncService, TRUE);
                             end;
     AsyncProtoName   : begin
                             FProto := pProtoEnt(@FAsyncBuff);
                             if FProto^.p_name = NIL then
                             begin
                               FStatus := Failure;
                               LookUpEvent(resProto,'',FALSE);
                               if FOKToDisplayErrors then
                                 raise ECsSocketError.create(WSAErrorMsg);
                               Exit;
                             end;
                             FAsyncProtoNo := IntToStr(FProto^.p_proto);
                             LookUpEvent(resProto, FAsyncProtoNo, TRUE);
                           end;
     AsyncProtoNumber : begin
                             FProto := pProtoEnt(@FAsyncBuff);
                             if FProto^.p_name = NIL then
                             begin
                               FStatus := Failure;
                               LookUpEvent(resProtoNo,'',FALSE);
                               if FOKToDisplayErrors then
                                 raise ECsSocketError.create(WSAErrorMsg);
                               Exit;
                             end;
                             FAsyncProtocol := StrPas(FProto^.p_name);
                             LookUpEvent(resProtoNo, FAsyncProtocol, TRUE);
                           end;
    end;
    if FNoOfBlockingTasks > 0 then
      dec(FNoOfBlockingTasks);
    end;
  end;
end;

function TCsSocket.GetAsyncHostName : String;
begin
  InfoEvent('Host resolved');
  Result := FAsyncRemoteName;
end;

procedure TCsSocket.SetAsyncHostName(ReqdHostName : String);
var
  IPAddress : TInaddr;
```

The Delphi Winsock Component

```
      SAddress: array[0..31] of char;
begin
 FillChar(FAsyncBuff, SizeOf(FAsyncBuff), #0);
 FAsyncRemoteName := ReqdHostName;
 StrPcopy(SAddress, FAsyncRemoteName);
 IPAddress.s_addr := inet_addr(SAddress);
 if IPAddress.s_addr <> INADDR_NONE then {this is a dotted address}
 begin
  FAddress := IPAddr;
  FAsyncType := AsyncAddr;
  if IPAddress.s_addr <> 0 then
  FTaskHandle := WSAAsyncGetHostByAddr(FAsyncHWND, ASYNC_EVENT,
                    pChar(@IPAddress), 4, PF_INET,
                    @FAsyncBuff[0], SizeOf(FAsyncBuff));
  if FTaskHandle = 0 then
  begin
   if FNoOfBlockingTasks > 0 then
    dec(FNoOfBlockingTasks);
   FStatus := Failure;
   ErrorEvent(FStatus,WSAErrorMsg);
   if FOKToDisplayErrors then
    raise ECsSocketError.create(WSAErrorMsg);
   Exit;
  end else FStatus := Success;
 end
 else {no, it looks like a human readable hostname}
 begin
  FAddress := HostAddr;
  FAsyncType := AsyncName;
  Inc(FNoOfBlockingTasks);
  FTaskHandle := WSAAsyncGetHostByName(FAsyncHWND, ASYNC_EVENT,
                                @FpHostName[0],
                                @FAsyncBuff[0], MAXGETHOSTSTRUCT);
  if FTaskHandle = 0 then
  begin
   FStatus := Failure;
   if FNoOfBlockingTasks > 0 then
    dec(FNoOfBlockingTasks);
   ErrorEvent(FStatus,WSAErrorMsg);
   if FOKToDisplayErrors then
    raise ECsSocketError.create(WSAErrorMsg);
   Exit;
  end else FStatus := Success;
 end;
end;
```

```
function TCsSocket.GetAsyncService : String;
begin
 InfoEvent('Service resolved');
 Result := FAsyncService;
end;

procedure TCsSocket.SetAsyncService(ReqdService : String);
var
 ProtoStr,
 ServStr : String;
begin
 ProtoStr := Copy(ProtoStrings[TProtoTypes(FProtocol)],1,Pos(' ',
                  ProtoStrings[TProtoTypes(FProtocol)])-1);
 StrPCopy(FProtoName, ProtoStr);
 //GetProt(FProtoName);
 FProto := getprotobyname(FProtoName);
 if FProto = NIL then
 begin { No service available }
  FStatus := Failure;
  InfoEvent(ProtoStr + ' not available!');
  if FOKToDisplayErrors then
   raise ECsSocketError.Create(WSAErrorMsg);
  Exit;
 end;
 ServStr := ReqdService;
 if Length(ServStr) = 0 then
 begin
  FStatus := Failure;
  ErrorEvent(FStatus,WSAErrorMsg);
   raise ECsSocketError.Create('No service name!');
  Exit;
 end;
 FillChar(FAsyncBuff, SizeOf(FAsyncBuff), #0);
 StrPCopy(FServName, ServStr);
 Inc(FNoOfBlockingTasks);
 FAsyncType := AsyncServ;
 FTaskHandle := WSAAsyncGetServByName(FAsyncHWND, ASYNC_EVENT, FServName,
                                      FProtoName,
                                      @FAsyncBuff[0], MAXGETHOSTSTRUCT);
 if FTaskHandle = 0 then
 begin
  FStatus := Failure;
  if FNoOfBlockingTasks > 0 then
```

```pascal
    dec(FNoOfBlockingTasks);
   if FOKToDisplayErrors then
     raise ECsSocketError.create(WSAErrorMsg);
   Exit;
 end else FStatus := Success;
end;

function TCsSocket.GetAsyncPort : String;
begin
 InfoEvent('Port resolved');
 Result := FAsyncPort;
end;

procedure TCsSocket.SetAsyncPort(ReqdPort : String);
var
 ProtoStr,
 PortStr : String;
begin
 ProtoStr := Copy(ProtoStrings[TProtoTypes(FProtocol)],1,Pos(' ',
                   ProtoStrings[TProtoTypes(FProtocol)])-1);
 StrPCopy(FProtoName, ProtoStr);
 FProto := getprotobyname(FProtoName);
 if FProto = NIL then
 begin { No service available }
  FStatus := Failure;
  InfoEvent(ProtoStr + ' not available!');
  ErrorEvent(Failure, ProtoStr + ' not available');
  raise ECsSocketError.create(ProtoStr + ' not available');
  Exit;
 end;
 PortStr := ReqdPort;
 if Length(PortStr) = 0 then
 begin
  FStatus := Failure;
  raise ECsSocketError.create('No port number!');
  Exit;
 end;
 FillChar(FAsyncBuff, SizeOf(FAsyncBuff), #0);
 FAsyncType := AsyncPort;
 FTaskHandle := WSAAsyncGetServByPort(FAsyncHWND, ASYNC_EVENT,
                                      htons(StrToInt(PortStr)),
                                      FProtoName,
                                      @FAsyncBuff[0], MAXGETHOSTSTRUCT);
 if FTaskHandle = 0 then
 begin
```

```
    FStatus := Failure;
    if FNoOfBlockingTasks > 0 then
     dec(FNoOfBlockingTasks);
    if FOKToDisplayErrors then
     raise ECsSocketError.create(WSAErrorMsg);
    Exit;
  end else FStatus := Success;
end;

function TCsSocket.GetAsyncProtoName : String;
begin
 InfoEvent('Protocol resolved');
 Result := FAsyncProtocol;
end;


procedure TCsSocket.SetAsyncProtoName(ReqdProtoName : String);
begin
 if Length(ReqdProtoName) = 0 then
  begin
   FStatus := Failure;
   ErrorEvent(FStatus, 'No protocol name!');
   raise ECsSocketError.create('No protocol name!');
   Exit;
  end;
 FillChar(FAsyncBuff, SizeOf(FAsyncBuff), #0);
 StrPCopy(FProtoName, ReqdProtoName);
 FAsyncType := AsyncProtoName;
 FTaskHandle := WSAAsyncGetProtoByName(FAsyncHWND, ASYNC_EVENT,
                                       @FProtoName[0], @FAsyncBuff[0],
                                       MAXGETHOSTSTRUCT);
 if FTaskHandle = 0 then
  begin
   FStatus := Failure;
   ErrorEvent(FStatus, WSAErrorMsg);
   if FNoOfBlockingTasks > 0 then
    dec(FNoOfBlockingTasks);
   if FOKToDisplayErrors then
    raise ECsSocketError.create(WSAErrorMsg);
   Exit;
  end else FStatus := Success;
end;

function TCsSocket.GetAsyncProtoNo : String;
begin
```

```
  InfoEvent('Proto Number resolved');
  Result := FAsyncProtoNo;
end;

procedure TCsSocket.SetAsyncProtoNo(ReqdProtoNo : String);
var
 ProtocolNo : Integer;
begin
 if Length(ReqdProtoNo) = 0 then
 begin
  FStatus := Failure;
  ErrorEvent(FStatus,'No protocol number!');
  raise ECsSocketError.create('No protocol number!');
  Exit;
 end;
 FillChar(FAsyncBuff, SizeOf(FAsyncBuff), #0);
 ProtocolNo := StrToInt(ReqdProtoNo);
 FAsyncType := AsyncProtoNumber;
 FTaskHandle := WSAAsyncGetProtoByNumber(FAsyncHWND, ASYNC_EVENT,
                                          ProtocolNo, @FAsyncBuff[0],
                                          MAXGETHOSTSTRUCT);
  if FTaskHandle = 0 then
  begin
   FStatus := Failure;
   ErrorEvent(FStatus,WSAErrorMsg);
   if FNoOfBlockingTasks > 0 then
    dec(FNoOfBlockingTasks);
   if FOKToDisplayErrors then
    raise ECsSocketError.create(WSAErrorMsg);
   Exit;
  end else FStatus := Success;
end;

function TCsSocket.CheckConnection : Boolean;
var
 peeraddr : tsockaddr;
 namelen : integer;
begin
 namelen := SizeOf(tsockaddr);
 Result := getpeername(FSocket, peeraddr, namelen) = 0;
end;

procedure TCsSocket.ConnEvent;
begin
 if Assigned(FOnConnEvent) then
  FOnConnEvent(Self, FSocket);
end;
```

```
procedure TCsSocket.CleanUpEvent;
begin
 if Assigned(FOnCleanUpEvent) then
  FOnCleanUpEvent(Self, FCleanUp);
end;

procedure TCsSocket.DisConnEvent;
begin
 if Assigned(FOnDisConnEvent) then
  FOnDisConnEvent(Self, FSocket);
end;

procedure TCsSocket.InfoEvent(Msg : String);
begin
 if Assigned(FOnInfoEvent) then
  FOnInfoEvent(Self, Msg);
end;

procedure TCsSocket.ErrorEvent(Status : TConditions; Msg : String);
begin
 if Assigned(FOnErrorEvent) then
  FOnErrorEvent(Self, Status, Msg);
end;

procedure TCsSocket.StatusEvent;
begin
 if Assigned(FOnStatusEvent) then
  FOnStatusEvent(Self, '','');
end;

procedure TCsSocket.BusyEvent;
begin
 if Assigned(FOnBusyEvent) then
  FOnBusyEvent(Self, FBusy);
end;

procedure TCsSocket.LookUpEvent(Value : TLookUpOp; Msg : String; Result :
                                Boolean);
begin
 if Assigned(FOnLookUpEvent) then
  FOnLookUpEvent(Self, Value, Msg, Result);
end;
```

```
procedure TCsSocket.SendDataEvent;
begin
 if Assigned(FOnSendDataEvent) then
   FOnSendDataEvent(Self, FSocket);
end;

procedure TCsSocket.RecvDataEvent;
begin
 if Assigned(FOnRecvDataEvent) then
   FOnRecvDataEvent(Self, FSocket);
end;

procedure TCsSocket.TimeOutEvent;
begin
 if Assigned(FOnTimeOutEvent) then
   FOnTimeOutEvent(Self, FSocket, FTimeOut);
end;

procedure TCsSocket.AbortEvent;
begin
 if Assigned(FOnAbortEvent) then
   FOnAbortEvent(Self);
end;

procedure TCsSocket.AsyncOpEvent;
begin
 if Assigned(FOnAsyncOpEvent) then
   FOnAsyncOpEvent(Self, FSocket);
end;

// Start of WinSock code - Implementation

{$INCLUDE CsSOCKIMP.PAS}

procedure Register;
begin
  RegisterComponents('CSWinsock', [TCsSocket]);
end;

end.
```

Under Unix, networking protocols typically are compiled directly into the operating systems kernel and thus always are initialized and available to applications. Under Windows, however, no such standard exists. Before an application uses any network services, the Winsock DLL requires that the application first make an initialization call. The CsSocket component performs this with its private method, **StartUp**. The constructor **TCsSocket.Create** sets the properties to their default values, as shown in Listing 5.2, then calls **StartUp**.

Listing 5.2 The TCsSocket.Create constructor.

```
constructor TCsSocket.Create(AOwner : TComponent);
begin
 inherited Create(AOwner);
 FParent         := AOwner;
 FValidSocket    := INVALID_SOCKET;
 FSockType       := SockDefault;
 FAddrType       := AddrDefault;
 FService        := ServDefault;
 FProtocol       := ProtoDefault;
 with FSockAddress do
 begin
  sin_family      := PF_INET;
  sin_addr.s_addr := INADDR_ANY;
  sin_port        := 0;
 end;
 FSocket         := INVALID_SOCKET;
 FLocalName      := '';
 FInfo           := '';
 FAccess         := Blocking;
 FStarted        := StartUp;
 if not FStarted then
 begin
  inherited Destroy;
  Exit;
 end;
 FHomeHostName      := 'local';
 FOKToDisplayErrors := TRUE;
 FConnected         := FALSE;
 FWSALastError      := 0;
 FTimeOut           := 0;
 FNoOfBlockingTasks := 0;
 InfoEvent(Concat('Version ',WSockVersionNo));
 FAsyncHWND         := AllocateHWND(AsyncOperation);
end;
```

StartUp determines whether the Winsock DLL is available as well as determining the status of the Winsock DLL. **StartUp** assigns values to the following properties:

FVendor, **FWSVersion**, **FWSStatus**, **FMaxNoSocks**, and **FMaxUDPPSize**, as shown in Listing 5.3. These properties are for information only and have no effect on the running of the main application. You can display the data returned by **StartUp** if desired. If **StartUp** is unable to initialize the Winsock DLL, it sets **FStatus** to "Failure", displays an error message, and exits. The calling application should always check the **Status** property during program initialization, usually in the application's **OnCreate** event handler.

Listing 5.3 The TCsSocket.StartUp function.

```
function TCsSocket.StartUp : Boolean;
var
 VersionReqd : WordRec;
begin
 with VersionReqD do
 begin
  Hi := 1;
  Lo := 1;
 end;
 Result := WSAStartUp(Word(VersionReqD),myWsaData) = 0;
 if not Result then
 begin
  FStatus := Failure;
  raise ECsSocketError.Create('Cannot start WinSock!');
  Exit;
 end
 else
 begin
  with myWsaData do
  begin
   FVendor       := StrPas(szDescription);
   FWSVersion    :=
Concat(IntToStr(Hi(wVersion)),'.',(intToStr(Lo(wVersion))));
   FWSStatus     := StrPas(szSystemStatus);
   FMaxNoSockets := IntToStr(iMaxSockets);
   FMaxUDPPSize  := IntToStr(iMaxUDPDg);
  end;
  InfoEvent('Started WinSock');
 end;
end;
```

The "clean up" task is just as important as initialization. When the client application completes its task—and thus its need for Winsock services—it must inform the

Winsock DLL to free the memory that was in use. CsSocket's **CleanUp** procedure takes care of this automatically when closing the Winsock DLL, as shown in Listing 5.4.

Listing 5.4   The TCsSocket.CleanUp procedure.

```
procedure TCsSocket.CleanUp;
begin
 if FStarted then
 begin
  FStarted := False;
  if WSACleanUp = SOCKET_ERROR then
   raise ECsSocketError.create('Cannot close WinSock!');
 end;
end;
```

Finally, a call to the Winsock DLL can fail to complete for a variety of network-related reasons. When this happens, CsSocket, via the **WSAErrorMsg** function, calls Winsock's **WSAGetLastError** function, reporting the error.

Running The RESOLVER32 Application

The RESOLVER32 program is a Winsock database conversion program that employs a few of the more interesting methods and properties provided by **TCsSocket**. RESOLVER32 can resolve a host name to its Internet (IP) address, and vice versa. Given either a port number or a service name, it can derive the other. And it can translate between protocol numbers and protocol names. These are practical demonstrations, for the resolution of a host name and a service name are the most common operations that a Winsock application ever performs.

The complete application as it appears in the Delphi IDE is shown in Figure 5.1. Click on the **CsSocket1** component and you'll see its properties in the Object Inspector, as shown in Figure 5.2. The default values, shown here, are fine for performing resolutions using blocking functions. The **Service** property is set to its default value of **NoService**, as there is no specific service to perform resolution tasks in our application.

Figure 5.3 shows the Events page, on which there are several event handlers. Whenever the status of the Winsock DLL changes, the **CsSocket1OnInfo** event procedure passes the information from CsSocket to the application. Similarly, the **CsSocket1LookUp**

The Delphi Winsock Component

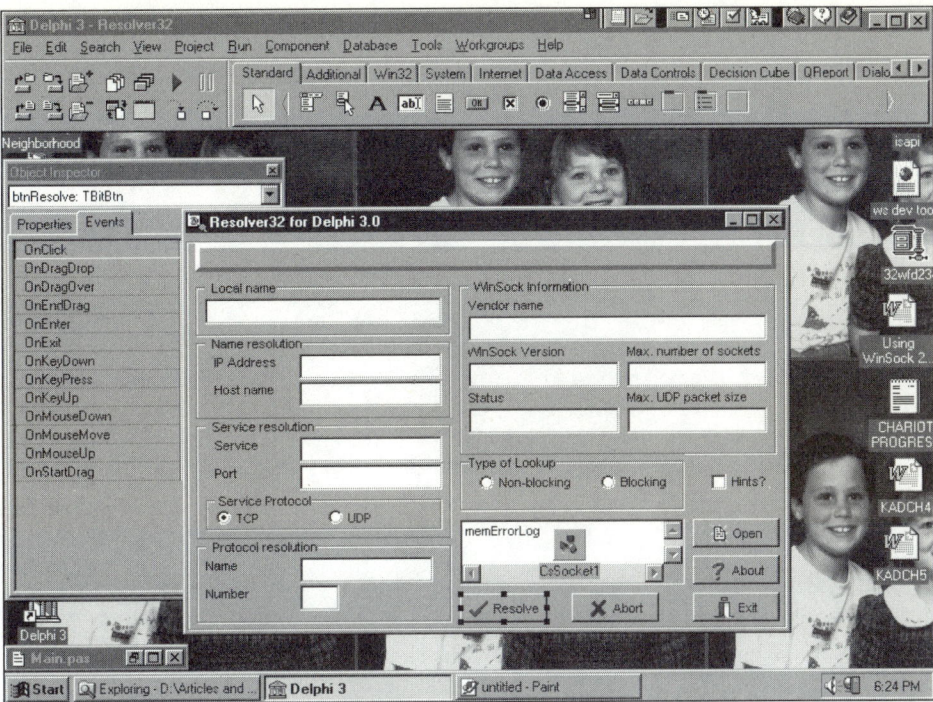

Figure 5.1
The RESOLVER32 application.

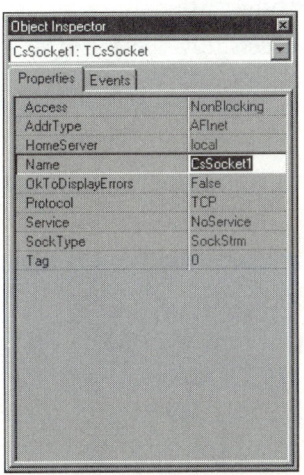

Figure 5.2
The CsSocket properties display.

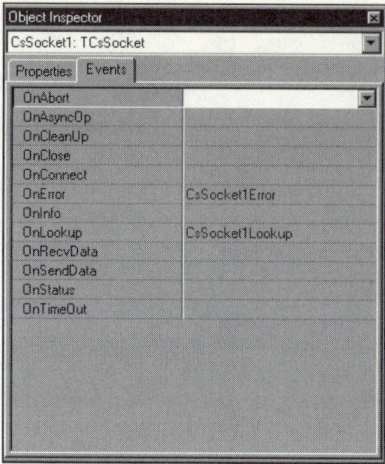

Figure 5.3
The CsSocket events display.

event procedure posts information whenever a lookup function completes its task. Another important event procedure is **CsSocket1Error**, which reports error messages from CsSocket to the application.

When you run the RESOLVER32 application, the **Application.CreateForm** procedure in RESOLVER32.DPR calls the constructor **TCsSocket.Create** to set CsSocket's properties to their default settings. After the constructor initializes the component and calls the Winsock DLL successfully, the **TFrmMain.FormCreate** procedure performs several tasks, as shown in Listing 5.5.

One of the necessary tasks that **TMainForm.FormCreate** has to perform is the checking of the **Status** property that is updated by CsSocket. If the **Status** property indicates a failure, RESOLVER32 disables the Resolve button and edit controls, sets the color property of **pnStatus**, a TPanel control, to clRed, and finally displays an error message in **pnStatus**'s caption property. Otherwise, RESOLVER32 proceeds to update the controls with values from Winsock in the **gbWSInfo** group box control on its form.

Listing 5.5 The main form's FormCreate procedure.

```
procedure TfrmMain.FormCreate(Sender: TObject);
begin
  tag := 1;
  memErrorLog.Clear;
```

```
memErrorLog.Visible := FALSE;
if CsSocket1.Status = Failure then
begin
  pnStatus.Color         := clRed;
  pnStatus.Caption       := 'Winsock not available!';
  btnResolve.Enabled     := FALSE;
  gbNameRes.Enabled      := FALSE;
  gbServiceRes.Enabled   := FALSE;
  gbProtoRes.Enabled     := FALSE;
  gbTypeOfLookUp.Enabled := FALSE;
  edMachineName.Text     := '';
  edVendorName.Text      := '';
  edVersionNo.Text       := '';
  edMaxNoSockets.Text    := '';
  edMaxUDPacketSize.Text := '';
  edWSStatusInfo.Text    := '';
end
else
begin
 with CsSocket1 do
 begin
   edMachineName.Text     := LocalName;
   edVendorName.Text      := WSVendor;
   edVersionNo.Text       := WSVersion;
   edMaxNoSockets.Text    := WSMaxNoSockets;
   edMaxUDPacketSize.Text := WSMaxUDPPSize;
   edWSStatusInfo.Text    := WSStatus;
   Access                 := Blocking;
   rgProtocol.ItemIndex   := 0; // Always default to TCP
 end;
 if CsSocket1.Access = Blocking then
 begin
   btnAbortRes.Enabled  := FALSE;
   rbBlocking.Checked   := TRUE;
 end;
 cbHint.Checked      := TRUE;
 frmMain.ShowHint    := TRUE;
 end;
end;
```

What's My Name?

RESOLVER32 reports the name that your machine presents to the network. It can do so because the **CsSocket1.LocalName** property assigns your machine's name to **Machine.Text**. The **TCsSocket.GetLocalName** method acts as a wrapper for the Winsock API's **gethostname** routine. It retrieves your machine's name from the local host's file (typically located in the Windows directory) and returns it in the **LocalName** property.

Listing 5.6 shows the code for the **TCsSocket.GetLocalName** method in **CSSOCKET.PAS**. It's important to note that **gethostname**, as with all Winsock routines, handles only ASCII strings. The **GetLocalName** method uses the **StrPas** function to convert the ASCII string to an Object Pascal string. The machine name then appears in the **edMachineName** edit control. If your machine is nameless, **GetLocalName** simply returns a blank string. Similarly, the miscellaneous information gathered by **TCsSocket.StartUp** about the particular Winsock DLL in use is passed back to RESOLVER32 by the properties **WSVendor**, **WSVersion**, **WSStatus**, **WSMaxNoSockets**, and **WSMaxUDPPSize** for display in the **gbWSInfo** group box.

Listing 5.6 The GetLocalName function.

```
function TCsSocket.GetLocalName : String;
var
 LocalName : array[0..MaxBufferSize] of Char;
begin
 if gethostname(LocalName, SizeOf(LocalName)) = 0 then
  Result := StrPas(LocalName)
 else
  Result := '';
end;
```

What's The Address?

The most common operation performed by a Winsock application is resolving a host name in blocking mode. In this case, blocking means that the application is waiting for a response from a remote computer—a response that may never come. Unable to proceed or respond to input until it receives a response, a blocked application often appears "dead" to the user.

Under operating systems like Unix, Windows 95, and Windows NT, this type of operation poses little problem. Even if an application blocks, the preemptive nature of these operating systems allows other applications to operate normally.

To allow a user to interact with any Winsock application in a blocking situation, Winsock replaces each blocking function with a pseudo blocking asynchronous equivalent. Instead of blocking, these routines enter a polling loop while waiting for the network event to complete. These nonblocking routines are identified by the **WSAAsync** prefix before the name. For example, **WSAAsyncGetHostByName** is the asynchronous version of **gethostbyname**. By using **WSAAsyncGetHostByName**, the user can abort the lookup operation at any time. In contrast, this flexibility is not possible with blocking functions.

We can determine the behavior of RESOLVER32 by adjusting the value of the **Access** property from Blocking to NonBlocking, and vice versa. Setting the property to NonBlocking tells CsSocket to use asynchronous functions for lookups.

Typically, an Internet host identifies itself over the network with a unique address in the form of a dotted decimal number quadruple such as 127.0.0.1. (Note that this is the special loopback address that you can use to test your Winsock applications on a nonnetworked machine.) Although highly convenient for computers, these addresses hold little appeal for humans. To reconcile this problem, a system was implemented that allows the creation of a unique human-readable name for each Internet address. For example, the name slipper109.iaccess.za is equivalent to the Internet address 196.7.7.109.

To resolve a host name, enter the name in RESOLVER32's **edHostName** edit control. After you press the Resolve button, RESOLVER32 assigns the name that you gave in the **edHostName** edit control to the **Hostname** property. Then the property calls **TCsSocket.SetRemoteHostName**. If the **NameReqd** string is empty, **SetRemoteHostName** reports the error and exits. Otherwise, CsSocket checks the **FAccess** variable, which is assigned a value of either Blocking or NonBlocking by the **Access** property, to determine the mode of conversion of a host name to its IP address. If **FAccess** is set to NonBlocking, **SetAsyncHostName** is called. If, however, **FAccess** is set to Blocking, then **StrpCopy** is used to convert **FRemoteName** from a Pascal string to an ASCII string. Listing 5.7 shows how CsSocket handles this.

Listing 5.7 TCsSocket.SetRemoteHostName—Mapping a host name to its Internet address.

```
procedure TCsSocket.SetRemoteHostName(NameReqd : String);
var
 P : Pointer;
 IPAddress : LongInt;
begin
```

```pascal
    FRemoteName := NameReqd;
    if Length(NameReqd) = 0 then
    begin
     FStatus := Failure;
     ErrorEvent(FStatus, 'No host name given!');
     case FLookUpOp of
      resHostName  : LookUpEvent(resHostName,FRemoteName, FALSE);
      resIPAddress : LookUpEvent(resIPAddress,FRemoteName, FALSE);
     end;// case
     raise ECsSocketError.Create('No host name given!');
     Exit;
    end;
    if FAccess = NonBlocking then
     SetAsyncHostName(FRemoteName)
    else
    begin
     InfoEvent('Resolving host');
     StrPCopy(FpHostName, FRemoteName);
     { check what type of address has been entered }
     IPAddress := inet_addr(FpHostName);
     if IPAddress <>INADDR_NONE then {this is a dotted address}
     begin
      FLookUpOp := resHostName;
      FAddress := IPAddr;
      P := addr(IPAddress);
      case AddrType of
       AFINET : FHost := gethostbyaddr(P, 4, AF_INET);
      end;
     end
     else {no, it looks like a human readable hostname}
     begin
      FLookUpOp := resIPAddress;
      FAddress := HostAddr;
      FHost    := gethostbyname(FpHostName);
     end;
     if FHost = NIL then
     begin{Unknown host, so aborting...}
      LookUpEvent(FLookUpOp, '', FALSE);
      FStatus := Failure;
      if FOkToDisplayErrors then
       raise ECsSocketError('Unable to resolve ' + FpHostName);
      Exit;
     end;
     InfoEvent('Host found');
     FStatus := Success;
     Move(FHost^.h_addr_list^, Fh_addr, SizeOf(FHost^.h_addr_list^));
```

```
    if FAddress = HostAddr then
    begin
     SetUpAddress;
     FRemoteName := StrPas(inet_ntoa(FSockAddress.sin_addr));
    end
    else
    if FAddress = IPAddr then
    begin
     FRemoteName := StrPas(FHost^.h_name);
     InfoEvent('Host found...');
    end;
    case FLookUpOp of
     resHostName  : LookUpEvent(resHostName,FRemoteName, TRUE);
     resIPAddress : LookUpEvent(resIPAddress,FRemoteName, TRUE);
    end;// case
   end;
end;
```

Next, the **SetRemoteHostName** method checks whether the string already contains a numeric Internet address using the **inet_addr** function. If not, the method assumes that the string contains a host name and calls the **gethostbyname** function to resolve it to an IP address. If the host name is not present in the local hosts file, **gethostbyname** looks for the name in a foreign hosts file elsewhere on the network.

If the name is not found, the lookup process times out and sets the private property **FHost**, which is a **pHostent** structure, to **NIL**. Then, **SetRemoteHostName** calls **LookUpEvent**, an event procedure, to post a failed lookup result, sets the **FStatus** flag to **Failure**, and exits back to the calling application. If the IP address is found, however, the **gethostbyname** function returns a pointer to **FHost**, which contains the IP address. The **SetUpAddress** procedure then extracts the IP address from the **FHost** structure. Finally, **SetRemoteHostName** sends back the dotted address as a Pascal string using the following statement:

```
FRemoteName := StrPas(inet_ntoa(FSockAddress.sin_addr));
```

The **inet_ntoa** function converts the returned IP address to an ASCII string in dotted format. The **StrPas** function finishes the conversion to a Pascal string. The address information for the socket is placed in **FSockAddress**, where it will later be used to set up a connection with a host machine. The **LookUpEvent** event procedure writes the IP address to the **edIPName** edit control, as shown in Figure 5.4. RESOLVER32 uses CsSocket's **OnLookUp** event handler, via the **LookUpEvent**

Chapter 5

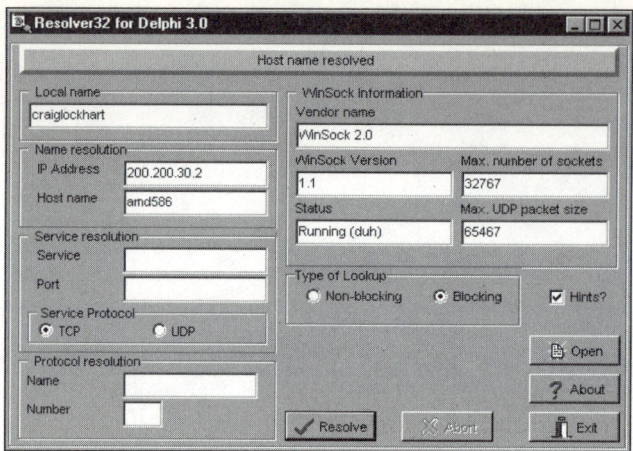

Figure 5.4
RESOLVER32 after resolving a host name.

event procedure, for the display of the results of lookup functions. Listing 5.8 shows how this is done.

Listing 5.8   TfrmMain.CsSocket1Lookup—RESOLVER32 displays the results of a lookup function.

```
procedure TfrmMain.CsSocket1Lookup(Sender: TObject; LookUpOp: TLookUpOp;
  Value: String; Result : Boolean);
begin
 btnResolve.Enabled   := TRUE;
 btnAbortRes.Enabled := FALSE;
 Screen.Cursor        := crDefault;
 if Result then
 begin
  pnStatus.Color := clLime;
  case LookUpOp of
   resHostName  : begin
                   edHostName.Text    := Value;
                   pnStatus.Caption   := 'IP address resolved';
                 end;
   resIPAddress : begin
                   edIpName.Text      := Value;
                   pnStatus.Caption   := 'Host name resolved';
```

The Delphi Winsock Component

```
                          end;
     resService    : begin
                       edPortName.Text     := Value;
                       pnStatus.Caption    := 'Service resolved';
                     end;
     resPort       : begin
                       edServiceName.Text  := Value;
                       pnStatus.Caption    := 'Port number resolved';
                     end;
     resProto      : begin
                       edProtoNo.Text      := Value;
                       pnStatus.Caption    := 'Protocol resolved';
                     end;
     resProtoNo    : begin
                       edProtoName.Text    := Value;
                       pnStatus.Caption    := 'Protocol number resolved';
                     end;
  end;// case
end
else
begin
  pnStatus.Color := clRed;
  case LookUpOp of
    resHostName  : begin
                     edHostName.Text := '';
                     pnStatus.Caption := 'IP address resolution failed.';
                   end;
    resIPAddress : begin
                     edIpName.Text    := '';
                     pnStatus.Caption := 'Host name resolution failed';
                   end;
    resService   : begin
                     edPortName.Text  := '';
                     pnStatus.Caption := 'Service resolution failed';
                   end;
    resPort      : begin
                     edServiceName.Text := '';
                     pnStatus.Caption := 'Port number resolution failed.';
                   end;
```

```
  resProto     : begin
                   edProtoNo.Text    := '';
                   pnStatus.Caption := 'Protocol resolution failed.';
                 end;
  resProtoNo   :
    begin
      edProtoName.Text := '';
      pnStatus.Caption := 'Protocol number resolution failed.';
    end;
  end;// case
 end;
end;
```

What's Your Name?

RESOLVER32 can also derive the name of a host from its numeric Internet address. The process begins when you enter an address into the **edIPName** edit control, as shown in Figure 5.5. When you click the Resolve button, RESOLVER32 passes the address string in **edIPName.Text** to the **SetRemoteHostName** method via the **Hostname** property.

As before, the **SetRemoteHostName** method uses the **inet_addr** function to check whether the string is in valid Internet address form. Before calling this function, however, the method assigns the address of the **IPAddress** string to a pointer, **P**, which **gethostbyaddr** requires as one of its parameters.

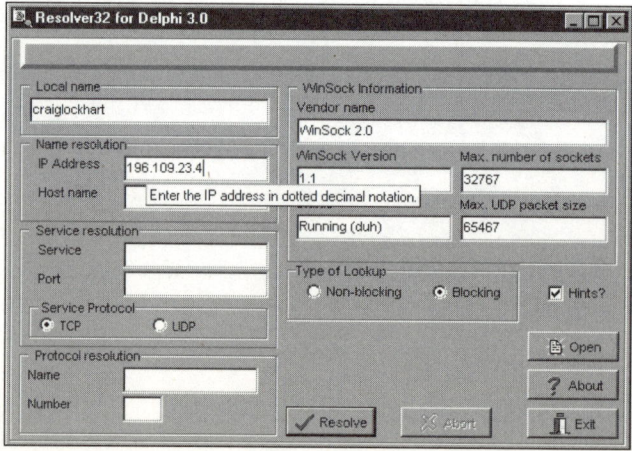

Figure 5.5
A dotted IP address ready to resolve.

The Delphi Winsock Component

If **inet_addr** returns a result other than **INADDR_NONE** (meaning that the string is a numeric Internet address), **SetRemoteHostName** calls **gethostbyaddr**. Like the call to **gethostbyname**, this call may also block. If **gethostbyaddr** is successful, it returns a pointer to the **pHostent** structure. If no corresponding name is found for the IP address, **FHost** is set to **NIL** and **SetRemoteHostName** calls **LookUpEvent** to report a failed lookup, sets the **FStatus** flag, and exits. On success, the **Hostname** property writes the host name obtained, using the statement below, back to the **edHostName** edit control via the **LookUpEvent** event procedure:

```
FRemoteName := StrPas(FHost^.h_name);
```

Getting The Name Asynchronously

Using the blocking lookup functions **gethostbyname** and **gethostbyaddr** is fairly straightforward. Employing the asynchronous versions of these functions, **WSAAyncGetHostByName** and **WSAAsyncGetHostByAddr**, is a little more complex. To understand the asynchronous process, let's go through the steps of calling **WSAAsyncGetHostByName** from the RESOLVER32 program.

First, change the **Access** property from **Blocking** to **NonBlocking** by selecting the **NonBlocking** radio button in the **TypeOfLookup** group box as shown in Figure 5.6. Pressing the Resolve button now assigns the name to the **HostName** property.

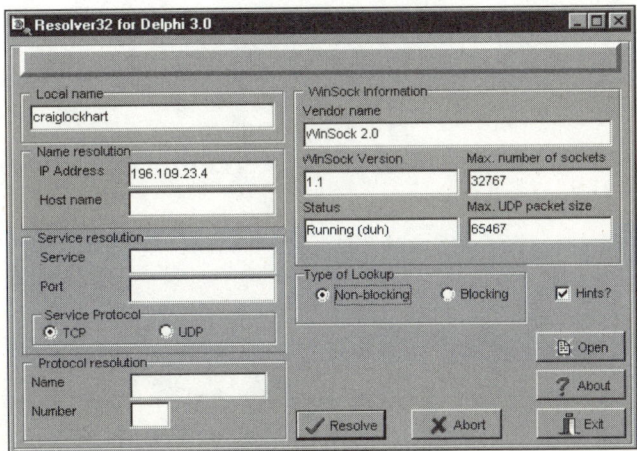

Figure 5.6
Changing from Blocking to NonBlocking.

183

Because **FAccess** is set to NonBlocking, **SetRemoteHostName** passes it to the **SetAsyncHostName** procedure as shown in Listing 5.9.

Listing 5.9 TCsSocket.SetAsyncHostName—Resolving the host name.

```
procedure TCsSocket.SetAsyncHostName(ReqdHostName : String);
var
 IPAddress : TInaddr;
 SAddress: array[0..31] of char;
begin
 FillChar(FAsyncBuff, SizeOf(FAsyncBuff), #0);
 FAsyncRemoteName := ReqdHostName;
 StrPcopy(SAddress, FAsyncRemoteName);
 IPAddress.s_addr := inet_addr(SAddress);
 if IPAddress.s_addr <> INADDR_NONE then {this is a dotted address}
 begin
  FAddress := IPAddr;
  FAsyncType := AsyncAddr;
  if IPAddress.s_addr <> 0 then
  FTaskHandle := WSAAsyncGetHostByAddr(FAsyncHWND, ASYNC_EVENT,
                                      pChar(@IPAddress), 4, PF_INET,
                                      @FAsyncBuff[0],
                                      SizeOf(FAsyncBuff));
  if FTaskHandle = 0 then
  begin
   if FNoOfBlockingTasks > 0 then
    dec(FNoOfBlockingTasks);
   FStatus := Failure;
   ErrorEvent(FStatus,WSAErrorMsg);
   if FOKToDisplayErrors then
    raise ECsSocketError.create(WSAErrorMsg);
   Exit;
  end else FStatus := Success;
 end
 else {no, it looks like a human readable hostname}
 begin
  FAddress := HostAddr;
  FAsyncType := AsyncName;
  Inc(FNoOfBlockingTasks);
  FTaskHandle := WSAAsyncGetHostByName(FAsyncHWND, ASYNC_EVENT,
                                      @FpHostName[0],
                                      @FAsyncBuff[0],
                                      MAXGETHOSTSTRUCT);
  if FTaskHandle = 0 then
```

```
begin
  FStatus := Failure;
  if FNoOfBlockingTasks > 0 then
    dec(FNoOfBlockingTasks);
  ErrorEvent(FStatus,WSAErrorMsg);
  if FOKToDisplayErrors then
    raise ECsSocketError.create(WSAErrorMsg);
  Exit;
 end else FStatus := Success;
end;
end;
```

SetAsyncHostName calls the **WSAAsyncGetHostByName** procedure with five important arguments. **FASyncHWND** is a handle to the window in which the asynchronous function will post its message on completion of the lookup operation. This window handle is initialized in the **TCsSocket.Create** constructor by a call to **AllocateHWND** with **AsyncOperation** as its procedural parameter. **ASYNC_EVENT** is the event notification constant used by **WSAAsyncGetHostByName**. **FAsyncBuff** is an array of characters that holds the result of the operation. Finally, **MAXGET- HOSTSTRUCT** is a Winsock constant representing the maximum size of the **FAsyncBuff** buffer. The **WSAAsyncGetHostByName** procedure returns the task number of the call as a **TaskHandle** type that is assigned to **FTaskHandle**.

WSAAyncGetHostByName returns immediately with a value of 0 if the call was unsuccessful or greater than 0 if successful. However, a nonzero value for **FTaskhandle** means only that the call to **WSAASyncGetHostByName** succeeded, not that the subsequent lookup operation (which continues to execute in the background) will be successful.

When the lookup does complete, the Winsock DLL triggers an **ASYNC_EVENT** event, notifying the **AsyncOperation** procedure that it should examine the **ASYNC_EVENT** message, as shown in Listing 5.10.

Listing 5.10 The AsyncOperation procedure.
```
procedure TCsSocket.AsyncOperation(var Mess : TMessage);
var
 MsgErr : Word;
begin
 if Mess.Msg = ASYNC_EVENT then
```

```
begin
 MsgErr := WSAGetAsyncError(Mess.lparam);
 if MsgErr <> 0 then
 begin
  FStatus := Failure;
  ErrorEvent(FStatus,WSAErrorMsg);
  if FOKToDisplayErrors then
   raise ECsSocketError.create(WSAErrorMsg);
  Exit;
 end
 else
 begin
  FStatus := Success;
  InfoEvent('WSAAsync operation succeeded!');
  case FAsyncType of
   AsyncName,
   AsyncAddr     : begin
                    FHost := pHostent(@FAsyncBuff);
                    if (FHost^.h_name = NIL) then
                    begin{Unknown host, so aborting...}
                     FStatus := Failure;
                     if FAsyncType = AsyncName then
                      LookUpEvent(resIPAddress,'',FALSE)
                     else
                      LookUpEvent(resHostName,'',FALSE);
                     if FOKToDisplayErrors then
                      raise ECsSocketError.create
                             ('Unable to resolve host');
                     Exit;
                    end;
                    if length(StrPas(FHost^.h_name)) = 0 then
                    begin
                     InfoEvent('Host lookup failed!');
                     FStatus := Failure;
                     if FAsyncType = AsyncName then
                      LookUpEvent(resIPAddress,'',FALSE)
                     else
                      LookUpEvent(resHostName,'',FALSE);
                     if FOKToDisplayErrors then
                      raise ECsSocketError.create
                             ('Unknown host');
                     Exit;
                    end;
```

```
                        case FAddress of
                          IPAddr   : begin
                                       Move(FHost^.h_addr_list^,
                                            Fh_addr,
                                            SizeOf(FHost^.h_addr_list^));
                                       FAsyncRemoteName :=
                                            StrPas(FHost^.h_name);
                                       LookUpEvent(resHostName,
                                                   FAsyncRemoteName,
                                                   TRUE);
                                     end;
                          HostAddr : begin
                                       Move(FHost^.h_addr_list^,
                                            Fh_addr,
                                            SizeOf(FHost^.h_addr_list^));
                                       SetUpAddress;
                                       FasyncRemoteName :=
                                         StrPas(inet_ntoa
                                                (FSockAddress.sin_addr));
                                       LookUpEvent(resIPAddress,
                                                   FAsyncRemoteName, TRUE);
                                     end;
                        end;{case}
                      end;
  AsyncServ         : begin
                        FServ := pServent(@FAsyncBuff);
                        if FServ^.s_name = NIL then
                        begin { No service available }
                          FStatus := Failure;
                          LookUpEvent(resService,'',FALSE);
                          if FOKToDisplayErrors then
                            raise ECsSocketError.create(WSAErrorMsg);
                          Exit;
                        end;
                        FAsyncPort := IntToStr(ntohs(FServ^.s_port));
                        LookUpEvent(resService, FAsyncPort, TRUE);
                      end;
  AsyncPort         : begin
                        FServ := pServent(@FAsyncBuff);
                        if FServ^.s_name = NIL then
                        begin { No service available }
                          FStatus := Failure;
                          LookUpEvent(resPort,'',FALSE);
                          if FOKToDisplayErrors then
                            raise ECsSocketError.create(WSAErrorMsg);
                          Exit;
                        end;
```

```
                        FAsyncService := StrPas(FServ^.s_name);
                        LookUpEvent(resPort, FAsyncService, TRUE);
                      end;
     AsyncProtoName    : begin
                          FProto := pProtoEnt(@FAsyncBuff);
                          if FProto^.p_name = NIL then
                          begin
                            FStatus := Failure;
                            LookUpEvent(resProto,'',FALSE);
                            if FOKToDisplayErrors then
                              raise ECsSocketError.create(WSAErrorMsg);
                            Exit;
                          end;
                          FAsyncProtoNo := IntToStr(FProto^.p_proto);
                          LookUpEvent(resProto, FAsyncProtoNo, TRUE);
                        end;
     AsyncProtoNumber  : begin
                          FProto := pProtoEnt(@FAsyncBuff);
                          if FProto^.p_name = NIL then
                          begin
                            FStatus := Failure;
                            LookUpEvent(resProtoNo,'',FALSE);
                            if FOKToDisplayErrors then
                              raise ECsSocketError.create(WSAErrorMsg);
                            Exit;
                          end;
                          FAsyncProtocol := StrPas(FProto^.p_name);
                          LookUpEvent(resProtoNo, FAsyncProtocol, TRUE);
                        end;
    end;
    if FNoOfBlockingTasks > 0 then
      dec(FNoOfBlockingTasks);
    end;
   end;
 end;
end;
```

The **WSAGetAsyncError** macro checks the **Mess** variable. If it indicates that an error occurred, **AsyncOperation** calls **ErrorEvent** to display the cause of the error, which is retrieved from **WSAErrorMsg**, then exits with the **FStatus** flag set to **Failure**. If no error has occurred, we parse the **FAsyncType** variable.

When we called **WSAASyncGetHostByName**, we set the **FAsyncType** to **AsyncName** to indicate that we were performing an asynchronous name lookup. The **case** statement now branches based on the value of **FAsyncType** to the **AsyncName** clause.

There, the character array **FAsyncBuff**, containing the result of the lookup, is typecast to a **pHostent** structure and stored in **FHost**. The address structure for the resolved host is read by **SetUpAddress** to get the corresponding IP address. The **LookUpEvent** event procedure returns the IP address back to RESOLVER32.

Who's At This Address?

To illustrate further the use of asynchronous mode, we'll examine how the **WSAAsyncGetHostByAddr** function retrieves a host name when given only an Internet address. To use this function in the RESOLVER32 application, set the **Access** property to **NonBlocking** in the **TypeOfLookUp** group box, and enter an Internet address in the **edIPName** edit control.

As before, we assign the name to the **HostName** property for handling by the **TCsSocket.SetAsyncHostName** method. If the name we passed is an empty string, **SetRemoteHostName** sets the **FStatus** flag to **Failure** and calls an error handler, **ErrorEvent**, which posts an error message. Next, we call another event handler, **LookUpEvent**, which posts a failed lookup result to RESOLVER32, and exits. After establishing that the **FRemoteName** is not empty, we call the **SetAsyncHostName** method, in which we use the **inet_addr** function to determine whether the string is a dotted decimal Internet address or host name. A return value different than **INADDR_NONE** indicates the string is in Internet address format.

This string is then passed to **WSAAsyncGetHostByAddr** to get the host information for the Internet address. A successful call to **WSAAsyncGetHostByAddr** sets the **FTaskHandle** to a number greater than zero, but doesn't ensure that we will get a valid result from **WSAAsyncGetHostByAddr** on completion. The method exits back to the RESOLVER32 application, and the lookup continues in the background.

When the lookup operation completes, the Winsock DLL posts a message to CsSocket by triggering the **ASYNC_EVENT** event. This trigger wakes up the **TCsSocket.- AsyncOperation** method, which examines the **Mess** variable. If **Mess** contains an error, the **AsyncOperation** method calls **ErrorEvent** to display the cause of the error from **WSAErrorMsg**, sets the **FStatus** flag to **Failure**, and exits.

If the **Mess** variable contains no error, a case statement parses **FAsyncType**. In this example, **FAsyncType** has the value **AsyncAddr**, so the same portion of code executes that handled the **AsyncName** case. Next, we parse **FAddress** to execute the section of code that handles the result of **WSAAsyncGetHostByAddr**. This setting is automatically determined by the **SetAsyncHostName** method by using the result of the **inet_addr** operation. That is, **FAddress** is set to **IPAddr** when a dotted decimal address is found, otherwise it is set to **HostAddr** for a host name. The host name is then extracted by the following code:

```
Move(FHost^.h_addr_list^, Fh_addr, SizeOf(FHost^.h_addr_list^));
FAsyncRemoteName := StrPas(FHost^.h_name);
```

This result is posted back to the application via the **OnLookUp** event handler.

Canceling A WSAAsync Operation

Because asynchronous operations run outside of normal program flow, canceling them poses a unique problem. To cancel any currently executing asynchronous operations, the Winsock API provides the **WSACancelAsyncRequest** function. (Note, however, that this function cannot cancel operations started by the **WSAAsyncSelect** function.) Listing 5.11 shows the **WSACancelAsyncRequest** function wrapped up inside the **FAsyncType** method.

Listing 5.11 TCsSocket.CancelAsyncOperation—Canceling an asynchronous operation.

```
procedure TCsSocket.CancelAsyncOperation(CancelOP : Boolean);
begin
 if WSACancelAsyncRequest(THandle(FTaskHandle)) = SOCKET_ERROR then
 begin
  FStatus := Failure;
  ErrorEvent(FStatus,WSAErrorMsg);
  if FOKToDisplayErrors then
   raise ECsSocketError.create(WSAErrorMsg);
 end
 else
 begin
  FStatus := Success;
  InfoEvent('WSAAsync lookup cancelled!');
 end;
end;
```

But the **WSACancelAsyncRequest** method is not visible to the RESOLVER32 application. So, how does RESOLVER32 cancel a **WSAAsyncGetHostByName** or

WSAAsyncGetHostByAddr call? By accessing the **CancelAsyncOperation** method using the public boolean property, **CancelAsyncOp**.

Listing 5.12 shows what happens when you press the **Abort** button in the **gbNameRes** group box in RESOLVER32. Because the call type is nonblocking, we assign the **CancelAsyncOp** to be **True**. This signals CsSocket, via the **CancelAsyncOperation**, to call the **WSACancelAsyncRequest** and thus to kill the asynchronous operation. Note that the Abort button is disabled during blocking calls.

Listing 5.12 TFrmMain.AbortAsyncHostBtnClick—Signaling a cancel operation.

```
procedure TfrmMain.btnAbortResClick(Sender: TObject);
begin
  CsSocket1.CancelAsyncOp  := TRUE;
  pnStatus.Color           := clYellow;
  pnStatus.Caption         := 'Operation aborted';
  btnAbortRes.Enabled      := FALSE;
  btnResolve.Enabled       := TRUE;
  Screen.Cursor            := crDefault;
end;
```

Resolving Ports And Services

As with name and address resolution, we can resolve a service name and a port using either a blocking or nonblocking (asynchronous) call. The Winsock API functions **getservbyname** or **getservbyport** provide these services in blocking mode.

Looking up the port associated with a particular service type is quite similar to the process of getting the host name. For example, if we wish to find the corresponding port number for FTP, we enter FTP in the **edServiceName** edit control, and then assign it to the **WSService** property. This passes the service name to the **TCsSocket.SetServiceName** method for conversion. After copying the **ReqdServiceName** to **ServName** using the Object Pascal function **StrPCopy**, the protocol string is set to "TCP", one of the required parameters for **getservbyname**. The protocol is set to "TCP" by default, which means that if you try to determine a port number for a service based on a different protocol, usually "UDP", the **getservbyname** function would return a **NIL** pointer. Some services use either "TCP" or "UDP", or both. To determine whether a service is available for the "UDP" protocol, we select the "UDP" radio button in the **rgProtocol** radio group control, and then click the Resolve button.

The **SetServiceName** method calls the **getservbyname** function to get the corresponding port number. If the service is found, the **getservbyname** function returns a pointer to **FServ**, a **pServent** structure. This structure now holds the port number. Otherwise, the function returns a null pointer, in which case the method calls **ErrorEvent** to display the cause of the error from **WSAErrorMsg**, sets the **FStatus** flag to **Failure**, and exits back to the calling application. The port number is extracted using the following statement:

```
FServiceName := IntToStr(ntohs(FServ^.s_port));
```

Figure 5.7 shows the result of the conversion.

Finding The Service

The process of translating a port number into its corresponding service is quite similar to the service lookup we just examined, except we use the blocking Winsock function **getservbyport**. Instead of tracing through that process, we'll look at the use of **WSAAsyncGetServByPort**, the asynchronous version of **getservbyport**.

To use the asynchronous mode, first change the **Access** property from blocking to nonblocking by selecting the Non-blocking radio button in the **TypeOfLookup** group box. Then enter a port number in the **edPortName** edit control and press the Resolve button.

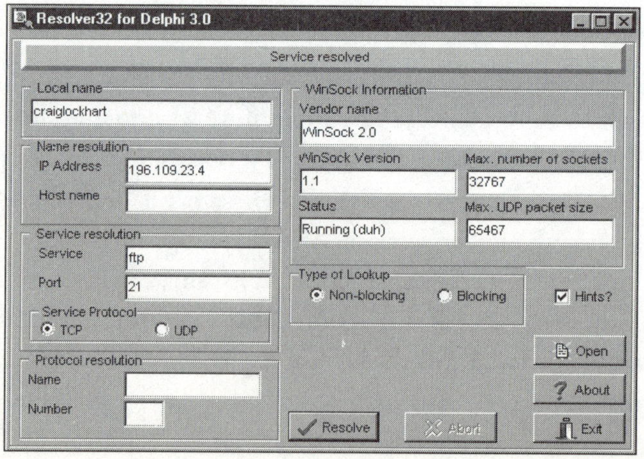

Figure 5.7
The result of the service conversion.

The port number, in **edPortName.Text**, is passed to the **TCsSocket.SetPortName** method as **ReqdPortName** when we assign it to the **WSPort** property. After verifying that the port number string is not empty, **SetPortName** calls **SetAsyncPort**. The **SetAsyncPort** method copies it to **FPortNo**, a null terminated string. Calling **WSAAsyncGetServByPort** then fetches the corresponding port number.

The result of the call is stored by **FTaskHandle**. If **FTaskHandle** is zero, then the call has failed. Otherwise, the call was successful, and the **SetAsyncPort** exits back to the application, leaving the lookup process to continue in the background. When the lookup process is complete, **AsyncOperation** is invoked by a message from the Winsock DLL. The **Mess** variable is examined for an error. If there is no error, the method returns the port number. Otherwise, the method calls **ErrorEvent** to display the cause of the error, sets the **FStatus** flag to **Failure**, reports the error, and exits back to the application.

Resolving Protocols

Getting the protocol name and number is not as common an operation as the other conversion functions, but the functions are supported in CsSocket for completeness. The Winsock API functions that perform these conversions are **getprotobyname**, **getprotobyno**, **WSAAsyncGetProtoByName** and **WSAAsyncGetProtoByNo**. The use and operation of these functions is similar to the previously discussed functions.

Using Tags

By now you might be wondering how RESOLVER32 determines which input to resolve. The solution is simple: Every control has a **Tag** property, which we use to distinguish what edit control will get the input string to resolve. To each edit control we assign an integer, starting with 1 for the **edIPName** edit control, through 6 for the **edProtoNo** in the Object Inspector. Then we use their **OnClick** event handler to assign the form's **Tag** property. The following code shows how this is done for the **edIPName** edit control:

```
procedure TfrmMain.edIPNameClick(Sender: TObject);
begin
 frmMain.tag := edIpName.tag;
end;
```

When we click the Resolve button RESOLVER32 parses the **frmMain.tag** in the case statement to assign a value to the target property for resolution. Listing 5.13 shows how this is done.

Listing 5.13 How RESOLVER32 uses the tag property for determining which input to resolve.

```
procedure TfrmMain.btnResolveClick(Sender: TObject);
begin
 btnResolve.Enabled := FALSE;
 Screen.Cursor      := crHourGlass;
 if CsSocket1.Access = NonBlocking then
  btnAbortRes.Enabled := TRUE;
 pnStatus.Color := clBtnFace;
 pnStatus.UpDate;
 case tag of
   1 : begin
         edHostName.Text     := '';
         edHostName.UpDate;
         pnStatus.Caption    := Concat('Resolving ',edIPName.Text);
         pnStatus.UpDate;
         CsSocket1.HostName  := edIPName.Text;
       end;
   2 : begin
         edIPName.Text       := '';
         edIPName.UpDate;
         pnStatus.Caption    := Concat('Resolving ',edHostName.Text);
         pnStatus.UpDate;
         CsSocket1.HostName  := edHostName.Text
       end;
   3 : begin
         edPortName.Text     := '';
         edPortName.UpDate;
         pnStatus.Caption := Concat('Resolving ',edServiceName.Text);
         pnStatus.UpDate;
         CsSocket1.WSService := edServiceName.Text
       end;
   4 : begin
         edServiceName.Text  := '';
         edServiceName.UpDate;
         pnStatus.Caption := Concat('Resolving ',edServiceName.Text);
         pnStatus.UpDate;
         CsSocket1.WSPort := edPortName.Text
       end;
```

```
    5 : begin
          edProtoNo.Text       := '';
          edProtoNo.UpDate;
          pnStatus.Caption     := 'Resolving protocol name.';
          pnStatus.UpDate;
          CsSocket1.WSProtoName := edProtoName.Text;
        end;
    6 : begin
          edProtoName.Text     := '';
          edProtoName.UpDate;
          pnStatus.Caption     := 'Resolving protocol number.';
          pnStatus.UpDate;
          CsSocket1.WSProtoNo  := edProtoNo.Text;
        end;
  end;
end;
```

To Block Or Not

If your application will use a local DNS, and the target host is on a local network, using blocking calls introduces far less overhead into your applications. However, if your application will connect to hosts beyond the local network, and the remote DNS is heavily used, asynchronous calls have a distinct advantage: Your application can perform other useful work while it's waiting.

CsSocket is not a perfect Winsock component, but it provides a reasonable framework upon which to build other Internet components. Having covered the CsSocket component in some detail, we can now go on to build more interesting applications using our daughter components based on CsSocket. In the chapter that follows, we'll build an FTP client application. After that, well, I leave it to your imagination.

CsShopper: An FTP Client Component

HIGH PERFORMANCE

CHAPTER 6

Go shopping for free stuff on the Internet with a Winsock FTP client component, and a complete FTP file transfer application written around it.

CsShopper: An FTP Client Component

John Penman

Much of the Internet's popularity is an outgrowth of its ability to share information among computers. The protocol that makes much of this sharing possible is the File Transfer Protocol (FTP), one of the oldest protocols in use on the Internet. Today's FTP is defined formally in the Internet Request for Comment document RFC959.

As with other Internet protocols, FTP is cast in the classic client/server transaction model. I like to picture an FTP server as the old-time shopkeeper that gets stuff from the shelves and hands them to the shopper, the FTP client. In this chapter, we'll implement an FTP client component for Delphi named, appropriately enough, CsShopper.

CsShopper depends on CsSocket, the simple component wrapper for Winsock API calls that we developed in Chapter 5. CsSocket sets up the basic functionality required by FTP to communicate using TCP/IP. With those details under control, we can begin immediately to take a closer look at the FTP process from the client side.

Are You Being Served?

By convention, an FTP server always listens for a client to set up a connection on TCP port number 21. This connection, known as the *control connection*, remains open until either the client or the server closes its side of the connection. The client and server exchange FTP commands and reply codes, respectively, over this link. Internet protocols generally use plain English text—usually in uppercase—for their commands. This holds true even for interactions between programs. This stems from the Internet's origins as a 7-bit, ASCII-only system, which was (and remains) the least common denominator for communications between two systems—computer or any other.

This doesn't do much for program speed, but it certainly makes the interaction between two Internet programs easier for human beings to follow. In general, for every command that is sent by the client, the server sends a three-digit reply code, followed by either a dash or a space, and then some text. The following two lines represent typical messages:

```
200 PORT command successful.
230-Welcome to your I-SITE Internet server!
```

The dash or space following the numeric code contains important information for the client. A dash following the code tells the client that the current message is a comment destined for human eyes, and may safely be ignored. A space after the code tells the client to proceed to the next step of the action. The text that follows is usually a status message or instruction to the user.

Figure 6.1 shows a finite state diagram representation of the interaction between the client and server during the login sequence. The FTP session begins with the client sending the USER command, followed by the user name to the server and listening

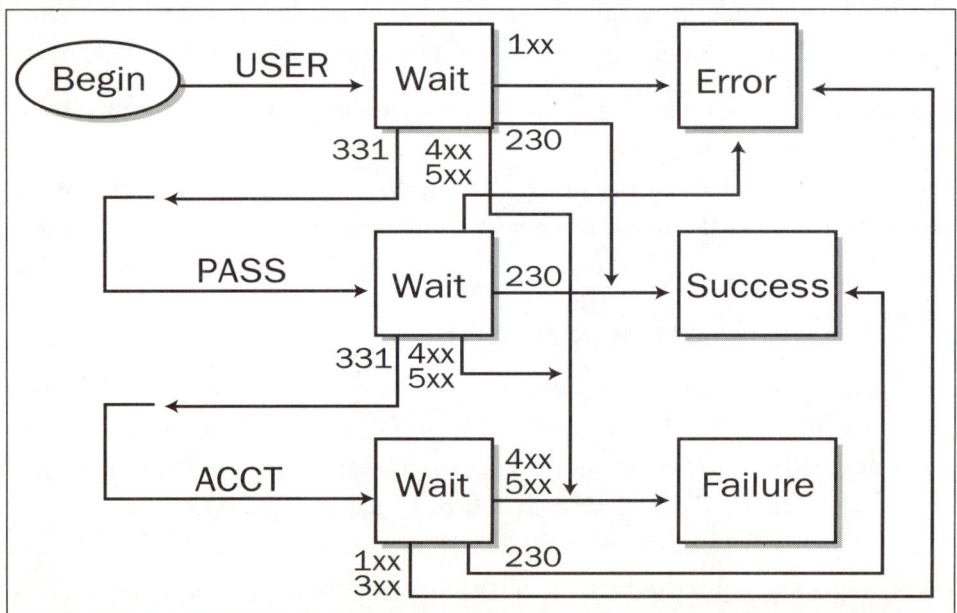

Figure 6.1
How the FTP client logs in to the FTP server.

for a three-digit reply code. If the user name is valid, the server responds with code 331 or 230. An invalid user name generates a response code of 4xx or 5xx, where "xx" is the subcode for the specific error in question

A response of 230 indicates that the user name is valid and no further information is needed to access the system. This server typically issues this code in response to the famous "anonymous" FTP login. A response of 331 indicates that the user name is valid, but a password is required. In this case, the client next sends the PASS command, followed by the password.

An incorrect password generates a 4xx or 5xx response, indicating an error. If the password is accepted by the server, the server may send a 230 code to indicate that the login sequence is complete. Alternately, if an account is required for login, the server sends another 331 code to tell the client to send the ACCT command and information.

Once it establishes a successful connection, the client can continue to issue commands. However, if there is a problem, such as a command with invalid syntax, or if there are too many users logged on to the system, the server sends a 4xx or 5xx code and closes the connection.

The CsShopper Component

CsShopper descends from the CsSocket VCL component developed in Chapter 5, and uses CsSocket's **TCsSocket** class for handling mundane housekeeping chores such as loading of the Winsock DLL, filling the data structures for setting up a connection with a host, transfer of data, ending the connection with the server, and closing down Winsock.

The foundation CsSocket VCL component has its **Service** property set to "NoService". As CsShopper always will be an FTP client component, we set the **Service** property to "FTP" in the **TCsShopper.Create** constructor. The FTP protocol uses the same CsSocket default settings—great things, these components! As shown in Figure 6.2, CsShopper has 10 other properties besides **Service: Access, AddrType, Asynchronous, Debug, HomeServer, LogOn, Password, Protocol, SockType,** and **UserName.**

Figure 6.2
CsShopper's properties in Delphi 3's Object Inspector.

The **Asynchronous** property can be used to operate CsShopper in either blocking or asynchronous mode. Though this property is not part of the FTP protocol, the choice of mode can affect data throughput, robustness, and the degree of flexibility. For example, when CsShopper is in asynchronous mode (that is, when **Asynchronous** is TRUE), the user can abort a file transfer that is taking forever. This flexibility is not possible in blocking mode. (Note, though, that if CsShopper is a multithreaded application, you can abort a lengthy file transfer in blocking mode, but that's another story.)

Because asynchronous operation is less straightforward than blocking operation, we will describe how CsShopper works in blocking mode first. We will examine how CsShopper operates in asynchronous mode later in this chapter.

CsShopper implements the more useful FTP commands, including USER, PASSWORD, RETR, and PUT, as individual properties. These FTP properties are in the public section of **TCsShopper**, where they are available to the component user. In blocking mode, each of these methods relies on the **FTPCommand** procedure, the heart of the CsShopper component. **FTPCommand** is a simple parser implemented as a large **case** statement. What the expression lacks in elegance, however, it makes up for in simplicity. In asynchronous mode, CsShopper uses a different approach.

Because the CSSHOPPER.PAS source code file for the component in its entirety is over 3,000 lines long, we won't be publishing it here within the chapter. Selected excerpts will be used to clarify certain points about its operation, and you can always print the full file from the CD-ROM for more leisurely perusal.

Displaying Output

Although CsShopper is a nonvisual component, it occasionally must communicate with the user's application to display messages passed between the client and the server. **TCsShopper**'s published property **OnInfo** (descended from the **TCsSocket** class in CsSocket) and private access procedure **InfoEvent** meet this need. The following code fragment illustrates the **InfoEvent** procedure:

```
procedure TCsSocket.InfoEvent(Msg : String);
begin
 if Assigned(FOnInfoEvent) then
  FOnInfoEvent(Self, Msg);
end;
```

When a message is sent or received over the control connection, **TempStr** in **FTPCommand** sets the **Info** property, and then **FTPCommand** calls the **InfoEvent** procedure. Inside **InfoEvent**, **Assigned** returns **True** and the **CsShopper1Info** procedure in the application displays **Info**.

To enable this communication between CsShopper and the client application, I created the **CsShopper1Info** procedure by using the Events page in the Object Inspector. The **memLog** window, in which these messages are displayed, gets updated whenever the **FOnInfoEvent** event occurs. **CsShopper1Info** contains the following code:

```
procedure TfrmMain.CsShopper1Info(Sender: TObject; Msg: String);
begin
 memLog.Lines.Add(Msg);
end;
```

Putting SHOPPER32 To Work

SHOPPER32, a basic FTP application created using the CsShopper component, is shown in Figure 6.3. To create this application, start a new project, SHOPPER32, call the main form **frmMain**, and store this in MAIN.PAS, shown in Listing 6.1.

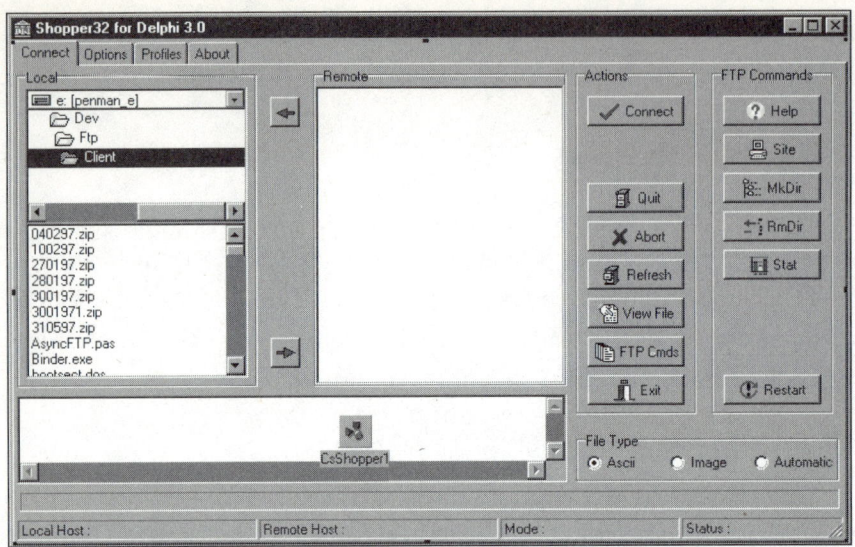

Figure 6.3
The finished SHOPPER32 application.

Listing 6.1 MAIN.PAS.

```
(*
   Main Unit
   Developed for High Performance Delphi 3 Programming—John C.Penman 1997
   For more information and help contact info@craiglockhart.com
*)

unit main;

interface

uses
  Windows, Messages, SysUtils, Classes, Graphics, Controls, Forms,
Dialogs, StdCtrls, Buttons, FileCtrl, ComCtrls, CsSocket, CsShopper,
  MkDirFrm, CsFtpMsg, ToolWin, Registry, ExtCtrls;

type
  TfrmMain = class(TForm)
    CsShopper1: TCsShopper;
    pcShopper: TPageControl;
    tsConnect: TTabSheet;
    tsOptions: TTabSheet;
    tsAbout: TTabSheet;
    gbLocal: TGroupBox;
```

```
gbRemote: TGroupBox;
gbActions: TGroupBox;
dcbLocal: TDriveComboBox;
dlbLocal: TDirectoryListBox;
flbLocal: TFileListBox;
sbStatus: TStatusBar;
pbDataTransfer: TProgressBar;
lbRemoteFiles: TListBox;
bbtnExit: TBitBtn;
bbtnConnect: TBitBtn;
bbtnAbort: TBitBtn;
gbUserName: TGroupBox;
gbPassword: TGroupBox;
gbDefLocalDir: TGroupBox;
gbDefTextEditor: TGroupBox;
edUserName: TEdit;
edPassword: TEdit;
edDefLocalDir: TEdit;
edDefTextEditor: TEdit;
bbtnFtpCmds: TBitBtn;
bbtnLocateTxtEditor: TBitBtn;
bbtnLocateDefLocalDir: TBitBtn;
gbMoreActions: TGroupBox;
bbtnRefresh: TBitBtn;
bbtnFTPHelp: TBitBtn;
bbtnSite: TBitBtn;
bbtnNewDir: TBitBtn;
bbtnDelDir: TBitBtn;
bbtnViewFile: TBitBtn;
memLog: TMemo;
rgFileType: TRadioGroup;
bbtnRestart: TBitBtn;
bbtnQuit: TBitBtn;
tsProfiles: TTabSheet;
gbSetProfile: TGroupBox;
gbPrName: TGroupBox;
gbPrHostName: TGroupBox;
gbPrUserName: TGroupBox;
gbPrPassWord: TGroupBox;
gbPrRemDir: TGroupBox;
gbPrLocDir: TGroupBox;
edPrName: TEdit;
edPrHostName: TEdit;
edPrUserName: TEdit;
edPrPassword: TEdit;
edPrRemDir: TEdit;
edPrLocDir: TEdit;
```

```
    gbPrList: TGroupBox;
    lbPrList: TListBox;
    bbtnPrNew: TBitBtn;
    bbtnPrSave: TBitBtn;
    bbtnPrDelete: TBitBtn;
    rgFTPMode: TRadioGroup;
    sbbtnRetr: TSpeedButton;
    sbbtnStor: TSpeedButton;
    Panel1: TPanel;
    Label1: TLabel;
    Label2: TLabel;
    Label3: TLabel;
    Label4: TLabel;
    Label5: TLabel;
    bbtnStat: TBitBtn;
    gbHints: TGroupBox;
    cbHints: TCheckBox;
    gbFTPOptions: TGroupBox;
    BitBtn2: TBitBtn;
    rgFileStructure: TRadioGroup;
    rgTransfer: TRadioGroup;
    bbtnAddNew: TBitBtn;
    procedure bbtnConnectClick(Sender: TObject);
    procedure FormCreate(Sender: TObject);
    procedure bbtnFtpCmdsClick(Sender: TObject);
    procedure CsShopper1Info(Sender: TObject; Msg: String);
    procedure CsShopper1UpDateList(Sender: TObject; List: TStringList);
    procedure lbRemoteFilesDblClick(Sender: TObject);
    procedure CsShopper1List(Sender: TObject; List: TStringList);
    procedure bbtnSiteClick(Sender: TObject);
    procedure bbtnFTPHelpClick(Sender: TObject);
    procedure CsShopper1Busy(Sender: TObject; BusyFlag: Boolean);
    procedure CsShopper1Progress(Sender: TObject; Position: Integer);
    procedure rgFileTypeClick(Sender: TObject);
    procedure CsShopper1FileType(Sender: TObject; FileType: TFileTypes);
    procedure CsShopper1Error(Sender: TObject; Status: TConditions;
                    Msg: String);
    procedure bbtnNewDirClick(Sender: TObject);
    procedure bbtnDelDirClick(Sender: TObject);
    procedure CsShopper1Connect(Sender: TObject; sSocket: Integer);
    procedure bbtnQuitClick(Sender: TObject);
    procedure rgFTPModeClick(Sender: TObject);
    procedure bbtnRefreshClick(Sender: TObject);
    procedure sbbtnRetrClick(Sender: TObject);
    procedure sbbtnStorClick(Sender: TObject);
    procedure CsShopper1DataDone(Sender: TObject; Done: Boolean);
```

```
    procedure bbtnStatClick(Sender: TObject);
    procedure bbtnRestartClick(Sender: TObject);
    procedure flbLocalDblClick(Sender: TObject);
    procedure lbRemoteFilesClick(Sender: TObject);
    procedure flbLocalClick(Sender: TObject);
    procedure lbPrListDblClick(Sender: TObject);
    procedure bbtnConnectMouseDown(Sender: TObject; Button: TMouseButton;
                          Shift: TShiftState; X, Y: Integer);
    procedure bbtnViewFileClick(Sender: TObject);
    procedure bbtnAbortClick(Sender: TObject);
    procedure bbtnPrSaveClick(Sender: TObject);
    procedure bbtnExitClick(Sender: TObject);
    procedure lbPrListClick(Sender: TObject);
    procedure bbtnPrNewClick(Sender: TObject);
    procedure bbtnAddNewClick(Sender: TObject);
    procedure edPrNameExit(Sender: TObject);
    procedure edPrHostNameExit(Sender: TObject);
    procedure edPrUserNameExit(Sender: TObject);
    procedure edPrPasswordExit(Sender: TObject);
    procedure edPrRemDirExit(Sender: TObject);
    procedure edPrLocDirExit(Sender: TObject);
    procedure bbtnPrDeleteClick(Sender: TObject);
    procedure bbtnLocateDefLocalDirClick(Sender: TObject);
    procedure bbtnLocateTxtEditorClick(Sender: TObject);
    procedure BitBtn2Click(Sender: TObject);
private
    { Private declarations }
public
    { Public declarations }
  HelpCmd   : String;
  UsedProfile,
  UsedQFTP,
  NewProfile : Boolean;
  OldTransferMode,
  OldFileStruct : String;
  OldProfiles,
  HostNameList,
  UsernameList,
  PasswordList,
  RemoteDirList,
  LocalDirList,
  CurrentProfiles,
  ProfileNameList : TStringList;
  NoOfUsers,
  LastProfileUsed,
  NoProfiles : Integer;
```

```pascal
    procedure LoadSettings;
    procedure SaveOptions;
    procedure SaveProfiles;
  end;

var
  frmMain: TfrmMain;

implementation

uses RMDirFrm, HelpFrm, QuickFTPfrm, LocateDirFrm, LocateEdFrm;

{$R *.DFM}


const
     FtpClientKey = 'Software\High Performance Delphi\Shopper32';

procedure TfrmMain.LoadSettings;
var
 Reg        : TRegistry;
 Count      : Integer;
 ProfileName   : String;
begin
 Reg := TRegistry.Create;
// read in default user name
 try
  Reg.OpenKey(FtpClientKey, TRUE);
  if Reg.ValueExists('UserName') then
   edUserName.Text := Reg.ReadString('UserName')
  else
   edUserName.Text := 'anonymous';
  finally
   Reg.CloseKey;
  end;
// read in default password
  try
   Reg.OpenKey(FtpClientKey, TRUE);
   if Reg.ValueExists('Password') then
    edPassword.Text := Reg.ReadString('Password')
   else
    edPassword.Text := 'guest';
   finally
    Reg.CloseKey;
   end;
// read in default local directory
```

CsShopper: An FTP Client Component

```
  try
   Reg.OpenKey(FtpClientKey, TRUE);
   if Reg.ValueExists('DefLocalDir') then
    edDefLocalDir.Text := Reg.ReadString('DefLocalDir')
   else
    edDefLocalDir.Text := 'C:\';
  finally
   Reg.CloseKey;
  end;
// read in default editor
  try
   Reg.OpenKey(FtpClientKey, TRUE);
   if Reg.ValueExists('Editor') then
    edDefTextEditor.Text := Reg.ReadString('Editor')
   else
    edDefTextEditor.Text := 'NOTEPAD ';
  finally
   Reg.CloseKey;
  end;
//Properties settings
 try
   Reg.OpenKey(FtpClientKey, TRUE);
    if Reg.ValueExists('Asynchronous') then
    begin
     with CsShopper1 do
     begin
      Asynchronous := Reg.ReadBool('Asynchronous');
      if Asynchronous then
       rgFTPMode.ItemIndex := 0
      else
       rgFTPMode.ItemIndex := 1;
     end;
    end
    else
    begin
     CsShopper1.Asynchronous := FALSE;
     rgFTPMode.ItemIndex := 0;
    end;
  finally
   Reg.CloseKey;
  end;
  try
   Reg.OpenKey(FtpClientKey, TRUE);
    if Reg.ValueExists('Hints') then
     cbHints.Checked := Reg.ReadBool('Hints')
    else
```

```
     cbHints.Checked := FALSE;
   finally
    Reg.CloseKey;
   end;
   try
    Reg.OpenKey(FtpClientKey, TRUE);
    if Reg.ValueExists('DTransferMode') then
    begin
     OldTransferMode := Reg.ReadString('DTransferMode');
     if UpperCase(OldTransferMode) = UpperCase(FtpTransferStr[STREAM]) then
     begin
      CsShopper1.Transfer := STREAM;
      rgTransfer.ItemIndex := 0;
     end;
     if UpperCase(OldTransferMode) = UpperCase(FtpTransferStr[BLOCK]) then
     begin
      CsShopper1.Transfer := BLOCK;
      rgTransfer.ItemIndex := 1;
     end;
     if UpperCase(OldTransferMode) = UpperCase(FtpTransferStr[COMPRESSED])
then
     begin
      CsShopper1.Transfer := COMPRESSED;
      rgTransfer.ItemIndex := 2;
     end;
    end else
    begin
     OldTransferMode := UpperCase(FtpTransferStr[STREAM]);
     CsShopper1.Transfer := STREAM;
     rgTransfer.ItemIndex := 0;
    end;
   finally
    Reg.CloseKey;
   end;
// File structure property
   try
    Reg.OpenKey(FtpClientKey, TRUE);
    if Reg.ValueExists('DFileStructure') then
    begin
     OldFileStruct := Reg.ReadString('DFileStructure');
     if UpperCase(OldFileStruct) = UpperCase(FtpFileStructStr[NOREC]) then
     begin
      CsShopper1.FileStruct := NOREC;
      rgFileStructure.ItemIndex := 0;
     end;
     if UpperCase(OldFileStruct) = UpperCase(FtpFileStructStr[REC]) then
```

```
    begin
      CsShopper1.FileStruct := REC;
      rgFileStructure.ItemIndex := 1;
    end;
    if UpperCase(OldFileStruct) = UpperCase(FtpFileStructStr[PAGE]) then
    begin
      CsShopper1.FileStruct := PAGE;
      rgFileStructure.ItemIndex := 2;
    end;
  end else
  begin
    OldFileStruct := UpperCase(FtpFileStructStr[NOREC]);
    CsShopper1.FileStruct := NOREC;
    rgFileStructure.ItemIndex := 0;
  end;

finally
  Reg.CloseKey;
end;
try
  Reg.OpenKey(FtpClientKey, TRUE);
  if Reg.ValueExists('LastProfileUsed') then
    LastProfileUsed := Reg.ReadInteger('LastProfileUsed')
  else
    LastProfileUsed := 0;
finally
  Reg.CloseKey;
end;
try
  Reg.OpenKey(FtpClientKey, TRUE);
  if Reg.ValueExists('NoProfiles') then
    NoProfiles := Reg.ReadInteger('NoProfiles')
  else
    NoProfiles := 1;
finally
  Reg.CloseKey;
end;
// List of profiles
for Count := 0 to NoProfiles - 1 do
begin
  ProfileName := Concat('ProfileName', IntToStr(Count));
  try
    Reg.OpenKey(FtpClientKey + '\Profiles' + '\' + ProfileName, TRUE);
    if Reg.ValueExists('ProfileName') then
      ProfileNameList.Add(Reg.ReadString('ProfileName'))
    else
```

```
      ProfileNameList.Add('PROFILE');
    OldProfiles.Add(Reg.ReadString('ProfileName'));
    if Reg.ValueExists('Host') then
      HostNameList.Add(Reg.ReadString('Host'))
    else
      HostNameList.Add('HOST');
    if Reg.ValueExists('User') then
      UserNameList.Add(Reg.ReadString('User'))
    else
      UserNameList.Add('ANONYMOUS');
    if Reg.ValueExists('Password') then
      PasswordList.Add(Reg.ReadString('Password'))
    else
      PasswordList.Add('GUEST');
    if Reg.ValueExists('RemoteDir') then
      RemoteDirList.Add(Reg.ReadString('RemoteDir'))
    else
      RemoteDirList.Add('\');
    if Reg.ValueExists('LocalDir') then
      LocalDirList.Add('LocalDir')
    else
      LocalDirList.Add('\');
   finally
    Reg.CloseKey;
   end;
 end;//for loop
 Reg.Free;
 lbPrList.Items         := ProfileNameList;
 lbPrList.ItemIndex     := LastProfileUsed;
 edPrName.Text          := ProfileNameList.Strings[lbPrList.ItemIndex];
 edPrHostName.Text      := HostNameList.Strings[lbPrList.ItemIndex];
 edPrUserName.Text      := UserNameList.Strings[lbPrList.ItemIndex];
 edPrPassword.Text      := PasswordList.Strings[lbPrList.ItemIndex];
 edPrRemDir.Text        := RemoteDirList.Strings[lbPrList.ItemIndex];
 edPrLocDir.Text        := LocalDirList.Strings[lbPrList.ItemIndex];
 CsShopper1.UserName    := edPrUserName.Text;
 CsShopper1.Password    := edPrPassword.Text;
 lbPrList.Refresh;
end;

procedure TfrmMain.SaveProfiles;
var
 Reg : TRegistry;
 Count : Integer;
 ProfileName : String;
begin
```

```pascal
Reg := TRegistry.Create;
try
 Reg.OpenKey(FtpClientKey, TRUE);
 Reg.WriteInteger('LastProfileUsed',LastProfileUsed);
finally
 Reg.CloseKey;
end;
NoProfiles := lbPrList.Items.Count;
try
 Reg.OpenKey(FtpClientKey, TRUE);
 Reg.WriteInteger('NoProfiles',NoProfiles);
finally
 Reg.CloseKey;
end;
for Count := 0 to NoProfiles - 1 do
begin
 ProfileName := Concat('ProfileName',IntToStr(Count));
 try
  Reg.OpenKey(FtpClientKey + '\Profiles' + '\' + ProfileName, TRUE);
  Reg.WriteString('ProfileName',lbPrList.Items.Strings[Count]);
  Reg.WriteString('ProfileName',ProfileNameList.Strings[Count]);
  Reg.WriteString('Host',HostNameList.Strings[Count]);
  Reg.WriteString('User',UserNameList.Strings[Count]);
  Reg.WriteString('Password',PasswordList.Strings[Count]);
  Reg.WriteString('RemoteDir',RemoteDirList.Strings[Count]);
  Reg.WriteString('LocalDir',LocalDirList.Strings[Count]);
 finally
  Reg.CloseKey;
 end;
end;
Reg.Free;
end;


procedure TfrmMain.SaveOptions;
var
 Reg : TRegistry;
begin
 Reg := TRegistry.Create;
// save default user name
 try
  Reg.OpenKey(FtpClientKey, TRUE);
  Reg.WriteString('UserName', edUserName.Text);
 finally
  Reg.CloseKey;
 end;
// save default password
```

```
 try
   Reg.OpenKey(FtpClientKey, TRUE);
   Reg.WriteString('Password', edPassword.Text);
 finally
   Reg.CloseKey;
 end;
// save default local directory
 try
   Reg.OpenKey(FtpClientKey, TRUE);
   Reg.WriteString('DefLocalDir', edDefLocalDir.Text);
 finally
   Reg.CloseKey;
 end;
// save default editor
 try
   Reg.OpenKey(FtpClientKey, TRUE);
   Reg.WriteString('Editor', edDefTextEditor.Text);
 finally
   Reg.CloseKey;
 end;
 try
   Reg.OpenKey(FtpClientKey,TRUE);
   case rgFTPMode.ItemIndex of
     0 : Reg.WriteBool('Asynchronous',TRUE);
     1 : Reg.WriteBool('Asynchronous',FALSE);
   end;
 finally
   Reg.CloseKey;
 end;
 try
   Reg.OpenKey(FtpClientKey, TRUE);
   if cbHints.Checked then
     Reg.WriteBool('Hints',TRUE)
   else
     Reg.WriteBool('Hints',FALSE);
 finally
   Reg.CloseKey;
 end;
 try
   Reg.OpenKey(FtpClientKey,TRUE);
   case rgTransfer.ItemIndex of
     0 :Reg.WriteString('DTransferMode',FtpTransferStr[STREAM]);
     1 :Reg.WriteString('DTransferMode',FtpTransferStr[BLOCK]);
     2 :Reg.WriteString('DTransferMode',FtpTransferStr[COMPRESSED]);
   end;
 finally
```

```
   Reg.CloseKey;
 end;
 try
  Reg.OpenKey(FtpClientKey,TRUE);
  case rgFileStructure.ItemIndex of
   0 :Reg.WriteString('DFileStructure',FtpFileStructStr[NOREC]);
   1 :Reg.WriteString('DFileStructure',FtpFileStructStr[REC]);
   2 :Reg.WriteString('DFileStructure',FtpFileStructStr[PAGE]);
  end;
 finally
  Reg.CloseKey;
 end;
 Reg.Free;
end;

procedure TfrmMain.bbtnConnectClick(Sender: TObject);
begin
 if (not UsedQFtp) and (not UsedProfile) then
 begin
  with CsShopper1 do
  begin
   HostName := HomeServer;
   if Status = Success then
    Start;
  end;
 end else
 if UsedQFtp then
  CsShopper1.Start
 else
 if UsedProfile then
 begin
  with CsShopper1 do
  begin
   UserName := edPrUserName.Text;
   Password := edPrPassword.Text;
   RemoteDir:= edPrRemDir.Text;
   LocalDir := edPrLocDir.Text;
   EditName := edDefTextEditor.Text;
   HostName := edPrHostName.Text;
   if Status = Success then
    Start;
  end;
 end;
end;

procedure TfrmMain.FormCreate(Sender: TObject);
begin
```

```
    bbtnQuit.Enabled        := FALSE;
    bbtnRefresh.Enabled     := FALSE;
    bbtnViewFile.Enabled    := FALSE;
    bbtnFtpCmds.Enabled     := FALSE;
    bbtnAbort.Enabled       := FALSE;
    rgFileType.Enabled      := FALSE;
    gbMoreActions.Visible   := FALSE;
    pbDataTransfer.Visible  := FALSE;
    sbbtnRetr.Enabled       := FALSE;
    sbbtnStor.Enabled       := FALSE;
    OldProfiles             := TStringList.Create;
    ProfileNameList         := TStringList.Create;
    HostNameList            := TStringList.Create;
    UserNameList            := TStringList.Create;
    PasswordList            := TStringList.Create;
    RemoteDirList           := TStringList.Create;
    LocalDirList            := TStringList.Create;
    LoadSettings;
    if CsShopper1.Asynchronous then
    begin
      sbStatus.Panels[2].Text := Concat('Mode : ','Asynchronous');
      rgFTPMode.ItemIndex := 0;
    end
    else
    begin
      sbStatus.Panels[2].Text := Concat('Mode : ','Non-Asynchronous');
      rgFTPMode.ItemIndex := 1;
    end;
    sbStatus.Panels[0].Text  := Concat( 'Local Host : ',
                                        CsShopper1.LocalName);
    sbStatus.Panels[3].Text  := Concat('Status : ', 'Idle');
    pcShopper.ActivePage := tsProfiles;
    UpDate;
end;

procedure TfrmMain.bbtnFtpCmdsClick(Sender: TObject);
begin
  gbMoreActions.Visible := not gbMoreActions.Visible;
  if gbMoreActions.Visible then
  begin
    bbtnFtpCmds.Hint    := 'Click here to close the panel of FTP commands';
    bbtnFtpCmds.Caption := 'Close';
  end
  else
  begin
    bbtnFtpCmds.Hint    := 'Click here to get more FTP commands';
```

```pascal
  bbtnFtpCmds.Caption := 'FTP Cmds';
 end;
end;

procedure TfrmMain.CsShopper1Info(Sender: TObject; Msg: String);
begin
 memLog.Lines.Add(Msg);
end;

procedure TfrmMain.CsShopper1UpDateList(Sender: TObject;
  List: TStringList);
begin
 LbRemoteFiles.Items := List;
 lbRemoteFiles.UpDate;
 gbRemote.Caption := Concat('Files on ',CsShopper1.HostName);
 sbStatus.Panels[1].Text := Concat('Remote Host : ',CsShopper1.HostName);
end;

procedure TfrmMain.lbRemoteFilesDblClick(Sender: TObject);
begin
 pbDataTransfer.Visible := TRUE;
 if lbRemoteFiles.ItemIndex <> -1 then
  CsShopper1.Get := lbRemoteFiles.Items.Strings[lbRemoteFiles.ItemIndex]
 else
  pbDataTransfer.Visible := FALSE;
end;

procedure TfrmMain.CsShopper1List(Sender: TObject; List: TStringList);
begin
 lbRemoteFiles.Clear;
 lbRemoteFiles.Items := List;
 lbRemoteFiles.UpDate;
 gbRemote.Caption := CsShopper1.RemoteDir;
end;

procedure TfrmMain.bbtnSiteClick(Sender: TObject);
begin
 CsShopper1.SiteFtp;
end;

procedure TfrmMain.bbtnFTPHelpClick(Sender: TObject);
var
 Counter : Integer;
begin
 frmHelp := TfrmHelp.Create(Application);
 for Counter := SFtpUser to SFtpNoop do
```

```
    frmHelp.lbHelpFtpCmds.Items.Add(LoadStr(Counter));
  frmHelp.ShowModal;
  CsShopper1.FtpHelp := HelpCmd;
  HelpFtpCmdList.Free;
  frmHelp.Free;
end;

procedure TfrmMain.CsShopper1Busy(Sender: TObject; BusyFlag: Boolean);
begin
  if BusyFlag then
  begin
   lbRemoteFiles.Enabled := FALSE;
   sbStatus.Panels[3].Text := Concat('Status : ','Busy');
  end else
  begin
   lbRemoteFiles.Enabled := TRUE;
   sbStatus.Panels[3].Text := Concat('Status : ','Idle');
  end;
  Update;
end;

procedure TfrmMain.CsShopper1Progress(Sender: TObject; Position:
                                     Integer);
begin
 pbDataTransfer.Position := Position;
 pbDataTransfer.UpDate;
end;

procedure TfrmMain.rgFileTypeClick(Sender: TObject);
begin
 with CsShopper1 do
  case rgFileType.ItemIndex of
   0 : FileType := ASCII;
   1 : FileType := IMAGE;
   2 : FileType := AUTO;
  end;
end;

procedure TfrmMain.CsShopper1FileType(Sender: TObject;
                                     FileType: TFileTypes);
begin
 case FileType of
  ASCII : rgFileType.ItemIndex := 0;
  IMAGE : rgFileType.ItemIndex := 1;
  AUTO  : rgFileType.ItemIndex := 2;
 end;
```

```
end;

procedure TfrmMain.CsShopper1Error(Sender: TObject; Status: TConditions;
                                   Msg: String);
begin
 memLog.Lines.Add(Msg);
end;

procedure TfrmMain.bbtnNewDirClick(Sender: TObject);
begin
 frmMkNewDir := TfrmMkNewDir.Create(Application);
 frmMkNewDir.ShowModal;
 if Length(NewDirName) > 0 then
   CsShopper1.MkDirName := NewDirName;
 frmMkNewDir.Free;
end;

procedure TfrmMain.bbtnDelDirClick(Sender: TObject);
begin
 if lbRemoteFiles.ItemIndex <> -1 then
   CsShopper1.RmDirName :=
lbRemoteFiles.Items.Strings[lbRemoteFiles.ItemIndex];
 CsShopper1.FilesList;
end;

procedure TfrmMain.CsShopper1Connect(Sender: TObject; sSocket: Integer);
begin
  bbtnQuit.Enabled         := TRUE;
  bbtnRefresh.Enabled      := TRUE;
  bbtnViewFile.Enabled     := TRUE;
  bbtnFtpCmds.Enabled      := TRUE;
  rgFileType.Enabled       := TRUE;
  if rgFTPMode.ItemIndex = 1 then
  begin
    sbbtnRetr.Enabled      := TRUE;
    sbbtnStor.Enabled      := TRUE;
  end
  else
  begin
    sbbtnRetr.Enabled      := FALSE;
    sbbtnStor.Enabled      := FALSE;
  end;
  bbtnConnect.Enabled      := FALSE;
  bbtnExit.Enabled         := FALSE;
  rgFTPMode.Enabled        := FALSE;
  gbRemote.Caption         := 'Remote : ' + CsShopper1.RemoteDir;
```

```pascal
  sbStatus.Panels[1].Text := 'Remote Host : ' + CsShopper1.HostName;
  sbStatus.Panels[3].Text := 'Status : Connected';
  Update;
end;

procedure TfrmMain.bbtnQuitClick(Sender: TObject);
begin
  bbtnQuit.Enabled        := FALSE;
  bbtnRefresh.Enabled     := FALSE;
  bbtnViewFile.Enabled    := FALSE;
  bbtnFtpCmds.Enabled     := FALSE;
  bbtnAbort.Enabled       := FALSE;
  rgFileType.Enabled      := FALSE;
  sbbtnRetr.Enabled       := FALSE;
  sbbtnStor.Enabled       := FALSE;
  gbMoreActions.Visible   := FALSE;
  pbDataTransfer.Visible  := FALSE;
  bbtnConnect.Enabled     := TRUE;
  bbtnExit.Enabled        := TRUE;
  rgFTPMode.Enabled       := TRUE;
  with sbStatus do
  begin
   Panels[1].Text := 'Remote Host : ';
   Panels[3].Text := 'Status : Idle';
  end;
  lbRemoteFiles.Clear;
  Update;
  CsShopper1.Finish;
end;
(*
procedure TfrmMain.Exit1Click(Sender: TObject);
begin
 Close;
end;
*)
procedure TfrmMain.rgFTPModeClick(Sender: TObject);
begin
 if rgFTPMode.ItemIndex = 0 then
 begin
   CsShopper1.Asynchronous := TRUE;
   sbStatus.Panels[2].Text := 'Mode : ' + 'Asynchronous';
   sbbtnRetr.Enabled       := FALSE;
   sbbtnStor.Enabled       := FALSE;
 end
 else
 begin
   CsShopper1.Asynchronous := FALSE;
```

```pascal
    sbStatus.Panels[2].Text := 'Mode : ' + 'Non-Asynchronous';
    sbbtnRetr.Enabled      := TRUE;
    sbbtnStor.Enabled      := TRUE;
  end;
  sbStatus.Update;
end;

procedure TfrmMain.bbtnRefreshClick(Sender: TObject);
begin
  CsShopper1.FilesList
end;

procedure TfrmMain.sbbtnRetrClick(Sender: TObject);
begin
  pbDataTransfer.Visible := TRUE;
  bbtnAbort.Enabled      := TRUE;
  CsShopper1.MGet;
end;

procedure TfrmMain.sbbtnStorClick(Sender: TObject);
begin
  pbDataTransfer.Visible := TRUE;
  bbtnAbort.Enabled      := TRUE;
  CsShopper1.MPut;
end;

procedure TfrmMain.CsShopper1DataDone(Sender: TObject; Done: Boolean);
begin
  if Done then
  begin
    pbDataTransfer.Visible := FALSE;
    bbtnAbort.Enabled      := FALSE
  end
  else
  begin
    pbDataTransfer.Visible := TRUE;
    bbtnAbort.Enabled      := TRUE
  end;
  pbDataTransfer.Update;
end;
procedure TfrmMain.bbtnStatClick(Sender: TObject);
begin
  CsShopper1.Stat;
end;

procedure TfrmMain.bbtnRestartClick(Sender: TObject);
begin
```

```
  ShowMessage('Not implemented in this version');
end;

procedure TfrmMain.flbLocalDblClick(Sender: TObject);
begin
 pbDataTransfer.Visible := TRUE;
 if flbLocal.ItemIndex <> -1 then
  CsShopper1.Put := flbLocal.Items.Strings[flbLocal.ItemIndex]
 else
 pbDataTransfer.Visible := FALSE;
end;

procedure TfrmMain.lbRemoteFilesClick(Sender: TObject);
begin
 CsShopper1.RemoteFiles.Add(lbRemoteFiles.Items.Strings[lbRemoteFiles.ItemIndex]);
end;

procedure TfrmMain.flbLocalClick(Sender: TObject);
begin
 CsShopper1.LocalFiles.Add(flbLocal.Items.Strings[flbLocal.ItemIndex]);
end;

procedure TfrmMain.lbPrListDblClick(Sender: TObject);
begin
 UsedProfile := TRUE;
 pcShopper.ActivePage := tsConnect;
 ActiveControl      := bbtnConnect;
 bbtnConnect.Click;
end;

procedure TfrmMain.bbtnConnectMouseDown(Sender: TObject;
   Button: TMouseButton; Shift: TShiftState; X, Y: Integer);
begin
 if Button = mbRight then // Get quickie ftp
 begin
  UsedQFtp := TRUE;
  UsedProfile := FALSE;
  frmQuickFtp := TfrmQuickFTP.Create(Application);
  frmQuickFtp.ShowModal;
  with CsShopper1 do
  begin
   UserName := frmQuickFtp.edUserName.Text;
   Password := frmQuickFtp.edPassword.Text;
   HostName := frmQuickFtp.edHostName.Text;
  end;
  frmQuickFtp.Free;
```

```
    ActiveControl := bbtnConnect;
    bbtnConnect.Click;
  end else
    UsedQFtp := FALSE;
end;

procedure TfrmMain.bbtnViewFileClick(Sender: TObject);
begin
  if lbRemoteFiles.ItemIndex <> -1 then
    CsShopper1.View :=
    lbRemoteFiles.Items.Strings[lbRemoteFiles.ItemIndex];
end;

procedure TfrmMain.bbtnAbortClick(Sender: TObject);
begin
  CsShopper1.Abort;
  bbtnAbort.Enabled := FALSE;
end;

procedure TfrmMain.bbtnPrSaveClick(Sender: TObject);
begin
  SaveProfiles;
end;

procedure TfrmMain.bbtnExitClick(Sender: TObject);
begin
  OldProfiles.Free;
  ProfileNameList.Free;
  HostNameList.Free;
  UserNameList.Free;
  PasswordList.Free;
  RemoteDirList.Free;
  LocalDirList.Free;
end;

procedure TfrmMain.lbPrListClick(Sender: TObject);
begin
  if lbPrList.ItemIndex <> -1 then
  begin
    LastProfileUsed   := lbPrList.ItemIndex;
    edPrName.Text     := ProfileNameList.Strings[LastProfileUsed];
    edPrHostName.Text := HostNameList.Strings[LastProfileUsed];
    edPrUserName.Text := UserNameList.Strings[LastProfileUsed];
    edPrPassword.Text := PasswordList.Strings[LastProfileUsed];
    edPrRemDir.Text   := RemoteDirList.Strings[LastProfileUsed];
    edPrLocDir.Text   := LocalDirList.Strings[LastProfileUsed];
    Update;
```

```
    end;
end;

procedure TfrmMain.bbtnPrNewClick(Sender: TObject);
begin
  NewProfile         := TRUE;
  edPrName.Text      := '';
  edPrHostName.Text  := '';
  edUserName.Text    := edUserName.Text;
  edPassword.Text    := edPassword.Text;
  edPrLocDir.Text    := edDefLocalDir.Text;
  edPrRemDir.Text    := '\';
  lbPrList.Visible   := FALSE;
end;

procedure TfrmMain.bbtnAddNewClick(Sender: TObject);
begin
  ProfileNameList.Add(edPrName.Text);
  HostNameList.Add(edPrHostName.Text);
  UserNameList.Add(edPrUserName.Text);
  PasswordList.Add(edPrPassword.Text);
  RemoteDirList.Add(edPrRemDir.Text);
  LocalDirList.Add(edPrLocDir.Text);
  lbPrList.Visible := TRUE;
  lbPrList.refresh;
  NewProfile := FALSE;
end;

procedure TfrmMain.edPrNameExit(Sender: TObject);
begin
  if (edPrName.Modified) and (not NewProfile) then
  begin
   lbPrList.Items.Strings[lbPrList.ItemIndex] := edPrName.Text;
   lbPrList.Refresh;
   ProfileNameList.Strings[lbPrList.ItemIndex] := edPrName.Text;
  end;
end;

procedure TfrmMain.edPrHostNameExit(Sender: TObject);
begin
  if (edPrHostName.Modified) and (not NewProfile) then
    HostNameList.Strings[lbPrList.ItemIndex] := edPrHostName.Text;
end;

procedure TfrmMain.edPrUserNameExit(Sender: TObject);
begin
```

```pascal
  if (edPrUserName.Modified) and (not NewProfile) then
    UserNameList.Strings[lbPrList.ItemIndex] := edPrUserName.Text;
end;

procedure TfrmMain.edPrPasswordExit(Sender: TObject);
begin
  if (edPrPassword.Modified) and (not NewProfile) then
    PasswordList.Strings[lbPrList.ItemIndex] := edPrPassword.Text;
end;

procedure TfrmMain.edPrRemDirExit(Sender: TObject);
begin
  if (edPrRemDir.Modified) and (not NewProfile) then
    RemoteDirList.Strings[lbPrList.ItemIndex] := edPrRemDir.Text;
end;

procedure TfrmMain.edPrLocDirExit(Sender: TObject);
begin
  if (edPrLocDir.Modified) and (not NewProfile) then
    LocalDirList.Strings[lbPrList.ItemIndex] := edPrLocDir.Text;
end;

procedure TfrmMain.bbtnPrDeleteClick(Sender: TObject);
var
  Reg : TRegistry;
  Profile : String;
begin
  Reg := TRegistry.Create;
  Profile := Concat('ProfileName',IntToStr(lbPrList.ItemIndex));
  if Reg.DeleteKey(FtpClientKey + '\Profiles\' + Profile) then
  begin
    ProfileNameList.Delete(lbPrList.ItemIndex);
    HostNameList.Delete(lbPrList.ItemIndex);
    UserNameList.Delete(lbPrList.ItemIndex);
    PasswordList.Delete(lbPrList.ItemIndex);
    RemoteDirList.Delete(lbPrList.ItemIndex);
    LocalDirList.Delete(lbPrList.ItemIndex);
    lbPrList.Items.Delete(lbPrList.ItemIndex);
    edPrName.Clear;
    edPrHostName.Clear;
    edPrUserName.Clear;
    edPrRemDir.Clear;
    edPrLocDir.Clear;
    NoProfiles := lbPrList.Items.Count;
    lbPrList.Refresh;
  end;
```

```
  Reg.Free;
end;

procedure TfrmMain.bbtnLocateDefLocalDirClick(Sender: TObject);
begin
  frmLocateDir := TfrmLocateDir.Create(Application);
  frmLocateDir.ShowModal;
  edDefLocalDir.Text := frmLocateDir.LocateDir;
  frmLocateDir.Free;
end;

procedure TfrmMain.bbtnLocateTxtEditorClick(Sender: TObject);
begin
  frmLocateEditor := TfrmLocateEditor.Create(Application);
  frmLocateEditor.ShowModal;
  edDefTextEditor.Text := frmLocateEditor.EditorPath;
  frmLocateEditor.Free;
end;

procedure TfrmMain.BitBtn2Click(Sender: TObject);
begin
  SaveOptions;
end;

end.
```

Be sure to install the CsSocket and CsShopper components in the component palette, and then pluck the CsShopper component from the palette onto the main form. Add a button for each FTP command to the form. For example, the Connect button calls up **CsShopper1.Start** as shown here:

```
procedure TfrmMain.bbtnConnectClick(Sender: TObject);
begin
  if (not UsedQFtp) and (not UsedProfile) then
  begin
    with CsShopper1 do
    begin
      HostName := HomeServer;
      if Status = Success then
        Start;
    end;
  end else
```

```
if UsedQFtp then
 CsShopper1.Start
else
if UsedProfile then
begin
 with CsShopper1 do
 begin
  UserName := edPrUserName.Text;
  Password := edPrPassword.Text;
  HostName := edPrHostName.Text;
  if Status = Success then
   Start;
 end;
end;
end;
```

SHOPPER32 Profiles

Before you connect to an FTP server, SHOPPER32 requires that you create a "profile" in which you enter the name of the FTP server, your user name, and your password in the Profiles tab sheet, as shown in Figure 6.4.

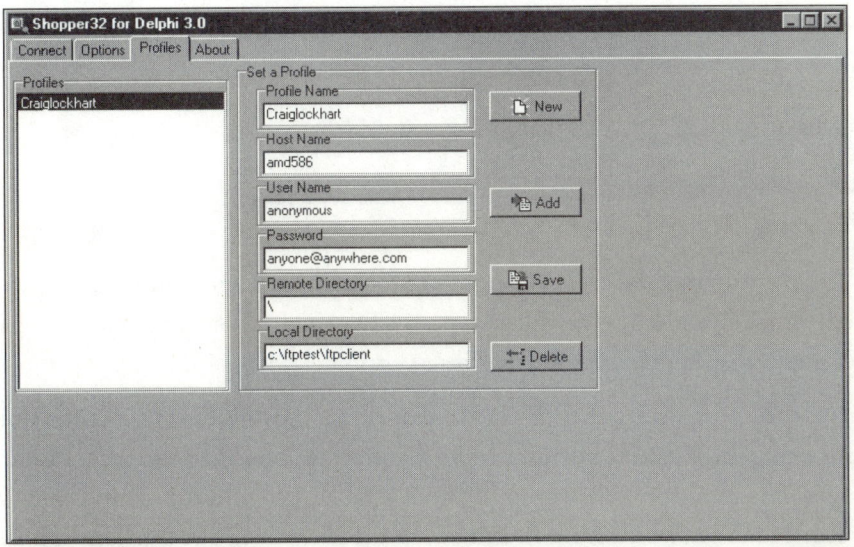

Figure 6.4
A typical profile, shown in the Profiles tab sheet.

We store these profiles in the Windows registry, from which we retrieve before login to save needless retyping of login information that is required to access the FTP server.

To add a new profile we first click the New button, which clears the edit boxes in the Profiles tab sheet. Then we add the name of the profile, the name of the FTP server, the user name, and password into the **edPrName**, **edPrHostName**, **edPrUserName**, and **edPrPassword** editboxes, respectively. In the case of anonymous login, enter "anonymous" in the **edPrUserName** editbox, and your email address into the **edPrPassword** editbox.

We click the Add button to add the new information to the string lists, and click the Save button to save the new settings in the registry. Should we need to remove a profile from the registry, we click the profile name in the Profiles list box, and click the Delete button. To select a profile to access an FTP server, we either click on the desired profile name in the Profiles list box, click the Connect tab, and finally click the Connect button, or easier still, we double-click the profile name in the same list box, which brings the Connect tab sheet to the focus, and further clicks the Connect button automatically, as shown in the following code for **lbPrList**'s OnDblClick event:

```
procedure TfrmMain.lbPrListDblClick(Sender: TObject);
begin
 UsedProfile := TRUE;
 pcShopper.ActivePage := tsConnect;
 ActiveControl       := bbtnConnect;
 bbtnConnect.Click;
end;
```

To further streamline the login process, we store the local and remote directories in the **edPrLocDir** and **edPrRemDir**, respectively, which CsShopper uses to change directories transparently without user intervention.

To access an infrequently used FTP site that doesn't justify having its own unique profile, bring the Connect button (in the Connect tab sheet) to the focus, and click the right mouse button to bring up the Quick FTP dialog. In this dialog enter your user name and password. Default values are supplied from the Options tab sheet, and if they're suitable you simply click the OK button to start the session.

CsShopper: An FTP Client Component

Note: *Some sites require account information (which is sent to the server using the ACCT command) to allow access and to use some FTP operations, such as the RMD command, to remove a directory. If you want to access such a site, you'll have to add an extra editbox in the Profiles tab sheet and modify CsShopper to send the ACCT command containing this additional information.*

Connecting In

Using the information you enter, the **CsShopper1.Start** method calls **GetHost** to open the connection to the remote host. If this fails, **WSAErrorMsg** displays the possible cause of the problem, and **Status** is set to **Failure**. Otherwise, **Status** is set to **Success**. If the connection succeeds, CsShopper calls the event procedure, **ConnEvent** (inherited from CsSocket) to notify SHOPPER32 to change the state of the buttons in the application. For example, the Quit button is disabled until a connection is created; then it becomes enabled. **Start** calls **FTPCommand** to send USER, PASS, SYST, and PWD commands—in that sequence—with their appropriate arguments. **Start** then starts a data connection to transfer the listing of the remote host's directories and files, using **GetPort** to set up the data port for the connection.

To retrieve the directory listing, **Start** sends the LIST command through **FTPCommand**. The result is stored for a later call to **Decode** to parse the returned data for directories and files.

Note: *The mechanics of parsing are simple, but the mapping of the directories and files varies among systems. The parser in CsShopper works with servers that run on Unix and Unix look-alikes. For other systems, the parser may occasionally return garbled directory listings.*

Decode checks the first character of each line in FTPFILE.TMP for a 'd', which denotes a directory, or the first two characters '-' and 'r', which denote a file. When a 'd' character is found, it is stripped out, and the line is scanned for the directory name and then converted to the familiar \ddd format. The backslash tells SHOPPER32 that this is a directory. Likewise, in the case of a file, the '-' and 'r' characters are removed, and the line is scanned for the name, time, date, and file size, which are chopped into substrings. These substrings are rearranged to form an acceptable string for viewing in SHOPPER32's listbox (see Figure 6.5).

The **FRemFiles.Add** method in **Decode** reads each line, formats it into a string, and adds it to the **FRemFiles** property. **FRemFiles** is a string list, derived from the **TStringList** class, created by the **TCsShopper.Create** constructor.

After the list is built by the Decode procedure, CsShopper passes **FRemFiles** to the **TCsShopper.ChangeList** procedure, which invokes the **OnList** event handler, shown here:

```
procedure TCsShopper.ChangeList(List : TStringList);
begin
 if Assigned(FUpDateList) then
  FUpDateList(Self, List);
end;
```

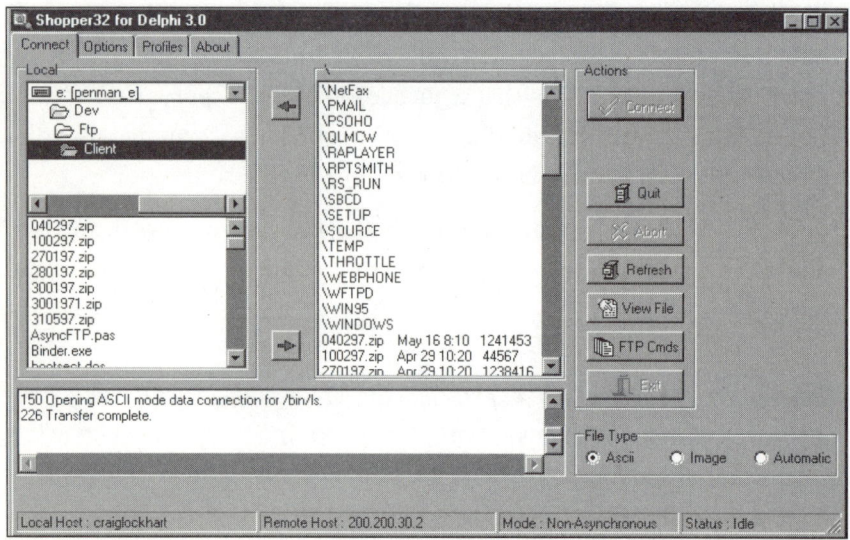

Figure 6.5
Files and directories displayed in SHOPPER32.

The **OnList** event handler in SHOPPER32 updates the **lbRemoteFiles** listbox like this:

```
procedure TfrmMain.CsShopper1List(Sender: TObject; List: TStringList);
begin
 lbRemoteFiles.Items := List;
 lbRemoteFiles.UpDate;
 gbRemote.Caption := CsShopper1.RemoteDir;
end;
```

Closing The Connection

To end our business with the FTP server, we need to kill the connection by sending a QUIT command. Clicking on the Quit button calls **CsShopper1.Finish** and terminates the session as shown here:

```
procedure TfrmMain.bbtnQuitClick(Sender: TObject);
begin
   bbtnQuit.Enabled          := FALSE;
   bbtnRefresh.Enabled       := FALSE;
   bbtnViewFile.Enabled      := FALSE;
   bbtnFtpCmds.Enabled       := FALSE;
   bbtnAbort.Enabled         := FALSE;
   rgFileType.Enabled        := FALSE;
   sbbtnRetr.Enabled         := FALSE;
   sbbtnStor.Enabled         := FALSE;
   gbMoreActions.Visible     := FALSE;
   pbDataTransfer.Visible    := FALSE;
   bbtnConnect.Enabled       := TRUE;
   bbtnExit.Enabled          := TRUE;
   with sbStatus do
   begin
    Panels[1].Text := 'Remote Host : ';
    Panels[3].Text := 'Status : Idle';
   end;
   lbRemoteFiles.Clear;
   CsShopper1.Finish;
  Update;
end;
```

Uploading And Downloading Files

There are two ways to go about downloading and uploading files: one at a time, or in batches of several. The first method I'll discuss is moving single files one at a time, by simply double-clicking on the file you wish to upload or download.

The key to making this technique work is to create a new event. When you add the **lbRemoteFiles** listbox to the Connect tab sheet, define a new **OnDblClick** event using the Events page in the Object Inspector. This event is handled by the **TfrmMain.lbRemoteFilesDblClick** procedure. The code fragment below shows that in response to the event, **CsShopper1.Get** is assigned a file name:

```
procedure TfrmMain.lbRemoteFilesDblClick(Sender: TObject);
begin
 pbDataTransfer.Visible := TRUE;
 if lbRemoteFiles.ItemIndex <> -1 then
  CsShopper1.Get := lbRemoteFiles.Items.Strings[lbRemoteFiles.ItemIndex]
 else
 pbDataTransfer.Visible := FALSE;
end;
```

Inside the CsShopper component, the **Get** property passes the file name as **Name** to **Retrieve**. To ensure that the file is sent and stored correctly, **SetUpFileTransfer** checks the file's extension. For a binary file (such as EXE, DLL, and ZIP), **SetUpFileTransfer** tells **FTPCommand** to send the TYPE IMAGE command, instructing the server to send the file as a stream of contiguous bytes. For nonbinary files, **SetUpFileTransfer** employs the TYPE A command. After the FTP server acknowledges the TYPE command, **SetUpFileTransfer** sends the RETR file name command through **FTPCommand**.

Changing Directories For File Transfers

When you double-click on a directory name such as \DELPHI, no download occurs. Instead, **SetUpFileTransfer** calls **ChangeDir** to handle a directory change. **ChangeDir** then calls **FTPCommand**, which then sends the CWD command, followed by the \DELPHI string, to the FTP server. If the server accepts the command, it returns a reply code of 250. **ChangeDir** next sends the LIST command, via **FTPCommand**, to update the remote file directory listbox. Finally, **Decode** creates a new directory listing for the changed directory.

Uploading Files

Internally, the process of uploading a file is similar to that of downloading, and the **CsShopper1.Put** property accomplishes this task using its **PutFile** method. On the main form, to facilitate uploading a file from the client to the server, I derived the following listboxes from the Windows 3.1 page in the components palette: **dcbLocal** from **TDriveComboBox**, **dlbLocal** from **TDirectoryListBox**, and **flbLocal** from **TFileListBox**.

Each of these listboxes is synchronized. When you select a different drive in **dcbLocal**, the contents of **dlbLocal** and **flbLocal** are updated transparently. As with the **lbRemoteFiles** listbox, I used the Events page in the Object Inspector to create a new OnDblClick event handler, **TfrmMain.flbLocalDblClick**, to handle a double click on a file in the **flbLocal** listbox. A double click on the file you wish to upload calls **TfrmMain.flbLocalDblClick** to assign the file name to the **CsShopper1.Put** property.

Transfer Of Multiple Files

The second file transmission method is to move a batch of files at one go. Before downloading we select some files in the **lbRemoteFiles** listbox by clicking on each file, by which action the file name is added to a string list property, **RemoteFiles**, in the **TfrmMain.lbRemoteFilesClick** handler. This is shown in the following code:

```
procedure TfrmMain.lbRemoteFilesClick(Sender: TObject);
begin
 CsShopper1.RemoteFiles.Add(lbRemoteFiles.Items.Strings[lbRemoteFiles.ItemIndex]);
end;
```

Figure 6.6 shows a number of files highlighted in the remote directory box, ready to be downloaded. After you've selected all the files in the group to be downloaded, click the top speed button, which is next to the **lbRemoteFiles** listbox, to initiate the download. This action causes a call to the **CsShopper1.MGet** method. The code looks like this:

```
procedure TfrmMain.sbbtnRetrClick(Sender: TObject);
begin
 pbDataTransfer.Visible := TRUE;
 bbtnAbort.Enabled      := TRUE;
 CsShopper1.MGet;
end;
```

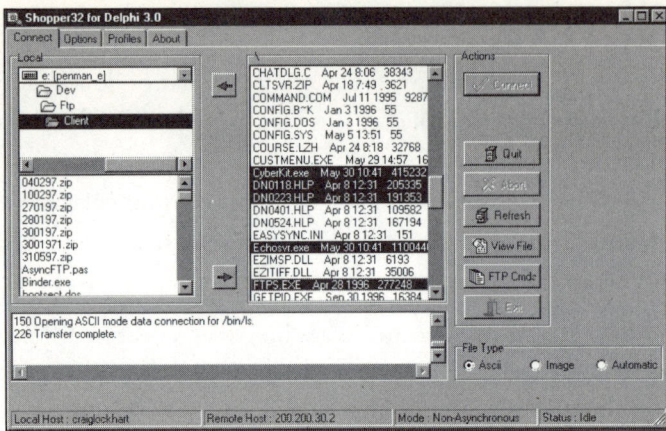

Figure 6.6
Multiple files selected for batch download.

However, to make this particular method work, we need to change two properties of the **lbRemoteFiles** listbox in the Object Inspector: (1) change **ExtendedSelect** from TRUE to FALSE, and (2) change **MultiSelect** from FALSE to TRUE. As we click on the desired name in **lbRemoteFiles** list box, the file name is added to **CsShopper1.- RemoteFiles**, which is a **TStringList** type. Similarly, for multiple uploads we need to change these two properties in the **flbLocal** listbox.

> **Note**: Be aware that the option to perform multiple file downloads and uploads is not available in asynchronous mode, because of the problem of synchronizing multiple file operations.

Asynchronous File Transfer

Having covered the FTP protocol from the blocking, or synchronous, perspective, we'll now take a brief look at how CsShopper operates in asynchronous mode. As we have examined the login process (in blocking mode) in detail, we will focus on file transfers, in particular the retrieval of a file from an FTP server in asynchronous mode.

Prior to connecting to an FTP server in asynchronous mode, we select the Asynchronous radio button in the FTP Mode radio group box on the Options tab sheet. This mode button governs the session for the life of the connection; once SHOPPER32 is connected to the FTP server, the FTP Mode radio group box is disabled for the duration of the session.

The process of selecting a file to download in asynchronous mode is the same as in blocking mode; that is, we assign the file name to the **Get** property before we call **Retrieve**. However, the process differs from this point on in **Retrieve**. After determining the file type, we set the state flag, **FFtpCmd**, to FTP_TYPEI, which tells the server to send the file as a contiguous stream of bytes. We send the TYPE command by calling the **SendFtpCmd** procedure.

When Winsock receives a **FD_READ** socket event, which is a result of the FTP server's response to the TYPE command, it sends a message containing the socket event to **FtpEvent**. In **FtpEvent**, the message is parsed for the following events: **FD_READ**, **FD_WRITE**, and **FD_CLOSE**. We use a *case* statement to discriminate among these socket events.

On receiving an **FD_READ** event, **InfoEvent** posts the entire contents of the **FRcvBuffer** for display in the SHOPPER32 application. The **FRcvBuffer** buffer, which contains a reply code from the server, is parsed for a 4 or a 5 for an FTP error. When this occurs, **FFtpCmd** is set to FTP_FAIL, which indicates an error condition to the application.

Otherwise, **ProcessRecvData**, which uses a *case* statement, processes **FRcvBuffer** and the **FFtpCmd** state flag. Because **FFtpCmd** is set to FTP_TYPEI, **ProcessRecvData** calls the **ProcessTypeI** procedure, in which the contents of the **FRcvBuffer** are parsed in detail. The following piece of code shows how parsing is performed in **ProcessTypeI**:

```
procedure TCsShopper.ProcessTypeI;
begin
 case GetReplyCode(FRcvBuffer) of
  200 : begin
         if Pos('200-',String(FRcvBuffer)) = 0
           then     //the server is waiting for us
                    //to create a data connection
                    //and send the PORT command
```

```
            begin
              ProcessPort;
            end
{rest of code not shown here}
  end;// case
  FillChar(FRcvBuffer, SizeOf(FRcvBuffer),#0);
end;
```

If the reply code is 200, then **ProcessPort** is called, from which **InitDataConn** is called to perform four tasks:

- Create a socket for the data connection;
- Call **WSAAsyncSelect** to create a handle to a window for **FtpDataEvent** to trap socket events on the data connection;
- Call **bind**, a Winsock API function, to bind the new data socket; and
- Call **listen** to put the data socket in a listening state.

If the data socket created by **InitDataConn** is a valid socket, **ProcessPort** creates a unique port number for the data connection, which is then sent by the **SendFtpCmd** procedure. Finally, the state flag, **FFtpCmd**, is set to **FTP_RETR** to signal to CsShopper that the next **FD_READ** socket event should be parsed in the context of a file download.

When the next **FD_READ** event occurs on the control connection, providing there are no socket errors or negative reply code, **ProcessRecvData** is called to dispatch the **ProcessGet** procedure.

In **ProcessGet**, on receipt of a 200 reply code (which signals success) the local file of the same name as the server-side file is created. A reply code of 150 thereafter signals the FTP client that the server has started to send data over the data connection.

As soon as the FTP server connects with the client over the data connection, Winsock notifies the **FtpDataEvent** procedure by posting an **FD_ACCEPT** event. In the **FD_ACCEPT** clause of the **case** statement, **WSAAsyncSelect** is called to reset the data socket to accept only the following events: **FD_READ, FD_WRITE** and **FD_CLOSE**. The following code fragment from **FtpDataEvent** shows how this is done:

```
FD_ACCEPT :   begin
                FStartTime := GetTickCount;
                FIntTime   := FStartTime;
                if FListenSocket <> INVALID_SOCKET then
                begin
                  nLen := SizeOf(TSockAddr);
                  FDataSocket := accept(FListenSocket,
                                        @FRemoteHost, @nLen);
                  if FDataSocket = SOCKET_ERROR then
                  begin
                    InfoEvent(Concat('Error : ',WSAErrorMsg));
                    FFtpCmd := FTP_FAIL;
                    Exit;
                  end;
                  nStat := WSAAsyncSelect(FDataSocket, FDataWnd,
                                          DATA_EVENT,
                                          FD_READ or
                                          FD_WRITE or
                                          FD_CLOSE);
                  if nStat = SOCKET_ERROR then
                  begin
                    InfoEvent(Concat('Error : ',WSAErrorMsg));
                    FFtpCmd := FTP_FAIL;
                    Exit;
                  end;
                  { rest of code }
                end;
              end;
```

When the first and later packets of data arrive on the data connection, Winsock posts an **FD_READ** notification to **FtpDataEvent**, which calls **RecvData** to pick up and save the incoming data to the local file. When the FTP server is done with the file transfer, it closes its end of the data connection, which signals Winsock to post an **FD_CLOSE** event. This would be a straightforward conclusion to the file transfer process, but in some cases there is still some data waiting to be read on the FTP client data socket. To avoid data loss, we set the boolean flag, **FTransferDone**, to TRUE. This is shown in the following code fragment from **FtpDataEvent**:

```
FD_CLOSE  :   begin
                FTransferDone := TRUE;
```

```
            if (FFTPCmd = FTP_RETR) or
               (FFTPCmd = FTP_LIST) then
          RecvData
          else
          if FFTPCmd = FTP_STOR then
            SendData;
        end;
```

The **FTransferDone** flag tells **RecvData** to continue reading the remaining data on the data socket in a **while** loop, as the following code fragment from **RecvData** shows:

```
FTP_RETR : begin
             { some code deleted }
             if FTransferDone then // FTP server is done, but must
                                   // read and save remaining data
                                   // on the data socket
             begin
               Done := FALSE;
               while not Done do
               begin
                 BlockWrite(FRetrFile, FDataBuffer, Response);
                 { some code deleted }
                 Response := recv(FDataSocket,
                                  FDataBuffer,
                                  SizeOf(FDataBuffer), 0);
                 if Response = SOCKET_ERROR then
                 begin
                   Done := TRUE;
                   WSAAsyncSelect(FDataSocket,
                                  FDataWnd, 0, 0); // don't post
                                                   // any more
                                                   // notifications
                   Closesocket(FDataSocket);
                   System.CloseFile(FRetrFile);
                   ChangeBusy(FALSE);
                   ChangeDataDone(TRUE);
                   InfoEvent(Concat('ERROR : ',WSAErrorMsg));
                 end;
                 if Response = 0 then // there is no more data
                 begin
                   { some code deleted }
                   Done := TRUE;
                   WSAAsyncSelect(FDataSocket, FDataWnd, 0, 0);
```

```
              Closesocket(FDataSocket);
              System.CloseFile(FRetrFile);
              ChangeBusy(FALSE);
              ChangeDataDone(TRUE);
              GetList;
            end;
          end;
        end else
          if Response > 0 then  // The FTP server is still
                                // sending data over to us,
                                // so process the data
          begin
            BlockWrite(FRetrFile, FDataBuffer, Response);
            { some code deleted }
          end;
      end;
```

Uploading a file to the FTP server using asynchronous mode follows the same logic as for downloading a file.

Put That Back On The Shelf!

Unlike blocking mode, we easily can cancel a file transfer that is taking too long to complete in asynchronous mode. We click the Abort button in the Connect tab sheet in the application during a file transfer. (Note this button is disabled in blocking mode.) Clicking the Abort button calls **CsShopper1.Abort** method, which sends the ABOR command to the server over the control connection. This is demonstrated in the following piece of code:

```
procedure TCsShopper.Abort;
begin
  ChangeBusy(TRUE);
  SendFtpCmd(LoadStr(SFtpAbor));
  FFtpCmd := FTP_ABORT;
  ChangeBusy(FALSE);
end;
```

On receipt of a 226 reply code, which indicates a successful cancellation of the file transfer, **CsShopper.ProcessAbort** closes the data connection and, if it was downloading a file, it discards the local file.

Gone Shopping

CsShopper is an FTP client and a nonvisual component, and has no provision for storing and retrieving host names, user names, passwords, and account information. Handling these is best left to the programmer, who can design these visible features to meet the needs of a specific application. However, the SHOPPER32 application demonstrates how easy it is to store and retrieve profiles, made feasible by CsShopper's published properties.

HIGH PERFORMANCE

An FTP Server Component

CHAPTER 7

It takes two to FTP, and by creating and customizing your own FTP server component, you can have full control over file transfer operations between your Internet-aware applications.

An FTP Server Component

John Penman

In Chapter 6 I described the Shopper component, which encapsulates the client side of the FTP protocol over the Internet. This is a common enough thing to want and use; in fact, Delphi 3 already includes an FTP client component among its many sample components. However, it takes more than a client to complete a transaction. As more and more people obtain around-the-clock (what is coming to be called 24×7) connections to the Net, more and more people will want to create their own server-side software with Delphi. Enter Keeper.

"Keeper" is my generic name for CsKeeper, a descendent of the CsSocket component I described in Chapter 5. CsKeeper is a VCL component that encapsulates the server side of the FTP protocol. CsKeeper is like the storekeeper of yesteryear, which fetches the files you require from the shelf and delivers them to you across the counter, but unlike the storekeeper of bygone days, it is a finite state automaton that strictly abides by the rules of the FTP protocol. (And as a bonus it won't attempt to engage you in small talk.)

Much of what you learned studying the CShopper component in Chapter 6 applies to Keeper as well, and if you haven't read Chapter 6 already, I would suggest that you pause here and do so. The two engage in a complex dance in accordance with the FTP protocol, and understanding one requires a certain level of understanding of the other.

If you feel you understand the client side reasonably well, we can begin here: An FTP server usually listens for a client connection on TCP port 21. On connection, the server initiates a login sequence by sending a USER command to the client. Since we have covered the login procedure in some detail in Chapter 6 regarding CsShopper, I'll skip over any detailed description of the login procedure. After a successful login, the server is ready to execute any FTP requests that come in from the client. The store is open at that point. Let's take a closer look.

The CsKeeper component embodies a simple and useful FTP server that complies with the minimal requirements formalized by RFC959. Therefore, some of the FTP commands like ACCT, NLIST, and PASV are not currently part CsKeeper's vocabulary. Table 7.1 provides a list of FTP commands, and commands not implemented in CsKeeper are marked with an asterisk in the table. When CsKeeper receives a command that is not implemented, it bounces back an error code with an informative message to the client.

Note well that CsKeeper is *not* a concurrent FTP server, which means it's capable of handling only one user at a time.

Table 7.1 The FTP command set.

Command	Description
ABOR	Requests the server to abort current file transfer
ACCT*	Sends the user's account
ALLO*	Requests the server to allocate storage space for a new file
APPE*	Requests the server to append data to an existing file
CDUP	Requests the server to change to the parent directory
CWD	Requests the server to change to a new directory
DELE	Requests the server to delete the user-specified file
HELP	Requests help information on any FTP command from the server
LIST	Requests a listing of files in the current directory
MKD	Requests the server to create a new directory
MODE	Requests the server to use a client-specified transfer mode
NLIST*	Requests a stream of file names from the server
NOOP	Requests the server to send an 'OK' reply
PASS	Sends a password to the server during the login phase
PASV*	Requests the server to listen on a unique data port
PORT	Requests the server to use the client specified data port
PWD	Requests the server to return current directory's name
QUIT	Ends FTP session
REIN*	Terminates a user, flushes all I/O and account
RMD	Requests the server to remove a directory
RNFR*	Sends a file name to be renamed

(continued)

Table 7.1 The FTP command set *(continued)*.

RNTO*	Sends a new file name. This command must be after RNFR
REST*	Restarts an interrupted file transfer
RETR	Retrieves a file from the server
SITE	Requests information on the server's specific services
SMNT*	Requests the server to mount a different file system
STAT*	Requests the server to send status information
STOR	Requests the server to store a file
STOU*	Stores a file under a unique name on the server
STRU*	Requests the server to use a client-specified file structure
SYST	Requests operating system type from the server
TYPE	Specifies the type of file to be transferred
USER	Sends the name of the user during the login phase

* Not implemented in this version of CsKeeper

Opening CsKeeper For Business

The KEEPER32 application (available on the CD-ROM in this chapter's subdirectory) demonstrates how to deploy the CsKeeper component in a complete application. The application has three TabSheet controls. The first tab sheet is **tsKeeper**, which is where all the main action takes place. This tab sheet is shown in Figure 7.1. Other tab sheets are **tsOptions** and **tsAbout**, which we'll discuss shortly.

But before we can run the KEEPER32 application we need to perform some preparations. We can determine the behavior of the **CsKeeper1** component by manipulating its properties in the Object Inspector at design time, which is shown in Figure 7.2.

However, whereas changing property values at design time is convenient for the designer, it's not so for the user, such as an FTP administrator who is not a programmer and does not have access to source code and the Delphi environment. That being the case, the FTP administrator can maintain the configuration of the FTP server in the **tsOptions** tab sheet. (Note that changes in the configuration are brought in from disk only when the app loads and runs, and thus will not take effect until the FTP server is stopped and restarted.) The **tsOptions** tab sheet is shown in Figure 7.3.

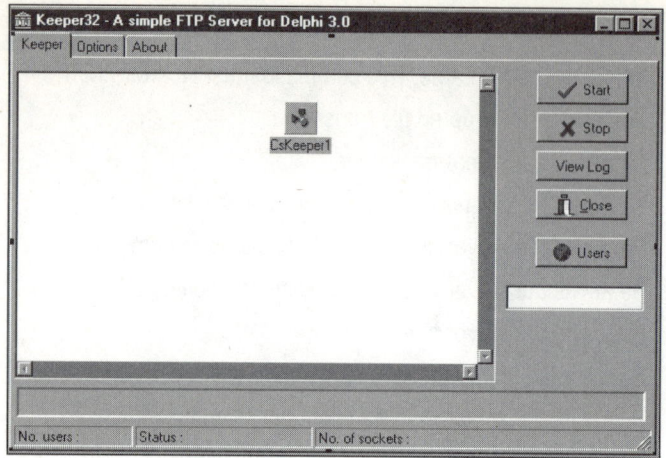

Figure 7.1
KEEPER32 at design time with the tsKeeper tab sheet in view.

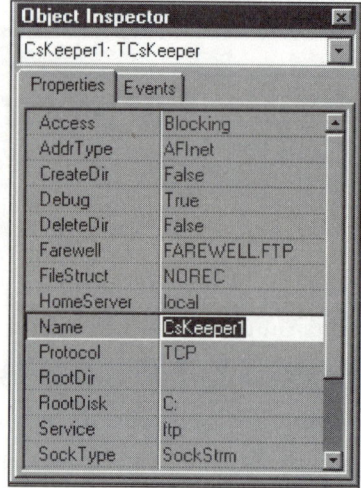

Figure 7.2
CsKeeper1's properties in the Object Inspector.

An FTP Server Component

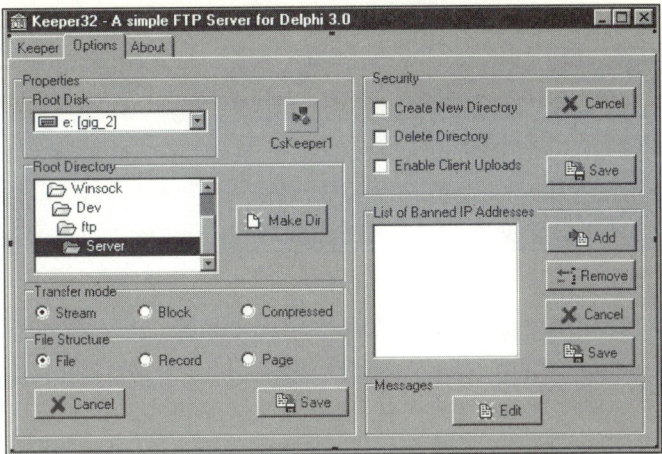

Figure 7.3
The Options tab sheet at design time.

Configuring KEEPER32 With The Options Tab

This is a very busy tab sheet and accomplishes quite a bit for us. Preventing clients from "wandering around" inside the server disk system is a prime example. We can restrict access by FTP clients to a specific disk drive and home directory on the machine that is running KEEPER32. That is, the FTP client cannot access other directories beyond that specified by the **CsKeeper1.RootDir** property, and its subdirectories.

To specify the root disk drive and the home directory, select a drive from the **dcbRootDisk**, which is a TDriveComboBox control. The location of the home directory is selected from **dlbRootDir**, a TDirectoryListBox control. Both controls are present in the **gbServerProperties** group box. Double-clicking the **dcbRootDisk** and **dlbRootDir** controls automatically assigns values to the **RootDisk** and **RootDir** properties. For example, the following piece of code shows how the **RootDisk** property is assigned a value in **dcbRootDisk**'s OnDblClick event handler:

```
procedure TfrmMain.dcbRootDiskDblClick(Sender: TObject);
begin
 CsKeeper1.RootDisk := dcbRootDisk.Drive;
end;
```

247

We also can create a new directory on the fly by clicking the Make Dir button, which calls up the **frmMkDir** form to allow edit of a directory name for the new directory. Then we double-click the new directory in the **dlbRootDir** control to assign the new name to the **RootDir** property.

We use **rgTransfer**, a radio group control, to select the default transfer mode for receiving and sending files. The default mode is Stream, which means that files are transferred as streams of bytes.

The Block and Compressed modes are necessary to implement the REST command, which enables an interrupted file transfer to restart at the point where the file transfer stopped. The Block and Compressed options, and hence the REST command, are not available in this version of **CsKeeper**. (The Block and Compressed buttons will be grayed out at runtime.) Therefore KEEPER32 will reject a MODE command with either the BLOCK or COMPRESSED option. I will probably add support for these two modes in the future—and of course you can too, if you're so inclined. They are not often used.

The FTP protocol allows the structure of a file to be specified, though the structures other than File are remnants of ancient times and are rarely used. There are three such structures. They are File (that is, no record structure), Record, and Page. **CsKeeper** defaults to the File type in the **rgFileStructure** radio group box. As with the MODE command, the present version of CsKeeper doesn't support the Record and Page structures, and it will reject a STRU command with either of these modes from the FTP client.

We can save the settings entered into the Options tab by clicking the Save button in the **gbServerProperties** group box. Doing this calls the **SavePropSettings** procedure. This procedure is shown in Listing 7.1. To cancel any changes, we click the Cancel button. (Note this will *not* recover previous settings if the new settings were already saved to the Registry.)

Listing 7.1 The SavePropSettings procedure.

```
procedure TfrmMain.SavePropSettings;
var Reg : TRegistry;
begin Reg := TRegistry.Create; try  Reg.OpenKey(FtpServerKey,TRUE);
Reg.WriteString('DRootDisk',dcbRootDisk.Drive);
 finally
```

```
   Reg.CloseKey;
 end;
 try
  Reg.OpenKey(FtpServerKey,TRUE);
  Reg.WriteString('DRootDir',dlbRootDir.Directory);
 finally
  Reg.CloseKey;
 end;
 try
  Reg.OpenKey(FtpServerKey,TRUE);
  case rgTransfer.ItemIndex of
   0 :Reg.WriteString('DTransferMode',FtpTransferStr[STREAM]);
   1 :Reg.WriteString('DTransferMode',FtpTransferStr[BLOCK]);
   2 :Reg.WriteString('DTransferMode',FtpTransferStr[COMPRESSED]);
  end;
 finally
  Reg.CloseKey;
 end;
 try
  Reg.OpenKey(FtpServerKey,TRUE);
  case rgFileStructure.ItemIndex of
   0 :Reg.WriteString('DFileStructure',FtpFileStructStr[NOREC]);
   1 :Reg.WriteString('DFileStructure',FtpFileStructStr[REC]);
   2 :Reg.WriteString('DFileStructure',FtpFileStructStr[PAGE]);
  end;
 finally
  Reg.CloseKey;
 end;
 Reg.Free;
end;
```

Security Settings

Security is a very big issue on the Internet. In KEEPER32 I've implemented some rather rudimentary forms of access security. If you wish to build on KEEPER32, this would be an excellent area to pursue.

In the **gbSecurity** group box, we can specify what actions FTP clients can and cannot perform. For example, we can prevent an incoming FTP client from deleting directories on the server by leaving the **cbDeleteDir**, a CheckBox control, unchecked. If we don't wish any FTP client to upload any files to KEEPER32, we simply leave the **cbUpload** checkbox unchecked. We save these settings by clicking the Save button, which calls the **SaveSecureSettings** procedure.

We can secure KEEPER32 against malicious hackers to some degree by maintaining a list of IP addresses of FTP clients that have a history of causing havoc. When an FTP client connects that originates from an IP address present in the **lbBadIPAddrs** list box, the **CsKeeper1** component disconnects the client. We can add, remove, and save "bad" IP addresses at will by clicking the Add, Remove, and Save buttons, respectively. Figure 7.4 shows the **tsOptions** tab sheet after setting up a list of unwanted IP addresses.

Informative Messages For Connecting Clients

Sometimes we might wish to alert incoming FTP client users of any changes in the FTP service that KEEPER32 provides, or provide some other informative messages or instructions. ("The pub/incoming directory has been eliminated...") Such messages typically are sent to users when they connect, or when they disconnect. They are called the Welcome message and the Farewell message, respectively.

We can maintain these messages by clicking the Edit button in the **gbMessages** group box, which brings up the **frmMessages** form. The **frmMessages** form has a **pcMessages** page control with two tab sheets, **tsWelcome** and **tsFarewell**. Both tab sheets contain Memo controls in which we can edit our messages. We click the Save button to save a message we're working on to a text file. This form is shown in Figure 7.5. We can provide file names in the **Welcome** and **Farewell** properties in the

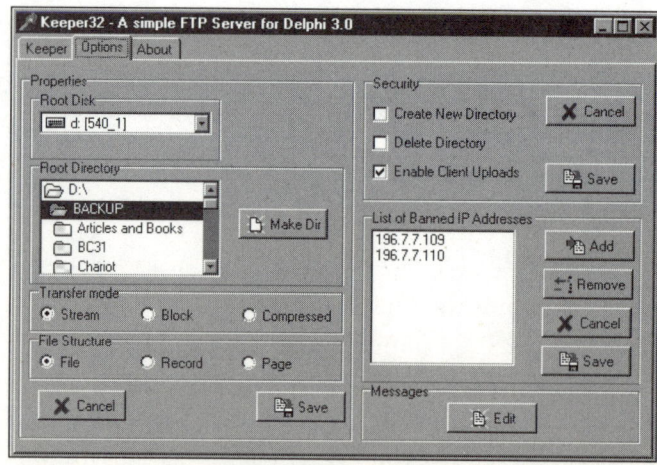

Figure 7.4
A list of unwanted IP addresses that KEEPER32 will refuse.

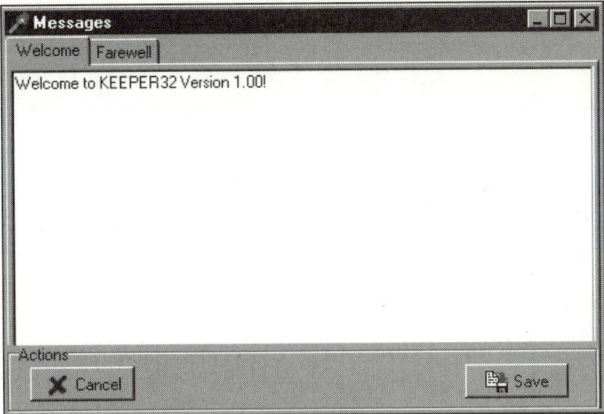

Figure 7.5
The form that edits Welcome and Farewell messages.

CsKeeper1 component to identify which text files store which messages. When KEEPER32 accepts a connecting client, the **CsKeeper1** component uses the **Welcome** property to locate and open the file for posting the message during the login phase.

Where And How Settings Are Stored

Except for the text files that hold the welcome and farewell messages, all of these settings are stored in the Windows 95 and NT 4.0 Registry. We make use of Delphi's **TRegistry** class to load and save these settings. When we start the KEEPER32 application, the **frmMain.OnCreate** event handler calls **LoadSettings** to read values from the Windows Registry. Listing 7.2 shows how this is done. After reading from the Registry, **LoadSettings** primes **CsKeeper1**'s properties with values retrieved from the Registry.

Listing 7.2 The LoadSettings procedure.

```
procedure TfrmMain.LoadSettings;
var Reg : TRegistry; Count : Integer; IPName : String;
begin Reg := TRegistry.Create;//Properties settings try
Reg.OpenKey(FtpServerKey, TRUE);
  if Reg.ValueExists('DRootDisk') then
   CsKeeper1.RootDisk := Reg.ReadString('DRootDisk')
  else
   CsKeeper1.RootDisk := '';
```

```
      if Reg.ValueExists('DRootDir') then
        CsKeeper1.RootDir := Reg.ReadString('DRootDir')
      else
        CsKeeper1.RootDir := '';
    finally
     Reg.CloseKey;
    end;
    try
     Reg.OpenKey(FtpServerKey, TRUE);
     if Reg.ValueExists('DTransferMode') then
     begin
       OldTransferMode := Reg.ReadString('DTransferMode');
       if UpperCase(OldTransferMode) =
           UpperCase(FtpTransferStr[STREAM]) then
       begin
        CsKeeper1.Transfer := STREAM;
        rgTransfer.ItemIndex := 0;
       end;
       if UpperCase(OldTransferMode) = UpperCase(FtpTransferStr[BLOCK]) then
begin
CsKeeper1.Transfer := BLOCK;
rgTransfer.ItemIndex := 1;
       end;
       if UpperCase(OldTransferMode) = UpperCase(FtpTransferStr
                                        [COMPRESSED]) then
begin    CsKeeper1.Transfer := COMPRESSED;
             rgTransfer.ItemIndex := 2;
             end;    end else
begin
OldTransferMode := UpperCase(FtpTransferStr[STREAM]);
      CsKeeper1.Transfer := STREAM;
     end;
    finally
     Reg.CloseKey;
    end;
// File structure
   try
     Reg.OpenKey(FtpServerKey, TRUE);
     if Reg.ValueExists('DFileStructure') then
     begin
      OldFileStruct := Reg.ReadString('DFileStructure');
      if UpperCase(OldFileStruct) = UpperCase(FtpFileStructStr[NOREC]) then
begin
CsKeeper1.FileStruct := NOREC;
             rgFileStructure.ItemIndex := 0;
end;
if UpperCase(OldFileStruct) = UpperCase(FtpFileStructStr[REC]) then
```

```
      begin
        CsKeeper1.FileStruct := REC;
        rgFileStructure.ItemIndex := 1;
      end;
      if UpperCase(OldFileStruct) = UpperCase(FtpFileStructStr[PAGE]) then
begin
CsKeeper1.FileStruct := PAGE;
              rgFileStructure.ItemIndex := 2;
      end;
    end else
    begin
      OldFileStruct := UpperCase(FtpFileStructStr[NOREC]);
      CsKeeper1.FileStruct := NOREC;
      rgFileStructure.ItemIndex := 0;
    end;
  finally
    Reg.CloseKey;
  end;
// Create new directory permission
  try
    Reg.OpenKey(FtpServerKey, TRUE);
    if Reg.ValueExists('DCreateNewDir') then
    begin
      OldMkDir := Reg.ReadBool('DCreateNewDir');
      CsKeeper1.CreateDir := OldMkDir;
      if OldMkDir then
        cbAllowMkDir.State := cbChecked
      else
        cbAllowMkDir.State := cbUnChecked;
    end else
    begin
      OldMkDir := FALSE;
      CsKeeper1.CreateDir := OldMkDir;
    end;
  finally
    Reg.CloseKey;
  end;
// Delete directory permission
  try
    Reg.OpenKey(FtpServerKey, TRUE);
    if Reg.ValueExists('DDeleteDir') then
    begin
      OldDeleteDir := Reg.ReadBool('DDeleteDir');
      CsKeeper1.DeleteDir := OldDeleteDir;
      if OldDeleteDir then
        cbDeleteDir.State := cbChecked
      else
```

```
    cbDeleteDir.State := cbUnChecked;
   end else
   begin
    OldDeleteDir := FALSE;
    CsKeeper1.DeleteDir := OldDeleteDir;
    cbDeleteDir.State := cbUnChecked;
   end;
  finally
   Reg.CloseKey;
  end;
 // Upload files permission
  try
   Reg.OpenKey(FtpServerKey, TRUE);
   if Reg.ValueExists('DUpLoads') then
   begin
    OldUpLoads := Reg.ReadBool('DUpLoads');
    CsKeeper1.UpLoads := OldUpLoads;
    if OldUpLoads then
     cbUpLoad.State := cbChecked
    else
     cbUpLoad.State := cbUnChecked;
   end else
   begin
    OldUpLoads := FALSE;
    CsKeeper1.UpLoads := OldUpLoads;
    cbUpLoad.State := cbUnChecked;
   end;
  finally
   Reg.CloseKey;
  end;
  try
   Reg.OpenKey(FtpServerKey, TRUE);
   if Reg.ValueExists('DNoBannedIPs') then
    NoOfBannedIPs := Reg.ReadInteger('DNoBannedIPs')
   else
    NoOfBannedIPs := 1;
  finally
   Reg.CloseKey;
  end;
 // List of banned IP addresses
  for Count := 0 to NoOfBannedIPs - 1 do
  begin
   IPName := Concat('IPName', IntToStr(Count));
   try
    Reg.OpenKey(FtpServerKey + '\IPs' + '\' + IPName, TRUE);
    if Reg.ValueExists('IPName') then
     lbBadIPAddrs.Items.Add(Reg.ReadString('IPName'))
```

```
    else
     lbBadIPAddrs.Items.Add('');
    OldBannedIPsList.Add(lbBadIPAddrs.Items.Strings[Count]);
   finally
    Reg.CloseKey;
   end;
 end;//for loop
 with CsKeeper1 do
 begin
  if Length(RootDisk) > 0 then
   dcbRootDisk.Drive := Char(RootDisk[1])
  else
   dcbRootDisk.Drive := 'C';
  if Length(RootDir) > 0 then
   dlbRootDir.Directory := RootDir;
  for Count := 0 to NoOfBannedIPs - 1 do
   BadIPs.Add(lbBadIPAddrs.Items.Strings[Count]);
 end;
 Reg.Free;
end;
```

Open And Running!

After configuring the FTP server component **CsKeeper1**, we are ready to start KEEPER32. We click the Start button to call **CsKeeper1.StartServer** method. Figure 7.6 shows the KEEPER32 Application after starting the FTP service.

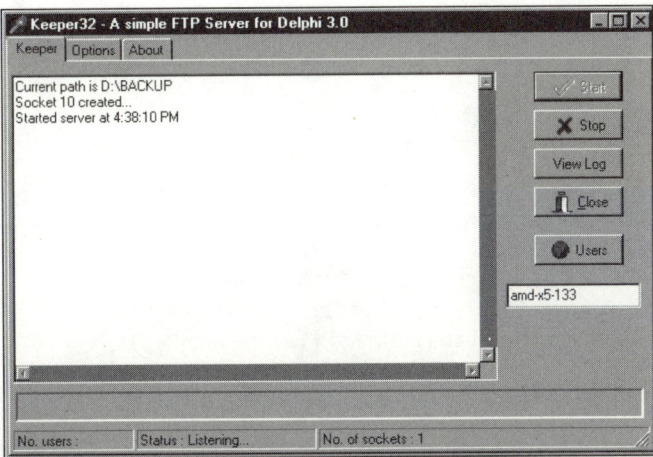

Figure 7.6
KEEPER32 after starting the FTP service.

The **CsKeeper1.StartServer** method calls the **GetHome** procedure to change the current drive and home directory as specified by **FRootDisk** and **FRootDir**, which are assigned by the **RootDisk** and **RootDir** properties as set by **LoadSettings**.

Showing The Client What's Available

The **GetDirList** method then is called to create a text file, INDEX.TXT, to contain the directories and files located in the home directory. The **GetDirList** method uses the **FindFirst** and **FindNext** functions to build a listing of directories and files in the home directory, the process of which is demonstrated in Listing 7.3.

Unfortunately, there is no truly standard format for presenting a list of directories and files. This varies from operating system to operating system, and is a problem that FTP clients must handle. For our server, **CsKeeper** uses the "standard" (more or less) Unix format to itemize the directories and files of the home directory in INDEX.TXT. This file is sent down the line to the client after the FTP client logs on successfully and whenever the FTP client changes directory, deletes a directory, or creates a directory.

Listing 7.3   The GetDirList procedure.

```
procedure TCsKeeper.GetDirList;
var F : TextFile;
 SearchRec : TSearchRec;
 SizeStr, FileName, S : String;
 TDate : TDateTime;
 Result, K, L : Integer;

begin
 AssignFile(F, DirListFile);
 Rewrite(F);
 if Pos('\',FDirPath) = length(FDirPath) then
  FileName := Concat(FDirPath,'*.*')
 else
 if Pos('\',FDirPath) < length(FDirPath) then
  FileName := Concat(FDirPath,'\*.*');
 Result := FindFirst(FileName, faAnyFile, SearchRec);
 try
  TDate := FileDateToDateTime(SearchRec.Time);
  except
```

An FTP Server Component

```
     on EConvertError do
     begin
       Status := Failure;
       Data := '500 Internal error';
       closesocket(FSocket);
       Exit;
     end;
  end;
  S := FormatDateTime('mmm dd hh'':''mm',TDate);
  if DirectoryExists(SearchRec.Name) then
   writeln(F,
   'drwxrwxrwx    1 noone     nogroup          ','0',' ',S,' ',SearchRec.Name)
  else
  begin
   {calculate length of size}
   SizeStr := IntToStr(SearchRec.Size);
   L := Length(SizeStr);
   for K := 9 - L downto 1 do
     SizeStr := ConCat(' ',SizeStr);
   write(F,'-rwxrwxrwx    1 noone     nogroup');
   writeln(F, SizeStr,' ',S,' ',SearchRec.Name);
  end;
  while Result = 0 do
  begin
   TDate := FileDateToDateTime(SearchRec.Time);
   S := FormatDateTime('mmm dd hh'':''mm',TDate);
   if DirectoryExists(SearchRec.Name) then
     writeln(F,'drwxrwxrwx    1 noone     nogroup
             ','0',' ',S,' ',SearchRec.Name)
   else
   begin
     SizeStr := IntToStr(SearchRec.Size);
     L := Length(SizeStr);
     for K := 9 - L downto 1 do
       SizeStr := ConCat(' ',SizeStr);
     write(F,'-rwxrwxrwx    1 noone     nogroup');
     writeln(F, SizeStr,' ',S,' ',SearchRec.Name);
   end;
   Result := FindNext(SearchRec);
  end;
  SysUtils.FindClose(SearchRec);
  CloseFile(F);
end;
```

As with **CsShopper**, the **CsKeeper1.OnInfo** event procedure passes messages to KEEPER32 for display in the **memStatus** Memo control, as shown in Figure 7.7. Any FTP errors are posted by **CsKeeper1.OnError** event handler to **pnErrorMsg**, a Panel control.

Creating A Listening Socket

Everything up to this point has really been preparation and mostly textual in nature. Now we get ready to make use of Windows Sockets. The first step is to call **CsSocket.GetServer** to initialize the necessary data structures required to start an FTP service with their appropriate values. This procedure is shown in full in Listing 7.4.

Listing 7.4 The CsSocket.GetServer method.

```
procedure TCsSocket.GetServer;
begin GetServ; if Status = Failure then Exit;
 FSockAddress.sin_family         := PF_INET;
 FSockAddress.sin_port           := FServ^.s_port;
 FSockAddress.sin_addr.s_addr    := htonl(INADDR_ANY);
 FRemoteName                     := LocalName;
 FSocket                         := CreateSocket;
end;
```

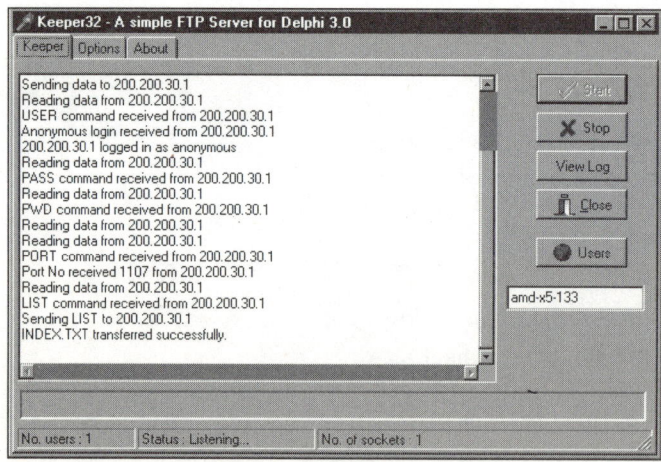

Figure 7.7
KEEPER32 with FTP transaction messages after a LIST command.

After initializing the required data structures with this call, **GetServer** calls **CreateSocket** to create a listening socket, **FSocket**. Next, we call **WSAAsyncSelect**, a Winsock API function, in order to instruct the Winsock DLL to notify **CsKeeper** of a socket event by posting a message to the **Wnd**, a windows handle of type **HWND**. This is shown in the following statement:

```
if WSAAsyncSelect(FSocket, Wnd, FTP_EVENT, FD_ACCEPT)
                = SOCKET_ERROR then {handle}
{rest of code}
```

We then call **bind**, another Winsock API function, to associate a local name with **FSocket**, an unnamed socket, and its host address and port number. This is required for listening on a port for an incoming connection. The **listen** function instructs **CsKeeper** to listen on port 21. After that call is made, KEEPER32 is now ready to accept a connection on that port

Are You Being Served?

When an incoming FTP client connects to TCP port 21, it causes the Winsock DLL to post an **FTP_EVENT** message to wake up **FtpEvent**, which then traps the **FD_ACCEPT** socket event notification. Inside the **FD_ACCEPT** clause of the **case** statement, the **FtpEvent** procedure calls the **accept** function to create a socket, **FClientSocket**, like this:

```
FClientSocket := accept(FSocketNo, @FClientSockAddr), @FAddrSize);
```

At this point we call the Winsock API function **getpeername** to retrieve the Internet address of the client. With the client IP address in hand, **CsKeeper** checks the IP address by comparing it to any of the strings representing "bad" clients that are stored in the **CsKeeper.FBadIPs** string list. If a match occurs, **CsKeeper** sends a warning message, disconnects the unwanted FTP client, and returns to the listening state. Otherwise, **CsKeeper** calls **LogInUser** to handle the rest of the login sequence.

One User At A Time

To prevent any more FTP clients from attempting to connect, **LogInUser** calls the **WSAAsyncSelect** function with the last parameter set to 0, which tells Winsock not to send any notifications on the listening socket, **FSocket**. This is shown in the following line of code:

```
if WSAAsyncSelect(FSocket, Wnd, FTP_EVENT, 0) = SOCKET_ERROR then
{rest of code}
```

This, in effect, shuts out any additional FTP clients until **CsKeeper** is done with the currently connected client.

Next, we make another call to **WSAAsyncSelect** in this form:

```
if WSAAsyncSelect(FClientSocket, Wnd, FTP_EVENT,
                 FD_READ OR FD_CLOSE OR FD_OOB OR FD_WRITE) =
                 SOCKET_ERROR then
begin
{and rest of code}
```

This call to **WSAAsyncSelect** ensures that Winsock notifies **CsKeeper1** of any socket event on the **FClientSocket** socket. When the login sequence is complete, the **CsKeeper1** awaits further FTP commands on the control connection.

When the FTP client issues a command such as RETR, **FtpEvent** catches the command by trapping the **FD_READ** event generated by the WinSock DLL. In the **FD_READ** clause of the **case** statement in **FtpEvent**, the **DecodeFTPCmd** is called to handle the command sent by the FTP client. **DecodeFTPCmd** decodes the command and executes the relevant routine. Otherwise, if the command request is not recognized, **CsKeeper1** posts an error code to the FTP client. Listing 7.5 shows how **DecodeFTPCmd** handles any FTP command. This is really the beating heart of the CsKeeper component.

Listing 7.5 The DecodeFTPCmd method.

```
procedure TCsKeeper.DecodeFTPCmd(SockNo : TSocket; CmdStr : CharArray; S
                                : String);
  var FtpCmd, Selector : TFtpCmds; DirStr, FileName, Port1Str, Port2Str,
  S1, TempStr : String; Finished : Boolean; Count : Byte;

begin
 FtpCmd := UNK;
 Finished := FALSE;
 Count := 1;
 S1 := '';
```

An FTP Server Component

```
       TempStr := StrPas(CmdStr);
       while not Finished do
       begin
         if (TempStr[Count] = ' ') or ((TempStr[Count] = #13) and
            (TempStr[Count + 1] = #10)) then
       begin
       Finished := TRUE;
     end
     else
     begin
     S1 := ConCat(S1,TempStr[Count]);
     Inc(Count);
     end;
      end;
       Selector := PWD;
       Status := Failure; {Assume we have failed}
       Finished := FALSE;
       if S1 = '' then Exit; {Must not process empty strings}
       while not Finished do
       begin
         if CompareText(S1, FtpCmdStr[Selector]) = 0 then
         begin
           FtpCmd := Selector;
           Status := Success;
          break;
         end else
         begin
           if Selector = UNK then
           begin
            Status := Failure;
            Finished := TRUE;
           end;
           if not Finished then Inc(Selector);
         end;
       end;
       if Status = Failure then
       begin
         Info := Concat('Unrecognised command received from ',FClientAddrStr);
              InfoEvent(Info);
              SendFtpCode(FClientSocket,'500 Unrecognised command');
              Status := Failure;
     Exit;
     end;
     case FtpCmd of   PWD  : begin
     Info := Concat('PWD command received from ',FClientAddrStr);
     InfoEvent(Info);
     GetDir(0, DirStr);
```

261

```
          SendFtpCode(FClientSocket,'257 Working directory is '+ DirStr);
end;
RETR : begin
Info := Concat('RETR command received from ', FClientAddrStr);
InfoEvent(Info);
FileName := Copy(TempStr, Pos(' ', TempStr)+1, Length(TempStr));
if Pos(#13, FileName) > 0 then FileName := Copy(FileName, 1, Pos(#13,
   FileName)-1);
          Info := Concat('Sending file ',FileName, ' to ', FClientAddrStr);
InfoEvent(Info);
if FFileType = IMAGE then
begin
          Info := Concat('Using IMAGE type');
          InfoEvent(Info);
          SendFtpCode(FClientSocket,'150
                    Opening BINARY data connection for ' + FileName)
end
else
begin
Info := Concat('Using ASCII type');
          InfoEvent(Info);
          SendFtpCode(FClientSocket,'150   Opening ASCII data connection
                    for ' + FileName);
end;
             SendFile(FileName);
end;
             STOR : begin
Info := Concat('STOR command received from ', FClientAddrStr);
          InfoEvent(Info);
          FileName := Copy(TempStr, Pos(' ', TempStr)+1,
                       Length(TempStr));
          if Pos(#13, FileName) > 0 then
           FileName := Copy(FileName, 1, Pos(#13, FileName)-1);
          Info := Concat('Sending file ',FileName, ' to ',
                    FClientAddrStr);
          InfoEvent(Info);
          if FFileType = IMAGE then
          begin
           Info := Concat('Using IMAGE type');
           InfoEvent(Info);
           SendFtpCode(FClientSocket,
                    '150   Opening BINARY data connection for ' +
                    FileName)
          end
          else
          begin
```

An FTP Server Component

```
              Info := Concat('Using ASCII type');
              InfoEvent(Info);
              SendFtpCode(FClientSocket,
                          '150  Opening ASCII data connection for ' +
                          FileName);
            end;
            GetFile(FileName);
          end;
USER : begin
         {Decode string}
         if Pos('ANONYMOUS',UpperCase(TempStr)) > 0 then
         begin
           Info := Concat('USER command received from ',
                          FClientAddrStr);
           InfoEvent(Info);
           Info := Concat('Anonymous login received from ',
                          FClientAddrStr);
           InfoEvent(Info);
           FUserType := ANONYMOUS;
           SendFtpCode(FClientSocket,
                        '331- Anonymous user accepted.');
           SendFtpCode(FClientSocket,
                        '331  Send in your password, please');
           Info := Concat(FClientAddrStr,
                          ' logged in as anonymous');
           InfoEvent(Info)
         end else
         begin
           FUserType := ACCOUNT;
           SendFtpCode(FClientSocket,'500 ' + FtpCmdStr[ACCT] +
                       ' command not implemented');
         end;
       end;
QUIT : begin
         Info := Concat('QUIT command received from ',
                        FClientAddrStr);
         InfoEvent(Info);
         SendFtpCode(FClientSocket,'221  Goodbye from Keeper!');
         Info := FClientAddrStr;
         Info := ConCat(Info, ' logged out');
         InfoEvent(Info);
         closesocket(FClientSocket);
         FClientSocket := INVALID_SOCKET;
         if FNoOfUsers >= 1 then
          Dec(FNoOfUsers);
         {now change to root disk and directory}
```

```
                GetHome;
                GetDirList;
                {return to listening state}
                if WSAAsyncSelect(FSocket, Wnd, FTP_EVENT, FD_ACCEPT)
                                = SOCKET_ERROR then {handle}
                begin
                  Info := Concat('ERROR : 11 [',FClientAddrStr,'] ',
                                WSAErrorMsg);
                  InfoEvent(Info);
                  Status := Failure;
                  Exit;
                end;
              end;
       PASS : begin
                {Type of user? }
                if FUserType = ANONYMOUS then
                begin
                  Info := Concat('PASS command received from ',
                                FClientAddrStr);
                  InfoEvent(Info);              {get email address of user}
                  SendFtpCode(FClientSocket,
                            '230  User logged in. Go ahead!');
                end;
              end;
       CDUP : begin
                Info := Concat('CDUP command received from ',
                              FClientAddrStr);
                InfoEvent(Info);
                SendFtpCode(FClientSocket,'500 ' + FtpCmdStr[CDUP] +
                            ' command not implemented');
              end;
       CWD  : begin
                Info := Concat('CWD command received from ',
                              FClientAddrStr);
                InfoEvent(Info);
                {$I-}
                { Change to directory specified in Edit1 }
                FileName := Copy(TempStr, Pos(' ', TempStr)+1,
                              Length(TempStr));
                if Pos(#13, FileName) > 0 then
                  FileName := Copy(FileName, 1, Pos(#13, FileName)-1);
                If DirectoryExists(FileName) then
                  ChDir(FileName)
                else
                begin
                  Status := Failure;
                  SendFtpCode(FClientSocket,'500 Not a directory');
```

```
              Exit;
            end;
            if IOResult <> 0 then
              SendFtpCode(FClientSocket,'500 Cannot find directory')
            else
            begin
              SendFtpCode(FClientSocket,'200 Changed directory');
              GetDir(0,FDirPath);
              GetDirList;
            end;
          end;
LIST : begin
         Info := Concat('LIST command received from ',
                        FClientAddrStr);
         InfoEvent(Info);
         GetDirList;
         Info := Concat('Sending LIST to ',FClientAddrStr);
         InfoEvent(Info);
         SendFtpCode(FClientSocket,
                     '150  Opening Ascii connection');
         SendFile(DirListFile);
       end;
PORT : begin
         Info := Concat('PORT command received from ',
                        FClientAddrStr);
         InfoEvent(Info);
         Count := Length(TempStr);
         Port1Str := '';
         Port2Str := '';
         if (TempStr[Count] = #10) and (TempStr[Count-1] = #13)
           then
           Dec(Count,2); { we do not want to include the CRLF!}
         while TempStr[Count] <> ',' do
         begin
           Port2Str := Concat(TempStr[Count], Port2Str);
           Dec(Count);
         end;
         Dec(Count);
         while TempStr[Count] <> ',' do
         begin
           Port1Str := Concat(TempStr[Count], Port1Str);
           Dec(Count);
         end;
         FPort2 := StrToInt(Port2Str);
         FPort1 := StrToInt(Port1Str);
         FPortNo := FPort2 + 1024;
         Info := Concat('Port No received ',IntToStr(FPortNo),
                        ' from ', FClientAddrStr);
```

```
              InfoEvent(Info);
              SendFtpCode(FClientSocket,'200 PORT command okay');
              FClientSockAddr.sin_port := FPortNo;
              {Open data connection }
           end;
   SYST : begin
             Info := Concat('SYST command received from ',
                          FClientAddrStr);
             InfoEvent(Info);
             SendFtpCode(FClientSocket,'215  Unix Keeper 1.0');
          end;
   HELP : begin
             Info := Concat('HELP command received from ',
                          FClientAddrStr);
             InfoEvent(Info);
             SendFtpCode(FClientSocket,
                '211- HELP Commands implemented at this site:');
             SendFtpCode(FClientSocket,
                '211- QUIT RETR USER PASS LIST PORT CWD TYPE PWD');
             SendFtpCode(FClientSocket,'211   ');
          end;
   FTYPE: begin
            if Pos('A', UpperCase(TempStr)) > 0 then
            begin
             FFileType := ASCII;
             SendFtpCode(FClientSocket,'200  TYPE ASCII');
            end
            else
            if Pos('I', UpperCase(TempStr)) > 0 then
            begin
             FFileType := IMAGE;
             SendFtpCode(FClientSocket,'200 TYPE BINARY');
            end;
          end;
   MODE : begin
             Info := Concat('MODE command received from ',
                          FClientAddrStr);
             InfoEvent(Info);
             if Pos(' S', Uppercase(TempStr)) > 0 then
              FTransfer := STREAM
             else
             if Pos(' B', Uppercase(TempStr)) > 0 then
              FTransfer := BLOCK
             else
              FTransfer := COMPRESSED;
          end;
   NLST : begin
```

AN FTP SERVER COMPONENT

```
              Info := Concat('NLST command received from ',
                             FClientAddrStr);
              InfoEvent(Info);
              SendFtpCode(FClientSocket,'500 ' + FtpCmdStr[NLST] +
                          ' command not implemented');
            end;
    QUOTE : begin
              Info := Concat('QUOTE command received from ',
                             FClientAddrStr);
              InfoEvent(Info);
              SendFtpCode(FClientSocket,'500 ' + FtpCmdStr[QUOTE] +
                          ' command not implemented');
            end;
    PASV  : begin
              Info := Concat('PASV command received from ',
                             FClientAddrStr);
              InfoEvent(Info);
              SendFtpCode(FClientSocket,'500 ' + FtpCmdStr[PASV] +
                          ' command not implemented');
            end;
    SITE  : begin
              Info := Concat('SITE command received from ',
                             FClientAddrStr);
              InfoEvent(Info);
              SendFtpCode(FClientSocket,'500 ' + FtpCmdStr[SITE] +
                          ' command not implemented');
            end;
    MKD   : begin
              Info := Concat('MKDIR command received from ',
                             FClientAddrStr);
              InfoEvent(Info);
              SendFtpCode(FClientSocket,'500 ' + FtpCmdStr[MKD] +
                          ' command not implemented');
            end;
    RMD   : begin
              Info := Concat('RMDIR command received from ',
                             FClientAddrStr);
              InfoEvent(Info);
              SendFtpCode(FClientSocket,'500 ' + FtpCmdStr[RMD] +
                          ' command not implemented');
            end;
    STRU  : begin
              Info := Concat('STRU command received from ',
                             FClientAddrStr);
              InfoEvent(Info);
              if Pos(' F', Uppercase(TempStr)) > 0 then
                FFileStruct := NOREC
```

```
              else
              if Pos(' R', Uppercase(TempStr)) > 0 then
                FFileStruct := REC
              else
                FFileStruct := PAGE;
            end;
    STAT  : begin
              Info := Concat('STAT command received from ',
                             FClientAddrStr);
              InfoEvent(Info);
              SendFtpCode(FClientSocket,'500 ' + FtpCmdStr[STAT] +
                          ' command not implemented');
            end;
    ACCT  : begin
              Info := Concat('ACCT command received from ',
                             FClientAddrStr);
              InfoEvent(Info);
              SendFtpCode(FClientSocket,'500 ' + FtpCmdStr[ACCT] +
                          ' command not implemented');
            end;
    NOOP  : begin
              Info := Concat('NOOP command received from ',
                             FClientAddrStr);
              InfoEvent(Info);
              SendFtpCode(FClientSocket,'200 ' + FtpCmdStr[NOOP] +
                          ' command received OK');
            end;
  end;
end;
```

When **CsKeeper** receives the LIST command from the FTP client, it calls **SendFile** to send the INDEX.TXT file over the data connection. After **CsKeeper** has sent the data, it closes the data connection. The data connection is always *transient*, unlike the control connection, which is *persistent*.

I'll Take One Of Those...

Obviously, the *raison d'être* for the whole FTP protocol is the transfer of files, so it's no surprise that the retrieve and store commands, RETR and STOR, are the most commonly used in the entire FTP command set. RETR retrieves a file from the server, and STOR instructs the server to accept and store a file sent by the client.

When **CsKeeper** receives a RETR command, the **DecodeFTPCmd** routine parses the RETR command string, and in the RETR clause of the big **case** statement, the code extracts the file name of the file to be retrieved. This file name is then sent to the **SendFile** procedure for actual transmission. To synchronize the receipt of the file by the FTP client, **CsKeeper** calls **SendFTPCode** to issue a 150 reply code, which informs the client to listen for data on the port set previously by the client.

There's nothing especially magical about actually sending the file. **SendFile** creates a local socket, called **LocalSocket**, and then calls **connect** to open the data connection. Once the connection is made, **CsKeeper** opens the file from which the data is read for transmission. A **repeat..until** loop executes the **BlockRead** procedure to read the data block by block, and the **send** function to send the data as it is read by **BlockRead**. When there is no more data to send, **CsKeeper** closes the file and kills the data connection by calling **closesocket** to close **LocalSocket**. **CsKeeper** calls **SendFtpCode** to send a 226 reply code to tell the FTP client that the server has completed sending the data in the requested file.

Can You Store This For Me?

STOR is a mirror of the RETR command, but instead of *sending* the file to the client, **CsKeeper** *stores* the file from the client, hence the name STOR. When **CsKeeper** receives the STOR command, the **DecodeFTPCmd** parses and passes the command string to the STOR clause of the **case** statement that parses out all the various commands. If **FUpLoads** is **TRUE** (remember we can restrict uploading of files to the server by deselecting the check box in the Options tab sheet), then **TCsKeeper.GetFile** is called. Otherwise, **DecodeFTPCmd** sends a 500 reply code responding in the negative.

TCsKeeper.GetFile creates a local socket, **LocalSocket**, for the data connection, which is done by a call to the **connect** Winsock API function, as shown below:

```
if connect(LocalSocket, DataS, SizeOf(TSockAddrIn)) = SOCKET_ERROR then
{rest of code}
```

After opening the file, we store the incoming data using **recv**, which is another Winsock function, and the **BlockWrite** function, which writes the data using a **while..do** loop as shown:

```
while not Finished do
begin
 Response := recv(LocalSocket, Buffer, SizeOf(Buffer, 0);
{rest of code}
 if Response > 0 then
 BlockWrite(F, Buffer, Response);
end;
```

When there is no more data to receive from the client, **TCsKeeper.GetFile** closes the data connection on **LocalSocket**, and sends a positive 226 reply code to the client through the **SendFtpCode** procedure.

Taking Inventory

And there you have it—your own functioning FTP server. It's a relatively straightforward task to build such a server. Indeed, my own experience indicates that an FTP server component is far easier to develop than an FTP client component, especially if you omit the more arcane and little-used FTP commands from the server's vocabulary.

However, one enhancement that would definitely make **CsKeeper** far more useful is concurrency. This would allow the simultaneous connection and servicing of more than one FTP client by our server. Virtually all servers in daily use today support concurrency, especially given the dominance of Windows NT and Unix in the server marketplace, both of which support concurrent connections. To implement concurrency in a server we would need to explore multithreading from Delphi, a worthy project but one which is outside the bounds of this chapter.

3D Fractal Landscapes

HIGH PERFORMANCE

CHAPTER 8

HIGH PERFORMANCE

Big Sur too expensive for you? Create your own Virtual Sur, and make it as big as you like, using fractal techniques and that old Delphi magic.

3D Fractal Landscapes

Jon Shemitz

The first time I heard the word "fractal" was back in 1983 or so, when I was still a mainframe programmer. A co-worker and I were talking about our spiffy new IBM PCs, and he asked me if I had any fractal software.

"No," I said. "What are fractals?"

He explained that you made a fractal by applying some geometric operation to a simple figure, and then repeatedly applying the same operation to the result. While this explanation doesn't even begin to touch on the sort of mathematical properties of fractals that interest mathematicians, it remains a good summary of how most fractals are generated.

It certainly describes 3D fractal landscape generation.

Bending And Dividing

To generate a landscape, simply assign random heights to the three vertices of an equilateral triangle, then "bend" each of the edges by raising or lowering the midpoint by some random amount. If you draw lines between each of the three midpoints, you have carved the initial triangle into four triangles. If you apply this bending and dividing operation to each new triangle as you create it, before long you will end up with something that looks surprisingly like a real landscape. (See Figures 8.1, 8.2, and 8.3.)

The Shared Edges Problem

Now, of course, fractal landscape generation's not *quite* as simple as "bend, divide, repeat"—you have to make sure that you only bend a given line once, and, of course, you generally do want to display the landscape—but those are the details.

Chapter 8

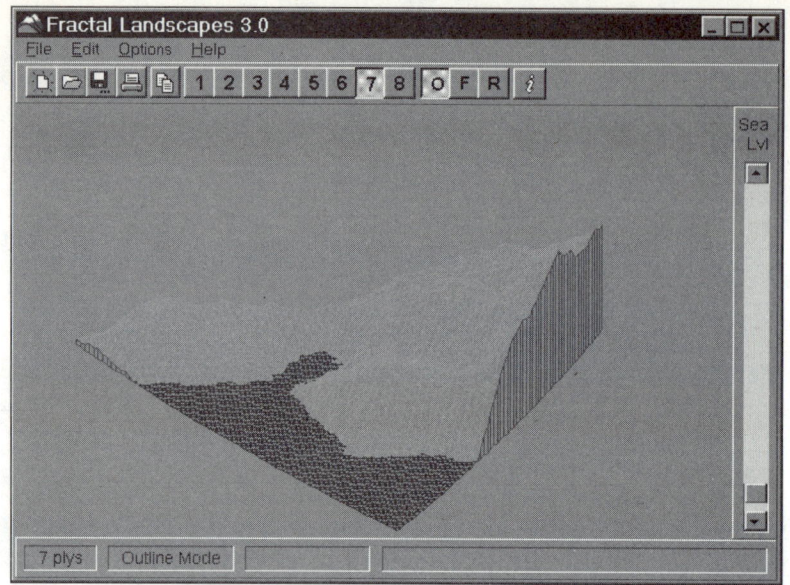

Figure 8.1
An outline fractal landscape.

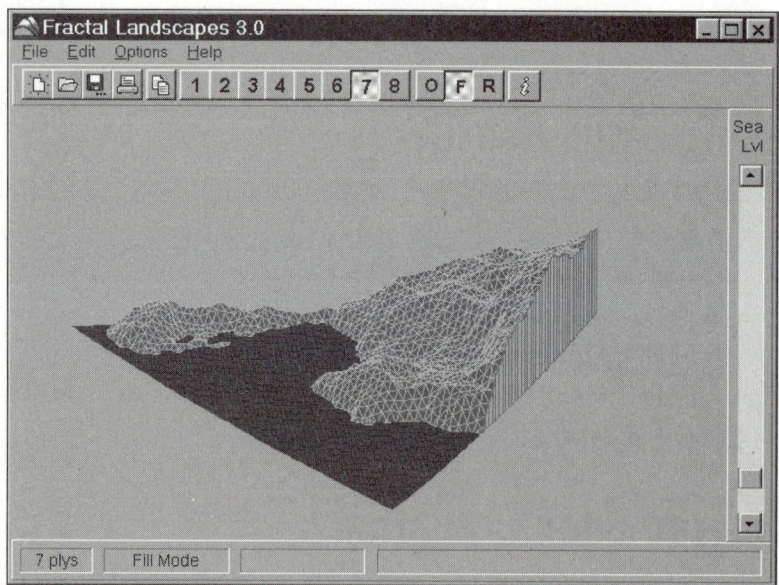

Figure 8.2
A filled fractal landscape.

3D Fractal Landscapes

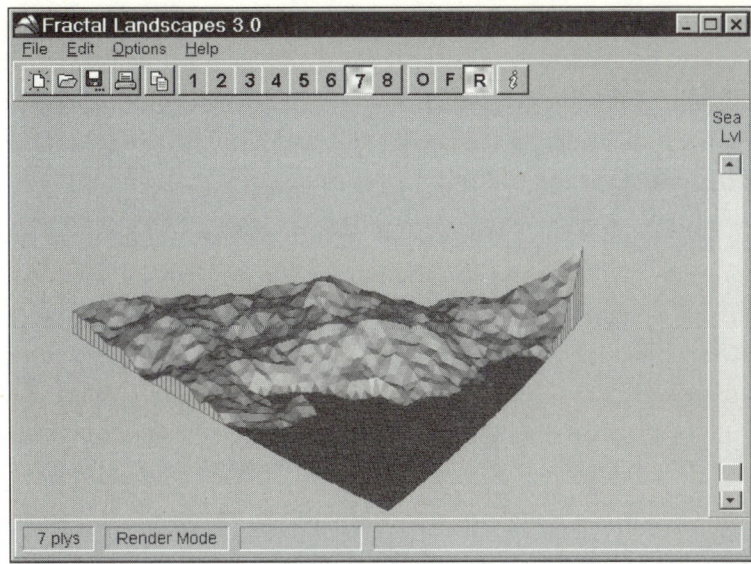

Figure 8.3
A rendered fractal landscape.

The first and most important detail is that you have to keep track of what you're doing. If you straightforwardly write the **FractureTriangle**() routine to bend each edge, you will end up with something like that shown in Figure 8.4. Your triangles won't form a smooth mesh; each group of four triangles will "float" with each vertex at a different height than its neighbors'.

Figure 8.4
When edges don't meet.

A look at Figure 8.5 may help make clear what's going on. Interior edges are shared by two triangles, which do not necessarily agree on how much to bend them. Vertex I is the midpoint of the line DF, which is shared by triangles CDF and DEF. If both triangles try to set the height of I, triangles 1, 2, and 3 will be given a different height for I than triangles 4, 5, and 6!

Clearly, we need to maintain a database of vertices, so that we can set vertex I when we fracture triangle CDF—and use the same value for vertex I when we fracture triangle DEF. We might try to say that triangle DEF is an "inside" triangle, and that therefore we will fracture it last and use the "outer" triangles' values for vertices G, H, and I—but look at triangles GEH and LMN. Lines GE and EH are shared with "outside" triangles, so we should use the outside triangles' values for vertices L and M, but line GH is "all inside," so we need to bend it. We could undoubtedly elaborate the scheme of inside and outside triangles to handle these "outside-inside subtriangles" properly, but we'd end up with code that was hard to read and liable to break whenever it was changed.

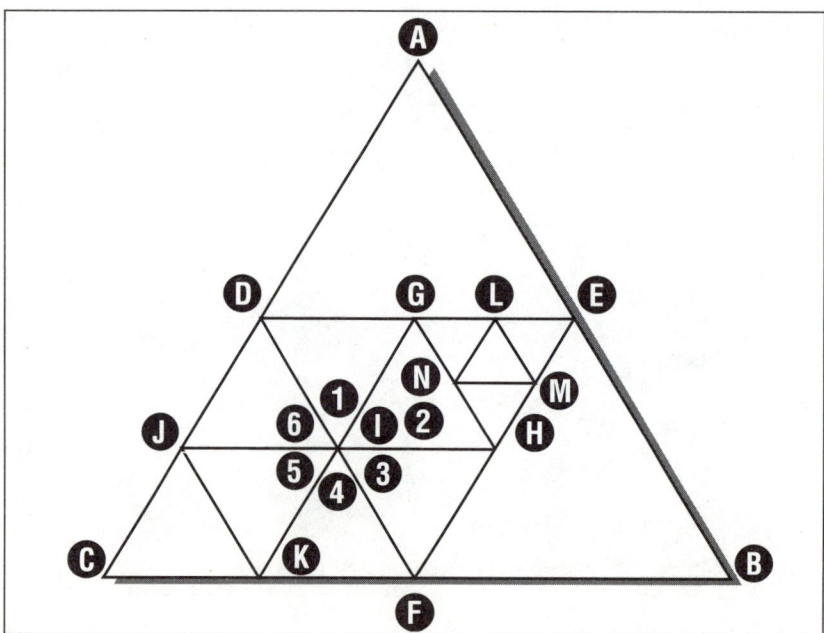

Figure 8.5
How triangles "fight" over edges.

It's far simpler to define a special value that only uninitialized vertices will have and make **FractureTriangle**() look to see if any given midpoint has already been set. If a midpoint has been set, **FractureTriangle**() uses that height; if no midpoint has been set, **FractureTriangle**() gives it a new height. It may be a *bit* slower to calculate and look up the midpoints of inside triangles than simply to pass in the right arguments, but the code is smaller and clearer—and displaying a landscape certainly takes *much* longer than generating it.

A Triangular Array

Now, when we bend a line, we are only changing the midpoint's *z* value, so in principle, we could somehow use the [*x*, *y*] coordinate pair as an index into a table of *z* values. However, this would turn out to be a *very* sparse array, and the code will run a lot faster if we can use a normal, contiguous array than if we have to keep walking a sparse array's lists. This is why Listing 8.1 defines a system of 2D logical addresses—the **TVertex** data type—which "name" the actual 3D coordinates in the **TTriple** data type.

Listing 8.1 GLOBAL.PAS.

```
unit Global; {Fractal Landscapes 3.0-Copyright © 1987..1997, Jon
              Shemitz}

interface

uses WinTypes;

type
  Int16 = {$ifdef Ver80} integer {$else} SmallInt {$endif} ;

const
  MaxPlys                = 8;
  MaxEdgeLength          = 1 shl (MaxPlys - 1);
  UnitLength: LongInt    = 5000;
  ShadesOfGray           = 64;

type
  TCoordinate = -30000..30000;
```

```
  TTriple = record
            X,              { Width:  0 (left) to UnitLength (right)      }
            Y,              { Depth:  0 (front) to VanishingPoint.Y (back) }
            Z: TCoordinate; { Height: 0 (bottom) to UnitLength (top)       }
            end;

function Triple(X, Y, Z: TCoordinate): TTriple;

type
  TPixel = TPoint;

type
  GridCoordinate = 0..MaxEdgeLength; { Triangular grid space }
  TVertex = record
            AB, BC, CA: GridCoordinate;
            end;

function Vertex(AB, BC, CA: GridCoordinate): TVertex;

type
  DrawModes = (dmOutline, dmFill, dmRender);
  DrawRates = (drLow, drMedium, drHigh);

const
  Envelope = 3000;
  SeaLevel: word = 100;      { 0 (bottom) to UnitLength (top) }
  VanishingPoint: TTriple = ( X:  1500 ;
                              Y: 25000 ; { Apparent depth of vanishing
                                           point }
                              Z: 15000 );
  LightSource: TTriple = ( X:  2500;
                           Y: +7500;
                           Z: 25000 );
  DrawMode: DrawModes    = dmOutline;
  DrawRate: DrawRates    = drHigh;

const
  Uninitialized = -30000;

var
  A, B, C: TVertex;
  Plys:      1..MaxPlys;
  EdgeLength: Int16;

  DisplayHeight,
  DisplayWidth: Int16;
```

3D Fractal Landscapes

```
implementation

function Triple(X, Y, Z: TCoordinate): TTriple;
begin
  Result.X := X;
  Result.Y := Y;
  Result.Z := Z;
end;

function Vertex(AB, BC, CA: GridCoordinate): TVertex;
begin
  Result.AB := AB;
  Result.BC := BC;
  Result.CA := CA;
end;

end.
```

Perhaps the simplest naming scheme is to simply number each vertex along the outermost triangle's three edges, as in the left half of Figure 8.6, and use all three coordinates to refer to each edge. While we really only need two coordinates and the third is redundant, I find it a bit clearer to be able to refer to the three outermost vertices as [1, 0, 0], [0, 1, 0], and [0, 0, 1] rather than as [1, 0], [0, 1], and [0, 0]. That's why a **TVertex** is defined as a coordinate triple, even though the third coordinate is not really necessary and does slow things down somewhat.

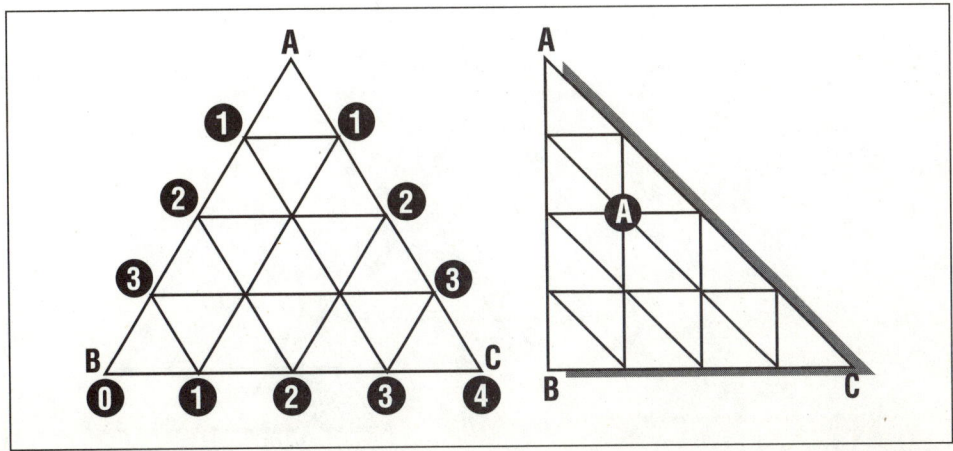

Figure 8.6
Storing vertices in a "square" array.

When it comes to the database of vertices, though, the third coordinate *is* ignored. As you can see from the right half of Figure 8.6, each vertex has the same coordinates if we make the equilateral triangle into an isosceles triangle. This lets us use the AB and BC coordinates much as if they were the normal row and column coordinates of a square array.

However, if we *did* store our triangular array in a square array, we would be wasting nearly half the space. This wouldn't be such a big deal, except that in 16-bit segmented environments we run smack into the 64K segment size barrier. Each **TTriple** consists of three 16-bit fixed-point numbers, so a square array for an eight-ply database (Figure 8.7) would take $(2^{8-1}+1)^2$ vertices, or 99,846 bytes. If we store only the cells on and below the diagonal, we can pare this to 50,310 bytes. This lets us use simple array indexing instead of arrays or huge pointers. Similarly, at least in this demo program, the database will fit in the data segment, which does make for faster access than if we had to use heap blocks and pointers.

Since eight ply is hardly too fine a resolution for, say, a 1280 × 1024 screen, the demo program for this chapter, Fractal Landscapes 3.0 (a.k.a. FL3, a Delphi port of a Windows port of a DOS program, which was originally written as a "cute hack" in Turbo Pascal 4.0) uses the triangular database code in Listing 8.2. The basic idea is that each row of vertices follows right after the previous row. Since there is only one vertex on the first row, the second row starts in **DB**'s second "cell." Since the second row has two vertices, the third row starts in **DB**'s fourth cell, and so on.

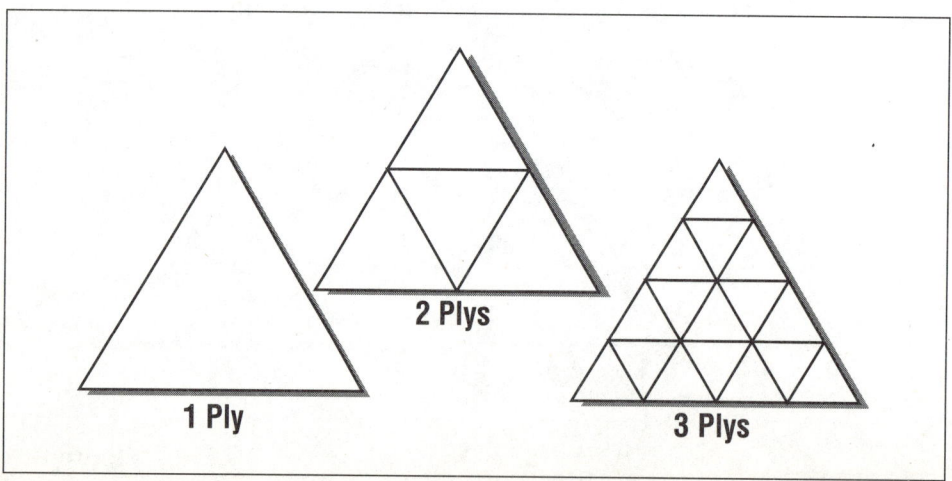

Figure 8.7
Ply versus number of triangles.

Listing 8.2   DATABASE.PAS.

```pascal
unit Database; {Fractal Landscapes 3.0—Copyright © 1987..1997, Jon
  Shemitz}

{Database and landscape generation}

interface

uses SysUtils, Global;

{ Misc math fns and such }

function IDIV(Numerator: LongInt; Denominator: Int16): Int16;
{$ifdef Ver80} {Delphi 1.0 still supported InLine fns}
InLine(
        $5B /                   { POP   BX ; Denominator    }
        $58 /                   { POP   AX ; Lo word of Num }
        $5A /                   { POP   DX ; Hi word of Num }
        $F7 / $FB               { IDIV  BX ; Mixed DIV      }
      );
{$endif}

function IMUL(A, B: Int16): LongInt;
{$ifdef Ver80} {Delphi 1.0 still supported InLine fns}
InLine(
        $5B /                   { POP   BX }
        $58 /                   { POP   AX }
        $F7 / $EB               { IMUL  BX }
      );
{$endif}

function Rand(Envelope: integer): integer;

{database}

procedure ResetDB;

function GetTriple(const V: TVertex): TTriple; { DB[V] }

procedure SwapTriples(var A, B: TTriple);

function Midpoint(A, B: TVertex): TVertex;

function LoadLandscape(const FileName: TFileName): boolean;
```

```pascal
function SaveLandscape(const FileName: TFileName): boolean;

{calculation}

procedure FractureTriangle(const A, B, C: TVertex; Plys: word);

function Unscale(ScaledCoordinate: LongInt): TCoordinate;
{$ifdef Ver80} {Delphi 1.0 still supported InLine fns}
InLine(
        $58 /                         { POP   AX              ; Lo word of SC   }
        $5A /                         { POP   DX              ; Hi word of SC   }
        $8B / $1E / UnitLength /      { MOV   BX,[UnitLength] ; Lo word of
scale }
        $F7 / $FB                     { IDIV  BX              ; Unscale         }
      );
{$endif}

implementation

{ Misc math fns and such }

{$ifNdef Ver80} {32-bit Delphi  doesn't support InLine fns}
function IDIV(Numerator: LongInt; Denominator: Int16): Int16;
begin
  Result := Numerator div Denominator;
end;
{$endif}

{$ifNdef Ver80} {32-bit Delphi  doesn't support InLine fns}
function IMUL(A, B: Int16): LongInt;
begin
  Result := Longint(A) * B;
end;
{$endif}

function Rand(Envelope: integer): integer;
{ Pseudonormal distribution, in range Envelope }
begin
  Rand := integer(Random(Envelope)) + integer(Random(Envelope)) -
                Envelope;
end;
```

3D Fractal Landscapes

```
{$ifNdef Ver80} {32-bit Delphi  doesn't support InLine fns}
function Unscale(ScaledCoordinate: LongInt): TCoordinate;
begin
  Result := ScaledCoordinate div UnitLength;
end;
{$endif}

{ Database }

var
  DB: array[0..8384] of TTriple; { Triangular array: Vertices(MEL+1)
                                      entries }

  NumberOfVertices, TopRow: word;

  Envelopes:   array[1..MaxPlys] of word;

function Vertices(N: word): word;
{ Vertices in an equilateral triangle with edgelength = N-1 }
begin
  Vertices := (Sqr(N) + N) shr 1;
end;

function Midpoint(A, B: TVertex): TVertex;
begin
  Result := Vertex( (A.AB + B.AB) shr 1, { Average }
                    (A.BC + B.BC) shr 1,
                    (A.CA + B.CA) shr 1 );
end;

function Loc(const V: TVertex): word;
begin
  Loc := NumberOfVertices - Vertices(TopRow - V.AB) + V.BC;
  {         ^^^^^^^^^^^^^^^^^ This is actually NOT necessary and just
                              wastes cycles, but I have retained it
                              for compatability with FL2.FL files. }

end;

procedure SetTriple(var V: TVertex; var T: TTriple);    { DB[V] := T }
begin
  DB[Loc(V)] := T;
end;

function GetTriple(const V: TVertex): TTriple; { DB[V] }
```

Chapter 8

```pascal
begin
  Result := DB[Loc(V)];
end;

procedure SwapTriples(var A, B: TTriple);
var
  Tmp: TTriple;
begin
  Tmp := A; A := B; B := Tmp;
end;

procedure SwapZ(var A, B: TTriple);
var
  C: TCoordinate;
begin
  C := A.Z; A.Z := B.Z; B.Z := C;
end;

const
  Uninitialized = -30000;

procedure ResetDB;
var
  T:            TTriple;
  R, Theta:     double;
  I, Offset:    integer;
  tA, tB, tC: TTriple;
const
  Base_Rotation = - Pi / 2.1; {Rotate point counterclockwise a bit}
  RotateBy      = Pi * 2 / 3; {120°}
begin
  { Set Plys dependent stuff }
  EdgeLength := 1 shl (Plys - 1);
  TopRow := EdgeLength + 1; { A "fencepost" situation }
  NumberOfVertices := Vertices(TopRow);
  for I := Plys downto 1 do
    Envelopes[I] := Envelope shr Succ(Plys - I);
  { Then reset NumberOfVertices vertices in DB }
  T.X := Uninitialized;
  T.Y := Uninitialized;
  T.Z := Uninitialized;
  for I := Low(DB) to High(DB) do DB[I] := T;
  { Now, set "defining" (outside) points A, B, and C }
  A.AB := 0;           A.BC := EdgeLength; A.CA := 0;
  B.AB := 0;           B.BC := 0;          B.CA := EdgeLength;
  C.AB := EdgeLength;  C.BC := 0;          C.CA := 0;
```

```
  { Then, assign them triples }
  Offset := UnitLength div 2;
  R      := UnitLength / 2;

  Theta := Base_Rotation;
  tA := Triple( Round(R * Cos(Theta)) + Offset,
                Round(R * Sin(Theta)) + Offset,
                SeaLevel + Rand(Envelope) );

  Theta := Theta + RotateBy;
  tB := Triple( Round(R * Cos(Theta)) + Offset,
                Round(R * Sin(Theta)) + Offset,
                SeaLevel + Rand(Envelope) );

  Theta := Theta + RotateBy;
  tC := Triple( Round(R * Cos(Theta)) + Offset,
                Round(R * Sin(Theta)) + Offset,
                SeaLevel + Rand(Envelope) );

  { At least one point above sealevel }
  if (tA.Z < SeaLevel) AND (tB.Z < SeaLevel) AND (tC.Z < SeaLevel) then
    repeat
      tB.Z := SeaLevel + Rand(Envelope);
    until tB.Z > SeaLevel;
  { Force A the lowest ... }
  if tA.Z > tB.Z then SwapZ(tA, tB);
  if tA.Z > tC.Z then SwapZ(tA, tC);

  SetTriple(A, tA);
  SetTriple(B, tB);
  SetTriple(C, tC);
end;

function SaveLandscape(const FileName: TFileName): boolean;
var
  Handle: integer;
begin
  Result := False;
  try
    Handle := FileCreate(FileName);
    try
      Result := (FileWrite(Handle, Plys, SizeOf(Plys)) = SizeOf(Plys))
                and
                (FileWrite(Handle, DB, NumberOfVertices *
                  SizeOf(TTriple))
                  = NumberOfVertices * SizeOf(TTriple));
```

```pascal
      finally
        FileClose(Handle);
      end;
    except
      on {any} Exception do Result := False;
    end;
end;

function LoadLandscape(const FileName: TFileName): boolean;
var
  Handle:  integer;
begin
  Result := False;
  try
    Handle := SysUtils.FileOpen(FileName, fmOpenRead);
    try
      if FileRead(Handle, Plys, SizeOf(Plys)) = SizeOf(Plys) then
        begin
        ResetDB;
        LoadLandscape := FileRead( Handle, DB,
                            NumberOfVertices * SizeOf(TTriple))
                       = NumberOfVertices * SizeOf(TTriple);
        end;
    finally
      FileClose(Handle);
    end;
  except
    on {any} Exception do Result := False;
  end;
end;

{ Action }

procedure FractureLine( var vM: TVertex;
                        const vA, vB: TVertex;
                        Envelope: integer );
var
  A, B, M: TTriple;
begin
  vM := Midpoint(vA, vB);
  M  := GetTriple(vM);
  if M.X = Uninitialized then { Not set yet }
    begin
    A := GetTriple(vA); B := GetTriple(vB);
    M := Triple( A.X + (B.X - A.X) div 2,
                 A.Y + (B.Y - A.Y) div 2,
                 A.Z + (B.Z - A.Z) div 2 + Rand(Envelope) );
```

```
      { Mean height _ Random(Envelope) }
      SetTriple(vM, M);
      end;
end;

procedure FractureTriangle(const A, B, C: TVertex; Plys: word);
var
  Envelope: word;
  AB, BC, CA: TVertex;
begin
  if Plys > 1 then
    begin
    Envelope := Envelopes[Plys];
    FractureLine(AB, A, B, Envelope);
    FractureLine(BC, B, C, Envelope);
    FractureLine(CA, C, A, Envelope);
    Dec(Plys);
    FractureTriangle(CA, BC, C, Plys);
    FractureTriangle(AB, B, BC, Plys);
    FractureTriangle(BC, CA, AB, Plys);
    FractureTriangle(A, AB, CA, Plys);
    end;
end;

end.
```

Bending

Another subtlety that I didn't discover until I actually wrote the code is that you shouldn't apply the same amount of randomness when you bend the larger-scale lines as when you bend the smaller-scale lines. If you do, you either end up with a bumpy plane or a spiky landscape. You need to apply more randomness to the large outer triangles, which produce the overall shape of the landscape, and to apply less randomness to the smaller inner triangles, which basically control the smoothness of your landscape.

What I ended up using is a function that generates something vaguely like a normal distribution:

```
function Rand(Envelope: integer): integer;
{ Pseudonormal (sawtooth) distribution,
  in range ±Envelope }
```

```
begin
  Rand := integer(Random(Envelope)) +
          integer(Random(Envelope)) -
          Envelope;
end;
```

Here, the **Envelope** value for each ply is half that of the next larger ply. This certainly produces plausible-looking landscapes, but real landscapes aren't always as smooth as FL3s. Real landscapes do have the occasional sharp edge—cliffs, mesas, canyons, and so on—while FL3 never really produces anything more abrupt than a steep slope.

One approach you may want to experiment with is to replace **Rand**'s pseudonormal distribution within a constricting envelope with an exponential function. On smaller scales, the function would be more *likely* to produce a number close to 0 than on larger scales, but it might throw out a large number on any scale.

Draw, Then Display

In the first incarnation of this program, the same recursive routine that built the landscape was responsible for drawing it. If the **Plys** argument was greater than 1, it broke its input triangle into four new triangles, and then decremented **Plys** and applied itself to each new triangle. When the **Plys** argument was equal to 1, it called a routine that drew the triangle.

This was certainly simple enough, but it meant that changing from a "wire mesh" rendering to a filled-triangle rendering required generating a whole new landscape. Similarly, using this simple design in a Windows version would mean that changing the window size also generates a whole new landscape. Clearly, a better approach is to generate the landscape first and then draw it. This requires two parallel recursions from the outermost triangle to the innermost ones (which are the only ones which are actually drawn), but the second recursion doesn't cost much compared to actually drawing the rectangles, so the price of flexibility is fairly low.

Generating And Displaying The Landscape

After all that prologue, the actual generation code may seem refreshingly simple. **FractureTriangle**() (present in Listing 8.2) takes a triangle and the number of **Plys** remaining. If **Plys** is greater than 1, **FractureTriangle**() calls **FractureLine**() to create (or retrieve) a midpoint value, then calls itself on each of the four triangles that these midpoints define. **FractureLine**() calls **Midpoint**() (both in Listing 8.2) to calculate the vertex between its two input vertices, and then checks to see if it has been set yet. If the midpoint is still uninitialized, **FractureLine**() bends the line between the endpoints by raising or lowering its midpoint.

Once the landscape has been generated, FL3 uses the code in Listing 8.3 to display it in the current window, in the current display mode. If the user changes the window size or the display mode, FL3 redraws the landscape.

Listing 8.3   DISPLAY.PAS.

```
unit Display; {Fractal Landscapes 3.0—Copyright © 1987..1997, Jon
  Shemitz}

interface

uses WinTypes, WinProcs,
     SysUtils, Graphics, Forms,
     Global, Database;

const
  DrawingNow: boolean = False;
  AbortDraw:  boolean = False;

type
  EAbortedDrawing = class (Exception) end;

procedure ScreenColors;

procedure PrinterColors;

procedure DrawTriangle(       Canvas:   TCanvas;
                        const A, B, C:  TVertex;
                              Plys:     word;
                              PointDn:  boolean);
```

```pascal
procedure DrawVerticals(Canvas: TCanvas);

{$ifdef Debug}
const DebugString: string = '';
{$endif}
implementation

uses Main;

type
  Surfaces = record
             Outline, Fill: TColor;
             end;

const
  scrnLand:     Surfaces = (Outline: clLime;  Fill: clGreen);
  scrnWater:    Surfaces = (Outline: clBlue;  Fill: clNavy);
  scrnVertical: Surfaces = (Outline: clGray;  Fill: clSilver);

  prnLand:     Surfaces = (Outline: clBlack; Fill: clWhite);
  prnWater:    Surfaces = (Outline: clBlack; Fill: clWhite);
  prnVertical: Surfaces = (Outline: clBlack; Fill: clWhite);

var
  Land, Water, Vertical: Surfaces;

procedure ScreenColors;
begin
  Land     := scrnLand;
  Water    := scrnWater;
  Vertical := scrnVertical;
end;

procedure PrinterColors;
begin
  Land     := prnLand;
  Water    := prnWater;
  Vertical := prnVertical;
end;

function Surface(Outline, Fill: TColor): Surfaces;
begin
  Result.Outline := Outline;
  Result.Fill    := Fill;
end;
```

```
{ $define Pascal} {$define Float}
{$ifdef Pascal}
  {$ifdef Float}
  type
    TFloatTriple = record X, Y, Z: double; end;

  function FloatTriple(T: TTriple): TFloatTriple;
  begin
    Result.X := T.X / UnitLength;
    Result.Y := T.Y / UnitLength;
    Result.Z := T.Z / UnitLength;
  end;

  function Project(const P: TTriple): TPixel; { 3D transform a point }
  var
    Delta_Y: double;
    Tr, V:   TFloatTriple;
  begin
    Tr := FloatTriple(P);
    V  := FloatTriple(VanishingPoint);

    Delta_Y  := Tr.Y / V.Y;
    Result.X := Round( DisplayWidth *
                    ((V.X - Tr.X) * Delta_Y + Tr.X));
    Result.Y := DisplayHeight -
                Round( DisplayHeight *
                    ((V.Z - Tr.Z) * Delta_Y + Tr.Z));
  end;
  {$else}
  function Project(const Tr: TTriple): TPixel; { 3D transform a point }
  var
    Delta_Y: integer;
  begin
    Delta_Y := MulDiv(Tr.Y, UnitLength, VanishingPoint.Y);
    Result.X := MulDiv( MulDiv( VanishingPoint.X - Tr.X,
                            Delta_Y, UnitLength) + Tr.X,
                            DisplayWidth, UnitLength);
    Result.Y := DisplayHeight -
                MulDiv( MulDiv( VanishingPoint.Z - Tr.Z,
                            Delta_Y, UnitLength) + Tr.Z,
                            DisplayHeight, UnitLength );
  end;
  {$endif}
```

```
{$else}
function Project(const Tr: TTriple): TPixel; assembler; {3D transform a
                                                                 point}
asm
{$ifdef Ver80} {Delphi 1.0; 16-bit}
        les     di,[Tr]
        mov     si,word ptr UnitLength   { Scaling factor }

        mov     ax,[TTriple ptr es:di].Y{ Tr.Y }
        imul    si                       { Scale by LoWord(UnitLength) }
        idiv    VanishingPoint.Y         { Scaled(depth/vanishing.depth) }
{DeltaY         equ     bx }
        mov     bx,ax                    { preserve Delta.Y }

        mov     ax,VanishingPoint.Z
        sub     ax,[TTriple ptr es:di].Z{ Delta.Z }
        imul    bx                       { Delta.Z * Delta.Y }
        idiv    si                       { Unscale(Delta.Z * Delta.Y) }
        add     ax,[TTriple ptr es:di].Z{ Tr.Z + Unscale(Delta.Z *
                                                  Delta.Y) }
        mov     cx,[DisplayHeight]       { We'll use it twice here ... }
        imul    cx                       { (Tr.Z+Delta.Z*Delta.Y)*Screen.Row }
        idiv    si                       { Unscale }
        sub     cx,ax                    { Px.Y }

        mov     ax,VanishingPoint.X
        sub     ax,[TTriple ptr es:di].X{ Delta.X }
        imul    bx                       { Delta.X * Delta.Y }
        idiv    si                       { Unscale(Delta.X * Delta.Y) }
        add     ax,[TTriple ptr es:di].X { Tr.X + Unscale(Delta.X * Delta.Y) }
        imul    [DisplayWidth]           { (Tr.X+Delta.X*Delta.Y)*Screen.Col }
        idiv    si                       { Px.X := Unscale(above) }

        mov     dx,cx                    {Return (X,Y) in ax:dx}
{$else} {Delphi 2.0 or better; 32-bit}
        push    ebx                      { Delphi 2.0 requires that we }
        push    esi                      { preserve these registers    }
        push    edi
        mov     edi,eax                  { lea edi,[Tr]}
        push    edx                      { Save @ Result }
        mov     si,word ptr UnitLength   { Scaling factor }

        mov     ax,TTriple[edi].Y        { Tr.Y }
        imul    si                       { Scale by LoWord(UnitLength) }
        idiv    VanishingPoint.Y         { Scaled(depth/vanishing.depth) }
{DeltaY equ     bx }
```

```
        mov     bx,ax                       { preserve Delta.Y }

        mov     ax,VanishingPoint.Z
        sub     ax,TTriple[edi].Z           { Delta.Z }
        imul    bx                          { Delta.Z * Delta.Y }
        idiv    si                          { Unscale(Delta.Z * Delta.Y) }
        add     ax,TTriple[edi].Z           { Tr.Z + Unscale(Delta.Z *
                                              Delta.Y) }
        mov     cx,[DisplayHeight]          { We'll use it twice here ... }
        imul    cx                          {
                                            (Tr.Z+Delta.Z*Delta.Y)*Screen.Row }
        idiv    si                          { Unscale }
        sub     cx,ax                       { Px.Y }

        mov     ax,VanishingPoint.X
        sub     ax,TTriple[edi].X           { Delta.X }
        imul    bx                          { Delta.X * Delta.Y }
        idiv    si                          { Unscale(Delta.X * Delta.Y) }
        add     ax,TTriple[edi].X           { Tr.X + Unscale(Delta.X *
                                              Delta.Y) }
        imul    [DisplayWidth]              {
                                            (Tr.X+Delta.X*Delta.Y)*Screen.Col }
        idiv    si                          { Px.X := Unscale(above) }
// Now ax=x, cx=y; we want to make them longints and save them to Result
        mov     ebx,$0000FFFF
        and     eax,ebx                     {clear the high word}
        and     ecx,ebx
        pop     edx                         { restore @ Result }
        mov     TPixel[edx].X,eax
        mov     TPixel[edx].Y,ecx
        pop     edi
        pop     esi
        pop     ebx
{$endif}
end;
{$endif}

procedure DrawPixels(const Canvas:        TCanvas;
                     const A, B, C, D:    TPixel;
                     const N:             word;
                     const Surface:       Surfaces);
```

```
begin
  if AbortDraw then raise EAbortedDrawing.Create('');

  Canvas.Pen.Color := Surface.Outline;
  if DrawMode = dmOutline
    then if N = 3
      then Canvas.PolyLine( [A, B, C, A] )
      else Canvas.PolyLine( [A, B, C, D, A] )
    else begin
        Canvas.Brush.Color := Surface.Fill;
        if N = 3
          then Canvas.Polygon( [A, B, C] )
          else Canvas.Polygon( [A, B, C, D] )
        end;
end;

procedure CalcCrossing(var Low, High, Crossing: TTriple;
  SetLow: boolean);
var
  CrossOverRatio: LongInt;
begin
CrossOverRatio := (SeaLevel - Low.Z) *
  UnitLength div (High.Z - Low.Z);
{ Distance of crossing point from A, as ratio of total line AB length, }
   { times UnitLength                                                  }
   Crossing := Triple( Low.X + Unscale((High.X - Low.X) *
                       CrossOverRatio),
                       Low.Y + Unscale((High.Y - Low.Y) *
                       CrossOverRatio),
                       SeaLevel );
   if SetLow then Low.Z := SeaLevel;
end;

procedure DrawVertical(Canvas: TCanvas; const A, B: TTriple;
                                        var pA, pB: TPixel);
var
  pC, pD: TPixel;
  tC, tD: TTriple;
begin
  tC   := A;
  tC.Z := SeaLevel;
  pC   := Project(tC);

  tD   := B;
  tD.Z := SeaLevel;
  pD   := Project(tD);
```

```
      DrawPixels(Canvas, pA, pB, pD, pC, 4, Vertical);
end;

procedure DrawVerticals(Canvas: TCanvas);
type
  Triad = record
          T: TTriple;
          V: TVertex;
          P: TPixel;
          end;
var
  Work: Triad;

  procedure Step( const Start: TVertex;
                  var Front:   Triad;
                  var StepDn:  GridCoordinate
                );
  var
    Idx: word;
    Back, Interpolate: Triad;
  begin
    Back.V := Start;
    Back.T := GetTriple(Back.V);
    if Back.T.Z > SeaLevel then Back.P := Project(Back.T);
    for Idx := 1 to EdgeLength do
      begin
      Front.V := Back.V;
      Inc(Work.V.BC);
      Dec(StepDn);
      Front.T := GetTriple(Front.V);
      if Front.T.Z > SeaLevel then Front.P := Project(Front.T);
      case (ord(Back.T.Z > SeaLevel) shl 1) + ord(Front.T.Z > SeaLevel)
        of
        1: begin { Back below, front above }
           CalcCrossing(Back.T, Front.T, Interpolate.T, False);
           Interpolate.P := Project(Interpolate.T);
           DrawVertical(Canvas, Interpolate.T, Front.T, Interpolate.P,
              Front.P);
           end;
        2: begin { Back above, front below }
           CalcCrossing(Front.T, Back.T, Interpolate.T, False);
           Interpolate.P := Project(Interpolate.T);
           DrawVertical(Canvas, Back.T, Interpolate.T, Back.P,
              Interpolate.P);
           end;
```

```
            3: DrawVertical(Canvas, Back.T, Front.T, Back.P, Front.P);
                  { Both above }
          end;
        Back := Front;
        end;
    end;

begin
  Step(C, Work, Work.V.AB );
  Step(B, Work, Work.V.CA );
end;

  function InnerProduct({const} A, B: TTriple): LongInt;
  begin
    InnerProduct := IMUL(A.X, B.X) + IMUL(A.Y, B.Y) + IMUL(A.Z, B.Z) ;
    { Damn but this >should< be Unscaled ...                          }
  end;

  function Delta(A, B: TTriple): TTriple;
  begin
    Result := Triple(A.X - B.X, A.Y - B.Y, A.Z - B.Z);
  end;

function LandColor(const A, B, C: TTriple): TColor;
var
  Center, ToA, ToLight: TTriple;
  Cos, Angle:          double;
  GrayLevel:           integer;
begin
  Center := Triple( (A.X + B.X + C.X) div 3,
                    (A.Y + B.Y + C.Y) div 3,
                    (A.Z + B.Z + C.Z) div 3 );
  ToA := Delta(A, Center);
  ToLight := Delta(Center, LightSource);

  {$ifopt R-} {$define ResetR} {$endif}
  {$R+}
    try
      Cos := InnerProduct(ToA, ToLight) /
             (Sqrt({Abs(}InnerProduct(ToA, ToA){)}) *
              Sqrt({Abs(}InnerProduct(ToLight, ToLight){)}) );
      try
        Angle := ArcTan (Sqrt (1 - Sqr (Cos)) / Cos);
```

```
    except
      on Exception do Angle := Pi / 2; {ArcCos(0)}
    end;
    {$ifdef HighContrast}
    GrayLevel := 255 - Round(255 * (Abs(Angle) / (Pi / 2)));
    {$else}
    GrayLevel := 235 - Round(180 * (Abs(Angle) / (Pi / 2)));
    {$endif}
  except
    on {any} Exception do GrayLevel := 255; {division by 0 ...}
  end;
{$ifdef ResetR} {$R-} {$undef ResetR} {$endif}

  Result := PaletteRGB(GrayLevel, GrayLevel, GrayLevel);
end;

procedure Draw3Vertices( Canvas: TCanvas;
                         const A, B, C: TVertex; Display: boolean);
var
  Color: TColor;
  pA, pB, pC, pD, pE: TPixel;
  tA, tB, tC, tD, tE: TTriple;
  aBelow, bBelow, cBelow: boolean;
begin
  tA := GetTriple(A); tB := GetTriple(B); tC := GetTriple(C);
  {$ifdef FloatingTriangles}
  ta.z := ta.z + random(Envelope shr Plys) - random(Envelope shr Plys);
  tb.z := tb.z + random(Envelope shr Plys) - random(Envelope shr Plys);
  tc.z := tc.z + random(Envelope shr Plys) - random(Envelope shr Plys);
  {$endif}
  aBelow := tA.Z <= SeaLevel;
  bBelow := tB.Z <= SeaLevel;
  cBelow := tC.Z <= SeaLevel;
  case ord(aBelow) + ord(bBelow) + ord(cBelow) of
    0:      if Display then {All above}
              begin
                pA := Project(tA); pB := Project(tB); pC := Project(tC);
                if DrawMode = dmRender
                  then begin
                    Color := LandColor(tA, tB, tC);
                    DrawPixels( Canvas,
                                pA, pB, pC, pC, 3, Surface(Color,
                                Color));
                  end
                  else DrawPixels( Canvas,
                                   pA, pB, pC, pC, 3, Land);
              end;
```

```
  3:         if Display then {All below}
               begin
               tA.Z := SeaLevel; tB.Z := SeaLevel; tC.Z := SeaLevel;
               pA := Project(tA); pB := Project(tB); pC := Project(tC);
               DrawPixels( Canvas, pA, pB, pC, pC, 3, Water);
               end;
  2:         begin {One vertex above water}
             { First ensure it's tA }
             if aBelow then
               if bBelow
                 then SwapTriples(tA, tC)
                 else SwapTriples(tA, tB);
             CalcCrossing(tB, tA, tD, True);
             CalcCrossing(tC, tA, tE, True);
             pA := Project(tA); pB := Project(tB); pC := Project(tC);
             pD := Project(tD); pE := Project(tE);
             DrawPixels( Canvas, pD, pB, pC, pE, 4, Water);
             if Drawmode = dmRender
               then begin
                    Color := LandColor(tD, tA, tE);
                    DrawPixels( Canvas, pD, pA, pE, pE, 3,
                                Surface(Color, Color));
                    end
               else DrawPixels( Canvas, pD, pA, pE, pE, 3, Land);
             end;
  1:         begin {One vertex below water}
             { First ensure it's tA }
             if bBelow
               then SwapTriples(tA, tB)
               else if cBelow then SwapTriples(tA, tC);
             CalcCrossing(tA, tB, tD, False);
             CalcCrossing(tA, tC, tE, True);
             pA := Project(tA); pB := Project(tB); pC := Project(tC);
             pD := Project(tD); pE := Project(tE);
             DrawPixels( Canvas, pD, pA, pE, pE, 3, Water);
             if DrawMode = dmRender
               then begin
                    Color := LandColor(tD, tB, tC);
                    DrawPixels( Canvas,
                                pD, pB, pC, pE, 4, Surface(Color,
                                Color));
                    end
               else DrawPixels( Canvas, pD, pB, pC, pE, 4, Land);
             end;
    end;
end;
```

```
procedure DrawTriangle(      Canvas:    TCanvas;
                       const A, B, C:   TVertex;
                             Plys:      word;
                             PointDn:   boolean);
var
  AB, BC, CA: TVertex;
begin
  if Plys = 1
    then Draw3Vertices(Canvas, A, B, C, (DrawMode <> dmOutline) OR
                                        PointDn)
    else
      begin
        AB := Midpoint(A, B);
        BC := Midpoint(B, C);
        CA := Midpoint(C, A);
        if Plys = 3 then FractalLandscape.DrewSomeTriangles(16);
        Dec(Plys);
        if PointDn
          then begin
                 DrawTriangle(Canvas, CA, BC, C, Plys, True);
                 DrawTriangle(Canvas, AB, B, BC, Plys, True);
                 DrawTriangle(Canvas, BC, CA, AB, Plys, False);
                 DrawTriangle(Canvas, A, AB, CA, Plys, True);
               end
          else begin
                 DrawTriangle(Canvas, A, CA, AB, Plys, False);
                 DrawTriangle(Canvas, BC, CA, AB, Plys, True);
                 DrawTriangle(Canvas, CA, C, BC, Plys, False);
                 DrawTriangle(Canvas, AB, BC, B, Plys, False);
               end;
      end;
end;

begin
  ScreenColors;
end.
```

There are three display modes: Outline, Filled, and Rendered. All three display the landscape as a collection of triangles by doing a single-point perspective transform of the triangle's three **TTriple**s to screen **TPixel**s, then doing either a **PolyLine** or **Polygon** draw. The only difference between the Outline mode and Filled and Rendered modes is that while Outline mode draws a simple "wire mesh" picture of the landscape with no hidden line removal, Filled and Rendered modes rely on drawing order and polygon filling to do a brute force hidden line removal. (This is the so-called Painter's Algorithm.) Rendered mode in turn differs from Filled mode in basing each triangle's color on the angle it presents to a ray from the "sun."

Draw3Vertices() implements a simplistic concept of "sea level" to lend a bit of verisimilitude to the display. Any triangle that's completely above sea level is drawn normally, while any triangle that's completely below sea level is drawn in blue, at sea level. If the triangle crosses sea level, FL3 interpolates the crossing points, and draws part of the triangle above water and part below. While this is plausible enough for "coastlines," it's a bit less plausible for lakes: FL3 doesn't detect the lowest lip of a basin, but colors as water only the part(s) of a basin that is under sea level.

Once all the triangles are drawn, FL3 draws vertical lines along the two front edges from sea level to any vertices which are above sea level. This is particularly effective in the two filled modes, where the filled vertical quadrilaterals obscure the underside of the landscape surface.

The Project() Routine

The **Project**() routine is the workhorse on which all drawing operations depend. It converts a 3D **TTriple** to a 2D **TPixel** using single-point perspective and the current window dimensions.

In effect, it draws a line through the point and a vanishing point, and marks the intersection of that line and the screen. Most of the complexity in Listing 8.3 comes from the use of fixed-point math. (This is primarily a legacy of FL3's origins in the days when floating-point math was very slow, but it *does* also serve to reduce the vertex database's size to the point where it fits in the data segment.) If we strip away the fixed point math, we end up with this:

```
{ 3D transform a point: }
function Project(const P: TTriple): TPixel;
var
  Ratio: double;
  Pt, V: TFloatTriple;
begin
  Pt := FloatTriple(P);
  V  := FloatTriple(VanishingPoint);
```

```
Ratio     := Pt.Y / V.Y;
Result.X  := Round( DisplayWidth *
                   ((V.X - Pt.X) * Ratio + Pt.X));
Result.Y  := DisplayHeight -
             Round( DisplayHeight *
                   ((V.Z - Pt.Z) * Ratio + Pt.Z));
end;
```

That is, it calculates the ratio of the point's depth to the vanishing point's depth, and applies this to the difference between the point's *x* and *z* coordinates and the vanishing point's *x* and *z* coordinates. Since the **TTriple** coordinate system ranges from 0 to 1, we simply can multiply the projected coordinates by the window size to obtain the proper screen coordinates.

Outline Mode

Outline mode is the simplest of all the drawing modes. It simply outlines "land" triangles in green and water triangles in blue. (See Figure 8.1; alas, we don't have color here.) About all that's really worth noting here is how simple and clear Delphi makes **DrawPixels**(). The API version of **DrawPixels** (for either C or Borland Pascal) would replace the single, simple statement **Canvas.PolyLine**([A, B, C, A]) with a local array declaration and four assignments—not to mention all the bother creating and destroying Windows device contexts (DCs) and pens.

Filled Mode

Outline mode is relatively fast and does a pretty good job of suggesting texture, but it has one big problem: You can see right through it. This means that the mesh on the backside of a hill, say, shows through to the front side.

Sophisticated graphics applications have complicated algorithms for "hidden line removal," but FL3 is *not* sophisticated, and relies on brute force techniques to remove hidden lines by drawing over them. (See Figure 8.2.)

That is, **DrawTriangle**() takes care to draw the rearmost triangles first, so that any triangles in front will be drawn later, obscuring the triangles in back. On the initial call to **DrawTriangle**(), the triangle is "point down." Vertex A is closest to the front and the bottom of the window, and B and C are in back, towards the top of the window. (See Figure 8.8.) Thus

```
DrawTriangle(Canvas, CA, BC, C, Plys, True);
DrawTriangle(Canvas, AB, B, BC, Plys, True);
DrawTriangle(Canvas, BC, CA, AB, Plys, False);
DrawTriangle(Canvas, A, AB, CA, Plys, True);
```

draws the leftmost subtriangle first, then the rightmost. Both of these "outside" subtriangles face the same way as triangle ABC, and the order of the parameters to the recursive call to **DrawTriangle**() ensures that the new A will also be in front, with the new B and C in back.

The third call draws the "inside" subtriangle, as this is visually in front of the second, right-most triangle. In every triangle, the inside subtriangle is upside down to its outer triangle, so on this initial call, the inside triangle is "point up." The parameter ordering ensures that on point-up calls, A is still the "point" facing up, with B and C in front, towards the bottom of the screen. If you step through **DrawTriangle**()'s **not PointDn** set of recursive calls, you'll see that point-up triangles are drawn back-to-front, right-to-left.

The fourth call draws the last, front-most subtriangle.

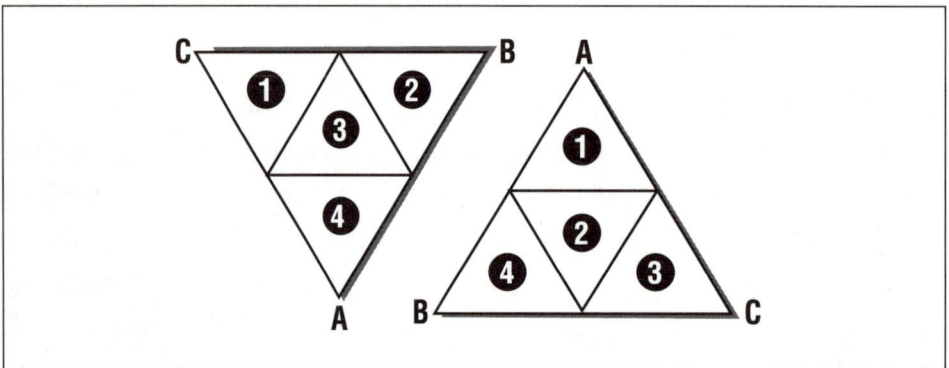

Figure 8.8
Drawing order and triangle orientation.

Rendered Mode

Rendered mode attempts to look more realistic than filled mode by coloring each triangle based on the angle between the triangle and a ray from the "sun," so that triangles orthogonal to the rays from the sun are lighter than triangles that present a more oblique angle to the sun's rays. (See Figure 8.3.) While it *does* seem to do a good job of showing, say, the curvature of a basin, overall it's a bit...gray. You may wish to experiment with a palette and some sort of **LandColor**() function that use a little false color.

Create Your Own Worlds

In summary, FL3 is a simple demo of fractal landscape generation techniques. You may wish to try to improve the random number distribution or the rendering code, or to modify the algorithm so as to generate entire fractal planets.

It may not be obvious that "plasma" routines are basically just rectangular versions of a fractal landscape generation algorithm: They fracture rectangles instead of triangles, and use color to show the third dimension instead of perspective.

The full source code suite, which includes all Delphi 3 files necessary to build and run Fractal Landscapes 3, is present on the CD-ROM in the directory for this chapter.

HIGH PERFORMANCE

Problems With Persistents, And Other Advice

CHAPTER 9

HIGH PERFORMANCE

*Sometimes you'll discover that Delphi sets a component property's value with its **read** method and not its **write** method. Creating these methods carelessly means big trouble! Jon and Ed share their thoughts on avoiding hassles like this and making the most of what Delphi offers.*

Problems With Persistents, And Other Advice

Jon Shemitz and Ed Jordan

Delphi properties have a simple, powerful interface: They look like variables, but you have full control over how (and whether) your class's users can read and write your class's properties. You can allow direct read access, just as if the property were a variable, or you can specify a **read** method that will be called whenever the property's value is read. You can allow direct write access, or you can specify a **write** method that will be called whenever the property's value is set.

Right?

Wrong.

Reading To Write?

What actually happens is this: While the simple model described above does apply in most cases, things get weird when the property is a **TPersistent** descendent like a **TBitmap** or a **TFont**. For **TPersistent** descendents, the **write** method is called when you set the property at design time or change it at runtime—but *not* when a component is created and loaded from its form's DFM stream. Instead, the runtime library calls the property's **read** method to get a pointer to the property's private field variable, then uses that pointer to call the property's read-from-stream method. The **write** method is not called when the component is loaded!

Of course, in most cases this doesn't matter—the property gets loaded, and it has the same value at runtime as it had at design time. However, there *are* a couple of ways this can affect you.

First, the **read** method should never return **Nil**. While it may seem sensible to use a strategy of not actually creating a private field variable until the **write** method supplies an actual value to copy, Delphi's component loading code is not quite smart enough to notice that it has no **TPersistent** to tell to load. If your **read** method returns **Nil**, you will get GPFs when the component is loaded. (For what it's worth, this behavior is what alerted me to the problem, though I'll confess that it took me a while to find out what was going on.)

Second, don't rely on your **write** method to extract information from the field variable and save it in runtime-only fields elsewhere in your component. The **write** method will be called when you set the property directly at design time or at runtime, but *not* when you indirectly set the property at component load time. If you expect your **write** method to update your component's internal state, your component will not load properly.

Reasonable Workarounds

Now, while this read-to-write behavior has lasted through three releases of Delphi, it's still not impossible that Borland will someday conclude that read-to-write *is* a bug, and will change this behavior in future releases of Delphi. That is, you should avoid any solutions to the problems of GPF-on-load or partial-loading that will fail if the **write** method *does* get called at component load time.

It's easy to prevent GPF-on-load in a "forward-compatible" way. We now know that if a **TPersistent** property is stored, Delphi will call its **read** method when the object is loaded from a stream. So, as shown in Listing 9.1, the object's **Create** constructor must create an object of the appropriate type, and set the property's private field variable. This *is* a bit wasteful if the property is not always set or stored, but a few hundred bytes of storage or a few hundred instructions of **Create** code are just plain insignificant to a 16 or 32MB Pentium.

Listing 9.1 PERSIST.SRC.

```
{interface}
type DemoComponent =
  class(TComponent)

    private
      fGlyph:        TBitmap;
      fGlyphWritten: boolean;
```

Problems With Persistents, And Other Advice

```
      procedure SetGlyph(Glyph: TBitmap); {not shown}

   protected
      constructor Create(Owner: TComponent); override;
      procedure Loaded; override;

   public

   published
      property Glyph: TBitmap read fGlyph write SetGlyph;

   end;

{implementation}

constructor DemoComponent.Create(Owner: TComponent);
begin
   inherited Create(Owner);
   fGlyph := TBitmap.Create;
   {Be sure to fill in the field with an empty object}
end;

procedure DemoComponent.SetGlyph(Glyph: TBitmap);
begin
   if fGlyph <> Glyph then     { fGlyph = Glyph when SetGlyph is  }
      begin                    { called by the Loaded procedure   }
      fGlyph.Free;     {Assign can fail if the target is not Empty:}
      fGlyph := TBitmap.Create; {Free/Create/Assign is a lot safer}
      fGlyph.Assign(Glyph);
      end;
   {Extract any necessary data ... set the PropertyWritten flag}
   fGlyphWritten := True;
end;

procedure DemoComponent.Loaded;
begin
   inherited Loaded; {Don't forget to do this!}
   if (not fGlyphWritten) and (not fGlyph.Empty) then
      SetGlyph(fGlyph); {Extract any necessary data from the bitmap}
end;
```

Partial-loading is a little more complex. Fortunately, Delphi components have a **Loaded** method which you can override to perform any necessary post-processing. You can overcome partial-loading by taking advantage of the **Loaded** method, and by making a few small changes to your code.

309

The first thing to do is to add an **fPropertyWritten** boolean flag for every **TPersistent** property that might be stored. (See Listing 9.1.) The flag will be set to **False** when the object is created, and should be set to **True** only by the **write** method.

Second, you must override (using the **override** directive) your component's **Loaded** method, and add a line like this

```
if not fPropertyWritten then
  SetProperty(fProperty);
```

so that **Loaded** calls your **write** method if (and *only* if) the component-loading code didn't call it.

Third, you generally *don't* want to **Assign** a **TPersistent** to itself, and you *certainly* don't want to **Free** it, **Create** a new instance, then **Assign** the old (freed) instance to the new instance. It's best to use code like that shown in Listing 9.2. This way, you only reset the private field variable if the new value does not equal the existing field. Adding this test ensures that **SetProperty(fProperty)** will not cause a GPF now, and won't constitute much overhead if read-to-write *does* go away.

Listing 9.2   PERSIST2.SRC.

```
if fProperty <> NewPropertyValue then
  begin
    fProperty.Free;                        {Assigning 'over' a }
    fProperty := TPropertyType.Create;     {TPersistent can fail:}
    fProperty.Assign(NewPropertyValue)     {Free/Create/Assign's safer}
  end;

{Extract any necessary data from NewPropertyValue}
fPropertyWritten := True;
```

A Little Perspective

My personal suspicion is that read-to-write is the result of a bit of overzealous optimization by the Delphi team. While it seems like it would be pretty hard to make a case for its not being a bug, whenever I run into a bug or bit of poor design in Delphi, I like to ask myself how many apps I've ever used or written that are more stable than Delphi, or have a higher ratio of good to bad design decisions. The answer is always "Few, if any."

It's also worth bearing in mind that the **write** method *is* called at load time for simple types like integers, enums, and strings—and that read-to-write for **TPersistent** objects and descendents is pretty easy to deal with.

Using RDTSC For Pentium Benchmarking

Back in ancient times, writing fast code wasn't just a matter of choosing the right algorithm; you had to know your instruction times, and you had to benchmark different sequences. Of course, because the system timer only ticked every 55 milliseconds, benchmarking meant either repeating your code hundreds of thousands of times, or pulling hackerish tricks like reading the timer chip's internal registers to get the time in 838 nanosecond increments.

Nowadays, of course, compilers are so good and processors are so fast that it's gotten pretty hard to come up with a piece of "brain-damaged" brute force code that's going to noticeably slow your programs. It seems more than a little ironic, then, that Intel waited for the Pentium to introduce a benchmarking instruction. RDTSC—Read Time Stamp Counter—returns the number of clock cycles since the CPU was powered up or reset. Where was RDTSC back when we *really* needed it?

Still, better late than never. RDTSC is a two-byte instruction: $0F 31. It returns a 64-bit count in EDX:EAX. Since the 8087 **comp** datatype is a 64-bit integer, we can use the Delphi code in Listing 9.3 to read the current value.

Listing 9.3   RDTSC.SRC.

```
const
   D32 = $66;

function RDTSC: comp;
var
    TimeStamp: record
                    case byte of
                        1: (Whole:  comp);
                        2: (Lo, Hi: LongInt);
                    end;
begin
   asm
```

```
            db $0F; db $31;      // BASM doesn't support RDTSC
            {Pentium RDTSC - Read Time Stamp Counter - instruction}
{$ifdef Cpu386}
            mov      [TimeStamp.Lo],eax   // the low dword
            mov      [TimeStamp.Hi],edx   // the high dword
{$else}
            db D32
            mov      word ptr TimeStamp.Lo,AX
            {mov     [TimeStamp.Lo],eax - the low dword}
            db D32
            mov      word ptr TimeStamp.Hi,DX
            {mov     [TimeStamp.Hi],edx - the high dword}
{$endif}
   end;
   Result := TimeStamp.Whole;
end;
```

One problem you may run into when you use RDTSC is that both **IntToStr** and **Format**('%d') can only handle **LongInt** values, not **comp** values. While you can pass a **comp** value to one of these functions, it cannot be any larger than **High(LongInt)**, which is 2,147,483,647. While that would be a mighty satisfying number of dollars to see on your brokerage statement, it's only a little over 16 seconds of clock ticks to a 133MHz Pentium. If you need to compare two long-running processes, the difference between the start ticks and the stop ticks can easily exceed **High(LongInt)**.

The key here is that while a **comp** is a 64-bit *integer*, it is actually an 80×87 datatype. To format a **comp** with **Format**(), we need to use the floating-point format types. The **CompToStr** function in Listing 9.4 hides the messy details, and using it will produce smaller object code than several inline **Format**() calls.

Listing 9.4   COMP2STR.SRC.

```
function CompToStr(N: comp): string;
begin
  Result := Format('%.0n', [N]);
end;
```

In the end, I guess you could say this is just another case of "The rich get richer"—we need to do a lot less benchmarking than we ever did before, while at the same time, the RDTSC instruction makes benchmarking easy and reliable.

And on that note, I turn control of this chapter over to my collaborator, Ed Jordan. Take it, Ed.

Drag-and-Drop Text For A Delphi Listbox

Thanks, Jon. When a user drags an item in Delphi, the mouse cursor changes; by default, it becomes an arrow with a small box clinging to its tail. Signifying drag and drop like this works with no fuss—after all, the mouse was going to be there anyway.

It is possible, however, to give users more assurance that something is happening. For example, when dragging an item from a listbox, the mouse could carry around a transparent image of the item text surrounded by a dotted rectangle. As it turns out, doing this in Delphi 3 is easy. Listing 9.5 presents the complete source code for a listbox component that adds the feature.

Unlike Delphi 1, Delphi 2 and 3 have built-in support for image dragging; all you need to do is supply the image. To supply an image, you draw the image on a bitmap, place the bitmap into a TImageList component, and then make the image list available to Delphi. Delphi code in the Controls unit is then responsible for drawing and erasing the image as the mouse moves.

As you can see in Listing 9.5, the listbox creates a private image list to hold the image. It creates this image list as soon as it can, but it doesn't add an image until a drag starts. The listbox senses the start of a drag by overriding the DoStartDrag method. It also overrides GetDragImages, since Delphi actually obtains the image list by calling that method.

Why wait until the last second to draw the image? Waiting lets you customize the drag image depending on which part of your control is moused around with. How could you know what text to draw on your bitmap, for example, if you tried to draw it before you knew which item was being dragged?

Listing 9.5 TXTDRGBX.PAS.

```
unit TxtDrgBx;

interface
uses
  Windows, Messages, SysUtils, Classes, Graphics, Controls,
  Forms, Dialogs, StdCtrls, ExtCtrls;

type
  TTextDragListBox = class( TListBox )
```

```pascal
  private
    FDragImage: TImageList;
  protected
    procedure CreateDragImage;
    procedure DoStartDrag( var DragObject: TDragObject );
      override;
  public
    constructor Create( AnOwner: TComponent ); override;
    destructor Destroy; override;
    function GetDragImages: TCustomImageList;
      override;
  end;

implementation

constructor TTextDragListBox.Create( AnOwner: TComponent );
begin
  inherited Create( AnOwner );
  ControlStyle := ControlStyle + [ csDisplayDragImage ];
  FDragImage := TImageList.CreateSize( 32, 32 );
end;

destructor TTextDragListBox.Destroy;
begin
  FDragImage.Free;
  inherited Destroy;
end;

procedure TTextDragListBox.CreateDragImage;
var
  Bitmap: TBitmap;           // The image to be dragged
  AnItemRect: TRect;         // Rectangle where item is located
  MousePt: TPoint;           // Location of mouse
begin
  // Empty the image list and exit if no item is selected
  FDragImage.Clear;
  if ItemIndex = -1 then Exit;

  // Create the bitmap, size it to the selected item, draw it
  AnItemRect := ItemRect( ItemIndex );
  Bitmap := TBitmap.Create;
  try
    with Bitmap do
    begin
      Width := AnItemRect.Right - AnItemRect.Left;
      Height := AnItemRect.Bottom - AnItemRect.Top;
```

```
      Canvas.Font := Font;
      Canvas.DrawFocusRect( Rect( 0, 0, Width, Height ) );
      Canvas.Brush.Style := bsClear;
      Canvas.TextOut( 1, 1, Items[ ItemIndex ] );

   // Size the image list, add the image, set transparent color
      FDragImage.Width := Width;
      FDragImage.Height := Height;
      FDragImage.AddMasked( Bitmap, clWhite );

   // .. Set the image hotspot
      GetCursorPos( MousePt );
      with ScreenToClient( MousePt ), AnItemRect do
        FDragImage.SetDragImage( 0, X - Left, Y - Top );
    end;
  finally
    Bitmap.Free;
  end;
end;

procedure TTextDragListBox.DoStartDrag( var DragObject:
  TDragObject );
begin
  inherited DoStartDrag( DragObject );
  CreateDragImage;
end;

function TTextDragListBox.GetDragImages: TCustomImageList;
begin
  Result := nil;
  if FDragImage.Count > 0 then Result := FDragImage;
end;

end.
```

The longest routine in Listing 9.5 is CreateDragImage, which shows how to work with an image list. After a bitmap is created and drawn, the image list is set to be the same size as the bitmap—always necessary!—and then the bitmap is added and the transparent color is set using the AddMasked method.

The SetDragImage call, two statements later, sets the image hotspot. The hotspot determines where the mouse will "hold" the image as it is dragged. Setting the hotspot ensures that if the mouse grabs the middle of the text rectangle, it will keep hold of the middle as it moves around.

These Delphi 2 and 3 techniques are certainly less direct than drawing on the screen, but they allow controls to cooperate in powerful ways. For example, when you drag an image from one list view to another, the second list view is able to hide the drag image, highlight its own target item, and then show the drag image again. And now any list view will do the same for items dragged from our listbox.

Making String Collections More List-Like

When I moved to Delphi from Borland Pascal, I wished that string lists were a little more like string collections—where were my **ForEach** iterators?

Now, though, as I port a Delphi application *back* to Turbo Vision, I'm wishing that string collections were a lot more like string lists.

Moving strings into and out of collections is like mixing concrete compared to the same smooth operations with lists—mainly because the new Object Pascal syntax is so much cleaner.

Compare this code, for adding an item to Turbo Vision collection

```
AStringColl^.AtInsert(AStringColl^.Count, NewStr(S));
S := PString(AStringColl^.At(Index))^;
```

to this code, which does the same thing for a Delphi string list

```
StringList.Add(S);
S := StringList[Index];
```

and you'll see what I mean. Not only are the string collection operations practically unreadable, the second line of code above is simply wrong. If the **PString** being indexed is **NIL**, signifying that we put an empty string into the collection, we'll read garbage into our string variable **S**.

Fortunately, a descendent of **TStringCollection** can make strings and collections mix more gracefully. The new object type shown in Listing 9.6 creates a pointer-safe **StrAt** method and a simple **Add** method. Now we can cleanly code things like this:

```
StrList^.Add(S);
S := StrList^.StrAt(Index);
```

And this similar syntax will ease our trips back and forth between the new and old worlds—as long as that old DOS world still matters.

Listing 9.6 STRLIST.PAS.

```
{ Create a friendlier, TStringList-like string collection.}
unit StrList;
interface
uses Objects;

type
  PStrListCollection = ^TStrListCollection;
  TStrListCollection = object(TStringCollection)
    function StrAt(Index: Integer): string;
    procedure Add(const S: string);
  end;

implementation

{ Translate a pointer into a string, handling the nil case. }
function PtrToStr(P: Pointer): string;
begin
  if P = nil then PtrToStr := '' else PtrToStr := PString(P)^;
end;

{ Safely return a string from the string collection. }
function TStrListCollection.StrAt(Index: Integer): string;
begin
  StrAt := PtrToStr(At(Index));
end;

{ Add a string to the end of the string collection. }
procedure TStrListCollection.Add(const S: string);
begin
  AtInsert(Count, NewStr(S));
end;

end.
```

Letting Delphi Applications Set Up Themselves

Since I develop shareware in Delphi, I wanted to use it to create a simple setup program for people who download my software from online services or bulletin boards. Unfortunately, because of the considerable resources Delphi provides nearly automatically, even a simple setup program can run nearly 200K (of course, the increase in program size levels off very quickly after that). Now, this size is unremarkable for a normal Windows application, but setup programs should be as small as possible—especially when the user is paying for every second of download time, or when I am paying to email a registered version to a subscriber.

Happily, though, I have hit on a way to use the full resources of Delphi for my setup program, with a minimal increase in download size: I use my main application as its own setup program. The application is initially named SETUP.EXE, and when run under that name, it installs itself. As far as users can tell, they are running a separate setup program. After installation, the program renames itself, and ceases to be an installer.

Here's how it works. Listing 9.7 shows the main block of a typical unmodified Delphi application's project (DPR) file. Listing 9.8 shows the same main block with additions that make it function as a setup program. Note that we test to see whether the application's .EXE name is SETUP.EXE—if it is, we run a form, or a series of forms, to let the user choose the program directory, program group, and other setup options.

Listing 9.7   BEFORE.SRC.

```
{ The main block of an application's DPR file, before
  being changed to function as a setup program. }
begin
  Application.Initialize;
  Application.CreateForm( TMainForm, MainForm );
  Application.Run;
end.
```

Listing 9.8   AFTER.SRC.

```
{ The main block of an application's DPR file, after being
  changed to function as a setup program. }
```

```
{ Note that SYSUTILS.PAS must be added to this unit's USES clause. }
begin
  Application.Initialize;
  if UpperCase( ExtractFileName( Application.ExeName ) ) =
     'SETUP.EXE' then
  begin
    Application.CreateForm( TSetupForm, SetupForm );
  end
  else
    Application.CreateForm( TMainForm, MainForm );
  Application.Run;
end.
```

Before I zip up my software (EXE file, help file, read-me file, and so on) to upload it, I rename my EXE file SETUP.EXE. After the user downloads the software, unzips it, and runs SETUP.EXE, the application copies itself and the auxiliary files to the final directory, renaming itself to its proper name. The next time it is run, it will find that it is *not* named SETUP.EXE, and so will behave normally.

In exchange for an inconsequentially small increase in program size and download time, users get a helpful setup program, and I get (I hope) a few more sales.

Using inherited With Redeclared Properties In Delphi

Suppose you're developing a Delphi VCL component—a descendent of **TDrawGrid**, let's say—and you need to take some special action when the component user (in this case, a programmer) changes the **ColCount** property. There are two ways to do this; the best way for you depends on whether you want mere notification of the change, or whether you want to control what the value of **ColCount** can be.

The **ColCount** property determines the number of columns in a grid. Like most properties, its value is stored in a private field (**FColCount**, in this case), and it is changed by way of a private access method (**SetColCount**). Thus, when a programmer writes

```
ColCount := AValue;
```

in his code, or when he changes **ColCount** in the Object Inspector at design time, **SetColCount** is called, and with the help of other private methods, changes the value of the **FColCount** field, and makes adjustments in the grid as needed. All this is encapsulated, out of reach.

But the original developers of **TDrawGrid** anticipated that developers of **TDrawGrid** descendents might want notification of a change in the number of columns—so after the change is made, but before it is shown, the **SizeChanged** method is called. **SizeChanged** is a dynamic method, which means we can override it, and our own **SizeChanged** will be called every time the number of columns (or the number of rows) changes. See Listing 9.9.

Listing 9.9 SIZECHAN.SRC.

```
{ A descendent of TDrawGrid that overrides the SizeChanged
  method.  This lets the descendent component be aware of
  when its number of columns or rows has changed. }

{ In unit's interface... }

type
  TMyGrid = class(TDrawGrid)
  protected
    procedure SizeChanged(OldColCount, OldRowCount: Longint);
      override;
  end;

{ In unit's implementation... }

procedure TMyGrid.SizeChanged(OldColCount, OldRowCount: Longint);
begin
  { Take whatever actions necessary }
end;
```

Overriding **SizeChanged** provides all the notification we need, but if we want control over the number of columns—for example, if we're developing a grid that should have no more than three columns—**SizeChanged** is not a satisfactory place to shoehorn in our veto. By the time **SizeChanged** is called (note the past tense in the name), the change has already been made. The best we can do then, if **ColCount** was set to 4, is change it to 3, requiring the whole private process of change to be repeated.

What we want is front-end control, and we can get this by redeclaring the **ColCount** property with our own access methods (see the **TMyGrid** declaration in Listing 9.10). Our redeclaration of the property will hide our ancestor's **ColCount**, so that when a programmer writes

```
ColCount := AValue;
```

our own nonvirtual **SetColCount** access method will be called. As you can see from the **SetColCount** method in Listing 9.10, we first check to see whether the suggested value for the number of columns is less than or equal to 3. If it is, we make the change.

Listing 9.10 SETCOLCT.SRC.

```
{ A descendent of TDrawGrid that redeclares the ColCount
  property with new access methods.  This lets the descendent
  component control the number of columns. }

{ In unit's interface... }

type
  TMyGrid = class(TDrawGrid)
  private
    function GetColCount: LongInt;
    procedure SetColCount(Value: LongInt);
  published
    property ColCount: LongInt read GetColCount
      write SetColCount default 0;
  end;

{ In unit's implementation... }

function TMyGrid.GetColCount: LongInt;
begin
  Result := inherited ColCount;
end;

procedure TMyGrid.SetColCount(Value: LongInt);
begin
  if Value <= 3 then inherited ColCount := Value;
end;
```

But how we make the change is perhaps the most interesting part of redeclaring a property. We can't directly change the **FColCount** field—and we wouldn't want to if we could—because the other adjustments needed in the grid would not get made. We can't call our ancestor's **SetColCount** method—that's private. And if we write

```
ColCount := Value;
```

within our own **SetColCount** method, we will create endless recursion and crash the stack.

The answer is to use the **inherited** keyword with the property name:

```
inherited ColCount := Value;
```

The ability to use **inherited** with an ancestor's property name is not as well documented as its use with an inherited public or protected method. It's a pleasant surprise, but it is entirely consistent with Object Pascal's other pleasant surprises.

Taking Snapshots Of The Screen With Delphi

In Delphi, if we want to capture the image of a form's client area, we can call **GetFormImage**. But sometimes we want a snapshot of the entire form—title bar, frame, and all. Or we want a snapshot of the entire screen. If we were desperate, we might pop up a message box that says, "Press Print Screen button NOW!" and then figure out a way to get the screen's mug off the clipboard.

But we're not *that* desperate. Combining Delphi canvases with a few GDI functions makes capturing the screen in code a snap. **CaptureScreenRect**, in Listing 9.11, demonstrates this. It gets the screen's device context with **GetDC(0)**, and then it copies a rectangular area from that DC to a bitmap's canvas. To do the copying, it uses **BitBlt**. The key to using **BitBlt**—or any GDI function—with Delphi is remembering that a canvas's handle is the DC that Windows needs.

Listing 9.11   SCRNCAP.PAS.

```
{ Screen capture functions for Delphi }
unit ScrnCap;

interface
uses WinTypes, WinProcs, Forms, Classes, Graphics, Controls;
```

```pascal
function CaptureScreenRect( ARect: TRect ): TBitmap;
function CaptureScreen: TBitmap;
function CaptureClientImage( Control: TControl ): TBitmap;
function CaptureControlImage( Control: TControl ): TBitmap;

implementation

{ Use this to capture a rectangle on the screen... }
function CaptureScreenRect( ARect: TRect ): TBitmap;
var
  ScreenDC: HDC;
begin
  Result := TBitmap.Create;
  with Result, ARect do
  begin
    Width := Right - Left;
    Height := Bottom - Top;

    ScreenDC := GetDC( 0 );
    try
      BitBlt( Canvas.Handle, 0, 0, Width, Height, ScreenDC,
        Left, Top, SRCCOPY );
    finally
      ReleaseDC( 0, ScreenDC );
    end;
  end;
end;

{ Use this to capture the entire screen... }
function CaptureScreen: TBitmap;
begin
  with Screen do
    Result := CaptureScreenRect( Rect( 0, 0, Width, Height ));
end;

{ Use this to capture just the client area of a form
  or control... }
function CaptureClientImage( Control: TControl ): TBitmap;
begin
  with Control, Control.ClientOrigin do
    Result := CaptureScreenRect( Bounds( X, Y, ClientWidth,
              ClientHeight ));
end;

{ Use this to capture an entire form or control... }
function CaptureControlImage( Control: TControl ): TBitmap;
```

```
begin
  with Control do
    if Parent = nil then
      Result := CaptureScreenRect( Bounds( Left, Top, Width,
                 Height ))
    else
      with Parent.ClientToScreen( Point( Left, Top )) do
        Result := CaptureScreenRect( Bounds( X, Y, Width,
                   Height ));
end;

end.
```

The remaining screen capture functions in Listing 9.11 cobble up rectangles and farm out the real work to **CaptureScreenRect**. **CaptureScreen** throws together a rectangle for the whole screen. **CaptureClientImage** and **CaptureControlImage** throw together rectangles for the client area and for the entire area of a control, respectively.

These four functions can be used to capture any arbitrary screen area, as well as the screen images of forms, buttons, memos, combo boxes, and so on. We just tell the little buggers to say *cheese*—and free the bitmaps when we're done.

Delphi RadioGroup Buttons You Can Disable

When I am designing forms, nothing is quite so comforting as controls that know how to snap into place, spring out to size, and arrange their contents into columns: Hey, I feel as though I'm not fighting the battle alone. And the benefit of these size-wise controls is not just emotional; how many lines of code has a panel's **Align** property saved me? Tens? Hundreds? That's why, when I need to disable individual radio buttons, I am reluctant to heave the springy little RadioGroup control over the side. **TRadioGroup** automatically arranges its child buttons into columns, spaces them evenly, and lets them be named with one string list.

What it does *not* do is allow access to individual buttons—and for good reason, I'm sure. But since I trust myself to disable responsibly, I derived an enhanced component from **TRadioGroup**, as shown in Listing 9.12. **TRadioBtnGroup** has a new property, **ItemEnabled**, that lets us get and set the enabled status of individual buttons.

Listing 9.12   RBTNGRPS.PAS.

```pascal
{ A radio group with buttons that can be disabled }
unit RBtnGrps;
interface
uses StdCtrls, ExtCtrls;

type
  TRadioBtnGroup = class( TRadioGroup )
  private
    function GetItemEnabled( Index: Integer ): Boolean;
    procedure SetItemEnabled( Index: Integer; Value: Boolean );
    function GetButtons( Index: Integer ): TRadioButton;
  protected
    function CheckAnyBut( NotThisIndex: Integer ): Boolean;
    property Buttons[ Index: Integer ]: TRadioButton
      read GetButtons;
  public
    property ItemEnabled[ Index: Integer ]: Boolean
      read GetItemEnabled write SetItemEnabled;
  end;

implementation

function TRadioBtnGroup.CheckAnyBut;
var
  Index: Integer;
begin
  Result := True;
  for Index := NotThisIndex + 1 to Items.Count - 1 do
    if Buttons[ Index ].Enabled then
    begin
      Buttons[ Index ].Checked := True;
      Exit;
    end;
  for Index := 0 to NotThisIndex - 1 do
    if Buttons[ Index ].Enabled then
    begin
      Buttons[ Index ].Checked := True;
      Exit;
    end;
  Result := False;
end;

function TRadioBtnGroup.GetItemEnabled;
```

```
begin
  Result := Buttons[ Index ].Enabled;
end;

procedure TRadioBtnGroup.SetItemEnabled;
begin
  if ( not Value ) and ( Index = ItemIndex ) and
      Buttons[ Index ].Checked and
      ( not CheckAnyBut( Index )) then
    ItemIndex := -1;
  Buttons[ Index ].Enabled := Value;
end;

function TRadioBtnGroup.GetButtons;
begin
  Result := Components[ Index ] as TRadioButton;
end;

end.
```

Internally, **TRadioBtnGroup** uses the **GetButtons** method to gain access to its radio buttons. **GetButtons** relies on the fact that, since a radio group owns its child buttons, it holds them in its **Components** array. All **GetButtons** does is index into the **Components** array and safely typecast the result.

The new control tries its best to be an intelligent helper. If a checked button is disabled, the control tries to check another button; if all the buttons are disabled, it unchecks all the buttons. Depending on your needs, you might want to change this latter behavior.

Capturing The System Palette With Delphi

Earlier in this chapter I showed how to take a snapshot of the screen with Delphi. This works perfectly if we use the bitmap soon after we create it. If we save the bitmap to a file and load it later, however, the image may be full of black specks.

The problem is that when we capture the screen in a palettized video mode, the pixels we get are merely indexes into a table of colors; these indexes are guaranteed to be correct *only* if we display the bitmap while the system palette remains the same.

Problems With Persistents, And Other Advice

What we need to do after we capture the screen is create a new palette containing the system colors and assign this to the bitmap's **Palette** property. Then, when the bitmap is saved, the color values will be saved along with it. **GetSystemPalette**, in Listing 9.13, creates such a palette and returns a handle for it. **CaptureScreenRect**, in the same listing, shows how to use **GetSystemPalette** with a newly captured bitmap.

Listing 9.13   SYSPAL.SRC.

```
function GetSystemPalette: HPalette;
var
  PaletteSize: Integer;
  LogSize: Integer;
  LogPalette: PLogPalette;
  DC: HDC;
  Focus: HWND;
begin
  Result := 0;
  Focus := GetFocus;    { ...Needed for GetDC }
  DC := GetDC( Focus ); { ...Needed for GetDeviceCaps }
  try
    PaletteSize := GetDeviceCaps( DC, SIZEPALETTE );
    LogSize := SizeOf( TLogPalette ) + ( PaletteSize - 1 ) *
               SizeOf( TPaletteEntry );
    GetMem( LogPalette, LogSize );
    try
      with LogPalette^ do
      begin
        palVersion := $0300;
        palNumEntries := PaletteSize;
        GetSystemPaletteEntries( DC, 0, PaletteSize,
          palPalEntry );
      end;
      Result := CreatePalette( LogPalette^ );
    finally
      FreeMem( LogPalette, LogSize );
    end;
  finally
    ReleaseDC( Focus, DC );
  end;
end;

{ Use this to capture a rectangle on the screen... }
function CaptureScreenRect( ARect: TRect ): TBitmap;
```

```
var
  ScreenDC: HDC;
begin
  Result := TBitmap.Create;
  with Result, ARect do
  begin
    Width := Right - Left;
    Height := Bottom - Top;

    ScreenDC := GetDC( 0 );
    try
      BitBlt( Canvas.Handle, 0, 0, Width, Height, ScreenDC,
        Left, Top, SRCCOPY );
    finally
      ReleaseDC( 0, ScreenDC );
    end;

    { Save system palette also... }
    Palette := GetSystemPalette;
  end;
end;
```

Palettes are created with the API function **CreatePalette**. **CreatePalette** takes one argument: a record that contains the palette version, the number of colors, and an array of entries specifying each color.

Oddly enough, the type for this "logical palette" record contains only enough room for one palette entry, but this is practical—the number of entries we need varies with the video mode. So first, we find out the palette size for the current video mode. Then we use a pointer type, **PLogPalette**, and allocate just enough room for the record and all the entries. As Listing 9.13 shows, **GetDeviceCaps** tells us how many entries are in the palette.

After the rigamarole required to allocate the logical palette record, the rest is easy. We obtain the color values themselves with **GetSystemPaletteEntries**. Then we call **CreatePalette** with the logical palette record as the argument, and we have the palette handle we need.

Treating The Clipboard Like A Stream

In my pre-Delphi days, I used **BlockWrite** and **BlockRead** to move data to and from a binary file. But in these enlightened times I have come to prefer using streams and their **Write** and **Read** methods. For one thing, Delphi's components already store themselves on streams; so an object that saves and loads itself with **TStream.Write** and **TStream.Read** is well prepared to hitch a ride.

Another reason I favor streams is that once an object can move on a stream, it can communicate itself to any device a stream represents: it can write just as easily to RAM—via a **TMemoryStream**—as it can to disk.

When we create streams to represent new devices, streaming code becomes even more versatile—and the devices often become easier to use. Communicating with the clipboard, for example, is no picnic; Delphi's **TClipboard** object helps, but to copy and paste custom formats or huge amounts of data we are still required to call strange API functions whose names begin with the word "Global." In contrast, the stream in Listing 9.14 lets us manipulate the clipboard with familiar **Write** and **Read** methods.

Listing 9.14   CLIPSTRM.PAS.

```
unit ClipStrm;

interface
uses Classes, Clipbrd, Consts, WinProcs, WinTypes;

type
  TClipboardMode = ( cmRead, cmWrite );
  TClipboardStream = class( TMemoryStream )
  private
    FMode: TClipboardMode;
    FFormat: Word;
  public
    constructor Create( Format: Word; Mode: TClipboardMode );
    destructor Destroy; override;
  end;

implementation

constructor TClipboardStream.Create;
var
  Handle: THandle;
  MemPtr: Pointer;
begin
  inherited Create;
  FMode := Mode;
  FFormat := Format;
```

```
{ In "read mode," immediately read clipboard data
  into the stream... }
  if ( FMode = cmRead ) and Clipboard.HasFormat( FFormat ) then
  begin
    Clipboard.Open;
    try
      Handle := Clipboard.GetAsHandle( FFormat );
      MemPtr := GlobalLock( Handle );
      try
        Write( MemPtr^, GlobalSize( Handle ));
      finally
        GlobalUnlock( Handle );
      end;
      Position := 0;
    finally
      Clipboard.Close;
    end;
  end;
end;

destructor TClipboardStream.Destroy;
var
  P: PChar;
begin
  { In "write mode," copy to the clipboard whatever the
    stream contains... }
  if FMode = cmWrite then
  begin
    P := GlobalAllocPtr( HeapAllocFlags, Size );
    try
      Position := 0;
      Read( P^, Size );
      Clipboard.SetAsHandle( FFormat, GlobalHandle( P ));
    except
      GlobalFreePtr( P );
    end;
  end;
  inherited Destroy;
end;

end.
```

TClipboardStream is easy to use. When we create it, we specify a format and whether we will be reading or writing it. A clipboard stream created in "read mode" immediately loads what is on the clipboard so we can use **Read** to get at the data. A clipboard stream created in "write mode" waits until it is being destroyed and then copies to the clipboard whatever we have written to it.

The result is that a streamable object can use the same code to save itself to disk (**TFileStream**), to memory (**TMemoryStream**), or to the clipboard, and can use the same code to read itself back again.

Changing Hints On The Fly

I sometimes want to display different hints for different parts of a control. This is true especially for grids, since information varies so much from cell to cell. Suppose, for example, that one grid column contains a baseball player's name, and another his team, and I want to change the hint based on which column the mouse is over.

Unfortunately, hints don't work that way. An application doesn't reevaluate which hint to show until the mouse moves to a different control.

However, the Application object has a public method named CancelHint that lets us put the current hint window away and restart the hint timer. If we change the grid's Hint property after we call CancelHint and before the hint window reappears, we can change hints without moving off the grid.

Listing 9.15 contains a sample OnMouseMove handler for a StringGrid, on which you can closely model your own code. The event handler is called every time the mouse moves over the grid, of course, but the event handler cancels the hint window and changes the grid hint only when the mouse moves to a different cell.

Listing 9.15 HINTPROC.SRC.

```
{ An example of changing hints for a grid }
procedure TForm1.StringGrid1MouseMove( Sender: TObject;
  Shift: TShiftState; X, Y: Integer );
const
  LastMCol: LongInt = -2;
  LastMRow: LongInt = -2;
var
  MCol, MRow: LongInt;   // Mouse column and mouse row
  NewHintText: string;
  Grid: TStringGrid;
begin
  Grid := Sender as TStringGrid;
  Grid.MouseToCell( X, Y, MCol, MRow );
```

```
    if ( MCol <> LastMCol ) or ( MRow <> LastMRow ) then
    begin
      Application.CancelHint;
      if ( MCol = -1 ) or ( MRow = -1 ) then
        NewHintText := 'Not over cell'
      else
        NewHintText := Format( 'Col %d, Row %d', [ MCol, MRow ]);
      Grid.Hint := NewHintText;
    end;
    LastMCol := MCol;
    LastMRow := MRow;
end;
```

You can use this code in all three versions of Delphi, although you get slightly different hint window behavior in each version. In Delphi 1 and 2, the hint window remains at the bottom of the grid no matter where the mouse is located. In Delphi 3, the hint window follows the mouse and locates itself on or near each cell—exactly what you would hope.

Using Macros With Delphi's Code Editor

The Delphi code editor contains a macro facility that can automate repetitive typing chores—but unless you've stumbled across it you probably don't know about it; it's undocumented in the Delphi help files.

While you edit your code, you can use the macro facility to record a series of keystrokes and then play back the keystrokes to automatically perform an identical editing task later on. To start recording, hold down the Ctrl and Shift keys and type R. Type the sequence of keys you want to record. To stop recording, press Ctrl+Shift+R again. To play the macro, press Ctrl+Shift+P.

The Delphi code editor isn't WinWord or WordPerfect, and its macro facility has several shortcomings: It remembers only one set of keystrokes at a time, and any keystroke that causes focus to jump to a window other than the code editor aborts the recording process. For example, if the last Find operation was a simple search, then pressing the F3 key does not cause a dialog box to appear (as long as the search is successful), and the F3 key can be included in the macro recording. But if the last

Find operation was a search-and-replace, then F3 will cause a confirmation dialog to appear and the recording will stop.

Even given these limitations, the macro facility can be powerful. Bookmarks can be set and jumped to, incremental searches can be run, and text can be copied and pasted.

For example, after I type a method heading into a class declaration, I often find myself pasting that heading into the implementation section of the unit, inserting the class name and period, and typing a **begin..end** pair. If I am careful about the keystrokes I use, I can record this action in a general purpose macro. Listing 9.16 shows one possible set of keystrokes to accomplish this task starting with the text cursor on the line that contains the method heading.

By the way, I use the code editor's default key mapping; if you use a different mapping, the keystrokes you need may differ.

Listing 9.16   HEADING.TXT.

```
{The following illustrates keystrokes that paste a method
heading into the implementation section of a unit and
add a begin-end pair. Special keystrokes are shown in
braces. Comments are shown after double slashes. This
assumes that the final line in the unit contains "end."}

{Ctrl+Shift+R}         // Start recording
{HOME}                 // Move to start of line
{Shift+DOWN}           // Block line
{Ctrl+C}               // Copy block
{Ctrl+END}             // Move to end of unit
{Ctrl+LEFT}            // Move left of "end."
{Ctrl+V}               // Insert copied line
{UP}                   // Move to start of inserted line
{Ctrl+T}               // Remove indentation
{Ctrl+RIGHT}           // Move to method name
TMyClass.              // Type class name and period
{END}                  // Move to end of heading line
{ENTER}                // Insert a new line
begin                  // type "begin"
{ENTER}{ENTER}         // Insert two new lines after "begin"
end;                   // type "end;"
{ENTER}                // Insert a new line after the method
{UP}{UP}               // Move back up to method body
{RIGHT}{RIGHT}         // Indent two spaces, ready to type
{Ctrl+Shift+R}         // Stop recording
```

Streaming TPersistent

Persistence is the ability to last, so Delphi has given the name **TPersistent** to the class of objects that are especially designed to last for more than one run of a program. To make the objects endure, the crucial information about each **TPersistent** is written to a stream and read back later.

Delphi's streams know how to work closely with a **TPersistent** so that its contents are read and written nearly automatically. However, not all **TPersistent** objects are equal. Components—which descend from **TPersistent**—can be read and written individually with the convenient **TStream.WriteComponent** and **ReadComponent** methods. But other descendents of **TPersistent** can only be streamed if components publish them as properties—they are, in other words, second-class citizens.

This is inconvenient if we want to, for example, save a font object to a stream. To do this, we must first declare a new component type that publishes a **TFont** property, then create an instance of the component, assign our font to its font property, and write the component to the stream.

Actually, however, if all we want is a sort of burro that carries a **TPersistent** on its back, we don't have to declare a new class of component each time. All we need is one component class that publishes a **TPersistent** property; then polymorphism will let us assign any **TPersistent** to that published property and our **TPersistent** will be written or read with the component.

The **TCarrier** component, in Listing 9.17, is just such a pack animal. It is tucked away in the implementation section of the **StrmPers** unit, and the **WritePersistent** and **ReadPersistent** procedures take care of creating, using, and destroying a temporary instance of it. Be sure to create your **TPersistent** before you use it in a call to **ReadPersistent**; **ReadPersistent** requires that the object already exists.

Listing 9.17   STRMPERS.PAS.

```
unit StrmPers;

interface
uses Classes;

procedure WritePersistent( Stream: TStream;
  Persistent: TPersistent );
```

```
{ NOTE: the TPersistent should be created before
  sending it to this procedure... }
procedure ReadPersistent( Stream: TStream;
  Persistent: TPersistent );

implementation

type
  TCarrier = class( TComponent )
  private
    FPersistent: TPersistent;
  published
    property Persistent: TPersistent
      read FPersistent write FPersistent;
  end;

procedure WritePersistent( Stream: TStream;
  Persistent: TPersistent );
var
  Carrier: TCarrier;
begin
  Carrier := TCarrier.Create( nil );
  try
    Carrier.Persistent := Persistent;
    Stream.WriteComponent( Carrier );
  finally
    Carrier.Free;
  end;
end;

procedure ReadPersistent( Stream: TStream;
  Persistent: TPersistent );
var
  Carrier: TCarrier;
begin
  Carrier := TCarrier.Create( nil );
  try
    Carrier.Persistent := Persistent;
    Stream.ReadComponent( Carrier );
  finally
    Carrier.Free;
  end;
end;

end.
```

Enabling Drag Image Display For Delphi 2 And 3

When you drag an item away from a TreeView or ListView, a partially transparent image of the item tags along with the mouse. This wonderful visual feedback continues until you drag the image to the edge of the control. At that point—zap!—the image disappears and won't reappear unless you move the mouse back into the original control, or unless you reach another TreeView or ListView.

Why does this happen? One of the things that determines a control's behavior is its **ControlStyle** property. In Delphi versions 2 and 3, a new predefined **ControlStyle** value has been added: **csDisplayDragImage**. If **csDisplayDragImage** is included in a **ControlStyle**, drag images will appear on top of the control. However, if **csDisplayDragImage** is not included, drag images will disconcertingly vanish until the mouse reaches friendlier territory. By default, unfortunately, most controls don't include the necessary **ControlStyle** value. So, if you want to let images be dragged across your forms, you need to adjust every form and every control in your project so that its **ControlStyle** includes **csDisplayDragImage**.

Listing 9.18 contains a routine named **EnableDisplayDragImage** that fixes the **ControlStyle** of a control, its children, its children's children, and so on.

To make every control on a form friendly to drag images, add the following statement to the form's **FormCreate** event handler:

```
EnableDisplayDragImage( Self, True );
```

And if you create controls on the fly, remember to call **EnableDisplayDragImage** for them as well.

Listing 9.18   ENABDISP.PAS.

```
unit EnabDisp;

interface
uses Controls;

procedure EnableDisplayDragImage( Control: TControl;
  ChildrenToo: Boolean );

implementation
```

```
procedure EnableDisplayDragImage( Control: TControl;
  ChildrenToo: Boolean );
var
  Index: Integer;
begin
  with Control do
    ControlStyle := ControlStyle + [ csDisplayDragImage ];

  if ChildrenToo and ( Control is TWinControl ) then
    with TWinControl( Control ) do
      for Index := 0 to ControlCount - 1 do
      begin
        EnableDisplayDragImage( Controls[ Index ],
          ChildrenToo );
      end;
end;

end.
```

HIGH PERFORMANCE

Models, Views, And Frames

CHAPTER 10

Here's a creative way of looking at program functionality that allows you to embed one form within another. Delphi 3's new interfaces feature makes it considerably easier.

Models, Views, And Frames

Jon Shemitz

One of Delphi's subtler virtues is the way it simplifies many aspects of the Windows API. Things that once required lots of cumbersome code have been reduced to a property assignment. What was so arcane as to be unimaginable is now quite simply trivial. While the **Canvas** property is probably the most familiar example of this, the **Parent** property deserves our attention, too. When you set a control's **Parent** property, you have told Windows to make that control a child window of its new **Parent**. It is now visible and enabled whenever its parent is visible and enabled. (This is how tabbed notebooks work: Each page is, in effect, a panel. All the components on it are children of the notebook page. When a page is brought to the front, over the other pages, it becomes visible, and so do all the components on it.) If you set the **Parent** property at runtime, you can get all sorts of special effects, from dynamic creation of notebook-like controls to placing one form on a blank area of another form.

Why might you want to embed one form in another form? Consider these four scenarios:

1. You are building wizards to walk users through the creation of an object. You also want to give your users property sheets with tabbed notebooks, so that they have random access to the object's properties and don't have to go through each step of the wizard to change a single property. The only real difference between a wizard and a property sheet is that a wizard walks the user from one page to the next (and will only allow the user to move on when each page contains valid data), while a property sheet allows the user to access pages in any order he or she likes. That is, as in Figures 10.1 and 10.2, the tabs of a property sheet contain the exact same view of a part of the object as the pages of a wizard. If you can use the same code for wizard pages as for property sheet tabs, there is no possibility of the two getting out of synch.

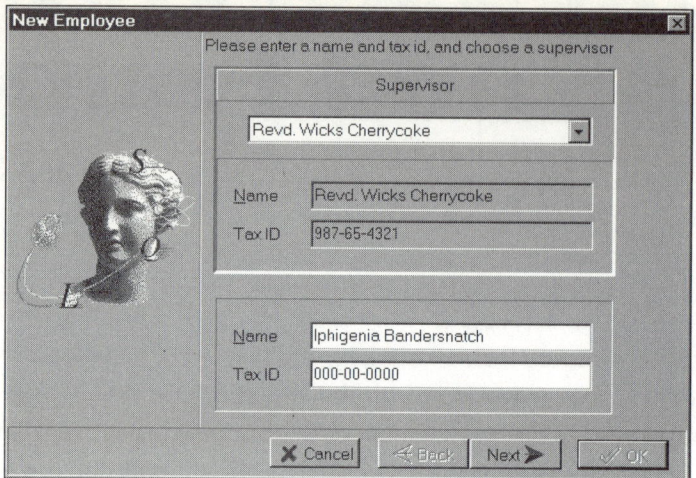

Figure 10.1
Wizard sharing "view" code with Figure 10.2 property sheet.

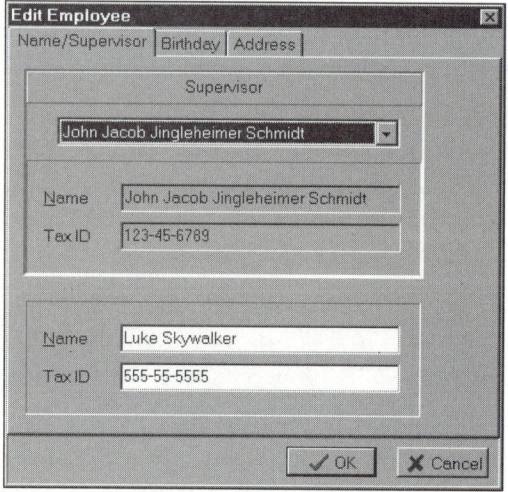

Figure 10.2
Property sheet sharing "view" code with Figure 10.1 wizard.

2. You have objects that can appear in more than one context. For example, a Person may be an Employee and an Employee's Supervisor. If you can use the same code to display the supervisor record as to display the employee record, you can save code and, again, eliminate the possibility of the two getting out of synch.

3. You are part of a team developing a large and complicated tabbed dialog. Because it is so big, the team has decided to put several people to work on the same dialog, with each person working on one or more of the tabs. Rather than always merging changes into a single humongous unit, you would like each tab to "live" in its own unit. This will keep you from stepping on each other's toes, and it will also keep the code clearer and more focused.

4. You have an object hierarchy, and you need a form that lets your users see and/or change any member of the hierarchy. Some things can be done to all members of the hierarchy; other actions are only possible on some members of the hierarchy. You would like to have a single form with the controls appropriate to the common actions. At runtime you will add the specialized controls appropriate to each object type, and change them as you change objects.

The first two cases are clearly the most similar. You have objects and standardized ways for your user to examine and manipulate the objects: models and views. What you need now is a *frame*. A frame can hold any view. When a frame is visible, so is the view it contains. The same view can be placed in more than one frame. Views may, in turn, act as frames for views of embedded or referenced objects.

Frames can handle the third scenario rather neatly, too. If you build a tabbed dialog with a frame on each tab, you have a generic tabbed dialog that can hold any views that you need it to hold. The form's unit has been pared down from an unwieldy unit containing all sorts of (at least potentially) unrelated code to a simple container with little more than the code to fill each frame and, perhaps, some OnChanging logic that tells the active frame to ask its view if it's okay to change to another tab. Your large tabbed dialog can now be split into multiple units, so that each member of a team can check in his or her own updates. No more frustrating losses of updates or reversal of bug fixes due to sloppy merging.

Somewhat similarly, a form for editing the class hierarchy in scenario four might contain a few controls for the things that can be done to all members of the hierarchy and a frame where you can place the view specific to each member of the hierarchy. (You could make the object responsible for telling the editing form which view to use.) To switch from one type of object to another, you'd simply put a different view in the frame.

Implementing Views As Real Live Code

This chapter might have seemed a bit abstract, so far. Day in, day out, you work with objects, components, forms, and event handlers—not models, views, and frames. But these abstractions are useful and even necessary. The standard model/view abstraction helps us avoid the "RAD trap" of scattering our applications' logic throughout a bunch of event handlers where it's hard to follow, hard to modify, and hard to reuse. Adding the notion of a frame helps us avoid the similar trap of tying a view to a particular container object, like a form, panel, or notebook page. Still, the theory's only as good as the code it helps you write—how *do* you implement a view so that you can plop it into more than one frame?

Component Templates And Compound Components

One approach might be to use the new Delphi 3 notion of *component templates*. These let us bundle up a group of interacting components—complete with names and event handlers—and place them on the component palette for reuse. This is a great idea, but it doesn't quite do what we want, here, because what we end up with is simply components on a form. When we want to put the same view on two different forms, we find that the collection as a whole is not an object that we can give methods to—so how can we tell the view to read or write its model?

When we have, say, two different Person views in the same Employee view, we find that placing two instances of a component template on the same form means that all the controls in the second instance lose their saved names and end up as **Label1**, **Edit1**, and so forth. When we want to perform team development of complex dialogs, we find both that all the pages end up in the same unit, and also that changing the template doesn't change the instance.

A similar but "stronger" approach is to make a view into a compound component, with private variables including other visual components. However, if you've ever actually done this, you know that creating and resizing the component is a real nightmare. Instead of simply placing components on a form the way we've grown used to, we have to explicitly create each subcomponent. Instead of dragging components around and setting properties in the Object Inspector until things look right, we have to manually set each and every property. This is doable, of course, but it's very slow, tedious, and error-prone, and we can end up with a *lot* of code that's hard to read and/or maintain. Worse, because the process is so painful, one tends to try to do as little as possible and the result is a lot of ugly, poorly laid out messes. Views built this way may "have all the widgets they need," but often aren't very usable.

We could avoid all the pain and ugliness of manually building compound components if we could build a form visually and then turn it into a component. Delphi does, in fact, allow us to do just this, but it's not particularly easy or straightforward. You have to buy or build a special design-time-only component to set the form's undocumented **IsControl** property, add some code to the form, and manually edit the DFM file to change the form object's parent class. If you really want to do this, Ray Lischner's excellent book *Secrets Of Delphi 2* (Waite Group Press, 1996) supplies the special component to tweak **IsControl**, and tells you step-by-step how to proceed—but while I found this section of his book fascinating reading, I've never actually used the technique and recommend that you don't either. Why? Because you have to go through the same procedure each time you create a new view, or change an existing one. Turning a form into a component in this way seems to make more sense for really generic components—such as bundling a **TMemo** or a **TRichEdit** with a toolbar—than for views.

Form Inheritance

Instead, I use form inheritance to derive perfectly ordinary forms from **TEmbedded Form**. As you can see in Listing 10.1 (which is an extract from EMBEDDED.PAS), embedded forms have a special constructor which lets them be treated as "lightweight controls" which can be placed on any container control—panel, notebook page, or group box—at runtime. Since forms are themselves objects, you can freely add any methods you need to make them act like views. Since these lightweight controls are normal forms, it's just as easy to change an embedded form as your project evolves as it is to change any other form.

Listing 10.1   A special constructor for embedded forms.

```
type
  EmbeddedFormMode = (efmZoomed, efmTopLeft, efmCentered);

function ALZ(Number: integer): Cardinal; // At Least Zero
begin
  if Number > 0
    then Result := Number
```

```
      else Result := 0;
end;

constructor TEmbeddedForm.CreateEmbedded(
  _Owner: TComponent;
  Frame:  TWinControl;
  Mode:   EmbeddedFormMode );
begin
  Inherited Create(_Owner);

  Parent      := Frame;
  BorderIcons := [];
  BorderStyle := bsNone;

  case Mode of
    efmZoomed:   Align := alClient;
    efmTopLeft:  begin
                   Top  := 0;
                   Left := 0;
                 end; // efmTopLeft
    efmCentered: begin
                   Top  := ALZ((Frame.Height - Height) div 2);
                   Left := ALZ((Frame.Width  - Width)  div 2);
                 end; // efmCentered
    else         Assert(False);
  end; // case
  Visible := True;
end; // TEmbeddedForm.CreateEmbedded
```

The most important line in Listing 10.1 is **Parent := Frame**, which makes the **Frame** control the embedded form's parent. This is just like what is done "behind the scenes" for a form's design-time controls when a form is loaded, and it has three consequences. First, a child control is visible whenever its parent is visible. Thus, hiding the frame hides the view, while making the frame visible or bringing it to the front also makes the view it contains visible. Second, child controls are clipped to their parent's client area; large views are automatically clipped to fit within their frame. Third, the child control is positioned relative to its parent's client area; just as with any other control, the embedded form's **Top** and **Left** properties are relative to the container it's placed on.

This last point means that when an embedded form is zoomed by setting **Align** equal to **alClient**, it acts just like any other **alClient**-aligned control: It sizes itself to fill its frame, and automatically resizes itself (and calls any **OnResize** handler) whenever the frame is resized. Conversely, unzoomed views retain their design-time size, and may be centered or placed at the top-left corner of their frame. You can match the view's starting size to its frame's starting size by setting its **ClientHeight** and **ClientWidth** properties at design time—or you can size frame windows based on the design size of their embedded forms, as the generic wizard and property sheets I'll talk about in the "Model Editors" section of this chapter do.

Before we get too far from Listing 10.1, though, I should point out that the lines **BorderIcons := []** and **BorderStyle := bsNone** mean that what actually appears at runtime is the view form's client area—there's no border or caption to show that the frame actually contains a whole independent form. Thus, as you can see in Figures 10.3 and 10.4, a view's design-time **Caption** property will have no effect at all at runtime.

From Embedded Forms To Views

The ability to use a form as a lightweight control is obviously a good start. We can place the form wherever we like. We can make as many copies of the form as we need. We can add methods to the form object so that it "acts like" a view.

So—how should a view act?

- It needs to be able to read data from a model object, and it needs to be able to write data back to a model object.

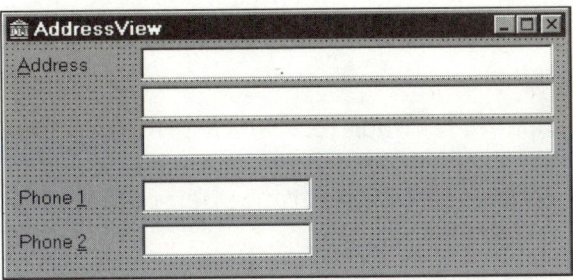

Figure 10.3
A view at design time, looking identical to a form.

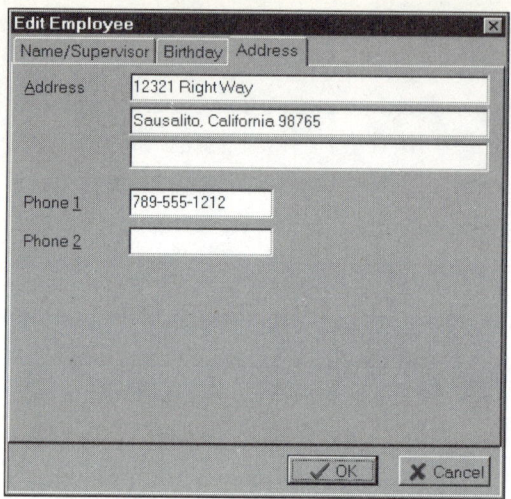

Figure 10.4
A view at runtime, looking unlike a form.

- It may need to be able to validate itself—a wizard typically doesn't let the user move to the next page until the current one is valid, and a property sheet usually won't let you save invalid data. Then again, it may not—you may not care whether a free-form "Notes" field is filled in or not.

- It needs some way to tell its frame when its **Valid** property changes, so the frame can enable or disable a Next or OK button.

- It may need the ability to display data without allowing the user to edit it. A property sheet may be read-only if the current user doesn't have permission to edit a model object, or simply because the user hasn't locked that object so as to avoid race conditions.

These "rules" are captured in Listing 10.2, which is an extract from MODELS.PAS.

Listing 10.2   Model, view, and frame behavior.
```
type
  TModel    = TObject;

  // Both IView and IModelEdit have a ReadOnly property
  IReadOnly = interface
              function  GetReadOnly: boolean;
```

```
                procedure SetReadOnly(Value: boolean);
                property  ReadOnly: boolean read  GetReadOnly
                                            write SetReadOnly;
                end;

// Fill a view from a model & write changes back;
// frame/view interactions
IFrame  =       interface;
IView   =       interface (IReadOnly)
                procedure ReadFromModel(Model: TModel);
                procedure WriteToModel(Model: TModel);

                function  GetValid: boolean;
                procedure SetValid(Value: boolean);
                property  Valid: boolean read GetValid
                                         write SetValid;


                procedure AddNotifiee(   Notify: IFrame);
                procedure RemoveNotifiee(Notify: IFrame);
                end;
IFrame  =       interface
                procedure OnValidChanged(
                  ChangingObject: TObject;
                  View:           IView );
                end;

// Wizards and Property Sheets are "model editors"
IModelEdit = interface (IReadOnly)
                // Low level routines that allow an app to setup
                // an editor once, and run it several times.
                procedure Initialize;
                function RunEditor(Model: TModel): boolean;
                procedure Finalize;
                // Initialize/RunEditor/Finalize
                function EditModel(Model: TModel): boolean;
                end;
```

It's probably pretty clear that we're working with a simple architecture here. Models are totally passive containers of data that are usually created, loaded, or stored by a data module. Views can read and write models on command, and can tell their frames when they become valid or invalid. Model editors—both wizards and property sheets—simply set up and run, and report back on whether they've actually made any changes to the model object because the user hit OK.

What we *don't* have is a full-blown Model-View-Controller architecture, where models can tell views to update themselves because the model has changed, and so on. It certainly wouldn't be all that hard to add this, but it would only further complicate a chapter on embedded forms—and it's not as if this simple Model-View-Frame architecture is weak or simplistic. I've used it with great success in several different projects.

The Interfaces Rationale

Before we move on, you may be wondering why I use Delphi 3 interfaces, instead of simply defining view objects and frame objects and deriving from them. Am I just using interfaces for the sake of using the new whiz-bang features in Delphi 3?

Not really. To start with, views and frames have a circular relationship. Frames need to tell their views when to read or write models; views need to tell frames when their **Valid** property changes. Obviously, I could have implemented this circularity using forward class declarations instead of a forward interface declaration, but I think using interfaces makes the interactions more obvious than when they're obscured by various unrelated object properties and methods. Also, though I don't take advantage of this in EMBEDDEDFORMS.DPR, using interfaces means that a view might be implemented in several different ways; views don't *have* to be descendents of **TEmbeddedForm**. The most important reason, though, is that *a view may also be a frame.*

For example, an **Employee** object might contain references to "employee" and "supervisor" **People** objects, each of which contains name and address information. A view of the **Employee** object might contain a view of the employee or supervisor field. Delphi doesn't support multiple inheritance, so an object can't simultaneously be a **TView** and a **TFrame**, but an object can easily implement both the **IView** and **IFrame** interfaces.

Before Delphi supported interfaces, the best way to implement something like the **INotify** protocol was to use procedural types:

```
type
  TOnValidChanged = procedure(ChangingObject: TObject) of object;

procedure TView.AddNotifiee(Callback: TOnValidChanged);
```

This worked, but **TOnValidChanged** is basically the same as **TNotifyProc**, and obviously every Delphi program has a lot of those. You can pass *any* **TNotifyProc** to this **AddNotifiee**, and the compiler has no way to prevent you from passing the wrong one by mistake. With interfaces, the frame's callback has to have the right name and the right signature, and it has to be in an object that has promised to implement the **IFrame** protocol—so it's much harder to make a careless mistake.

Interfaced Forms

When I began to implement the interfaces in Listing 10.3, I ran into a snag. Though the resolution was simple, it took me many hours of generating and testing hypotheses before I could stop my system from crashing whenever I called **AddNotifiee(Self)** from a form that implemented **IFrame**. To understand what was going on, you're going to need a bit of background.

The Delphi 3 documentation is quite clear that any object that implements an interface must also implement the **IUnknown** interface, which supports reference counting and interface querying. If you declare

```
type
  IFoo = interface
         procedure Foo;
         end;
  TFoo = class (TObject, IFoo)
         procedure Foo;
         end;

procedure TFoo.Foo; begin end;
```

the compiler will complain about the undeclared identifiers **QueryInterface**, **_AddRef**, and **_Release**. You have to explicitly implement **IUnknown**, or you have to derive your object from **TInterfacedObject** instead of from **TObject**. On the other hand, the compiler won't complain at all about

```
type
  TFoo = class (TForm, IFoo)
         procedure Foo;
         end;

procedure TFoo.Foo; begin end;
```

That means that Borland implemented **IUnknown** somewhere in the VCL, and we're home free, right?

Well, no. Whenever you pass a **TForm** as an interface reference, you get GPFs in the VCL. It turns out that while **TComponent** does implement **IUnknown**'s methods, it does so in a way which isn't very useful to those of us who want to use interfaces within an application. **IUnknown** calls are delegated to **FVCLComObject**, which is a pointer that is only set when you call **GetComObject** to get an interface reference for the object. What's more, **GetComObject** only sets **FVCLComObject** if you have used **VCLCom** in your project. If you do that, your call to **GetComObject** generates complaints about class factories not being registered—at which point I stopped caring. This is probably great if you are sharing COM objects with other applications, but not if all you wanted was to add interfaces to your forms.

It's far simpler to just look at the implementation of **TInterfacedObject** and add a simple, self-contained **IUnknown** implementation to **TForm**, and then just derive from **TInterfacedForm** instead of from **TForm.**

Listing 10.3 INTERFACEDFORMS.PAS.

```
unit InterfacedForms;

// Copyright © 1997 by Jon Shemitz, all rights reserved.
// Permission is hereby granted to freely use, modify, and
// distribute this source code PROVIDED that all six lines of
// this copyright and contact notice are included without any
// changes. Questions? Comments? Offers of work?
// mailto:jon@midnightbeach.com

// ---------------------------------------------------

// Adds a functional IUnknown implementation to TForm.

interface

uses Classes, Forms;

type
  TInterfacedForm =
    class (TForm, IUnknown)
    private
      fRefCount: integer;
```

```
    protected
      function QueryInterface( const IID: TGUID;
                                out Obj): Integer; stdcall;
      function _AddRef: Integer;                   stdcall;
      function _Release: Integer;                  stdcall;
    public
      property RefCount: integer read fRefCount write fRefCount;
    end;

implementation

uses Windows; // for E_NOINTERFACE

// IUnknown code based on the TInterfacedObject source

function TInterfacedForm.QueryInterface( const IID: TGUID;
                                          out Obj): Integer;
begin
  if GetInterface(IID, Obj)
    then Result := 0
    else Result := E_NOINTERFACE;
end;

function TInterfacedForm._AddRef: Integer;
begin
  Inc(fRefCount);
  Result := fRefCount;
end;

function TInterfacedForm._Release: Integer;
begin
  Dec(fRefCount);
  Result := fRefCount;
  if fRefCount = 0 then Destroy;
end;

end.
```

Pretty simple, actually. In retrospect, I don't know what took me so long, though I suppose I was sort of blindsided by the assumption that adding interfaces to a form wouldn't compile unless it was safe. While I was experimenting, however, I discovered one more problem with Delphi 3's implementation of interfaces that I should mention before we move on.

Delphi 3's Reference Count Gotcha

Interface references are reference-counted, just as huge strings are. Every time you make a copy of an interface reference variable (either by direct assignment, or by passing it to a procedure), the object's **_AddRef** method gets called to increment the reference count. Every time you remove a reference to the interface (either by explicitly reassigning a variable, or when it goes out of scope), the object's **_Release** method gets called to decrement the reference count. When the reference count goes to 0, the object frees itself. "Old-style" object references *don't affect the reference count at all.*

This works perfectly—if you only ever interact with the object through interface references. For example, if you have this

```
type
  IFoo = interface
         procedure Foo;
         end;
  TFoo = class (TForm, IFoo)
         procedure Foo;
         end;

procedure TFoo.Foo; begin end;

procedure Bar(InterfaceReference: IFoo); begin end;

begin
  Bar(TFoo.Create);
end.
```

the **TFoo** created in the call to **Bar** will be automatically freed when **Bar** returns. But consider a slightly different scenario, where we mix object reference and interface references:

```
var
  ObjectReference: TFoo;

begin
  ObjectReference := TFoo.Create;
  try
    Bar(ObjectReference);
  finally ObjectReference.Free; end;
end.
```

The problem is that setting **ObjectReference** to **TFoo.Create** does not affect the object's reference count. After we set **ObjectReference**, the **RefCount** property is still 0, just as it was when the object was created. However, when we call procedure **Bar**, we do an implicit assignment to its **InterfaceReference** parameter. This generates a call to **_AddRef**, which sets **RefCount** to 1. When **Bar** returns, **Interface Reference** goes out of scope. This in turn generates a call to **_Release**, which sets **RefCount** back to 0, and thus frees the object. **ObjectReference** is now invalid! The next time we refer to it—when we call **Free** on it, in this case—we will get a GPF.

Obviously, this scenario is a bit contrived, but it serves to illustrate the sort of problems you'll face if you start adding interfaces to legacy code. For that matter, even in new code there will be times when you find that the most natural way to work with an object is through a mixture of object and interface references. (In particular, there's nothing like **TList** that works with interface references.)

In these cases, what you'll need to do is to set the object's reference count artificially to 1, before you ever use an interface reference to it. For example, the next section's **TAbstractView** class has the following **OnCreate** handler:

```
procedure TAbstractView.FormCreate(Sender: TObject);
begin
  inherited;
  _AddRef;  // so can pass Self as an interface reference
end;
```

Explicitly calling **_AddRef** this way means that the first interface reference sets **RefCount** to 2, and that **RefCount** will never go to 0. Thus, the object will never destroy itself and invalidate your object references; it will survive until you explicitly free it, in the old-fashioned way.

Of course, you only need to call **_AddRef** explicitly if you will be mixing object and interface references. If you will only interact with the object *via* interface references, you should be very chary of explicitly calling **_AddRef** lest you mess up the reference counting so that your object doesn't free itself when it should. Conversely, when you do have such a "pure interface" object, you should be careful never to create an object reference to it, lest that object reference become invalid when the interface reference count goes to 0 and the object frees itself. One simple precaution you can take is to make all the interfaced methods **protected**—they will still be publicly accessible *via* the interface, but if you can't access them from an object reference, you're not particularly likely to ever create one.

Abstract, Valid, And Fickle Views

As you can see from the inheritance tree in Figure 10.5, the EmbeddedForms project uses interfaced forms to build two basic sorts of views: *valid* views, whose **Valid** property is always **True**, and *fickle* views, whose **Valid** property may change. You might use a valid view for something like a memo field, where you don't care about the contents in any way, or perhaps for an initial or final panel of a wizard. You would use a fickle view any time it's possible for users to enter invalid data that they should not be allowed to save—a date like February 31st, proposed expenditures that exceed the budget, and so on. Since both implement the **IView** interface, both can be handled identically by generic code that knows only that it has a collection of views to deal with.

Both types of view descend from Listing 10.4's **TAbstractView**.

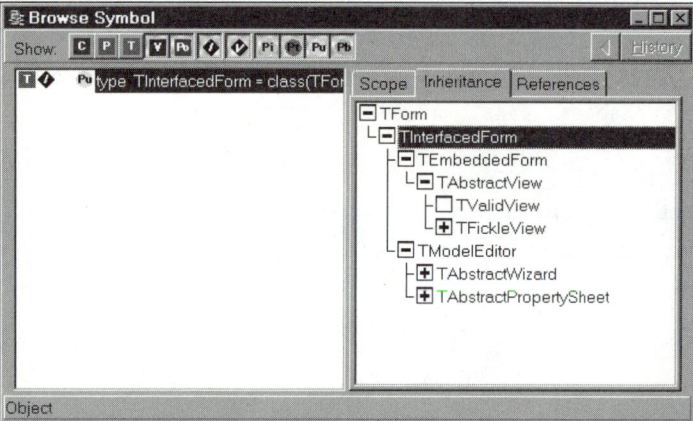

Figure 10.5
Interfaced forms in the sample project.

Listing 10.4   VIEWS.PAS.

```pascal
unit Views;

// Copyright © 1997 by Jon Shemitz, all rights reserved.
// Permission is hereby granted to freely use, modify, and
// distribute this source code PROVIDED that all six lines of
// this copyright and contact notice are included without any
// changes. Questions? Comments? Offers of work?
// mailto:jon@midnightbeach.com

// -----------------------------------------------------------

// Maps the IView contract onto an embedded form. Typically,
// you would derive views from TValidView or TFickleView.

interface

uses
  Models, Embedded;

type
  TAbstractView = class(TEmbeddedForm, IView)
    procedure FormCreate(Sender: TObject);
  private
    fReadOnly: boolean;
  protected
    function  GetValid: boolean;             virtual; abstract;
    procedure SetValid(Value: boolean);      virtual; abstract;

    function  GetReadOnly: boolean;          virtual;
    procedure SetReadOnly(Value: boolean);   virtual;
  public
    procedure ReadFromModel(Model: TModel);  virtual;
    procedure WriteToModel(Model:  TModel);  virtual;

    procedure AddNotifiee(   Notify: IFrame); virtual; abstract;
    procedure RemoveNotifiee(Notify: IFrame); virtual; abstract;

    property Valid:    boolean read GetValid write SetValid;
    property ReadOnly: boolean read  fReadOnly
                               write SetReadOnly;
  end;

  TViewClass = class of TAbstractView;

implementation
```

```
{$R *.DFM}

function TAbstractView.GetReadOnly: boolean;
begin
  Result := fReadOnly;
end; // TAbstractView.GetReadOnly

procedure TAbstractView.SetReadOnly(Value: boolean);
begin
  fReadOnly := Value;
  Enabled   := not Value;
            // A read only view will display information but not
            // let users change it; you can override SetReadOnly
            // to change the appearance of read only views.
end; // TAbstractView.SetReadOnly

procedure TAbstractView.ReadFromModel(Model: TModel);
begin
end; // TAbstractView.ReadFromModel

procedure TAbstractView.WriteToModel(Model: TModel);
begin
end; // TAbstractView.WriteToModel

procedure TAbstractView.FormCreate(Sender: TObject);
begin
  inherited;
  _AddRef;  // so can pass Self as an interface reference
end;

end.
```

TAbstractView effectively splits the **IView** protocol into three parts—read-only, validation, and model I/O—and handles each a little differently:

- It implements the basic read-only functionality—users can't change the data on a disabled form—though actual views will typically override **SetReadOnly** so as to change the visual appearance of read-only views.

- It defers all implementation of validation to its **TValidView** and **TFickleView** descendents.

- It provides do-nothing stub code for **ReadFromModel** and **WriteToModel**. Since these typically are overridden by each actual view object, it seemed desirable to let views *always* call **inherited**.

As you might imagine from the name, you're not meant to actually use a **TAbstract View** nor to inherit directly from one. Rather, you would use a **TValidView** or a **TFickleView**.

Obviously, I could simply have collapsed all "abstract," "valid," and "fickle" views into a single **TView** class. Splitting them up as I did has two main benefits: First, because valid views have special code to flat-out ignore the validation parts of the **IView** protocol, they are a trifle faster and take a bit less memory. More importantly, when you have derived a particular view from **TValidView** instead of **TFickleView**, its **Valid** property is always **True**, even if you carelessly set it to **False**. (Compare Listings 10.5. and 10.6.)

Listing 10.5   The IValid methods in VALIDVIEWS.PAS.

```
function TValidView.GetValid: boolean;
begin
  Result := True;
end; // TValidView.GetValid

procedure TValidView.SetValid(Value: boolean);
begin
  // A TValidView is always Valid - ignore the Value
end; // TValidView.SetValid

procedure TValidView.AddNotifiee(Notify: IFrame);
begin
  // A TValidView is always Valid - ignore the Add request
end; // TValidView.AddNotifiee

procedure TValidView.RemoveNotifiee(Notify: IFrame);
begin
  // A TValidView is always Valid - ignore the Remove request
end; // TValidView.RemoveNotifiee
```

Listing 10.6   Extracts from FICKLEVIEWS.PAS.

```
type
  TFickleView = class(TAbstractView)
  private
    fValid:  boolean;
    fNotify: IFrame;
    // This implementation of IValid only supports 1 Notifiee
  public
    procedure AddNotifiee(   Notify: IFrame); override;
```

```pascal
    procedure RemoveNotifiee(Notify: IFrame); override;

    function  GetValid: boolean;                override;
    procedure SetValid(Value: boolean);         override;
  end;

procedure TFickleView.AddNotifiee(Notify: IFrame);
begin
  fNotify := Notify;
end; // TFickleView.AddNotifiee

procedure TFickleView.RemoveNotifiee(Notify: IFrame);
begin
  fNotify := Nil;
end; // TFickleView.RemoveNotifiee

function  TFickleView.GetValid: boolean;
begin
  Result := fValid;
end; // TFickleView.GetValid

procedure TFickleView.SetValid(Value: boolean);
begin
  if Value <> fValid then
    begin
    fValid := Value;
    if Assigned(fNotify) then
      fNotify.OnValidChanged(Self, Self);
    end; // Value <> fValid
end; // TFickleView.SetValid
```

Model Editors

Wizards and property sheets are both *model editors*: You pass them a model object, they run, and then they return control. If the user pressed the OK button and changed the model, they return **True**; otherwise they return **False**. The abstract wizard and property sheet in the EMBEDDEDFORMS.DPR project let you create actual wizards and property sheets that can share model objects and views. All you have to do is:

- Create a new form that inherits from **TAbstractWizard** or **TAbstractPropertySheet**.
- Set the caption.

- For wizards, supply an image and adjust the image panel's width.
- Write a small **Initialize** procedure that supplies page captions and view classes as in the following snippet from TESTSHEET.PAS:

```
procedure TPropertySheet.Initialize;
begin
  InitializeSheet(
    ['Name/Supervisor', 'Birthday', 'Address'],
    [TEmployeeIdView, TBirthdayView, TAddressView] );
end; // TPropertySheet.Initialize
```

The abstract wizard and property sheet code does all the rest: Both automatically size themselves to fit the largest view. The wizard has standard Prev/Next/OK button logic; the property sheet will disable the OK button whenever a page is invalid, unless at least one page was already invalid when you called EditModel. Both call all views' **ReadFromModel** method on entry, and call all views' **WriteToModel** method if the user clicks OK. The property sheet has a **ReadOnly** property so you can let users look at objects without being able to edit them. Both are "pure interface" objects with no public methods, so that you don't have to bother with **Free** or **try..finally**. Listing 10.7, for example, is the code from MAIN.PAS that actually creates and runs the sample wizard and property sheet.

Listing 10.7 Running model editors.

```
procedure TTestForm.EditModel(Editor: IModelEdit; Model: TModel);
begin
  {$ifdef ReadOnly}
    Editor.ReadOnly := True;
  {$endif} // ReadOnly
  if Editor.EditModel(Model)
    then ShowMessage('OK!')
    else ShowMessage('Abort ...');
end; // TTestForm.EditModel

procedure TTestForm.RunWizard(Sender: TObject);
var
  Employee: TEmployee;
begin
  Employee := DataModel.NewEmployee;
  try
    EditModel(TWizard.Create(Self), Employee);
  finally Employee.Free; end;
end;
```

```
procedure TTestForm.RunSheet(Sender: TObject);
var
  Employee: TEmployee;
begin
  Employee := DataModel.LoadEmployee(3);
  try
    EditModel(TPropertySheet.Create(Self), Employee);
  finally Employee.Free; end;
end;
```

To me, the really amazing part of the wizard and property sheet code is how *simple* such generic code is in Delphi. The key is the **array of TViewClass** argument to **InitializeSheet()** and **InitializeWizard()**, shown in Listing 10.8.

Listing 10.8 TAbstractPropertySheet.InitializeSheet.

```
// From PropertySheets.pas

procedure TAbstractPropertySheet.InitializeSheet(
  Captions:   array of string;
  Views:      array of TViewClass );
var
  MaxSpan:    TSpan;
  Index:      integer;
  Sheet:      TTabSheet;
  ActualView: TAbstractView;
begin
  Assert( fViews.Count = 0,
          'Should only call ' + Name + '.InitializeSheet once' );
  Assert( High(Captions) >= Low(Captions), // can use Slice() to
          'Must have at least one tab' );  // pass empty arrays
  Assert( High(Captions) = High(Views),
          'Must have same number of Captions as of Views' );

  MaxSpan := Point(0, 0);

  for Index := Low(Captions) to High(Captions) do
    begin
    Sheet := TTabSheet.Create(Self);
    with Sheet do
      begin
      PageControl := Self.PageControl;
      Caption     := Captions[Index];
      end; // with Sheet
    ActualView := Views[Index].CreateEmbedded( Self,
```

```
                                            Sheet,
                                            efmTopLeft );
    fViews.Add(ActualView);
    ActualView.AddNotifiee(Self);
    MaxSpan := UnionSpan(MaxSpan, ActualView.Span);
    end; // for

  Sheet  := PageControl.ActivePage;
  Width  := (Width  - Sheet.Width)  + MaxSpan.X;
  Height := (Height - Sheet.Height) + MaxSpan.Y;
end; // TAbstractPropertySheet.InitializeSheet
```

The three **Assert** statements check that this property sheet hasn't been set up already, that there is at least one caption, and that there are the same number of captions as view classes. (I really love **Assert**—I never quite realized just how cumbersome {$IfOpt D+} {$endif} was until I didn't have to use it anymore. Assertions are easier to type, as well as being smaller and easier to read.)

Spans are defined in EMBEDDED.PAS. They're just a width/height pair, the **BottomRight** of a **TRect** whose **Top** and **Left** are 0:

```
function TEmbeddedForm.Span: TSpan;
begin
  Result.X := Width;
  Result.Y := Height;
end; // TEmbeddedForm.Span
```

UnionSpan is very similar to the Windows API's **UnionRect** except that it works on spans instead of rectangles. Setting **MaxSpan** to (0, 0) is just setup for calculating the smallest rectangle that will hold all the **Views**.

The real work is done in the loop on the **Captions** array. For each item in the array, we create a new tab sheet, place it on the page control, and set its caption. Then we use the array of class of **TAbstractView** argument, **Views**, to create a new view. We then add the new view to a **TList** of views, tell it to call its frame whenever **Valid** changes, and inflate **MaxSpan**.

Once we've added all the views, we calculate how much room to allow "around" **MaxSpan** for the frame, caption, buttons, and notebook tabs. We get this by looking at the difference between the form's height/width and the PageControl.ActivePage's height/width.

TAbstractWizard is very similar, but is a bit more complicated because instead of notebook pages, we use three panels: an outer panel, a top-aligned caption panel, and a client-aligned frame panel. Activating a particular page is simply a matter of bringing the appropriate outer panel to the front, as shown in Listing 10.9.

Listing 10.9 TAbstractWizard.SetCurrentPage.

```
// From Wizards.pas

property CurrentPage: integer read  fCurrentPage
                              write SetCurrentPage;

procedure TAbstractWizard.SetCurrentPage(Value: integer);
var
  LastPage, PageIsValid: boolean;
begin
  Assert(TObject(fPanels[Value]) is TPanel);
  Assert(TObject(fViews[Value]) is TAbstractView);
  // Using Assert(is) with 'blind' casts gives us the debugging
  // safety of "as" without the (modest) performance hit

  fCurrentPage := Value;
  TPanel(fPanels[Value]).BringToFront;

  LastPage := Value = fPageCount;
  PageIsValid := TAbstractView(fViews[Value]).Valid;

  PrevBtn.Enabled := Value > 0;
  NextBtn.Enabled := PageIsValid and (not LastPage);
  OkBtn.Enabled   := PageIsValid and LastPage;
end; // TAbstractWizard.SetCurrentPage
```

As you can see in Listing 10.9, another nice feature of **Assert** statements is the way the assert-and-blind-cast pair gives us all the development-time type checking of **as** without any deployment-time speed penalty. Otherwise, the code is pretty straightforward: We set **fCurrentPage** and bring the appropriate panel to the front. Then we check to see if it is the first or last page and if the page is **Valid**, and then we set the Previous, Next, and OK buttons accordingly.

The rest of the code in WIZARDS.PAS and PROPERTYSHEETS.PAS is pretty straightforward. While I'll be pleased and flattered if you think it's worth studying, you don't need to understand it to use it, and it's certainly not worth killing trees to print any more of it in this chapter. It's on the CD-ROM if you really want it.

The Sample Model

While the real point of EMBEDDEDFORMS.PAS is to give an extended example of embedded forms in action, and to give you a usable wizard and property sheet framework, it also contains a simplistic data model and four views, both to show you how to use the framework and to serve as an example of a view containing another view.

The **Data** unit is a skeletal data module that contains methods to create, "load," and "save" **Employee** objects (see Listing 10.10). In a real application, these methods would probably be wrappers around database access routines; here, the load method just retrieves some compiled-in dummy data and the save method does nothing at all. The **Employee** object contains references to two **People** objects, which contain personal data about the employee and his or her supervisor. The EmployeeIdView you saw back in Figures 10.1 and 10.2 allows the user to select the employee's supervisor from a pull-down list and to edit the employee's name and tax identification.

The interesting part of this is that we are displaying the same view of the supervisor field as of the employee field—and using two different copies of the same view object to do so. At design time, both views are just blank place holders (Figure 10.6). When we create the form, we create two instances of the PersonIdView of Figure 10.7 and place each on the appropriate panel of the EmployeeIdview form.

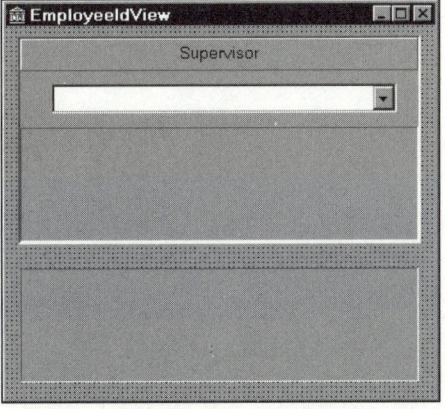

Figure 10.6
A view that is also a frame.

Chapter 10

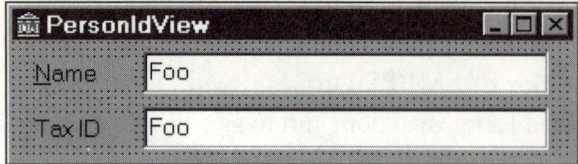

Figure 10.7
The PersonIdView at design time.

Listing 10.10   EMPLOYEEIDVIEWS.PAS.

```
unit EmployeeIdViews;

// Copyright © 1997 by Jon Shemitz, all rights reserved.
// Permission is hereby granted to freely use, modify, and
// distribute this source code PROVIDED that all six lines of
// this copyright and contact notice are included without any
// changes. Questions? Comments? Offers of work?
// mailto:jon@midnightbeach.com

// ----------------------------------------------------------

// A reasonably plausible employee id view - select/view the
// supervisor; set name and tax id.

interface

uses
  Windows, Messages, SysUtils, Classes, Graphics, Controls,
  Forms, Dialogs, StdCtrls, ExtCtrls,
  Models, Embedded, FickleViews, PersonIdViews;

type
  TEmployeeIdView = class(TFickleView, IFrame)
    SupervisorPnl: TPanel;
    SupervisorCaptionPnl: TPanel;
    SupervisorFrame: TPanel;
    SelectSupervisor: TComboBox;
    SupervisorLbl: TLabel;
    EmployeeIdFrame: TPanel;
    procedure FormCreate(Sender: TObject);
    procedure FormDestroy(Sender: TObject);
    procedure SelectSupervisorChange(Sender: TObject);
  private
    SupervisorView,
    EmployeeView:    TPersonIdView;
```

```
    protected
      procedure ReadFromModel(Model: TModel);    override;
      procedure WriteToModel(Model:  TModel);    override;
      procedure SetReadOnly(Value: boolean);     override;
      procedure OnValidChanged( ChangingObject: TObject;
                                View:           IView );
    end;

implementation

{$R *.DFM}

uses Data;

// create/destroy

procedure TEmployeeIdView.FormCreate(Sender: TObject);
var
  Index: integer;
begin
  inherited;
  SupervisorView :=
    TPersonIdView.CreateEmbedded( Self,
                                  SupervisorFrame,
                                  efmCentered );
  SupervisorView.ReadOnly := True;
  SupervisorView.AddNotifiee(Self);

  EmployeeView :=
    TPersonIdView.CreateEmbedded( Self,
                                  EmployeeIdFrame,
                                  efmCentered );
  EmployeeView.AddNotifiee(Self);

  with DataModel do
    for Index := 0 to SupervisorCount - 1 do
      SelectSupervisor.Items.Add(
        GetEmployeeName(Supervisor[Index]) );
end; // TEmployeeIdView.FormCreate

procedure TEmployeeIdView.FormDestroy(Sender: TObject);
begin
  inherited;
  SupervisorView.RemoveNotifiee(Self);
  SupervisorView.Free;
```

```
    EmployeeView.RemoveNotifiee(Self);
    EmployeeView.Free;
end; // TEmployeeIdView.FormDestroy

// IView overrides

procedure TEmployeeIdView.ReadFromModel(Model: TModel);
begin
  Assert(Model is TEmployee);

  with TEmployee(Model) do
    begin
    SupervisorView.ReadFromModel(Supervisor);
    EmployeeView.ReadFromModel(Employee);

    SelectSupervisor.ItemIndex :=
      DataModel.IndexOfSupervisor(Supervisor.ID);
    end; // with
end; // TEmployeeIdView.ReadFromModel

procedure TEmployeeIdView.WriteToModel(Model:  TModel);
begin
  Assert(Model is TEmployee);

  with TEmployee(Model) do
    begin
    SupervisorView.WriteToModel(Supervisor);
    EmployeeView.WriteToModel(Employee);
    end; // with
end; // TEmployeeIdView.WriteToModel

procedure TEmployeeIdView.SetReadOnly(Value: boolean);
begin
  inherited;
  EmployeeView.ReadOnly   := ReadOnly;
  SelectSupervisor.Color := ShowReadOnly_EditColors[ReadOnly];
end; // TEmployeeIdView.SetReadOnly

// change supervisor

procedure TEmployeeIdView.SelectSupervisorChange(Sender: TObject);
var
  ID:         TPersonID;
  Supervisor: TPerson;
begin
```

Models, Views, And Frames

```
  inherited;
  ID := DataModel.Supervisor[SelectSupervisor.ItemIndex];
  Supervisor := DataModel.LoadPerson(ID);
  try
    SupervisorView.ReadFromModel(Supervisor);
  finally Supervisor.Free; end;
end; // TEmployeeIdView.SelectSupervisorChange

// frame notification

procedure TEmployeeIdView.OnValidChanged(
  ChangingObject: TObject;
  View:           IView );
begin
  Valid := SupervisorView.Valid and EmployeeView.Valid;
end; // TEmployeeIdView.OnValidChanged

end.
```

FormCreate creates the two **TPersonID** views and registers itself as their frame. The supervisor view is read-only; the only way to change it is via the drop-down box. **FormDestroy** undoes the registration (that is, releases the interface reference) and frees the embedded forms.

ReadFromModel and **WriteToModel** basically just delegate their jobs to the embedded views. In general, it's a good idea for all model I/O functions to do as these do, and **Assert** that their model argument is of the type that they expect. This will cause a runtime error during development if you pass the wrong model type to the model editor, or pass the wrong view type to the model editor's setup routine.

Other Applications

EMBEDDEDFORMS.DPR really only illustrates the first two scenarios that I laid out at the beginning of this chapter: using the same form in a wizard and a property sheet, and using forms as lightweight components. I haven't shown you any actual examples of the second two scenarios: using embedded forms for team development of a tabbed dialog, or to build a generic editor that can handle any member of an object hierarchy. However, I *have* illustrated the techniques you would need to handle these less common cases.

To build a dialog out of multiple independent forms, just have each derive from **TEmbeddedForm**. Create a tab for each page, and in the dialog's OnCreate handler, call **CreateEmbedded** for each page's form. I generally make a point of freeing each page in the OnDestroy handler, honoring the general Free What You Create rule, but this isn't strictly necessary, as freeing the dialog will free all its child components. If you need any sort of *per page* validation—perhaps you won't let users tab off of invalid pages—you can derive from **TFickleView** instead of **TEmbeddedForm**.

You could model a generic editor on the abstract model editors: a container object with all the standard controls you need, and a blank frame panel where the object-specific controls will go. Each member of the object hierarchy might have a **class function** which returns a **TViewClass**. This would let the generic editor fill the frame with the right view for each object it's asked to edit.

I've gotten a lot of mileage out of embedded forms over the last year or so. They have considerable ability to make your code simpler and clearer, more reliable and more flexible. They're yet another example of the sort of thing that's always been possible under Windows, but which was impossibly complex until Delphi made it easy.

HIGH PERFORMANCE

The Shadowy Math Unit

CHAPTER 11

Explore the new Delphi unit no one knows about—and harness it to do all sorts of statistical dirty work on your data.

The Shadowy Math Unit

Terence Goggin

Delphi 2 and Delphi 3 contain a first-class utility unit that, so far, has received only second-class attention. It's in the documentation (sort of), and people seem to know it's there (some people, at least), but most of them don't have the first notion how to use it. It's called the Math unit, and it's an excellent collection of financial, statistical, and general arithmetic and trigonometric functions.

Using some of these functions, this chapter will show you how to build—and use—a data-aware statistical reporting component, TDBStatistics. This component will allow you to give your users a complete data profile of up to 13 different statistics.

Three Good Reasons To Use The Math Unit

There are actually three good reasons to use the Math unit. First and foremost is speed. The Math unit's routines are *fast*. Many of them are coded in assembly language specifically optimized for the Pentium's Floating-Point Unit (FPU). Unless you've got a Pentium II and a lot of free time, it probably doesn't get much faster than that!

Second, the alternative of using SQL's statistical routines is unacceptable. SQL only offers four or five statistical functions—far too few to provide a complete statistical picture.

Third, choosing the Math unit over SQL or BDE-based solutions ensures that the TDBStatistics component should work with replacement database engines such as Apollo, Titan, or Direct Access.

Dynamic Data And Static Declarations

The Math unit *is* fast and comprehensive, but there's a catch. You'll need a trick or two to make the most of the statistical functions. You see, many of the Math unit's routines take a parameter declared as:

```
const Data: array of Double
```

Functions like this can be difficult to use because arrays passed via these parameters must be *statically declared*. At first glance, then, there doesn't appear to be a way to pass dynamic data to these functions. Most programmers assume that they've got to use one of two partial solutions to solve this dynamic data dilemma. They can:

1. Hard-code values into the program; or
2. Make the array as large as possible and hope no user ever exceeds that limit.

Hard-coding values into a program *occasionally* is necessary, but most of the time it turns out to be a very bad idea. In fact, that's exactly what happens here. Consider this call to the **Mean** function:

```
Mean([3, 2, 1, 5, 6]);
```

Essentially, what we have in this line of code is a calculator that gives the same result each time, no matter what values are entered. That's not exactly a useful result, is it?

Obviously, the idea of hard-coding data just won't cut it. This leaves the option of "overdeclaring" the size of the array. While this technique is typically very useful in some situations—if not downright necessary at times—it can introduce unseen complications.

This is especially true in the case of the Math unit. Again, consider the **Mean** function. The "mean" is defined as the sum of N terms / N. Let's assume we have a 10,000-element array that we're going to pass to the **Mean** function. If the user were to enter only 50 values, the denominator—that's N—would be off by 9,950! Whoops!

Slice To The Rescue

Overdeclaring doesn't appear to be such a good idea either. So, how do we pass dynamic data to these otherwise excellent routines? The answer lies in an all but unknown function buried in the System unit called **Slice**:

```
function Slice(var A: array; Count: Integer): array;
```

Slice takes an array of any size and type and returns **Count** elements as though they were a *separate and distinct array*. With **Slice**, we can declare a very large array and use as many or as few elements as we want.

The **Slice** function, then, allows us to revive the idea of "overdeclaring," such that we no longer need to be concerned about the problem of the inaccurate denominator. This, in turn, makes it possible for us to pass dynamic data to these functions.

Armed with our newfound solution, we can now proceed with the creation of our quick and easy statistical reporting component.

Creating The DBStatistics Component

We've just discovered—thanks to **Slice**—how to pass dynamic data to the functions of the Math unit. So, now what we need is a way to make these routines work efficiently for database analysis. The simplest and friendliest way to do this is by wrapping the routines up as a component—a component called, appropriately enough, DBStatistics.

Defining The Component's Tasks

When you're building components, it's usually a good idea to begin by defining the component's tasks. As you might expect, that's just what we'll do for DBStatistics.

DBStatistics' main task is to provide us with easy access to one, several, or all of the 13 possible statistics, given a field name and a DataSource. In order to do this, the component will need the following inner workings:

1. Access to data, preferably via a DataSource;
2. A place to store large amounts of data locally;

3. A way to extract the data from a DataSource; and

4. A way to make the 13 statistics easily available.

In the next four sections, we'll discuss these inner workings in detail.

Getting Access To The Data

To extract the data our new class **TDBStatistics** is to analyze, it must first have a way to link to some **TTable** or **TQuery** component. The easiest and simplest way to do this is to provide our component with a DataSource property. And that's exactly what we do. The **private** section contains the following declaration:

```
fDataSource : TDataSource;
```

which, of course, is made available at design-time via the **published** qualifier.

We also need a way for DBStatistics to know which field it is to analyze. This can be provided easily via a **DataField** property. There's nothing new to this; you can see it in any component on the "Data Controls" palette tab. Because these two properties are so common, including them in DBStatistics helps to create a familiar design-time feel.

Storing Data Locally

Now that we have access to data, we need a place to store this data once we extract it. The Math unit's routines require a statically declared array; therefore, we must have just such an array. Our array is called, appropriately enough, **Data**.

The question that remains, then, is what the maximum number of elements in **Data** should be. When choosing this value, there are two factors to consider. First, we must consider the number of records in our average table. If our tables generally don't exceed 4,000 records, then 4,500 would be a good maximum elements value.

The other factor to take into account is the amount of available memory. If memory is not an issue, then we can make the array as large as we like. If memory is an issue, however, trial and error is the way to find the optimum size for the array.

For the purposes of illustration, though, let's declare our **Data** array to have 10,000 elements. (Naturally, the 10,000 value will be declared as a constant, **MaxValues**.) This should give us plenty of space for most everyday applications.

Extracting Data

The next two pieces of **TDBStatistics** are very tightly interrelated, so we'll try to develop both of them at the same time. The first of these two areas of interest is the error checking routine, **GetRange**. When the component extracts data, the error-checking routine must ensure that everything is done "legally." In most cases, "legally" means nothing more than preventing the component from, say, reading beyond the last record.

However, in the case of **TDBStatistics**, it's a little more subtle than that. Because users might want to analyze a set of records that is larger than our array, we should allow them to select a subset of their data. This is done through two properties: **UpperBound** and **LowerBound**. These properties provide the component with starting and ending record numbers. The job of the error-checking routine then, is to monitor these two values. The simplest way to accomplish this is through a function that:

1. Checks the values for possible errors;
2. Makes any necessary adjustments; and
3. Returns the (adjusted) difference between the two values.

The first two tests ensure that **LowerBound** is greater than zero, and that **UpperBound** is at least **LowerBound + 1**:

```
if (LowerBound < 1) then
    LowerBound := 1;
if (UpperBound < 1) then
    UpperBound := LowerBound + 1;
```

The next test ensures that **UpperBound** is greater than **LowerBound**. If it's found that **LowerBound** is greater than **UpperBound**, the two values are swapped:

```
if (LowerBound > UpperBound) then
  begin
    TempInt := UpperBound;
    UpperBound := LowerBound;
    LowerBound := TempInt;
  end;
```

Then, we test and adjust the values of **UpperBound** and **LowerBound** to make sure that they do not exceed the number of records in the DataSource (the

DataSource.DataSet.RecordCount value has already been retrieved and stored in the **Records** variable):

```
if (LowerBound > Records) then
    LowerBound := 1;
if (UpperBound > Records) then
    UpperBound := Records;
```

The last test makes sure that the difference between **UpperBound** and **LowerBound** doesn't exceed the number of elements in the **Data** array. In other words, we can't store more values than we have elements in the array:

```
if (UpperBound - LowerBound > MaxValues) then
  UpperBound := LowerBound + MaxValues;
```

Finally, the **GetRange** function returns the difference between the now adjusted **UpperBound** and **LowerBound**:

```
Result := UpperBound - LowerBound;
```

And that's our error-checking routine.

Now that we have our error checking done, we can proceed to the task of extracting the data from the DataSource and storing it in our **Data** array. This is done in a procedure called **FillArray**.

The real work of **FillArray** begins with a call to **GetRange**. Then, once the bounds have been adjusted (as described above), we can extract the data and store it locally. First, we open the DataSource and go to the record number specified by **LowerBound**:

```
fDataSource.DataSet.Open;
fDataSource.DataSet.MoveBy(LowerBound);
```

Next, we test the type of **fDataField**. If the field contains numerical values, then we just extract the data, one record at a time, placing each value into the **Data** array:

```
if ((fDataSource.DataSet.FieldByName(fDataField) is TCurrencyField) or
(fDataSource.DataSet.FieldByName(fDataField) is TFloatField) or
(fDataSource.DataSet.FieldByName(fDataField) is TIntegerField) or
(fDataSource.DataSet.FieldByName(fDataField) is TSmallIntField))then
begin
  for I := LowerBound to UpperBound do
```

```
      begin
        if not (fDataSource.DataSet.FieldByName(fDataField).IsNull) then
          Data[Index] :=
              fDataSource.DataSet.FieldByName(fDataField).Value
            else
          Data[Index] := 0;
        Inc(Index);
        fDataSource.DataSet.Next;
      end;
end;
```

If the field is a character field, though, we should extract the data in a slightly different manner. The only character field data that the component expects to deal with are ZIP codes. There are two possible types of ZIP codes: the older five-digit kind, and the newer five "plus four" kind.

As far as **TDBStatistics** is concerned, if the field contains five-digit ZIP codes, the value can be converted to a numeric type without additional handling. If the value is a nine-digit, hyphenated ZIP code, though, the hyphen must first be changed to a "." character so that the value can be converted to a numeric type:

```
else if (fDataSource.DataSet.FieldByName(fDataField) is TStringField)
  then
  begin
    for I := LowerBound to UpperBound do
      begin
        TempString :=
          fDataSource.DataSet.FieldByName(fDataField).Value;
        if (Pos('-', TempString) > 0) then
          TempString[Pos('-', TempString)] := '.';
        Data[Index] := StrToFloat(TempString);
        Inc(Index);
        fDataSource.DataSet.Next;
      end;
  end;
```

Finally, we close the DataSource and reset two boolean flags:

```
fDataSource.DataSet.Close;
IsArrayFilled := True;
DidGetAll := False;
```

The **IsArrayFilled** variable lets the other methods of the component know if the data has been extracted from the DataSource. If it is set to **False**, the other routines can call **FillArray** before completing their work. The **DidGetAll** variable is another boolean flag used by access methods. (Its purpose will become clear momentarily.)

Making The Data Available

Now that we've done all the background work, the only thing left is to provide a way for us to retrieve the statistics. There are two ways to do this:

1. A method that retrieves all of the 13 results at once; and

2. Individual access methods for each of the 13 results, made available via properties.

In this component we use both ideas.

To retrieve all of the statistics at once, we have the **GetAllStats** procedure. **GetAllStats** passes the **Data** array to all 13 statistical functions and stores the results in variables defined in the **private** section of our component. In addition, it sets the boolean variable **DidGetAll** to **True**, indicating to other methods that all of the statistics have already been retrieved.

The individual access methods, of course, can then check the value of the **DidGetAll** variable. If it is set to **True**, the access method simply can return the already stored result. On the other hand, if **DidGetAll** is set to **False**, the access method can call its related Math function directly and return the result from the Math unit. As an example of a typical access method, let's look at **GetMean**, which returns the mean of the selected DataField's values.

First, we make sure that the data has been extracted from the DataSource and stored in the **Data** array:

```
if not (IsArrayFilled) then
   FillArray;
```

Now, another test—this time to make sure that the statistical result we're looking for hasn't already been retrieved. The idea here is that if the result already has been obtained and stored, there's no reason to get it again; the access method should simply return the already-stored value to save time.

On the other hand, if it hasn't yet been retrieved, we call the relevant Math unit function, using **Slice** and the **GetRange** function. Lastly, we return the statistic given to us by the Math unit:

```
if not (DidGetAll) then
   fMean := Math.Mean(Slice(Data,GetRange));
Result := fMean;
```

Now that we've provided a quick and easy way to access the statistical results, **TDBStatistics** is ready to be plugged into any project.

Test Driving The DBStatistics Component

Well, now that we've built this wonderful component, let's put it to work. In this section, we'll create a program that allows the user to select any field in any table, and get a complete statistical report displayed neatly in a Memo component. Figure 11.1 shows the **StatsProject** at runtime.

(All associated files for this project are on the CD-ROM in the subdirectory for Chapter 11. Only the code under immediate discussion will be printed here.)

You'll notice that everything on the form is pretty standard—there are a few ordinary visual controls, along with a **TTable**, a **TDataSource**, a **TOpenDialog**, and, of course, a **TDBStatistics**. When the user starts the **StatsProject**, he/she must first select a table. This is done through **BtnTableSelect**, the **TButton** control marked "1. Select a table & field". In the **BtnTableSelect**'s **OnClick** event, a table name is retrieved via the TOpenDialog component, **OpenDialog1**.

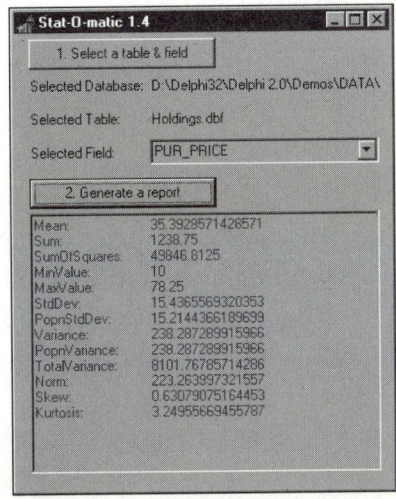

Figure 11.1
StatsProject at runtime.

First, the **Execute** method is called. If a valid file name was selected, then we proceed:

```
with OpenDialog1 do
  begin
    Execute;
    if FileName = '' then
      exit;
```

We now set the properties of the **TTable** component based on the user's file selection. In addition, we display the relevant information via two **TLabel** controls:

```
Table1.DatabaseName := ExtractFilePath(FileName);
LblDatabase.Caption := ExtractFilePath(FileName);
Table1.TableName := ExtractFileName(FileName);
LblTable.Caption := ExtractFileName(FileName);
```

Because **TDBStatistics** only operates on one field at a time, we must provide a way for the user to select a field. This is done by retrieving the field names of the **TTable** and placing them into a ComboBox component:

```
CBFields.Items.Clear; {reset TComboBox}
CBFields.Text := '';
Table1.Open;
for I := 0 to Table1.FieldDefs.Count-1  do
  begin
    Application.ProcessMessages;
    CBFields.Items.Add(Table1.Fields[I].FieldName);
  end;
Table1.Close;
```

And that's all there is to selecting a table and field name.

Once the user has selected a field to be analyzed, he/she can generate a statistical report in the Memo control by clicking the **BtnReports** button. (It's the one marked "2. Generate a report".) In the **BtnReports.OnClick** event, then, we first set the appropriate properties for the DBStatistics component, **DBStatistics1**:

```
DBStatistics1.LowerBound := 1;
Table1.Open;
DBStatistics1.UpperBound := Table1.RecordCount;
Table1.Close;
DataSource1.DataSet := Table1;
```

```
DBStatistics1.DataSource := DataSource1;
DBStatistics1.DataField := CBFields.Text;{user-selected field}
```

Then, we call **DBStatistics1.GetAllStats** and print the results to the Memo component:

```
DBStatistics1.GetAllStats;
Memo1.Text := '';
Memo1.Lines.Add('Mean: ' + #09 + #09 + FloatToStr(DBStatistics1.Mean));

{etc......}

Memo1.Lines.Add('Kurtosis: ' + #09 + #09 +
  FloatToStr(DBStatistics1.Kurtosis));
```

And that's about all there is to it. We now have a complete statistical report generator.

Bugs In The Delphi 2 Math Unit

Yes, believe it or not, there is a bug in the Math unit for Delphi 2. But it's probably better you hear it now than find out the hard way, right? (Better still, upgrade to Delphi 3!)

So here goes: In Math unit of Delphi 2, **MinValue** and **MaxValue** are reversed. **MinValue** actually returns the largest value in the array, while **MaxValue** returns the smallest value in the array. While this bug isn't a showstopper, it does deserve mentioning. (Of course, the DBStatistics component fixes this problem with regards to its own **MaxValue** and **MinValue** properties.)

Note well that this bug *has* been fixed in the Delphi 3 version of the Math unit. The DBStatistics component has been updated to reflect this. Thanks to a few judicious {$IFDEF} statements, the TDBStatistics component will work with either Delphi 2 or Delphi 3.

Poly: The Function That Got Away

While I was preparing the complete list of the Math unit's functions presented at the end of this chapter, there was one function that was omitted intentionally. Why? Because Borland didn't document it either! So it isn't clear whether it's "really" supposed to be in the Math unit at all. (In fact, the only way anyone would ever find it is if they were studying the source for the Math unit while preparing a chapter for *High Performance Delphi 3*....)

What's this mysterious function all about? Here it is:

```
function Poly(X: Extended; const Coefficients: array of Double):
  Extended;
```

Basically, **Poly** solves polynomial equations for you. The only limitation is that they must be polynomials in *one* variable. You pass **Poly** two pieces of information: a value, X, at which you want the polynomial evaluated, and the coefficients of the polynomial's terms. The coefficients should be ordered in increasing powers of X.

What this means is that if you have a polynomial such as

$4x^4 \; [+ \; 0x^3] \; - \; x^2 \; + \; 3x \; + \; 34$

the values in your coefficients array should be ordered like this:

34, 3, -1, 0, 4.

If you were to put an interface on the **Poly** function, you'd probably end up with something like Figure 11.2, which shows PolyProject running.

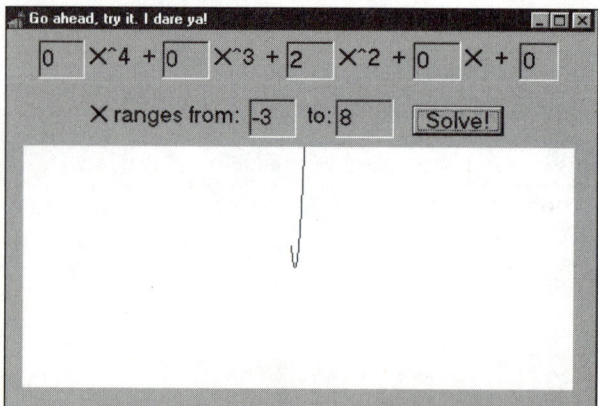

Figure 11.2
Graphing a polynomial function with Poly.

PolyProject (on the CD-ROM for this chapter) is just such an application. It allows the user to enter a polynomial, and then actually graphs it. You'll notice that the PolyProject's main window has a few edit controls, along with some labels, set up so that the user can enter coefficients for a generic polynomial. However, all of the significant work of the PolyProject is done in the OnClick event of the "Solve!" Button:

```
procedure TForm1.SolveButtonClick(Sender: TObject);
var
   i : Integer;
   XCoes : array[0..4] of double;
   X,Y, OffsetX, OffsetY : Integer;
   NewRect: TRect;
```

Our first job is to fill the **XCoes** array with the coefficient values the user has entered:

```
begin
  XCoes[0] := StrToFloat(TxtX0.Text);
  XCoes[1] := StrToFloat(TxtX1.Text);
  XCoes[2] := StrToFloat(TxtX2.Text);
  XCoes[3] := StrToFloat(TxtX3.Text);
  XCoes[4] := StrToFloat(TxtX4.Text);
...
```

That done, we now have to set the center for our graphing area. I prefer to use the center of the **TImage** control, but you could just as easily use any point you like:

```
OffsetX := Image1.Width div 2;
OffsetY := Image1.Height div 2;
```

Next, we initialize our X-coordinate value and clear the graph by essentially filling **Image1** with a solid white rectangle. Then, we reset **Image1.Canvas.Brush.Color** so that our graph will be drawn in black:

```
X := 0; {Initialize X just to be safe}
NewRect := Rect(0, 0, Image1.Width, Image1.Height);
Image1.Canvas.Brush.Color := clWhite;
Image1.Canvas.FillRect(NewRect);
Image1.Canvas.Brush.Color := clBlack;
```

Here's where the calculations are done. We first generate a starting point for the line. Note that we don't actually draw anything until we're inside the **for** loop. This is because we need a point at which to position the "pen" before we do any serious drawing. So we call the **Poly** function, passing the value contained in the lower bound range editbox (**TxtRangeStart**) and the **XCoes** array:

```
with Image1.Canvas do
  begin
    Y := Trunc(Poly(StrToInt(TxtRangeStart.Text), XCoes));
...
```

You may be surprised to see that I've truncated the result of the **Poly** function. This is for graphing purposes only; although the **Poly** function returns a floating-point (**Extended** type) value, the Windows API only understands integer coordinates.

Next, we convert the result we just got to an (X, Y) pair that corresponds to our center, and we move the "pen" to that point:

```
X := StrToInt(TxtRangeStart.Text) + OffsetX;
Y := OffsetY - Y;
MoveTo(X,Y);
```

We then use a **for** loop to iterate through the X-range values, one at a time, starting with the lower bound plus 1 (we just did the lower bound value a moment ago), and continuing through to the value contained in the upper bound editbox (**TxtRangeEnd**):

```
for i := StrToInt(TxtRangeStart.Text) + 1 to
StrToInt(TxtRangeEnd.Text) do
  begin
    Y := Trunc(Poly(I, XCoes));
    X := I + OffsetX;
    Y := OffsetY - Y;
    LineTo(X,Y);
    MoveTo(X,Y);
  end;
```

While **Poly** appears to be the only *publicly* available, undocumented function in the Math unit, there are a few routines declared in the **implementation** section that look interesting. (One actually determines if value A is "small" relative to value B!) While they can't be discussed here due to space constraints, I'd recommend reading them over if you've got the source code—and the patience, of course!

Filling The Pascal Power Gap

The Math unit introduces something Pascal has never had: an official power (exponent) function. In fact, the Math unit contains *two* power functions.

The first power function, **Power**, takes two **Extended** type values; one is the base, the other is the exponent. The second power function, **IntPower**, takes one **Extended** type parameter and one integer parameter; the **Extended** value is the base, the integer is the exponent.

The difference between the two routines is that **IntPower**, like many of the Math unit's routines, is coded entirely in Pentium FPU optimized assembler, making it quite fast.

If you're concerned about which one your app should use, don't be.

Although it's not explained or documented, **Power** itself will decide whether the exponent is an integer. If it is, **Power** calls **IntPower**. If, on the other hand, the exponent is a true floating-point value, **Power** uses the canonical natural log/base *e* method of calculating its result.

Math Unit Function Summary

To close out this chapter, I'll present a complete list of the functions and procedures presented in the Math unit. Although the math unit has changed very little from Delphi 2 to Delphi 3, Borland did add three new functions for Delphi 3: **MaxIntValue**, **MinIntValue**, and **SumInt**. The only real difference between these routines and their cousins (**MaxValue**, **MinValue**, and **Sum**) is that these routines are strictly integer-only and do not accept or return floating-point values. As for the other routines, most of them are reasonably self-explanatory. Those that aren't—well, sit yourself down and do some sleuthing. Not all Delphi knowledge will be handed to you on a silver-plated Help screen!

Trigonometric Functions And Procedures

ArcCos—Inverse Cosine.

ArcCosh—Inverse Hyperbolic Cosine.

ArcSin—Inverse Sine.

ArcSinh—Inverse Hyperbolic Sine.

ArcTanh—Inverse Hyperbolic Tangent.

ArcTan2—Inverse Tangent with corrections for the proper quadrant. (The function can be found in the System unit.)

Cosh—Hyperbolic Cosine.

Cotan—Cotangent.

CycleToRad—Converts Cycles to Radians.

DegToRad—Converts Degrees to Radians.

GradToRad—Converts Grads to Radians.

Hypot—Calculates the length of the hypotenuse of a triangle given the length of the two sides.

RadToCycle—Converts Radians to Cycles.

RadToDeg—Converts Radians to Degrees.

RadToGrad—Converts Radians to Grads.

SinCos—Calculates both the Sine and Cosine for a given angle. Just as with **SumAndSquares** and **MeanAndStdDev**, it is faster to generate both values at once.

Sinh—Hyperbolic Sine.

Tan—Tangent.

Tanh—Hyperbolic Tangent.

Arithmetic Functions And Procedures

Ceil—Rounds up.

Floor—Rounds down.

Frexp—Calculates the Mantissa and exponent of a given value.

IntPower—Raises a number to an integral power. If you're not going to use Float-based exponents, this function is to be highly recommended because of its speed.

Ldexp—Calculates X times 2 to a given power.

LnXP1—Calculates the natural log of X + 1. This is intended for estimating Xs close to zero.

LogN—Given a base and an X value, calculates the base N log of X.

Log10—Calculates the natural log of X.

Log2—Calculates the log in base two of X.

Power—Raises a number to an exponent. This one isn't as fast as IntPower, but if you need Float-type exponents, it'll do quite well.

Financial Functions And Procedures

DoubleDecliningBalance—Calculates depreciation using the double-declining balance formula.

FutureValue—Calculates the future value of an investment.

InterestPayment—Calculates the amount of the loan payment that is interest.

InterestRate—Calculates the interest rate necessary to earn a specified amount.

InternalRateOfReturn—Calculates a rate of return based on cash-flow data.

NetPresentValue—Calculates the current value of a set of cash-flow values, taking the interest rate into account.

NumberOfPeriods—Calculates the number of periods for an investment to reach a specified value.

Payment—Calculates the amount of loan payments, given the amount borrowed, the interest rate, and present and future values of the investment.

PeriodPayment—Calculates the amount of the loan payment that is principal.

PresentValue—Calculates the present value of an investment.

SLNDepreciation—Calculates the Straight-Line Depreciation of an investment.

SYDDepreciation—Calculates the Sum-of-Years-Digits Depreciation.

Chapter 11

Statistical Functions And Procedures

MaxIntValue—Finds the largest value in a set of *integer* data. New to Delphi 3, does not exist in Delphi 2.

MaxValue—Finds the largest value in a set of data. Under Delphi 2, finds the *smallest* value.

Mean—Calculates the Mean for a set of values.

MeanAndStdDev—Calculates *both* the Mean and standard deviation for a set of data. This is faster than calculating each value separately.

MinIntValue—Finds the smallest value in a set of *integer* data. New to Delphi 3, does not exist in Delphi 2.

MinValue—Finds the smallest value in a set of data. Under Delphi 2, finds the *largest* value.

MomentSkewKurtosis—Calculates the skew and kurtosis for a given set of data.

Norm—Calculates the norm for a given set of data. The norm is the square root of the sum of squares.

PopnStdDev—Calculates the population standard deviation, which differs from the standard deviation in that it uses the population variance (**PopnVariance**), defined below.

PopnVariance—Calculates the population variance for a given set of data. This routine uses the TotalVariance / n or "biased" formula.

RandG—Generates "fake" data points given a mean and a standard deviation.

StdDev—Calculates the standard deviation for a set of data.

Sum—Calculates the sum of a set of values.

SumsAndSquares—Calculates *both* the sum and the sum of squares for a given set of data. As with several of the Math unit's routines, it is faster to generate these two results at once, rather than first generating the sum and then the sum of squares.

SumInt—Calculates the sum of a set of *integer* values. New to Delphi 3, does not exist in Delphi 2.

SumOfSquares—Calculates the sum of the squares of a set of values.

TotalVariance—Calculates the total variance for a given set of data. Total variance is the sum of every value's distance from the mean squared.

Variance—Calculates the sample variance for a given set of data. This routine uses the TotalVariance / (n-1) or "unbiased" formula.

HIGH PERFORMANCE

Dynamic User Interfaces

CHAPTER 12

If your users don't like the user interface you hand them, well, why not hand them a user interface that they can modify at runtime? Emulating design time at runtime is easier than you think, and can add tremendously to an application's appeal.

Dynamic User Interfaces

Terence Goggin

Let's face it: No two people look at data in the same way. After all, if everybody had the same idea of how data should be presented, there would only be one "Personal Information Manager" program. But that's not the case; the world is littered with PIMs of all shapes and sizes.

Some PIMs are lucky accidents in interface design and receive immediate widespread acceptance. Others are difficult to use and probably only intuitive to their creators. The problem seems to be that there's no in-between.

Occasionally, users will find one of these difficult-to-use programs so beneficial that they will force themselves to use it, no matter how difficult a task learning it might be. However, you can't count on this when you're designing a program. Mostly, you can count on complaints.

A perfect example of this is the MS Word 6.0 toolbar. Maybe the purpose of those curvy arrow buttons has always been clear to you. On the other hand, you might think the whole thing is far too cluttered and confusing. Again, there's really no middle ground: It's either intuitive or it isn't.

Since the goal of any software company is, in the end, to sell as many units as possible, the designers of graphical interfaces can't ignore these "everything is in the wrong place" customers—yet they can't alter the entire design to suit the quirks of individual end users.

Until now, this problem hasn't really been properly addressed. *No one has attempted a do-it-yourself design for end users.* But, with Delphi 2 or Delphi 3, a little bit of creative coding, and a runtime Object Inspector, you can!

First, we'll take a look at what a simple database application with dynamic design capabilities might look like. Then, we can examine some of the mechanics that make this on-the-fly user interface design possible in the first place.

CHAPTER 12

An Example "UI-It-Yourself" Application

Figure 12.1 is a "composite" screen shot of a sample database application that shows all of the options you can offer to the end user.

The selected item from the form's main menu offers three options:

- Adjust All Fonts (pick a new font for all of the controls);
- Tab Order (set the Tab Orders of the controls); and
- Show Properties (show the Object Inspector).

There's also a pop-up menu that offers the ability to change the form's background color.

In addition, there is another pop-up menu that offers four choices:

- Escape/No changes (cancels possible changes);
- Adjust Size & Position (resize and move the control);
- Change Font (change the individual control's font); and
- View Properties (show the Object Inspector).

Every control's **PopupMenu** property points to this pop-up menu.

On the left side of the screen is a runtime Object Inspector that allows users to view and change some of the additional properties of the controls.

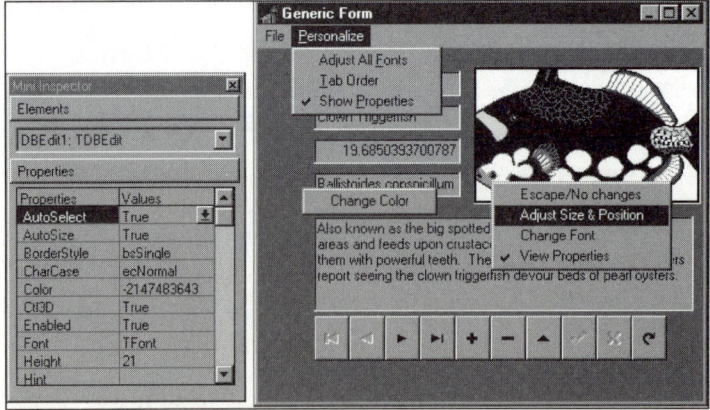

Figure 12.1
Custom UI options.

The greatest part about this dynamic, do-it-yourself interface is that there's a simple "jumping-off point" boilerplate project included on the CD-ROM (STARTER.DPR). You can add this project to your Object Repository and simply draw on it when you need to. It's that easy!

As you can see from this first example UI, we'll end up capturing many of Delphi's design-time features and making them available to the end user at runtime.

Building In A "Delphi" For Your Users

When you design a program using Delphi, you need a few tools to define the look and feel you want. Similarly, users will need the following tools to help them define the look and feel *they* want:

- A way to move controls at runtime;
- A way to resize controls at runtime;
- A way to change the Tab Order of the controls as they move them around;
- A way to change additional properties of controls, such as color or border style; and
- A way to automatically save and load the changes they've made.

Of course, it's vital that we make each of these tools fast, simple, and easy-to-use. What we want is for our users to have much (if not all) of the same flexibility that we programmers have at design time. In a sense, we're giving them their own, somewhat limited version of Delphi in our apps, to be used at runtime. Explaining how to accomplish each of the points listed above is what this chapter is about.

Moving Controls

While there are several ways to move controls at runtime, the best method for our purposes involves an almost undocumented **WM_SYSCOMMAND** trick. In order to move a **TWinControl**, you call **ReleaseCapture** and send the control a **WM_SYSCOMMAND** message, specifying the literal $F012 as the **wParam** parameter. Or, in code terms:

```
ReleaseCapture;
SendMessage(SomeWinControl.Handle, WM_SYSCOMMAND, $F012, 0);
```

Figure 12.2
Moving a Windows button.

The results of this code, as seen by the user, are shown in Figure 12.2.

Visually, the effect is the same as moving a modal dialog box—a thin, dotted outline of the control follows the cursor until the mouse button is released.

As you may have noticed, however, this method does have a limitation: It requires a window handle to work. TWinControl descendents have a window handle, TGraphic Control descendents do not. Therefore, components of type **TGraphicControl** (such as **TLabel**) are not supported. Obviously, for our dynamic forms solution to be truly useful and complete, we must find a way to support TGraphicControl descendents.

In order to get around this, then, we must enhance the **WM_SYSCOMMAND** mechanism just described. Of course, **WM_SYSCOMMAND** can't be used on GraphicControl components directly, but there *is* a way to fake it by creating a transparent **TWinControl** that will sit above the control being moved.

When a user selects the Adjust Size & Position pop-up menu option in the sample application, we'll place our transparent **TWinControl** above the selected control. The user will be able to drag the transparent control around (via **WM_SYSCOMMAND** using the $F012 parameter) as if it were the "selected" control. In other words, when the user clicks the "selected" control and begins to drag it somewhere, they'll really be dragging our transparent **TWinControl**. Then, when the user opts to keep the changes they've made (again by selecting the Adjust Size & Position option), we'll hide the transparent **TWinControl** and programmatically move the "selected" control to the new location.

In fact, this is exactly what Delphi does at design time. If you look closely, you can see that when you drag a control around in Delphi, you're really dragging a thick-bordered transparent rectangle. This is shown in Figure 12.3.

Dynamic User Interfaces

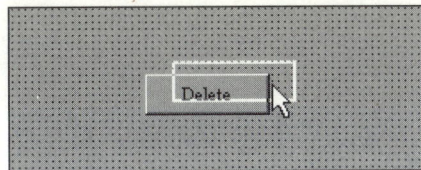

Figure 12.3
Dragging a control within Delphi at design time.

In essence, this transparent rectangle appears above the control you wish to move. From the time you click the "selected" control until you let the mouse button up, the transparent rectangle follows your cursor. As soon as you release the mouse button, though, the transparent rectangle disappears, and the control you intended to move jumps to the new location.

We will create our own transparent **TWinControl** derivative, called the SizingRect component, of class **TSizingRect**. Again, the **TSizingRect** class will serve as a control's stand-in while that control is being dragged around.

The important methods of class **TSizingRect** are **CreateParams** and **Paint**. The **CreateParams** method is used to set up certain behavioral aspects of the control before it's actually created. We'll use the **CreateParams** method to make our control transparent, as shown in Listing 12.1.

Listing 12.1 The TSizingRect.CreateParams method.

```
procedure TSizingRect.CreateParams(var Params: TCreateParams);
begin
     inherited CreateParams(Params);
     Params.ExStyle := Params.ExStyle + WS_EX_TRANSPARENT;
end;
```

The **Paint** method, shown in Listing 12.2, draws the thick rectangle border our users will see when a SizingRect is being used. When drawing this three-pixel-wide rectangle, we set the canvas's **Pen.Mode** property to **pmNot**. This ensures that, just as with Delphi's resizing mechanism, the rectangle drawn will always be a different color than the form.

Listing 12.2 The TSizingRect.Paint Method.

```
procedure TSizingRect.Paint;
begin
    inherited Paint;
    if fVisible = False then
        Exit;
    Canvas.Pen.Mode := pmNot;
    Canvas.Pen.Width := 3;
    Canvas.Brush.Style := bsClear;
    Canvas.Rectangle(0, 0, Width, Height);
end;
```

Resizing Controls

Resizing controls is even easier than moving them. Again, we'll use Delphi's design-time mechanisms as a guide. Delphi allows you to resize a selected control by clicking on one of the six black handles at the control's edges, and dragging that handle until the altered size of the control suits you.

We'll take the same approach to our runtime resizing. The only difference is that for the sake of simplicity (and to reduce the amount of coding needed) we'll limit ourselves to just one of the six possible resizing handles.

Since we're already using the **TSizingRect** class to manage the movement of the control, we'll use it to manage the resizing of controls as well. We'll simply designate the lower right-hand corner of **TSizingRect** to be a "hot spot" where users can click to resize the control.

Also, to make this design easier to use, we'll indicate which corner is "hot" by drawing a small white box there, and by changing the cursor every time the mouse passes over the white box. The action happens in the handler for the MouseMove event, which is shown in its entirety in Listing 12.3. I'll be discussing the handler piece by piece in the text that follows.

Listing 12.3 SizingRect's MouseMove Event Handler.

```
procedure TFrmMain.SizingRect1MouseMove(Sender: TObject;
                                       Shift: TShiftState;
                                       X, Y: Integer);
begin
{ControlDC and ControlRect are globally declared variables used
 by several procedures. These two lines, then, are just setup.}
    ControlDC := GetDC(TWinControl(Sender).Handle);
```

```
  GetWindowRect(TWinControl(Sender).Handle, ControlRect);

  if ((X > TControl(Sender).Width -SizeVal) and
     (Y > TControl(Sender).Height -SizeVal)) then
  begin
    TWinControl(Sender).Cursor := crSizeNWSE;
    Rectangle(ControlDC, TWinControl(Sender).Width - SizeVal,
              TControl(Sender).Height -SizeVal,
              TControl(Sender).Width, TControl(Sender).Height);
  end
    else
  begin
    TWinControl(Sender).Cursor := crDefault;
  end;

  if ((TWinControl(Sender).Cursor = crSizeNWSE) and
     (ssLeft in Shift)) then
  begin
    TWinControl(Sender).Width := X;
    TWinControl(Sender).Height := Y;
  end;
end;
```

After some initial setup, the handler tests to see if the mouse is within the sizing area. The **SizeVal** constant, which determines the area of the white sizing box, is defined in the **TSizingRect** unit. If the mouse is in the sizing area, the handler changes the cursor to the appropriate "sizing" cursor, and, of course, draws the rectangle:

```
if ((X > TControl(Sender).Width -SizeVal) and
   (Y > TControl(Sender).Height -SizeVal)) then
  begin
    TWinControl(Sender).Cursor := crSizeNWSE;
    Rectangle(ControlDC,
              TWinControl(Sender).Width - SizeVal,
              TControl(Sender).Height - SizeVal,
              TControl(Sender).Width, Control(Sender).Height);
  end
```

If the mouse is outside the sizing area, the routine simply changes the cursor back to the default style:

```
else
  begin
    TWinControl(Sender).Cursor := crDefault;
  end;
```

Finally, we check to see if the user is still resizing the control: If the cursor is equal to **crSizeNWSE** and the left mouse button is depressed, then the user is still resizing. The routine then sets the control's bottom-right corner to the mouse position:

```
if ((TWinControl(Sender).Cursor = crSizeNWSE) and
(ssLeft in Shift)) then
  begin
    TWinControl(Sender).Width := X;
    TWinControl(Sender).Height := Y;
  end;
end;
```

The overall effect here is that as long as the mouse button is depressed and the cursor is in the hot spot, the sizing corner will follow the mouse's movements.

Responding To The Pop-Up Menu

In our sample app, the **TSizingRect** component is activated by **PopupMenu1**, which is set as the pop-up menu for each of the controls on the form. Figure 12.4 shows **Popup menu1** at runtime, after a user has right-clicked the DBImage.

At this point, the user can make the following choices:

- Do nothing (by selecting the Escape/No changes item);
- Resize or move the control (the Adjust Size & Position item);
- Change the control's font (Change Font); or
- Display the MiniInspector (View Properties).

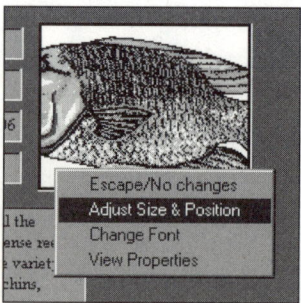

Figure 12.4
The pop-up menu for a right mouse click.

Selecting the Adjust Size & Position item invokes the **TFrmMain.AdjustClick** procedure, shown in Listing 12.4.

Listing 12.4 The Adjust Size & Position OnClick Handler.

```
procedure TFrmMain.AdjustClick(Sender: TObject);
begin
  if (Adjust.Checked = True) then
    begin
      if ((PopupMenu1.PopupComponent <> ComponentBeingAdjusted) and
          (PopupMenu1.PopupComponent <> SizingRect1)) then
        begin
          MessageDlg('You can only adjust one element at a time.' +
          #13#10 +
          'Please unselect the current element before continuing.',
          mtWarning, [mbOK], 0);
          Exit;
        end;
      Adjust.Checked := False;
      With TWinControl(ComponentBeingAdjusted) do
        begin
          Top := SizingRect1.Top;
          Left := SizingRect1.Left;
          Width := SizingRect1.Width;
          Height := SizingRect1.Height;
        end;
      SizingRect1.Cursor := crDefault;
      SizingRect1.Visible := False;
      SizingRect1.Top := -40;
      SizingRect1.Left := -40;
      SizingRect1.Width := 40;
      SizingRect1.Height := 40;
      MiniInspector1.ShowThisComponent(ComponentBeingAdjusted);
      ComponentBeingAdjusted := Self; { i.e., no control is }
    end                               { currently selected. }
  else
    begin
      if ((ComponentBeingAdjusted <> Self) and
          (PopupMenu1.PopupComponent <> ComponentBeingAdjusted))
          then
        begin
          MessageDlg('You can only adjust one element at a time.'
          + #13#10 +
          'Please unselect the current element before continuing.',
          mtWarning, [mbOK], 0);
          Exit;
        end;
```

```
      Adjust.Checked := True;
      ComponentBeingAdjusted := PopupMenu1.PopupComponent;
      With TWinControl(PopupMenu1.PopupComponent) do
        begin
          SizingRect1.Top := Top;
          SizingRect1.Left := Left;
          SizingRect1.Width := Width;
          SizingRect1.Height := Height;
        end;
      SizingRect1.Visible := True;
      MiniInspector1.ShowThisComponent(ComponentBeingAdjusted);
    end;
end;
```

Once various checks are performed to be sure the operation is legal, the **TSizingRect** is moved to the same position as the control being adjusted. (The variable **ComponentBeingAdjusted** exists for the benefit of additional routines that may not be able to rely on **PopupMenu1.PopupComponent**.) It's done like this:

```
ComponentBeingAdjusted := PopupMenu1.PopupComponent;

With TWinControl(PopupMenu1.PopupComponent) do
  begin
    SizingRect1.Top := Top;
    SizingRect1.Left := Left;
    SizingRect1.Width := Width;
    SizingRect1.Height := Height;
  end;
SizingRect1.Visible := True;
MiniInspector1.ShowThisComponent(ComponentBeingAdjusted);
```

At this point, the SizingRect component is active and can be moved and resized by the mouse, as shown in Figure 12.5.

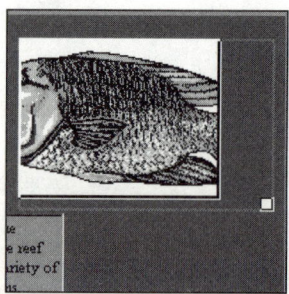

Figure 12.5
The SizingRect's rectangle.

Dynamic User Interfaces

When the user has finished adjusting the control, they can again right-click the control to save or discard their changes, as shown in Figure 12.6.

If the user does wish to move ahead with the adjustment, and thus selects the second option, the control being adjusted is moved and resized to the new specifications, after which the SizingRect is again hidden (this code is also part of **TFrm-Main.AdjustClick**):

```
With TWinControl(ComponentBeingAdjusted) do
    begin
      Top := SizingRect1.Top;
      Left := SizingRect1.Left;
      Width := SizingRect1.Width;
      Height := SizingRect1.Height;
    end;
SizingRect1.Cursor := crDefault;
SizingRect1.Visible := False;
SizingRect1.Top := -40;
SizingRect1.Left := -40;
{...}
```

Abandoning Changes

If the user doesn't want to keep any changes, and thus chooses the first pop-up menu option, the **TSizingRect** is hidden and the selected control remains unchanged. This is done in **TFrmMain.Escape1Click**, as shown in Listing 12.5.

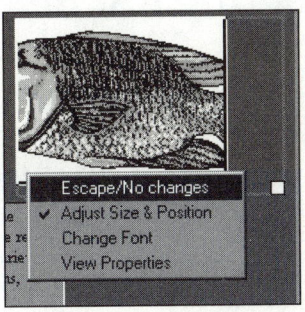

Figure 12.6
Saving or discarding changes.

Listing 12.5   The Escape/No Changes OnClick Handler.

```
procedure TFrmMain.EscapeClick(Sender: TObject);
begin
  {if we were just now resizing a component, then...}
  if (Adjust.Checked = True) then
    begin
      Adjust.Checked := False;
      SizingRect1.Cursor := crDefault;
      SizingRect1.Visible := False;
      SizingRect1.Top := -40;
      SizingRect1.Left := -40;
      SizingRect1.Width := 40;
      SizingRect1.Height := 40;
      ComponentBeingAdjusted := Self; {i.e., no control is  }
    end;                              { currently selected. }
end;
```

Note: *In the STARTER.DPR project, the SizingRect component is hidden off to the top right of the main form to prevent it from being accidentally shown at the wrong time. When using the project as a starting point for your own apps, be sure to locate the SizingRect component and, from Delphi's main menu, select Edit/Bring To Front after you have added all of your own controls. Also, be sure that all of the controls' PopupMenu properties point to **PopupMenu1**.*

Changing The Tab Order At Runtime

If users are going to move controls around, chances are they'll want to be able to adjust the tab order as well. After all, our do-it-yourself design would completely fail the ease-of-use test if users were locked into the original tab order. Navigating from one control to another would be a very confusing task.

In Delphi, you set the tab order of the controls via the Tab Order dialog box, which consists primarily of a listbox component, an up-arrow button, and a down-arrow button. Since this seems to work well for Delphi, we'll use the same kind of dialog box in our system. Figure 12.7 shows our FrmTabOrder component at runtime.

FrmTabOrder itself, however, is just a friendly interface. What actually manages the tab order is the code that shows FrmTabOrder. This is the **TFrmMain.TabOrder1Click** method, shown in Listing 12.6. I'll discuss this handler in detail next.

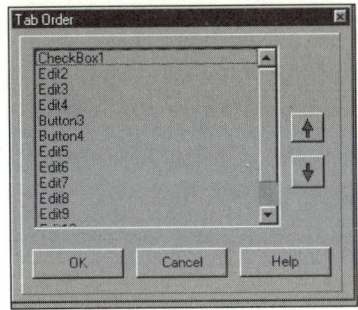

Figure 12.7
The FrmTabOrder component at runtime.

Listing 12.6 The tab order menu item's OnClick Handler.

```
procedure TFrmMain.TabOrder1Click(Sender: TObject);
var
   i : Integer;
begin
  FrmTabOrder.LBControls.Items.Clear;
  for i := 0 to ComponentCount -1 do
  begin
    if ((Components[i] is TWinControl) and
       not (Components[i] is TSizingRect)) then
       FrmTabOrder.LBControls.Items.Add(Components[i].Name);
  end;
  FrmTabOrder.ShowModal;
  if FrmTabOrder.ModalResult = mrOK then
  begin
    for i := 0 to FrmTabOrder.LbControls.Items.Count -1 do
      TWinControl(FindComponent(
                  FrmTabOrder.LbControls.Items[i])).TabOrder := i;
  end;
end;
```

Now, in detail. First, the routine clears the listbox. Then it iterates through all of the form's controls, adding every control that's a **TWinControl** to the listbox, except for the SizingRect:

```
FrmTabOrder.LBControls.Items.Clear;
for I := 0 to ComponentCount -1 do
  begin
    if ((Components[I] is TWinControl) and
    not (Components[I] is TSizingRect)) then
       FrmTabOrder.LBControls.Items.Add(Components[I].Name);
  end;
```

Next, the routine shows the form. (**FrmTabOrder.LBControls** handles the reordering of the items itself.) If the user clicks the OK button, our program goes through **FrmTabOrder.LBControls.Items**, extracting the index of each item, assigning that value to the related control's **TabOrder** property:

```
FrmTabOrder.ShowModal;
if FrmTabOrder.ModalResult = mrOK then
  begin
    for I := 0 to FrmTabOrder.LbControls.Items.Count -1 do
      TWinControl(FindComponent(
                FrmTabOrder.LbControls.Items[I])).TabOrder := I;
  end;
```

Pretty simple, isn't it? That's all there is to runtime control of component tab order.

Changing Other Properties

Now we've got to tackle the issue of changing some of the other properties of the controls on the form. For instance, what if a user wanted to change the font or color of some DBEdit components to indicate that they were required fields? Well, there are a few simple things that we can do for some of these additional properties. As we've just discovered, it's relatively easy to change the tab order for all of the controls. It's also quite simple to change other individual properties of a control.

Changing Control Fonts At Runtime

For instance, in our sample app, we offer the user the ability to change every control's character font via a main menu item, Adjust All Fonts. The code to do this is relatively simple, as shown in Listing 12.7.

Listing 12.7 Changing fonts of all controls on a form.

```
procedure TFrmMain.AdjustMenu2Click(Sender: TObject);
var
  i : Integer;
begin
  {multiple Font changes}
  if FontDialog1.Execute then
```

```
      begin
        for i := 0 to ComponentCount - 1 do
          begin
            try
              if ((Components[i] is TWinControl) or
                  (Components[i] is TGraphicControl)) and
                  not ((Components[i] is TMenu) and
                  (Components[i] is TMenuItem)) then
                    TMagic(Components[i]).Font := FontDialog1.Font;
            except
              Continue;
            end;
          end;
      end;
end;
```

Something interesting is going on here. Note the **TMagic** typecast in the actual assignment statement. **TMagic** is a control class defined in the **TSizingRect** unit that does absolutely nothing from a code action standpoint. The only reason it exists at all is to publish certain protected properties; namely, the **Font** property. Since the **Font** property of most controls is protected, we can't change it at runtime without performing just such a typecast. Therefore, **TMagic** makes it possible to change a control's font at runtime.

Our sample application also offers users the ability to change a single control's font via the Change Font option of the popup menu. This, too, is a relatively simple process, as shown in Listing 12.8.

Listing 12.8 Changing the font for a single control at runtime.

```
procedure TFrmMain.ChangeFont1Click(Sender: TObject);
begin
  if FontDialog1.Execute then
    try
      TMagic(PopupMenu1.PopupComponent).Font := FontDialog1.Font;
    except
      Exit;
    end;
end;
```

Note: *Even with the help of **TMagic**, there are some control classes—for instance, **TMenu**—that will raise an exception if you try to change their* *fonts, "magic" typecast or not. Therefore, it's usually best to test the type of the control before attempting to change its font. In the above example, though, there was no need to filter out the "no-font" controls. This is because the code is launched via a pop-up menu. The controls that have a pop-up menu property do not object if you change their fonts—even if they don't display any text. (An example of this would be a ScrollBar component.)*

Changing Properties In An Object Inspector

We must now provide the users with a way to edit additional properties such as **Caption**, **CharCase**, or **Color**. It's not unreasonable for a user to expect the ability to change any of these items, considering that we're letting them change everything else.

How does Delphi allow us to change these properties at design time? Through the Object Inspector. So, for our project, we'll use an Object Inspector of our own.

Note: Because the Object Inspector presented in this chapter has been previously available as a commercial product, only a demo version (that is, without source code) is provided on the CD-ROM. Basically, this version limits the type of properties and controls available. However, it's otherwise fully functional, and there are no "nag screens." Please consult the licensing agreement for more details. Information about the full version of the **TMiniInspector** *class, which includes all source code, can be found on the CD-ROM accompanying this book, or by clicking the MiniInspector component's* **About_This_Component** *property at design time. Please note that both the Delphi 2 and Delphi 3 versions of the MiniInspector are provided on the CD. They are located in the Chapter 12 directory, under \Delphi2Lib\ and \Delphi3Lib\, respectively.*

To install **TMiniInspector** to your component palette, choose Components|Install and add **MINIOI.DCU**. You will also want to ensure that the following three files are in the same directory as **MINIOI.DCU**:

- OICOMPDEMO.DCU
- OICOMPDEMO.DFM
- MINIOI.DCR

Dynamic User Interfaces

The Object Inspector in our project works exactly like the Object Inspector supplied with Delphi. The user selects a component via the combo box at the top. He or she can then edit the properties by either typing in a value or by clicking on a button to select a separate property editing form, where one is available. Figure 12.8 shows **TMiniInspector** at runtime.

In our sample app, when the user selects either the **Show Properties** option from the main menu, or the **View Properties** option from the pop-up menu, we display the Object Inspector with a simple call to its **Show** method.

```
MiniInspector1.Show;
```

Then, if the user activated the Object Inspector via the popup menu, we'll tell the **TMiniInspector** component to show the control that was right-clicked in the first place.

```
if PopupMenu1.PopupComponent <> nil then
  MiniInspector1.ShowThisComponent(PopupMenu1.PopupComponent);
```

The **ShowThisComponenent** method is a function that takes a **TComponent** parameter and returns a boolean value. If the component type passed to the function can be found in the combo box, it will be displayed and the function will return a value of **True**. If the component can't be found, or if the MiniInspector is not visible, the function will return a value of **False**.

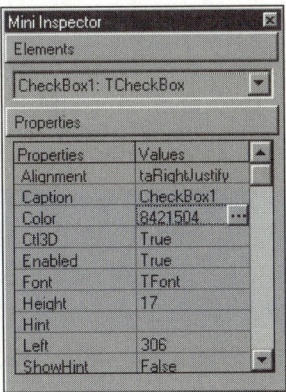

Figure 12.8
The MiniInspector component at runtime.

Saving Component Changes Made At Runtime

Now that we have methods for changing just about all of the elements of a user interface, we'd better come up with a way to save the changes so that they can become "persistent" across sessions. Users will *not* be amused if they're forced to alter the UI each time they run the application! While we might be tempted to just plunge in and use INI files—or maybe the Windows 95 Registry if we're brave enough—there are some serious drawbacks to both of these approaches. The problem is that since each component has numerous properties of different types, there's no straightforward way to write a generic "**Save_This_Component**" method.

If we tried, we'd probably end up testing each component's type, and then saving certain properties based on that type. This isn't very efficient, you'll agree. On the other hand, we could decide to save only those properties which are common to all components. Since the **TComponent** type—the ancestor of all other component types—has only nine properties (not including the **Left**, **Top**, **Width**, and **Height** properties), this, too, would be useless.

However, all is not lost! There are several very good mechanisms for saving and loading the properties of components. All you have to do is dig through Borland's documentation and experiment a little bit.

In this expedition into the documentation, our final destination is the **TFiler** / **TWriter** / **TReader** family of objects. According to the Delphi help files, **TFiler** is "the abstract base object for the reader objects and writer objects that Delphi uses for saving (and loading) forms and components in form files."

That definition says something very important to us: namely, that the **TWriter** and **TReader** objects can be used to save and load a component's properties from a file. By associating an instance of the **TWriter** or **TReader** class with an instance of **TFileStream**, we can, in fact, use the **WriteRootComponent** and **ReadRootComponent** methods to do exactly what we want.

Snag: Components With Components As Properties

The only limitation of these methods is that there are a few types of components that cannot be saved directly. The components in question are those that have *other* components as properties.

The problem occurs when trying to load these component properties from the file. Since these components are saved on their own, loading them as *properties of another component* raises an exception with a message to the effect of "A component named Widget1 already exists."

Thankfully, this behavior seems to be limited to only four types of components: **TMainMenu**, **TMenuItem**, **TPopupMenu**, and **TForm**.

For our purposes, the first three don't really matter. However, we probably should give users the power to save some of the form's properties. Since there aren't likely to be that many **TForm** properties we really need to be concerned with, it's simpler just to save the ones we *do* care about.

In Listing 12.9 is the code to save a form's properties, as executed in the FormCloseQuery event. As is my style, I'll discuss pertinent portions of the event handler in detail shortly.

Listing 12.9   The event handler for the FormCloseQuery event.

```
procedure TFrmMain.FormCloseQuery(Sender: TObject;
                                  var CanClose: Boolean);
var
  Writer : TWriter;
  FileStream : TFileStream;
  i : Integer;
  TempRect : TRect;

begin
  {File extension of .HPD == High Performance Delphi}
  {Just to be on the safe side, we delete the old *.HPD file:}
  DeleteFile(ExtractFilePath(Application.ExeName) +
```

```
            TObject(Self).ClassName + '.HPD ');
    {Then, go ahead & rewrite it:}
    FileStream :=
      TFileStream.Create(ExtractFilePath(Application.ExeName)
      + TObject(Self).ClassName + '.HPD',fmOpenWrite or fmCreate);
    for i := 0 to ComponentCount-1 do
      begin
        {There are some controls that should not (or cannot) be
        saved in this manner. Luckily, they're ones you're not likely to
        want to save anyhow:}
        if ((Components[i] is TSizingRect) or
            (Components[i] is TMenu) or
            (Components[i] is TMenuItem) or
            (Components[i] is TPopupMenu) or
            (not(Components[i] is TControl))) then
          Continue;
        Writer := TWriter.Create(FileStream, SizeOf(Components[i]));
        Writer.WriteRootComponent(Components[i]);
        Writer.Free;
      end;
    {Save & Load form properties here:}
    TempRect.Top := Self.Top;
    TempRect.Left := Self.Left;
    TempRect.Bottom := TempRect.Top + Self.Height;
    TempRect.Right := TempRect.Left + Self.Width;
    FileStream.Write(TempRect, SizeOf(TRect));
    FileStream.Write(Self.Color, SizeOf(TColor));
    FileStream.Free;
    {Don't forget to 'OK' the closing of the form!}
    CanClose := True;
end;
```

Now, let's take a detailed look at how all this works. First, just to be on the safe side, we delete the old *.HPD file. Next, we recreate it:

```
FileStream := TFileStream.Create(ExtractFilePath
                        (Application.ExeName) +
                        TObject(Self).ClassName +
                        '.HPD',fmOpenWrite or fmCreate);
```

Then, we filter out the types that can't be saved, taking no action when those types are encountered:

```
for i := 0 to ComponentCount-1 do
  begin
    if ((Components[i] is TSizingRect) or
        (Components[i] is TMenu) or
        (Components[i] is TMenuItem) or
        (Components[i] is TPopupMenu) or
        (not(Components[i] is TControl))) then
      Continue;
```

Each time we discover a component that can be saved, we write it out to the stream:

```
Writer := TWriter.Create(FileStream, SizeOf(Components[i]));
Writer.WriteRootComponent(Components[i]);
Writer.Free;
```

After iterating through the form's components and saving any pertinent ones, we save any of the form's own properties that are important to the application:

```
TempRect.Top := Self.Top;
TempRect.Left := Self.Left;
TempRect.Bottom := TempRect.Top + Self.Height;
TempRect.Right := TempRect.Left + Self.Width;
FileStream.Write(TempRect, SizeOf(TRect));
FileStream.Write(Self.Color, SizeOf(TColor));
FileStream.Free;
```

Finally, we set the flag allowing the form to be closed:

```
CanClose := True;
```

Alternate Paths To A Stream

You may have noticed that the **TFileStream** class also appears to have methods that will save and restore a component's properties. While **TFileStream** has, in fact, two different sets of methods for saving and loading components to and from files, these routines do some additional processing that makes them somewhat less efficient than the **TReader/TWriter** implementation we've chosen.

The **WriteComponentRes** and **ReadComponentRes** methods read and write the component as a standard windows resource. This adds some processing overhead to the equation. In addition, these routines save data that is simply of no use to us, making our properties files larger than they really need to be.

The **WriteComponent** and **ReadComponent** methods also achieve the same end result as we do, but with an additional function call or two. Our method is more efficient and slightly faster.

Toward More Flexible User Interfaces

Runtime-definable user interfaces really deserve more than a single book chapter to treat them in full detail. We've looked at giving users control over the most common UI elements, including control position and size, fonts, and tab order, as well as other properties that may be displayed in a commercial property-editor component. That's only scratching the surface, especially when you consider that a really good user interface customization system should itself have a careful UI, as well as guidelines and checks to ensure that the user does not somehow render the application unusable. Consider this chapter as a jumping-off point from which you can explore the matter as far as you (and your users) need to take it.

HIGH PERFORMANCE

Hierarchical Data In Relational Databases

CHAPTER 13

HIGH PERFORMANCE

Data isn't always expressed as rows and columns. Here are some pointers on handling hierarchical data within Delphi databases, and some VCL components to shoulder the bulk of the load.

Hierarchical Data In Relational Databases

Richard Haven

The real world contains lots of hierarchical data. This broad category includes companies, and within companies, divisions, departments, and teams; parts which make up parts which make up parts; specialties, subspecialties, and skills; employees and supervisors; and on and on. A group of items where one item can own or be the "parent" of any number of other items is organized in a *tree hierarchy*. The VCL object hierarchy is an immediate example: A **TEdit** is a **TControl** because **TEdit** descends from **TControl**. **TEdit** is also a **TWinControl** and a **TCustomControl** because they are intermediate ancestors in the VCL hierarchy.

Such relationships are not represented intuitively by the relational database model. Often, these hierarchical relationships are recursive (in that any row can own any other row) and arbitrarily nested (any row can own another row no matter who owns it). Simple navigation and display of a tree hierarchy can be difficult in the two-dimensional landscape of rows and columns, and querying is especially confusing. You often want to extract an item's *lineage* (the list of its owner and its owner's owner, and so on) or *progeny* (the list of all its descendents and its descendents' descendents) to use as criteria for a query. This chapter will provide some mechanisms for dealing with such hierarchical relationships within the relational database mindset familiar to Delphi programmers.

One-To-Many Hierarchies

Delphi deals well with traditional relational databases: These are tables (sometimes called *relations*) with rows (records) and columns (fields) that link to one another by matching common column values (see Figure 13.1). To link rows this way is also called *relating* the tables. The relational model is not the only model used in database management. The *hierarchical* and *network* database models were standard before the relational model, and the *object-oriented* database model is a modern alternative.

The value of any of these models lies in how they help the database designer to create databases to fit the data. The relational model fits many kinds of real-world data structures: many invoices to each customer, many parts to many vendors, many members each having many characteristics, and so on. Delphi's **TTable.MasterSource** and **TQuery.DataSource** properties let you show related subsets of a table or query based on linking values in another table. This is one way to establish a *master/detail* relationship within Delphi, where *master* is the "one" and *detail* is the "many."

Simple Recursive Hierarchical Data

The relational model works well for master/detail data in the same table as long as there is only a single level of ownership: that is, when any single row either is owned by one other row or owns another row. The boss and staff rows shown in Table 13.1

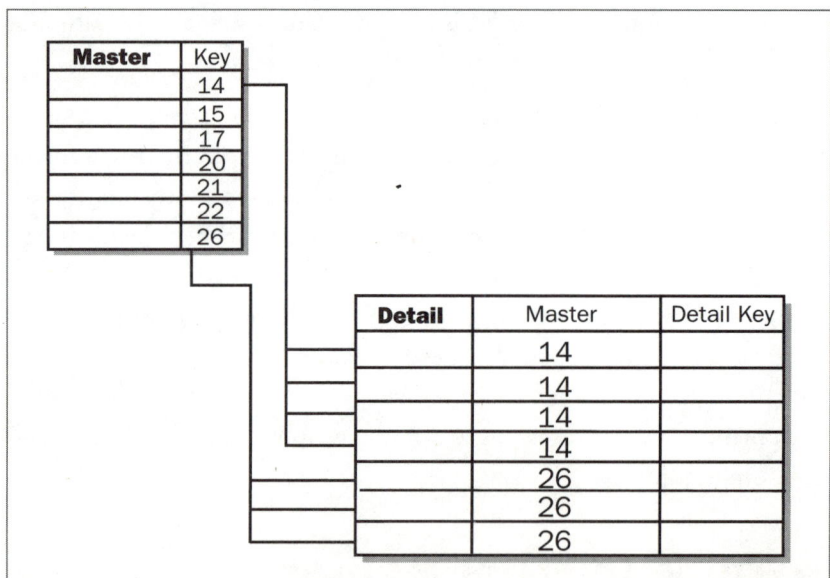

Figure 13.1
Master/detail tables.

Table 13.1 Simple recursive hierarchical data.

Emp_ID	Boss_ID	Emp_Name
Boss 1	<nil>	Frank Eng
Boss 2	<nil>	Sharon Oakstein
Boss 3	<nil>	Charles Willings
Staff 1	Boss 1	Roger Otkin
Staff 2	Boss 1	Marilyn Fionne
Staff 3	Boss 1	Judy Czeglarek
Staff 4	Boss 2	Sean O'Donhail
Staff 5	Boss 3	Karol Klauss
Staff 6	Boss 3	James Riordan

might as well be in two separate tables at this single level of recursion because each grid has a separate connection to the data.

Table 13.2 summarizes the property values necessary to have two sets of **TTable**, **TDataSource**, and **TDBGrid** components, where both sets point to the same physical table. One set will show parent rows while the other set will show the child rows that belong to the currently selected parent row. The **MasterSource** and **MasterFields** properties of the child **TTable** automatically restrict it to the rows belonging to the current row in the parent Table.

Table 13.2 Property setup for parent or child row display.

Parent Component Set	Child Component Set
Table1.TableName = 'employees'	Table2.TableName = 'employees'
Table1.IndexFieldName = 'Boss_ID;Emp_ID'	Table2.MasterSource = 'DataSource1'
DataSource1.DataSet = 'Table1'	Table2.MasterFields = 'Emp_ID'
DBGrid1.DataSource = 'DataSource1'	Table2.IndexFieldName = 'Boss_ID;Emp_ID'
Table1.SetRange([''],['']);	DataSource2.DataSet = 'Table2'
	DBGrid2.DataSource = 'DataSource2'

To restrict the parent Table so that it does not show any child rows, place an explicit filter on it so it only shows rows that have nothing in their **Boss_ID** column. These are parent rows.

> **Note**: You can use the **SetRange** method instead of the **Filter** property. This is a method that you call to make **Table1** display only boss rows (i.e., those where **Boss_ID** = **nil**). A good place to put the call to **Table1.SetRange** is in the **Table1.AfterOpen** handler so it executes whether the table is left open at design time or opened at runtime.

Figure 13.2 shows a Delphi form containing two **TDBGrid** components, set up according to the properties summarized in Table 13.2. The boss rows are shown in one grid, and the staff rows in the other. All rows are, in fact, present in one physical table.

Whenever **DataSource1** (connected to **Table1**) changes, **Table2** will automatically set its range just as though you had executed the code in Listing 13.1.

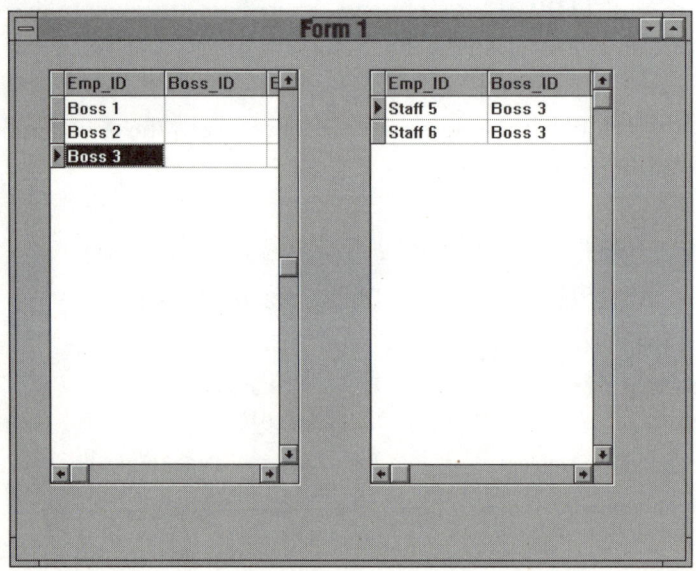

Figure 13.2
A master/detail relationship between rows of the same table.

Listing 13.1 Equivalent code for automatic range updates by MasterSource.

```
procedure TForm1.DataSource1DataChange(Sender : TObject;
                                      Field : TField);
begin
  if (Field = nil) or (Field.FieldName = 'Emp_ID') then
    Table2.SetRange([Table1.FieldByName('Emp_ID').AsString],
                    [Table1.FieldByName('Emp_ID').AsString]);
end;
```

Note: It can only do this if there is an index on **Table2** for **Boss_ID** so it can filter all the rows where **Table1.Boss_ID** for one grid contains the null string and **Table2.Boss_ID = Table1.Emp_ID** for the other. This index can have extra columns that are not part of the range, which determine the sequence of the rows in the filtered set. In this case, only staff for one boss will appear in **Table2**, and those rows will be in **Emp_ID** sequence. If the table is on a SQL Server, all non-BLOB (Binary Large Objects) columns are considered indexed, although performance will suffer if you use columns that don't actually have physical indexes. The **Filter** property does not require indexes, but will use them if available.

Using TQuery As A Detail DataSet

A **TQuery** can be a detail DataSet as well by letting its master data set (a **TTable** or **TQuery**) send its values to its SQL property as parameters to a dynamic query. In the example above, the **SQL** property of the detail **TQuery** would look something like this:

```
SELECT *
FROM Employee T1
WHERE T1.Boss_ID = :Emp_ID
```

The **TQuery.DataSource** property indicates where the parameter value comes from. In the SQL query shown above, the parameter named **Emp_ID** gets its value from **TQuery.DataSource.DataSet.FieldByName('Emp_ID')** (the parameter name must match the field name of the source). Anytime the master field changes, the query reexecutes with its new parameter value.

Detail **TQuerys** have to use dynamic SQL and the **DataSource** property together. The query is *dynamic* because it uses a parameter instead of recreating the full SQL text each time the criteria changes. However, if there are several possible statement structures for the query, you will have to create the entire SQL statement textually; parameters will only take you so far.

You can use code instead of the **MasterSource** property if you want more control over how ranges appear or you want to send customized SQL through a **TQuery** instead of letting **TQuery.DataSource** do it for you. For example, you might want to include certain rows besides the ones specified by the range. This is best done when an **OnDataChange** event handler is attached to the *master* **TDataSource**, as shown in Listing 13.2.

Listing 13.2 Special handling in range updates for values outside the range.

```
procedure TForm1.DataSource1DataChange(Sender : TObject; Field : TField);
begin
  if (Field = nil) or (Field.FieldName = 'Emp_ID') then
    begin
      Query2.DisableControls;
      Query2.Close;
      with Query2.SQL do
        begin
          Clear;
          Add('SELECT *');
          Add('FROM employees T1');
          Add('WHERE T1.Boss_ID =
              ' + Table1.Field ByName('Emp_ID').AsString);
          Add('OR T1.Boss_ID IS NULL');  {// extra code }
        end;
      Query2.Open;
      Query2.EnableControls;
    end;
end;
```

This will retrieve the rows owned by the current **Boss_ID** as well as those who are not owned by any **Boss_ID** (for example, unassigned staff).

Nested Recursive Hierarchical Data

Recursively hierarchical data means that the owner and the owned rows are all in the same table: One nonkey column of a row contains the key value of another row, indicating that that row is owned by the other row. This nonkey column is called a *foreign key* even if it links the row with another row in the same table. The examples described earlier reflect one level of ownership: Each row is either a boss or a staffer. To allow a staffer to also be a boss, make the table fully recursive: Any row can both *be* a boss and *have* a boss. Note that the only field in the key is **Emp_ID**; you do not have to add the **Boss_ID** column to the key in order to manage the relationship as long as you have a secondary index starting with **Boss_ID**. (See Table 13.3.)

This data has three levels: Boss, Manager, and Staff. Rather than adding another **TDBGrid** for the new level, Form2 (see Figure 13.3) shows two levels at a time. By showing any two levels at a time, the data can be arbitrarily nested without changing the visual interface at all.

You can change the range of the master table **Table1** so it only shows employees with **Boss_ID** of some chosen value, and the detail table **Table2** dutifully will show only details rows linked to that master row (for example, the employees working for a

Table 13.3 A recursive table.

Emp_ID	Boss_ID
<nil>	Boss 1
<nil>	Boss 2
<nil>	Boss 3
Boss 1	Manager 1
Boss 1	Manager 2
Boss 2	Manager 3
Boss 1	Staff 1
Manager 1	Staff 2
Manager 1	Staff 3
Manager 3	Staff 4
Boss 3	Staff 5
Boss 3	Staff 6

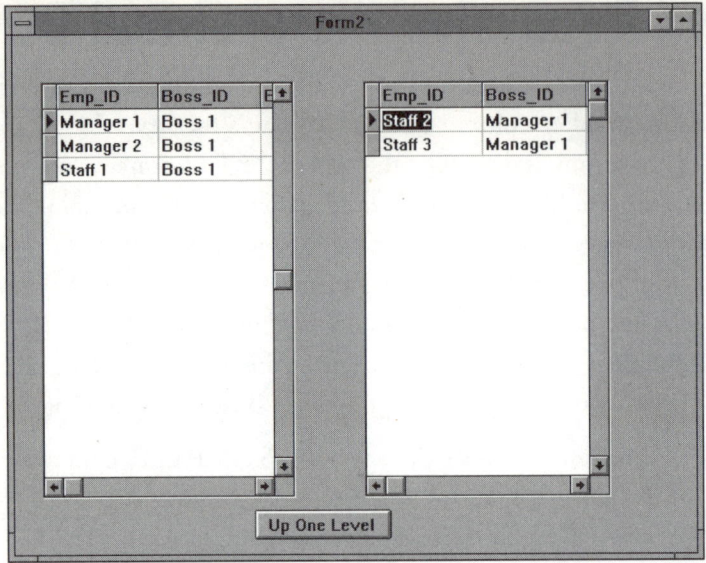

Figure 13.3
A recursive master/detail relationship between rows of the same table.

manager). The details don't know or care that their owner row is itself owned and filtered. Each level has a master and detail sets, and drilling-down to see the details of a specific detail row does not change this—only the specific data changes.

This "step" type of interface is fine for shallow hierarchy trees, but when there are many paths to follow, it's easy for a user to get lost. The least you can do is show a label with the lineage, as Figure 13.3 does. This not only shows who the current master row belongs to, but it shows how many levels down it is. The label at the top of the form (**Label1**) shows the lineage of the current record in **Table1**.

Hierarchy Navigation

To navigate up and down the hierarchy, you need to offer two additional functions. In the example we've been following, the user goes down the branch when they double-click on a detail row of the right-hand (child) grid. This changes the filter on the table connected to the left-hand (parent) grid so that it shows the same rows as the right-hand grid. This new filter then changes the rows in the right-hand grid: It now shows child rows of the current parent row. This is a difficult business to describe in plain text, so Listing 13.3 shows an event handler for the **OnDoubleClick** event that demonstrates this action. Read the code closely to make sure you understand how it works.

Listing 13.3 Double-click handler for recursive relationship navigation.

```
procedure TForm2.DBGrid2DblClick(Sender : TObject);
var
  NewRangeID, SelectedEmployeeID : String;

begin
{ show the user the current range }
  if Table1.FieldByName('Boss_ID').AsString = '' then
    Label1.Caption := Table2.FieldByName('Boss_ID').AsString
  else
    Label1.Caption := Label1.Caption + ':' +
                      Table2.FieldByName('Boss_ID').AsString;

{ Assume that Table1.IndexFieldNames is still Boss_ID;Emp_ID }

  SelectedEmployeeID := Table2.FieldByName('Emp_ID').AsString;
  NewRangeID := Table2.FieldByName('Boss_ID').AsString;
  Table1.SetRange([NewRangeID],[NewRangeID]);
  Table1.FindKey([NewRangeID,SelectedEmployeeID]);
end;

procedure TForm2.UpOneLevelButtonClick(Sender : TObject);
var
  PrevPos : Integer;
  NewRangeID : String;

begin
{We want to filter on the selected employee's Boss_ID }
  NewRangeID := Table1.FieldByName('Boss_ID').AsString;
  Table1.CancelRange;
  Table1.IndexFieldNames := 'Emp_ID';
  Table1.FindKey([NewRangeID]);
  NewRangeID := Table1.FieldByName('Boss_ID').AsString;
  Table1.IndexFieldNames := 'Boss_ID';

{ This will resynchronize Table2 }
  Table1.SetRange([NewRangeID],[NewRangeID]);

  if Table1.FieldByName('Boss_ID').AsString = '' then
    Label1.Caption := '<Top level>'
```

```
    else
      begin
        PrevPos := 0;
        while Pos(':',Copy(Label1.Caption,PrevPos + 1,999))<>0 do
            PrevPos :=
                Pos(':',Copy(Label1.Caption,PrevPos + 1,999)) +
                PrevPos;
        Label1.Caption := Copy(Label1.Caption,1,(PrevPos - 1));
      end;
end;
```

The left-hand grid's table is filtered on the current filter's **Boss_ID** value when the user clicks the Up One Level button. While this allows infinite recursion, it does not allow an easy way to get a list of *all* members of a boss's staff's staff, and so on down the hierarchy. It also gives you no way to get a staff member's bosses' bosses. You have to iterate through the linking values in either direction and you don't know how many levels of ownership you'll have to go through.

But hierarchies like this are useful in allowing a user to pick an item from any level of detail while giving an application the right level of data. For example, you could have geographical regions broken down into smaller and smaller areas, but the application would still want to know what region those areas are in (what is the top-level parent).

You might also want to have general categories broken into specialties, but still allow the choice of a general category to include all the specialized ones. For example, choosing all Painters automatically includes Painters:Decorative, Painters:Commercial, Painters:Marine, and so on. This way, you don't have to list members of every specialty separately in a general category to get all of the members of the general category. In this case, you want to get all the descendents of an item.

Displaying The Data

While there is no clever way to avoid walking up and down the hierarchy tree, you can use tools that do all that walking for you. Think about how your users want to use the data. They may not care if it is hierarchical or not, but they may want to find an item by looking for its ancestor. They may want to search for items by name wherever they appear in the hierarchy, or only in the descendents of the current item. They may want the ID of the item they choose, or the entire lineage or progeny of that item.

For example, a basic question you will confront in building applications is what to do when the user asks for the "next" item. This could be the next sibling of the current item's parent; it could be the first child; it could be the next parent if there are no siblings; it could even be the first child of the next sibling. With a visual interface, the user's expectations are going to be based on position, display, and their own actions, not necessarily on a logical protocol based on the application's abstract data design.

Besides the one-level relationship described earlier involving two **TDBGrid** components, the obvious controls to use with hierarchical data are the **TOutline** and **TTreeView** components because they were created specifically to show trees of related items rather than simple linear lists. They tend to take up a lot of screen area, so you cannot use them everywhere you want the user to choose an item from a hierarchy. They also encourage you to load the entire structure into memory at once (which can be memory wasteful). You *can* configure them to load branches as the user opens those branches, but that flexibility comes with a performance penalty.

Listing 13.4 is an example of how such controls may be loaded. You should have a working familiarity with the general operation of the **TOutline** component before trying to follow this code.

Listing 13.4 Loading an Outline component from a list of items.

```
procedure LoadItemStringsFromTop(ListOfItems : TListOfItems);
var
  Counter : Integer;

procedure LoadOutline(StartIndex : Integer; StartItem : TItem);
var
  NewIndex : Integer;
begin
  NewIndex := MyOutline.AddChildObject(StartIndex,
                                       StartItem.Description,
                                       StartItem);
  if StartItem.FirstChildItem <> nil then
    LoadOutline(NewIndex,StartItem.FirstChildItem);
  if StartItem.FirstSiblingItem <> nil then
    LoadOutline(StartIndex,StartItem.FirstSiblingItem);
end;
```

```
begin
  MyOutline.Clear;
  for Counter := 0 to ListOfItems.Count - 1 do
    if ListOfItems[Counter].Level = 1 then
      LoadOutline(0,ListOfItems[Counter]);
end;
```

To load an Outline, you can go from the top to the bottom, adding children to each *node*, assuming that each node knows whether it's a top-level node and what its children are. **TListOfItems** and **TItem** (present in Listing 13.4) are fictitious classes that contain this information (see the TreeData Components, below).

Unfortunately, the standard hierarchical model does not keep an explicit list of children, but rather determines the set of children as those items that have the same item as a parent. Unless you preload the entire set into memory (like a **TListOfItems**) and establish the parent-to-child links, you have to load from the bottom to the top. That is, as you add each item's parent item, you have to check if a sibling has added the parent already, and if the parent is loaded, tell the control that your new item is part of that parent's branch.

Using The Data

The point of any user interface should be to communicate effectively with the user. The user needs to see enough of the data to make a choice (or see enough to know that a choice cannot be made), and then make that choice. With graphical trees, it's easy to use the double-click or the spacebar to choose the current item.

Once the user makes a choice, your application has to identify it. The visible text in the control for an item may not uniquely identify it (it may be duplicated in different branches), so most strategies use a unique ID code in addition to the text. These IDs should be short and are usually numerical. This makes it easy to ensure that they are unique by adding one to the highest existing value.

> **Note**: Just because you use the **Index** value to set up the hierarchy in the control does not mean that you can automatically get it back out again. The **Index** property of the **TOutline** class changes for each item as you modify the **TOutline's** contents; it's a relative value and not specifically associated with any particular item.

You must link the ID with the item itself so you can retrieve it and identify the user's choice. Most controls that store a number of string items also store an object pointer associated with each string item. This is part of the **TStrings** interface that many controls use. You can store a pointer to any object, or you can store a value that just *looks* like a pointer. You can cast a positive integer (also known as a cardinal) to a **TObject** and store it in this pointer property (usually named **Objects**). If you have anything except an integer value, you have to create a custom class to hold the data:

```
type
  TMyIDClass = class(TObject)
  public
    ID : String;
  end;
begin
...
  NewIDObject := TMyIDClass.Create;
  NewIDObject.ID := ItemTable.FieldByName('ID').AsString;
  MyOutline.AddChildObject(0,
ItemTable.FieldByName('Description').AsString, NewIDObject);
```

The **TOutline** component offers these pointers as **Items[Index].Data** instead of calling the property **Objects** as most controls do. (Another anomaly: The **Index** value starts from 1 instead of 0, as most lists do.) This pointer will link an object descended from **TObject** (that is to say, any class instance) to an item. You have to define a new class that holds your ID value, create an instance of it for every item you load, put the ID in that instance, and set the pointer.

To get your ID back, your code might look like this:

```
with MyOutline do
  ThisID := (Items[SelectedItem].Data as TMyIDClass).ID;
```

Your application may need more information than just the ID. You can use the ID to look up that other information in a table, and you can also store more information in the objects that hold the IDs by expanding the **TMyIDClass** definition.

Remember that the **Objects** or **Data** property will not free these objects just because they point to them. Either make them descend from **TComponent**, which will let their component owner free them, or iterate through the list on the **destructor** or on **FormDestroy** and free each item yourself. As long as you respect the **Count** property, you can safely **Free** items in one section of code that may or may not have been created in another.

```
with MyOutline do
  for Counter := Count downto 1 do
    (ata[Counter] as TMYIDClass).Free;
```

Note in the code above that freeing items from the bottom of a list to the top using a **for..downto** loop is slightly more efficient because the list does not have to shuffle items up to fill an empty space.

Finding Rows

You need to identify which item in a control the user chooses, but you will also need to locate an item within a control programmatically. Depending on your control, you may have to iterate through the entire structure until you find the item you are looking for. If your hierarchy subdivides a sorted list into sorted groups (for example, a parent item for each letter of the alphabet and all the items with descriptions starting with that letter as its children), you can take advantage of the grouping to narrow down your search by finding the parent you want and iterating through just its children.

One pitfall is examining the same items more than once during the search. If you search from an item up through its parent, you will examine the same parent item for each of its children. Unless the contents of the items create some groupings that narrow your search, checking the list of items linearly is always the safest way to find an item.

Sometimes, it's worth making a index or cross-reference for your code to use. The **TTreeView** component is very slow, even iterating through its nodes. A sorted **TStringList** will make binary, case-insensitive searches which are very fast. They can connect an ID value with a pointer to the **TTreeNode** or **TOutline.ID** (get this **ID** after you have loaded all the nodes).

```
Result := nil;
Index := LookupStringList.IndexOf(IntToStr(FindThisValue));
if Index > -1 then
  Result := TTreeNode(LookupStringList[Index]);
```

Using Hierarchical Data In Queries

A hard place to reconcile the hierarchical and relational models is in the area of queries. The relational model is good at identifying rows by their attributes (columns) or common values in other tables (joins). Such a query is often a short, self-evident string in SQL.

SQL, however, is *not* good at expressing concepts like "somewhere in your lineage, there is a green box." It is good at finding green boxes, but has no idea what a "lineage" is. The section discussing SQL later on in this chapter has some solutions for finding rows iteratively, but if you have the hierarchy in memory, you can get the lineage as a set of IDs and use it in a query with the **IN** criteria operator. It looks for a field's value in a delimited list of alternatives. Listing 13.5 demonstrates how this is done by creating an SQL query programmatically in the **TQuery.SQL** property. Notice here that SQL does not do all the work itself; the hierarchy object first identifies the lineage using its own machinery.

Listing 13.5 Using SQL to search a lineage.

```
procedure TForm1.FindColoredBoxes(ColorName : String;
                                  StartingID : Integer);
var
  DescendantList : String;

begin
  DescendantString := HierarchyObject.GetDescendants(StartingID);
  with Query1 do
    begin
      DisableControls;
      Close;
      with SQL do
        begin
          Clear;
          Add('SELECT *');
          Add('FROM BoxList T1');
          Add('WHERE T1.BoxColor = ''' + ColorName + '''');
          { This assumes that the IDs in DescendantString
            are delimited with commas }
          if DescendantString <> '' then
            Add('AND T1.BoxID IN (' + DescendantString + ')');
        end;
      Open;
      EnableControls;
    end;
end;
```

As an example: If your query is looking for all painters, you can go to your hierarchy, find the parent of all painters, programmatically extract all the descendent IDs of that item, and use those ID values as criteria. This allows you to use a single ID to identify a row, allow that ID to be very specialized, and still retrieve that row when you ask for the general category. Because you use the hierarchy, you don't have to know how many descendents the Painter item has—you will get them all.

If you have a hierarchy in a **TOutline** or **TTreeView** component, you can use the navigational properties of those components to iterate through the descendents of any given item. Otherwise, you have to load it into memory and set pointers between parents and children, or use the iterative or recursive query techniques described below.

Referential Integrity And Circular References

Ironically, a recursive hierarchy in a single table makes referential integrity easy: One column in the table refers to another column in the table. Within the table, every **Boss_ID** value will be another row's **Emp_ID**, or else nil (indicating a top-level item). This protects all of the descendents of an item because no **Emp_ID** can change if any other row depends upon it. If the lookup values are in several columns or tables to allow multilevel groupings or relationships, referential integrity becomes more complicated.

The most dangerous thing for code that controls a hierarchy is a circular reference. If one item refers to a nonexistent ancestor item, that is a detectable problem; however, if an item refers to an ancestor item that is also a descendent item (which is hard to see if the items are separated by several generations), the code will loop endlessly, looking for a parent item without a parent itself.

The answer? Apart from checking each candidate ancestor item to see if any of its ancestors are already in the family (which can be expensive in performance terms), your code can have a burnout counter that throws an exception if the code processes through an excessive number of search cycles. One advantage to graphical hierarchical controls is there is no way the end user can set up a circular reference because it clearly violates the graphical rules of the control.

Using SQL

If your hierarchies are huge and cannot operate entirely within memory, investigate an SQL solution. If you know how many levels of recursion are involved, you can use SQL subqueries to bridge generations, as shown here in Listing 13.6.

Listing 13.6 Using SQL to bridge a known number of generations: 3.

```
SELECT *
FROM Items T1
WHERE T1.Parent_ID IN
  (SELECT T2.Item_ID
   FROM Items T2
   WHERE T2.Parent_ID IN
     {SELECT T3.Item_ID
      FROM Items T3
      WHERE T3.Parent_ID = 'Fred'))
```

This requires exactly three generations: The only rows returned are the grandchildren of Fred. To get children and grandchildren, run two queries, and either use **UNION** or add the result sets together using **INSERT INTO** or temporary tables.

To find an item's parent item, simply query for the one row where the **Item_ID** is equal to the **Parent_ID**. To find all the children of an item, query for all the rows that have the **Item_ID** value as their **Parent_ID**. To find all the siblings, find all the items that have the same **Parent_ID**. (Note here that the original item will also be a part of the set unless you specifically exclude it.) Once you have a child or sibling set, to find all the descendents, you have to iterate through each row of that set and run a query to find its children. Iterate through *that* set to find any children of the children, and so on.

Solving The Problem Of Arbitrary Nesting

The big problem comes in when the nesting is arbitrary and you don't know how many levels a lineage might have. There is no conditional branching in SQL; either a subquery finds rows or it does not. Joe Celko devotes two chapters of his book *SQL for Smarties* (Morgan Kaufman Publishers, 1995) to trees and graphs; that is, the data that goes into visual graphs, including hierarchical trees. His techniques are advanced and demonstrate what you have to do to correctly associate one item (or *node*) to another.

If you want a simpler though possibly inefficient (and certainly less elegant) solution, consider using a temporary table (the "Final" table) to hold the cumulative results of many queries, and another temporary table (the "Working" table) to hold the results of the most recent one. You may have to use two Working tables and alternate between them depending on which SQL server you are using. The algorithm looks like this:

1. Query for children of the starting item;
2. Copy the item IDs to the Working table;
3. Query for children of any of the item IDs in the Working table;
4. If there are no child rows, exit;
5. Add the Working table to the Final table;
6. Erase the Working table and add all the query's item IDs to it;
7. Go back to step 3.

Each cycle retrieves the next generation, and the Final table will contain all the child rows in generation sequence.

Using Stored Procedures

Stored procedures resemble SQL with conditional and looping logic, which SQL itself lacks. InterBase allows stored procedures, called *select procedures*, which return any number of rows just as an SQL query would. Its procedure language allows you to iterate over a result set (using a query or another select procedure inside the procedure) and operate on it, as shown in Listing 13.7, which is in the InterBase command language. (The line numbers are significant in the discussion that follows.)

Listing 13.7   InterBase select procedures.

```
1.  CREATE PROCEDURE GETCHILDREN (STARTING_ITEM_ID SMALLINT,
                                 THISLEVEL SMALLINT)
2.  RETURNS(ITEM_ID SMALLINT, DESCRIPTION CHAR(30),
            ITEMLEVEL SMALLINT) AS
3.  BEGIN
4.    FOR
5.      SELECT T1.ITEM_ID, T1.DESCRIPTION
6.      FROM ITEMS T1
```

```
7.        WHERE T1.PARENT_ID = :STARTING_ITEM_ID
8.      INTO :ITEM_ID, :DESCRIPTION
9.    DO BEGIN
10.       ITEMLEVEL = THISLEVEL + 1;
11.       SUSPEND;
12.       FOR
13.         SELECT T1.ITEM_ID, T1.DESCRIPTION, T1.ITEMLEVEL
14.         FROM  GETCHILDREN(:ITEM_ID, :ITEMLEVEL) T1
15.         INTO :ITEM_ID,  :DESCRIPTION, :ITEMLEVEL
16.       DO BEGIN
17.           SUSPEND;
18.       END
19.    END
20. END;
```

This sort of recursive iteration is exactly what you need to walk up and down the branches of hierarchical data because these stored procedures are recursive: You can call them from within themselves to get children of children, and so on. Instead of getting all the rows in a generation, and then getting the next generation, this strategy gets the first child of the first child, then the first grandchild of the first child, and so on until the last descendent is found.

In the InterBase language, **SUSPEND** means to return the **RETURNS** variables as the next row in the result set. The first **SUSPEND** (line 11) returns the values from the first row of the query on the immediate children of **STARTING_ITEM_ID** (lines 5 through 8). The next **SUSPEND** (line 17) returns whatever comes back from a recursive call to the **GETCHILDREN** select procedure. As long as that second call returns rows (that is, as long as it still has grandchildren and descendents to report), the second **SUSPEND** will keep passing the return values back to the original caller. When it has no more return values, the calling code continues and uses the first **SUSPEND** to return the second row of the original query. If you don't reset the **ITEMLEVEL** in the outer loop (line 10), it will contain the value from the last iteration of the inner loop (line 15).

Use a **TQuery** to call InterBase select procedures, not a **TStoredProc**. The syntax is simple:

```
with Query1 do
begin
  SQL.Clear;
```

```
    SQL.Add('SELECT * FROM
          GetChildren(' + IntToStr(CurrentItemID) + ',0)');
  Open;
end;
```

The result set will have all the children of the current item and will identify their level.

The TreeData Components

The TreeData components are components I've created that allow you to view, navigate, and manage hierarchical data. They will display the rows in a graphical tree form with each level indented to show its ownership, show the entire lineage of an item by concatenating all the parent names, and give your application a list of all the ancestor or descendent IDs. There are several components in the family, and I've summarized them in Table 13.4.

Table 13.4 The TreeData family of components.

Control	Description	Use
TreeDataComboBox	Displays the items in an indented tree layout on the drop-down list; displays the lineage in the edit control.	Get a single choice from the user: Get the ID or all the ancestor or descendent IDs.
	Allows incremental searching on both the edit and the drop-down.	
	Data-aware to link to chosen IDs to a DataSource.	
TreeDataOutline	Displays the entire tree graphically and allows expansion and contraction of various branches.	Get a single choice from the user: Get the ID or all the ancestor or descendent IDs.
	Data-aware to link to chosen IDs to a DataSource.	

(continued)

Table 13.4 The TreeData family of components *(continued)*.

Control	Description	Use
TreeDataList	Combines a TreeDataComboBox with a data-aware listbox. Data-aware to link all chosen IDs to a DataSource.	Allows user to pick any number of tree items and save them to a table as a set or load them as a set.
TreeDataUpdate	Combines a TreeOutline. with editing functions to edit and update the rows that make up the hierarchy. Immediate or cached updates to DataSource.	Maintains a hierarchical dataset.

The TreeData controls crystallize a lot of what I've been discussing in this chapter so far. Unfortunately, they represent thousands of lines of source code (available on the CD-ROM accompanying this book). They use a common set of routines to load the entire tree into a memory structure from a table, and then modify the display behavior of the base controls to show the data hierarchically.

TreeData Property Management

Certain properties are very important in this operation. All the TreeData controls take the design-time properties: **LookupDatabaseName**, **LookupTableName**, **LookupSQL** (mutually exclusive with **LookupTableName**), **LookupDisplayField**, **LookupIDField, LookupParentIDField,** and if used with Delphi 2.0, **LookupSessionName**. (See Figure 13.4.) Using these properties, a TreeData control loads all the data into memory and displays it as a hierarchical tree, then closes the connection.

As an alternative, the TreeData controls also have a **LookupDataSource** property that can use an open DataSource to get the data. This lets you filter, range, or query the **DataSource.DataSet** property to control what items go into the control. The **LookupAutoRefresh** property specifies whether or not you want to reload the lookup data if the **LookupDataSource** changes.

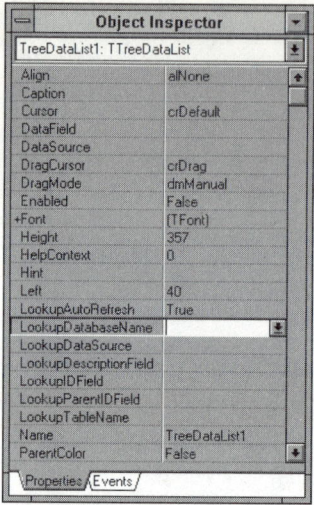

Figure 13.4
Properties of the TreeData components.

TreeData Component Internals

All these components share a base code unit TREEUTIL.PAS, which holds the definition of the various internal classes that manage the data. TREEUTIL.PAS defines a class named **TTreeDataItem**, which holds information about an item, and a class named **TTreeDataItems**, which is a **TList** descendent that keeps track of all the **TTreeDataItem** objects. Each of the controls exposes a **TTreeDataItems** object as the property **ItemList**. You can call the public methods of this object to load, save, find, move, or delete an item. You can also get all ancestor or descendent IDs for an item, or get the top-level ID in an item's lineage.

TTreeDataItems descends from class **TStringList**, which holds all the item IDs. The **Objects** property of each **TStringList** item points to the **TTreeDataItem** object for that item. The pointers to the control's items are in a separate **TList** and synchronized with the **TTreeDataItems** list. Sorted **TStrngLists** will use case-insensitive, binary searching within the **IndexOf** method, so they easily can find IDs. After it loads all the items and sorts the IDs, class **TTreeDataItems** iterates through all of them and puts the index for the first child and the next sibling in each item's data structure. This allows easy iteration down and across the hierarchy.

With all that said of the TreeData family as a whole, I'll briefly discuss each control in the family separately.

TreeDataComboBox

This control is data-aware as well as getting its data from a lookup table, so you can use it to save the user's choices to a table. It stores the single value to **LookupIDField**. The drop-down portion of the display shows the items indented under their owners, and the editbox shows the hierarchy of the current item by joining all the descriptions, separated by colons. The editbox also allows incremental type-in that displays the first match to text already entered. When a match is found, typing the colon (or semicolon) locks that item and moves the search point to text entered after the colon or semicolon. This allows you to continue typing to search that item's children. This is shown in Figure 13.5.

The TreeDataComboBox component has properties for the description, ID, and **Item.FullDescription**, which contains the delimited descriptions as displayed in the edit control. It has additional properties that return a string with all the parent or child IDs concatenated together.

TreeDataListBox

This control incorporates both a **TTreeDataComboBox** at the top and a data-aware **TListBox** beneath it (see Figure 13.6). The **TListBox** acts on all the rows in its DataSource instead of just the current row. You can use the combo box to pick items and then add them to the list. When you call **SaveIDs** or exit the control with the **SaveOnExit** flag set, the control writes all the IDs to the DataSource, one per row. The DataSource can incorporate a range (for example, a MasterSource) or filter so it presents detail rows for only master items in the MasterSource or filter.

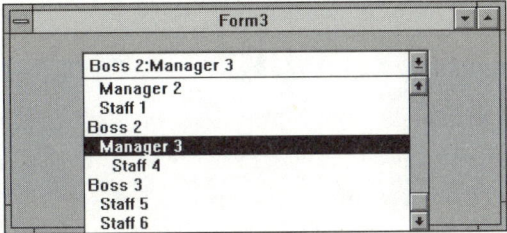

Figure 13.5
The TreeDataComboBox component.

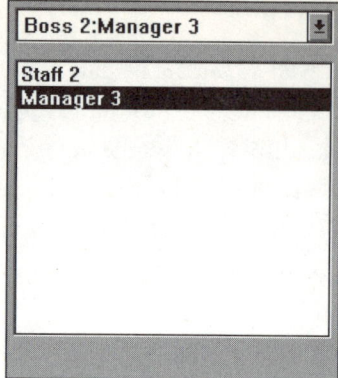

Figure 13.6
The TreeDataListBox component.

The effect is something like a **TTreeDataCombo** with the list permanently dropped down.

TreeDataOutline And TreeDataUpdate

TreeDataOutline displays the hierarchy in a graphical structure resembling the Windows 95 Explorer interface. As with the other controls, you can get the current item's ID, description, and **Item.FullDescription**, as well as a string list of all the parent or child IDs.

The TreeDataUpdate component (see Figure 13.7) combines this functionality with some additional behavior to manage a hierarchical data structure from a table. It will let you add, modify, and delete items as well as move them within the hierarchy.

Hierarchical Wisdom

Hierarchies use the terminology of family relationships (parents, grandchildren, ancestors, descendents) because families are the most universal example of a gathering of individual entities—here, human beings—relating to other entities in hierarchical ways. Ironically, it is also a reminder that while you may build systems to

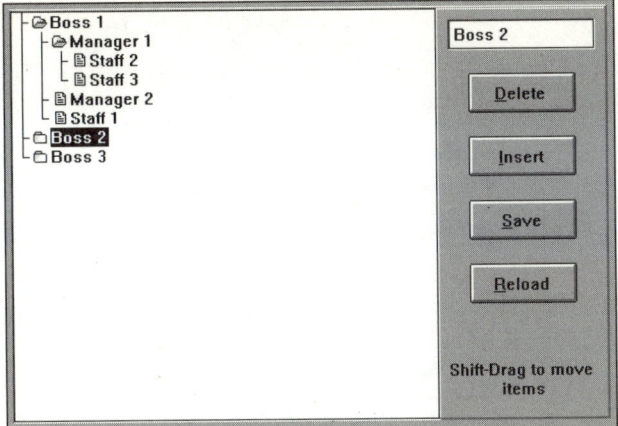

Figure 13.7
The TreeDataUpdate component.

handle recursive hierarchies generically, each item's value lies in the unique information that it contains; its *place* in the family tree is valuable only as it relates to other members. Hierarchical structuring is a means of holding and finding an item; it's up to you to ensure that the item is worth it.

HIGH PERFORMANCE

The Oracle Vanishes

CHAPTER 14

Ace Breakpoint has returned—but his casebook is missing, and larceny is suspected. Ace begins the hunt for the Mysterious Stranger, who has in turn been hunting for Delphi Wisdom. The plot thickens!

The Oracle Vanishes

Don Taylor

You're about to embark on a journey that some might call strange. I guess I would be among the first to agree with them.

It was only two years ago that both Delphi and Ace Breakpoint first came upon the scene. Delphi was, of course, the product of the extremely creative team of developers at Borland International. Ace was—well, the product of necessity.

While learning Delphi, it became obvious that no amount of words could ever describe every aspect of this incredible product. One could never just read about Delphi and learn it—one had to discover it firsthand. My assignment: to write the tutorial map, to lead the expedition, and to create a detailed example, using Delphi in a real-world situation. And oh, yes—to hold the readers' attention for some 200+ pages!

My proposed solution was to write an adventure story that carried the reader through the entire tutorial, featuring one of the most unusual programming consultants of all time. I pitched the idea to Jeff Duntemann, then held my breath. In case you're not aware, Jeff is just as daring and fun-loving as he is brilliant. He gave me the thumbs-up, and I created Ace Breakpoint, hard-hitting fictional private investigator-turned-programmer....

As a boy growing up in Hackensack, Ace dreamed of becoming a P.I., just like his heroes in the classic 1940 movies—Phil Marlowe, Sam Spade, and Ellery Queen. But after years of study and hard work learning investigative techniques and snappy dialog, Ace discovered there was little demand for a 1940s-style P.I. in today's world.

Undaunted, Ace decided to make a serious career change. This time, Ace would choose a profession that would be in demand for a lifetime—he would become a Windows programmer. But in addition to becoming today's professional, he also wanted to become a "person of the '90s." So he moved to Poulsbo, Washington, and for two long years he attended night classes in computer programming at the

Chapter 14

Suquamish School of Art. On graduation day, he was awarded an Associate of Arts in Programming Appropriateness. He promptly rented an office and hung out his shingle.

As with most heroes, Ace has his minor flaws. In spite of all his formal education, he is still a little rough around the edges. Although he does his best to care about the needs of others, there are times when sensitivity hangs on him like a cheap suit. He frequently makes mistakes. But he has a tenacious quality about him, and you've got to love him for that. When faced with problems, he will doggedly pursue them until he digs out the answers.

Oh, yes—just one little matter. Although the Breakpoint adventures are fictional, one thing is true. The location—Poulsbo—is a real town, situated about 15 miles (as the crow swims) west of Seattle. At its inception, it was a fishing village, founded by a hardy group of Norwegian immigrants. Today Poulsbo is largely a tourist town, with marinas and a winding street full of quaint shops and restaurants. (You don't want to move there, though. It's too crowded already. And it rains nearly all the time. Honest.)

Very little else in the Breakpoint adventures bears any connection to reality. And of course, unless stated otherwise, characters in the stories are purely fictional, and are not meant to represent any person, living or dead.

So don't touch that dial! Grab your favorite snack, turn down the lights, slide up close to your screen, and prepare yourself for the adventure I call...

Ace Breakpoint in...

"The Case of the Missing Ink!"

An Evening At The Office

I stepped inside my office and slammed the door behind me so hard that I could hear a thud outside as my shingle fell to the ground. It had been pouring all day, and now it seemed to be raining even harder. The excessive rain of the past few days had turned the field next to my office complex into a thick, muddy paste that was now relentlessly encroaching on the asphalt parking lot like a television news crew heading for a disaster scene. I scraped my shoes on the mat inside the door in a futile attempt to remove the sticky brown goo.

I stripped off my hat and coat and tossed the soaking armload on the couch, missing Mewnix by a whisker. The fatigued feline didn't so much as flinch, but he did manage to pop open one eye and fire a dirty look in my direction. I plunked down in the chair in front of my computer and switched it on. Having just returned from the regular Tuesday night meeting of my Win95 codependency group, I needed to lighten up a little. I decided to go online and pick up my mail.

The only item waiting for me was a note from my mom, Queenie Breakpoint, reminding me to call my sister on her birthday, and to be sure to invite all my friends to the party celebrating the anniversary of the adventure that took place in *Delphi Programming EXplorer*.

I rapped out an email invitation and sent it to the list marked "friends," and then found myself reminiscing. Although that adventure had taken place only two years ago, it already seemed like a lifetime. It had started out innocently enough, with Melvin Bohacker and myself competing for a potential contract. Bohacker was a tall, pencil-necked geek with a propensity for snack food and programming in C and C++, using a multitude of libraries. Up to that time he had beaten me out of every consulting job I had gone after.

The competition sounded straightforward. But when the smoke cleared just 24 hours later, I was a physical wreck—beaten, bloodied, and bewildered. If it hadn't been for my friends, I don't know what I would have done.

We had all gotten to know each other at the art school, and we had stuck together like glue ever since. As close friends, even they had been to some extent subjected to the heat of the competition. Bruiser Buckendorf-Rabinowicz (the former pro football player) was taken in for psychological evaluation. Biff Murphy, the Business Ethics major, was in fear for my life. Muffy Katz, the professional part-time psychic and Fashion Therapy major, was in fear of—well, to tell the truth, she was probably most in fear of breaking a nail.

And then there was Helen Highwater. For nearly five years, Helen had stuck by me, through thick and thin. She was the love of my life. But in the midst of the adventure, I almost lost her. Although I been devastated as a result of the competition (I still bear the coffee stains on my hands as testimony), I managed to get in my licks with Bohacker the following afternoon. In fact, I hit him so hard that some of the blood from his pummeled nose splattered on the trenchcoat I was wearing. That bloodstained memento still hangs in the back of my closet.

Chapter 14

I had to chuckle. A lot of water had gone under the bridge in the past year. I was now using Delphi 3 almost exclusively, and my consulting practice was steadily growing. Biff was still working the takeout window at Buck McGawk's Norwegian Fried Chicken Haus. Helen was now the day manager at the Hardanger World outlet at the local mall. Muffy left her job to start her own line of designer clothes and accessories, under the Pure Prophet label. And then there's Bruiser's tragic story. He was diagnosed as a codependent megalomaniac and committed to a state institution. Two months later, after intense study, he had learned to tune a guitar. Then one night he and four other inmates escaped and started a grunge band called Not Ourselves Today. Their first CD went platinum. Their second album is scheduled for release this week. (I don't plan to buy either of them. There are, after all, limits to every friendship.)

An Urgent Plea

I wandered over to the TV and flipped to the Shopping Channel for some background noise, then picked up the latest volume of my Casebook and began dutifully recording the details of the day's events. I had written only two paragraphs when the telephone rang.

"Breakpoint. What can I do for ya?"

"Mr. Breakpoint—thank goodness you're there!" said the voice coming from the receiver. "I truly don't know what I'd have done if you hadn't answered your phone."

It was an unusual voice, to say the least. Certainly, it was desperate. And it was definitely female. Hot and cold, breathy and chilling all at the same time. Sort of like Lauren Bacall, with ice cubes. She was in a near panic.

"Slow down," I said. "Just take it easy, and explain your situation in detail."

"I'm an heiress," she replied, her voice still breathless. "For the past week I've been followed at a distance by a very large man whom I believe is intending to kidnap me and hold me for ransom. A few moments ago when I stopped at a traffic light, he jumped out of his car and tried to force open my door. I sped off and managed to lose him temporarily, but he may catch up with me any minute. I found your name in the phone book. I have nowhere else to turn."

"Okay. Keep calm," I said reassuringly. "Can you describe this man? Did he have a beard or mustache?"

"I couldn't tell," she replied. "His head was covered with a nylon stocking."

"Seamed or seamless?" I queried.

"Seamless, I think."

"What shade?"

"Natural. No, no—it may have been sand. Oh, I don't know! Listen, Mr. Breakpoint," she pleaded, "you're my only hope. He's liable to show up at any moment. I need you right now."

"Just hold on," I said. "Where are you?"

"I'm at a pay phone on the highway, at a place called Ole's Espresso Bar and Tire Emporium. I desperately need your protect—"

My heart fell as I heard the unmistakable sounds of a struggle, followed by a crash, a muffled scream, and the hiss of steam escaping from an espresso machine. Then the line went dead.

I glanced at my watch. It was 10:13 P.M. I tossed my Casebook on the desk, grabbed my keys and rain gear, and raced for the car. The pouring rain mingled with a fog that had begun to roll in, making it difficult to find my car, parked only 50 feet away. I flipped on my headlights, but even their powerful halogen beams could barely penetrate the steamy curtain in front of me. The row of shrubs planted alongside my office looked like a group of Angry White Males standing in the shadows, waiting for a bus. I backed out of my space and managed to find my way to the street. Then I slammed the accelerator to the floor.

The Disappearance

At 10:57 P.M., I pulled back into the parking lot at my office. The mud had become so thick that the car skidded across the pavement like an elephant on ice skates, stopped only by the tires smashing into the curbing in front of space #132.

I had been stood up by the woman on the phone. When I arrived at the phone booth, there was no one in sight. Ole said he hadn't seen anyone near the pay phone

Chapter 14

all evening. It was a perplexing situation. The only thing I had gotten out of this wild goose chase was a free tire rotation while I waited for my latté order.

I stumbled to the edge of the parking lot, slipping and sliding all the way. I turned the corner and headed down the walkway.

And then my heart stopped.

The door to my office was standing wide open. As I ran the last few steps, I specifically remembered having locked the door when I left. Nevertheless, it was open, and all the lights were on inside. As I crossed the threshold, my eyes scanned the entire room with lightning speed. *Nothing missing*, I thought. No—Mewnix was nowhere in sight, but he probably just wandered out the open doorway. Then my eyes fell on my desk, and a lump the size of a large fur ball suddenly stuck in my throat: My Casebook was gone!

Moving quickly to the desk, I frantically thrashed through the papers on top, then searched each of the drawers, and in total desperation, I examined the floor around the desk. But the Casebook was nowhere to be found.

I slumped down in my chair. The phone call had been merely a ruse to get me out of the office. Thanks to the woman on the phone (and quite likely an accomplice), I had just been promoted to Chump First Class.

I had been so engrossed in looking for the missing Casebook that I hadn't noticed the thick carpet of carbon dioxide fog that had rolled into the room. It now covered the entire floor, spilling over the tops of my running shoes. The room had gone dim, the only lighting in the room now seeming to come up through the fog from the floor beneath. My eyes were drawn like a magnet to a mysterious figure framed in the doorway. It was a wispy creature, definitely humanoid, but not clearly male or female. Sensing I had noticed it, it spoke out in an announcer-like voice, with entirely too much reverberation to suit my comfort.

Welcome back, Mr. Breakpoint. You have been expected.

"Wait a second," Ace demanded. "Who—or what—are you?"

First things first. As you have discovered, your Casebook has indeed been stolen. The entire contents will be read by someone else. Not just your technical notes, but all your personal writings as well. The Author felt you needed some help in conveying the remainder of this story. He has therefore provided you with a narrator.

Ace removed his fedora and scratched the top of his head. "A narrator?"

The Third Person.

"A politically correct, 1990s version of Harry Lime, the famous detective called The Third Man?" Ace asked.

No. The Third Person. The one you studied in English Comp. Remember?

"Sort of," Ace replied. "I don't know your name, Mr. or Mrs.... Hey—are you a man or a woman?"

Third Persons don't have names. Being merely a literary device, a Third Person has no gender. Nor does a Third Person have a life of its own, for that matter.

"I can kinda identify," Ace observed. "But answer me this: How come I have lost control of the narration of this story?"

It is only a temporary situation. Control will automatically revert to you near the end of the story. Until then, it is the job of the narrator to describe the flow of events. Pretend you're watching an episode of The Outer Limits.

"I don't know if I'm gonna like this."

At The Sleeveless Arms

In The Sleeveless Arms, a shabby, brick-faced building across town, a shadowy figure slipped from the hallway into a recently rented second-story apartment and locked the door. Inching through the darkness, the tall, lanky form found its way to a small desk in the corner, where it snapped on the familiar banker's lamp, bathing the desktop in a warm glow. The figure carefully removed a hardbound leather notebook from the inside pocket of a full-length raincoat, and pushing aside several unopened packages of snack food, laid it on the desk. The light reflecting from the desktop illuminated the small portion of face exposed between an upturned collar and the wide brim of a dirt-brown hat: two blazing, close-set eyes and a sharp nose that barely extended beyond a thick, perfectly manicured mustache.

"So this is it, eh?" said the rain-soaked figure, in a voice dripping with anticipation. "Let's just see what we have here."

The mysterious figure sat down at the desk, paused for just a moment, and then turned to the first page and began to read from Ace Breakpoint's Casebook.

Doing The Old Drag/Drop

Casebook No. 16, March 19: Sometimes the things that look the simplest can be the most difficult. Then again, the opposite can be true. At least that's the case with intra-application drag and drop operations in Delphi applications.

I was creating an application in which I wanted to select an item and relate it to a date by dragging it over and dropping it on a calendar on the same form. First, I had to investigate what that would entail. I found there to be four primary steps to any drag and drop operation:

1. Initiating the **BeginDrag** method of the originating (source) component, by handling mouse-related events occurring within that component;

2. Creating a handler for the destination component's OnDragOver event, to indicate where within the component a drop is permissible;

3. Creating a handler for the destination component's OnDragDrop event, to determine what action is taken as a result of the dropping action; and

4. Optionally, creating a handler for the originating component's OnDragEnd event. While the other three steps are required in any drag/drop, this step is needed only if some housekeeping is required on the originating component when the drag ends—housekeeping that will be performed even if the operation was aborted.

Kind Of A Drag

My first challenge was the calendar component. Although a good one is provided with Delphi, it did not provide an easy way to relate a position on the calendar to a date. Because the sample calendar component shows only the days in the current month (leaving blank entries everywhere else in its grid), I would have to write code that computed the dates relating to those blanks. Not a pretty situation.

My solution turned out to be the OvcCalendar component provided with TurboPower Software's Orpheus VCL package. This powerful little component relates a date to every cell in the grid, displaying days from the previous and/or following month. By eliminating the default header on the calendar, I know that every square on the calendar represents a valid date. Since each square is the same size as the others, relating an absolute date to a position on an OvcCalendar is a straightforward process.

Note: *The OvcCalendar component, along with the rest of the components in the Orpheus collection, have all been included in a special trial version located in the \ORPHEUS directory on the CD-ROM that accompanies this book. The latest trial version is always available on TurboPower's website, located at http://www.turbopower.com.*

For my investigation, I created an application with a single form that contained an edit box, a string grid, and a calendar (and the ever-present button to exit the application). The idea would be to enter a string in the edit box, and then drag and drop the string on the calendar, where it would be associated with a date. A string containing the date and the entered string would then be added to the string grid. A snapshot of the running version of the experiment is shown in Figure 14.1.

I started with Step 1. It seemed logical to look for a mouse-down message arriving in the edit box, which turned out to be a good idea—more or less. By setting up a drag from an edit box, I had unknowingly put myself at cross purposes: The OnMouseDown event already had a standard meaning in the context of an edit box, that of selecting text. By using that event to enable a drag, I would lose the ability to select a portion of the text by dragging the I-beam cursor over it.

The OnMouseDown event handler is provided with several pieces of information—a reference to the object originating the message; a parameter that indicates which mouse button is down; another parameter that indicates the state of the Shift, Ctrl,

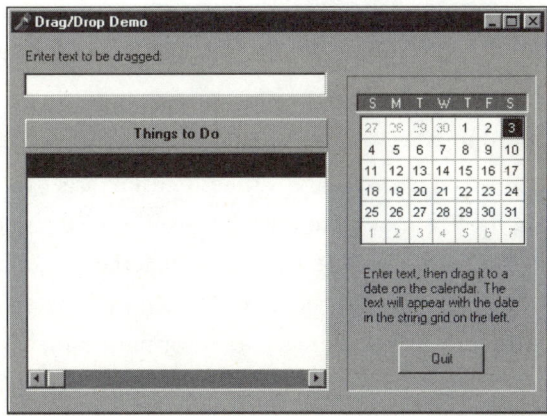

Figure 14.1
Ace's drag and drop experiment.

and Alt keys; and finally, x-y position information on the cursor. In this case, the originator (sender) would be the edit box, because that is where I wanted the drag to begin. I could ignore the positioning information, since I didn't care where the drag could begin within the simple rectangle of an edit box. And I wanted to start a drag only when the left mouse button was pressed. (I later discovered I had to filter out double-clicks, too, because allowing them to initiate drags caused some strange side effects.)

Pretty simple. My final code appears in Listing 14.1.

Listing 14.1   An event handler to begin the drag.

```
procedure TDDDemoForm.EditBoxMouseDown(Sender: TObject;
  Button: TMouseButton; Shift: TShiftState; X, Y: Integer);
begin
 if (Button = mbLeft)
   and (EditBox.Text <> '')
   and not (ssDouble in Shift)
  then TEdit(Sender).BeginDrag(False);
end;
```

While testing my original version of the handler, I discovered there are two ways to initiate the drag. Using **True** as the argument of the **BeginDrag** method starts the drag as soon as the mouse is pressed, while selecting **False** delays until the mouse is actually moved a few pixels. The second choice felt far more natural. After some bumbles, I also added the line of code that blocks out any attempt to drag an empty string. The typecast used to call the **BeginDrag** method is typically required when working with the **Sender** and **Source** object references provided to event handlers.

Step 2 was next. The handler for OnDragOver events brings with it several parameters. **Source** specifies the object where the drag started (in this case, the edit box). **Sender** is the object sending the message—the potential target for the drop. In this case it's the calendar. The **X** and **Y** parameters give the relative coordinates of the mouse cursor within the **Sender**, and **State** specifies whether the object being dragged is entering, leaving or moving across the **Sender**. Although default cursors are provided for the drag/drop process, this drag state information makes it easy to specify your own cursors for each part of the process. Finally, there is the **Accept** parameter, a boolean passed by reference.

The object of the game is to decide, based on the information provided, whether or not it is acceptable to complete the drop. The process is sort of like a pilot of a small plane (the **Source**) radioing to a controller on the ground, saying, "Here are my coordinates over the field in which you're standing. Is it okay to drop my payload?"

It turned out that by selecting the OvcCalendar, I had made my work exceedingly simple: Everything within the calendar's client area was fair game for a drop. The code appears in Listing 14.2.

Listing 14.2   Checking for the acceptability of a drop.

```
procedure TDDDemoForm.CalendarDragOver(Sender, Source: TObject; X,
  Y: Integer; State: TDragState; var Accept: Boolean);
begin
  Accept := True;
end;
```

Dropping The Payload

I proceeded to Step 3. The strategy was to figure out the row and column locations of the first day of the month and the cursor position. From that, a little arithmetic would give me the number of day's difference between the two dates, which I could then add to the first day's date to obtain the *absolute* date.

Obviously, that first day will always appear in the first row, no matter which day of the week it falls on. So much for the row. Since I hadn't changed the calendar from the standard Sunday through Saturday format, getting the day of the week for the first day gave me a column reference position. From there, I just had to advance the number of days into the calendar. Fortunately, the Orpheus package comes with some powerful date conversion and arithmetic routines that helped greatly. My calculation routine for the date pointed at is shown in Listing 14.3.

Listing 14.3   Calculating the date from the mouse position.

```
function DatePointedTo : TOvcDate;
  var
    Idx : Longint;
    DOW : Integer;
    Day1 : TOvcDate;
  begin
   { Compute first day as Row = 1, Col = DOW, then
     calculate an offset to the date pointed to. Then
     add the two. }
```

```
  Day1 := DMYToDate(1, Calendar.Month, Calendar.Year);
  DOW := Ord(DayOfWeek(Day1)) + 1;
  Idx := (RNum - 1) * 7;
  if CNum < DOW
   then Idx := Idx - (DOW - CNum)
   else if CNum > DOW
         then Idx := Idx + (CNum - DOW);
  Result := IncDate(Day1, Idx, 0, 0);
end; { DatePointedTo }
```

All that was left was some simple housekeeping—converting the date and edit box text to a string, and adding that string to the string grid. I also found it handy to clear out the edit box once the drop was complete; with the editing capabilities of the edit box somewhat hampered by the dragging support, it became cumbersome to clear it manually.

Note to myself: In this case, it was appropriate to clear the edit box as part of the drag/drop event handler, because I wanted it performed only if the drop was performed. Had I wanted to clear the edit box whether or not the drop succeeded, I would have done so in an OnEndDrag handler for the edit box.

Reminders to myself: 1) Make sure the OvcCalendar's **Initialize** property is set to **True**. Otherwise, it comes up in an undefined state! 2) Make sure to set the **DrawHeader** property to **False**, so the calendar displays nothing but dates.

Listing 14.4 shows the code for the entire unit.

Listing 14.4   Code for the drag/drop demo.

```
{—————————————————————————————————}
{             Drag/Drop Demonstration              }
{       DRAGMAIN.PAS : Drag/Drop Main Unit         }
{           By Ace Breakpoint, N.T.P.              }
{            Assisted by Don Taylor                }
{                                                  }
{ Application that demonstrates dragging and       }
{ dropping within the single application.          }
{                                                  }
{ Written for *High Performance Delphi 3 Programming* }
{ Copyright (c) 1997 The Coriolis Group, Inc.      }
{            Last Updated 5/3/97                   }
{—————————————————————————————————}
```

```
unit DragMain;

interface

uses
  SysUtils, WinTypes, WinProcs, Messages, Classes, Graphics, Controls,
  Forms, Dialogs, Grids, StdCtrls, OvcBase, OvcCal, OvcData, OvcDT,
  ExtCtrls;

type
  TDDDemoForm = class(TForm)
    Calendar: TOvcCalendar;
    OvcController1: TOvcController;
    EditBox: TEdit;
    StringGrid: TStringGrid;
    Label1: TLabel;
    Bevel1: TBevel;
    QuitBtn: TButton;
    Panel1: TPanel;
    Label2: TLabel;
    Label3: TLabel;
    Label4: TLabel;
    Label5: TLabel;
    Panel2: TPanel;
    procedure QuitBtnClick(Sender: TObject);
    procedure EditBoxMouseDown(Sender: TObject; Button: TMouseButton;
      Shift: TShiftState; X, Y: Integer);
    procedure CalendarDragOver(Sender, Source: TObject; X, Y: Integer;
      State: TDragState; var Accept: Boolean);
    procedure CalendarDragDrop(Sender, Source: TObject; X, Y: Integer);
  private
    { Private declarations }
  public
    { Public declarations }
  end;

var
  DDDemoForm: TDDDemoForm;

implementation

{$R *.DFM}

procedure TDDDemoForm.QuitBtnClick(Sender: TObject);
begin
 Close;
end;
```

```
procedure TDDDemoForm.EditBoxMouseDown(Sender: TObject;
  Button: TMouseButton; Shift: TShiftState; X, Y: Integer);
begin
  if (Button = mbLeft)
    and (EditBox.Text <> '')
    and not (ssDouble in Shift)
    then TEdit(Sender).BeginDrag(False);
end;

procedure TDDDemoForm.CalendarDragOver(Sender, Source: TObject; X,
  Y: Integer; State: TDragState; var Accept: Boolean);
begin
  Accept := True;
end;

procedure TDDDemoForm.CalendarDragDrop(Sender, Source: TObject; X,
  Y: Integer);
var
  RHeight : Integer;
  CWidth  : Integer;
  RNum    : Integer;
  CNum    : Integer;
  s       : String;

  function DatePointedTo : TOvcDate;
  var
    Idx : Longint;
    DOW : Integer;
    Day1 : TOvcDate;
  begin
    { Compute first day as Row = 1, Col = DOW, then
      calculate an offset to the date pointed to. Then
      add the two. }
    Day1 := DMYToDate(1, Calendar.Month, Calendar.Year);
    DOW := Ord(DayOfWeek(Day1)) + 1;
    Idx := (RNum - 1) * 7;
    if CNum < DOW
      then Idx := Idx - (DOW - CNum)
      else if CNum > DOW
           then Idx := Idx + (CNum - DOW);
    Result := IncDate(Day1, Idx, 0, 0);
  end; { DatePointedTo }

begin
  RHeight := Calendar.ClientHeight div 6;
  RNum := Y div RHeight + 1;
```

```
CWidth := Calendar.ClientWidth div 7;
CNum := X div CWidth + 1;

{ Put the date and task in the string list }
s := DateTimeToStr(OvcDateToDateTime(DatePointedTo))
     + ' - ' + EditBox.Text;
StringGrid.Cells[0, StringGrid.RowCount - 1] := s;

{ Add a blank row to the string list }
StringGrid.RowCount := StringGrid.RowCount + 1;

EditBox.Text := '';

end;

end.
```

End of entry, March 19.

The sinister figure leaned forward, intently reading the purloined Casebook. The dark eyes swept across the gutter to the next page.

Packing Paradox And dBASE Tables

Casebook No. 16, March 20: When I was growing up, my mother constantly hounded me to put away bits and pieces that had not gotten incorporated into various projects I was working on. "Clean up your mess!" was a phrase I heard at least once a day. Perhaps the Bag Man had a mother like that, too—maybe that's why he approached me with a request for an easy way to delete the excess space in Paradox and dBASE tables from a Delphi application.

I guess, like my strange client, the Bag Man, I had just assumed there would be a **TTable** method for accomplishing this. After all, both dBASE and Paradox offer that functionality. I suppose Delphi's design team was looking at a bigger picture, one that included large client/server databases that wouldn't recognize such commands from an application.

Although Delphi's designers didn't provide a direct way to pack tables, they *did* provide an easy way to "get under the hood" and access lots of low-level stuff. Not just Windows' internals. We're talking any old application program interface (API) that wants to make itself available—including the Borland Database Engine (BDE).

Chapter 14

The BDE provides a lot of low-level services to programs. It is the basis for the methods associated with Delphi's data-aware components. And the BDE units are available to any Delphi program.

A little searching on the Internet rewarded me with a routine that used the BDE routines to pack both Paradox and dBASE tables. Unfortunately, the routine appeared to have been written anonymously, so I can't credit the original author here. I modified the code just a bit, to place it in a unit and incorporate some exception handling. I saved the modified version in a file named PAKTABLE.PAS, which can be seen in Listing 14.5.

Listing 14.5 A unit for packing Paradox and dBASE tables.

```
{——————————————————————————————————————————}
{             Data Table Packing Demo                   }
{            PAKTABLE.PAS : Packing Routine             }
{               By Ace Breakpoint, N.T.P.               }
{                Assisted by Don Taylor                 }
{                                                       }
{ A unit containing a specialized procedure for         }
{ "packing" Paradox and dBASE tables to eliminate       }
{ wasted space.                                         }
{                                                       }
{ Written for *High Performance Delphi 3 Programming*   }
{ Copyright (c) 1997 The Coriolis Group, Inc.           }
{              Last Updated 4/22/97                     }
{——————————————————————————————————————————}

unit PakTable;

interface

uses
  SysUtils, Dialogs, DBTables, DBiTypes, DBiProcs, DBiErrs;

function PackTable(var ATable : TTable) : Boolean;

implementation

type
  EDBPackMisc = class(Exception);

var
  ActiveStatus : Boolean;
```

```
    ExclusiveStatus : Boolean;
    Error : DBiResult;
    ErrorMsg : DBiMsg;
    pTableDesc : pCRTblDesc;
    AHandle : hDBiDB;

{ PackTable packs the records (and in the case of dBASE
  tables, actually removes records previously marked
  for deletion) in Paradox and dBASE tables. The
  TableType property of the table to be packed must
  be either ttParadox or ttDBase; ttDefault will not
  work. Also, the table must not be in use by anyone
  else, because it has to be put in Exclusive mode. }
function PackTable(var ATable : TTable) : Boolean;
begin
 Result := False;
 try
   with ATable do
     begin
       { Save the current status of the table }
       ActiveStatus := Active;
       ExclusiveStatus := Exclusive;

       { Disconnect the table from controls and make it exclusive }
       DisableControls;
       Active := False;
       Exclusive := True;
     end; { with }

   try
     { Pack the table, depending on the table's type }
     case ATable.TableType of
       ttParadox :
         begin
           { Create a description table and prepare it for use }
           GetMem(pTableDesc, SizeOf(CRTblDesc));
           FillChar(pTableDesc^, SizeOf(CRTblDesc), 0);

           with pTableDesc^ do
             begin
               StrPCopy(szTblName, ATable.TableName);
               StrPCopy(szTblType, szParadox);
               bPack := True;
             end; { with }
```

```
        { Get the table's database handle }
        with ATable do
         begin
          Active := True;
          AHandle := ATable.DBHandle;
          Active := False;
         end; { with }

        try
         { Attempt a restructure/pack and handle any error }
         Error := DBiDoRestructure(AHandle, 1, pTableDesc, nil, nil, nil,
                                   False);
         if Error = DBIERR_NONE
          then Result := True
          else begin
                DBiGetErrorString(Error, ErrorMsg);
                raise EDBPackMisc.Create(ErrorMsg);
               end;
        finally
         FreeMem(pTableDesc, SizeOf(CRTblDesc));
        end; { try }
      end;

     ttDBase :
      with ATable do
       begin
        Active := True;
        Error := DBiPackTable(DBHandle, Handle, nil, nil, True);
        if Error = DBIERR_NONE
         then Result := True
         else raise EDBPackMisc.Create('Could not pack this dBASE table');
       end;

     else raise EDBPackMisc.Create('Cannot pack this table type');
    end; { case }
   except
    on E:EDBPackMisc do
     MessageDlg(E.Message, mtError, [mbOK], 0);
   end; { try }

  finally
   { Restore the original condition of the table }
   with ATable do
```

```
    begin
      Active := False;
      Exclusive := ExclusiveStatus;
      Active := ActiveStatus;
      EnableControls;
    end; { with }
  end; { try }
end;

end.
```

Deleted records are treated differently by Paradox and dBASE. When dBASE "deletes" a record, it doesn't physically remove it. It just marks the record for deletion, by placing an asterisk in the first byte of the record. The advantage is that records can be easily "undeleted." The disadvantage is that zero space is recovered when a record is deleted. On the other hand, Paradox really does delete the record, and it reuses the space when new records are added.

The mechanics of packing the two flavors of tables are different, as well. dBASE tables are packed with a **DBiPackTable** command. In contrast, Paradox tables are packed as part of a restructuring process (a relationship that may explain why the pack option was placed on Paradox's restructure dialog).

Most of the machinations in **PackTable** center around capturing the state of the table (so it can be restored on exit) and getting the table in the proper state prior to making the appropriate call to the BDE's API. The only way **PackTable** can differentiate between the two table styles is by the value given to the **TableType** property. When setting the table's properties, either **ttParadox** or **ttDBase** must be selected; the standard **ttDefault** won't cut the mustard. And no matter which type of table is being packed, it *must* be operated on in the Exclusive mode. No one else can be accessing the table while the packing operation is taking place.

The Packing Demo

I needed a simple program to demonstrate the functionality of the PakTable unit. The running version of what I came up with is shown in Figure 14.2. The code for the program can be seen in Listing 14.6.

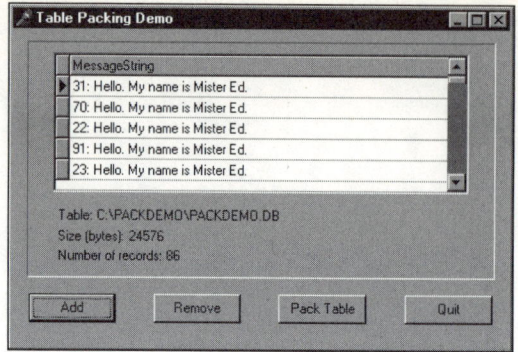

Figure 14.2
The Packing Demo program.

Listing 14.6   Code for the packing demo.

```
{---------------------------------------------------------------}
{              Data Table Packing Demo                          }
{              PackMain.PAS : Main Form                         }
{              By Ace Breakpoint, N.T.P.                        }
{              Assisted by Don Taylor                           }
{                                                               }
{ A program demonstrating the use of the PakTable               }
{ unit for packing Paradox and dBASE tables.                    }
{                                                               }
{ Written for *High Performance Delphi 3 Programming*           }
{ Copyright (c) 1997 The Coriolis Group, Inc.                   }
{              Last Updated 5/3/97                              }
{---------------------------------------------------------------}
unit PackMain;

interface

uses
  Windows, Messages, SysUtils, Classes, Graphics, Controls, Forms,
  Dialogs, DB, DBTables, StdCtrls, Grids, DBGrids, PakTable, ExtCtrls;

type
  TForm1 = class(TForm)
    AddBtn: TButton;
    RemoveBtn: TButton;
    PackBtn: TButton;
    QuitBtn: TButton;
```

```
    Table1: TTable;
    DataSource1: TDataSource;
    DBGrid1: TDBGrid;
    Label1: TLabel;
    TableNameLabel: TLabel;
    Label2: TLabel;
    FileSizeLabel: TLabel;
    Label3: TLabel;
    NumRecsLabel: TLabel;
    Bevel1: TBevel;
    Table1MessageString: TStringField;
    Table1ID: TAutoIncField;
    procedure QuitBtnClick(Sender: TObject);
    procedure FormCreate(Sender: TObject);
    procedure AddBtnClick(Sender: TObject);
    procedure RemoveBtnClick(Sender: TObject);
    procedure PackBtnClick(Sender: TObject);
    procedure FormActivate(Sender: TObject);
  private
    TablePathName : ShortString;
    procedure UpdateFileLabels;
  public
    { Public declarations }
  end;

var
  Form1: TForm1;

implementation

{$R *.DFM}

procedure TForm1.QuitBtnClick(Sender: TObject);
begin
 Close;
end;

procedure TForm1.FormCreate(Sender: TObject);
var
 s : ShortString;
begin
 Table1.Active := True;
 s := Application.ExeName;
 TablePathName := Copy(s, 1, pos('.', s)) + 'DB';
 TableNameLabel.Caption := TablePathName;
end;
```

```
procedure TForm1.UpdateFileLabels;
var
 f : File of Byte;
begin
 { Can't have the table open during the Reset }
 Table1.Close;
 AssignFile(f, TablePathName);
 {$I-}
 Reset(f);
 {$I+}
 if IOResult = 0
  then begin
        FileSizeLabel.Caption := IntToStr(FileSize(f));
        CloseFile(f);
       end
  else FileSizeLabel.Caption := 'I/O error!';

 { Re-open the table }
 Table1.Open;
 NumRecsLabel.Caption := IntToStr(Table1.RecordCount);
end;

procedure TForm1.AddBtnClick(Sender: TObject);
var
 i : Integer;
begin
 with Table1 do
  begin
   for i := 1 to 100 do
    begin
     Append;
     Table1.FieldByName('MessageString').AsString
       := IntToStr(i) + ': Hello. My name is Mister Ed.';
     Post;
    end; { for }
  end; { with }

 UpdateFileLabels;
end;

procedure TForm1.RemoveBtnClick(Sender: TObject);
begin
 with Table1 do
  begin
   First;
   while not EOF do
    begin
```

```
        Edit;
        Delete;
        MoveBy(3);
      end; { while }
   end; { with }

  UpdateFileLabels;
end;

procedure TForm1.PackBtnClick(Sender: TObject);
begin
  if not PackTable(Table1)
    then MessageDlg('Error packing the table', mtError, [mbOK], 0);

  UpdateFileLabels;
end;

procedure TForm1.FormActivate(Sender: TObject);
begin
  UpdateFileLabels;
end;

end.
```

This simple application demonstrates the packing of Paradox files. Clicking the Add button adds 100 new records to the table; clicking Remove deletes every third record. By hitting the Add and Remove buttons a few times while monitoring the display, it becomes obvious that not all the space is being recovered by the delete operation. Clicking the Pack Table button doesn't change the number of records, but it can certainly reduce the total file size.

End of entry, March 20.

Back At Ace's Office

He had been so engrossed with the loss of his Casebook, Ace hadn't even noticed the morning light streaming in through the venetian blinds. Although he had paced the small room until he had nearly worn a hole in the carpet, he was no closer to a solution to the whereabouts of his Casebook than when he started.

Defeated, he flopped down in his chair. *If I'm such a great detective, why can't I solve this simple mystery*? he thought. During the past nine hours, he had gone over the scenario a thousand times, but still there were no answers. Only questions. He had

Chapter 14

even dusted the room for fingerprints, and found none other than his own. There didn't seem to be a single clue.

Ace sat there for nearly an hour, drowning in the gloom. His Casebook, the repository of all technical knowledge he had gained while working with Delphi, was gone. Someone out there was reading his secret aspirations. His innermost thoughts. He felt naked and exposed. And in all likelihood he would never see the Casebook again. *If only there were even a glimmer of hope,* he thought.

His eyes popped wide open. There *was* a glimmer. He had seen it last night, as his headlights swept across the shrubbery in the hasty departure from his office. He remembered seeing the two tiny reflections from one of those trees that could have come from only one thing—the eyes of a human being!

The former detective leaped to his feet. *If there was a man, he must have left footprints in the soft, soggy soil!* He rushed outside, and was in the midst of painstaking examination of the ground around the shrubbery when he was startled by the sound of a familiar voice.

"Hi, neighbor."

Ace whirled around. "Uh—Hi, Marge," he replied. "I didn't hear you."

Marge Reynolds was a frumpy, middle-aged widow and a socially responsible member of the Save the Polyester Knit movement. She had been Ace's neighbor for nearly two years, and her cat, Charmin, was one of Mewnix's most ardent admirers. Marge was someone who kept her ear to the ground and her eyes fixed in the gap between the drapes she never quite closed. Very little escaped her notice.

"Looking for anything in particular?" she asked, her squinty eyes peering out from underneath a camouflage-colored sou'wester.

Ace decided to take her into his confidence, and told her the entire sordid tale. She was particularly interested in the part where Ace thought he saw a man in the bushes.

"You know," she said thoughtfully, "when I opened the door to let Charmin out last night, there was a man moving about in the bushes near the door. When I asked him what he was doing out there at that time of night, he took off like a shot. I'll bet it was the same man you saw."

"What time was that?" Ace queried.

"Oh, I would say it was about ten or ten-thirty," she replied.

"Can you describe him?"

"He was rather tall and slender," she said. "He was wearing a long raincoat and a hat that totally hid his face. He was holding something in his hand. Could have been a tool. Maybe even a weapon. You know, someone else might have seen him. I think we should ask the manager."

"Great idea!"

The two would-be sleuths strode across the parking lot to the manager's office. But when they got there, they found the door standing wide open and no one in sight! They exchanged questioning glances. Then Marge voiced the concern that was weighing heavily on both their minds:

"I wish Frank and Joe Hardy were here right now," she said grimly.

Different Strokes

Across town, the exhaust fumes from the last bus leaving for Bayport drifted in through a broken pane in the only window in the shabby, one-room apartment. Oblivious to the noise from the street below, the mysterious figure reached for the corner of the hardbound Casebook and turned the page.

Casebook No. 16, March 21: Got a new client today, a man by the name of Barry Mountebank. As the chief Spin Doctor for a prominent politician, Barry wants me to develop a word processor that can create different descriptions of the same events, depending on which way the wind is blowing on a given day.

I thought it might be profitable to create a demo that would show how you can filter and translate the keystrokes arriving at a Delphi application, turning keystrokes received into whatever keystrokes you please. When I proposed this to the client, he got very excited.

The technique is exceedingly simple. The Delphi application object recognizes an OnMessage event that lets anyone tie directly into the message chain for all components in that application.

I set out to create a simple application that would demonstrate three points:

1. It is an easy process to exchange one keystroke for another;
2. All key swaps performed in this manner are automatically sent to all components within the application, even other forms; and

Chapter 14

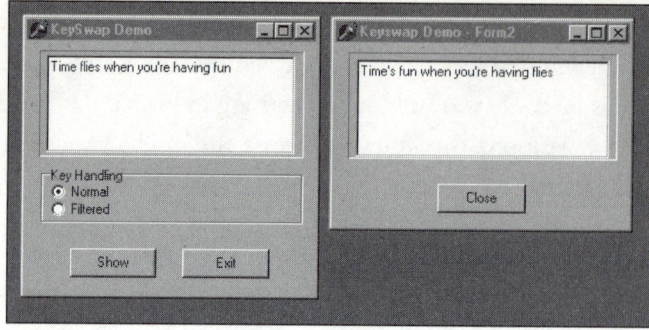

Figure 14.3
Filtering Delphi's keystrokes.

3. Swapping can be turned on and off on the fly.

Figure 14.3 shows the example I created, with two forms up on the screen. Selecting the appropriate radio button switches filtering off and on. When filtering is on, the capital and lowercase "a" are reversed, the backspace key acts as the delete key, and the delete key and Shift+F5 combination both take on the former role of the backspace key. The code is included in KSMAIN.PAS and KSFORM2.PAS, shown as Listings 14.7 and 14.8.

Listing 14.7 Main form of the key swapping demo.

```
{-----------------------------------------------}
{              Key Swapping Demo                }
{            KSMAIN.PAS : Main Form             }
{           By Ace Breakpoint, N.T.P.           }
{             Assisted by Don Taylor            }
{                                               }
{ A simple application that demonstrates the    }
{ selective filtering and substitution of one   }
{ key for another, throughout an application.   }
{                                               }
{ Written for *High Performance Delphi 3 Programming* }
{ Copyright (c) 1997 The Coriolis Group, Inc.   }
{             Last Updated 4/22/97              }
{-----------------------------------------------}
```

```pascal
unit KsMain;

interface

uses
  Windows, Messages, SysUtils, Classes, Graphics, Controls, Forms,
  Dialogs, StdCtrls, KSForm2, ExtCtrls;

type
  TForm1 = class(TForm)
    ExitBtn: TButton;
    ShowBtn: TButton;
    Form1Memo: TMemo;
    Bevel1: TBevel;
    KeyHandlerRBGroup: TRadioGroup;
    procedure FormCreate(Sender: TObject);
    procedure ExitBtnClick(Sender: TObject);
    procedure ShowBtnClick(Sender: TObject);
  private
    procedure OnAppMessage(var Msg : TMsg; var Handled : Boolean);
  public
    { Public declarations }
  end;

const
 Shifted : Boolean = False;

var
  Form1: TForm1;

implementation

{$R *.DFM}

procedure TForm1.OnAppMessage(var Msg : TMsg; var Handled : Boolean);
begin
 if KeyHandlerRBGroup.ItemIndex = 1
 then with Msg do
  begin
   case Message of
    WM_KEYDOWN :
```

```
      begin
        case WParam of
          VK_SHIFT : Shifted := True;
          VK_F5 : if Shifted then WParam := VK_BACK;
          VK_DELETE : WParam := VK_BACK;
          VK_BACK : WParam := VK_DELETE;
        end; { case }
      end;

    WM_CHAR :
      begin
        case chr(WParam) of
          'a' : WParam := ord('A');
          'A' : WParam := ord('a');
        end; { case }
      end;

    WM_KEYUP :
      begin
        case WParam of
          VK_SHIFT : Shifted := False;
        end; { case }
      end;
    end; { case }
  end; { with }
end;

procedure TForm1.FormCreate(Sender: TObject);
begin
  Application.OnMessage := OnAppMessage;
  KeyHandlerRBGroup.ItemIndex := 0;
end;

procedure TForm1.ExitBtnClick(Sender: TObject);
begin
  Close;
end;

procedure TForm1.ShowBtnClick(Sender: TObject);
begin
  Form2.Show;
end;
```

end.

Listing 14.8 Secondary entry form for the key swapping demo.

```
{─────────────────────────────────────────────────────}
{                  Key Swapping Demo                  }
{          KSFORM2.PAS : Secondary Entry Form         }
{               By Ace Breakpoint, N.T.P.             }
{                Assisted by Don Taylor               }
{                                                     }
{ A simple application that demonstrates the          }
{ selective filtering and substitution of one         }
{ key for another, throughout an application.         }
{                                                     }
{ Written for *High Performance Delphi 3 Programming* }
{ Copyright (c) 1997 The Coriolis Group, Inc.         }
{               Last Updated 4/22/97                  }
{─────────────────────────────────────────────────────}

unit KsForm2;

interface

uses
  Windows, Messages, SysUtils, Classes, Graphics, Controls, Forms,
  Dialogs, StdCtrls, ExtCtrls;

type
  TForm2 = class(TForm)
    CloseBtn: TButton;
    Bevel1: TBevel;
    Form2Memo: TMemo;
    procedure CloseBtnClick(Sender: TObject);
  private
    { Private declarations }
  public
    { Public declarations }
  end;
```

```
var
  Form2: TForm2;

implementation

{$R *.DFM}

procedure TForm2.CloseBtnClick(Sender: TObject);
begin
 Close;
end;

end.
```

It was helpful to dig into the source code for the **TApplication** object, to see just how messages were processed by default, and how any OnMessage event handler I might create should participate in the overall process. Specifically, what should I do (if anything) with the **Handled** variable passed to the event handler? Listing 14.9 reveals the source for the **TApplication**'s **ProcessMessage** method, which is called as part of any application's endless message processing loop.

Listing 14.9 Source code for TApplication's ProcessMessage method.

```
function TApplication.ProcessMessage: Boolean;
var
  Handled: Boolean;
  Msg: TMsg;
begin
  Result := False;
  if PeekMessage(Msg, 0, 0, 0, PM_REMOVE) then
  begin
    Result := True;
    if Msg.Message <> WM_QUIT then
    begin
      Handled := False;
      if Assigned(FOnMessage) then FOnMessage(Msg, Handled);
      if not IsHintMsg(Msg) and not Handled and not IsMDIMsg(Msg) and
        not IsKeyMsg(Msg) and not IsDlgMsg(Msg) then
      begin
        TranslateMessage(Msg);
        DispatchMessage(Msg);
```

```
      end;
    end
  else
    FTerminate := True;
  end;
end;
```

Listing 14.9 reveals the source of the **Handled** variable. As can be seen, the **ProcessMessage** method is called to detect and process any message waiting in the queue. If a message is present, it is removed from the queue. If the message is **WM_QUIT**, the **FTerminate** field is set **True**; otherwise, **Handled** is set to **False**, and if it is defined, the OnMessage handler is called. If the message comes back with **Handled** set to **False**, and it is not one of several message types (a hint message, an MDI-related message, a control notification message or a dialog message), then the standard **TranslateMessage** and **DispatchMessage** routines are called to process the message. It is evident that setting **Handled** to **True** in the OnMessage event handler would halt any further processing of the message. I just wanted to substitute one keystroke for another, and let processing go on as usual. Therefore, I did not touch the **Handled** variable.

My OnMessage handler is straightforward. If the Filtered radio button is selected, the case statement picks off selected messages and substitutes key values, using Windows-defined virtual key constants for the control keys. One item of note: Detecting a shifted character is a two-step process. Since this routine only receives single keystrokes, it doesn't know whether any of the shift keys (Alt, Ctrl and Shift) are being held down when other keys are pressed. I had to detect the shift presses and releases by first looking for a **VK_SHIFT** as the **wParam** value passed during **WM_KEYDOWN** and **WM_KEYUP** messages, and then on detection of a **VK_SHIFT**, storing the shift status in a boolean variable.

The OnMessage handler belongs to the application and not the main form, so there is no provision for setting it as a property during program design. Instead, it gets installed at runtime as part of the main form's OnCreate handler.

End of entry, March 21.

Playing A WAV File

The sinister character in the long raincoat began to quiver, as at last it looked up from the Casebook. A high-pitched cackle began to emanate from the twisted mouth, daring the mustache to stay in synchronization with the lips directly below it.

"Now I can absorb all the material in this Casebook—information so powerful, it can only be used for Good or for Evil. I will become the most respected and powerful Windows programmer on the face of the earth. Thanks to Ace Breakpoint, I will no longer be known merely as 'Bohacker' or 'Hey—you.' Instead, I will become known far and wide by another name: *The Delphi Avenger*. With my newly found programming knowledge *I'll rule the world!* Ha ha ha ha!...."

The fit of uncontrolled laughter lasted for nearly 10 minutes. Then the Avenger opened a fresh pack of HoHos and smugly leafed to the next page.

Some Sound Advice

Casebook No. 16, March 22: Today, I discovered how to play a WAV file from my Delphi applications. Not that it's at all difficult. But I was thinking how great it would be to have one of my biggest heroes—Humphrey Bogart—speak when I clicked a button in an application.

Figure 14.4 shows an executing version of the form I created to test my experiments. Listing 14.10 contains the code.

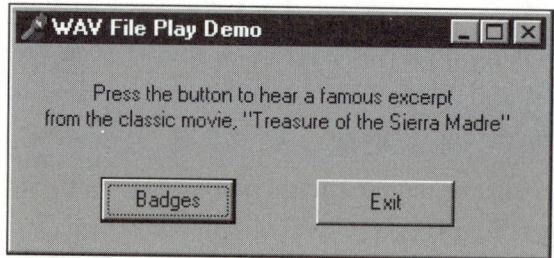

Figure 14.4
Ace's WAV form.

Listing 14.10 A demo program that plays WAV files.

```
{------------------------------------------------------------}
{              The WAV File Player Demo                      }
{                PLAYMAIN.PAS : Main Unit                    }
{              By Ace Breakpoint, N.T.P.                     }
{                Assisted by Don Taylor                      }
{                                                            }
{ Application that demonstrates how to play a WAV            }
{ file in a Delphi application.                              }
{                                                            }
{                                                            }
{ Written for *High Performance Delphi 3 Programming*        }
{ Copyright (c) 1997 The Coriolis Group, Inc.                }
{                Last Updated 5/3/97                         }
{------------------------------------------------------------}

unit playmain;

interface

uses
   Windows, Messages, SysUtils, Classes, Graphics, Controls, Forms,
   Dialogs, StdCtrls, MMSystem;

type
   TForm1 = class(TForm)
     BadgeBtn: TButton;
     ExitBtn: TButton;
     Label1: TLabel;
     Label2: TLabel;
     procedure BadgeBtnClick(Sender: TObject);
     procedure ExitBtnClick(Sender: TObject);
   private
     { Private declarations }
   public
     { Public declarations }
   end;

var
   Form1: TForm1;

implementation

{$R *.DFM}
```

```
procedure TForm1.BadgeBtnClick(Sender: TObject);
begin
 if not PlaySound('badges.wav', 0, SND_FILENAME)
   then MessageDlg('Problem playing sound file', mtError,
        [mbOK], 0);
end;

procedure TForm1.ExitBtnClick(Sender: TObject);
begin
 Close;
end;

end.
```

At first, I had assumed I would have to use a MediaPlayer component to play a file. I soon discovered an alternative low-level function called **PlaySound** in the MMSystem unit. I simply gave it the name of the file and the constant **SND_FILENAME**, which indicated I wanted the routine to play a sound stored in a file. It doesn't get much easier than that.

Note to myself: The file used for my experiment (BADGES.WAV) is an edited excerpt from the famous "Stinking Badges" dialog in the classic 1948 Bogie movie, *The Treasure of the Sierra Madre*. It's one of my faves.

End of entry, March 22.

A Disconcerting Discovery

The Avenger closed the Casebook and leaned back, considering the events of the last several hours. It had been a long night, and one fraught with peril. But the ruse had worked perfectly. Just as expected, Breakpoint had been lured away by the sound of a helpless female voice. As soon as the former private detective had left his office, the Delphi Avenger was waiting in perfect coordination to break in and steal the precious Casebook.

Breakpoint was probably a basket case by now. But what became of him was of no concern. The only thing that mattered was the Casebook and the intelligence it contained. The end most certainly justified the means. If that meant the end of Ace Breakpoint, so much the better.

The Oracle Vanishes

The Avenger rubbed a hand across the leather-covered oracle and started to pat it lovingly, then suddenly froze. It was now apparent that all had not gone according to plan, and that something was missing. A frantic search through the pockets of the raincoat came up empty.

Beads of nervous sweat began to pop out on the Avenger's forehead. *Maybe it had merely fallen out of a pocket, and it was still in the car. Perhaps it had been left on the top of the vehicle and had slipped off, and was now floating in a gutter somewhere.*

But there remained a chance—perhaps a likelihood—that the missing object was lying somewhere near Breakpoint's office. And that would mean it was...evidence. Very *important* evidence.

So important, it would be worth the risk of getting caught to retrieve it.

HIGH PERFORMANCE

A Revelation In The Mud

CHAPTER 15

HIGH PERFORMANCE

With Ace hard in pursuit, the nefarious Delphi Avenger soaks up Ace's hard-won programming expertise in every area from splash screens to preemptive multitasking.

A Revelation In The Mud

Don Taylor

Helen rushed into Ace's office. "I'm so sorry you lost your Casebook. It's gonna be all right, Baby," she said, slipping her arms around Ace and pressing her cheek against his. "I would have been here sooner, but the streets are treacherous."

Helen Highwater had come from a well-to-do family, but insisted on making her own way in the world. To look at her slender, feminine five-foot-five frame and the strawberry blond hair falling just above her shoulders, few would suspect just how determined Helen could be. So far, she had made it through college to a management position at an outlet store at the mall. But her bigger dream—as yet unfulfilled—was to spend the rest of her life as the wife of Ace Breakpoint.

"Not lost, Helen. That Casebook was *stolen*. It was a con from start to finish, and I fell for it like some rube from Bayport."

Ace related the entire story of what had happened the night before, and of his conversation earlier that morning with Marge Reynolds.

"So at least we have a fairly good description of the perpetrator," he concluded. "I'm just not sure it leads anywhere. We left a note on the manager's door, asking him to call when he returns."

"Don't you see?" Helen asked incredulously. "It's got to be Melvin Bohacker. The description fits. I'm sure he is just being vindictive about what happened in *The Case of the Duplicitous Demo*, and he's trying to get back at both of us. He probably hired that woman to make the bogus phone call for him. I'll bet he's sitting at home right now, gloating over the whole situation."

"I don't think it's that simple, Helen," Ace replied. "You didn't see Bohacker's face when I—"

Ace's attention had suddenly been stolen by something outside. Through the blinds in the side window, he could make out the shape of a man moving about in the

Chapter 15

bushes. He was a tallish man, wearing a brimmed hat and a long, khaki-colored raincoat. He moved closer to the window and peered inside.

"That's him!" Ace shouted. "That's the man Marge described, and undoubtedly the man who stole my Casebook. He has returned, just as sure as another sequel to *Nightmare on Elm Street*—and I've got some *very* pointed questions to ask him!"

Hearing Ace's cry, the intruder's eyes shot wide open and he bolted from the shrubbery, heading diagonally across the parking lot. Ace raced to the door and followed in hot pursuit, hampered greatly by the slippery mud that now completely covered the asphalt.

"Stop!" Ace commanded. But the raincoated figure just scrambled faster. Ace managed an extra surge, lunging forward and tackling the stranger in front of the manager's office. The tall interloper hit the ground with a resounding thud that took his breath away. Together, they slid a full six feet in the mud before coming to a stop.

"Hey—what's goin' on here?" came a voice from behind. Ace wrenched his head around far enough to see Marvin Gardens, the property manager, walking up behind him.

"I've caught the intruder Marge saw last night," Ace replied, vainly trying to keep the rain out of his eyes. "The guy who lifted my Casebook." With some effort, Ace managed to stand up, still maintaining an iron grip on the arm of the man in the raincoat. Both men were covered with mud from head to toe.

"Yeah, I got yer note," said Gardens, chewing on the stogie clamped between his crooked, yellow teeth. "I was gonna call ya. But dis is no intruder, Breakpoint. Say 'Hello' ta my new groundskeeper, Sergei Stakupopov. He don't speak much English, but dat much he'll understand."

"Wait a second," Ace protested. "Last night this man was seen brandishing some sort of weapon. He was confronted twice, and each time he ran away. Gardener or not, that tells me he's guilty."

"Where he's from, people live in fear of da secret police," Gardens replied, taking a drag off the cheap stogie as he talked. "In his country, a challenge yelled by someone could be da last thing ya ever hear. He's here onna Green Card, and he's deathly afraid he's gonna lose it, which would mean his family would have ta return to da homeland. That's why he's willing ta work long, hard hours. He was trimmin' da

A Revelation In The Mud

bushes by your apartment last night—Marge probably saw him holdin' a pairra shears, dat's all."

Ace loosened his grip on the immigrant, then sheepishly shook hands with the groundskeeper and apologized profusely. Sergei watched him guardedly, then smiled politely and said, "Hello."

The former P.I. trudged back to his office, where Helen was waiting with a million questions. He related his experiences of the past few minutes, then just stood there, hanging his head.

"Hey, it's going to be okay," Helen affirmed once again. "This is just a temporary setback. Now get out of that muddy trenchcoat before you catch a cold."

Reluctantly, Ace complied. "I wish I could believe it's only temporary," he said, choosing a fresh trenchcoat and hat from the row of identical outfits in his closet.

"Of course it is, Sweetheart," she replied. "Listen, my lunch hour is over, and I've got to get back to the shop. But give me a call this afternoon. I'll stop by after work, to see how things are going."

She gave him a kiss on the cheek and then slipped out into the pouring rain.

Resizing Forms

The Avenger popped open another pack of HoHos and took a big bite. The decision not to return to Breakpoint's apartment office had been a gamble, but hopefully it would pay off. After all, the chances of the has-been detective finding any incriminating evidence accidentally left behind were slim to none. It was better to absorb as much information as quickly as possible.

Casebook No. 16, March 25: I had often wondered how some applications were able to limit the minimum size of a resizable window, so I determined to find out how it was done. I didn't have any idea how easy that task would be. I did suspect the process had something to do with messages, however. By this time, I had realized that nearly everything that takes place within the Windows environment is somehow related to messaging.

I was also intrigued by the ability of some rather complex forms to maintain an integrity of their component parts, even if those forms were resized. That would also be part of today's independent investigations.

I wanted a form with a minimum of four major components. I created a rough form containing a speedbutton, a memo, and two regular buttons. It's shown in Figure 15.1. My first goal was to limit the resizing process to a minimum form size specified by the programmer. The answer came in a message called **WM_GETMINMAXINFO**.

WM_GETMINMAXINFO is a Windows message that notifies an application when the system is checking the size of a window, so it has an opportunity to change default values. Among these values are the minimum and maximum "tracking sizes," which determine the horizontal and vertical ranges for the width and height of a window. The default minimum is the size of an icon; the default maximum is the size of the entire screen.

The actual parameter passed to the message handler for **WM_GETMINMAXINFO** is a point that represents the X,Y offset from the upper-left corner of the window, measured in pixels.

The challenge, then, would be to write a replacement message handler, defining points that would describe minimum and maximum window sizes. I first declared variables for the minimum height and width, so I could easily manipulate these values.

The next step was to determine the point representing the lower-right corner of the form. The **lParam** of the default **WM_GETMINMAXINFO** handler is a pointer to an array of five point structures. Thankfully, the wizards at Borland thoughtfully provided a **TWMGetMinMaxInfo** message type that hides most of the complexity.

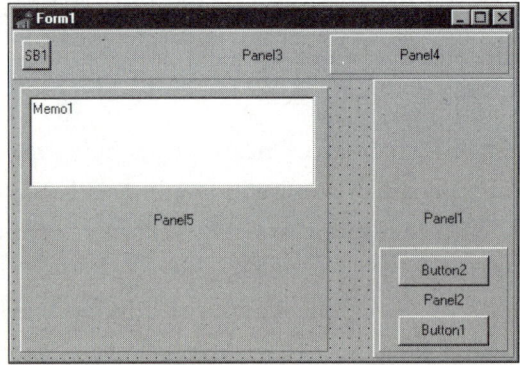

Figure 15.1
The Resize Demo form at design time.

Listing 15.1 contains the complete source for my resizing experiment. The listing includes the handler that resulted after several head-scratching attempts (I was surprised by the "interesting" effects that could be attained by forgetting such frivolities as calling the inherited handler). As can be seen in the listing, simply dereferencing the **MinMaxInfo** portion of the message gives quick and easy access to the points defined by **ptMinTrackSize** and **ptMaxTrackSize**. I added some code in the form's OnCreate handler to compute values for **MinWidth** and **MinHeight**, based on the sizes of the form's components at startup.

Listing 15.1   Source code for the Form Resize Demo.

```
{-------------------------------------------------------------}
{                    Form Resize Demo                         }
{                   RS.PAS : Main Form                        }
{                By Ace Breakpoint, N.T.P.                    }
{                  Assisted by Don Taylor                     }
{                                                             }
{ This application demonstrates how a combination             }
{ of panels with alignments set, along with gaining           }
{ control of Windows' resizing messaging can create           }
{ flexible forms that follow and limit resizing               }
{ commands.                                                   }
{                                                             }
{                                                             }
{ Written for *High Performance Delphi 3 Programming*         }
{ Copyright (c) 1997 The Coriolis Group, Inc.                 }
{                 Last Updated 4/23/97                        }
{-------------------------------------------------------------}

unit Rs;

interface

uses
  SysUtils, WinTypes, WinProcs, Messages, Classes, Graphics, Controls,
  Forms, Dialogs, StdCtrls, ExtCtrls, Buttons;

type
  TRSMainForm = class(TForm)
    ControlPanel: TPanel;
    RSMemoPanel: TPanel;
    RSMemo: TMemo;
    BtnPanel: TPanel;
```

```
    SBPanel: TPanel;
    QuitSB: TSpeedButton;
    QuitBtn: TButton;
    SBComboPanel: TPanel;
    ComboBox1: TComboBox;
    SpeedButton1: TSpeedButton;
    Button1: TButton;
    procedure QuitBtnClick(Sender: TObject);
    procedure FormCreate(Sender: TObject);
    procedure FormResize(Sender: TObject);
  private
    { Private declarations }
    procedure WMGetMinMaxInfo(var Msg: TWMGetMinMaxInfo); message
    WM_GETMINMAXINFO;
  public
    { Public declarations }
  end;

var
  RSMainForm: TRSMainForm;
  MinWidth : Integer;
  MinHeight : Integer;

implementation

{$R *.DFM}

procedure TRSMainForm.QuitBtnClick(Sender: TObject);
begin
 Close;
end;

procedure TRSMainForm.FormCreate(Sender: TObject);
begin
 MinWidth := RSMemoPanel.Width + BtnPanel.Width + 10;
 MinHeight := RSMainForm.Height
    - (RSMainForm.ClientHeight - (RSMemo.Top + RSMemo.Height)) + 10;
end;

procedure TRSMainForm.WMGetMinMaxInfo(var Msg: TWMGetMinMaxInfo);
begin
 inherited;
   with Msg.MinMaxInfo^ do
   begin
     with ptMinTrackSize do
```

```
      begin
        X := MinWidth;
        Y := MinHeight;
      end;  { with }

      with ptMaxTrackSize do
      begin
        X := Screen.Width;
        Y := Screen.Height;
      end;  { with }
    end;  { with }
end;

procedure TRSMainForm.FormResize(Sender: TObject);
begin
 RSMemo.Height := RSMemoPanel.Height - (2 * RSMemo.Top);
 RSMemoPanel.Width := RSMainForm.ClientWidth - BtnPanel.Width;
 RSMemo.Width := RSMemoPanel.Width - (2 * RSMemo.Left);
end;

end.
```

Now it was time to play with the arrangement of components on the form, so their positioning would be consistent even if the form containing them was resized.

When I first started working with panels, they gave me headaches. But as I got to know them better, I fell in love with three cool characteristics they share. First, they can, with the **Alignment** property, be forced into absolute correspondence with their parents. If you set a panel's **Alignment** to **alTop**, it will take over the entire top of the form it's placed on. Second, other components (memos, buttons, etc.) placed on a panel will stay in a fixed position relative to that panel, as long as it is not resized. Finally, a panel placed on another panel has the same characteristics as a panel placed on a form: If the **Alignment** is set to **alBottom**, it will spread out and glue itself across the bottom of the parent panel.

All of this creates a neat little set of behaviors that makes consistent form resizing possible. I had several goals for the form shown in Figure 15.1:

- Panel3 would have a fixed height and occupy the entire top of the form, so its length would always track the width of the form;

- SB1 would remain in a fixed position relative to the left side of Panel3 (and thus the upper-left corner of the window);

- Panel4 would be aligned with the right side of Panel3, so Panel4 would not change in size, but would track the right side of Panel3 as the length of Panel3 changed;

- Panel5 (which contains Memo1) would be aligned with the left side of the form, and its height would track with form resizing;

- Panel1 (which contains Panel2) would be aligned with the right side of the form, and its height would also track with form resizing;

- Panel2 (which contains Button1 and Button2) would be aligned with the bottom of Panel1, so it would remain the same size and follow the bottom of Panel1 (and thus the form) during a resize; and

- Button1 and Button2 would be placed in a fixed position on Panel2, so they would each remain fixed with respect to both the bottom and right side of the form.

Whew! I got to work setting the properties of the various panels. It's a little confusing working with panels, until you learn the rules of etiquette. Panel alignments set to **alTop** or **alBottom** will always take precedence over those set **alLeft** or **alRight**. Anyway, I set Panel3 to **alTop**, Panel1 and Panel4 to **alRight**, Panel5 to alLeft, and Panel2 to **alBottom**. I set the **BevelOuter** properties on Panel4 and Panel2 to **bvNone**, so they would "disappear," and I set the color of Panel3 and Panel4 to **clGray**, to set them off aesthetically from the rest of the form. I also added a combobox and a speedbutton to Panel4, so I could verify that tracking was working properly. I then renamed the panels and blanked out all their captions.

I decided I wanted the overall panel containing the buttons (formerly Panel1) to remain a constant width, while enabling the panel holding the memo to take up the rest of the available width. I would then automatically resize Memo1 to take up all of its parent panel, less some margins on each side. I was able to accomplish this with a little arithmetic in the form's OnResize event handler.

After several tries, I got everything just the way I wanted it. Figure 15.2 shows the demo form as it appears at the start of the program; Figure 15.3 is a shot of how the form looks when it has been resized to the specified limits.

End of entry, March 25.

Figure 15.2
The Resize Demo form at program startup.

Figure 15.3
The Resize Demo form after resizing to the limits.

Making A Splash

The mysterious figure closed the Casebook and reached for the telephone. The instrument readily accepted the seven digits keyed in, then produced a series of soft buzzes that indicated the line was ringing at the other end. There was a click. Then the Avenger began to speak to an intimately familiar voice on the other end of the line.

"Hello, Baby Cakes.... Yes, it's me. Just thought you'd like to know how things went last night. I broke into Ace Breakpoint's apartment as planned, and stole his Casebook right out from under his nose. The whole thing was nearly flawless.... Uh-huh....I want you to know the invaluable part you played in last night's plan.

Chapter 15

I couldn't have done it without you.... What? Yes, it's been a long time coming—and believe me, revenge is sweet. Right. Listen, Baby Cakes—drop everything and meet me tonight at nine o'clock at the Gates Motel, just off Highway 101. Right—up on the hill, just outside of Norton City. Uh-huh.... Tonight I'll show you the book that will change both our lives, and make me the world's preeminent Windows programmer.... That's right, Baby, *me*—the Delphi Avenger. 9:00 P.M. Don't be late. Bye."

The Avenger cradled the phone and picked up the Casebook, and chuckling loudly, began once again to peruse its pages.

Casebook No. 16, March 26: Today the Bag Man called me again. This time he wants me to create a "splash screen" component he can use in a variety of programs. He basically wants to drop a component on the main form of an application, set a few properties, and have it pop up a screen before the main form shows up.

I got to thinking about what I would like to see in a generic splash screen. Not a great deal. I would probably make it modal, so I could prevent the program from executing until the screen had properly displayed its contents to the user. I would want to kill the screen with a click of a button, a timeout, or both. And of course, I would want the ability to include a graphic on the screen. I sat down at the computer and created the initial design shown in Figure 15.4.

Now, how was I going to turn this into a component? After a couple of false starts, I decided the best approach would be to create a new component with a **TForm** object as its core, but with another object "wrapped" around the **TForm** to manage

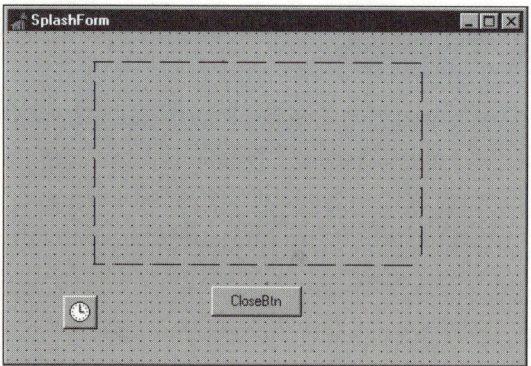

Figure 15.4
A first cut at the splash screen, shown at design time.

it. This wrapper object could manage only the properties associated with the splash screen object, giving the splash screen a simple user interface. The wrapper could also manage the creation and destruction of the form, all from one simple command issued by the owner of the wrapper object. I decided to call the wrapper a **TSplashDialog**.

As part of my initial specification, I decided to write a simple test application—a form containing only a button—that would eventually contain a **TSplashDialog**. The code for the test application is shown in Listing 15.2.

Listing 15.2 The test application for TSplashDialog.

```
{-----------------------------------------------------------------}
{            Splash Screen Component                              }
{         SPLSHMN.PAS : Demo Program Main Form                    }
{              By Ace Breakpoint, N.T.P.                          }
{              Assisted by Don Taylor                             }
{                                                                 }
{ A simple program that demonstrates the use of                   }
{ the TSplashDialog component. Try combinations                   }
{ of time delays, sizes, graphics and such to see                 }
{ the flexibility provided.                                       }
{                                                                 }
{ Written for *High Performance Delphi 3 Programming*             }
{ Copyright (c) 1997 The Coriolis Group, Inc.                     }
{              Last Updated 5/3/97                                }
{-----------------------------------------------------------------}

unit SplshMn;

{$define Test }

interface

uses
  Windows, Messages, SysUtils, Classes, Graphics, Controls, Forms,
  Dialogs, StdCtrls, SplshDlg;

type
  TForm1 = class(TForm)
    QuitBtn: TButton;
    procedure QuitBtnClick(Sender: TObject);
    procedure FormCreate(Sender: TObject);
```

```
  private
    { Private declarations }
    {$ifdef Test }
    SplashDialog1: TSplashDialog;
    {$endif }
  public
    { Public declarations }
  end;

var
  Form1: TForm1;

implementation

{$R *.DFM}

procedure TForm1.QuitBtnClick(Sender: TObject);
begin
 Close;
end;

procedure TForm1.FormCreate(Sender: TObject);
begin
 {$ifdef Test}
 SplashDialog1 := TSplashDialog.Create(Application);
 {$endif}
 SplashDialog1.Execute;
end;

end.
```

This brings up something noteworthy: Never test a component under construction by placing it in Delphi's library. Bad—very bad—stuff can happen if things aren't right. Plus, it's a slow, tedious process to update the component library for each and every run. Instead, include the component's unit in a test program, and then create an instance of the component as the object it is.

That is what is done here. Through the use of a conditional compiler directive and a constant I called **Test**, this simple program has been given two modes. As shown, the conditional code is enabled, which in this program declares a **TSplashDialog** with the same name (SplashDialog1) that the IDE will give the finished component when it is dropped on the form. Use of the conditional test in the OnCreate handler also creates an instance of SplashDialog1. When compiled in this condition, the program will use the straight (non-component) TSplashDialog object from the compiled unit (SplshDlg).

When the component is finalized and installed in the library, a period will be added, immediately preceding the "$" in the directive. Under these conditions the "$define" becomes merely a comment, and the program can be used to test the installed version of the component.

As can be seen, I decided to put the dialog into action with a method called **Execute**, in the proud tradition of the specialized system dialogs like **TOpenDialog**.

I had set the stage for a **TSplashDialog**. Now, what properties should it have? It must enable the programmer to specify its size, although I would assume it would always be displayed at the center of the user's screen. The screen needs to be told whether it has a button, and if so, the caption on that button. It needs to know if the dialog is to have a timeout, and if so, what the time delay will be. It needs a **TPicture** object to plug into the **TImage** component. And to give it some flexibility with that graphic, the programmer should be able to specify the alignment, whether or not the **TImage** is to be autosized to the graphic's dimensions, and whether or not the graphic is to be stretched to fit the **TImage** dimensions.

A couple of hours later, I had a more-or-less finished component. The source code appears in Listing 15.3.

Listing 15.3   Source code for the TSplashDialog component.

```
{-----------------------------------------------------------}
{              Splash Screen Component                      }
{           SPLSHDLG.PAS : Component unit                   }
{              By Ace Breakpoint, N.T.P.                    }
{              Assisted by Don Taylor                       }
{                                                           }
{ This unit describes a specialized component that          }
{ pops up a "splash screen" whenever your program           }
{ wants to display one (usually at program startup)         }
{                                                           }
{ Written for *High Performance Delphi 3 Programming*       }
{ Copyright (c) 1997 The Coriolis Group, Inc.               }
{              Last Updated 5/3/97                          }
{-----------------------------------------------------------}

unit SplshDlg;
```

```
{$define Test }

interface

uses
  Windows, Messages, SysUtils, Classes, Graphics, Controls, Forms,
  Dialogs, ExtCtrls, StdCtrls;

type
  ESplashConflict = class(Exception);

  TImageAlign = (iaNone, iaTop, iaBottom, iaLeft, iaRight,
     iaClient, iaAllAboveButton);

  { TSplashForm is the actual form displayed to the user. It contains
    a TImage, a TButton and a TTimer, so the programmer can vary how
    the splash screen is used. }
  TSplashForm = class(TForm)
    CloseBtn: TButton;
    Image: TImage;
    DelayTimer: TTimer;
    procedure CloseBtnClick(Sender: TObject);
    procedure Button1Click(Sender: TObject);
    procedure DelayTimerTimer(Sender: TObject);
  private
    { Private declarations }
  public
    { Public declarations }
  end;

  { TSplashDialog is the wrapper that surrounds the TSplashForm.
    The form is owned by the TSplashDialog, so it can "automatically"
    be created, set up, executed and destroyed at any time. The
    TSplashDialog makes available only those properties used for the
    splash dialog, then passes them on to the TSplashForm when it
    it created. }
  TSplashDialog = class(TComponent)
  private
    FAlign : TImageAlign;
    FAutoSize : Boolean;
    FButtonCaption : String;
    FCaption : String;
    FDelay : Word;
    FHasButton : Boolean;
    FHasDelay : Boolean;
```

```pascal
    FHeight : Word;
    FPicture : TPicture;
    FStretch : Boolean;
    FWidth : Word;
    procedure SetCaption(Value : String);
    procedure SetDelay(Value : Word);
    procedure SetHasButton(Value : Boolean);
    procedure SetHasDelay(Value : Boolean);
    procedure SetHeight(Value : Word);
    procedure SetPicture(Value : TPicture);
    procedure SetWidth(Value : Word);
  public
    constructor Create(AOwner : TComponent); override;
    destructor Destroy; override;
    function Execute : Boolean; virtual;
  published
    property Align : TImageAlign read FAlign write FAlign;
    property AutoSize : Boolean read FAutoSize write FAutoSize;
    property ButtonCaption : String read FButtonCaption write
FButtonCaption;
    property Caption : String read FCaption write SetCaption;
    property Delay : Word read FDelay write SetDelay;
    property HasButton : Boolean read FHasButton write SetHasButton;
    property HasDelay : Boolean read FHasDelay write SetHasDelay;
    property Height : Word read FHeight write SetHeight;
    property Picture : TPicture read FPicture write SetPicture;
    property Stretch : Boolean read FStretch write FStretch;
    property Width : Word read FWidth write SetWidth;
  end;


procedure Register;

implementation

{$R *.DFM}

procedure TSplashDialog.SetCaption(Value : String);
begin
 if Value <> FCaption
   then FCaption := Value;
end;

{ Set the value of FHasButton. If the user has specified he
  wants no button and no delay timer, raise an exception -
  without both, the screen has no way to be cleared! }
procedure TSplashDialog.SetHasButton(Value : Boolean);
```

```
begin
  if not Value and not FHasDelay
    then raise ESplashConflict.Create('Must have either a button or a
                                      delay!')
    else FHasButton := Value;
end;

{ Set the value of FHasDelay, protecting against the anomaly
  cited above. }
procedure TSplashDialog.SetHasDelay(Value : Boolean);
begin
  if not Value and not FHasButton
    then raise ESplashConflict.Create('Must have either a button or a
                                      delay!')
    else FHasDelay := Value;
end;

procedure TSplashDialog.SetHeight(Value : Word);
begin
  if (Value <> FHeight) and (Value > 10)
    then FHeight := Value;
end;

procedure TSplashDialog.SetWidth(Value : Word);
begin
  if (Value <> FWidth) and (Value > 20)
    then FWidth := Value;
end;

procedure TSplashDialog.SetDelay(Value : Word);
begin
  if (Value <> FDelay) and (Value > 0)
    then FDelay := Value;
end;

procedure TSplashDialog.SetPicture(Value : TPicture);
begin
  if Value <> nil then FPicture.Assign(Value);
end;

constructor TSplashDialog.Create(AOwner : TComponent);
begin
  inherited Create(AOwner);

  { Set defaults }
  FAlign := iaAllAboveButton;
```

```
  FAutoSize := False;
  FStretch := False;
  FButtonCaption := 'OK';
  FCaption := copy(ClassName, 2, Length(ClassName) - 1);
  FDelay := 3500;
  FHasButton := True;
  FHasDelay := True;
  FHeight := 200;
  FWidth := 300;
  FPicture := TPicture.Create;

  {$ifdef Test }
  FPicture.LoadFromFile('splash.bmp');
  FAlign := iaClient;
  FHasDelay := False;
  {$endif }

end;

destructor TSplashDialog.Destroy;
begin
  FPicture.Free;
  inherited Destroy;
end;

{ The Execute method is the primary focus. It's the method
  called by the owner of the TSplashDialog when the splash
  screen is desired. Execute creates a SplashForm and modifies
  it according to the parameters given to the SplashDialog.
  The SplashForm is destroyed when it has closed. }
function TSplashDialog.Execute : Boolean;
var
  SplashForm : TSplashForm;
begin
  try
    SplashForm := TSplashForm.Create(Application);
  except
    on E:Exception do
      begin
        MessageBeep(MB_ICONERROR);
        Result := False;
        Exit;
      end;
  end; { try }
```

```
with SplashForm do
  begin
    Position := poScreenCenter;
    Caption := FCaption;
    Height := FHeight;
    Width := FWidth;

    if FAlign = iaAllAboveButton
      then begin
            if FHasButton
              then begin
                    Image.Align := alTop;
                    Image.Height := ClientHeight - CloseBtn.Height - 15;
                  end
              else Image.Align := alClient;
           end
      else Image.Align := TAlign(Ord(FAlign));
    Image.AutoSize := FAutoSize;
    Image.Stretch := FStretch;
    if Image.Picture <> nil
      then Image.Picture.Assign(FPicture);

    if FHasButton
      then begin
            CloseBtn.Caption := FButtonCaption;
            CloseBtn.Left := (ClientWidth - CloseBtn.Width) div 2;
            CloseBtn.Top := ClientHeight - CloseBtn.Height - 10;
           end
      else CloseBtn.Visible := False;

    if FHasDelay
      then begin
            DelayTimer.Interval := FDelay;
            DelayTimer.Enabled := True;
           end;

    try
      ShowModal;
    finally
      Free;
      Result := True;
    end; { try }
  end; { with }
end;
```

```
procedure TSplashForm.CloseBtnClick(Sender: TObject);
begin
 Close;
end;

procedure Register;
begin
 RegisterComponents('Ace''s Stuff', [TSplashDialog]);
end;

procedure TSplashForm.Button1Click(Sender: TObject);
begin
 Close;
end;

procedure TSplashForm.DelayTimerTimer(Sender: TObject);
begin
 Enabled := False;
 Close;
end;

end.
```

Several comments need to be made about this code. Here again, I used a conditional directive to give the component two modes. When in the test mode (as shown in Listing 15.3), it automatically loads a special test bitmap and disables the timer. Adding the period before the "$" turns the directive into a comment, rendering the file suitable for compiling into a Delphi component package that can be installed in the library.

I added some code to prevent the condition where neither a button nor a timer was selected. (This would mean there would be no way to end the modal dialog!) I also declared an enumerated type (**TImageAlign**) to functionally extend the **TAlign** type by adding a value called **iaAllAboveButton**. This new value would indicate the user wanted to use the form's client area, but only that portion above the button. Oh, yes—I also declared a special exception class as a catchall for problems detected when the programmer was setting properties.

By far, the most interesting part of this project was selecting the **TPicture** and placing it in the **TImage**. After triggering several exceptions for system access violations, I finally found myself combing through the VCL source code, looking for instances of selecting and assigning bitmaps. Once the answers were found, I realized how easy the process had been made, thanks to the foresight of Delphi's designers. When you declare a property of type **TPicture**, Delphi's IDE already knows how to work with it. You create an instance of a **TPicture**, and the IDE will call up the Picture Editor. Once a bitmap is selected by the Picture Editor, it will automatically be stored in the stream when the form file is closed, which means the bitmap will be there the next time the file is opened.

True to its design goals, the **TSplashDialog** wrapper manages the critical properties of the form. When its **Execute** method is called, **TSplashDialog** creates an instance of the form, sets its properties accordingly, and then calls **ShowModal** to halt all other processing in the program. When execution resumes, the form is destroyed. The test splash screen is shown in Figure 15.5.

End of entry, March 26.

Ace Gets An Answer

"Hello, Helen? Yeah, Baby. Just calling to let you know there's nothing new. It's a brick wall. I've gone over everything a hundred more times, and I'm right back where I started. No clues whatsoever. I feel absolutely helpless. Some detective *I* am!..."

"Ace, you know you're still a good P.I.— one of the best," Helen said. "It just so happens you can't do this one on your own."

"I suppose you're right," he admitted. "I could use a little help."

"Why don't you talk to The Author," Helen suggested. "Remember how he helped you before?"

Figure 15.5
The splash screen making a splash at runtime.

"Yeah, I suppose you're right. Guess it's worth a try. Thanks, Baby. Love you."

"Love you, too," she replied.

Ace hung up the phone and grabbed the phone directory. Running his finger down the page, he found the number he sought. He quickly dialed, and the line was as quickly answered.

"Hello, Ace," said the voice.

"Uh, hello," Ace replied. "I guess you already know why I'm calling."

"You're looking for some answers regarding the theft of your Casebook."

"Yeah, I'm feeling totally helpless here. I decided to give you a call."

"I haven't heard from you in quite some time, Ace," said the voice. "Not since *The Case of the Duplicitous Demo*. I gave you some help that night, didn't I?"

"Oh, yes," Ace replied. "You reminded me how special I was, and you gave me the courage to keep going. I don't think I would have made it without your help."

"I wonder why you never thanked me."

"Uh, I suppose it was a combination of things," Ace replied sheepishly. "Once I had the problem solved, I guess I thought I didn't need any help from anyone else." He paused momentarily. "And I didn't want to bug you. After all, I'm just one of your many characters."

"All of my characters are special. You are one of my *favorite* characters. I've missed hearing from you. Sometimes it makes me sad when you try to accomplish everything on your own. Remember, you can call on me anytime, day or night. It doesn't matter how big the problem is—or how small. But as to your question at the moment. You want to know who stole your Casebook."

"Right. Helen thinks it was Melvin Bohacker and a female accomplice. At first I didn't think so, but now I'm not so sure. *Was* it Bohacker who stole the Casebook?"

"There are three possible answers to that question: 'Yes,' 'No,' and the answer I have for you, 'Not right now.'"

"But I've got to know who took my most valuable possession. I don't know how I'm going to go on without it. And my reputation with Helen as a P.I. is on the line, as well."

"Ace, in your case, life is definitely *not* like a box of chocolates. For you, it's more like event-driven programming: You see, it's not only important that an event occurs, it's equally as important *when* it occurs. Life is a mystery. And in any mystery, the timing of events is critical. Besides, sometimes you learn more by *discovering* things than by just being given the answer."

"So what should I do?" Ace asked plaintively.

"Go to the parking lot and thoroughly search the area near where your car is parked. You'll find the key that will unlock this whole mystery."

"Thanks," Ace replied excitedly. "I won't forget this." He was barely able to get the phone back in the cradle before he was out the door.

Making Data Global To An Application

In the shabby little apartment, the Avenger stuffed down a whole Twinkie and continued to read Ace's purloined Casebook.

Casebook No. 16, March 27: With Delphi 1.0, sharing tables between forms was always bothersome. Although there was an alternative to placing tables and datasources on every form that needed data from a table, it was a clumsy process that involved temporarily creating extra datasources and then later deleting them. I had on many occasions wished for an easier way. Later releases of Delphi include objects called data modules that greatly simplify the process. I decided to investigate.

A data module, as it turns out, is basically a specialized form that will accept only the standard items on Delphi's Data Access palette. You can build the entire database for an application, including tables, sources, queries and whatever—all in a data module. To make the whole kit and caboodle available to a form, you just include the data module in the form's *implementation* section (*not* the interface section). Components and fields on the data module then become available to data-aware components on the form (and to the Object Inspector as well).

I decided to try a simple example using some data for a client, The Chichen Itza Pizza Company. The data is stored in a Paradox table in a file named PIZADATA.DB. The table contains three fields: the name, retail price and actual cost of the company's best-selling products. To this mix, I wanted to add a calculated field to display the percent profit generated by each item.

Figure 15.6
A data module at design time.

I first created a DatabaseName alias called "Pizza" to point to the table's directory. Then I created a new data module and gave it the name PizzaData. Onto that module, (see Figure 15.6) I dropped a Table and a DataSource, giving them the names ProductTable and ProductSource. I connected ProductSource to ProductTable, and set **AutoEdit** to **False**. I opened the Fields Editor in the table and added all the available fields. Next, I added a new calculated field to hold the percent profit, and then wrote a handler for ProductTable's OnCalc event. The data module can be seen in Figure 15.6. The code for PizzaData is shown in Listing 15.4.

Listing 15.4 Code for the Data Module Demo.

```
{—————————————————————————————————}
{                Data Module Demo                 }
{             PIZADAT.PAS : Data Module           }
{             By Ace Breakpoint, N.T.P.           }
{             Assisted by Don Taylor              }
{                                                 }
{ This data module contains a simple Table/       }
{ Datasource combination that links to a Paradox  }
{ data table. A calculated field is provided to   }
{ users of this module.                           }
{                                                 }
{ Written for *High Performance Delphi 3 Programming* }
{ Copyright (c) 1997 The Coriolis Group, Inc.     }
{             Last Updated 4/23/97                }
{—————————————————————————————————}
```

```
unit PizaDat;

interface

uses
  Windows, Messages, SysUtils, Classes, Graphics, Controls, Forms,
  Dialogs, DB, DBTables;

type
  TPizzaData = class(TDataModule)
    ProductTable: TTable;
    ProductSource: TDataSource;
    ProductTableName: TStringField;
    ProductTablePrice: TCurrencyField;
    ProductTableCost: TCurrencyField;
    ProductTablePctProfit: TFloatField;
    procedure ProductTableCalcFields(DataSet: TDataSet);
  private
    { Private declarations }
  public
    { Public declarations }
  end;

var
  PizzaData: TPizzaData;

implementation

{$R *.DFM}

procedure TPizzaData.ProductTableCalcFields(DataSet: TDataSet);
begin
 ProductTablePctProfit.Value := 100.0 *
   ((ProductTablePrice.Value - ProductTableCost.Value) /
     ProductTableCost.Value);
end;

end.
```

I had the data. Now it was time for the demo. I decided to play with two forms. The first form would simply access the data through ProductSource on the data module. This form would display the product's name and the calculated field, and I would give it a Navigator so I could browse through the data.

The other form (which would be the application's main form) would have its own Table and DataSource, plus a DBGrid and a Navigator. In addition, I would

A Revelation In The Mud

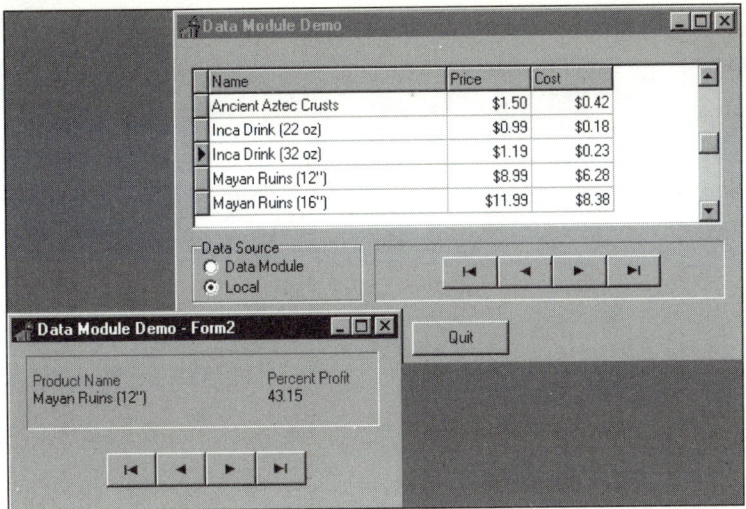

Figure 15.7
The Data Module Demo at runtime.

provide a set of radio buttons that would permit dynamic switching between the data module and the local source. By selecting the local source, the Navigators on the two forms (see Figure 15.7) would work independently, since they would be working with different table objects.

Figure 15.7 shows the two forms up and running. Listing 15.5 illustrates the code for the demo's main form, while Listing 15.6 contains the code for the secondary form.

Listing 15.5   Code for the Data Module Demo's main form.

```
{------------------------------------------------------------}
{               Data Module Demo                             }
{             PIZAMAIN.PAS : Main Form                       }
{            By Ace Breakpoint, N.T.P.                       }
{             Assisted by Don Taylor                         }
{                                                            }
{ This demo shows how a form can be connected to             }
{ a data module constructed for a project. This              }
{ form provides a switch to select the source of             }
{ its data - the module or a local Table/Datasource          }
{ combination.                                               }
```

```
{                                                          }
{ Written for *High Performance Delphi 3 Programming* }
{ Copyright (c) 1997 The Coriolis Group, Inc.              }
{              Last Updated 4/23/97                        }
{----------------------------------------------------------}

unit PizaMain;

interface

uses
  Windows, Messages, SysUtils, Classes, Graphics, Controls, Forms,
  Dialogs, Grids, DBGrids, ExtCtrls, DBCtrls, DBTables, DB, StdCtrls;

type
  TForm1 = class(TForm)
    DBGrid: TDBGrid;
    Navigator: TDBNavigator;
    DataSourceRBGroup: TRadioGroup;
    QuitBtn: TButton;
    LocalTable: TTable;
    LocalDataSource: TDataSource;
    LocalTableName: TStringField;
    LocalTablePrice: TCurrencyField;
    LocalTableCost: TCurrencyField;
    Bevel1: TBevel;
    procedure FormShow(Sender: TObject);
    procedure FormCreate(Sender: TObject);
    procedure DataSourceRBGroupClick(Sender: TObject);
    procedure QuitBtnClick(Sender: TObject);
  private
    { Private declarations }
  public
    { Public declarations }
  end;

var
  Form1: TForm1;

implementation

uses
 PizaDat, PizaFrm2;
```

```
{$R *.DFM}

procedure TForm1.FormShow(Sender: TObject);
begin
 Form2.Show;
end;

procedure TForm1.FormCreate(Sender: TObject);
begin
 DataSourceRBGroup.ItemIndex := 0;
end;

procedure TForm1.DataSourceRBGroupClick(Sender: TObject);
begin
 if Tag > 0
 then case DataSourceRBGroup.ItemIndex of
       0 : begin
             DBGrid.DataSource := PizzaData.ProductSource;
             Navigator.DataSource := PizzaData.ProductSource;
           end;
       1 : begin
             DBGrid.DataSource := LocalDataSource;
             Navigator.DataSource := LocalDataSource;
           end;
      end { case }
 else Tag := 1;
end;

procedure TForm1.QuitBtnClick(Sender: TObject);
begin
 Close;
end;

end.
```

Listing 15.6 Code for the Data Module Demo's secondary form.

```
{-------------------------------------------------}
{              Data Module Demo                   }
{         PIZAFRM2.PAS : Secondary Form           }
{           By Ace Breakpoint, N.T.P.             }
{            Assisted by Don Taylor               }
{                                                 }
```

```
{ This demo shows how a form can be connected to      }
{ a data module constructed for a project. This       }
{ form receives its data from the project's data      }
{ module.                                             }
{                                                     }
{ Written for *High Performance Delphi 3 Programming* }
{ Copyright (c) 1997 The Coriolis Group, Inc.         }
{             Last Updated 4/23/97                    }
{─────────────────────────────────────────────────────}

unit PizaFrm2;

interface

uses
   Windows, Messages, SysUtils, Classes, Graphics, Controls, Forms,
   Dialogs, StdCtrls, DBCtrls, ExtCtrls, DB;

type
   TForm2 = class(TForm)
     NameDBText: TDBText;
     PctDBText: TDBText;
     Label1: TLabel;
     Label2: TLabel;
     Navigator: TDBNavigator;
     Bevel1: TBevel;
   private
     { Private declarations }
   public
     { Public declarations }
   end;

var
   Form2: TForm2;

implementation

uses
 PizaDat;

{$R *.DFM}

end.
```

Before compilation, I set the **Active** property for all the table objects to **True**. I guess that's just force of habit.

Both forms declare PizaDat (the data module's unit name) in their implementation section. Once that is done, the fields from the data module become selectable through the Object Inspector for any data-aware component.

As can be seen, it was a straightforward exercise to make the switch between the two data sources with the radio buttons. Well, almost...

It seems that the OnClick event handler for radio buttons gets called during the creation of a form. In this case, the data sources weren't fully constructed and connected, which generated an exception. I chose to avert this situation by using the form's **Tag** property. On initialization, it is zero and there is no attempt to connect the sources. The next time through is a different story, because **Tag** has been set equal to one.

Sure enough, the demo works as designed. When the main form is connected to the data module, the main form displays the percent profit field, and both forms synchronize on the same record, no matter which form is controlling the browsing. When the main form is switched to the local data source, the two forms operate independently. Switching back to the data module instantly synchronizes the two forms.

Of course, a data module is not limited to something as simple as a calculated field. A data module is, after all, an Object Pascal unit that can contain newly defined objects, methods, and handlers for every event in a Table, DataSource, SQL Query, or whatever. In fact, a programmer can implement an entire set of business rules for a company's data. Pretty cool. And very, very powerful.

End of entry, March 27.

An Exciting Discovery!

Ace Breakpoint finished dialing Helen's work number. She picked up on the second ring.

"Hardanger World. May I help you?" she said.

"Helen—I've got some really exciting news. I wanted you to be the first to hear it," he said.

Chapter 15

"That's wonderful, Sweetheart," Helen replied. "What's happened?"

"I've found an important clue—er, I mean The Author led me to an important piece of evidence."

"I'm so glad you got in touch with him, Ace. What did you find?"

"It's a single leather glove. It was lying on the ground in the parking space next to mine, nearly buried in the mud. Only the tip of the thumb was sticking up. If I hadn't known to look there, I never would have found it."

"That means it was probably dropped by someone who parked next to you," Helen observed.

"Dang!" he exclaimed. "You know, there *was* a car parked there last night. I noticed it only because that spot is normally empty. But I was in such a hurry to get out of here, it didn't really register. In fact, I can't even remember what make the car was. I only remember it was large and kind of boxy—a dirty white color, I think. May have been a four-wheel-drive job. By now, there's not a snowball's chance of getting a tread imprint."

"How about the glove? Can you tell anything from it?" Helen asked.

Ace examined the glove closely. "Needless to say, it's covered with mud and a complete mess. There's no possibility of lifting any fingerprints from it. Let's see the inside... totally soaked with water... no lining.... Wait! Wait just a second! Part way down inside, I can see a couple of hairs. Probably from the back of the thief's hand."

"It's *Bohacker*, Ace," Helen said in an excited whisper.

"Sweetheart, it can't be. For a while I did think it might be him. But I tried to call him several times earlier today at his home, and there was no answer. Besides, now that I have the glove—"

"Call it 'woman's intuition,' or call it anything you like," Helen interrupted. "I just *know* that's Bohacker's glove," she insisted.

"If I just had another hair—one I knew was his, we could know for sure by performing a DNA test," Ace observed.

"I suppose we may never know. It's just... Ace! Don't you still have that trenchcoat with some of Melvin Bohacker's blood on it? Wouldn't that work for a DNA test?"

"Sure I do!" he exclaimed. "It's still in my closet. I can take it and the glove down to Crime City."

"Huh? What's that?" she asked.

"Crime City," he replied. "It's one of those all-night criminal laboratory chain stores. They can do a DNA match test and fax the results to my office in a couple of hours. I think I may even have a coupon for two dollars off the regular price. Tell you what: I'll drop off the stuff and then pick you up when you get off work. We can catch a quick burger somewhere. By that time, the test results should be in. That okay with you?"

"Count on it," she said.

Taking Win95 For A Walk

Ace swallowed the last bite of his hamburger and sat deep in thought, staring unexpressively across the table at his dinner partner. Realizing she wasn't likely to get any more conversation out of him for awhile, Helen suggested they head back to his office to see if the test results had come in.

"While you're taking care of the check, I have a stop to make," she said, gracefully getting up from the table.

"Okay," he said absent-mindedly. His eyes automatically followed her as she meandered toward the front of the restaurant. The *Maison de Mort Rouge Viande* was one of those upscale, bovine-centric joints that virtually dripped with class. The kind of place Helen liked best. Of course, she had grown up eating in places like this.

Ace partially snapped out of his trance. *If there's a chance this guy really is Bohacker,* he thought, *I want to know it now. And with Helen out of earshot for the moment, this might be a good time to check in with my Man on the Street, to see what's happening.*

He pulled the trusty cell phone from his coat pocket and dialed the number for Buck McGawk's Norwegian Fried Chicken Haus—a place, he remembered, that dripped with something other than class.

"Welcome to Buck's," the voice said. "Our special tonight is the Pullet Surprise. May I take your order?"

Chapter 15

"Is that you, Biff?" Ace asked.

"Ace—how's it going, Buddy?"

"I need some information, and I need it fast. Have you seen Melvin Bohacker recently?"

"You know, it's funny you should mention him. Something really weird happened today."

"Spill it," Ace said.

"Well, I may have told you before that Bohacker has a standing order for a tub of Extra Greasy on Tuesdays and Fridays. So normally he would have come by tonight to pick up his dinner."

"Uh-huh."

"Well, he called in earlier this afternoon and canceled," Biff continued. "Said he was going out of town on an unexpected trip, and didn't know for sure when he'd be back."

"Was that all?" Ace prompted.

"It was kind of noisy, with cars pulling through here and all. But it sounded sorta like he said he was meeting some woman over in Norton City. Whaddya think? That little receptionist dumped him?"

"I wouldn't know, Biff," Ace replied. "Listen. Gotta go. I'll talk to you later." Ace switched off the phone, slipped it in his pocket, and headed for the register.

Meanwhile, across town, the missing Casebook was still being scrutinized....

Casebook No. 16, March 28: Ever since its initial release, I've heard that one thing that sets Delphi apart from other visual programming tools is its ability to make all the difficult Windows stuff easy to work with, while affording programmers the ability to work at the nuts-and-bolts level. I decided to investigate some of the inner workings of Windows 95, and how they could be accessed from a Delphi application.

One of the major differences between Windows 3.1 and Win95 is the changes resulting from the addition of preemptive multitasking. Under Windows 3.1, the multitasking was cooperative, which meant only one task could execute at a time, and no other task could get control of the CPU until the current task yielded control in a cooperative manner. Among other things, this meant that one program could always prevent another program from accessing system data structures until it was good and ready to allow that access. But Win95, with its multithreading and *preemptive* multitasking, creates quite a different scenario, where the operating system is in absolute control, parceling out CPU time slices on a prioritized basis.

Microsoft quietly included a Dynamic Link Library called TOOLHELP.DLL with Windows 3.1. Although it received little coverage in books or magazines (and the documentation for it was almost nonexistent), Borland did provide an interface unit for it as part of Delphi 1.0. ToolHelp provided several interesting "under-the-hood" routines, including **TaskFirst** and **TaskNext** routines that enabled a programmer to "walk" the list of currently active tasks within the system. I was pleased to see a similar interface unit, called TLHELP32, included with later releases of Delphi aimed at the 32-bit world, and I decided to concentrate today's investigations in that area.

Just Say "Cheese"

At first, I was rather surprised by the difference between the 16-bit and 32-bit versions of ToolHelp. Several of the routines (including **TaskFirst** and **TaskNext**) were missing in the 32-bit version. Was it an oversight?

As it turns out, it was not. The implementation of preemptive, multithreaded multitasking has created a situation so dynamic, it has established the software equivalent of the Heisenberg Uncertainty Principle: You can't let a system that is continuously managing tasks and creating, prioritizing, scheduling and destroying threads do its thing and also dynamically report on the system at the same time. By the time you would get a report, the system's state would quite likely have changed.

My fondest desire would be that Win95 would hand over control for a few CPU cycles, so I could get an absolutely accurate report of the state of the system. But that would put the entire system at the mercy of one application, and that's in total disagreement with what preemptive multitasking is all about.

So what's the solution? It's to take a "snapshot" of the entire system, scheduled at Win95's discretion. We can then analyze that snapshot to our hearts' content without interfering with system operation. It's certainly not a perfect solution, but at least it's workable.

The snapshot capability is included in the 32-bit version of ToolHelp, in a function called **CreateToolHelp32Snapshot**. This function requires two parameters. The first is a mask that determines what kind of information to collect. Table 15.1 details the masks and their values. The second parameter is a handle to a process within the system. This handle—to an object called a *process ID*—gives us access to a single process; by examining that process, several pieces of information can be obtained. In general, it works like this:

- Make a call to get a list of all current processes, using the appropriate mask to collect the desired data. This returns a handle to a memory record maintained by KERNEL32, the source of all knowledge regarding system status.

- Use the **Process32First** and **Process32Next** routines to walk down the list of processes, examining various aspects of each process. The information about each process will be placed in a variable specified in the call to the walking routines.

Even though this was an investigation and not a formal exercise, it was time to make a few design decisions. First, I had to determine my overall goal. I decided I wanted to create an application that would display the names of all active processes in the system. In addition, I wanted to show the names of every module (that is, collection of code, data, bitmaps, device drivers, etc. that make up a process) in the system. I also wanted the option of listing only the modules that are associated with a specified process. Finally, I wanted to see the count of how many system-wide instances there were of every module displayed.

Table 15.1 Masks for CreateToolHelp32Snapshot.

Name	Value	Collects data for
TH32CS_SNAPHEAPLIST	1	Memory heaps within a process
TH32CS_SNAPPROCESS	2	All processes, system-wide
TH32CS_SNAPTHREAD	4	Threads within a specified process
TH32CS_SNAPMODULE	8	Modules within a specified process
TH32CS_SNAPALL	15	All of the above

The WalkStuf Unit

After several hours of thrashing and many false starts, I created the unit shown in Listing 15.7. This bit of code provides several general-purpose routines that make it pretty straightforward to get lists of modules and procedures from Win95.

Listing 15.7 Code for the WalkStuf unit.

```
{-------------------------------------------------------------}
{                   The Walking Demo                          }
{              WALKSTUF.PAS : Utilities Unit                  }
{                 By Ace Breakpoint, N.T.P.                   }
{                  Assisted by Don Taylor                     }
{                                                             }
{ This unit contains some routines for returning              }
{ specific results from the TlHelp32 unit.                    }
{                                                             }
{ Written for *High Performance Delphi 3 Programming*         }
{ Copyright (c) 1997 The Coriolis Group, Inc.                 }
{                 Last Updated 4/23/97                        }
{-------------------------------------------------------------}

unit WalkStuf;

interface

uses
  Windows, Classes, Dialogs, SysUtils, TLHelp32;

const
  ws_FullPath = True;
  ws_NoDirectory = False;
  ws_Unique = True;
  ws_DupesOK = False;
  ws_InstanceCount = True;
  ws_NoInstanceCount = False;

  function GetSystemProcessList(FullPath : Boolean;
                                Unique : Boolean) : TStringList;

  function GetSystemModuleList(FullPath : Boolean;
                               Unique : Boolean;
                               IncludeData : Boolean) : TStringList;
```

```delphi
function GetProcessModules(ProcName : String;
                           FullPath : Boolean;
                           IncludeData : Boolean) : TStringList;

function GetLocalModuleList : TStringList;
function ModuleSysInstCount(ModuleName : String) : Integer;

implementation

{
Return a string with the path information removed.
}
function ChopPath(PathName : String) : String;
var
 s : String;
begin
 s := PathName;
 if Length(s) > 0
  then begin
        while Pos(':', s) > 0 do Delete(s, 1, Pos(':', s));
        while Pos('\', s) > 0 do Delete(s, 1, Pos('\', s));
        Result := s;
        end
  else Result := '';

end;

{
Return a String List containing the names of all active
processes in the system.
}
function GetSystemProcessList(FullPath : Boolean;
                              Unique : Boolean) : TStringList;
var
 AList : TStringList;
 ProcHandle : THandle;
 AProcEntry : TProcessEntry32;
begin
 AList := TStringList.Create;
 Result := AList;
 AList.Sorted := True;
 if Unique
  then AList.Duplicates := dupIgnore
  else Alist.Duplicates := dupAccept;
```

```
    ProcHandle := CreateToolHelp32Snapshot(TH32CS_SNAPPROCESS, 0);
    if ProcHandle = -1 then Exit;

    AProcEntry.dwSize := sizeof(TProcessEntry32);

    if Process32First(ProcHandle, AProcEntry)
     then begin
          { Add the first process }
          if FullPath
           then AList.Add(AProcEntry.szExeFile)
           else AList.Add(ChopPath(AProcEntry.szExeFile));

          { Add any other processes }
          while Process32Next(ProcHandle, AProcEntry) do
           if FullPath
            then AList.Add(AProcEntry.szExeFile)
            else AList.Add(ChopPath(AProcEntry.szExeFile));
          end;

    CloseHandle(ProcHandle);
end;

{
Return a String List containing the names of all active
modules in all processes in the system.
}
function GetSystemModuleList(FullPath : Boolean;
                             Unique : Boolean;
                             IncludeData : Boolean) : TStringList;
var
 s : String;
 AList : TStringList;
 ProcHandle : THandle;
 ModHandle : THandle;
 AProcEntry : TProcessEntry32;
 AModEntry : TModuleEntry32;
begin
 AList := TStringList.Create;
 Result := AList;
 AList.Sorted := True;
 if Unique
  then AList.Duplicates := dupIgnore
  else Alist.Duplicates := dupAccept;

 ProcHandle := CreateToolHelp32Snapshot(TH32CS_SNAPPROCESS, 0);
 if ProcHandle = -1 then Exit;
```

```
AProcEntry.dwSize := sizeof(TProcessEntry32);
AModEntry.dwSize := sizeof(TModuleEntry32);

if Process32First(ProcHandle, AProcEntry)
  then begin
         { Work on the first process }
         ModHandle := CreateToolHelp32Snapshot(TH32CS_SNAPMODULE,
                                               AProcEntry.th32ProcessID);
         if Module32First(ModHandle, AModEntry)
           then begin
                  { Work on the first module in the first process }
                  if IncludeData
                   then s := '<' + IntToStr(AModEntry.GlblcntUsage)
                   else s := '';

                  if FullPath
                   then s := AModEntry.szExePath + s
                   else s := AModEntry.szModule + s;
                  AList.Add(s);

                  { Work on any remaining module in first process }
                  while Module32Next(ModHandle, AModEntry) do
                   begin
                     if IncludeData
                      then s := '<' + IntToStr(AModEntry.GlblcntUsage)
                      else s := '';

                     if FullPath
                      then s := AModEntry.szExePath + s
                      else s := AModEntry.szModule + s;
                     AList.Add(s);
                   end;
                CloseHandle(ModHandle);

                { Work on any remaining processes }
                while Process32Next(ProcHandle, AProcEntry) do
                 begin
                   ModHandle := CreateToolHelp32Snapshot(TH32CS_SNAPMODULE,
                                                         AProcEntry.th32
                                                         ProcessID);
                   if Module32First(ModHandle, AModEntry)
                     then begin
                            { Work on first module in this process }
                            if IncludeData
                             then s := '<' + IntToStr(AModEntry.GlblcntUsage)
                             else s := '';
```

```
                        if FullPath
                          then s := AModEntry.szExePath + s
                          else s := AModEntry.szModule + s;
                        AList.Add(s);

                        { Work on remaining modules in this process }
                        while Module32Next(ModHandle, AModEntry) do
                          begin
                            if IncludeData
                              then s := '<' + IntToStr(AModEntry.GlblcntUsage)
                              else s := '';

                            if FullPath
                              then s := AModEntry.szExePath + s
                              else s := AModEntry.szModule + s;
                            AList.Add(s);
                          end;
                        end;
                        CloseHandle(ModHandle);
                  end; { while }

              end;
        end;

  CloseHandle(ProcHandle);
end;

{
Return a String List containing the names of all active
modules in the current process.
}
function GetLocalModuleList : TStringList;
var
  AList : TStringList;
  ModHandle : THandle;
  AModEntry : TModuleEntry32;
begin
  AList := TStringList.Create;
  AList.Sorted := True;
  Result := AList;
  ModHandle := CreateToolHelp32Snapshot(TH32CS_SNAPMODULE, 0);
  if ModHandle = -1 then Exit;

  AModEntry.dwSize := sizeof(TModuleEntry32);
```

```
    if Module32First(ModHandle, AModEntry)
     then begin
            { Add the first module }
            AList.Add(AModEntry.szModule);

            { Add any remaining modules }
            while Module32Next(ModHandle, AModEntry) do
              AList.Add(AModEntry.szModule);
          end;

 CloseHandle(ModHandle);
end;

{
Return a String List containing the names of all active
modules in the process specified by name.
}
function GetProcessModules(ProcName : String;
                           FullPath : Boolean;
                           IncludeData : Boolean) : TStringList;
var
 s : String;
 Found : Boolean;
 Done : Boolean;
 AList : TStringList;
 ProcHandle : THandle;
 ModHandle : THandle;
 AProcEntry : TProcessEntry32;
 AModEntry : TModuleEntry32;

begin
 AList := TStringList.Create;
 Result := AList;
 AList.Sorted := True;

 ProcHandle := CreateToolHelp32Snapshot(TH32CS_SNAPALL, 0);
 if ProcHandle = -1 then Exit;

 AProcEntry.dwSize := sizeof(TProcessEntry32);
 AModEntry.dwSize := sizeof(TModuleEntry32);

 if Process32First(ProcHandle, AProcEntry)
   then begin
          { Examine processes until a match is found }
          Found := UpperCase(AProcEntry.szExeFile) = UpperCase(ProcName);
```

```
        if not Found
          then repeat
                 Done := not Process32Next(ProcHandle, AProcEntry);
                 if not Done
                   then Found := UpperCase(AProcEntry.szExeFile) =
                                           UpperCase(ProcName);
               until Done or Found;

        if Found
          then begin
                 ModHandle := CreateToolHelp32Snapshot(TH32CS_SNAPMODULE,
                                                      AProcEntry.th32
                                                      ProcessID);
                 if Module32First(ModHandle, AModEntry)
                   then begin
                          { Work on the first module in the first process }
                          if IncludeData
                            then s := '<' + IntToStr(AModEntry.GlblcntUsage)
                            else s := '';

                          if FullPath
                            then s := AModEntry.szExePath + s
                            else s := AModEntry.szModule + s;
                          AList.Add(s);

                          { Work on any remaining module in first process }
                          while Module32Next(ModHandle, AModEntry) do
                            begin
                              if IncludeData
                                then s := '<' + IntToStr(AModEntry.GlblcntUsage)
                                else s := '';

                              if FullPath
                                then s := AModEntry.szExePath + s
                                else s := AModEntry.szModule + s;
                              AList.Add(s);
                            end;
                        end;
                 CloseHandle(ModHandle);

               end;
      end;
  CloseHandle(ProcHandle);
end;
```

```
{
Return a count of the total number of times the specified
module appears in all processes in the system.
}
function ModuleSysInstCount(ModuleName : String) : Integer;
var
 Idx : Integer;
 p : Integer;
 s : String;
 ModList : TStringList;
 MatchFound : Boolean;
begin
 Result := -1;
 ModList := GetSystemModuleList(ws_NoDirectory, ws_DupesOK,
                                ws_InstanceCount);
 if ModList = nil then Exit;

 Idx := 0;
 p := 0;
 MatchFound := False;
 while (Idx < ModList.Count) and not MatchFound do
  begin
   s := ModList.Strings[Idx];
   p := pos('<', s);
   MatchFound := Uppercase(copy(s, 1, p - 1)) = Uppercase(ModuleName);
   if not MatchFound then Inc(Idx);
  end; { while }

 if MatchFound
   then Result := StrToInt(copy(s, p + 1, Length(s) - p))
   else Result := 0;
end;

end.
```

WalkStuf provides five useful functions that make exploring Win95's operations a lot easier. GetSystemProcessList returns a string list containing the names of all active processes in the system. An option is provided to list only the process name (without its full path) and to suppress multiple instances of the same process. GetSystemModuleList returns a string list of all modules from all processes in the system. The same options are provided for suppressing path information and multiple instances; in addition, there is a provision to append the number of system-wide instances of the module to each entry's string. GetProcessModules returns a string list of all modules for a specified process. GetLocalModuleList brings back a string list of only the modules in the current process. Finally, ModuleSysInstCount returns an integer representing the number of system-wide instances of a specified module.

There are a few items of interest in the WalkStuf routines that bear some explanation. GetSystemProcessList illustrates how to "walk" the list of processes. ProcHandle is assigned a handle to an area within KERNEL32 that is set up to contain a list of all the processes. Next, the dwSize field of the TProcessEntry32 (a record designed to handle process information) is set to the size of that data type. (Although this seems almost silly, it is critical to the operation!) Process32First is then called, using the ProcHandle to the KERNEL32 information and the variable (AProcEntry) where the data is to be dumped.

If Process32First returns True, several pieces of information about the first process in the list have been copied to the fields of AProcEntry. Perhaps the two most interesting are szExeFile and th32ProcessID. The szExeFile field contains a string which identifies the complete path to the EXE file the process was created from. The th32ProcessID field is a unique ID value for the process being examined; it can be passed on to other functions within ToolHelp. More on that in a moment.

After the szExeFile is added to the string list, a while loop is used to repeatedly call Process32Next. This routine takes the same parameters, and if it returns True, another process's data will be placed in AProcEntry. (If you've ever used FindFirst and FindNext under DOS, you already know this drill.) When all is finished, there is one last housekeeping chore to perform. The call to CreateToolHelp32Snapshot created a Win95 object that must be disposed. This is done with a call to CloseHandle.

GetSystemModuleList is a more extensive example of walking. For each process, the complete list of modules for that process is examined with Module32First and Module32Next. For each process, a handle is obtained using CreateToolHelp32Snapshot. This time, the unique process ID of the process currently being examined (AProcEntry.th32ProcessID) is used in the call, resulting in a handle referring to module information for that process only. Note the use of the mask TH32CS_SNAPMODULE, which limits the data retreived to that for modules.

TModuleEntry32 records contain several fields. For our purposes, the three most interesting are szExePath, a string containing the complete path to the module;

szModule, a string containing the base name of the module; and GlblcntUsage, a double word field containing the number of system-wide instances of this module.

Note once again that the size of the TModuleEntry32 record must be entered in AModEntry's dwSize field, and that every call to CreateToolHelp32Snapshot must have a matching CloseHandle to dispose of the object created.

The remaining routines are, for the most part, variations on a theme. GetLocalModuleList walks the list of only the modules belonging to the current process, obtained by using a zero as the process ID number. GetProcessModules walks through the module list, seeking a match for the specified process. If found, it walks through the modules for that process. And ModuleSysInstCount uses a customized call to GetSystemModuleList to get a system-wide list of modules, from which it searches for a match for the specified module. From the string entry for the matching module, it converts the number of instances and returns that number as an integer.

Stepping Out

They say when the going gets tough, the tough make coffee. I was at that point, so I brewed a pot of Scandinavian blend and set to designing a demo application that would use several of the WalkStuf routines. A running version of what I came up with is shown in Figure 15.8. The code appears in Listing 15.8.

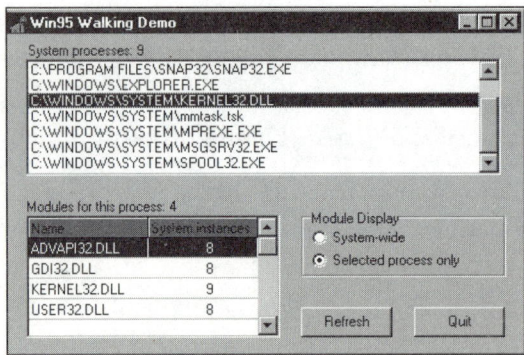

Figure 15.8
The Windows 95 Walking Demo taking a walk.

Listing 15.8 Code for the Walking Demo.

```
{————————————————————————————————————}
{              The Walking Demo                     }
{            WALKMAIN.PAS : Main Unit               }
{             By Ace Breakpoint, N.T.P.             }
{              Assisted by Don Taylor               }
{                                                   }
{ This program demonstrates some techniques for     }
{ "walking" through the Win95 system fo get         }
{ specific system-wide information.                 }
{                                                   }
{                                                   }
{ Written for *High Performance Delphi 3 Programming* }
{ Copyright (c) 1997 The Coriolis Group, Inc.       }
{              Last Updated 4/23/97                 }
{————————————————————————————————————}

unit WalkMain;

interface

uses
  Windows, Messages, SysUtils, Classes, Graphics, Controls, Forms,
  Dialogs, WalkStuf, Grids, StdCtrls, ExtCtrls;

type
  TForm1 = class(TForm)
    ModuleGrid: TStringGrid;
    RefreshBtn: TButton;
    QuitBtn: TButton;
    ModuleRBGroup: TRadioGroup;
    ProcessesLabel: TLabel;
    ProcessListBox: TListBox;
    ModulesLabel: TLabel;
    procedure QuitBtnClick(Sender: TObject);
    procedure RefreshBtnClick(Sender: TObject);
    procedure FormCreate(Sender: TObject);
    procedure ModuleRBGroupClick(Sender: TObject);
    procedure ProcessListBoxClick(Sender: TObject);
  private
    TheList : TStringList;
    procedure RefreshForm;
    procedure DisplayProcessModules;
    procedure ClearModuleGrid;
    procedure FillProcessList;
    procedure FillModuleGrid;
```

```
  public
    { Public declarations }
  end;

var
  Form1: TForm1;

implementation

{$R *.DFM}

{
Return a string of spaces of the specified length.
}
function Spaces(Size : Integer) : String;
begin
 Result := '';
 while Length(Result) < Size do Result := Result + ' ';
end;

{
Clear the screen elements, retrieve data and
update the screen.
}
procedure TForm1.RefreshForm;
begin
 ClearModuleGrid;
 ProcessListBox.Clear;
 TheList := GetSystemProcessList(ws_FullPath, ws_DupesOK);
 FillProcessList;
 ProcessesLabel.Caption := 'System processes: ' +
IntToStr(TheList.Count);
 TheList.Free;

 case ModuleRBGroup.ItemIndex of
  0 : begin
       TheList := GetSystemModuleList(ws_NoDirectory, ws_Unique,
                                ws_InstanceCount);
       FillModuleGrid;
       ModulesLabel.Caption := 'System-wide modules: ' +
                                IntToStr(TheList.Count);
       TheList.Free;
      end;

  1 : begin
       TheList := GetSystemModuleList(ws_NoDirectory, ws_Unique,
                                ws_InstanceCount);
```

```
            if TheList.Count > 0
              then begin
                    ProcessListBox.ItemIndex := 0;
                    DisplayProcessModules;
                   end;
         end;
  end; { case }
end;

{
Special screen update procedure that retrieves
the module data for the currently selected
process.
}
procedure TForm1.DisplayProcessModules;
var
 Idx : Integer;
 s : String;
 p : Integer;
begin
 if ProcessListBox.Items.Count > 0
   then begin
         ClearModuleGrid;
         Idx := ProcessListBox.ItemIndex;
         TheList := GetProcessModules(ProcessListBox.Items[Idx],
           ws_NoDirectory, ws_InstanceCount);

         if TheList.Count > 0
           then for Idx := 1 to TheList.Count do
             begin
               s := TheList.Strings[Idx - 1];
               p := pos('<', s);
               ModuleGrid.Cells[0, Idx] := copy(s, 1, p - 1);
               delete(s, 1, p);
               s := Spaces(15) + s;
               ModuleGrid.Cells[1, Idx] := s;
               ModuleGrid.RowCount := ModuleGrid.RowCount + 1;
             end;

         ModulesLabel.Caption := 'Modules for this process: '
             + IntToStr(TheList.Count);
         TheList.Free;
        end;
end;
```

```
{
Clear all rows in the Module String Grid, and reset the
number of rows to one.
}
procedure TForm1.ClearModuleGrid;
var
 Idx : Integer;
begin
 for Idx := 1 to ModuleGrid.RowCount - 1 do
  begin
   ModuleGrid.Cells[0, Idx] := '';
   ModuleGrid.Cells[1, Idx] := '';
  end;
 ModuleGrid.RowCount := 2;
end;

{
Fill in the Process listbox, line by line, from the
global String List.
}
procedure TForm1.FillProcessList;
var
 Idx : Integer;
begin
 if TheList.Count > 0
  then for Idx := 0 to TheList.Count - 1 do
    ProcessListBox.Items.Add(TheList.Strings[Idx]);
end;

{
Fill in the Module String Grid, line by line, from the
global String List.
}
procedure TForm1.FillModuleGrid;
var
 s : String;
 p : Integer;
 Idx : Integer;
begin
 if TheList.Count > 0
  then begin
       for Idx := 1 to TheList.Count do
         begin
          s := TheList.Strings[Idx - 1];
          p := pos('<', s);
```

```
            ModuleGrid.Cells[0, Idx] := copy(s, 1, p - 1);
            delete(s, 1, p);
            s := Spaces(15) + s;
            ModuleGrid.Cells[1, Idx] := s;
            ModuleGrid.RowCount := ModuleGrid.RowCount + 1;
          end; { for }
      end;
end;

procedure TForm1.QuitBtnClick(Sender: TObject);
begin
 Close;
end;


procedure TForm1.RefreshBtnClick(Sender: TObject);
begin
 RefreshForm;
end;

procedure TForm1.FormCreate(Sender: TObject);
begin
 ModuleGrid.Colwidths[1] := ModuleGrid.Width - ModuleGrid.ColWidths[0] -
 22;
 ModuleGrid.Cells[0, 0] := 'Name';
 ModuleGrid.Cells[1, 0] := 'System instances';
 ModuleRBGroup.ItemIndex := 0;
end;

procedure TForm1.ModuleRBGroupClick(Sender: TObject);
begin
 RefreshForm;
end;

procedure TForm1.ProcessListBoxClick(Sender: TObject);
begin
 if ModuleRBGroup.ItemIndex > 0 then DisplayProcessModules;
end;

end.
```

There's nothing really special about the code in the demo. The upper window always shows all active processes in the system snapshot. If the radio button marked "System-wide" is selected, the lower window lists all modules in the system, including the number of instances of each. If the "Selected process only" button is selected, the lower window lists only the modules for the process highlighted in the upper window. And of course, the Refresh button takes a new snapshot and updates the screen. The main thing to remember is that every call to a WalkDemo routine that returns a string list does so by creating a new object; that object must later be disposed exactly once.

This was all quite instructional, and a lot of fun as well. But my investigations only scratched the surface, and there are many more things to learn. One of the things I discovered is that the ToolHelp routines are compatible only with Win95 and not NT, at least for now.

I get the distinct impression that I'll be able to use some of this stuff in my applications. And I'll certainly have to come back and investigate more thoroughly when I have more time.

End of entry, March 28.

When Ace and Helen arrived at the office, there was still no word on the DNA test. Ace took out a bottle of Purely Poulsbo from the refrigerator, and blew the dust from a couple of glasses he found in the cupboard. He poured two fingers' worth into each glass, then handed one to Helen. He had no more than touched the glass to his lips when there came a sharp rap at the door.

It was Marge Reynolds. Ace could hear a quiet excitement in her voice as she exchanged pleasantries with Helen. Marge quickly came to the point.

"I know you've been looking for clues to last night's robbery," she began. "I saw you out there digging through the mud in the parking lot this afternoon. But I've been keeping my eyes open, too—looking for anything suspicious." Her eyes were locked on Ace's as she paused, looking for an acknowledgment of interest.

"Go on," he urged.

"This evening, as I was walking past the public phone booth on the other side of the courtyard—you know, the one that faces your kitchen window—I found a piece of paper stuck in a bush, about a foot above the ground."

Marge fumbled around in the pocket of her bulky knit sweater. "I'm sure it's here somewhere. I put it—oh, here it is," she said, pulling out a lavender-colored scrap of paper and examining it one more time. "It looks like it was written by a woman. It's got your name and phone number on it, and two other words: 'kidnapped heiress.' Do you think it means anything?"

HIGH PERFORMANCE

The Oracle Returns

CHAPTER 16

HIGH PERFORMANCE

While the Delphi Avenger discovers how to make Delphi apps detect both themselves and Delphi (floating a toolbar as a bonus), Ace detects one too many Xs in a very strange equation—but ultimately drags the case to a jaw-dropping conclusion.

The Oracle Returns

Don Taylor

Ace switched on the halogen lamp on his desk and held the lavender remnant up to the light.

"Pretty expensive stuff," he said. "It's fine linen. I can just make out what appears to be the edge of a watermark." He turned the scrap so the light coming from the lamp reflected off the paper. "The writing's in a feminine hand, all right," he said. "By the size of the loops, I'd say the woman who wrote this has a strong personality, consistent with the woman who had the bravado to call me last night. And this was definitely written with a very expressive pen, probably a Habasher No. 4374 tip, using what appears to be Mandolay's 'Nightshade' ink. Other than that, there's not much I can deduce."

"May I see it?" asked Helen.

"Sure," Ace replied. Handing over the note, he added, "One more thing. You'll notice the paper has been scented with perfume."

Helen's eyes widened as she passed the paper scrap under her nose. "This is not just ordinary perfume," she said. "It's a very expensive fragrance. *Chez Monieux.*"

"Okay, so it's expensive perfume," he said, a bit testily.

"I didn't mean to belittle you in any way, Sweetheart. It's just that women notice little things that men often don't. You see, only a sophisticated, well-to-do woman would wear this scent—*Chez Monieux.*"

"Hey, lighten up already. I said she used expensive paper, and a very nice pen and ink, didn't I? Just because I'm not a perfume expert—"

"I think what Helen is trying to say," Marge interjected, "is the *name of the perfume* is *Chez Monieux.*"

Chapter 16

Ace froze for a moment, as if wondering what to say. His eyes darted quickly between those of Marge and Helen. Something his friend Muffy had once said came to mind. "I knew that," he replied guardedly.

"Remember?" Helen said. "It's part of that new exclusive line of fashion accessories produced for Muffy. You know, the Pure Prophet collection?"

"I knew that, too," Ace said. "But where does all this get us?"

"Well, I have a theory," Helen began. "I think Melvin Bohacker has for some time been looking to get even with you. He has probably recently gotten involved with a woman of means—a woman used to having her own way about things, and someone to whom pride is a precious commodity."

She looked to her companions for a confirmation to continue. Ace rolled his eyes, but Marge was obviously hanging on Helen's every word.

"When this woman—let's call her 'Madame X'—found out about how Melvin had lost face because of you, she coaxed him to get even. Together, they concocted the plan they executed last night: Driving her car, they pulled in here and parked in the space next to yours. He got out and hid in the shadows somewhere while she walked to the pay phone on the other side of the courtyard. From there, she was able to watch you through your kitchen window as she dialed the number she had earlier scrawled on a corner of her personal notepaper."

"So how did the note get where it was found?" Ace asked.

"I have a theory about that, too. The pay phone is one of those open types, mounted on a pole. Madame X probably laid the note down and it was blown away by a puff of wind. There's a light by the pole. But if the note was blown even a few feet away, it could have been lost in the darkness. She was probably in a hurry, and may not even have missed the note."

"And the glove?"

"Bohacker undoubtedly wore gloves to break into your apartment, so he wouldn't leave any fingerprints. He probably took them off as he was getting back into the car, and dropped one on the ground. He may have run over it with the car, burying it in the mud."

"I'm sorry," Ace said, waving her off. "It all sounds plausible enough, except for one thing: Bohacker isn't capable of doing it, even with the goading of some rich babe—heiress or not."

Helen sighed. "I guess we'll just have to wait for the results from the DNA testing. That should prove who is right, once and for all."

"DNA testing?" Marge asked. "What DNA testing? And what is this business about a glove?"

Ace recounted the story of the glove to Marge. It took nearly half an hour to detail all the events to her satisfaction.

"It's sure been an exciting day," she said. "I wish I could sit around here with you kids and wait for the test results. But there's a new tenant moving into #193 tonight—a bachelor—and I want to see what brand of appliances he owns."

Marge Reynolds rustled to the front door, her polyester knit pants hugging every bulge, looking like a sack full of cats on their way to the pound. She squeezed through the door and quietly closed it behind her.

Sharing Event Handlers

In an untidy little room across town, an ominous figure was bent over a book, reading intently.

Casebook No. 16, March 29: Among the bills in today's mail, I found a wedding invitation from Blade Porter and Cinder Holte-Mullingham-LaFong, a couple Helen and I had gotten to know while we were attending art school. The announcement read "Come and share our joyous event with us." We had always assumed they would get married. Now it was official.

As I tossed the card on my desk, I got to thinking about ways it's possible to "share events" in an entirely different way—by using common handlers to deal with events that require similar actions.

I decided to create a simple application that would let me explore this concept. After a little pondering, I settled on a little "To Do List" program that would be a spin-off of the Drag/Drop Demo I had written a few days ago.

As in the earlier demo, the new program would feature an edit box in which the user could type a comment. Instead of dragging it to a calendar, this time I would provide three separate string grids—one for morning tasks, another for afternoon duties, and a final one for evening activities. The three grids would be placed on separate pages of a tabbed notebook. I created a design model of the form, which can be seen in Figure 16.1.

Taking A First Run

The scenario would be to select the proper page and then drag the task description string from the edit box to the grid on that page. The operation would be virtually identical for each of the three pages, the only difference being which grid would receive the string. There should therefore be a way for the three string grids to share their OnDragOver and OnDragDrop event handlers in common.

I suppose this is a personal preference, but I would like shared event handlers to have a more generic name than what is automatically generated by Delphi. I decided to call the two handlers **GridDragOver** and **GridDragDrop**.

Before proceeding any further, I want to document the 8-step method I used to create generic-sounding routine names for the handlers:

1. Double-click on the name of the event to be handled, as it appears in the Object Inspector.

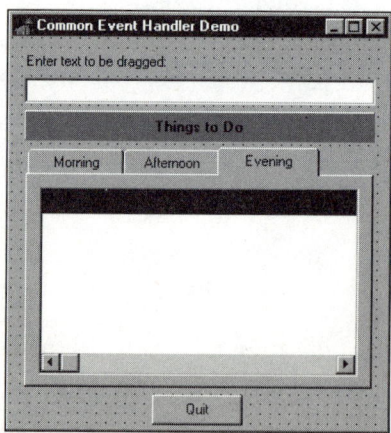

Figure 16.1
The shared events demo.

2. Delphi automatically names the routine, combining the names of the component and the event to produce a unique identifier. More importantly, it automatically generates the call parameter list for the specific event. (Being lazy, I would much rather have Delphi do this for me than create it from scratch.)

3. Type anything (a semicolon does nicely) between the **begin** and **end** of the empty routine created by Delphi. This will prevent Delphi from automatically deleting the routine if you try to save it.

4. Edit the name of the routine, then double-click to highlight it, and press Ctrl+C to copy the new name to the clipboard.

5. Jump to the beginning of the file, and find the original handler declaration within the form's declaration. Highlight the original name there, and tap Ctrl+V to replace it with the new name.

6. At some point in the process, Delphi will complain that the name it originally assigned (still present in the Object Inspector) can't be found. Give Delphi the okay to remove it.

7. Move the cursor to the event slot in the Object Inspector, where this all began. Use the Ctrl+V combination to paste in the new name.

8. Save the file.

The routines I wrote appear in Listing 16.1.

Listing 16.1 Common handlers for OnDragOver and OnDragDrop events.

```
{ Common event handler for all the grids' OnDragOver event. }
procedure TShareEventDemoForm.GridDragOver(Sender, Source: TObject;
  X, Y: Integer; State: TDragState; var Accept: Boolean);
begin
 { We can accept anything, but only from the EditBox. }
 Accept := Source is TEdit;
end;

{ Common event handler for all the grids' OnDragDrop event. }
procedure TShareEventDemoForm.GridDragDrop(Sender, Source : TObject;
  X, Y : Integer);
begin
 { Drop the load on the currently selected grid. }
 DropEditString(CurrentGrid);
end;
```

```
{ Common event handler support routine that drops the string
  in the EditBox onto the specified grid. Also clears the EditBox. }
procedure TShareEventDemoForm.DropEditString(AGrid : TStringGrid);
begin
 if AGrid <> nil
   then with AGrid do
     begin
       Cells[0, RowCount - 1] := EditBox.Text;
       RowCount := RowCount + 1;
       EditBox.Text := '';
     end; { with }
end;

{ Return a pointer to the grid on the currently selected tab sheet. }
function TShareEventDemoForm.CurrentGrid : TStringGrid;
begin
 Result := nil;
 if PageControl.ActivePage = MorningSheet
   then Result := MorningGrid else
 if PageControl.ActivePage = AfternoonSheet
   then Result := AfternoonGrid else
 if PageControl.ActivePage = EveningSheet
   then Result := EveningGrid;
end;
```

The OnDragOver routine is very straightforward. As long as the source object for the drag is the edit box, it can be accepted by any of the grids. I chose to split the OnDragDrop handling into two routines: a main handler and a support method. The handler merely calls the support routine, using a function which returns a pointer to the grid on the currently selected tabsheet. Delphi's ability to mask the use of pointers really comes into play here, making it very straightforward to pull some shenanigans with pointers, while keeping the program exceedingly readable. Given the pointer, the **DropEditString** routine adds the string from the edit box to the appropriate string grid, updating the grid's row counter and clearing out the edit box.

The handlers worked as expected for the grid on the first tabsheet (**MorningGrid**). I went back to the Object Inspector and selected the same handlers for the other two grids. Again, everything worked perfectly.

Down A Crooked Path

It must be a quirk in my personality (or maybe I'm just a nerd at heart), but this was just too easy. I wanted to take the process a step further, where I could drop a string from the edit box onto any of the string grids, simply by dropping it onto the appropriate tab. In a way, I wish I had never started down this road.

I first learned that TabSets have a method that will tell you the index of a tab, given an x-y position. The wrapper-relationship of PageControls gives most of the power to the TabSheets, leaving little to the PageControl, which is pretty well limited to knowing which is the currently selected sheet.

I would need to calculate where the tabs were, so I could know which tab the mouse was pointing to. From that information, I could easily determine the associated tabsheet. But there was another problem: PageControls automatically size each tab's width individually, based on the length of its caption string. What to do?

I decided to support drops onto tabs only if the tabs had been manually sized by setting the PageControl's TabHeight and TabWidth properties to some value other than zero. I should have stopped there. But I decided I also wanted to provide a feature that would automatically size the tabs at equal width, based on the length of the longest caption. That eventually led me to a much longer version of the code, the complete version of which is shown in Listing 16.2.

Listing 16.2 Complete code for the common event handler demo application.

```
{—————————————————————————————————}
{            Event Handler Sharing Demonstration         }
{                 SHARMAIN.PAS : Main Unit               }
{                 By Ace Breakpoint, N.T.P.              }
{                  Assisted by Don Taylor                }
{                                                        }
{ Application that demonstrates the sharing of           }
{ event handlers within an application, as part          }
{ of a drag/drop operation.                              }
{                                                        }
{ Written for *High Performance Delphi 3 Programming*    }
{ Copyright (c) 1997 The Coriolis Group, Inc.            }
{                   Last Updated 4/30/97                 }
{—————————————————————————————————}
```

```
unit SharMain;

interface

uses
  SysUtils, WinTypes, WinProcs, Messages, Classes, Graphics, Controls,
  Forms, Dialogs, Grids, StdCtrls, ExtCtrls, ComCtrls;

type
  TShareEventDemoForm = class(TForm)
    EditBox: TEdit;
    Label1: TLabel;
    QuitBtn: TButton;
    Panel1: TPanel;
    PageControl: TPageControl;
    MorningSheet: TTabSheet;
    AfternoonSheet: TTabSheet;
    EveningSheet: TTabSheet;
    MorningGrid: TStringGrid;
    AfternoonGrid: TStringGrid;
    EveningGrid: TStringGrid;
    procedure FormCreate(Sender: TObject);
    procedure QuitBtnClick(Sender: TObject);
    procedure EditBoxMouseDown(Sender: TObject; Button: TMouseButton;
      Shift: TShiftState; X, Y: Integer);
    procedure GridMouseDown(Sender: TObject; Button: TMouseButton;
      Shift: TShiftState; X, Y: Integer);
    procedure GridDragOver(Sender, Source: TObject;
      X, Y: Integer; State: TDragState; var Accept: Boolean);
    procedure GridDragDrop(Sender, Source : TObject;
      X, Y : Integer);
    procedure PageControlDragOver(Sender, Source: TObject; X, Y: Integer;
      State: TDragState; var Accept: Boolean);
    procedure PageControlDragDrop(Sender, Source: TObject; X, Y: Inte
                                   ger);
  private
    CopyDrag : Boolean;
    function ManualTabsSet : Boolean;
    function CurrentGrid : TStringGrid;
    function TabGrid(X : Integer) : TStringGrid;
    procedure SetTabSizes;
    procedure DropEditString(AGrid : TStringGrid);
    procedure DropGridString(TargetGrid : TStringGrid);
  public
    { Public declarations }
  end;
```

```
var
   ShareEventDemoForm: TShareEventDemoForm;

implementation

{$R *.DFM}

{ Return the length in pixels of a string for display,
  given a handle to the window in which it will appear,
  along with a handle to the window's font. }
function StringWidth(WinHnd : HWND; FntHnd : HWND; Text : String) :
Integer;
var
 DCHnd : HWND;
 StrSize : TSize;
 TextArr : array[0..127] of char;
begin
 Result := -1;
 DCHnd := GetDC(WinHnd);
 if GetMapMode(DCHnd) = MM_TEXT
   then begin
        SelectObject(DCHnd, FntHnd);
        StrPCopy(TextArr, Text);
        if GetTextExtentPoint32(DCHnd, @TextArr, Length(Text), StrSize)
          then Result := StrSize.Cx
        end;
 ReleaseDC(WinHnd, DCHnd);
end;

{ Return the height in pixels of a font for display,
  given a handle to the window in which it will appear,
  along with a handle to the window's font. The height
  must include the ascent, descent and inner leading. }
function FontHeight(WinHnd : HWND; FntHnd : HWND) : Integer;
var
 DCHnd : HWND;
 TextMex : TTextMetric;
begin
 Result := -1;
 DCHnd := GetDC(WinHnd);
 if GetMapMode(DCHnd) = MM_TEXT
   then begin
        SelectObject(DCHnd, FntHnd);
        GetTextMetrics(DCHnd, TextMex);
        Result := TextMex.tmHeight;
        end;
```

```
    ReleaseDC(WinHnd, DCHnd);
end;

procedure TShareEventDemoForm.FormCreate(Sender: TObject);
begin
  PageControl.ActivePage := MorningSheet;
  SetTabSizes;
  CopyDrag := False;
end;

procedure TShareEventDemoForm.QuitBtnClick(Sender: TObject);
begin
  Close;
end;

procedure TShareEventDemoForm.EditBoxMouseDown(Sender: TObject;
  Button: TMouseButton; Shift: TShiftState; X, Y: Integer);
begin
 { Before initiating a drag, make sure the left button
   is pressed, the EditBox has text in it, and that we're
   not in a double-click situation. }
 if (Button = mbLeft)
   and (EditBox.Text <> '')
   and not (ssDouble in Shift)
   then TEdit(Sender).BeginDrag(False);
end;

{ Common event handler for all the grids' OnMouseDown event. }
procedure TShareEventDemoForm.GridMouseDown(Sender: TObject;
  Button: TMouseButton; Shift: TShiftState; X, Y: Integer);
var
  TheGrid : TStringGrid;
begin
 { We're initiating a drag from whichever string grid
   is currently selected. Set the CopyDrag flag if the
   control key is down. Before starting the drag, make
   sure the left mouse button is pressed, there is text
   in the selected row of the grid, and we're not in
   a double-click situation. }
 TheGrid := CurrentGrid;
 CopyDrag := ssCtrl in Shift;
 if (Button = mbLeft)
   and (TheGrid.Cells[0, TheGrid.Row] <> '')
   and not (ssDouble in Shift)
   then TStringGrid(Sender).BeginDrag(False);
end;
```

The Oracle Returns

```
{ Common event handler for all the grids' OnDragOver event. }
procedure TShareEventDemoForm.GridDragOver(Sender, Source: TObject;
  X, Y: Integer; State: TDragState; var Accept: Boolean);
begin
 { We can accept anything, but only from the EditBox. }
 Accept := Source is TEdit;
end;

{ Common event handler for all the grids' OnDragDrop event. }
procedure TShareEventDemoForm.GridDragDrop(Sender, Source : TObject;
  X, Y : Integer);
begin
 { Drop the load on the currently selected grid. }
 DropEditString(CurrentGrid);
end;

procedure TShareEventDemoForm.PageControlDragOver(Sender, Source:
TObject; X, Y: Integer; State: TDragState; var Accept: Boolean);
begin
 { A drop on a tab is acceptable if it comes from the EditBox,
   or if it comes from a grid -- as long as the tab isn't the
   one for the grid originating the drag. In either case, tabs must
   have been manually set. }
 Accept := ManualTabsSet and
           (
            (Source is TEdit)
              or
            ((Source is TStringGrid) and (CurrentGrid <> TabGrid(X)))
           );
end;

procedure TShareEventDemoForm.PageControlDragDrop(Sender, Source:
TObject; X, Y: Integer);
begin
  { Get the string from the proper source and drop it on the grid
    associated with the tab at position X. }
  if (Source is TEdit) then DropEditString(TabGrid(X));
  if (Source is TStringGrid) then DropGridString(TabGrid(X));
end;

{ Return True only if both tab height and width have been set manually. }
function TShareEventDemoForm.ManualTabsSet : Boolean;
begin
 Result := (PageControl.TabHeight > 0) and (PageControl.TabWidth > 0);
end;
```

```pascal
{ Return a pointer to the grid on the currently selected tab sheet. }
function TShareEventDemoForm.CurrentGrid : TStringGrid;
begin
 Result := nil;
 if PageControl.ActivePage = MorningSheet
   then Result := MorningGrid else
 if PageControl.ActivePage = AfternoonSheet
   then Result := AfternoonGrid else
 if PageControl.ActivePage = EveningSheet
   then Result := EveningGrid;
end;

{ Return a pointer to the grid on the tab sheet associated with
  the tab located at position X. }
function TShareEventDemoForm.TabGrid(X : Integer) : TStringGrid;
var
 Idx : Integer;
begin
 Result := nil;
 with PageControl do
  begin
   Idx := X div TabWidth;
   case Idx of
    0 : Result := MorningGrid;
    1 : Result := AfternoonGrid;
    2 : Result := EveningGrid;
   end; { case }
  end; { with }
end;

{ Adjust tab height and width as required to give a pleasing
  appearance, and to ensure tabs each have the same height and
  width. }
procedure TShareEventDemoForm.SetTabSizes;
var
 i : Integer;
 Len : Integer;
 MaxWidth : Integer;
 s : String;
begin
 with PageControl do
  begin
   if TabWidth > 0
     then begin
           MaxWidth := -1;
           for i := 0 to PageCount - 1 do
             begin
```

```
            s := Pages[i].Caption;
            Len := StringWidth(Handle, Font.Handle, s);
            if Len > MaxWidth then MaxWidth := Len;
          end;
        if MaxWidth > 0 then TabWidth := MaxWidth + 10;
      end;

    if TabHeight > 0
      then PageControl.TabHeight := FontHeight(Handle, Font.Handle) + 5;

  end; { with }
end;

{ Common event handler support routine that drops the string
  in the EditBox onto the specified grid. Also clears the EditBox. }
procedure TShareEventDemoForm.DropEditString(AGrid : TStringGrid);
begin
 if AGrid <> nil
   then with AGrid do
     begin
       Cells[0, RowCount - 1] := EditBox.Text;
       RowCount := RowCount + 1;
       EditBox.Text := '';
     end; { with }
end;

{ Common event handler support routine that drops the string
  in the selected row of the currently selected grid onto
  the specified grid. If it is a "move" operation, the current
  grid is purged of the string and the grid is compressed. }
procedure TShareEventDemoForm.DropGridString(TargetGrid : TStringGrid);
var
 i : Integer;
begin
 if TargetGrid <> nil
   then begin
        with TargetGrid do
          begin
            Cells[0, RowCount - 1] := CurrentGrid.Cells[0,
              CurrentGrid.Row];
            RowCount := RowCount + 1;
          end; { with }

        if not CopyDrag
          then with CurrentGrid do
            begin
              Cells[0, Row] := '';
```

```
          if Row < RowCount - 1
            then for i := Row to RowCount - 1 do
              Cells[0, i] := Cells[0, i + 1];
          RowCount := RowCount - 1;
        end; { with }
      end;
end;

end.
```

To properly compute the height and width of the string that would be written on a tab, I had to resort to routines within the Win95 API. I learned a couple of interesting things in the process. First, the **Height** sub-property of the **Font** property in a component includes the height of a character (ascender part plus descender part), but not the internal leading which is used for special purposes, like displaying umlauts (those two little dots) above some international characters.

I wanted to know the true height, which is provided by a call to **GetTextMetrics**. I created a general-purpose function called **FontHeight** that would return the height of the font on a component, given a handle to that component and a handle to its associated font. A check is made within **FontHeight** to make sure the map mode is **MM_TEXT**, meaning the value returned is for the screen and will be measured in pixels.

The companion routine, **StringWidth**, uses a similar technique to pass a string to **GetTextExtentPoint32**. The return value is the approximate length (in pixels) that will be required to display the string. (The value is only approximate because it doesn't account for any kerning done within a font.)

The **SetTabSizes** method is called by the form's **OnCreate** handler to see if the tabs need adjusting. If this routine determines that both **TabHeight** and **TabWidth** properties for the PageControl have been set to a non-zero value during design, **SetTabSize** takes over and adjusts the sizes according to the font metrics and the longest caption.

The **TabGrid** function uses the **TabWidth** and X-coordinate information provided during the drag to determine the tab being referenced, and from that, it returns a pointer to the associated string grid. **PageControlDragDrop** also uses **TabGrid** to determine which string grid will receive the string that will be dropped.

Just One More Thing…

Listing 16.2 reflects some additional capability I just couldn't resist adding to this example: the ability to drag an item from a string grid and copy or move it to one of the other grids by dropping it on the grid's tab. This required writing a common OnMouseDown handler for the grids, and extending the OnDragOver and OnDragDrop handlers for the PageControl. I also added **CopyDrag**, a boolean flag that is set whenever the Ctrl key is pressed and a drag is started in any of the grids.

DropGridString performs the lion's share of the work when items are dragged from a string grid to a tab. If the control key was not held down during the drag, **DropGridString** executes some extra steps that turn a straight copy into a move, clearing out the selected item from the source grid and then squeezing out the dead space.

An executing version of the demo is shown in Figure 16.2. This little application is really a lot of fun to play with. You can easily drag items back and forth between the pages, copying and moving, zigging and zagging. I think sharing event handlers are a lot more fun than attending a wedding. Especially my own.

End of entry, March 29.

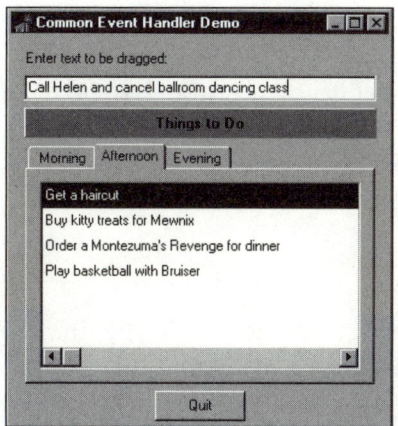

Figure 16.2
The shared events demo app in action.

Chapter 16

The fax machine in Ace's office began to whirr. Helen immediately jumped to her feet.

"Ace, there's a fax coming in," she said. "Hurry—it must be the test results!"

Breakpoint crossed the room and deftly ripped the page from the machine, just as the beep indicated it had finished printing. "Now we'll see which one of us is right about this Bohacker accusation," he said smugly.

He stood there, staring at the page and fidgeting for several seconds. Finally Helen couldn't stand it any longer.

"Well, what does it say?" she demanded. "Was it Bohacker, or wasn't it?"

"Uh, it isn't completely clear. You see, these quick tests aren't always conclusive, and—"

"Let me see that," she said, grabbing the page from his hand. She quickly absorbed the information and then turned to her companion.

"It says right here—and I quote: 'The test results indicate a nearly point-for-point match between the two samples, with a congruence in the 95th percentile, perfectly consistent with DNA tests of this type.' That means the hair and blood samples match, doesn't it?"

"Well, yes," Ace admitted. "But—"

"Then it *must* be Melvin Bohacker, just as I said. And wherever he is, you can bet Madame X is right there with him. Now all we have to do is find out where he has gone."

"Norton City."

"What?"

"Norton City," Ace repeated. "Biff told me earlier this evening that Bohacker was going to Norton City sometime tonight. Trust me on this."

"But *where* in Norton City?" she asked. "He could be in any one of a hundred places."

"I think I have a way to find that out, too," Ace said, as he strode across the room and flipped on his computer. "I'm going online—and I'm going to get some answers, pronto!"

Using Memory Files

Casebook No. 16, April 1: I guess one of the most-often-asked questions about Delphi is how to write an application that can limit itself to one instance in the system. During the past year, I've discovered several ways to accomplish that goal. But one of them was so much fun I thought I would document it here.

For an application to detect another instance of itself, it must be able to query the system in some way. Under Windows 3.1, an application could check a handle called **hPrevInst** to see if there was already an instance running. But that all changed with Win95.

One way to accomplish the goal would be to use the WalkStuf unit I developed earlier. Using the **ModuleSysInstCount** function would return a value that would indicate how many copies of the program were already running. It would be simple for the application to abort execution if that count was something other than zero. But that wouldn't work with NT.

A common technique for communicating information between applications is the use of a unique global key that is accessible to multiple instances of a program. A classic example is the use of a unique file. When an application starts up, it checks for the presence of a file with a certain name (e.g., FOOBAR99.DAT). If the file is present, there is another instance of the program already running. If the file is not found, the newly instantiated program creates it. When the program shuts down, it deletes the file.

One problem with this approach is caused by anomalies such as system crashes and power failures. Since the "flag" (in this case, a file) has been stored on a non-volatile medium, it's still there when the errant system is rebooted. Under those conditions, the first instance that comes along will see the file, assume another instance is running, and shut down. That means exactly zero instances of the program will run. Some manual housekeeping is required to remove the file and get everything back to normal.

Win95 offers a much nicer alternative through its shared memory files. This time, the files are in volatile memory (or at least it's treated that way, even if it's being swapped between RAM and the hard disk). And unlike many of the operations within Win95, memory files can be shared between processes.

Chapter 16

I created a simple application to test the theory that memory files could be used to detect multiple instances of a program. The running application is shown in Figure 16.3, and its code appears in Listing 16.3.

Listing 16.3 A simple single-instance program.

```
{-------------------------------------------------------}
{                 The One Instance Demo                 }
{                INSTMAIN.PAS : Main Form               }
{                By Ace Breakpoint, N.T.P.              }
{                  Assisted by Don Taylor               }
{                                                       }
{ Application that demonstrates how to prevent          }
{ more than one instance of a program from running      }
{ in the Win95 environment.                             }
{                                                       }
{ Written for *High Performance Delphi 3 Programming*   }
{ Copyright (c) 1997 The Coriolis Group, Inc.           }
{                 Last Updated 4/30/97                  }
{-------------------------------------------------------}

unit InstMain;
interface
uses
  Windows, Messages, SysUtils, Classes, Graphics, Controls, Forms,
Dialogs, StdCtrls;
type
  TForm1 = class(TForm)
    ExitBtn: TButton;
    Label1: TLabel;
    procedure ExitBtnClick(Sender: TObject);
  private
    { Private declarations }
  public
    { Public declarations }
  end;
var
  Form1: TForm1;
implementation
{$R *.DFM}
procedure TForm1.ExitBtnClick(Sender: TObject);
begin
 Close;
end;

end.
```

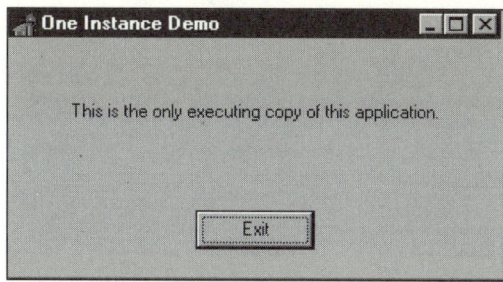

Figure 16.3
The single-instance program at runtime.

Of course, the form does nothing by itself. The idea is for a multiple instance to detect the presence of a previous instance and then shut itself down. And while this could be done in the startup code of the form, it is much more polite to accomplish this work in a way that doesn't display the new instance at all. That means taking care of it before the application even begins.

Before The Beginning

A lot of people don't seem to know that it's possible to execute code in the project file, even before the application is initialized. That's the case here. The project file for this experimental application is shown in Listing 16.4.

Listing 16.4 Project file for the One Instance Demo.

```
{-----------------------------------------------------------}
{               The One Instance Demo                       }
{            ONEINST.DPR : Project File                     }
{              By Ace Breakpoint, N.T.P.                    }
{               Assisted by Don Taylor                      }
{                                                           }
{ Application that demonstrates how to prevent              }
{ more than one instance of a program from running          }
{ in the Win95 environment.                                 }
{                                                           }
{ Written for *High Performance Delphi 3 Programming*       }
{ Copyright (c) 1997 The Coriolis Group, Inc.               }
{              Last Updated 4/30/97                         }
{-----------------------------------------------------------}
program OneInst;
uses
  Windows,
```

```
  Forms,
  InstMain in 'InstMain.pas' {Form1};

const
 MemFileSize = 1024;
 MemFileName = 'one_inst_demo_memfile';

var
 MemHnd : HWND;

{$R *.RES}

begin
 { Attempt to create a file mapping object }
 MemHnd := CreateFileMapping(HWND($FFFFFFFF),
                             nil,
                             PAGE_READWRITE,
                             0,
                             MemFileSize,
                             MemFileName);
 { If it didn't already exist, then run the app... }
 if GetLastError <> ERROR_ALREADY_EXISTS
   then begin
        Application.Initialize;
        Application.CreateForm(TForm1, Form1);
        Application.Run;
        end;

 CloseHandle(MemHnd);

end.
```

This is a kick. First, an attempt is made to create a file mapping object with the **CreateFileMapping** API call. Whether the object already exists or is actually created, a handle to the object is returned and assigned to **MemHnd**. Calling **CreateFile Mapping** with a handle value of $FFFFFFFF causes the operating system to use its own paging file instead of the conventional file system, so the file can be shared between processes; all the process needs to know is the name of the file. Although the file is set up for read/write, a call is not made here to **MapViewOfFile**, which would give the program access to the file's contents through a pointer. For the purpose of this example, it's sufficient just to check for the file's existence.

If the memory file already existed at the time of the call to **CreateFileMapping**, a handle to the file is returned to the caller, and an error value of **ERROR_ALREADY**

_EXISTS is sent to the system. If that error isn't found by **GetLastError**, it means there isn't an instance already running, and it's safe to go ahead.

Because a handle was returned whether or not the file was created, the handle must be closed before the application finally shuts down. The first program to call **CreateFileMapping** creates the file mapping object; the last program to close a handle to it causes the system to destroy the object. This is the equivalent of deleting the file.

End of entry, April 1.

Ace clicked the Print button on a dialog and his laser printer came alive. He printed four pages of information, then pulled the sheets from the tray and examined them.

"Now there's no doubt in my mind," he said with a newly found determination in his voice.

Helen was tempted to say something about her being right after all, but thought better of it. Besides, Ace was heading for the door.

"I'm coming with you," she said, picking up her raincoat and purse.

"Sorry, Baby," Ace replied. "This one might be dangerous, so you're staying here. Wait by the phone in case something goes wrong."

"I suppose you're right," she said reluctantly. "But be careful, Sweetheart." Then she tenderly kissed him on the lips.

"I should be back in an hour or so," he said. "If you haven't heard from me by then, call the cops. Tell them I'm on a mission to bring in Bohacker!" One more kiss and he was gone.

Preventing Program Execution

Casebook No. 16, April 2: It was interesting to explore how to shut down a program when it finds a previous instance running. But something kept bugging me. What about the times you don't want an application to run unless another program *is* running?

This is the case with several demo versions of components, such as the Orpheus VCL library. If you create an application using what TurboPower Software calls the "trial" version of its components, they require Delphi to be running in order for the application to execute. How could something like this be accomplished?

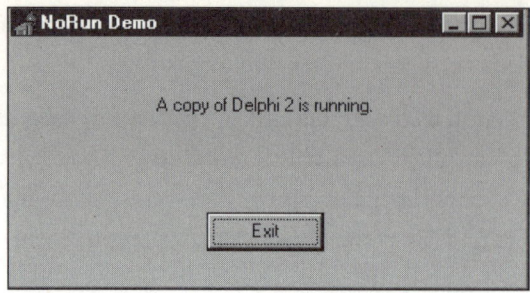

Figure 16.4
The Delphi Environment Detector running.

The answer was so simple I almost couldn't believe it. The running version of this experiment is shown in Figure 16.4. The main form's code is shown in Listing 16.5, and the project source is detailed in Listing 16.6.

Listing 16.5 Code for the No Run Demo's main form.

```
{------------------------------------------------------------}
{                   The No Run Demo                          }
{              NRUNMAIN.PAS : Main Form                      }
{              By Ace Breakpoint, N.T.P.                     }
{                 Assisted by Don Taylor                     }
{                                                            }
{ Main form for the application that demonstrates            }
{ how to prevent execution if a 32-bit version of            }
{ Delphi isn't running.                                      }
{                                                            }
{ Written for *High Performance Delphi 3 Programming*        }
{ Copyright (c) 1997 The Coriolis Group, Inc.                }
{              Last Updated 4/30/97                          }
{------------------------------------------------------------}

unit NRunMain;

interface

uses
  Windows, Messages, SysUtils, Classes, Graphics, Controls, Forms,
  Dialogs, StdCtrls, WalkStuf;

type
```

```
  TForm1 = class(TForm)
    ExitBtn: TButton;
    Label1: TLabel;
    procedure ExitBtnClick(Sender: TObject);
  private
    { Private declarations }
  public
    { Public declarations }
  end;

var
  Form1: TForm1;
implementation

{$R *.DFM}

procedure TForm1.ExitBtnClick(Sender: TObject);
begin
 Close;
end;

end.
```

Listing 16.6   No Run Demo project file.

```
{------------------------------------------------------}
{                  The No Run Demo                     }
{              NORUN.DPR : Project File                }
{               By Ace Breakpoint, N.T.P.              }
{                 Assisted by Don Taylor               }
{                                                      }
{ An application that demonstrates how to prevent      }
{ execution if a 32-bit version of Delphi isn't        }
{ running.                                             }
{                                                      }
{ Written for *High Performance Delphi 3 Programming*  }
{ Copyright (c) 1997 The Coriolis Group, Inc.          }
{              Last Updated 4/30/97                    }
{------------------------------------------------------}

program NoRun;

uses
  Forms, Dialogs,
  NRunMain in 'NRunMain.pas' {Form1},
  WalkStuf in 'WalkStuf.pas';
```

```
{$R *.RES}

begin
  Application.Initialize;
  { If there isn't a copy of a 32-bit version of Delphi running,
    display an error message and kill the program. Otherwise, let
    this application execute. }
  if ModuleSysInstCount('DELPHI32.EXE') < 1
    then MessageDlg('Delphi 32 must be running to execute this program',
         mtError, [mbOK], 0)
    else begin
         Application.CreateForm(TForm1, Form1);
         Application.Run;
         end;
end.
```

The goal is to kill the application without the user even seeing the main form. So once again, code is added to the project file to accomplish the task. This time the **ModuleSysInstCount** function from the **WalkStuf** unit is used to make sure at least one instance of a 32-bit version of Delphi (DELPHI32.EXE) is running. If so, the program continues. If not, an error message is displayed.

One note: Because WalkStuf relies on ToolHelp32, this technique will only work with programs running under Win95.

End of entry, April 2.

Floating Toolbars

Casebook No. 16, April 3: I've always liked programs with toolbars that can be moved around on the screen. They're especially handy in artwork and page makeup programs, because you can have a tool palette right next to where you're working.

I sifted through the various components provided with Delphi, looking for something that could be used as the basis for a "floating" toolbar. I suppose I could have used an additional form, but I didn't need anything fancy. Something that would be limited to the main form's client area would be just fine.

It seemed that panels would do the trick nicely, except for one thing: They aren't movable at runtime. But a little investigation revealed they have the provision for mouse event handling. After a few bumps and blind alleys, I came up with the demo program documented in Listing 16.7.

Listing 16.7 Code for the Floating Toolbar demo.

```
{—————————————————————————————————}
{           The Floating Toolbar Demo             }
{           TOOLMAIN.PAS : Main Form              }
{           By Ace Breakpoint, N.T.P.             }
{              Assisted by Don Taylor             }
{                                                 }
{ An application that demonstrates the use of     }
{ moveable TPanel objects as floating toolbars.   }
{                                                 }
{ Written for *High Performance Delphi 3 Programming* }
{ Copyright (c) 1997 The Coriolis Group, Inc.     }
{              Last Updated 4/30/97               }
{—————————————————————————————————}

unit ToolMain;

interface

uses
   Windows, Messages, SysUtils, Classes, Graphics, Controls, Forms,
   Dialogs, StdCtrls, FileCtrl, ExtCtrls, Buttons;

type
   TDirection = (otHorizontal, otVertical);

   TForm1 = class(TForm)
     Toolbar: TPanel;
     ExitSB: TSpeedButton;
     ZoomInSB: TSpeedButton;
     ZoomOutSB: TSpeedButton;
     ControlPanel: TPanel;
     GranRBGroup: TRadioGroup;
     MarginRBGroup: TRadioGroup;
     OrientRBGroup: TRadioGroup;
     ExitBtn: TButton;
     LEDSB: TSpeedButton;
     procedure ExitBtnClick(Sender: TObject);
```

```
    procedure ToolbarMouseDown(Sender: TObject; Button: TMouseButton;
      Shift: TShiftState; X, Y: Integer);
    procedure ToolbarMouseUp(Sender: TObject; Button: TMouseButton;
      Shift: TShiftState; X, Y: Integer);
    procedure ToolbarMouseMove(Sender: TObject; Shift: TShiftState; X,
      Y: Integer);
    procedure FormCreate(Sender: TObject);
    procedure GranRBGroupClick(Sender: TObject);
    procedure MarginRBGroupClick(Sender: TObject);
    procedure ExitSBClick(Sender: TObject);
    procedure OrientRBGroupClick(Sender: TObject);
  private
    DraggingPanel : Boolean;
    DragStartX : Integer;
    DragStartY : Integer;
    GridSize : Integer;
    MarginSize : Integer;
    procedure OrientToolBar(Direction : TDirection);
  public
    { Public declarations }
  end;

var
  Form1: TForm1;

implementation

{$R *.DFM}

procedure TForm1.ExitBtnClick(Sender: TObject);
begin
 Close;
end;

procedure TForm1.ToolbarMouseDown(Sender: TObject; Button: TMouseButton;
  Shift: TShiftState; X, Y: Integer);
begin
 if Button = mbLeft
   then begin
        DraggingPanel := True;
        DragStartX := X;
        DragStartY := Y;
        end;
end;
```

```
procedure TForm1.ToolbarMouseUp(Sender: TObject; Button: TMouseButton;
  Shift: TShiftState; X, Y: Integer);
begin
 DraggingPanel := False;
end;

procedure TForm1.ToolbarMouseMove(Sender: TObject; Shift: TShiftState; X,
  Y: Integer);
var
 DeltaX : Integer;
 DeltaY : Integer;
 SafetyMargin : Integer;
begin
 if DraggingPanel
   then with Toolbar do
    begin
      DeltaX := X - DragStartX;
      DeltaY := Y - DragStartY;
      if GridSize > MarginSize
        then SafetyMargin := GridSize
        else SafetyMargin := MarginSize;

      if (abs(DeltaX) > GridSize - 1)
       then if DeltaX > 0
              then begin
                     if (ControlPanel.Left - Left) > SafetyMargin
                       then Left := Left + DeltaX
                       else Left := ControlPanel.Left - SafetyMargin;
                   end
              else begin
                     if (Left + Width) > SafetyMargin
                       then Left := Left + DeltaX
                       else Left := SafetyMargin - Width;
                   end;

      if (abs(DeltaY) > GridSize - 1)
       then if DeltaY > 0
              then begin
                     if (Form1.ClientHeight - Top) > SafetyMargin
                       then Top := Top + DeltaY
                       else Top := Form1.ClientHeight - SafetyMargin;
                   end
```

```
            else begin
              if Top + Height > SafetyMargin
                then Top := Top + DeltaY
                else Top := SafetyMargin - Height;
            end;
    end; { with }
end;

procedure TForm1.FormCreate(Sender: TObject);
begin
 GranRBGroup.ItemIndex := 0;
 MarginRBGroup.ItemIndex :=0;
 OrientRBGroup.ItemIndex := 0;
end;

procedure TForm1.GranRBGroupClick(Sender: TObject);
begin
 case GranRBGroup.ItemIndex of
  0 : GridSize := 1;
  1 : GridSize := 10;
  2 : GridSize := 20;
 end; { case }
end;

procedure TForm1.MarginRBGroupClick(Sender: TObject);
begin
 case MarginRBGroup.ItemIndex of
  0 : MarginSize := 5;
  1 : MarginSize := 10;
  2 : MarginSize := 15;
 end; { case }
end;

procedure TForm1.ExitSBClick(Sender: TObject);
begin
 Close;
end;

procedure TForm1.OrientRBGroupClick(Sender: TObject);
begin
 case OrientRBGroup.ItemIndex of
  0 : OrientToolBar(otHorizontal);
  1 : OrientToolBar(otVertical);
```

```
    end; { case }
end;

procedure TForm1.OrientToolbar(Direction : TDirection);
begin
 with Toolbar do
   begin
     Left := 20;
     Top := 20;

     case Direction of
      otHorizontal :
        begin
          Width := (4 * ExitSB.Width) + 20;;
          Height := ExitSB.Height + 10;
          ExitSB.Top := 6;
          ZoomInSB.Top := 6;
          ZoomOutSB.Top := 6;
          LEDSB.Top := 6;

          ExitSB.Left := 11;
          ZoomInSB.Left := ExitSB.Left + ExitSB.Width;
          ZoomOutSB.Left := ZoomInSB.Left + ZoomInSB.Width;
          LEDSB.Left := ZoomOutSB.Left + ZoomOutSB.Width;
        end;

      otVertical :
        begin
          Width := ExitSB.Width + 10;
          Height := (4 * ExitSB.Height) + 20;
          ExitSB.Left := 6;
          ZoomInSB.Left := 6;
          ZoomOutSB.Left := 6;
          LEDSB.Left := 6;

          ExitSB.Top := 11;
          ZoomInSB.Top := ExitSB.Top + ExitSB.Height;
          ZoomOutSB.Top := ZoomInSB.Top + ZoomInSB.Height;
          LEDSB.Top := ZoomOutSB.Top + ZoomOutSB.Height;
        end;
     end; { case }
   end; { with }
end;

end.
```

As can be seen, the panel (Toolbar) must handle three mouse events—OnMouse Down, OnMouseMove and OnMouseUp. The OnMouseDown handler simply makes sure it's the left mouse button that has been pressed. If so, it documents the initial position of the mouse and it sets a status variable that indicates a dragging process is underway.

The OnMouseMove handler is quite a bit more complex, mainly because it's making sure the panel doesn't move outside the client area of the form, where it might get lost. Basically, the ToolbarMouseMove handler computes the difference between the original mouse position and the current mouse position, and then it adds the differential to the original Left and Top properties of Toolbar to move it. A provision has been made to move Toolbar by jumps of 1, 10 or 20 pixels, giving it the same feeling as moving it in the "lock to grid" mode when designing with Delphi. I also added a margining capability, to make sure a piece of the toolbar can always be grabbed with the mouse, in those cases when the toolbar gets shoved off in a corner.

The OnMouseUp handler is obvious: All it has to do is turn off the status variable.

I added three radiobutton groups to the form, so grid and margin sizes can be set on the fly. I also included a capability for switching the toolbar between horizontal and vertical orientations.

An executing version of the program is shown in Figure 16.5. It's kind of fun to drag the toolbar around, and the first button on the toolbar is actually functional—it ends the program.

End of entry, April 3.

Ace Gets The Goods

As the Delphi Avenger glanced up from the Casebook, it was obvious that something had gone awry. The temperature had dropped and the air stung the nostrils with each breath. The room had become enveloped in a cloudy mist, a thick carpet of carbon-dioxide fog now hugging the floor like a basset hound on its day off. A brilliant white light managed to half-penetrate the cloud, giving an eerie cast to everything in the room. Something was very, very wrong. Then suddenly, from across the room there came a violent explosion, as the rickety door blew off its hinges and

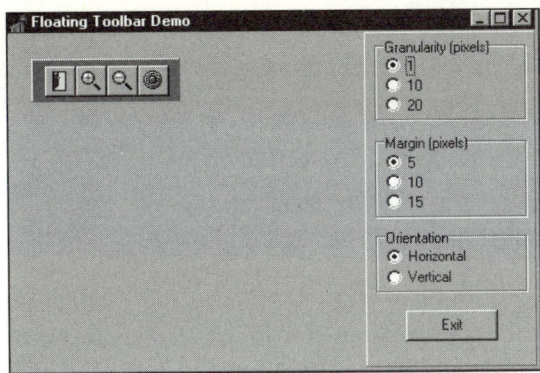

Figure 16.5
Floating a Delphi toolbar.

crashed inward to the floor. In the open doorway, illuminated from behind by the neon bug zapper in the hallway, stood a triumphant Ace Breakpoint!

* * *

The odor permeating the seedy little apartment was unmistakable, a veritable snack-food smorgasbord. I crossed the room powerfully, knowing I had not only solved this case, but I had wrested complete control of the story from The Third Person. Three giant steps, and I had closed the gap between myself and the pathetic creature cowering against the opposite wall—the now-defeated entity that once dared to call itself the Delphi Avenger.

"Breakpoint!" Bohacker hissed, dropping my Casebook on the floor. "How did you know?"

"Easy," I snarled. "From the very beginning of this case, I knew something was amiss. It just took me a while to realize the "miss" was you…

"Miss Bohacker! " I shouted, as I tore the false mustache from her upper lip.

"Cursors!" she spat through clenched teeth. Her wide eyes were sizing me up, like a wild animal trapped in a corner. The look of defeat was entirely gone, and in its place was a twisted smile that quite unnerved me. "Yes, it's me," she grinned. "Melvin Bohacker's evil twin sister, Mevlyn."

A chill ran down my spine. Suddenly I felt like I was playing a scene in a very bad "B" movie. How did I get myself into these situations? I just shook my head.

Chapter 16

"Sure," she said disdainfully. "Be *Mr. High and Mighty*. But imagine for just one minute what your life would be like, spending every day of your childhood following in Melvin Bohacker's footsteps."

And following his nutritional guidelines as well, I mused, noticing the mass of Twinkie and HoHo wrappers strewn all over the apartment. But strangely, I did feel a twinge of empathy. She looked like someone who was about to spill her guts.

"He was exactly eight minutes older," she said. "So *he* got all the good stuff. I got whatever was left. And when it came time for college, there was only enough money to send one of us. So of course it was Melvin who went off to school, while I stayed home. I probably would have starved to death, if I hadn't started the designer clothes business."

"Wait a second," I interrupted. "You mean you're the 'Bohacker' of Bohacker Industries? The people who make Bohacker Blues jeans?"

"You hadn't made the connection?" she asked wryly. "Then you're also not aware that my company produces the Pure Prophet designer line for your little friend, Muffy Katz."

"Why, you must be worth a bundle!" I exclaimed.

"Oh, yes—I have a net worth of several million. Which is fine, I suppose—if you're merely interested in money. But Melvin is the one who got all the *love*. He got the *accolades*. He's the one who got the college education. And he's the one who went on to become one of the most esteemed and revered members of the entire scientific community—a Windows 95 programmer."

Her eyes now burned with hatred. "Since childhood, I've been a dysfunctional, codependent victim, and I've sworn I would get even with Melvin, no matter how long it took. Then a few weeks ago, it became obvious," she said, staring dreamily off into the distance. "I would steal your Casebook, and armed with the secrets it contains, I would become the best Windows programmer in the world—better even than Melvin. And certainly better than you," she said, reaching out and poking me in the chest with a long, slender index finger.

"Don't poke that thing at me," I warned. "It's got a nail on the end."

"The thing that would make the theft even sweeter," she continued, "was to frame Melvin for the robbery. I called him earlier today, to torment him and then lure him out of town tonight, so everyone would think he had taken it on the lam. It was a perfect plan. But something went wrong. Evidently I underestimated you."

"You forgot I used to be a detective," I replied. "And you left a trail of clues so transparent that even an MIS manager from Bayport could have followed them."

"Like the glove?" she asked. "Losing it was an accident. I thought of trying to get it back. But even so, it should have pointed to Melvin, not me."

"Sure it did. The muddy glove left at the crime scene contained some hair that was a nearly exact DNA match with Melvin's. But at that point, I knew this had to be a frame, albeit a very sophisticated one. There were two reasons for that conclusion. You see, after the drubbing I gave him when he tried to double-cross me a year ago, I knew Melvin would never have the nerve to try anything underhanded with me again. I broke his spirit."

"And the second reason?" she queried.

"Whatever I might think of your brother, I didn't believe he was in the habit of wearing *ladies' gloves*," I chuckled. "They were simply too small for him. So I queried the Department of Licensing computer and got a copy of his driver's license. That netted me his birth date. I knew he was originally from California. So my next link was to a large database, where I searched through all the California county records."

She was one step ahead of me. "So you found our birth certificates," she said.

"Yeah. That's when I discovered there were actually *two* babies born to Chester and Martha Bohacker that night—a boy named Melvin, and a *girl* they called Mevlyn, born a few minutes later. Twins. That's why the DNA samples matched almost perfectly."

"All right. So you found out I was a twin. How did you trace me to this dump?" she asked.

"I guessed you had been in town for at least a couple of weeks to implement your plan. There were no new guests registered at the Gooey Duck Grill and Motel, the only place in town to stay. So I examined the local phone company's records, looking for new service connections made in the last couple of weeks. This is a small town. It wasn't long before my search led me here to the Sleeveless Arms. One final link to California gave me your car registration. When it matched your vehicle parked out front, I knew I had the goods. Typical gumshoe stuff."

Chapter 16

"Gumshoe, perhaps. But typical? I don't think so," Mevlyn said, the tone of her voice suddenly becoming soft and low. The sudden change in her tenor caught my attention. Her eyes no longer filled with hatred but with icy fire, she removed her dark, wide-brimmed hat and flung it lazily across the room, carelessly tossing her head. Her silky, brunette tresses spilled over her shoulders, flowed down her back, turned at her heels, and rolled across the three-foot expanse of floor to the wall, where they lapped up onto the molding. It was obvious I would have to watch my step with this woman, or I might get tripped up.

Someone next door began to play an alto saxophone. Mevlyn picked up my Casebook from the floor where she had dropped it. "Listen, Ace," she said, lifting her eyes to mine and tossing me a coquettish smile. "Maybe we just got off to a bad start, you and I. Maybe you could just leave this itsy-bitsy book with me, and we could get to be *really close friends*."

She pursed her lips, and I noticed she was caressing the buttery-smooth leather cover on my hardbound Casebook as if it were a prize-winning Pomeranian. This situation had all the earmarks of something that could turn ugly very fast. I had to keep my distance. Three bass saxophones had joined the alto, and now they were so loud it seemed they were right there in the room. *These cheap apartments really do have thin walls*, I thought.

"I'm afraid I can't do that," I said, stepping back. "I already have a really close friend. Her name is Helen."

"I know," she replied, advancing steadily toward me. "I've seen her. Nice girl, kind of...country. Sweet face. Cute little figure. But tell me," she said, a wry little smile spreading across her mouth in anticipation, "how do you think she'd like to have *these?!*"

Still holding the Casebook, she grabbed both of her lapels and, with a single motion, threw open her full-length raincoat. I gasped and reeled backward, my wide-eyed gaze fixed upon the two objects inside the open raincoat: Protruding from the inside pocket were a pair of front-row tickets for the Seattle concert on the Stones' 1999 "Old Rocker" Tour. She smoothly removed the passes and pressed them into my palm, closing my fingers around them.

"I'm glad you like them," she said.

"How—how did you manage to get these?" I stammered, trying to regain my composure.

"Money talks, Baby Cakes," she replied. "Go on. Take them. They're yours."

I stared at the tickets in my fist for what seemed like an hour. "I'm—I'm sorry, I, uh, just can't accept a bribe," I said, still visibly shaken. I reluctantly tossed the ill-gotten booty on the floor. "I have no choice. I'll have to turn you in."

"Can't blame a girl for trying," she said, rather matter-of-factly. "So what do you say, Ace...how about a little kiss, just to show there's no hard feelings? Just for old times' sake?"

She flashed me a devilish smile and pressed close to me. She slipped her arms under mine and pulled me to her, still maintaining a tight grip on the Casebook in her right hand. "A...*kiss*?" I asked stupidly, trying to stall for enough time to come up with a plan. A tenor sax had now joined the others to form a quintet, and some idiot had started accompanying them on a kettle drum that resonated inside my chest.

The ice had melted, and her liquid, steel-gray eyes were now riveted on mine. "Of course, silly," she replied playfully. "You know what a kiss is, don't you? It's when two people each press their lips together, and then *together* they press their lips together... like...this...."

Until now, I hadn't really noticed her mouth. But as her moist, ruby lips inched their way toward mine, her breath laden with the sweet scent of creme-filled sponge cake, I could think of nothing else. I found myself in a trance, suspended in time with a small orchestra playing Barry Manilow's greatest hits, all at the same time. What could I do? What about Helen? The voluptuous, trembling lips came closer and closer....

Just as our lips were about to meet, I heard a muffled *thump* behind me, and a small explosion went off in my brain. Everything slowly melted from Technicolor into black and white and then into a palette of grays. Mevlyn's lips became twisted in a maniacal laugh that seemed to echo from every wall. I caught a whiff of the distinctive perfume she wore, the same scent that had permeated the scrap of notepaper. Now it completely filled my nostrils and burned indelibly into my brain.

Chapter 16

"*Chez Monieux,*" I heard myself say to Mevlyn in a half-whisper. My knees turned to rubber. Then the whole eerie scene faded to black.

* * *

When I came to, my head was pounding and I had a mouth full of cotton candy. Struggling to my feet, I threw away the paper cone and swallowed the sticky pink ball. I glanced at my watch. It was 7:34 P.M. There was no sign of either Mevlyn or the Casebook, but downstairs I could hear the telltale sound of a racing engine as her slow-moving white Bronco lumbered away from the curb.

On the desk was a lavender-colored envelope, on its face a message written in a familiar feminine hand. I picked it up, and after a few seconds I managed to focus on the words in front of me:

> *Dearest Ace,*
>
> *Inside you'll find a little something just for you.*
>
> *I think we really could have hit it off together. But a girl's gotta do what a girl's gotta do. Perhaps we will meet again.*
>
> *I suppose it's like this: You can't always get what you want. But if you try sometimes, you get what you need.*
>
> *Always,*
> *Mevlyn*

I eagerly tore open the scented envelope and emptied its contents on the desk—a single strip of thin, white cardboard with a perforation near one end.

I picked up the ticket and stared at it, reviewing the whole crazy scene in my mind. First I had been struck with her beauty, which had left a permanent impression on my psyche. Then I had been struck with my hardbound Casebook, which had left a considerable goose egg on the back of my head. The lump would eventually heal. Right now I had to get my life back together.

I guessed that when my socially conscious friends heard about this incident, they would all encourage me to try to better understand Mevlyn and to forget the pain and suffering she had caused me. And I supposed I would eventually be able to do that. But it would be a long time before I would again trust any woman with a twisted grin and a maniacal laugh.

Epilogue

Casebook No. 17, April 13: It was the best of times. It was the worst of times. For me, the past 24 hours had been a Dickens of a time. It had been an adventure I never wanted to repeat.

Helen was waiting for me when I got back from The Sleeveless Arms. At least she had been partially right—the perpetrator was a Bohacker. But I had been right, too—he would never have had the courage to try anything with me.

My watch told me it was 11:39 P.M. I poured a cup of Dark Roast and took a big gulp of the hot brew. I now knew what it was like to have my office ransacked and my property stolen. It's not an experience I want to have again. Like my Dad, Jack Breakpoint, always told me, "Take care of your stuff, son. There's always someone out there who wants it more than you do." Then Mom would add, "And always wear your best underwear, in case you get hit by a bus."

One thing was for sure: I wouldn't leave my Casebooks lying around any more. In all probability I would never see the stolen one again. Thankfully, it was only my most recent Casebook, one of several. Someone told me the best parts of it are on a CD-ROM included with a new book on Delphi programming.

Before she left, Helen and I had a long talk about The Author. She convinced me that if I really do appreciate what The Author has done for me, I need to talk to him more often and to tell others about him. All things considered, I guess that's the least I can do.

Against my better judgment, I picked up a copy of the latest CD from Not Ourselves Today at a convenience store on the way home. It's entitled "Transcend Dental Medication." I hit the stop button halfway through the first track, "Rinse and Spit." It was too much like sitting through a root canal to suit my taste.

I sat down at my kitchen table and took a sip of the bitter brown water. Outside I could hear the sounds of the relentless rain as it pounded against the window. I

Chapter 16

pulled out my wallet and extracted the lone ticket found in the envelope left at The Sleeveless Arms. For some reason I just couldn't get it off my mind.

Perhaps I *would* go to that concert. It would be a good opportunity to get away from the hustle and bustle of life in a small town. It was my kind of music. It could even be an adventure.

After all, you never know who may show up in the seat beside you.

End of entry, April 13.

HIGH PERFORMANCE

An Age-Old Problem

CHAPTER 17

Ace takes the stage to explain the machineries of Windows 95 broadcast messaging to an extremely mature audience, at least one member of which seems remarkably familiar.

An Age-Old Problem

Don Taylor

I awoke with a start. The clock by my recliner told me it was 1:23 P.M., which meant I had only seven minutes to make it all the way across town. I tossed the pizza box off my lap, and in what seemed only a few seconds later, I found myself in an unfamiliar part of town. I somehow managed to find the address I had penciled in my day planner.

The sign at the parking lot entrance read "Hacker Haven—An Upward-Compatible Digital Retirement Community." I vaguely remembered hearing rumors about the construction of an Old Programmers Home here in Poulsbo. But as I pulled into the parking lot, I wondered why I hadn't noticed the place before. It was a huge two-story complex that must have covered the better part of an entire city block.

I held my attaché case above my head and vainly tried to dodge the raindrops as I raced for the main entrance. I hustled through the automatic doors and checked my watch. 1:30 P.M. exactly — I had just made it.

There was no one to be seen in the lobby, so I decided to poke around a bit to satisfy my curiosity. Who knows, I thought, someday maybe I'll be living here myself. I picked the second of three corridors leading from the lobby.

The first six doors down that hallway were all marked "Restroom." I quietly slipped inside the seventh door, under a sign that read "Recreation Room." I guess I expected the place to be full of ex-programmers working out on exercise equipment. To my surprise, I found a room containing 30 individual cubicles, each with its own client PC, all connected to a network server running the multiplayer version of Doom.

I walked completely around the room, but couldn't find one person. I supposed a bunch of old programmers might be insular enough to socialize only through games over a network. But why was the room empty? It wasn't mealtime. Where was everybody? I was standing there scratching my head when a voice came from behind me.

Chapter 17

"May I help you?"

I whirled around to face the questioner. She was a relatively young woman, probably early thirties, a tad on the hefty side.

"My name's Breakpoint," I said. "Ace Breakpoint."

"I thought so," she replied. "You're here to present the in-service lecture on programming for Windows 95. I'm Dinah Setz, the Volunteer Coordinator," she said, extending her hand. After a few pleasantries, she invited me to follow her to the multipurpose room where the lecture was to be held.

"I'll be your guide while you're here," Dinah said, as we walked down the long hallway. "If you have any needs, or if there are any questions I can answer, please feel free to ask."

"There is one thing," I said. "We just passed four more restrooms. Why so many?"

"Having them helps alleviate some of the little problems that burden many of our guests," she replied, flashing me a knowing smile.

"Oh, I get it," I said. "The old geezers can't pack the mail any more."

"We prefer to call them our 'Legacy Application Developers' or more simply, 'guests,'" she said. "We have both men and women here, by the way. And yes, many of our guests experience some common challenges due to the number of their years. Since they are all programmers, we euphemistically refer to the results of these problems as 'errors,' and we have assigned standard error numbers to most of them. It makes it easier, and less embarrassing for everyone concerned."

"I don't think I understand," I said.

"Well, the most common occurrence is *Error 214: collection overflow error*. It frequently cascades from an *Error 11: line too long*. That's why we have included a large number of restrooms in the facility."

"I see. Uh, listen," I said, noticing we had come to the dining room. "If you don't mind, I'd like to get a little something to bring in with me. Just in case I need some extra energy during the lecture."

"Certainly," she said. "Help yourself."

I expected to get a snack from the kitchen. On entering the dining room, I was surprised to find there was no kitchen—only a series of vending machines that encircled the room full of tables and chairs. Dinah said the place saved a lot of money by just ordering takeout food and billing it to the guests' accounts. I walked up to one of the machines and dropped in four quarters.

"Ready to go," I said, slipping a candy bar into my pocket. We walked past an expanse of windows, where Dinah pointed out Hacker Haven Cemetery, located at the rear of the property.

"Nice place," I commented, noticing the immaculately manicured lawns. "Beautiful place. I'll bet you charge an arm and a leg to get in there."

"It's largely a matter of convenience," she said. "With the cemetery right here on the property, our guests never have to leave us. We like to think of it as our way of enabling our programmers to terminate and stay resident. Well, here is the multipurpose room."

Facing The Situation

Dinah opened the door and motioned for me to go in. "I'll stay with you," she said, "in case you have any problems. Just walk up on the stage."

The whole place was buzzing with excitement. So this is where everyone had gone, I thought. This was truly going to be an event. I cautiously made my way up the aisle, past rows full of gray-haired programmers seated in ergonomic easy chairs. On the stage was a complete 5GHz Pentagram server with 64 gig of RAM, full T-5 net access, and a 64 million color projection system. I fished around in my pocket until I located the Delphi system CD and the floppy that contained the entry-level code examples I had prepared for today's lecture. I sat down at the server and installed Delphi. Then I slipped the floppy into the powerful machine and waited in anticipation. I didn't have to wait long.

Dinah picked up the microphone, and a hush fell over the room. "We are very fortunate today," she began, "to have with us Mr. Ace Breakpoint, an expert who is going to share with us some of the finer points of programming under Windows 95 with 32-bit Delphi." She glanced my way and smiled, and I shot back a look of near panic. This was not what I had intended. Not at all.

"I'm sure we all remember," she continued, "the lecture Mr. Bohacker gave us last week on entry-level programming. So now, let's welcome Mr. Breakpoint, as he presents more advanced topics."

Chapter 17

I'm sure she must have motioned to me to take the floor. All I remember was the sick feeling in the pit of my stomach, and some guy in the third row shouting, "Yeah—let's see if he can top Bohacker!" I suddenly felt I was having a bad dream—like the one where you walk into class on the day of the final exam, and it's the first time you've ever attended the class. But this was even worse. Why had I volunteered to do this gig? I honestly couldn't remember even talking to anyone about it.

I stepped up to the microphone and tried to get a grip on myself. "What we'll be covering today won't quite be 'finer points' of Win95 programming. Instead you'll hear some really basic information I'm sure you'll all want to know—"

I felt a dull pain between my ribs, and looked down to see an old coot who had gotten up from his seat in the front row. "Listen, Sonny," he said, poking me in the chest with the tip of his telescoping presentation pointer. "All I want to know is how you would have two different Win95 applications communicate between themselves, using standard Windows messaging."

Specifying The Problem

"Yeah!" someone else shouted. Then, one by one, residents began to voice their requirements for a problem specification.

"What if you've got multiple instances of sender and receiver apps—how are you going to satisfy them all?" yelled a shriveled little man in the fourth row. "And how are you going to make sure any message you're broadcasting throughout the system won't trigger an unwanted side effect on some other application that happens to use the same message ID?"

"How about the ability to selectively send a message to a single form, all forms, or certain classes of forms with reception capability?" added the man in the first row with a bag over his head. He looked somehow familiar....

"Make it a component, make it a component!" shouted another man. One by one, every person in the audience began to pick up the chant. Pandemonium reigned for several minutes. I tried to get my bearings and come up with some sort of approach.

As luck would have it, several staff members came in, rolling carts loaded with take-out pepperoni pizza. Within two or three minutes, the entire room had quieted down once again, as the residents munched on the tasty fare. I was able to use those precious moments to create the diagram shown in Figure 17.1.

"Ladies and gentlemen," I began, as I projected my bitmap on the screen. "Here is one possible approach to the problem you've described. We could create two separate components, a sender component and a receiver component. Each of these components would share some common routines contained in a Dynamic Link Library (DLL). On creation, each receiver component would register itself with the DLL, which would maintain in shared memory an array of records. Each record would contain the handle values and class names of all active receivers, along with a boolean that indicates whether or not that record was occupied. A receiver would unregister itself with the DLL as part of the receiver's destructor routine."

I swept my eyes across the crowd, looking for major objections. Seeing none, I continued. "Sender components can have access to the handles of the receivers by querying the DLL. By calling routines included in the DLL, a sender can send a message selectively to any or all of the handles it gets from the query."

"Wait a second," came a voice from the back of the room. "You skipped over a very important point. You're talking about sending messages to a form in another process. How are you going to make sure the message IDs you're going to broadcast aren't used by some other process?"

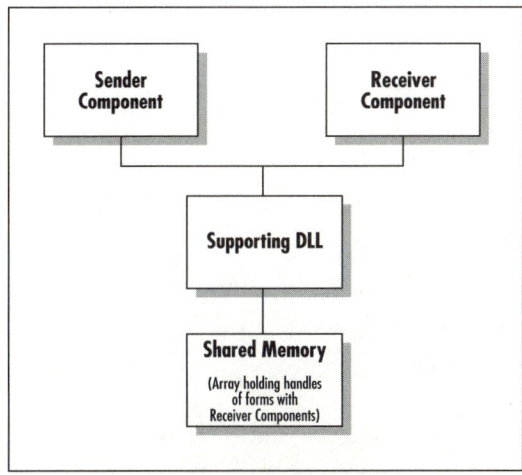

Figure 17.1
Relationship of entities comprising of Sender and Receiver components.

"By being unique," I replied. "Windows gives us an API call named **RegisterWindow Message**. This function accepts a string and returns a message ID that is guaranteed to be unique throughout the system. If a second application tries to register the same string, it is given the same unique message ID. This is how the sender and receiver components can share a unique message—by simply sharing a string that is made a property of each component."

"There's a serious flaw in your logic, Kid," said a totally bald-headed codger sitting in front of me. "You may have a unique message, all right. But you won't be able to create a handler for it, because you won't know the message ID until runtime."

I thought for a moment. *How am I going to handle this one?* Then it came to me.

"A radio wave," I said.

"What? Are you crazy?" shouted some curmudgeon in the third row.

"No, really. We can send out a message the way a transmitter sends a modulated signal to a receiver. The transmitter impresses a signal—information—onto a carrier wave of a designated frequency. Because the receiver is tuned to that same designated frequency and is constantly monitoring the incoming signal, it's able to pick off the information from the carrier wave, process it, and extract the information."

Dead silence. I looked out over the crowd. But all I could see was 249 eyes staring back at me.

"Thanks to a call to **RegisterWindowMessage**," I continued, "both the sender and receiver of our intended message will wind up with the same unique message ID—call it **FMessageID**. That's like the frequency of the carrier wave. The real message will be sent as a package inside the message with the unique ID—sort of a private message. The sender will transmit a message to the receiver with the standard **SendMessage** function, using the receiver form's handle and the unique "carrier" message ID. But the private message ID and any additional message information will be packed into **wParam** and **lParam**. It will look something like this." I typed in the function shown in Listing 17.1.

Listing 17.1   Prototype of a message transmission routine.

```
function TMsgSender.DoBroadcast(Handle : Integer;
                               wParam : Word;
                               iParam : Integer) : Integer;
```

```
begin
  Result := BroadcastIt(FMessageID, Handle, wParam, iParam);
end;
```

They looked skeptical, but they were still hanging in there. "On the receiver side, we declare as a property a generic event that can be called whenever the form containing the receiver detects the unique message ID. If we call the event **FOnIDMessage**, the routine might look something like this," I said, punching in the procedure shown in Listing 17.2.

Listing 17.2 Prototype of a message reception routine.

```
procedure TMsgReceiver.WndProc(var Msg : TMessage);
begin
  if Msg.Msg = FMessageID
    then begin
         if Assigned(FOnIDMessage)
           then Msg.Result := FOnIDMessage(Msg.wParam, Msg.lParam);
         end
    else Dispatch(Msg);
end;
```

"Hold on, Wizard Boy," came a voice from somewhere off to the left. "Now you've overstepped your bounds. You're presuming the receiver component has somehow taken over the message processing for the form's window. But you haven't subclassed the window."

"It will be part of the component's design for it to automatically subclass the form on which it resides," I explained. "But enough of this talk. Let's write some code so we can explore this whole concept."

I looked around the room. For the first time, they had all sat back in their chairs. I had their undivided attention. Now I just had to do the impossible: make them happy.

Designing The DLL

By far, the DLL would be the biggest challenge. It was also the centerpiece of the whole process, so it seemed like a logical place to start. With the residents shouting out their own ideas for what needed to be included in the DLL, we hammered out a rough version. I couldn't believe how quickly we came up with the final version of the code, shown in Listing 17.3.

Listing 17.3 DLL for sender/receiver component support.

```
{------------------------------------------------------------}
{         Message Broadcasting in 32-bit Delphi              }
{              BCASTDLL.DLL : Library File                   }
{               By Ace Breakpoint, N.T.P.                    }
{                 Assisted by Don Taylor                     }
{                                                            }
{ DLL that provides the underlying function of               }
{ managing a list of registered components in                }
{ shared memory.                                             }
{                                                            }
{ Written for *High Performance Delphi 3 Programming*        }
{ Copyright (c) 1997 The Coriolis Group, Inc.                }
{                 Last Updated 4/30/97                       }
{------------------------------------------------------------}

library BcastDll;

uses
  SysUtils,
  Classes,
  Windows;

type
 PMsgReceiverRec = ^MsgReceiverRec;
 MsgReceiverRec =
  record
    Assigned : Boolean;
    WndHandle : HWND;
    WndClassName : ShortString;
  end; { record }

const
 MaxReceivers = 100;
 ArraySize = MaxReceivers * SizeOf(MsgReceiverRec);
 MemFileName = 'msg_reg_array';
 SemaphoreName = 'msg_bcast_semaphore';

var
  ArrayHnd     : HWND;
  ArrayBasePtr : PMsgReceiverRec;
  SemaphoreHnd : HWND;
  DLLValid     : Boolean;
  SaveExit     : Pointer;
  LastErr      : Longint;
```

An Age-Old Problem

```
{ BcastDLLValid returns a Boolean that lets the caller know
  that the shared memory and semaphores are operational, so
  all of the other exported routines are valid. }
function BcastDLLValid : Boolean;
begin
 Result := DLLValid;
end;

{ RegisterReceiver adds the specified handle and class name
  to the array of receivers in shared memory. It returns the
  index (plus 1) of the new entry, or -1 if it couldn't be found. }
function RegisterReceiver(Hnd : THandle; CName : ShortString) : Integer;
var
 Idx : Integer;
 Found : Boolean;
 RecPtr : PMsgReceiverRec;
begin
 Idx := 0;
 Result := -1;
 RecPtr := ArrayBasePtr;
 WaitForSingleObject(SemaphoreHnd, INFINITE);

 { Find an unused slot }
 repeat
  Found := RecPtr^.Assigned = False;
  if not Found
   then begin
         Inc(Idx);
         Inc(RecPtr);
        end;
 until Found or (Idx >= MaxReceivers);

 if Found
  then begin { Put the record in the slot }
        FillChar(RecPtr^, 0, SizeOf(MsgReceiverRec));
        with RecPtr^ do
         begin
          Assigned := True;
          WndHandle := Hnd;
          WndClassName := CName;
         end; { with }
        Result := Idx + 1;
       end;

 ReleaseSemaphore(SemaphoreHnd, 1, nil);
end;
```

```pascal
{ UnregisterReceiver removes the record with the specified
  handle from the array. It returns the former index (plus 1)
  of the specified receiver, or -1 if it couldn't be found. }
function UnregisterReceiver(Hnd : THandle) : Integer;
var
 Idx : Integer;
 Found : Boolean;
 RecPtr : PMsgReceiverRec;
begin
 Idx := 0;
 Result := -1;
 RecPtr := ArrayBasePtr;
 WaitForSingleObject(SemaphoreHnd, INFINITE);

 { Locate the record }
 repeat
  Found := RecPtr^.Assigned and (RecPtr^.WndHandle = Hnd);
  if not Found
   then begin
         Inc(Idx);
         Inc(RecPtr);
        end;
 until Found or (Idx >= MaxReceivers);

 if Found
  then begin
        RecPtr^.Assigned := False;
        Result := Idx + 1;
       end;

 ReleaseSemaphore(SemaphoreHnd, 1, nil);
end;

{ BroadcastToClass uses SendMessage to broadcast the specified
  message to all registered components with the specified class.
  Returns as a result the value from the first message that
  returns a non-zero result. }
function BroadcastToClass(CName : ShortString;
                          MessageID : Word;
                          wParam : Word;
                          lParam : Longint) : Longint;
var
 Idx : Integer;
 RecPtr : PMsgReceiverRec;
```

```
begin
 Idx := 0;
 Result := 0;
 RecPtr := ArrayBasePtr;
 WaitForSingleObject(SemaphoreHnd, INFINITE);

 { Send the message to all matching entries }
 repeat
  if RecPtr^.Assigned and (RecPtr^.WndClassName = CName)
    then begin
         if Result = 0
           then Result := SendMessage(RecPtr^.WndHandle, MessageID,
                                     wParam, lParam)
           else SendMessage(RecPtr^.WndHandle, MessageID, wParam, lParam);
         end;

  Inc(Idx);
  Inc(RecPtr);
 until Idx >= MaxReceivers;
 ReleaseSemaphore(SemaphoreHnd, 1, nil);
end;

{ BroadcastToAll uses SendMessage to broadcast the specified
  message to all registered components. Returns as a result
  the value from the first message that returns a non-zero result. }
function BroadcastToAll(MessageID : Word;
                       wParam : Word;
                       lParam : Longint) : Longint;
var
 Idx : Integer;
 RecPtr : PMsgReceiverRec;
begin
 Idx := 0;
 Result := 0;
 RecPtr := ArrayBasePtr;
 WaitForSingleObject(SemaphoreHnd, INFINITE);

 repeat
  if RecPtr^.Assigned
    then begin
         if Result = 0
           then Result := SendMessage(RecPtr^.WndHandle, MessageID,
                                     wParam, lParam)
           else SendMessage(RecPtr^.WndHandle, MessageID, wParam, lParam);
         end;
```

```
    Inc(Idx);
    Inc(RecPtr);
   until Idx >= MaxReceivers;
  ReleaseSemaphore(SemaphoreHnd, 1, nil);
end;

{ BroadcastToOne uses SendMessage to broadcast the specified
  message to only one specified registered component. Returns as
  a result the value received from the component. }
function BroadcastToOne(MessageID : Word;
                       RcvNum : Integer;
                       wParam : Word;
                       lParam : Longint) : Longint;
var
 RecPtr : PMsgReceiverRec;
begin
 Result := 0;
 RecPtr := ArrayBasePtr;
 if (RcvNum > 0) and (RcvNum <= MaxReceivers)
   then begin
        WaitForSingleObject(SemaphoreHnd, INFINITE);

        Inc(RecPtr, RcvNum - 1);
        if RecPtr^.Assigned
          then Result := SendMessage(RecPtr^.WndHandle, MessageID, wParam,
                                     lParam);

        ReleaseSemaphore(SemaphoreHnd, 1, nil);
        end;
end;

{ NumClassMsgReceivers returns the quantity of registered
  receivers of the specified class. }
function NumClassMsgReceivers(CName : ShortString) : Integer;
var
 Idx : Integer;
 RecPtr : PMsgReceiverRec;
begin
 Idx := 0;
 Result := 0;
 RecPtr := ArrayBasePtr;
 WaitForSingleObject(SemaphoreHnd, INFINITE);

 repeat
   if RecPtr^.Assigned and (RecPtr^.WndClassName = CName) then
```

```
    Inc(Result);
     Inc(Idx);
     Inc(RecPtr);
   until Idx >= MaxReceivers;

   ReleaseSemaphore(SemaphoreHnd, 1, nil);
 end;

 { NumMsgReceivers returns the total quantity of registered
   receivers, regardless of class. }
 function NumMsgReceivers : Integer;
 var
  Idx : Integer;
  RecPtr : PMsgReceiverRec;
 begin
  Idx := 0;
  Result := 0;
  RecPtr := ArrayBasePtr;
  WaitForSingleObject(SemaphoreHnd, INFINITE);
  repeat
   if RecPtr^.Assigned then Inc(Result);
   Inc(Idx);
   Inc(RecPtr);
  until Idx >= MaxReceivers;
  ReleaseSemaphore(SemaphoreHnd, 1, nil);
 end;

 { First ReceiverAssigned returns the index + 1
   of the first registered receiver in the list.
   If the list is empty, -1 is returned. }
 function FirstReceiverAssigned : Integer;
 var
  Idx : Integer;
  Found : Boolean;
  RecPtr : PMsgReceiverRec;
 begin
  Idx := 0;
  RecPtr := ArrayBasePtr;
  WaitForSingleObject(SemaphoreHnd, INFINITE);

  repeat
   Found := RecPtr^.Assigned;
   if not Found
    then begin
          Inc(Idx);
          Inc(RecPtr);
         end;
```

```
    until Found or (Idx >= MaxReceivers);

  if Found
    then Result := Idx + 1
    else Result := -1;

  ReleaseSemaphore(SemaphoreHnd, 1, nil);
end;

{ NextReceiverAssigned returns the index number + 1
  of the next registered receiver in the list, following
  a specified "receiver number" (i.e., the starting
  index + 1). If there are no more receivers in the
  list, -1 is returned. }
function NextReceiverAssigned(RcvrNum : Integer) : Integer;
var
 Idx : Integer;
 Found : Boolean;
 RecPtr : PMsgReceiverRec;
begin
  if (RcvrNum >= 1) and (RcvrNum < MaxReceivers)
    then begin
         Idx := RcvrNum;
         RecPtr := ArrayBasePtr;
         Inc(RecPtr, Idx);
         WaitForSingleObject(SemaphoreHnd, INFINITE);

         repeat
          Found := RecPtr^.Assigned;
          if not Found
            then begin
                 Inc(Idx);
                 Inc(RecPtr);
                 end;
         until Found or (Idx >= MaxReceivers);

         if Found
           then Result := Idx + 1
           else Result := -1;
         ReleaseSemaphore(SemaphoreHnd, 1, nil);
         end
    else Result := -1;
end;
```

An Age-Old Problem

```pascal
{ Finalize unmaps and releases the shared memory, then
  releases the semaphore. If there is another instance of
  this DLL active at the moment, the memory and semaphore
  will not go away. When all other instances of the DLL
  have been closed, the OS will destroy the reserved
  memory and semaphore. }
procedure FinalizeLibrary;
begin
 UnmapViewOfFile(ArrayBasePtr);
 CloseHandle(ArrayHnd);
 CloseHandle(SemaphoreHnd);

 { Restore the exit chain }
 ExitProc := SaveExit;
end;

exports
 BcastDLLValid index 1,
 RegisterReceiver index 2,
 UnregisterReceiver index 3,
 BroadcastToClass index 4,
 BroadcastToAll index 5,
 BroadcastToOne index 6,
 NumClassMsgReceivers index 7,
 NumMsgReceivers index 8,
 FirstReceiverAssigned index 9,
 NextReceiverAssigned index 10;

begin
 { Library initialization code }

 DLLValid := False;


 {Attempt to create a memory-mapped file. If it already exists,
  that's fine. In either case we will get a valid handle. }
 ArrayHnd := CreateFileMapping(HWND($FFFFFFFF),
                               nil,
                               PAGE_READWRITE,
                               0,
                               ArraySize,
                               MemFileName);

 { If we failed, we're done. }
 if (ArrayHnd = 0) then Exit;
```

```
    { Map the file by getting a pointer to it }
    LastErr := GetLastError;
    ArrayBasePtr := MapViewOfFile(ArrayHnd, FILE_MAP_WRITE, 0, 0, 0);

    { If we didn't get a valid pointer, we're done. }
    if ArrayBasePtr = nil
     then begin
            CloseHandle(ArrayHnd);
            Exit;
          end;

    { If we actually created the mapped memory, clear it. }
    if LastErr <> ERROR_ALREADY_EXISTS
     then FillChar(ArrayBasePtr^, 0, ArraySize);

    { Create a semaphore to control access to the mapped memory. If
      the handle comes back zero, we failed for some reason. }
    SemaphoreHnd := CreateSemaphore(nil, 0, 1, SemaphoreName);
    LastErr := GetLastError;
    if (SemaphoreHnd = 0)
     then begin
            CloseHandle(ArrayHnd);
            UnmapViewOfFile(ArrayBasePtr);
            Exit;
          end;

    { Save then exit chain and insert the finalization routine. }
    SaveExit := ExitProc;
    ExitProc := @FinalizeLibrary;

    { If we created the semaphore, then force it to its "signaled" state. }
    if LastErr <> ERROR_ALREADY_EXISTS
     then ReleaseSemaphore(SemaphoreHnd, 1, nil);

    DLLValid := True;
end;
```

Startup Code

Perhaps the most interesting part of the DLL is what happens when it starts and ends. It was pointed out by several of the residents that each process which employs a sender or receiver component would undoubtedly load its own copy of the DLL, meaning there could be several DLL instances loaded and running simultaneously. To allow that, several things must be true:

- There must be only one (global) memory area containing the references to which form handles have been registered;
- All instances of the DLL must be capable of cooperatively managing the global memory area;
- There must be a mechanism for a DLL instance to create the shared memory area if there is none, and to destroy the memory area when there is no longer a need for it; and
- Only one DLL at a time can be allowed to change the contents of the memory.

As it turns out, this gnarly little problem was not as bad as it sounded. Win95 provides some good tools not only for creating shared memory, but for managing access to it as well.

The **CreateFileMapping** function returns a handle to a memory file object. If the object doesn't exist, it gets created, and a chunk of the system's paging file—in this case, a chunk of memory big enough to hold the data for 100 receivers—is reserved. The "file" is given a name to ensure it is exclusive to this DLL.

If the memory file already exists, the handle to it is returned, but an **ERROR _ALREADY_EXISTS** error value is generated. By testing for this value, an instance of the DLL can determine if it has created the memory file. If so, it is free to use **FillChar** to clear the entire area—once we know its location. (Since the memory file can be considered merely as a chunk of memory, that's how it will be treated from here on.)

The location of the memory is mapped to a pointer within the application through a call to **MapViewOfFile**, using the handle returned by **CreateFileMapping**. In this example, the value is assigned to **ArrayBasePtr**. The combination of calling **CreateFileMapping** and **MapViewOfFile** is a lot like making a call to **GetMem**.

Signals From A Semaphore

"Okay, Wunderkind," said the old guy wearing the shopping bag. "How are you gonna keep multiple instances of the DLL from clobbering the shared memory?

What if one instance adds something, and then another instance comes in right behind it and adds it again?"

"That's a fair question," I replied. "I think this situation calls for a semaphore."

Win95 provides several synchronization objects, ranging from the trivial to the complex—semaphores, events, and mutexes. But for restricting access to the memory in this situation, the clear choice would be a semaphore. This puppy would enable different processes to cooperatively use the memory through a signal-and-counter system. Like the call to **CreateFileMapping**, the call to **CreateSemaphore** either returns the handle to a newly created object (in this case a semaphore), or the handle to an existing object, while generating an **ERROR_ALREADY_EXISTS** error code. If a new instance of the DLL creates the semaphore, it is given the sole responsibility for setting the semaphore to its signaled state.

By "signaled," it means the semaphore's counter has a non-zero value. Each time a process executes a call to **WaitForSingleObject** using the semaphore's handle, the semaphore's counter is examined. If it is non-zero, the counter is decremented by one and the next program statement in the process is executed. If the counter is already zero, the process goes into an efficient time-wasting loop, waiting for the counter to change to a non-zero value (or a timeout value to be exceeded).

The code in this example permits only two values (0 and 1) for the semaphore counter, effectively turning it into an off/on switch. One of our design goals was that, as long as one instance of a DLL was accessing the shared memory—for any purpose—no other instance could gain access at the same time. Listing 17.4 is an example routine that shows how we could use a semaphore to achieve that goal.

Listing 17.4   Using a semaphore to control memory access.

```
procedure DoSomething;
begin
 WaitForSingleObject(SemaphoreHnd, INFINITE);
 DoSomeStuffWithTheMemory;
 ReleaseSemaphore(SemaphoreHnd, 1, nil);
end;
```

In this simple example, we first test the value of the semaphore. If another process is accessing the memory at the moment, the semaphore will be in its non-signaled state (0), and we will wait until forever (as specified by the **INFINITE** timeout constant), if necessary, for the semaphore to change to its signaled state (1).

Once the semaphore is signaled, its counter is automatically decremented by one (to zero), and our process goes ahead and **DoSomeStuffWithThe Memory** executes. While this is going on, any other process that examines the semaphore will find it unsignaled and (if the process has properly used a call to **WaitForSingleObject**) it will bide its time until we're through.

When we're all done with the memory, we place a call to **ReleaseSemaphore**, which will increment the semaphore's counter by the amount we specify. We use a value of one, in effect turning "on" the semaphore "switch."

Shutdown Code

If we make it all the way through the DLL startup code without error, we set a variable (**DLLValid**) to attest to our success. But if we have succeeded, several handles have been created that must be released when Win95 unloads the library.

This is taken care of by creating **FinalizeLibrary**, an exit routine that will be executed when the DLL is shut down. The procedure is inserted in the program's chain of events by saving the pointer to the normal exit routine (**ExitProc**) in the variable **SaveExit**, and then pointing **ExitProc** to **FinalizeLibrary**.

When the library is unloaded, **FinalizeLibrary** will execute. It will release the map view assigned to **ArrayBasePtr**, and then release the handles to the memory file object and the semaphore. Finally, it will restore the link to the standard exit procedure, so the program will terminate normally.

And what about the memory file object itself? Win95 automatically takes care of that for us. Like many of the system calls that create objects, Win95 associates a counter with the memory file object. Each time a **CreateFile Mapping** call is executed, the system increments a counter for the associated object. Whenever a handle to that object is released, the counter is decremented. When the count reaches zero, Win95 knows the object is no longer being used, so it destroys it. Last one out, turn out the lights.

Examining The DLL Routines

Most of the routines exported by the DLL busy themselves with stepping through the records in the memory array. Since we know the base address of the array, the size of a record, and the maximum number of records, we can easily tiptoe our way through the array using the pointer arithmetic provided by Object Pascal.

The **NumMsgReceivers** function provides a good example of this technique. A pointer of type **PMsgReceiverRec** is assigned to the base address. Each time a record is examined, the **Inc** procedure is used to advance the pointer by exactly the size of a **TMsgReceiverRec**. Tracking the process with an index variable prevents us from accessing memory outside the bounds of the memory block we have been allocated. The **NumMsgReceivers** function simply counts all the records that have their **Assigned** field set **True**.

The **Assigned** field is managed by two routines, **RegisterReceiver** and **Unregister Receiver**. **RegisterReceiver** looks for the first unused record and, after clearing it, stores the handle value and class name passed into **RegisterReceiver**. It also sets the record's **Assigned** field **True**. **UnregisterReceiver**, to no great surprise, does pretty much the opposite. It searches the fields with **Assigned** set **True**, looking for a handle value that matches the one specified. If the record is found, it sets the **Assigned** field **False**.

BroadcastToOne, **BroadcastToClass**, and **BroadcastToAll** use the **SendMessage** API function to transmit a message to the handle of a specific form, handles of all active forms of a given class name, or the handles of all active forms in the list. **BroadcastToOne** returns the value returned to it from the call to **SendMessage**; the other two return the first non-zero value returned by a call to **SendMessage**.

FirstReceiverAssigned and **NextReceiverAssigned** together provide a way for a user of the DLL to construct a list of all currently active record numbers in the array. It works a bit like the DOS **FindFirst** and **FindNext** routines. In this case, **FirstReceiverAssigned** returns an index to the first active form in the array. If that index value is then passed to **NextReceiverAssigned**, it will return an index to the next form, starting its search from the specified index. If no active form is found, these routines return a negative one.

Finally, **BcastDLLValid** returns a boolean that indicates whether or not the DLL was able to set up (or connect to) the required shared memory and the semaphore.

Creating The Sender Component

The residents were quietly buzzing among themselves. In a back corner, the murmuring broke out into shouting, as two nearly bald-headed programmers began arguing the various merits of their favorite programming languages at the tops of their lungs. The altercation soon turned to fisticuffs, and it took three staff members to pull the septuagenarians apart.

"Is it always like this around here?" I asked Dinah.

"No," she replied. "But yesterday one of the guests asked for a cup of java with creamer, and someone else thought he said the Java language was for dreamers, and clobbered the poor man alongside the head with his standard-issue wrist brace. That one took five stitches."

I examined the crowd more carefully. Sure enough, nearly everyone was wearing an identical brace.

She had apparently noticed my look of dismay. "Carpal Tunnel Syndrome," she sighed, with a look full of sorrow. "It gets even the best of them, sooner or later. Researchers are still looking for a cure."

I nodded in sympathy. The dispute now under control, I decided it would be an opportune time to segue back to developing the program.

With the DLL now under my belt, I was able to move to the next piece of the puzzle. I chose what I would call the MsgSender component. This component would, on command, take a snapshot of the list of registered form handles maintained by the DLL. The component would also be able to call selected DLL routines to broadcast messages and to determine the number of receiver components registered at any given time.

The MsgSender component, I reasoned, would need only one property: the unique message string that would be set to match a corresponding receiver component. The unique message ID, returned by using the message string in a call to **RegisterWindow Message**, would not be made available outside the component.

Listing 17.5 illustrates the final version of the code for the MsgSender component.

Listing 17.5 Code for the MsgSender component.

```
{----------------------------------------------------------------}
{           Message Broadcasting in 32-bit Delphi                }
{           MSGSENDR.PAS : MsgSender Component                   }
{                 By Ace Breakpoint, N.T.P.                      }
{                  Assisted by Don Taylor                        }
{                                                                }
{ This component registers a special system-wide                 }
{ message with Win95, and then is able to send                   }
{ system-wide messages to other forms in the                     }
{ system via MsgReceiver components.                             }
{                                                                }
{ Written for *High Performance Delphi 3 Programming*            }
{ Copyright (c) 1997 The Coriolis Group, Inc.                    }
{                 Last Updated 4/30/97                           }
{----------------------------------------------------------------}

unit MsgSendr;

interface

uses
  Windows, Messages, SysUtils, Classes, Graphics, Controls,
  Forms, Dialogs;

type
  TBcastDLLValid = function : Boolean;
  TRegisterReceiver = procedure(Hnd : THandle; CName : ShortString);
  TUnregisterReceiver = procedure(Hnd : THandle);
  TBroadcastToClass = function(CName : ShortString;
                               MessageID : Word;
                               wParam : Word;
                               lParam : Longint) : Longint;

  TBroadcastToAll = function(MessageID : Word;
                             wParam : Word;
                             lParam : Longint) : Longint;


  TBroadcastToOne = function(MessageID : Word;
                             RcvNum : Integer;
                             wParam : Word;
                             lParam : Longint) : Longint;
```

```
    TNumClassMsgReceivers = function(CName : ShortString) : Integer;
    TNumMsgReceivers = function : Integer;
    TFirstReceiverAssigned = function : Integer;
    TNextReceiverAssigned = function(RcvrNum : Integer) : Integer;

    TMsgSender = class(TComponent)
    private
      FIDString : ShortString;
      FMessageID : Word;
      LibraryHandle : THandle;
      DLLValid : Boolean;
      BcastDLLValid : TBcastDLLValid;
      BroadcastToClass : TBroadcastToClass;
      BroadcastToAll : TBroadcastToAll;
      BroadcastToOne : TBroadcastToOne;
      NumClassMsgReceivers : TNumClassMsgReceivers;
      NumMsgReceivers : TNumMsgReceivers;
      FirstReceiverAssigned : TFirstReceiverAssigned;
      NextReceiverAssigned : TNextReceiverAssigned;
      procedure SetIDStr(NewID : ShortString);
      procedure RegisterIDStr;

    public
      ReceiverList : TStringList; { Read only - do not modify! }
      constructor Create(AOwner : TComponent); override;
      destructor Destroy; override;
      function ClassBroadcast(CName : ShortString;
                              wParam : Word;
                              lParam : Longint) : Longint;

      function AllBroadcast(wParam : Word; lParam : Longint) : Longint;
      function OneBroadcast(RcvNum : Integer; wParam : Word; lParam :
                            LongInt) : Longint;
      function NumClassReceivers(CName : ShortString) : Integer;
      function NumReceivers : Integer;
      procedure UpdateReceiverList;

    published
      property IDString : ShortString read FIDString write SetIDStr;
    end;

procedure Register;

implementation

constructor TMsgSender.Create(AOwner : TComponent);
```

```
begin
 DLLValid := False;
 inherited Create(AOwner);
 FMessageID := 0;

 if not (csDesigning in ComponentState)
   then begin
        LibraryHandle := LoadLibrary('BCASTDLL.DLL');
        if LibraryHandle > HINSTANCE_ERROR
          then begin
              @BroadcastToClass := GetProcAddress(LibraryHandle,
                                           'BroadcastToClass');
              @BroadcastToAll := GetProcAddress(LibraryHandle,
                                           'BroadcastToAll');
              @BroadcastToOne := GetProcAddress(LibraryHandle,
                                           'BroadcastToOne');
              @NumClassMsgReceivers := GetProcAddress(LibraryHandle,
                                           'NumClassMsg
                                            Receivers');
              @NumMsgReceivers := GetProcAddress(LibraryHandle,
                                           'NumMsgReceivers');
              @FirstReceiverAssigned := GetProcAddress(LibraryHandle,
                                           'FirstReceiver
                                            Assigned');
              @NextReceiverAssigned := GetProcAddress(LibraryHandle,
                                           'NextReceiver
                                            Assigned');
              @BcastDLLValid := GetProcAddress(LibraryHandle,
                                           'BcastDLLValid');
              DLLValid := BcastDLLValid;
              RegisterIDStr;
            end
         else MessageDlg('Could not load DLL "BCASTDLL.DLL"', mtError,
                    [mbOK], 0);
      end;
 ReceiverList := TStringList.Create;
end;

destructor TMsgSender.Destroy;
begin
 ReceiverList.Free;
 if not (csDesigning in ComponentState)
   then if LibraryHandle > HINSTANCE_ERROR then
   FreeLibrary(LibraryHandle);
 inherited Destroy;
end;
```

```pascal
procedure TMsgSender.SetIDStr(NewID : ShortString);
begin
 if NewID <> FIDString
   then begin
          FIDString := NewID;
          RegisterIDStr;
        end;
end;

procedure TMsgSender.RegisterIDStr;
var
 IDStr : Array [0..255] of Char;
begin
 if not (csDesigning in ComponentState) and (Length(FIDString) > 0)
   then begin
          StrPCopy(IDStr, FIDString);
          FMessageID := RegisterWindowMessage(IDStr);
        end
   else FMessageID := 0;
end;

function TMsgSender.ClassBroadcast(CName : ShortString;
                                   wParam : Word;
                                   lParam : Longint) : Longint;
begin
 if DLLValid
   then Result := BroadcastToClass(CName, FMessageID, wParam, lParam)
   else Result := -1;
end;

function TMsgSender.AllBroadcast(wParam : Word; lParam : Longint) :
Longint;
begin
 if DLLValid
   then Result := BroadcastToAll(FMessageID, wParam, lParam)
   else Result := -1;
end;

function TMsgSender.OneBroadcast(RcvNum : Integer;
                                 wParam : Word;
                                 lParam : Longint) : Longint;
begin
 if DLLValid
   then Result := BroadcastToOne(FMessageID, RcvNum, wParam, lParam)
   else Result := -1;
end;
```

```
function TMsgSender.NumClassReceivers(CName : ShortString) : Integer;
begin
 if DLLValid
   then Result := NumClassMsgReceivers(CName)
   else Result := -1;
end;

function TMsgSender.NumReceivers : Integer;
begin
 if DLLValid
   then Result := NumMsgReceivers
   else Result := -1;
end;

procedure TMsgSender.UpdateReceiverList;
var
 RcvrNum : Integer;
begin
 ReceiverList.Clear;
 if DLLValid
   then begin
        RcvrNum := FirstReceiverAssigned;
        if RcvrNum > 0
          then begin
               ReceiverList.Add(IntToStr(RcvrNum));
               repeat
                RcvrNum := NextReceiverAssigned(RcvrNum);
                if RcvrNum > 0 then ReceiverList.Add(IntToStr(RcvrNum));
               until RcvrNum < 0;
               end;
        end;
end;

procedure Register;
begin
  RegisterComponents('Ace''s Stuff', [TMsgSender]);
end;

end.
```

For the most part, this component was a simple interface between the form that would own the component and routines in the DLL. **DLLValid** is a boolean, set to indicate the result of attempting to load the DLL. **DLLValid** is checked by methods that call DLL routines. The DLL itself is not loaded if Delphi is in the design state.

Broadcast functions were implemented using the corresponding DLL routines, returning a value of minus one if they failed. **UpdateReceiverList** uses the DLL's **FirstReceiverAssigned** and **NextReceiverAssigned** functions to prepare a fresh snapshot of the state of the registered receiver list. I decided to give the MsgSender's owner the sole responsibility for calling **UpdateReceiverList**.

For a finishing touch, I used Delphi's Image Editor to create a resource file containing a bitmap for the face of the component. Although the process was easy, it had to be done exactly right or it wouldn't work. So I'll document the process here.

After opening the Image Editor, I selected the New option from the File menu. From the choices, I selected "Component Resource File (.dcr)". I then selected the New option from the Resource menu, and selected "Bitmap". I specified a bitmap size of 24 by 24 pixels, and VGA (16-color) resolution.

Before creating the artwork itself, I saved the resource file with the still-blank bitmap. This is the most critical part of the process. First, I clicked on the default name given to the bitmap resource ("Bitmap1") and changed the name to "TMSGSENDER". Although the tradition is to use all caps, it isn't necessary. But the name must *exactly* match the type identifier given to the component. Next, I saved the file, with the name "MsgSendr.dcr". Once again, this is critical: The file name must exactly match the DCU file (which is the same as the PAS file) that contains the code for the component. Figure 17.2 shows the state of the Image Editor once I had saved the file. From that point, I was able to create my beautiful piece of artwork and save it.

Creating The Receiver Component

The pizza now entirely consumed, the natives once again became restless. I was about to suggest an intermission when I looked at my watch in horror: It still read 1:30! Absolutely no time had passed!

I made a mental note to get the watch to the local jeweler. When I glanced up, I saw that one of the residents had his hand up. *Finally*, I thought. *Decorum is about to break out.*

"Excuse me," the man said.

I nodded for him to proceed with his question.

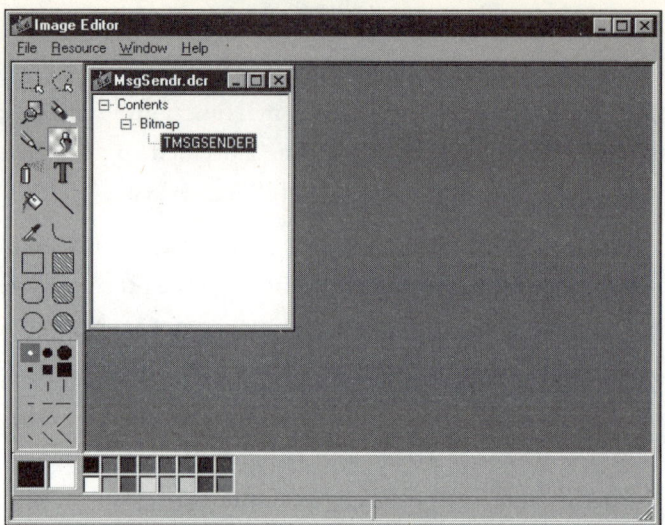

Figure 17.2
The Delphi Image Editor and the blank bitmap.

"Who are you? And what are you doing here?" he asked. He looked around at the other programmers and continued. "And where is Arnold? Isn't Arnold supposed to be here?"

A titter drifted through the audience, and some jerk in the third row holding a bucket of extra greasy chicken began to guffaw. Totally confused, I looked to Dinah for a clue.

"Who's Arnold?" I asked her.

"One of the guests," she replied. "An inveterate troublemaker. He's been put in detention for violating the Internet curfew," she said.

I pointed with my thumb to the man who had raised his hand. "And what about this guy?" I asked, trying hard not to move my mouth.

She didn't make a sound, but I could read her lips. "That's Bernie," she said. "*Error 1: out of memory.*"

Whoever said that truth was stranger than fiction certainly hadn't experienced this place. I sighed and began the task of creating the receiver component.

An Age-Old Problem

TMsgReceiver turned out to be more of a challenge than **TMsgSender**. I should have expected that, since I knew going in I would have to subclass the window of the component's owner.

The MsgReceiver component would have to perform only four basic tasks:

1. Register itself with the DLL when it's created, if the application is executing;
2. Register the unique message string with Windows to obtain the unique message ID;
3. Unregister itself with the DLL when the component is destroyed; and
4. Call a specified handler procedure when the component receives the unique message ID.

The final version of **TMsgReceiver**'s code is shown in Listing 17.6.

Listing 17.6 Code for the MsgReceiver component.

```
{─────────────────────────────────────────────────}
{         Message Broadcasting in 32-bit Delphi   }
{         MSGRCVR.PAS : MsgReceiver Component     }
{               By Ace Breakpoint, N.T.P.         }
{                Assisted by Don Taylor           }
{                                                 }
{ This component effectively subclasses the form  }
{ it is placed on, replacing the form's WndProc   }
{ and registering a special system-wide message   }
{ with Win95. Only one of these components is     }
{ allowed per form.                               }
{                                                 }
{ Written for *High Performance Delphi 3 Programming* }
{ Copyright (c) 1997 The Coriolis Group, Inc.     }
{                Last Updated 4/30/97             }
{─────────────────────────────────────────────────}

unit MsgRcvr;

interface

uses
  Windows, Messages, SysUtils, Classes, Graphics, Controls,
  Forms, Dialogs;
```

```
type
  EOwnerNotWinControl = class(Exception);
  EMultipleMsgReceivers = class(Exception);

  TBcastDLLValid = function : Boolean;
  TRegisterReceiver = function(Hnd : THandle; CName : ShortString) :
Integer;
  TUnregisterReceiver = function(Hnd : THandle) : Integer;

  TMsgReceiverEvent = function(wParam : Word; iParam : Integer) : Integer
    of object;

  TMsgReceiver = class(TComponent)
   private
    FIDString : ShortString;
    FMessageID : Word;
    FReceiverNum : Integer;
    LibraryHandle : THandle;
    DLLValid : Boolean;
    OriginalWndProc : TFarProc;
    NewWndProc : TFarProc;
    WndProcHooked : Boolean;
    OwnerHandle : THandle;
    BcastDLLValid : TBcastDLLValid;
    RegisterReceiver : TRegisterReceiver;
    UnregisterReceiver : TUnregisterReceiver;
    procedure SetIDStr(NewID : ShortString);
    procedure RegisterIDStr;

   protected
    FOnIDMessage : TMsgReceiverEvent;
    procedure WndProc(var Msg : TMessage); virtual;
    procedure DefaultHandler(var Msg); override;
    procedure HandleWMDestroy(var Msg : TWMDestroy); message WM_Destroy;

   public
    constructor Create(AOwner : TComponent); override;
    destructor Destroy; override;

   published
    property IDString : ShortString read FIDString write SetIDStr;
    property ReceiverNum : Integer read FReceiverNum;
    property OnIDMessage : TMsgReceiverEvent read FOnIDMessage write
FOnIDMessage;
  end;
```

```
        procedure Register;

implementation

constructor TMsgReceiver.Create(AOwner : TComponent);
var
 i : Integer;
begin
 DLLValid := False;
 FReceiverNum := -1;

 if not (AOwner is TWinControl)
   then raise EOwnerNotWinControl.Create('Owner must be TWinControl or
                                          descendant');

 for i := 0 to AOwner.ComponentCount - 1 do
   if AOwner.Components[i] is TMsgReceiver
     then raise EMultipleMsgReceivers.Create('Only one TMsgReceiver allowed
                                        per form');

 inherited Create(AOwner);
 OwnerHandle := (AOwner as TWinControl).Handle;
 NewWndProc := MakeObjectInstance(WndProc);
 FMessageID := 0;

 if not (csDesigning in ComponentState)
   then begin
         OriginalWndProc := TFarProc(GetWindowLong((AOwner as
                                   TWinControl).Handle,
             gwl_WndProc));
         SetWindowLong((AOwner as TWinControl).Handle, gwl_WndProc,
             Longint(NewWndProc));
         WndProcHooked := True;

         LibraryHandle := LoadLibrary('BCASTDLL.DLL');
         if LibraryHandle > HINSTANCE_ERROR
           then begin
             @RegisterReceiver := GetProcAddress(LibraryHandle,
                                            'RegisterReceiver');
             @UnregisterReceiver := GetProcAddress(LibraryHandle,
                                            'Unregister
                                             Receiver');
             @BcastDLLValid := GetProcAddress(LibraryHandle,
                                            'BcastDLLValid');
             DLLValid := BcastDLLValid;
             RegisterIDStr;
```

```
              end
           else MessageDlg('Could not load DLL "BCASTDLL.DLL"', mtError,
                      [mbOK], 0);
        end;

  if DLLValid then FReceiverNum := RegisterReceiver(OwnerHandle,
                                            AOwner.ClassName);
end;

destructor TMsgReceiver.Destroy;
begin
  if WndProcHooked
    then SetWindowLong((Owner as TWinControl).Handle, gwl_WndProc,
            Longint(OriginalWndProc));

  FreeObjectInstance(NewWndProc);
  if DLLValid then UnregisterReceiver(OwnerHandle);

  if not (csDesigning in ComponentState)
    then if LibraryHandle > HINSTANCE_ERROR then
    FreeLibrary(LibraryHandle);

  Inherited Destroy;
end;

procedure TMsgReceiver.HandleWMDestroy(var Msg : TWMDestroy);
begin
  SetWindowLong((Owner as TWinControl).Handle, gwl_WndProc,
Longint(OriginalWndProc));
  WndProcHooked := False;
end;

procedure TMsgReceiver.WndProc(var Msg : TMessage);
begin
  if Msg.Msg = FMessageID
    then begin
         if Assigned(FOnIDMessage)
           then Msg.Result := FOnIDMessage(Msg.wParam, Msg.lParam);
         end
    else Dispatch(Msg);
end;

procedure TMsgReceiver.DefaultHandler(var Msg);
begin
  with TMessage(Msg) do
```

```
      Result := CallWindowProc(OriginalWndProc, (Owner as
      TWinControl).Handle, Msg, wParam, lParam);
end;

procedure TMsgReceiver.SetIDStr(NewID : ShortString);
begin
 if NewID <> FIDString
   then begin
          FIDString := NewID;
          RegisterIDStr;
        end;
end;

procedure TMsgReceiver.RegisterIDStr;
var
 IDStr : Array [0..255] of Char;
begin
 if not (csDesigning in ComponentState) and (Length(FIDString) > 0)
   then begin
          StrPCopy(IDStr, FIDString);
          FMessageID := RegisterWindowMessage(IDStr);
        end
   else FMessageID := 0;
end;

procedure Register;
begin
 RegisterComponents('Ace''s Stuff', [TMsgReceiver]);
end;

end.
```

Subclassing The Owner Window

All Delphi objects (that is, those based on **TObject** and hence part of the VCL) have inherent messaging capability. Figure 17.3a shows the event processing chain for a **TObject**, with its built-in **Dispatch** and **DefaultHandler** routines.

The job of the **Dispatch** routine is to examine any event reaching it, first checking to see if the event's message ID matches those of any special event handlers. These special handlers are the ones added to the **TObject** descendent by the programmer, and are of the form:

```
procedure HandleMyEvent (var Msg : TMessage);
   message MyEventMessageID;
```

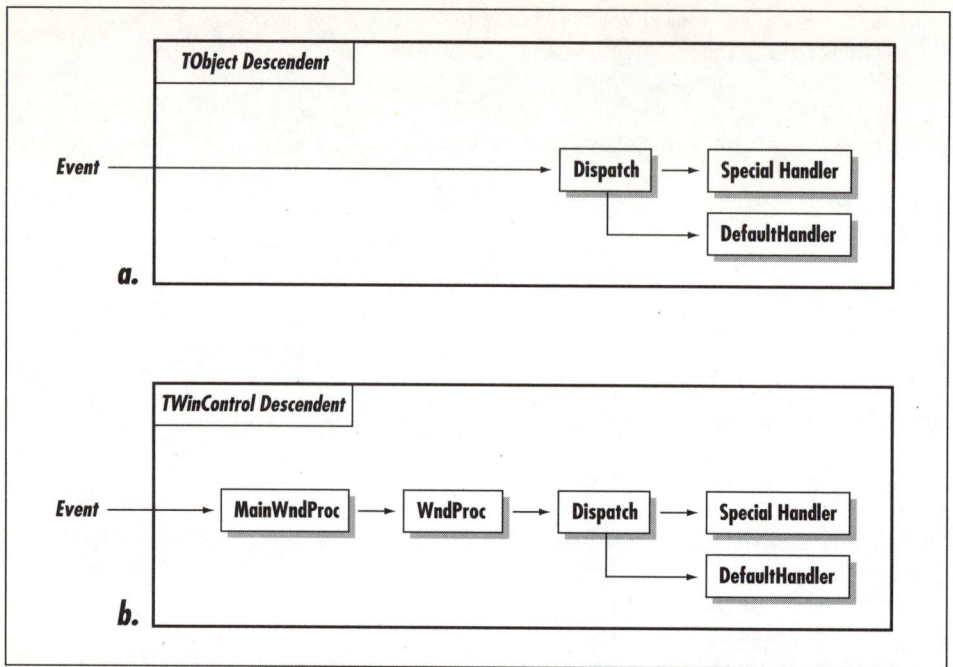

Figure 17.3 a and b
The event handling process for TObject and TWinControl types.

If a match is found, the special handler corresponding to the event's message ID is called. Otherwise, the built-in **DefaultHandler** routine gets called. Unless modified, the standard **DefaultHandler** does nothing.

Standard event processing for a **TWinControl** descendent is slightly more sophisticated, as can be seen in Figure 17.3b. This time there are two more methods involved, **MainWndProc** and **WndProc**. **MainWndProc** is the main window procedure for each type of component in an application. When a message is received by any **TWinControl** descendent, it is first checked by **MainWndProc** to see if the message relates to an exception. If not, the message is passed to the virtual method **WndProc**.

Classically, a window's **WndProc** routine is sort of "Message Central." It is within this routine that certain messages can be trapped or handled in a special way. The **WndProc** method for a **TWinControl** descendent, for example, passes keyboard events to **Dispatch** only if the component isn't being dragged.

An Age-Old Problem

Under normal circumstances, Delphi provides a great deal of flexibility for handling special events. The ability to create special handlers for any **TObject** descendent as described above is a simple and powerful technique, as long as you know the message IDs of the events you want to handle at compile time.

But what we want here cannot be done that simply, for two reasons. First, we won't know the message ID we're looking for until the program is executing and has called **RegisterWindowMessage**. And second, the component must receive the event first, before its owner form sees it. In other words, we must break into the message chain of the owner, handle anything corresponding to the special message ID, and then pass everything else back to the owner to process in the normal manner.

Figure 17.4 illustrates this process. Here we have broken the chain in the form, so **MainWndProc** passes events to a new **WndProc** method written for the MsgReceiver component. The MsgReceiver's **WndProc** is aware of the special message ID and the procedure assigned to handle that ID.

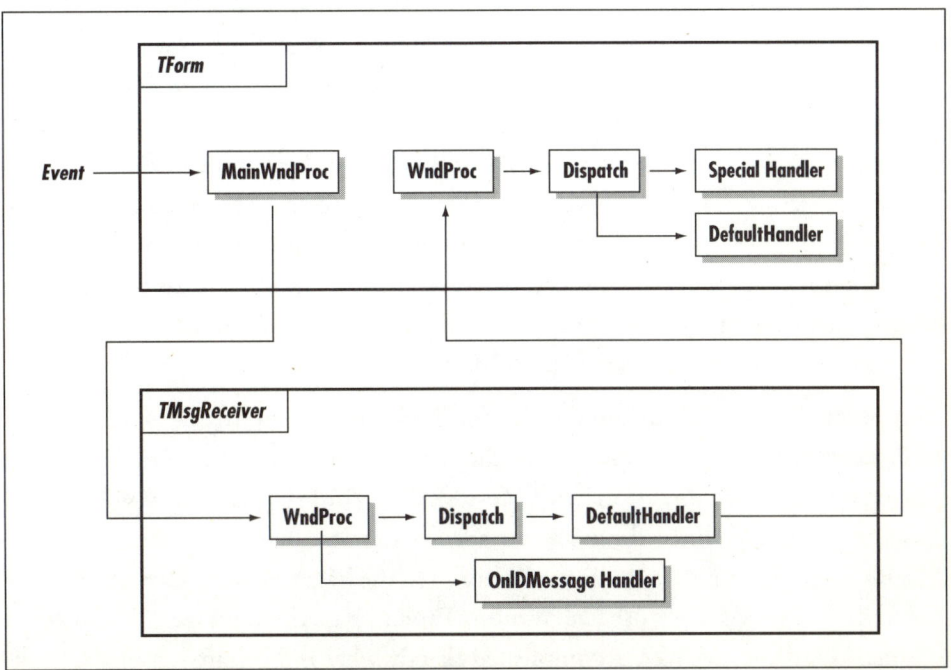

Figure 17.4
Subclassing the TForm's window with TMsgReceiver.

If the ID of the event matches the special message ID, the assigned **OnIDMessage** handler gets called. Otherwise, MsgReceiver's **Dispatch** method is called. Since there are no special handlers defined for MsgReceiver, the event is passed on to **DefaultHandler**. **DefaultHandler** has been modified to simply send the event back to the form's original **WndProc**, where processing resumes normally. That means any special event handlers written for the form will execute as if nothing had been changed.

This process of breaking into a window's message chain and inserting an additional **WndProc** is called *subclassing*. It's a standard technique used all the time in Windows programming. There is just less need for it when programming with Delphi.

In this example, the subclassing is performed dynamically in the MsgReceiver's constructor. The call to **MakeObjectInstance** creates **NewWndProc**, a pointer to a procedure of the form

```
procedure AWndProc(var Msg : TMessage),
```

which is a prototype for a method used to handle messages sent to window procedures. If the application is executing (i.e., not in design mode), three statements are then performed to complete the subclassing process. First, a pointer to the owner's original **WndProc** is stored in **OriginalWndProc**. Next, **SetWindowLong** is used to tell Windows that the MsgReceiver's **WndProc** (pointed to by **NewWndProc**) is the new place to send messages to the owner. Finally, a boolean (**WndProcHooked**) is set to indicate the subclassing process has succeeded. If the DLL loads correctly, the MsgReceiver's **RegisterIDStr** method will be called, which will in turn call **RegisterWindowMessage** and set the **FMessageID** field.

The MsgReceiver's **WndProc** checks the incoming event to see if it matches **FMessageID**. If so, it attempts to call the handler specified in the **OnIDMessage** property. If the event doesn't match **FMessageID**, **WndProc** calls the MsgReceiver's **Dispatch** method. Since there are no special message handlers defined for the MsgReceiver, the event is automatically passed to the MsgReceiver's **DefaultHandler** method, where we simply use **CallWindowProc** to pass the message to the owner's original **WndProc**. We have accomplished exactly what is illustrated in Figure 17.4.

What has all this gained us? We've set up a pre-processing system for the form containing the MsgReceiver. Instead of having to know exactly what we're looking for (the message ID) and what we're going to do when we get it (the handler) at compile time, we have shifted the whole decision-making process to execution time. (In fact, we could even dynamically switch both the message ID string and the procedure chosen to handle it at any time during the program's execution—a frightening concept.)

Other Interesting Stuff

Just as there is a way to subclass a window, there must be a way to restore the system when the program terminates. This feat is accomplished in a couple of places. If the component receives a **WM_Destroy** message, it must immediately restore the original messaging, before anything else takes place; otherwise, there will be no valid window by the time execution gets to the MsgReceiver's **Destroy** destructor—an ugly situation. The **Handle WMDestroy** method takes care of this, setting the **WndProcHooked** variable **False** to indicate that subclassing has already been eliminated.

The **Destroy** destructor accomplishes the same task, assuming subclassing is still in place when it is called. Once subclassing has been eliminated, the destructor can safely free the object instance for **NewWndProc**. Before calling the inherited destructor, though, the component is unregistered and the DLL is unloaded.

Two other interesting things happen within MsgReceiver's **OnCreate** handler. First, before creating the component we must make sure the potential owner is a qualified, card-carrying member of the **TWinControl** family. If it isn't, we won't have a **MainWndProc** or **WndProc** to work with, and the results won't be pretty. If the owner is not a **TWinControl** or descendent, an exception is raised before the inherited **Create** constructor can be called.

Second, we only want to allow one MsgReceiver component per form. Can you imagine keeping track of *several levels* of subclassing? Only if you're a masochist. After the **TWinControl** test, a check is made for prior instances of a **TMsgReceiver** type in the owner's list of components. If one is found, an exception is raised, and we're outta here!

One last thing: MsgReceiver contains a read-only property called **Receiver Num**, the value returned when the component is registered with the DLL.

CHAPTER 17

Using the same overall procedure as I had used for the MsgSender, I created a bitmap for the **TMsgReceiver** object. Done at last—well, almost.

Creating A Receiver Demo

"You're really doing well," Dinah said. "I haven't seen our guests this interested in a long time. Even Mr. Bohacker wasn't able to command such attention."

I suppose I needed the encouragement. But I realized that this time I *really was* doing well. I couldn't believe how well the code was coming together. And to be able to pull this off under such extreme pressure made it all the sweeter.

And I really was commanding respect. Most of the programmers were intently watching my every move, hanging on every syllable leaving my mouth. Of course, there were a few exceptions. Probably 20 or 25 old fogies were napping at any given time. The three women sitting in the last row who I thought were knitting were actually surfing the Web through a wireless link to their laptop PCs. But there was one guy that *really* bugged me.

"Psssst. Pssssssst." I leaned away from the microphone, attempting to attract Dinah's attention. She finally looked up from the copy of *Weekly World News* she was perusing.

"What's with the guy in the leftmost seat in the front row?" I whispered. "He's been sitting there this whole time, just staring off into space. I haven't even seen him blink."

"That's Herbie," she whispered back. "He's a little, uh, you know.... We just say he's in permanent screen saver mode."

I pulled the candy bar out of my pocket and tore off the wrapper. I still had two applications to write, and I was in need of some extra energy. I bit off the end of the bar and nearly gagged. The Foo Bar was the candy confection universally chosen by programmers worldwide. Its delicate balance of fat calories, sugar, and caffeine made it the perfect productivity snack food. Today I had grabbed a Foo Bar++ from the machine, thinking it would have even more of the ingredients my body needed to make it through this endless afternoon. It wasn't until I had snarfed a big bite that I realized the ingredient that had been added for extra throughput was pulverized dried prunes. I took a gulp of water from the glass perched on the lectern and then shoved the remainder of the bar back in my pocket.

With the component design complete, I needed to create a demo application for each component—two programs that would highlight most of the features of the components.

From the several suggestions pitched at me by the audience, I chose a scenario where a sender application would send predetermined codes to a receiver, causing it to set a series of indicators. We decided to emulate those little lights on some automobile odometers that indicate when you should change your oil or filter, or rotate your tires. The receiver demo app would illuminate red or green indicators to indicate the condition, as transmitted by a sender app. In fact, we could have multiple instances of both sender and receiver apps if we wished; the methods we had chosen for communication should support that concept.

I decided to write the receiver demo first, because it seemed the easier of the two. In fact, it was pretty simple. The first thing was to come up with a set of command constants to use for private message IDs that could be used by both sender and receiver applications. By placing those constants in a single unit, they could be shared by the applications, eliminating a potential source of errors. The resulting unit is shown in Listing 17.7.

Listing 17.7 Constants for the Sender and Receiver demo applications.

```
{-------------------------------------------------------------}
{          Message Broadcasting in 32-bit Delphi              }
{             CONSTANT.PAS : Constants Unit                   }
{                By Ace Breakpoint, N.T.P.                    }
{                  Assisted by Don Taylor                     }
{                                                             }
{ Constants for use by the Sender and Receiver                }
{ applications.                                               }
{                                                             }
{ Written for *High Performance Delphi 3 Programming*         }
{ Copyright (c) 1997 The Coriolis Group, Inc.                 }
{               Last Updated 4/30/97                          }
{-------------------------------------------------------------}
```

Chapter 17

```
unit Constant;
interface

const
  { Command codes }
  mdSetAll = 100;
  mdSetChangeOil = 101;
  mdSetChangeFilter = 102;
  mdSetRotateTires = 103;

  mdResetAll = 200;
  mdResetChangeOil = 201;
  mdResetChangeFilter = 202;
  mdResetRotateTires = 203;

  { Status codes }
  mdNoReply = 0;
  mdReady = 1;
  mdSuccess = 2;
  mdRcvChange = 3;

implementation

end.
```

Creating the Receiver demo was a breeze. A picture of the design version, next to the Object Inspector, is shown in Figure 17.5. The code is shown in Listing 17.8.

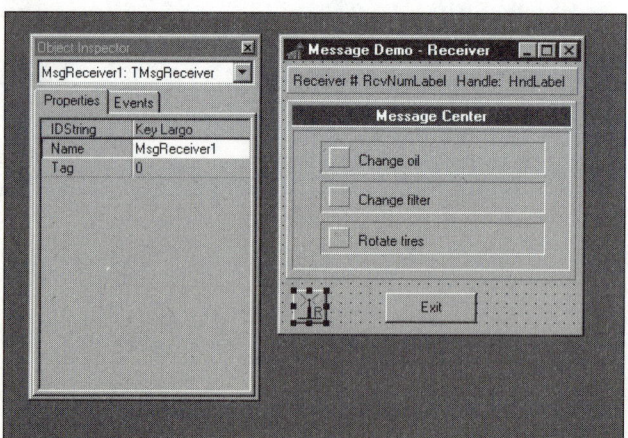

Figure 17.5
The Receiver demo at design time.

Listing 17.8 Code for the Receiver demo.

```
{─────────────────────────────────────────}
{         Message Broadcasting in 32-bit Delphi         }
{         RECVMAIN.PAS : Receiver Main Form             }
{              By Ace Breakpoint, N.T.P.                }
{                Assisted by Don Taylor                 }
{                                                       }
{ This demo application receives commands from          }
{ the Sender application, through the use of the        }
{ MsgSender and MsgReceiver components.                 }
{                                                       }
{ Written for *High Performance Delphi 3 Programming*   }
{ Copyright (c) 1997 The Coriolis Group, Inc.           }
{             Last Updated 4/30/97                      }
{─────────────────────────────────────────}

unit RecvMain;

interface

uses
  Windows, Messages, SysUtils, Classes, Graphics, Controls, Forms,
  Dialogs, StdCtrls, ExtCtrls, MsgRcvr, Constant;

type
  TReceiverForm = class(TForm)
    ExitBtn: TButton;
    Panel2: TPanel;
    HndLabel: TLabel;
    Label2: TLabel;
    RcvNumLabel: TLabel;
    Label1: TLabel;
    Panel1: TPanel;
    Panel3: TPanel;
    Bevel1: TBevel;
    Label3: TLabel;
    Label4: TLabel;
    Label5: TLabel;
    Bevel2: TBevel;
    ChangeOilInd: TPanel;
    Bevel3: TBevel;
    ChangeFiltInd: TPanel;
    Bevel4: TBevel;
    RotateInd: TPanel;
    MsgReceiver1: TMsgReceiver;
    procedure ExitBtnClick(Sender: TObject);
```

```
    procedure FormCreate(Sender: TObject);
    function MsgReceiver1IDMessage(wParam: Word; iParam: Integer):
Integer;
  private
    { Private declarations }
  public
    { Public declarations }
  end;

var
  ReceiverForm: TReceiverForm;

implementation

{$R *.DFM}

procedure TReceiverForm.ExitBtnClick(Sender: TObject);
begin
 Close;
end;

procedure TReceiverForm.FormCreate(Sender: TObject);
begin
 HndLabel.Caption := IntToStr(Self.Handle);
 RcvNumLabel.Caption := IntToStr(MsgReceiver1.ReceiverNum);
 ChangeOilInd.Color := clYellow;
 ChangeFiltInd.Color := clYellow;
 RotateInd.Color := clYellow;
end;

function TReceiverForm.MsgReceiver1IDMessage(wParam: Word;
  iParam: Integer): Integer;
begin
 case wParam of
  mdSetChangeOil : ChangeOilInd.Color := clRed;
  mdSetChangeFilter : ChangeFiltInd.Color := clRed;
  mdSetRotateTires : RotateInd.Color := clRed;
  mdResetChangeOil : ChangeOilInd.Color := clLime;
  mdResetChangeFilter : ChangeFiltInd.Color := clLime;
  mdResetRotateTires : RotateInd.Color := clLime;
 end; { case }

 Result := mdSuccess;
end;

end.
```

The centerpiece of the Receiver demo is the **MsgReceiverIDMessage** method. This is the handler specified in the **OnIDMessage** property of the MsgReceiver component. **MsgReceiverIDMessage** tests the **wParam** portion of the message to set the colors of the three indicators. It then returns a message result of **mdSuccess**, which will be returned to the MsgSender component issuing the command.

I could have simply defined a string constant for the **IDString** property of the MsgSender and MsgReceiver components in my Constants unit, and then assigned the string to the properties of each of the components at runtime. I guess after all this mysterious mumbo-jumbo, I was overcome by a fit of conformity to the standard way of doing things.

To demonstrate the ability of a MsgReceiver to get the index number assigned by the DLL, I displayed **ReceiverNum** in the top panel of the Receiver form. I also displayed the form's handle value, the same value that would be registered by the DLL.

Creating A Sender Demo

"That receiver demo-thingy isn't such a big deal," said the old man with the bucket of chicken, as he took a big bite out of a thigh. "I could do just as well—even on one of my 'bad' days."

"Me, too," said the bald and toothless old geezer sitting next to him, as he wiped off the grease running down his friend's chin with a paper towel.

"Any of us could, in the Old Days," someone agreed.

"Yeah, we didn't have it so easy back then," came another voice. "Didn't have all these new-fangled development tools. Had to walk 10 miles to school in the snow. And the only debugger we had was a can of Raid."

"You think that's bad?" someone else chimed in. "We had to walk 50 feet across ice-cold linoleum, just to get from our cubicles to the vending machines. And we had to write everything in assembly code."

I looked around the room. It was getting more tense by the moment.

"You're all a bunch of dweebs," said a heavy-set man in the fifth row, as he stood up and addressed the crowd. "You all go around humming the background tunes from Doom episodes. Where I was working, we didn't even have assemblers. We had to write everything with ones and zeros. There were times we ran out of ones, and we had to make do."

CHAPTER 17

The scene probably would have turned into a full-scale riot, except for a fortuitous event. Suddenly, the door at the back of the room flew open and hit the wall so hard it sounded like a small explosion. Everyone instantly stopped arguing and turned to the door to see who had made the noise, and as they did I could hear several people suck in their breath. Framed in the doorway was a tall, slender man with a grizzled face and a toothpick protruding from between his lips. His full-length coveralls were sky-blue, an insignia adorning the left breast pocket, and he wore a leather belt with a spray bottle hanging low from each side. In his right hand he held a rubber squeegee.

"All right. Where is he?" he growled, the toothpick following every delicate movement of his lower lip. He stood there for several seconds, pounding the business end of the squeegee against the palm of his other hand. "Anybody seen Eddie today?" he snarled. His tiny eyes oscillated left and right as he examined each of the wrinkled faces, but he received no response. He grunted something indiscernible, and then turned on his heel and ambled back down the hallway.

I shot Dinah a questioning glance, and she responded without my having to ask.

"That was Brad, Chief of Janitors," she explained. "He's looking for Eddie Rivers, one of our, well, problem guests."

"A man with a problem? Doesn't sound at all unusual. Everybody here seems to have some problem or another."

"Not Eddie. His is a *recurring* problem. *Error 212: stream registration error.* It happened three times, yesterday alone."

I turned to face the audience. The crowd had once again quieted down, and it was now time for the final piece of this whole puzzle—a demo that would transmit commands to the Receiver demo. But I wanted the Sender demo to be much more. After all, I was up against Bohacker again, and my reputation was on the line. I had to perform Big Time.

I decided to pop a timer on the form, to force a periodic query of what the DLL had registered. By monitoring that information, I could pull off some pretty cute stuff. A snapshot of the design version of the form is shown in Figure 17.6. The final version of the code is detailed in Listing 17.9.

An Age-Old Problem

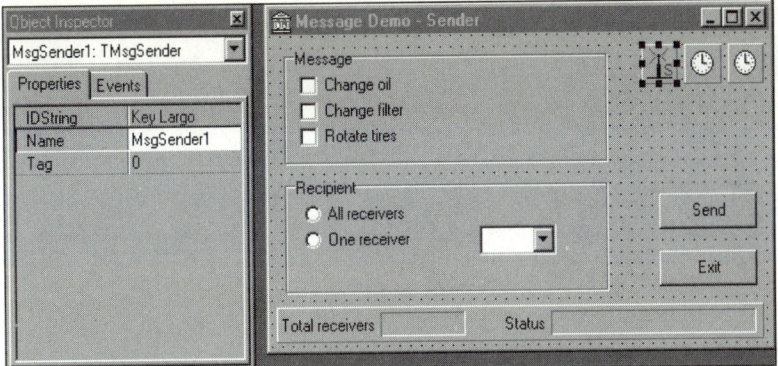

Figure 17.6
The Sender demo at design time.

Listing 17.9   Code for the Sender demo.

```
{——————————————————————————}
{         Message Broadcasting in 32-bit Delphi       }
{            SENDMAIN.PAS : Sender Main Form          }
{               By Ace Breakpoint, N.T.P.             }
{                Assisted by Don Taylor               }
{                                                     }
{ This demo application sends commands to the         }
{ Receiver application, through the use of the        }
{ MsgSender and MsgReceiver components.               }
{                                                     }
{ Written for *High Performance Delphi 3 Programming* }
{ Copyright (c) 1997 The Coriolis Group, Inc.         }
{              Last Updated 4/30/97                   }
{——————————————————————————}

unit SendMain;

interface

uses
  Windows, Messages, SysUtils, Classes, Graphics, Controls, Forms,
Dialogs, tdCtrls, MsgSendr, ExtCtrls, Constant;

type
  TSenderMainForm = class(TForm)
    SendBtn: TButton;
    ExitBtn: TButton;
```

```pascal
    MsgSender1: TMsgSender;
    RefreshTimer: TTimer;
    RecipientGroup: TGroupBox;
    AllRB: TRadioButton;
    OneRB: TRadioButton;
    OneCombo: TComboBox;
    Panel1: TPanel;
    Label1: TLabel;
    NumRcvrsLabel: TLabel;
    Bevel1: TBevel;
    Bevel2: TBevel;
    Label2: TLabel;
    StatusLabel: TLabel;
    StatusTimer: TTimer;
    MsgGroup: TGroupBox;
    ChangeOilCB: TCheckBox;
    ChangeFiltCB: TCheckBox;
    RotateCB: TCheckBox;
    procedure ExitBtnClick(Sender: TObject);
    procedure FormCreate(Sender: TObject);
    procedure RefreshTimerTimer(Sender: TObject);
    procedure StatusTimerTimer(Sender: TObject);
    procedure SendBtnClick(Sender: TObject);
    procedure AllRBClick(Sender: TObject);
    procedure OneRBClick(Sender: TObject);
  private
    NumReceivers : Integer;
    procedure RefreshRecipientGroup;
    procedure ShowStatus(MsgNum : Integer);
  public
    { Public declarations }
  end;

var
  SenderMainForm: TSenderMainForm;

implementation

{$R *.DFM}

procedure TSenderMainForm.RefreshRecipientGroup;
var
 CurrReceivers : Integer;
 i : Integer;
```

```
begin
 CurrReceivers := MsgSender1.NumReceivers;
 if NumReceivers <> CurrReceivers
  then begin
        NumReceivers := CurrReceivers;
        NumRcvrsLabel.Caption := IntToStr(NumReceivers);
        if NumReceivers > 0
         then begin
               OneRB.Enabled := True;
               OneCombo.Items.Clear;
               MsgSender1.UpdateReceiverList;
               for i := 0 to MsgSender1.ReceiverList.Count - 1 do
                 OneCombo.Items.Add(MsgSender1.ReceiverList[i]);
               OneCombo.ItemIndex := 0;
               OneCombo.Enabled := OneRB.Checked;
              end
          else begin
               AllRB.Checked := True;
               OneRB.Enabled := False;
               OneCombo.Text := '';
               OneCombo.Enabled := False;
              end;
         ShowStatus(mdRcvChange);
       end;

end;

procedure TSenderMainForm.ShowStatus(MsgNum : Integer);
var
 Msg : ShortString;
begin
 case MsgNum of
  mdReady : Msg := 'Ready';
  mdSuccess : Msg := 'Complete';
  mdNoReply : Msg := 'No reply';
  mdRcvChange : Msg := 'Number of receivers changed';
 else
  Msg := 'Unknown status response';
 end; { case }
 StatusLabel.Caption := Msg;
 StatusTimer.Enabled := True;
end;

procedure TSenderMainForm.ExitBtnClick(Sender: TObject);
begin
 Close;
end;
```

```
procedure TSenderMainForm.FormCreate(Sender: TObject);
begin
 NumRcvrsLabel.Caption := IntToStr(MsgSender1.NumReceivers);
 AllRB.Checked := True;
 OneRB.Enabled := False;
 OneCombo.Enabled := False;
 ShowStatus(mdReady);
end;

procedure TSenderMainForm.RefreshTimerTimer(Sender: TObject);
begin
 RefreshRecipientGroup;
end;

procedure TSenderMainForm.StatusTimerTimer(Sender: TObject);
begin
 StatusTimer.Enabled := False;
 StatusLabel.Caption := '';
end;

procedure TSenderMainForm.SendBtnClick(Sender: TObject);
var
 Status : Integer;
 RcvrNum : Integer;
begin
 with MsgSender1 do
 if AllRB.Checked
  then begin
       if ChangeOilCB.Checked
         then AllBroadcast(mdSetChangeOil, 0)
         else AllBroadcast(mdResetChangeOil, 0);

       if ChangeFiltCB.Checked
         then AllBroadcast(mdSetChangeFilter, 0)
         else AllBroadcast(mdResetChangeFilter, 0);

       if RotateCB.Checked
         then Status := AllBroadcast(mdSetRotateTires, 0)
         else Status := AllBroadcast(mdResetRotateTires, 0);

       ShowStatus(Status);
      end
  else begin
       RcvrNum := StrToInt(OneCombo.Items[OneCombo.ItemIndex]);
       if ChangeOilCB.Checked
```

```
          then OneBroadcast(RcvrNum, mdSetChangeOil, 0)
          else OneBroadcast(RcvrNum, mdResetChangeOil, 0);

      if ChangeFiltCB.Checked
        then OneBroadcast(RcvrNum, mdSetChangeFilter, 0)
        else OneBroadcast(RcvrNum, mdResetChangeFilter, 0);

      if RotateCB.Checked
        then Status := OneBroadcast(RcvrNum, mdSetRotateTires, 0)
        else Status := OneBroadcast(RcvrNum, mdResetRotateTires, 0);

      ShowStatus(Status);
    end;

  ChangeOilCB.Checked := False;
  ChangeFiltCB.Checked := False;
  RotateCB.Checked := False;
end;

procedure TSenderMainForm.AllRBClick(Sender: TObject);
begin
  OneCombo.Enabled := False;
end;

procedure TSenderMainForm.OneRBClick(Sender: TObject);
begin
  OneCombo.Enabled := True;
end;

end.
```

Each time **RefreshTimer** fires, it calls the **RefreshRecipientGroup** method. **RefreshRecipientGroup** determines whether the number of registered receivers has changed since the last inquiry. If so, a status indicator is updated. If there is at least one receiver, the list of items in the combo box is updated with the indexes of the receivers. If there are no receivers registered, the combo box is disabled.

The Send button's OnClick handler is the busiest routine on this form. If commands are to be sent to all registered receivers, **SendBtnClick** simply composes three messages using commands from the Constants unit—one message for each check box—and uses the MsgSender's **AllBroadcast** method to send the messages on their way. If the commands are to be sent to a single receiver, **SendBtnClick** composes the messages, but sends them via the **OneBroadcast** method, computing the receiver's index number from the combo box's item index.

A **ShowStatus** method is provided to display the results of some of the operations, including a change in the number of receivers, and the response to a transmitted command. **StatusTimer** automatically blanks the status display after three seconds.

I fired off the Sender app, then brought up the Receiver app. They worked famously, as shown in Figure 17.7. At the urging of the crowd, I brought up more instances. At one point, I had two Senders and four Receivers on the screen, all working perfectly. Using the "One receiver" radio button and combo box, I could selectively send commands to any individual receiver.

A Rude Awakening

I had met the challenge of the day, and although it had been the longest afternoon of my life, I had performed well. I felt good.

"And in conclusion," I said to the assembled masses, "there isn't any problem that a combination of persistence and determination can't overcome. Thank you, ladies and gentlemen, for being here. You've been a wonderful audience."

I stood back from the microphone, ready to accept the inevitable applause. I had no idea what was about to happen.

"Sounds like 'Spam' to me," shouted the greaseball with the chicken in his lap.

"Yea—let's flame him!" yelled his toothless companion with the billiard-ball head.

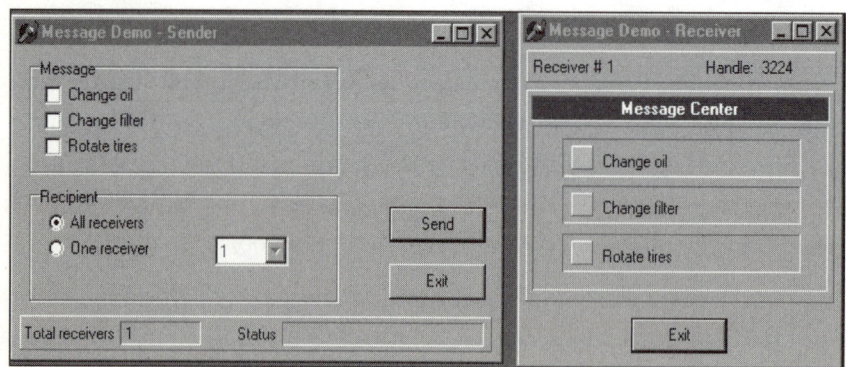

Figure 17.7
Sender and Receiver at runtime.

An Age-Old Problem

It was a matter of unfortunate timing that brought four staff members into the room at that moment, prepared to distribute the golden, finger-like sponge cakes bursting with creme filling intended for the residents' mid-afternoon snack. An instant later those palatable pastries had turned into weapons of wrath, filling the air, hundreds of them pelting my person.

Out of the corner of my eye, I saw the toothless old geezer heading in my direction, climbing up onto the stage, making his way right up to me, and finally, shoving his wrinkled face so close to mine that our noses touched. Whoever said that bad breath is better than no breath at all was overly optimistic. This guy was, for me, the ultimate argument against growing old.

"Whaddya want with me?" I asked him.

"I just want you to know what it's gonna be like for you, if you don't take better care of yourself," he said, looking me straight in the eye. "Count on it."

I stared back at his weak brown eyes through lenses as thick as soda bottles. There was something very familiar about those eyes. Then it struck me.

"You're...me!" I shouted.

"In yer dreams, Bud," he replied. Then he began to laugh....

My eyes snapped open and I sat bolt upright. Beads of sweat poured down my face as I fought to gain my bearings. I realized I had fallen asleep and had never left my office. I was still sitting in the recliner, the half-full pizza box sitting on my lap. I got up, wiping my forehead on my sleeve. I rushed to the sink and doused my face with cold water.

Whew! I hate dream sequences, I thought. But it was no use. I was just a two-bit character in an expensive technical book, and I knew it.

I grabbed a bottle of Purely Poulsbo from the fridge and started to contemplate what had happened. Maybe Helen had been right after all. Perhaps I should take better care of myself. Balanced meals. Vitamin supplements. More exercise. I picked up the pizza box and tossed it in the trash bin. I could do better.

This time out, The Author had given me a glimpse at one possible scenario. If that scenario was intended to be someone's future, I didn't want it to be mine.

Chapter 17

I guess time and cotton briefs are a lot alike—they can slowly creep up on you, and if you don't do anything about it, you can eventually find yourself in a really tight situation.

If I could just keep that concept firmly in mind, tomorrow would be a brighter day.

Index

32-bit console applications
    API functions, 8
    defined, 3
    hello world example, 5
    uses statement, 6
3D fractal landscape
    applying randomness, 287
    bending, 273, 287
    filled mode, 300
    FL3, 280, 288, 301
    fractal defined, 273
    generating a landscape, 273
    outline mode, 302
    rendered mode, 303

A

ActiveX. *See* OLE.
Add method, 119
Address space, Windows
    access, 3
API, 462
Application program interface. *See* API.
Applications
    common technique for communicating between, 553
    limiting itself to one instance in the system, 553
Applications, console
    and writing filter programs, 9
    definition, 3
    no extender software required, 4
    steps required to build, 7
Arbitrary nesting, 435
Asynchronous file transfer
    and CsShopper, 236
Asynchronous mode, 193, 194, 202

Asynchronous operations
    problems with canceling, 192
Asynchronous process
    understanding, 185

B

BDE, 462
BeginDrag method, 355, 454
Bitmaps
    using soon after creating, 326
Blocking
    definition, 178
Blocking mode, 202
Borland Database Engine. *See* BDE.
Borland's MAKE program, 13

C

Calendar component
    relating a position to a date, 454
CD-ROM
    fractal landscapes 3, 304
    KEEPER32, 245
    ORPHEUS, 455
    PolyProject, 385
    Starter.Dpr, 397
Celko, Joe, 435
Circular reference, 434
Clipboard stream, 331
Clone method, 114
Code
    importance of keeping in separate units, 23
    where to write, 6
Columns, 419
COM
    definition, 97
Command-line options
    kinds, 13

Index

Command-line parser
    developing a generalized, 14
Command-line parsing functions
    test program, 21
Compiler directive, 6
Compile-time dynamic linking
    and error recovery, 47
Component Object Model. *See* COM.
Component templates, 344
Component, "splash screen"
    creating, 494
Components
    defining tasks, 375
    problems testing, 496
    rearranging on the form, 491
    saving properties, 412
Components, compound, 344
Compound component, 344
Connections
    transient vs. persistent, 269
Console applications
    and writing filter programs, 9
    definition, 3
    no extender software required, 4
    steps required to build, 7
Console-specific functions, 8
Control
    determining behavior, 336
Control classes
    raising exception when trying to change fonts, 409
Control connection
    definition, 199
Control, front-end
    getting, 321
CreateParams method, 345
CsShopper
    and asynchronous file transfer, 236
CsSocket component
    benefits of creating, 131

D

Data Access palette, 506
Data loss
    avoiding, 239
Data Module
    definition, 506
Database model
    network, 420
    object-oriented, 420
Databases
    hierarchical, 419
    network, 419
    relational. *See* One-to-many hierarchies.
    tree hierarchy, 419
    VCL object hierarchy, 419
dBASE tables
    and deleted records, 466
    deleting excess space, 462
Debugging
    moving forms from programs into DLLs, 53
Debugging the Development Process, 12
Dialog
    building out of multiple independent forms, 370
Display modes, 300
DLLs, 6, 517, 581, 593
    biggest disadvantage, 50
    bug in Delphi's handling of initialization, 63
    definition, 40
    and Delphi's units, 40
    most common use of in Delphi programming, 50
    and multiple instances, 60
    order in which Windows searches for, 49
    parts, 41
    requirements for instances to be loaded and running simultaneously, 594
    and similarities to programs, 42
    using a form stored in, 53
    ways to tell programs to call functions, 41
DOS box, 3
DOS Protected Mode Interface. *See* DPMI.
Downloading files, 234
DPMI, 3
Drag and drop, 99, 313

Drag and drop interfaces
   supported by Delphi programs, 67
Drag and drop operations
   intra-application, 454
   primary steps, 454
Drag and drop server
   building, 110
   duties, 111
   interfaces required, 112
DragEnter method, 100
DragLeave method, 100
DragOver method, 100
Drag operation
   methods that must be defined, 100
Drop method, 100
Drop target
   requirements, 99
Dynamic Link Libraries. See DLLs.
Dynamic linking
   definition, 40
   and error recovery, 47
   runtime, 44
   vs. static linking, 40
Dynamic query, 424

E

Embedded spaces problem
   workable solution, 12
Embedding
   reasons for, 341
Error checking routine, 378
Error recovery
   and compile-time dynamic linking, 47
Event handlers
   steps to create generic-sounding routine names, 540
Execute method, 330, 382
Explicit filter, 422
Extenders
   16-bit, 4
   32-bit, 4
   DOS, 4
   and problems running, 4

F

Farewell message, 250
Fields, 419
File Manager Drag and Drop. See FMDD.
File names
   command-line options, 13
File Transfer Protocol. See FTP.
Files
   getting a listing of current directory, 13
   uploading and downloading in asynchronous mode, 241
   ways to download and upload, 234
Filled display mode, 300
Filter programs
   model to use, 13
   writing as console applications, 9
Filter, explicit, 422
Filters
   common functionality, 10
   definition, 4
   way of operating, 4
FL3, 280, 288, 301
   displaying landscape, 289
Floating-Point Unit. See FPU.
FMDD, 67
   functions defined by, 74
   implementation, 68
   steps required in implementation, 68
Foreign key
   definition, 425
Formats
   easiest way to add, 56
Forms
   designing, 324
   turning into components, 345
FPU, 373
Fractal Landscapes 3.0. See FL3.
Fractals
   definition, 273
Frames
   and views, 350
   definition, 343
Front-end control
   getting, 321

Index

FTP, 199
   command set, 244
FTP clients
   shutting out additional, 261
Functions
   C/C++ programs having access, 43
Functions, console-specific, 8

G

GetButtons method, 326
GetChar method, 35
GetData method, 109
GetDirList method, 256
Globally Unique Identifier. *See* GUID.
Grinzo, Lou, 12, 50
GUID
   definition, 108

H

Hard-coding, 374
Hello world program, 5
Hierarchies, one-to-many, 419
Hierarchy
   navigating up and down, 426
Hierarchy, tree
   definition, 419
Hints
   displaying for different parts of a control, 331
Home directory
   specifying, 247
Host name
   resolving, 179
HTTP, 132
   steps for creating a component, 132
Hypertext Transfer Protocol. *See* HTTP.

I

Image Editor
   using to create a resource file, 605
index clause
   and linking to DLL functions, 44
Inheritance
   in OLE parlance, 98
InterBase language, 437

Interfaces
   problems with implementation, 353
   similarity to classes, 109
Interfaces, drag and drop
   supported by Delphi programs, 67

K

KEEPER32, 245
   and security, 250
Keystrokes
   filtering and translating, 472

L

Landscape
   generating, 273
Lineage
   definition, 419
Lischner, Ray, 345

M

Macro facility, 332
Maguire, Steve, 12
MAKE program, 13
Math unit, Delphi 2
   bug, 383
Messages
   Welcome and Farewell, 250
Methods
   Add, 119
   BeginDrag, 355, 454
   Clone, 114
   CreateParams, 345
   DragEnter, 100
   DragLeave, 100
   DragOver, 100
   Drop, 100
   Execute, 330, 382
   GetButtons, 326
   GetChar, 35
   GetData, 109
   GetDirList, 256
   Loaded, 309
   Next, 114
   Paint, 346
   ProcessMessage, 361
   PutChar, 35

Read, 306
Reset, 114
SetRange, 352
SetTabSizes, 366
Show, 349
ShowStatus, 376
Skip, 114
StartUp, 167
TTable, 358
Write, 306
Multitasking, preemptive, 516
Multithreading, 517

N

name clause
   and linking to DLL functions, 44
Nesting, arbitrary, 435
Network database model, 420
Next method, 114
Nonblocking. *See* Asynchronous.
Numbers
   command-line options, 13

O

Object Linking and Embedding. *See* OLE.
Object Repository, 4, 7
   adding the filter, 34
   and storing objects in the directory, 8
   creating your own directory, 8
Object-oriented database model, 420
OCX. *See* OLE.
OLE, 67
   definition, 97
   ensuring libraries are properly initialized, 106
One-to-many hierarchies, 419
Orpheus VCL library, 558
Orpheus VCL package, 454
Outline display mode, 300
Outline mode, 302

P

Paint method, 346
Palettes
   creating, 328
Panels
   learning to work with, 492
Paradox tables
   and deleted records, 466
   deleting excess space, 462
Params program
   testing from within Delphi, 11
Parser, command-line
   developing a generalized, 14
Parsing functions, command-line
   test program, 21
Partial-loading, 309
Persistence
   definition, 334
Personal Information Manager. *See* PIM.
PIM, 395
Preemptive multitasking, 516
Procedures
   select, 436
   stored, 436
ProcessMessage method, 361
Progeny
   definition, 419
Program
   designing using Delphi, 397
Project file, 23
   and what it should contain, 25
Property
   redeclaring, 321
Property sheets, 360
PutChar method, 35

Q

Queries
   reconciling hierarchical and relational database models, 433
Query, dynamic, 424

R

Randomness
   importance of applying, 287
RDTSC, 311
   problem with, 312
Read method, 306

Index

Read Time Stamp Counter. *See* RDTSC.
Read-to-write behavior
    and problems with, 308
Reason parameter
    constants, 61
Records, 419
    variant, 20
Recursively hierarchical data
    definition, 425
Reference count
    setting artificially, 355
Referential integrity, 434
Relations
    definition, 419
Rendered display mode, 300, 303
Rendering
    changing from wire mesh to filled-triangle, 288
Reset method, 114
Resizing controls
    vs. moving controls, 400
RESOLVER32, 174
    and deriving name of host from numeric Internet address, 184
    determining behavior, 179
    determining which input to resolve, 195
Root disk drive
    specifying, 247
Rows, 419

S

SDK, 97
Secrets Of Delphi 2, 345
Security
    and KEEPER32, 249
Select procedures, 436
Semaphore
    definition, 595
Server, drag and drop
    building, 110
    interfaces required, 112
    what it has to do, 111
SetRange method, 352
SetTabSizes method, 366
Shared memory
    testing, 63
Shared memory block
    setting up, 61
ShareMem, 60
SHOPPER32
    requirements before connecting to FTP server, 228
Show method, 349
ShowStatus method, 376
Signaled
    definition, 595
Skip method, 114
Software Development Kit. *See* SDK.
"Splash screen" component
    creating, 494
SQL
    and solutions to huge hierarchies, 435
SQL for Smarties, 435
StartUp method, 167
Static declarations, 374
Static linking
    definition, 40
    problems with, 45
    vs. dynamic linking, 40
Statistics
    ways to retrieve, 380
Stored procedures, 436
Stream, clipboard, 331
Strings
    command-line options, 13
    computing height and width, 550
Subclassing, 84, 615
    definition, 81
Superclassing
    definition, 82
Switches
    command-line options, 13
Synchronous. *See* Blocking.
System
    restoring when a program terminates, 616